D1621408

The **History** of **Handball** at Texas A&M University

DON JOHNSON

 FriesenPress

One Printers Way
Altona, MB R0G 0B0
Canada

www.friesenpress.com

Copyright © 2022 by Don Johnson
First Edition — 2022

All rights reserved.

No part of this publication may be reproduced in any form, or by any
means, electronic or mechanical, including photocopying, recording,
or any information browsing, storage, or retrieval system, without
permission in writing from FriesenPress.

ISBN
978-1-03-914989-2 (Hardcover)
978-1-03-914988-5 (Paperback)
978-1-03-914990-8 (eBook)

1. Sports & Recreation, History

Distributed to the trade by The Ingram Book Company

CONTENTS

Foreword

"Dr. Sheffield-Moore, um… a gentleman by the name of General Johnson stopped by the main office earlier to see you, and since you were out of the office, he asked if I would get him on your schedule for a meeting." A General, really? As a relatively new department head of Health & Kinesiology at Texas A&M, my first thought was *Damn, what did I do?* What I *did* was play handball from 1983-1987 at Texas A&M, and General Johnson, despite having graduated thirty-two years before me, was still playing, and now wanted to meet to discuss coaching a handball activity class. In my role as Department Head at Texas A&M University, I've had the pleasure to meet many current and former students who serve our great university in so many remarkable, selfless ways. General Don Johnson is one such Aggie. Though service is not unusual for Aggies, Don's love for Texas A&M and the sport of handball is evident not only in this enjoyable book, but also in the way he lives his life, serves his country, and continues to serve his university.

It is therefore not surprising that Don took on the monumental task to document and share the history of Texas A&M handball with us all in this book. It is a history that spans from the mid-1920s through today, and conveys the many handball successes and failures of Aggies throughout the years. Many of those Aggies had never heard of the game before attending Texas A&M University. He includes letters from former players who describe their experiences while playing handball at Texas A&M, told through their lens – or at least that which they can remember. The ease and informality of Don's prose makes readers feel like they have stepped back into Aggieland and are holding a conversation about handball, like the one we had in my office the day we met. Regardless of your class year, your success as an Aggie handballer on the team or in an activity class, or how well your memory serves you of your time playing handball at Texas A&M, this book will undoubtedly restore your memory of the coaches, teammates and friends you made while playing the sport of handball. Thank you, General Johnson, for reinvigorating the memories we all cherish from our time as members of the fighting Texas Aggie Handball team!

Preface

With a downtrodden walk and a scowl upon his face, I watched Ozzie Burke walk toward the handball courts in the Texas A&M Recreation Center. It took no imagination to realize Ozzie had a serious problem. So, I asked what was wrong. Ozzie replied that the keeper of his handball history during his time as coach of the Texas A&M handball team had somehow deleted all remnants of his history from the computer-not only this time, but this had happened once before.

To console a good friend and to help lighten his day, the author, who had always tried to reject attempts to write anything beyond letters and short versions of required text, spilled forth with the words, "Ozzie, if you will help, I will put your history in print so it can't be lost." Probably without thinking, he agreed.

On the way home from handball my offer began to sink in and I realized I was not prepared in any way to accomplish what I had offered. However, before reaching the safe confines of home I realized that my wife, Pam, had written and published several books so maybe all was not in vain.

When confronted with my seemingly impossible task, Pam confidently replied that I could do it without much of a problem. Wow! Now I had no choice but to go forward. Even though the commitment was given as a consoling thought, I have never been one to back away from my given word.

So, with a hopeful start, I left for Cushing Archives at Texas A&M University to begin researching data. Expecting to find a treasure trove of information to help Ozzie's history, I found essentially nothing. However, there were some newspaper clippings from the early stages of A&M handball, some photos and newspaper clippings of handball history during the time Lance Lowy was coach of the handball team, plus a couple of interesting handball articles, one of which really caught my attention. A couple of Aggies had won the National Collegiate Doubles Handball title back in the long-gone years of 1954-55. Finding my name in the Archives and that of my partner Jim Mathis, and so little about anyone else or handball at A&M was an unbelievably sobering thought. With so little in text or photos about this great game and its influence on so many Aggies, the need for a book on the history of handball at Texas A&M was a glaring fact that stared me straight in the face. It was at that moment that I realized that it had to be done. Without a recorded history, what we have done during our lifetime is not history but a happening that is gone when those who remembered cannot remember.

Having been invited some time ago into a small group called the "history group" I presented my problem to them. This group was not a group of unknowns interested in history, but a veritable source of history, not only Texas A&M, but many different subject areas. The health of Dr. Haskell Monroe prevented him from being present that day; however, Dr. Henry Dethloff, Dr. John Adams, Jerry Cooper, Maj. Gen. Tom Darling, Col. Jim Woodall, David Chapman and LTC Buck Henderson were there. All unanimously agreed that the history needed to be written. With special encouragement from Dr. Dethloff at the end of the meeting, I was off for home.

Upon hearing the decision to actually write the book, Pam said, "I will not write one sentence for you nor will I tell you how to organize it-it is your book; however, if you need help with the computer in how to do certain things, I am there to help." It was a promise she has kept to this day.

And so began a totally new and exciting, as it has turned out, adventure. No small part of this adventure has been the realization that this book will bring joy to those of us who have enjoyed the game of handball. Admittedly, some of the history in this book will not be in the least interesting and possibly boring to readers who have not played the game. However, for those who have been in the competitive arena of this supposedly oldest game with a ball known to mankind, it will bring back fond memories of times past. At some point in our playing, all of us have been there to make that incredible shot to get to 21 first. How could I ever forget the aces I served when Jim and I played World Doubles Handball champions and Handball Hall of Fame honorees, Sam Haber and Ken Schneider, at the Dallas Athletic Club in the spring of 1955? Or later that spring, our doubles match against Jimmy Jacobs and his partner in Houston? Or many years later, the non-believing look of incredulity on Charlie Bokleman's face when I served an ace to him on the 21st point for Marvin Harris and me to take a game of doubles from him and Ozzie Burke. No doubt, Charlie has long forgotten that shot but as I recall it even today, so many years and handball games since, I still remember the court and how I planned and executed that particular serve. All the others leading up to that point are not in my memory bank and no amount of effort can raise an inkling of how Marvin and I got to 20, but that 21st point, even now, I can remember almost every detail.

And so, it is hoped that this book will help unbind those special memories and bring our Aggie handball players back to Aggieland, even if only in memory. They were special times we spent on the handball court that should not be forgotten and this book will aid in being able to share with family and maybe others. This book is Aggie handball history.

So much of this book would not have been possible without the help of so many incredible people. None who were asked to contribute or help in any way hesitated-though some were quicker with their response than others. In making a decision who to contact for information and stories, it was quickly determined that it would be a near impossibility to contact all who have played the game at Aggieland. So, I made the decision, right or wrong, to contact those who lived in the Bryan/College Station area and who have played or are still playing handball at A&M, those former students prior to 1980 who were on the Aggie handball team/club and those 1980 and thereafter, who participated and met with some success at the National Collegiate Handball Tournament.

Having gone through more than one ream of paper in the letter writing process, I am so thankful for the insight, stories and information received from so many contacts. Unfortunately, and I do not use that term loosely, many did not answer my inquiry. Most of them, I am certain, never received the intended mailing. Few came back with "Undeliverable-Addressee Unknown" stamped on my mailing. I used an up-to-date Association of Former Students Directory for the addresses, and for many, I found that the former student had not updated to their current address. In some cases, the former student asked to not list an address. Based on this experience, I would suggest that ALL former students need to keep the Association notified of address changes, unless the former student no longer wants to remain in contact. Even though I personally know of some address changes, the Association will not make those changes unless the former student personally makes the request. Their stories, insights into the game and what they have done in life will, most likely, be the chapter most readers will enjoy and remember.

Bill Page, at the University Libraries and a former 'ol lady (roommate) to an Aggie from Cranfills Gap, Texas (my hometown), was very helpful early on and then Leslie Winters at Cushing Archives was there every time I needed access to information or have questions answered. Early on, my research took me to the Corps of Cadets Center, where many years of the *Longhorn* and *Aggieland* are in a library. Lt. Col. Jeff Gardner saw me there and asked what I was doing. He politely informed me that I could do that research at home on my computer by logging into the Texas A&M University Yearbook Collection. Former Aggie handball coach, Lance Lowy, loaned his complete library of USHA's *Handball* magazines. Mike Driscoll, Handball chair for the Southwest Region, provided me with information where a void existed. Vern Roberts, then Executive Director of the United States Handball Association, sent me, free of charge, the magazines that were missing from Coach Lowy's collection. As we all know, free is sometimes not free, as I agreed to provide a book to the USHA Handball Museum in Tucson, Arizona, when published. Matthew Krueger, the current Executive Director who replaced Vern, was there for help when needed. Mike Dau, handball coach seemingly forever at Lake Forest College, sent me the names representing College/Universities of all participants of the National Collegiate Handball Tournament hosted by Lake Forest in 1997. For reasons unknown, the names, game and match results were not published in the magazine that year. I want to issue a special thank you to James Welford at the Texas A&M Recreation Center, who provided me with copies of the intramural handball results from the very beginning to the end of their record keeping; Keith Joseph, who helped with the photography of trophies and banners; and Dennis Corrington, former Director, and Rick Hall, current Director of Recreational Sports, who provided me names of those placed in charge of keeping intramural sports running smoothly since 1979. And now I come back to Ozzie Burke who was very helpful in making sure my facts and stories were correct during his time as coach.

And now separately I need to say a special thanks to two who are key to the success of this book-Jerry Cooper who has made his living in the Journalism field and Dr. Melinda Sheffield-Moore, Head of Health and Kinesiology, who has agreed, whether or not she had the time available from a busy day of doing her job and raising a family, to write the Foreword. Jerry agreed to look over my writing and make recommendations before I took the big step of presenting to a publisher for printing.

Of course, the one person who has been there day and night for me is the lady who kept her original promise and has not badgered me into writing or doing anything to push me forward. However, her quiet tolerance and helpfulness with my computer issues of photo cropping, placement and other idiosyncrasies were invaluable. Her background in education is that of a teacher, and as such, agreed to be my proof reader. I continue to be so thankful that she came along and agreed to be a special part of my life.

CHAPTER 1
Historic Overview of Handball at Texas A&M

Handball???? It is a game using only the hands to send a ball against a wall in such a fashion not to be returned by an opponent. A game using only the hands is one of the oldest games known to man. Early records note a game using the hands as early as 2000 BC in Egypt. Over 700 handball court sites used by the Aztecs, some dating to 1500 BC, have been found throughout the area from Arizona to Nicaragua. Alexander the Great has been credited with spreading the game to Italy and from there to Spain, France and the rest of the Roman Empire.

The game of playing a ball with hands against a wall was mentioned in Scotland in 1427. Irish migrants spread the game to England and later to South Africa, America and Australia.

Given the nomadic lifestyle of the Native Americans, it is highly improbable there were any games of hitting a ball with the hands. There were no permanent structures to hit a ball against a wall. One favorite game was "stick toss" which probably dates back to the time the first baskets were woven. There is little record of using any type of ball in their games, although in the movie *Jeremiah Johnson* starring Robert Redford, there is a scene sequence of a game using sticks and a ball made with a furry cover from an animal. Although records indicate games using a ball hit with the hands early in the history of Central America and the southwest of North America, it was the Irish descendants who made the game of handball popular in this country.

Dr. Elaine Shapiro accurately describes handball in an article published in the USHA's *Handball*, May 1983, page 10. She writes: "Each time a handball player steps on the court, certain specific demands are made on the body. During just five minutes of a handball game, a player will probably run, squat, bend, lunge, dive, and stretch for a ball that must be kept in play by both his/her dominant and non-dominant hands. Obviously, handball is a total body sport involving the upper body as well as the lower body."

Texas A&M opened in October 1876 as a land grant college. With its military background, athletics were very important for the development of cadets. Football, baseball and track were the main organized sports being played. Basketball was introduced in 1908, but very little interest was shown so it was discontinued. Basketball was tried again in 1913 and soon became another of the major sports of athletic competition.

In March 1925, the Texas A&M Athletic Council met and named a committee to recommend improvements to the intramural program. The committee submitted their recommendations to the Athletic Council in May of 1925. Handball was one of the recommended sports to be added as part of the program. At the time there were no indoor handball courts in existence at A&M. It is likely, and I have been told, that handball was played using a wall and with a marked boundary. It is not known if this activity was part of the intramural program or was being played by the cadets simply as a game.

James Sullivan was hired as business manager of athletics in 1919. He inherited a department with a debt of $17,000 which was a huge sum for that era. In two years, he had the department out of debt and had started updating the athletic facilities. He added additional and better seating at Kyle Field, then built Memorial Gymnasium which was later changed in name to honor Charles A. DeWare who was one of the greatest tight ends in America during the first 25 years of the twentieth century. Mr. Sullivan felt very strongly that the College should provide all the facilities necessary for cadets to have a means of recreation. In 1926, he stated it was his aim to build indoor handball courts for play. According to an article in the Friday, 9 July, 1926, printing of *The Eagle* newspaper of Bryan, Texas (found in Cushing Archives, Texas A&M University), the north part of Memorial Gymnasium which had been left uncompleted earlier, was now being converted into two handball courts and space for punching bags, tumbling mats, parallel bars and other equipment. Due to an increasing number of students, especially entering freshmen, more physical activity facilities were needed. The new building, which was referred to as the auxiliary gym by administrators and as the "the Little Gym" by students, was reported as being completed and ready for the incoming freshmen class in the fall of 1929. In the new building were 5 new "regulation-sized" handball courts. Having played in those courts while a student, I know they were not regulation size by today's standard or even of those times. However, the courts were welcomed and served as handball courts for thousands of students.

With the new handball courts, one of the two courts in Memorial gymnasium was converted into lockers for cadets and the other into a wrestling room. Teaching of handball as a required Physical Education course would also have been moved to the new building. In addition to the new handball courts, the new building also had floor space for a basketball court and other athletic equipment. With the new handball courts, the game began to flourish. As my great friend George Harris, Class of 1941, told me years ago, "It was a very popular sport."

World events became one of the main concerns of Americans in the late 1930s. The daily routine of college life was interrupted in the early 1940s when America became a participant in World War II. Handball and other intramural athletics held little significance with the military staff. As a practical matter, the new direction beyond the academic day was preparing the cadets physically and mentally for the war effort. A new physical fitness program was installed and became the primary effort in preparing the cadets physically. Intramural athletics became secondary. During this period handball and other intramural activities were relegated to lesser importance and the "speed up" program in academic and physical fitness were at the forefront. Peace eventually prevailed and the academic year and intramural activities took on a more normal pace.

As A&M returned to its routine, so did the activities of intramural sports. Handball again became one of the preferred sports of the intramural program. For the first time in A&M's history, a handball club was organized. It can be ascertained that Herman Segrest was the first sponsor of the first handball club at Texas A&M. It is known that he was the club sponsor during the 1948-49 school year. He would remain the sponsor through the 1954-55 school year. During this time, he was instrumental in arranging for the first handball matches with other teams. The first record that can be found was against the University of Texas Longhorns. Jewell McDowell was the top Aggie handball player at the time and led the Aggies to a 3-1 victory over the Longhorns.

The United States Handball Association (USHA) was established in 1951 by Chicago business man, Robert Kendler. The purpose was to expand handball nationally and to provide handball tournaments to players throughout the land. The USHA was readily accepted by handball players and soon became the established authority in the game of handball throughout the nation. The USHA opened its competition at the college level in 1953. In late 1954, Phil Collins, an airman stationed at Bryan Air Force Base, suggested to two members of the A&M handball club, Jim Mathis and Don "Johnny" Johnson, that A&M should send a team to Chicago to participate in the intercollegiate championships. Herman Segrest was instrumental in helping arrange for the team to go. The result was the first national handball champions at Texas A&M. Jim and Johnny returned to Aggieland as National Collegiate Handball Doubles Champions. To participate as a team in the National Handball Collegiate Tournament, four players were required. To complete the 1954 team Don Grant played as the number 1 singles player and Paul Meiners played as the number 2 singles player. The team earned 3rd place in the tournament. It would be a few years before the Aggies would return to play in the National Collegiate Handball Tournament.

After Herman Segrest was no longer the sponsor for the handball team, the club continued without a sponsor. Handball was still a very popular sport. It is likely that Maj. Conoley, an Air Force officer, was the top handball player at A&M during the 1955-56 year. It is also likely that he brought the idea of a handball ladder with him. A handball ladder is a rank order listing of handball players of any local club or team. A player on the ladder can challenge a player who is listed on the ladder above him/her to a match. If the challenging player wins the match, then he/she can move their name up the ladder to the position of the challenged player. The defeated challenged player would then replace the challenger's spot on the ladder. It is a great method for determining the top players in the club and also a great way to challenge someone to a match who is very close in a skill level to your own. The handball ladder has survived throughout the 60 plus years since its introduction.

Barney Welch, then Director of Intramurals, played handball and likely learned of the handball skills that Maj. Conoley possessed. It can logically be assumed that Barney Welch asked Maj. Conoley to coach the handball club in 1956-57, and Maj. Conoley accepted the responsibility. The competitive record of the handball team during Maj. Conoley's year of being the coach is not available. There is no record of Maj. Conoley continuing to coach the team after 1957. There are no definitive records of continuance of the club between the years of 1957-61 although some students in their senior year listed in the *Aggieland* that they were a member of the handball club. In the *Aggieland* of 1961, Gary E. Staley listed that he was the president of the handball club. Based on that information, it is likely that the handball club continued during those years and the handball ladder continued to be used to show rank order in terms of skill level of the members of the club.

In 1959, the handball club lost an avid supporter when Barney Welch retired from his position as Director of Intramurals. It was through the teaching of classes and intramurals that the handball club relied to have a steady flow of talent into the club. Beginners would take the handball classes as a Physical Education requirement. At that time, the university required all students to take four semesters of Physical Education classes. Handball was one of the optional classes and also very popular. Some students would sign up for a second semester of handball. In addition to classes, handball was one of the most popular sports of the intramural program. Between the classes and the intramural program, especially in the spring, it was not easy to find an open court to play a handball match. The handball club had to reserve courts during specific times for practice as a club and for challenges to those on the handball ladder. A challenge to someone on the handball ladder did not have to be played during the time the club had the courts reserved.

Following the retirement of Barney Welch, Dr. Charles McCandless became the Director of Intramurals. He would continue to support the handball program in a similar fashion as Welch had.

A photo of the 1963 handball team in the *Aggieland* listed C. E. Evans as the sponsor of the team. The following quote from page 239 of the 1963 *Aggieland* indicates that the team was actively participating in tournaments and competitive matches with other teams:

A&M's newly-revived handball team took second place in the annual SWC Handball Tournament in Houston this year. Ed Merritt won the Class A singles for A&M and Jerry Levy turned in what Merritt called a "real fine performance" to take the Class B singles award.

The reference to the SWC would indicate the Southwest Conference of which A&M was a member; however, the NCAA and Southwest Conference had never had a handball league. It is likely that the Editor should have used the term "annual Southwest Handball Tournament" which was held during that time period.

Joe DePasqual, Class of 1965 and who was on the '63, '64, and '65 handball teams, reported that the handball team was very active in matches with the Rice Owls, winning decisively over the Owl handball team on more than one occasion. The club also traveled to the University of Texas, where the Texas coach, Pete Tyson, gave instructional pointers and paired the Aggie and Longhorn players evenly with no agenda toward a team victory. During that time period, Pete Tyson had developed the UT handball program into a power on the national collegiate handball scene.

In 1965, the A&M handball team once again competed in the National Collegiate Handball Tournament, which was held in Austin. The team did not place in any category but continued to be very competitive.

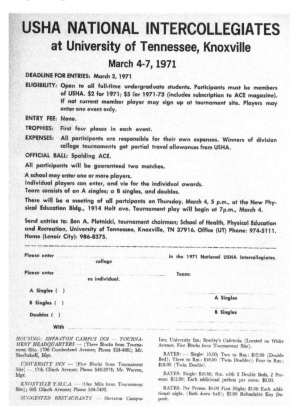

Entry form to participate in the National Intercollegiate Handball Tournament during the early years. This would have been the form Ozzie Burke completed to enter in 1971.

(The USHA's *Ace*, February 1971, page 69)

Arriving at Texas A&M in 1967 was a man who had grown up in the Bronx playing one wall handball. Stan Lowy came to Texas A&M as a professor in the Aerospace Engineering Department; however, his professorship was not the only talent he brought to A&M. He joined the handball club and immediately created a new energy within it. He was soon named sponsor to the club and remained so for many years. He continued playing until his health became a greater issue than handball.

The A&M club remained very active and continued to participate, when possible, in the National Collegiate Tournament. In the fall of 1967, a freshman, Ozzie Burke, who had played a lot of handball on the A&M courts while attending A&M Consolidated High School, joined the handball club and continued to play. In the spring of 1968, he teamed up with Dan Kennerly to become the second of A&M's national collegiate doubles champions. Dan Kennerly graduated and moved on to his life's profession. Ozzie was never able to repeat as a national champion although he and his brother Cyril came very close in 1969. Ozzie continued going to the National Collegiate Championships and, in his senior year, was the only member of the team to go to the national tournament. There, he came in 5th in Class A (Open) singles. He, just as Dan Kennerly had done earlier, graduated and moved on to his life's profession.

Arriving at A&M shortly after Stan Lowy was Dr. Jeff Bronson, a graduate of Rice University. Dr. Bronson was employed as a physicist with the Cyclotron. Dr. Bronson also brought a talent of handball with him. He and Stan Lowy would be co-faculty advisors to the club for many years and would provide valuable handball instruction to all of the club members.

In the fall of 1972 two young students arrived at A&M who would have a great impact on handball at Texas A&M. They were Charles "Charlie" Bokelman and Jack Gressett. Both became excellent handball players. Gressett moved away after graduation, but later returned to the Bryan/College Station area. Bokelman also left the area but returned later. Both continued their handball careers upon returning to the area and later became members of the Texas A&M handball club. In 1992, Bokelman was asked by some of the student members of the handball club to help with coaching. He accepted and has been an assistant coach until this day. He has helped many young players develop into excellent players, including some who have won championships. Today, he has no peer in the local area to match his handball skills although Jack Gressett can give him a creditable game. Gressett also volunteered to help with the coaching of our young Aggies. The two of them, along with myself, helped Ozzie Burke (coach 2007-2021) develop our young Aggie handball players. Jack Gressett took the reins as coach during the summer of 2021 and I continued as an assistant coach.

The handball team continued to participate in handball tournaments held in the state of Texas but did not make trips to the National Collegiate Handball Tournament. Then, in 1975, a major change happened to the composition of the handball club. For the first time, women became members of the club. Women had been enrolled in handball classes for a number of years before and it is not known why none had ever joined the club before 1975. The reason may have been as simple as "no one ever asked" but the opportunities for women to participate in tournaments were increasing. It has been a known fact for years that skill improvement occurs at a much greater rate and to a higher level when the competition is greater. That is one of the primary purposes for being and the reason for joining a handball club. So, the women made a great choice and "broke ground" for many to follow.

Another handball player arriving in the '70s would leave an enviable record as coach. Lance Lowy came to A&M in 1977 as a graduate assistant and was given a charge to help with the handball program. In 1978, he was given the responsibility to take charge of the handball program and to become the coach of the handball team. Under his leadership, A&M became a national collegiate power. It did not happen overnight, but as 1980 approached, Lowy knew he had some special handball players and would soon be competing for national championships.

As Lowy took control of the handball program, he knew that the team and club would need greater competition for improvement. Improvement was needed to compete at a higher level in tournaments around the state and especially in the National Collegiate Handball Tournament. He knew that a local tournament would help advance the skill level of his team, but it would also provide an incentive for those in the handball classes to enter "our own tournament". He took the step and started the Aggieland Classic to be held once near the end of the fall semester and once near the end of the spring semester.

Not only did the Aggieland Classic help to develop a higher skill level of players, but it also was a means to assist providing funds for the team to travel to the National Collegiate Handball Tournament. The tournament became very successful and became the largest handball tournament in the state. Some tournaments hosted as high as 300 entries. The tournament continued to be held twice a year through the spring of 2016. In early 2018, the Aggieland Classic was held in San Antonio and repeated in 2019, courtesy of Aggie handball players living in San Antonio.

In the decade of the 1970s, it became apparent that women had a strong interest in learning and playing the game of handball. Many in the sport felt that the hard ball was a detriment for women and juniors to learn and play the game, so a new "family" ball was developed for these participants. It was introduced at the 24th annual USHA national juniors-girls division in San Antonio. The ball acted like a handball, but was much softer and painless to the hands. It became an instant success. The new ball led to the development of coed doubles and was introduced in the same time period that A&M women were really becoming excited about playing the game of handball. The first coed doubles handball tournament was held at Southwest Texas State and Sue Oakleaf entered with a partner named Jim Sellars of Austin. Oakleaf and Sellars became the first coed champions and easily defended the title the following year, defeating Amy Morgan of Austin and National Master champion Jim Faulk of Dallas in the finals 21-5, 21-18.

Nineteen seventy-five was a breakout year for A&M women to join the A&M handball club, but 1980 was even bigger for women collegiate handball players. It was announced that women would be competing at the National Collegiate Handball Tournament for a national championship. The Aggies were ready. At the top of the list was Susan E. Oakleaf, who became the very first National Collegiate Women's Handball Champion. Also on the team was Glorian Motal. Glorian, nicknamed "Peanut," had her handball beginning at the very end of her college career but continued after leaving A&M to become the best women's handball player in America.

The 1980 team was made up of three women and one man, so they could not play for the team championship; however, that was the beginning to what became a remarkable record in collegiate handball. Lowy knew and predicted that it would be just a matter of time for the Aggies to reach the top as a team.

As women's handball began to take off nationally, helped with the introduction of the family ball, Aggie women were making their presence felt. Of the 40 handball players to participate in the third Women's National Four-Wall championships, which included women from Ireland and Canada; three were Aggies. In the singles matches Hilary Huffard was defeated in her first match, but Sue Oakleaf and Peanut Motal made it to the quarterfinals before being eliminated.

In the doubles division of the tournament, Aggies were in the headlines. Reenie Turek reported the doubles action and was recorded on page 27 of the September 1982 issue of the USHA's *Handball*:

> The women joined forces for only the second time in history for the women's doubles-and the same teams battled their way to the championship match.
>
> The field was larger this year than last, with 16 teams beginning competition mid-week of the tournament. The cast of players was truly international, with teams from all across the US, Mexico, Canada and a full contingent of players from Ireland.
>
> There were plenty of new faces, including Lupe Alvarado, wife of National Open champ Naty Alvarado. But when the fighting was through, it was the familiar faces dominating the division.
>
> Seeded first were the defending champs, Rosemary Bellini of New York and Sue Oakleaf of Texas. They won the title last year at Palatine in the first-ever women's doubles championships. Heading up the lower bracket was last year's other finalist team-Allison Roberts of Ohio and Glorian "Peanut" Motal of Texas.
>
> The first round went pretty much as expected except for something of a rarity; not one single tiebreaker in eight matches.

The quarters produced some fireworks as Susan Carey/Liz Nichol of Ireland slipped by the highly-regarded French Canadian team of Carole Faucher/Lucy Joyal 11-8 in the tiebreaker. The seeded teams advanced without incident with Bellini/Oakleaf defeating Denise Carideo/Deborak Marler of Tucson in two games; Roberts/Motal stopping Lynn Johnson/Andre Torrence of Illinois; and the California team of Rossanna Ettinger/ Diane Harmon ending the hopes of Hilary Huffard/Troy Hinnant of Texas.

Both of the top-seeded teams had a momentary struggle in the semis. Bellini/Oakleaf beat Ettinger/Harmon 21-6 in the first game, but found themselves locked up at 20-20 in the second game. Long rallies ensued with the defending champions coming out on top finally. In the other half of the draw, about the same sort of thing was happening. Roberts/Motal sailed through the first game 21-12 over the Irish team of Carey/Nichol. In game two, each side shot its way to 20 points, only to have the Americans' tournament experience gain the upper hand.

The finale was a textbook case of two women wanting the win so badly that nothing could stop them.

Roberts/Motal were hot from the start of game one, running off a 9-1 lead before Bellini/ Oakleaf took control and won 21-10. Stunned by the cold spell in the first game, Roberts/ Motal shot and rallied their way to 20-20 in game two. Facing match point, Roberts/ Motal called time out, which seemed to rattle the defending champs. The second game went to Roberts/Motal.

The tiebreaker was all Roberts/Motal, who simply overpowered the defending champs with speed and determination. The final score was 11-2.

The win resulted in Aggie women being on the first and the second women's national handball doubles championship teams.

Another first came to an Aggie during the weekend of 5-7 November 1982. In the first ever women's national YMCA handball tournament, Allison Roberts and Glorian "Peanut" Motal emerged champions once again as they took on all other doubles teams and added another national title to their resume. In the singles action, each of the finalists in doubles made it to the semifinals in singles. In the semifinals, Rosemary Bellini defeated her doubles partner, Sue Oakleaf, 21-6, 21-9. In the other semifinal, Peanut Motal defeated her doubles partner in a grueling match of 1 hour and 30 minutes 20-21, 21-15, 21-18. NOTE: the YMCA tournament was not yet using the tiebreaker to 11 points as was being done in the professional ranks and the National Collegiate Tournament. After the totally energy expending match with her partner and the doubles competition, Peanut was no match for Bellini in the finals as she was defeated 21-10, 21-6. At this point in the national women's competition, Bellini had won all of the national singles titles open to women. As time would tell, Peanut was an upcoming star and continued to improve each time she stepped on the court.

Aggies also were in the spotlight in two of the divisions of the 1982 Ace Mallory Y Seis Tournament held in San Antonio at the YMCA handball courts. Matt Pokryfki, who had just finished two years of handball at A&M, upset the number 1 seed in B singles division during the second match 21-10, 21-14. Matt earned his way to the finals where he came up just short to Bobby Pena 18-21, 21-19, 11-9. Two Aggies, Sue Oakleaf and Peanut Motal, met in the women's singles finals. This time, Sue prevailed by the score of 21-15, 21-19. These two Aggie women totally dominated women's handball in Texas during the early stages of women's handball.

The two Aggie women continued to play at a high level at the national women's championships in 1983. In singles, Sue Oakleaf was defeated during the round of 16 in a very close match coming out on the short end of an 11-9 tiebreaker. Peanut Motal still could not get past the past previous champion, Rosemary Bellini, and was defeated in the semifinal. As in the past couple of years, the two Aggies met in the finals of the women's doubles. Sue Oakleaf advanced to the finals this time with a new partner, LeaAnn Tyson; however, the duo of Allison Roberts and Motal totally dominated the finals and won by the score of 21-2, 21-10. The skill level of Roberts/Motal was reported on page 26 of the July 1983 issue of the USHA's *Handball*:

> Peanut and Allison complement each other to perfection to make for a dynamite doubles team. Motal is an aggressive, strong-armed right side player. She digs and drives everything that comes near her in the front court. Peanut could write the book on right side doubles play. Her partner is as stylish a left side player as any of the Roberts clan. Her two-handed play from deep court including a deadly right corner kill from anywhere on the court, supplies the needed offense. After Allison's tiebreaker loss to Diane Harmon, (during singles play in the semifinals) Fred Lewis said, "that Allison has the best strokes and shots of any of the women. If she lost the extra weight, she would win the singles." The extra weight wasn't as crucial in doubles, especially with Motal to cover the front like a vacuum. In a word, Motal and Roberts "jell" together. An average of just six points per game was allowed by the dynamic duo en route to the championship.

Thirty women signed up to play in the 1985 National Handball tournament. Five of the women were Aggies. They were: Peanut Motal, Sue Oakleaf, Julie Werner, Beth Rowley and Renee deLassus. Beth Rowley and Renee deLassus were defeated in the first round. Sue Oakleaf was defeated in the quarterfinals. Motal won her first National women's singles title. Pete Tyson reported the final on page 24 of the July–August 1985 issue of the USHA's *Handball*:

> From the outset of the tournament the 30 women who entered the Open singles knew there would be a new first-time national champion. The only two women to have won the title were not entered. Four-time and defending champ Rosemary Bellini had sustained a serious hand injury earlier this year and wasn't fully recovered. The 1983 champion and last year's runner-up, Diane Harmon, was pregnant and decided not to play.
>
> The question, "Would they have dominated this year's tournament?" can't be answered until next year. But everyone in attendance left this year's nationals impressed by the vast improvement in the quality of play displayed by the women.
>
> The final between Peanut Motal and LeaAnn Tyson (Mrs. Pete Tyson) figured to be an exciting match and an interesting contrast in styles. LeaAnn had defeated Peanut in March at the Bud Light tournament in Austin, but Peanut came to the nationals in top form. Tyson tallied the first point of the match, but a combination of the "National Finals Jitters," the glass court and Peanut's aggressive play caused the usually consistent LeaAnn to make too many errors. Peanut built up a large lead and LeaAnn couldn't get untracked and rolled to the first game win 21-7.

LeaAnn's strategy was to keep the ball high and to the left by using lobs and ceiling shots, but Peanut wasn't about to get involved in such tactics and brought the ball down at every opportunity. The second game started as a continuation of the first with Peanut controlling the tempo by serving well, including aces to the left-wall crotch, and by driving the ball down the left wall. Peanut mounted a 15-6 lead, when LeaAnn started to use a hard-hit Z-serve that gave Peanut trouble. The Z-serve forced Peanut to make defensive returns and LeaAnn was now in charge of the rallies, forcing the ceiling game, which is LeaAnn's specialty. But it was just too late. LeaAnn came back to 13-17, at which point Peanut called a timeout. Motal regained the serve and scored with her offensive attack following strong serves. At match point, LeaAnn hit what she thought was a perfect pass, but the always-hustling Motal made a great retrieve. LeaAnn could only watch as the ball floated to the front wall and rolled out of the left corner for game and match point.

A hard worker with 110 percent effort, Peanut Motal, one of the friendliest and most-liked of the women players, is now the national champ.

Two Aggies made the finals in the women's Consolation division. Pete Tyson wrote the story on page 41 of the July-August 1985 issue of the USHA's *Handball*:

There were 13 first-round victims in the women's Open who competed in the Consolation event. The victims included some very talented players, many of whom had lost in close contests.

In the top half of the draw, national collegiate champion Julie Werner got some revenge for her teammate from Texas A&M, Renee deLassus, who had lost to Lupe Alvarado in the quarters. Julie defeated Lupe in the semifinals to advance to the finals against former Aggie Beth Rowley.

Rowley advanced to the final with a quarterfinal win over Alaska state champ Dottie Watson and a semifinal win over Carrie Cooke. Rowley had played at A&M with Peanut Motal and Sue Oakleaf, and now lives in Dallas.

The final was a very-well played match with many long and hard-fought rallies. Rowley managed to pull out the tiebreaker with an 11-6 win over Werner.

As in the past, this year's women's doubles championship match featured the same two Aggies, Sue Oakleaf and Peanut Motal, but not as partners. The other three Aggies on doubles teams, Rene deLassus/Julie Werner and Beth Rowley/Shirley Holstadt from Oregon, were defeated in the first round. The final match action was described by Pete Tyson and recorded on page 25 of the July-August 1985 issue of the USHA's *Handball*:

The only finalist to return from last year's tournament was Peanut Motal who had teamed with Allison Roberts to win the last three national women's doubles titles. This year Peanut teamed with Nancy Molter and advanced to the final to face the established doubles team of LeaAnn Tyson and Sue Oakleaf. Both teams were devastating in reaching the final, allowing an average of just 8 points per game.

The final turned into a rout for Tyson and Oakleaf as they played their best handball of the tournament. LeaAnn took control of the rallies with wall-hugging ceiling shots and hard-hit passing shots down the left wall. Oakleaf seemed to score at will with superb serving and hard drives. Neither player attempted many kills as they were overpowering Molter and Motal, but when they did go for the bottom board, their percentage of success was phenomenal.

Motal and Molter just couldn't get anything going. The new champs wouldn't let up and made very few mistakes. They were able to make a run in the second game to tie the score at 11-all, but that was the end of the rally. Oakleaf and Tyson regained the serve and ran out the game, 21-11.

The year 1985 was a great year for Aggie handball. The Aggies won their first ever national collegiate handball team championship. Accolades followed after the win. Dr. Steve Smith, a professor at Texas A&M, an avid handball player and winner of the Open championship on more than one occasion in the Aggieland Classic, wrote the following article about the success of A&M handball, which was reported on pages 20, 21 of the October 1986 issue of the USHA's *Handball*:

> When I was first hired by Texas A&M University, located in some place called College Station, I figured it was the end of my handball-playing days, unless I could regularly drive the 100 miles to Austin or Houston for games.
>
> Actually, I wondered whether the Texas Aggies could do anything besides play football, ride horses, and grow hay. Well, I soon discovered that hay isn't all that's growing here in College Station. Handball is growing at Texas A&M, and faster, perhaps, than anywhere else on the planet.
>
> Most find it hard to believe, since most areas are more familiar with players in their seventies, and all the young athletes are taking up tennis and racquetball. Well, believe it. Refreshing news for most areas would be 10 or 12 new recruits over the course of a year. To see 100 new players would stagger most handball players, anywhere. But here, at Texas A&M University, they teach between 1,000 and 1,200 college students the game of handball every year. Hundreds of these new recruits participate in the campus handball club. Needless to say, I found the Aggie handball program amazing.
>
> The hope of those involved in the program is that these new handball fanatics will graduate, disseminate across the country, and teach the game to their friends and relatives. With these numbers, it's hoped that everyone in the country will soon be experiencing bone bruises and sore backs, but, most importantly, the excitement and camaraderie we share in handball.
>
> Even those who no longer play the game would be knowledgeable spectators, one of the most lacking commodities in our sport today. Perhaps the game will survive, perhaps it will grow, but either will be due in large part to efforts such as those at Texas A&M to get new players involved in the sport.
>
> Much of the credit for the explosive growth and participation in handball at Texas A&M is due to our quiet and little-sung hero, Coach Lance Lowy. Lance has drawn together an educational handball program, the campus club, championship collegiate teams, and a

strong Aggieland Classic tournament. All of these have given College Station an increasingly important place on the handball map.

Lance learned to play handball under the tutelage of his father, Stan, and Pete Tyson. From this start in the game, he developed a picture-perfect swing and that sense of camaraderie that keeps his students coming back to the campus courts. Lowy came to A&M in 1977 as a lecturer in the Physical Education Department to teach handball classes and coach the team. He now supervises, not only handball, but racquetball and badminton as well. Lance and three other instructors teach fourteen handball classes each semester. The annual spring and fall Aggieland Classic tournaments, also organized by Coach Lowy, draw over 200 players from around the state for the various divisions offered.

Although his programs and instruction are probably his most important successes in handball, Lance became known for the success of his Texas A&M handball teams. The Aggies won the national team title in 1985 and finished second in 1986. His teams have won the southwest regional title several times, and he has coached some of the best women ever to play the game. His female proteges include Peanut Motal, National Open singles champ in 1985 and 1986; Sue Oakleaf, National Open Doubles champ in 1985 and 1986; Julie Werner, the 1985 National Collegiate champ; and Renee deLassus, a top-ranked collegiate player.

Given these successes and more on the collegiate level, most expect Lance to be out recruiting players to attend Texas A&M. When asked how many of his team members, over his many years at A&M, were recruited for their talent or had played before, he answers without a moment of deliberation "Zero."

Coach Lowy doesn't recruit players. *He makes them.* Lance points to former team member Matt Pokryfki, who won the southwest regional A singles title, as an example of how good a player can get in four years at A&M, but adds that someone like that is unusual. Lance has yet to field an A (men's) singles entrant in the national tournament. Of course, winning is great for the team members at A&M, but it takes a backseat to participation and camaraderie, not to mention fun. Lance is often reminding his players, "If you win, I'm going to react the same as if you lose."

As coach and former national Collegiate Commissioner, Lance tries to stress the importance of participation for all skill levels and genders. More women play handball at Texas A&M than anywhere else. Somehow, the women here were never told to stick with racquetball and leave handball to the men. In fact, they've been beating male players and other college women for a long time. Some of the best female athletes on campus are now being attracted to this increasingly popular and competitive sport. And, having women in the handball club makes the meetings far more worth attending.

Handball success at Texas A&M isn't really a new thing-it's just the numbers of these players who are. Colonel Don "Johnny" Johnson was winning the Collegiate doubles back in the 1950s. Brothers Cyril and Ozzie Burke were collegiate doubles titlists in the 1960s. But it is especially heartening to see the game gaining new life, the way it is growing here in College Station. We can only hope that this type of program is contagious and spawning programs like it at other universities so that our sport will have future generations enjoying it as we do.

Note: Ozzie Burke and Dan Kennerly were collegiate doubles titlists in the 1960s, not brothers Cyril and Ozzie Burke.

At the national level Aggie women continued to make their mark. Peanut Motal proved that her singles championship in 1985 was no fluke, even though the clear champion, Rosemary Bellini, of the first few years, was not able to play. Motal and Sue Oakleaf advanced easily to the semifinals where they met to see who would continue to the championship final. Sue gave Peanut her toughest challenge on the way to the championship. Peanut won by the score of 21-17, 21-19. Pete Tyson wrote about the finals on page 16 of the August 1986 issue of the USHA's *Handball*:

> Since the inception of the women's championship seven years ago, it's been a battle for second place honors. New York's Rosemary Bellini has dominated the competition with the exception of Diane Harmon's upset win in 1983. Last year, Bellini was sidelined due to injury, throwing her title up for grabs. Peanut Motal won last year's event but honestly felt she earned only the No. 2 spot due to Bellini's absence. Peanut doesn't feel that way anymore as she downed Bellini in this year's final with a convincing 21-4, 21-15 win.

The two Aggies, with their respective doubles partners, would meet in the National Open Doubles finals. The defending champions, Sue Oakleaf and LeaAnn Tyson, were at the top of their game. Peanut Motal and her partner, Allison Roberts, had won three national doubles titles; however, could not overcome the teamwork of Oakleaf and Tyson. Oakleaf and Tyson won the championship in two games 21-16, 21-14.

One of the casualties of handball has always been a person's eyes. Getting hit in the eye by a handball can be a life changing event. Ask Dr. Lavon Anderson, '57, who was a member of the A&M handball club during his student days. He was hit in the eye with a handball and the damage resulted in being nearsighted in one eye and farsighted in the other. It could have been worse if he had lost his eyesight in the eye that was hit. Knowing the possibility and seeing the damage to the eye when hit with a handball caused alarms to be raised among handball enthusiasts. The possibility of eye damage was also known to exist in the games of racquetball and squash. For eye protection, developers came up with a lens-less pair of eye protective glasses. Many eye injuries continued even with the lens-less glasses. As a result, the USHA Board of Directors approved the funding for testing these protective glasses. The testing was done by the Detroit Testing Laboratory and the tests proved that the lens-less glasses were almost useless in protecting the eye from injury when hit with a handball. As a result, the USHA Board of Directors recommended the use of lensed eye guards constructed with polycarbonate lenses of at least three-millimeter thickness in the center. A report of the testing done with the lens-less eye guards can be found on pages 30 and 31 of the October 1989 issue of the USHA's *Handball* magazine. The Texas A&M Recreation Center requires the use of protective eye guards when playing handball or racquetball. The year that the Texas A&M Recreation Center required all players in handball and racquetball to use eye guards cannot be verified.

On 19 June 1988, the USHA Board of Directors followed in the footsteps of the Commissioners of the National Collegiate Handball Tournament, who made the ruling in 1987 that all play in collegiate sanctioned events would require eye guards to be worn properly. The newly adopted rules read: "Any player participating in an USHA-administered handball tournament or championship is required to wear protective eyewear. Protective eyewear is to be worn properly covering the eyes at all times during matches. Refusal to wear protective eyewear properly will result in the player's disqualification." The new ruling became effective 1 July 1988.

Since the introduction of the "family ball" in the early 1980s, the number of women playing handball has gradually increased, but many of the better women players prefer to play with the hardball. As the "family ball' evolved into a much better ball, it became known as the soft ball. A poll, whether to use the hard ball or soft ball for the national tournament, was given to the better women players. The poll proved to be inconclusive. So, the USHA held two distinctive tournaments for women at the national tournament. Those choosing to use the soft ball would be entered in one tournament and another tournament would be held for the women who preferred to use the hard ball. Glorian "Peanut" Motal-Hummel and LeaAnn Tyson won the 1988 National "Softball" Handball Doubles title. The two totally outclassed all competition, winning in the finals 21-3, 21-9. Afterward Motal said, "It was fun to be here and play with LeaAnn instead of against her. I just hope the women's brackets won't be separated next year." Most of the women there echoed her opinion.

Many changes in the formatting and scoring were implemented during the time Lowy was coach. One of the most popular changes was the "drop-down format" which is still being used today in the National Collegiate Handball Tournament and other tournaments around the country. Lowy developed the format as a means to ensure that every player, no matter their level, would be assured of at least three matches at any tournament. The concept was introduced and tried with the women at the 1987 National Collegiate Handball Tournament. In 1988, the format was also used for the men's competition.

The drop-down format did not come into being just as a spur of the moment idea. Lowy worked on a plan and then would meet with his good friend, Rick Hall, in Recreation Sports at A&M to discuss it. This experimentation continued until one day Lowy excitedly told Hall, "I've got it figured out." It was a great plan and has added much more enjoyment for all handball players at various skill levels during tournament play.

The progression of the handball teams and their records under Coach Lowy are covered in Chapters 9, 10 and 11.

February 1991 was another important date in Aggie handball history. For the first time the Aggies had a world champion handball player. Beth Rowley agreed to play doubles with Anna Engele at the World Handball Championships held in Phoenix, Arizona during 4-10 February 1991. Results of the doubles play were reported on page 15 of the April 1991 issue of the USHA's *Handball* magazine. In the first round, Anna Engele/Beth Rowley, the number 2 seeded team, received a bye. In the quarterfinals, Engele/Rowley defeated Drueger/Lohmuellar 21-12, 21-6. In the semifinals, Engele/Rowley defeated Halil/Vallee 21-18, 21-14. In the finals, Engele/Rowley defeated Fraser/Muloin 17-21, 21-18, 11-8 to become world champions. The article described the team's chemistry and strategy to become champions:

> Anna Engele made it a great week for the USA women, winning the women's Open doubles with Dallas' Beth Rowley in an exciting final tiebreaker over current Canadian and US National Champs Lavonah Muloin and Lisa Fraser.
>
> The dominating force in women's handball, Engele has won practically everything this year in singles, but her doubles record hasn't been so great. She may have found the perfect right-side compliment in the strong-armed Rowley. On the left side, Engele is free to roam and spread out with her fluid strokes. but the right-side players need to be able to work in close company. Rowley has a great deal of power with just a short stroke. Many experts, including John Bike (a top ranked pro), feel Rowley only needs a win or two to boost her confidence enough to challenge the top-ranking women in singles.

Whether this doubles pairing builds singles confidence is another question, but her doubles confidence was plenty high during the week in Phoenix. Thus, there was no weakness for the lefty-righty Muloin/Fraser tandem to exploit. Meanwhile, the up-and-back formation of the Canadian pair was caught off-guard by Engele and Rowley's blasts. Still, the match could have gone either way.

Perhaps it was fortunate for the newly formed Engele and Rowley duo to have a tough test in the semis. The No. 2 seeds had their teamwork tested by Diane Vallee and Nancy Kalil for two close games, 21-18, 21-14.

The USHA has always advocated increasing the number of handball players, especially in the United States. In the early 1990s, the USHA held a recruiting contest. It was announced on page 23 of the June 1991 issue of the USHA's *Handball* that the contest winner was the coach of the A&M handball team, Lance Lowy. Of the 250 new handball players recruited during the contest, Lowy recruited 91. Of course, getting new handball players at A&M was never a problem during that time period. The challenge was always the development of the players to a championship level. Coach Lowy was the main person developing the players, but not to be overlooked was the help of other members of the handball club. Of special note is the coaching assistance provided over many years by Stan Lowy, Jeff Bronson, Marvin Harris, Ozzie Burke, Charlie Bokelman, Jack Gressett and Don Johnson. Bokelman started his coaching duties in 1992. Ozzie Burke began his time coaching in 2002 and took over as the primary coach after Lance Lowy announced his retirement to Burke on 22 December 2007. Don Johnson started assisting in 2010 and Jack Gressett started in 2014.

In the April 1992 issue of the USHA's *Handball*, the women's Commissioner handball report was given by a newcomer. The new women's Commissioner was Aggie Beth Rowley who replaced Andra Torrence. As Commissioner, Rowley would also serve as a member of the Board of Directors for the USHA. This position, so important to the ever-increasing number of women handball players, was a great honor for Rowley and Aggies in general. She is the first and only Aggie, to this date, to serve in this prestigious position. She was the fourth women's Commissioner to serve on the Board. In her introductory article Rowley reported: (*Handball*, April 1992, page 28)

> As an introduction, I would like to open my first article as Women's Commissioner by thanking Andra Torrence for everything she has accomplished during her term as the commissioner. When I look at the contributions made by my predecessors (Andra, Nancy Kalil and Maria Higgins), I know I have my work cut out for me if I am to continue to boost the growth and progress that women's handball has made over the years. I look forward to the opportunity and the challenge.

> Three major goals I have are: To organize a ranking system of the women players, get a major sponsor for the Classic and to increase female participation.

> Andra passed ... (NOTE: the rest of her first article was about the routine surrounding women's handball and what has happened recently and what is to happen in the upcoming future).

In 1993, the USHA held its 43rd USHA National Four-Wall Championship. Beth Rowley and her doubles partner, Anna Engele, survived all comers to win the national doubles title.

Also in 1993, the USHA announced that the USHA would become the only distributor of handballs. The new ball would weigh about 58 grams. Spalding, the company that had been producing the handballs known as the Red and White Ace, announced that it would no longer produce those balls. The White Ace was known originally as the "family" ball but, as more players used it and refinements were made, the name gradually changed and became known as the White Ace.

In the 1995 USHA National Four-Wall Championship an Aggie newcomer, Priscilla Kojin, entered in the women's Pro division and got her first glimpse of the skill level of the pros on the women's circuit. In her first match, she was defeated by Jennifer Saunders from Albuquerque 21-7, 21-7. She was also entered in the women's B division. Kojin was seeded in the top four and easily made it into the semifinals. There she met the number 1 seed, Sasha Gawley. Gawley controlled the first game easily to win 21-18. Kojin settled down in the second game and started making some great pass shots and fly kills. Kojin defeated Gawley in the second game 21-16. The momentum of the second game carried over into the tiebreaker and Kojin won 11-7. Kojin dominated the final where she was pitted against Rachel Hall, a former University of Texas handball star. Kojin dominated the match and won going away 21-13, 21-10. Beth Rowley proved that she was still a handball force by winning the senior Women's Open easily dispatching Denise Carideo-Harrington in the final 21-8, 21-8.

The 1990s proved to be the golden years for Aggie women handball players. Not only were they a force at the collegiate level with all of their team championships but they also were a force at the USHA national three- and four-wall handball championships. At the 1995 USHA National Three-Wall Championships held in Toledo, Ohio, Priscilla Kojin showed continued improvement. Entered for the first time in the three-wall championship, she showed how much her game had improved. Beth Rowley reported the action of the women's Open singles. The story was published on page 22 of the October 1995 issue of the USHA's *Handball:*

> The best match of the first round, and arguably of the day, was between Priscilla Kojin of Texas A&M and a New Yorker, Sydell Smith. Playing three-wall for the first time, Priscilla used her height to her advantage, staying in the front court and taking the ball on the fly. She squeaked out the first game, 21-20. Sydell jumped out to a big lead in the second game with good serves followed up by one-wall dinks in the front. She won the second game 21-13. The tiebreaker was a battle, with Priscilla taking the match, 11-9.

Kojin gained valuable experience in her first match, but was not able to come up with a win in the quarterfinals. In the quarters, she was defeated by Yvonne August 21-4, 21-10. In the women's Senior Open, Beth Rowley defeated Kay Sleeper 21-8, 21-2. In the semifinals, Andra Torrence defeated Rowley 21-3, 21-11 to end Rowley's bid for a repeat championship. But Rowley did not leave the tournament without being a winner. She teamed with Yvonne August to take the Open doubles championship. Priscilla Kojin reported the story of the doubles championship. The part of the story referring to Aggies, reported on page 23 of the October 1995 issue of the USHA's *Handball*, follows:

> In the quarterfinals, New Yorkers Dori Ten and Barbara Canton beat Texans Rachel Hall and Priscilla Kojin, and Yvonne August and Beth Rowley beat Robin Sterrett and Tanya Dietzler.

> In the semis, Rosemary Bellini and Andra Torrence defeated Canton and Ten, 21-9, 21-7 and advanced to the final. The other finalist team was decided between August/ Rowley and Allison Roberts and Sheryl Kraft. August and Rowley played very well and took the match in two games 21-9, 21-8.

The final was a real war. On one side: Bellini and Torrence. On the other side: August and Rowley. In the first game, both teams were playing the same way, with the right-side player moving up a little and the left side player covering the back court. Because of this strategy, many rallies were fought in the back between August and Bellini, with deep, high shots hit by both. Bellini and Torrence played very well and took the first game 21-17. In the second game, the strategies seemed to shift. August and Rowley started shooting more and the game was no longer as deep or as high as the first. In this game, August, who played very well through the match with powerful fist shots and great control, consistently hit her kill shots. Rowley, who made very few mistakes throughout the match, started to take her shots in the front court and made numerous corner kills.

In the tiebreaker, Rowley and August established a solid lead, but Bellini and Torrence came back strong, tying the game at 9-9. Bellini hit perfect, very deep shots to both the right and the left, and Torrence served well, giving the other team a difficult time. But August and Rowley stayed in the game and ended up taking the match, 11-9.

Priscilla Kojin made the comment, "I'm a bad player with a good serve." Her handball playing record does not support that personal statement. In the 45th USHA National Championships, Kojin showed she was a budding star and continued to improve. As reported on pages 25 and 26 of the August 1996 issue of the USHA's *Handball*, her play showed the ability to adjust to different styles of play:

In the round of 16, there was only one upset (by seeding measures). Priscilla Kojin of Texas A&M/Dallas/Brazil, the No. 12 seed, defeated Lavonah Madden 21-10, 21-19. With powerful serves to Lavonah's right, Priscilla was able to get a lot of fly kills to end the rallies quickly.

Kojin continued her upset bids, this time against LeaAnn Tyson. After losing the first game 21-9 and being down 16-2 in the second, Kojin was completely frustrated and befuddled as to what to do against Tyson. With nothing to lose at that point, she changed the pace of the game by slowing it down, keeping the ball in play and not taking any chances. LeaAnn began to make errors and Kojin's confidence reappeared. In a very gutsy performance, Priscilla pulled out game two, 21-18. LeaAnn, not exactly sure of how she let that big game and lead slip away, played very cautiously in the tiebreaker. This allowed Priscilla to get into her groove of serving and fly-killing. While LeaAnn had two easy shots at match point, she did not execute and Priscilla won the tiebreaker 11-10.

Engele (Anna Engele, the eventual champ) put a stop to Kojin's "Cinderella" tournament by handily defeating her, 21-12, 21-3 in the semifinal. Priscilla was pleased with the way she played against Anna, claiming that the 15 total points were twice as many as she got against her in the women's Classic in February. She was very impressed with Anna's overall game, claiming she has the best serve she has ever seen and she never makes mistakes.

In the women's doubles Yvonne August and Beth Rowley were not able to repeat as champions. They were defeated in the quarterfinals by Rosemary Bellini and Lavonah Madden 21-7, 18-21, 11-3. Rowley was unable to take the Women's Senior title, losing a very close match in the final to Hall of Famer Rosemary Bellini 10-21, 21-16, 11-9.

As Beth Rowley's tenure as women's Commissioner came to an end she reflected on her accomplishments during her time and provided her last message in her last editorial on page 71 of the August 1996 issue of the USHA's *Handball*. In her last paragraph she wrote, "Finally, I would like to thank everyone for their help over the past four-and-one-half years during my tenure as women's Commissioner. The assistance the women have received from the USHA Board and from the USHA staff, has been remarkable. Every important issue concerning women's handball has been addressed and enthusiastically supported. I look forward to continuing to support handball in other capacities."

As 1997 approached, the A&M handball community was busy anticipating and preparing for the upcoming National Collegiate Handball Championships. This would be the first time this championship would be held on the Texas A&M campus. Displayed here is the information flyer about the tournament that was published on pages 62 and 63 of the February 1997 issue of the USHA's *Handball*.

There are many things for the host university to consider including insuring that all participants are eligible to enter and a full understanding of the rules surrounding the event. The following are the USHA collegiate rules and eligibility for the 1997 tournament:

Rule I: MATRICULATION: Participation is permitted in any collegiate handball contest provided the player is a bona fide matriculated student at any accredited university or college (not a business or trade school) and is regularly enrolled doing full-time work as defined by the regulation of the institution at which he/she is enrolled.

Eligibility of participants shall be verified by letter, with school seal affixed, from the Dean of the Office of Admissions or Registrar prior to the tournament.

Rule II: UNDERGRADUATE:

Participation in collegiate handball shall be limited to four varsity years over a period of five consecutive college years, beginning at the date of matriculation. The point of this rule is to accommodate the accelerated or interrupted student who may be a graduate student or skipped a year, but still fulfills the requirements of this rule. In the event a student's studies are interrupted by military service, the student will still have five years of eligibility exclusive of the time of military service. Freshmen are eligible for competition in handball with the one-year residence rule. Total years of competition shall not exceed four. Senior students requiring less than a full-time academic curriculum in order to graduate will be allowed to participate.

Rule III: GRADUATE PARTICIPATION:

Essentially same as above, but does not count toward a team's points except as provided by Rule II and competes only within the graduate competition.

Players may only participate in one singles event. The seeding committee shall seed the top 16 players in the men's and women's open events. B, C, contenders and novice titles will be decided by drop-down competition. Members of the doubles teams must be from the same institution. Players are permitted to participate in both singles and doubles. Players entered in both singles and doubles competition are eligible to compete in a contenders bracket if eliminated in both divisions in an early round. Players may compete in only one contenders event.

Rule V: SCORING:

Each school entered at the national tournament will be awarded points based on the achievements of its players. There is no limit to the number of participants from any school but a maximum of six men and six women scorers will count toward the men's, women's and combined championships. Players entering both singles and doubles can earn points in only one event. The determinant in awarding points to players competing in both singles and doubles will be the event where most points are won-i.e., combined singles or doubles points. Points awarded in both men and women's competition will be as follows: open singles: 100 for first, 96 for second, 92 for semifinalists, and 88 for quarterfinalists and 86 for round of 16.

B singles: 80 for first, 76 for second, 72 for semifinalists, 68 for quarterfinalists and 64 for round of 16.

C singles: 60 for first, 56 for second, 52 for semifinalists, 48 for quarterfinalists and 44 for round of 16.

Contenders: 40 for first, 36 for second, 32 for semifinalists, 28 for quarterfinalists and 25 for round of 16.

Novice: 20 for first, 16 for second, 12 for semifinalists, 8 for quarterfinalists and 5 for round of 16.

Doubles: 80 for first, 58 for second, 48 for semifinalists, 40 for quarterfinalists and 32 for round of 16.

When a player fails to win a match yet in a point-awarded round, they will receive one half the designated total for that round with half points to be rounded up.

With no recruiting outside the university or scholarships to offer, many wondered how Texas A&M could be so successful in fielding a competitive team at the national level year after year. Obviously, there was a method on how the program was run to be so successful. Those at the national level wanted to know so the United States Handball Association made the decision to report how the Aggies did it. In an article printed on pages 58 and 59 of the December 1997 issue of the USHA's *Handball,* Lance Lowy, handball coach and teacher of essentially all handball classes during his tenure, describes just that:

Anatomy of the Largest College Handball Program

By Lance Lowy, Texas A&M University

Since I have been teaching handball at Texas A&M University for 20 years it is reasonable to say that I have tried many methods to instill a love for the game in my players. To let you know more about the handball program at Texas A&M, let me give you an overview.

There are currently 11 handball classes offered, 10 beginning and one intermediate class. There are 36 students in each of the beginning classes and 24 students in the intermediate class due to the limited court space during a popular recreation time. We use 12 courts in the Student Recreation Center, which means I have three players in every court. Each of my classes lasts 40 minutes per day and meets twice a week. Students receive one hour of academic credit per semester for their handball class and may retake it as many times as they like.

When students want to retake their handball class and cannot take the intermediate class due to class conflicts, I end up with beginners and intermediates in the same class. This is a common occurrence. Of the 40 different activities offered in the Physical Education Activity Program at Texas A&M, handball is the most repeated sport.

My handball classes are an introduction on how to play with adequate time to demonstrate what I want my players to practice for that day and how to do it, but little time for them to practice. I have had to learn how to be very efficient with my use of time, allowing maximum time for my students to practice and play. Outside-of-class practice is highly recommended and my students find this out early as the challenge of playing handball becomes apparent.

In a 15-week semester, here is a progression of teaching that works very well for me: our first week of a semester is an administrative nightmare as the 43,000 students at Texas A&M re-adjust to school life, so no teaching takes place the first week. However, the second week we start in earnest. My beginners start throwing a ball with both hands. This is a character-building time as everyone goes through that awkward sensation ("I've never done anything with my other hand"). I stress five things at this point: Pivot (facing the front wall, pivot on one foot to face a side wall, left foot pivot to throw left-handed): Preparation (elbow pointed out to enhance the elbow in front of the hand for the whip action): Weight Transfer (from back to front foot): Point of Release (occurs just as the weight transfers): Follow Through (end of throwing motion).

I have beginners work on six areas, three with each hand. With their strong hand over throw, their target is the ceiling. With their strong hand sidearm throw, their target is the same height on the front wall that they release the ball. With their strong hand, low sidearm throw, their target is as low on the front wall or front side wall combination as they can get it. I ask them to do 25 repetitions of each drill. I ask only two players to practice in a court at a time for safety purposes.

My intermediate players are allowed to play, but may only use lob serves. The returner is reminded that their target is the ceiling. The second day of the first week, my beginners start bouncing the ball and with a cupped hand, stroking the ball to their target areas. The same strokes with both hands and the same number of repetitions as the first day are used. My intermediates play using three types of Z serves; overhand soft, overhand hard and sidearm hard. The returner is reminded that their return should move the server out of the front court.

The first day of the third week, we combine our second week progression. I have my beginners throw the ball to the front wall, then get in position and return the ball with whatever stroke is necessary. If the ball is above the shoulder, they return the ball with their overhand stroke to the ceiling. If the ball is between their waist and shoulder, they return the ball to the front wall with their sidearm stroke. If the ball is knee high or lower, they will attempt to hit it as low as possible to end the rally. One player at a time performs this drill for as long as necessary or until a hand error occurs. Players rotate as this happens.

The point to stress at this time is for the player to be in position prior to the ball arriving so they may execute their throwing motion properly. Intermediates hit low, power serves and fist-to-the-ceiling returns. Whoever loses the rally rotates out and the third person in the court rotates in. On the second day of the third week, we have one player bounce and hit the ball to the front wall or ceiling, have another player return it, then alternate hitting, to simulate playing. Whoever loses the rally rotates out and the third player rotates in. Intermediates continue their low power serves and fist returns.

The first day of the fourth week, we demonstrate the back-wall return. I stress a two slide-step technique that entails going back a step or two as the ball goes toward the back wall, stopping when the ball hits the back wall, and going forward with two slide steps as the ball rebounds off the back wall. I emphasize being very low with knees and back bent and to follow through with a low sidearm stroke parallel to the floor. We begin practicing this shot with a drill. We toss the ball softly against the back wall, allow it to bounce, and with two slide steps catch up with the ball in order to contact it as low as possible.

When my players become comfortable with their footwork and their results with this drill, then we attempt the real back wall shot. This is self-paced with everyone moving from the drill to the real shot as they are ready. I promote the sword and shield strategy at this point, Kill or pass with their strong hand and return the ball off the back wall with their weak hand. I have beginners and intermediates attend this demonstration because this is my favorite shot and is your back-wall game ever good enough? Everyone does 100 repetitions with both hands on both days of this week.

On the first day of the fifth week, I do an in-court discussion of the various serves and returns. We then go above the court to a viewing area and watch an exhibition match. I demonstrate refereeing essentials and talk about rules. This takes about 30 of our 40 minutes of class time. My intermediates are allowed to play cut-throat or California singles. The second day of the fifth week is spent practicing the low power, Z and lob serves with one person serving, one person returning and the third person rotating in. We do 25 repetitions of each serve with each player. Intermediates are allowed to play.

The seventh through the fourteenth week, we play a ladder-type tournament that keeps everybody busy. The order of the courts in descending order for the ladder tournament is court 1 through court 12. Players are seeded and assigned to a court where there will be two players playing singles and one player refereeing. Each player will play two games a day and referee one. The winner of the first game then plays the player who was refereeing and the loser of the first game becomes the referee. Then, the two players who haven't played each other yet play and the other player referees. The players' results dictate where they play next class. The winner of both games would move up to a court on the ladder next class. The player who wins one and loses one game would stay in that court and the loser of both games would move down a court next class. Two people stay in the top and bottom courts, otherwise only one player stays in a court.

Play is now maximized and the fun begins. In our final week of class, we take a skill test consisting of lob serves, Z-serves, strong hand back wall kills, strong and weak hand ceiling shots and a 30-second rally. We take a final exam on our last day.

In my intermediate class, each court is labeled to practice a serve and return or conditioning. Court One: lob serve-ceiling return. Court Two: four-corner conditioning drill. Court Three: low power serve-fist to the ceiling return. Court Four: conditioning. Court Five: Z-serve, sidearm return. Court Six: conditioning. Court Seven: "Sal" serve. Court Eight: conditioning. Every player changes courts every day and conditions one day a week for the first six weeks. Then, we move to a ladder tournament. With 36 different players coming to play every hour, totaling over 350 players, we definitely have a Handball Program at Texas A&M.

With the number of students Coach Lance Lowy has seen through his classes, it was just a matter of time until one or more of his players started winning at the professional level. In the April 1999 Women's Classic Handball Tournament, Priscilla (Kojin) Shumate, who had shown steady improvement in both her skill and ability to remain calm amid the stress of a close game, defeated Jennifer Roberts 21-20, 21-10 in the finals to earn her first championship check as a pro and became the first Aggie female to become a pro. The first Aggie male to enter the professional ranks was Sal SantaAna. On the weekend of 9-11 April 1999 at a pro qualifier in New York, he defeated Randy Morones, who was ranked number 6 on the pro tour at the beginning of the season but had dropped to number 17 due an eight-month absence. The number 17 ranking required Morones to enter the pro qualifier to get back on the active pro tour. SantaAna defeated Morones 21-9, 21-5 to earn his qualification to play in the upcoming pro stops at St Louis in April and Memphis in May.

Priscilla (Kojin) Shumate is arguably the best women's Aggie handball player to put on a pair of handball gloves. To help bolster that claim would be her dominance in her very first tournament at 1-wall handball. The October 1999 issue of the USHA's *Handball*, pages 8 and 9, describes her success at that tournament:

Shumate's win as big as Texas 1-wall rookie walks away a champ

The women who have dominated one-wall for the last several years have all been superb athletes. But this year's women's champion, new to the title as well as to the one-wall version of the sport, is truly phenomenal.

Fans gasped at the power and control exhibited by Priscilla Shumate of Houston in sub-duing all her opposition, including a 21-20 victory over defending champion Karen McConney in the first round.

Shumate's dominance might have been foreshadowed by her recent victories in the nation's biggest women's four-wall tournaments. Still, to be able to control the play against veteran one-wall players on their home courts makes her victory all the more amazing.

Priscilla Shumate,
2000 Four-Wall, One-Wall,
Three-Wall and World Champion

Gladys Miranda, who defeated Barbara Canton-Jackson 21-15, 21-19, became Shumate's second victim, falling 21-11, 21-12. This triumph placed the Texan in the final.

In a battle of former champions, Dori Ten outlasted Dee Stringfield 21-19, 21-12. After Tracy Davis bested Sydell Smith 21-15, 21-13, she edged Ten 21-19, 20-21, 11-6 to earn the right to challenge the newcomer.

But strong and fearless though she was, Davis could not surmount the awesome serves and overwhelming power of Shumate, who won the championship in two straight games 21-9, 21-16.

It should be noted that in the second game of her first match against the defending champ, Shumate defeated McConney 21-4. As the defending champ, McConney would have been seeded first and as a newcomer to the one-wall game, Shumate would have been pitted against the defending champ.

Priscilla Shumate did not participate in the 1999 Women's National Four-Wall due to a work conflict, but was there to participate in the first-ever pro stop in Dallas. There she met the current National Four-Wall Champion, Anna Christoff, in the finals. Christoff got off to a great start and won the first game 21-7. Shumate entered the second game more determined and focused. Shumate won the second game 21-19 setting up a tiebreaker for the championship. In the story written covering the tournament, the tiebreaker action was reported in the April 2000 issue of the USHA's *Handball,* page 40:

> The tiebreaker was close throughout. Christoff scored on several perfectly placed ceiling shots that fell into the left rear corner. Shumate smacked power serves to the right and left that resulted in aces. She had an opportunity to win at 10-7 but floored a kill attempt, relinquishing the serve.

> Christoff re-entered the service box and scored one point on a corner kill, but lost the serve on an attempted kill that rolled into the front wall. Shumate again served, this time ending a long rally with a corner kill to the right that won the tiebreaker 11-8.

> Shumate took home the $1,250 first prize, and Christoff left with the $1,000 second prize.

Just as Sue (Oakleaf) Sellars, an Aggie, became the first ever Women's National Collegiate Handball Singles Champion Priscilla (Kojin) Shumate, an Aggie, won the first ever women's pro stop in Dallas. And speaking of first ever, the Aggie men's team won its first ever team title at the USHA National Collegiate Championship held at the Texas A&M Recreation Center 21-24 February 2002. (*For the story see the Team Chapter 2000-2009.*)

Shumate wasn't through for the year, but continued winning to make 2000 a very memorable year.

The cover of the December 2000 issue of the USHA's *Handball* magazine and inside story states her dominance of women's handball for that time period.

WATERFORD CRYSTAL WORLD CHAMPIONSHIPS: WOMEN'S FOUR-WALL OPEN SINGLES

Simple adjective for Shumate: Best

By Jennifer Schmitt

Priscilla Shumate has stormed into dominance of women's handball in a way that has never been accomplished until now. She proved her amazing versatility in winning the national four-wall title, followed by the national one-wall and three-wall. This was a first in Women's open play in the same year.

What could possibly top this? Well, the World Championships, held every three years, completed this incredible year for Shumate.

She started the tournament cautiously, thinking maybe this dream couldn't come true. She hadn't cut her hair in a long time, thinking it had brought her luck. She was also nursing a shoulder that had been nagging her all year.

But no one could detect uncertainty from watching her play. She displayed crisp, clean shots, few emotions, and the same steady tenacity, regardless of the score.

Shumate said she had come to the tournament thinking: "I've had a great year. It's OK not to win this." She thought this was a good attitude, putting no pressure on herself and playing relaxed all the way to the final. But when the final came and she stepped into the court to play Anna Christoff for the world title, she realized: "It's not OK to lose. I do care, and I'm going to win this title."

Then the pressure was on. She said she had never been so focused as in this match.

Christoff started strongly and repeatedly passed her opponent on the tough left glass wall, going up 14-10. But nothing seemed to affect Shumate, who started chipping away at the deficit.

When Shumate closed within a point at 16-15, it was Christoff who started to get flustered and called time out. After Shumate delivered some great power serves to go ahead 19-16, her foe called time again. Then Shumate pounded another awesome serve for 20 before struggling through a tough rally, which she ended with a decisive right-side kill to win Game 1.

Shumate later cited her comeback as the turning point in the match. She was confident in the second game, even as Christoff got off to an early advantage. Trailing 7-6, Shumate called time to regroup, and she returned with a well-timed ace. It tied the game and restored her momentum as she forged ahead 17-9. Though Christoff flurried with a surge of flat kills, all she could muster was 13 points before Shumate closed out the match.

Brian Shumate couldn't wait to congratulate his wife, and he quickly entered the court. Priscilla said he had played her with the White Label to train for the tournament, even though he had to prepare for his events too. Now, that's love!

Christoff and Lisa Fraser Gilmore, who had met in the two prior world finals and in many other finals over the last 10 years, collided in one semifinal. Though Christoff led most of the first game, Fraser rallied to win 21-18. But Christoff rebounded by blasting to a 21-7 Game 2 win. Helped by some unusual Fraser errors, Christoff came out on top in the tiebreaker 11-4.

December 2000

On her feet or from her knees, Shumate wasn't shy about shooting against Christoff ... though some of the play did tend to take place in rather close quarters in the women's open four-wall final on the glass court.

In the other semi, Shumate defeated Fiona Shannon, Ireland's national champion. Shannon played well through the first half of Game 1, but then Shumate turned on her power serve and Shannon was left scrambling. The second game was more of the same.

The Irishwoman was the only semifinalist who was thoroughly pushed in the quarters, outlasting Jennifer Schmitt 11-4. The biggest first-round match was the Amber Rounseville-Jessica Gawley duel. This time Gawley came out on top 11-5.

Some new talent of note in this division:
■ Courtney Peixoto continues to improve and should be pushing the top players in no time.
■ This year's national B champion, Vanessa Kamp, gave Schmitt a bit of a struggle in the first round.
■ Ireland's Roisin Faulkner played well against Rachel Kos.

First round: Priscilla Shumate (Albuquerque) d. Courtney Peixoto (Watsonville, Calif.) 4, 6; Lavonah Madden (Antigonish, Canada) d. Julie Long (Dublin) 5, 4; Jennifer Schmitt (Tucson) d. Vanessa Kamp (Bloomfield Hills, Mich.) 15, 4; Fiona Shannon (Antrim, Ireland) d. Sabrina Zamora (Pasadena, Calif.) 4, 7; Lisa Fraser Gilmore (Winnipeg) d. Marla Higgins (Albuquerque) 4, 5; Rachel Kos (Round Rock, Texas) d. Roisin Faulkner (Cavan, Ireland) 9, 9; Jessica Gawley (Regina, Canada) d. Amber Rounseville (Sioux Falls, S.D.) 15, (10), 5; Anna Christoff (St. Paul, Minn.) d. Cherylann Mendonca (Sacramento) 2, 1.
Quarters: Shumate d. Madden 5, 16; Shannon d. Schmitt 10, (14), 4; Fraser d. Kos 4, 5; Christoff d. Gawley 7, 4.
Semis: Shumate d. Shannon 13, 4; Christoff d. Fraser (18), 7, 4.
Final: Shumate d. Christoff 16, 13.

Alesi drives from deep court with Roberts, Shumate and Schmitt in position.

Team Aggie averts agony

Priscilla Shumate's cry of "Go, Aggies!" resonated well after she and Lynn Alesi held on to tip sisters Allison Roberts and Jennifer Schmitt in an 11-10 tiebreaker in the women's doubles final.

"I thought Anna (Christoff, last year's singles and doubles champ) was going to play with Megan (Mehilos) again," Shumate said. "And I thought about how neat it would be for Lynn and me to team up–the up-and-comers with the established players. It didn't materialize, but it was still fun because Lynn's coached by Charlie Bokelman, who also coached me at Texas A&M."

Having never played together before, Shumate and Alesi watched the other teams to decide on a strategy.

"We watched Sabrina (Zamora) and Tracy (Davis) play their first match, and they looked really good," Shumate said. "We decided to play the same kind of up-and-back formation they used. After all, I'm 6 feet tall, so I'm a pain to have in the front."

Zamora/Davis couldn't get it past the lanky Shumate, and Alesi was there for everthing that did get by her.

However, the final was much closer.

"They beat us fairly easily in the first game," Shumate said. "Jen's defense was great and Allie was pumped, so we got pounded in spite of the fact that we thought we were playing well.

"We got off to a better start in the second game. Lynn was extremely reliable in the back court. She was out past 70 feet and making shots. So I knew I didn't have to force anything and was able to play very relaxed in the front court.

"We were up big in the tiebreaker and Lynn and I must have served five or six times at 10. It was a matter of survival. We just stayed in there a little longer to win."

It was another story for the Roberts sisters.

"That was so sad," Roberts said. "To come all the way back and get to 10 and then get them out so many times, that hurt. Jenny shouldn't have even been playing on her broken foot. To work that hard and get so close, it hurts."

The sisters found out early that there would be no picking on Shumate's inexperienced partner.

"Lynn played outstanding," Roberts said. "She hit the crack on the left on her pass shots about 10 times. She got everything back and hit some really good shots."

Roberts/Schmitt earned the final with a semifinal win over one-wall champs Theresa McCourt/Anna Calderon 21-17, 21-11.

First round: Sabrina Zamora/Tracy Davis (Calif./N.Y.) d. Debra Forrester/Maggie Grelle (N.M./Mass.) 17, 3; Theresa McCourt/Anna Calderon (N.Y.) d. Robin Sterrett/Andra Stapleton (Ill./Tenn.) 5, 7; Jennifer Schmitt/Allison Roberts (Ariz./Ill.) d. Carly Stickles/Melody Ruiz (Canada/N.Y.) 3, 4.
Semis: Priscilla Shumate/Lynn Alesi (Ind./Texas) d. Zamora/Davis 4, 0; Schmitt/Roberts d. McCourt/Calderon 17, 11.
Final: Shumate/Alesi d. Schmitt/Roberts (13), 8, 10.

Two Aggies team up to win the USHA National Three-Wall Doubles Championship.

(*Handball*, December 2002, page 7)

As the name Texas A&M became more frequent in the game of handball, another significant event added to the Aggie history. The Aggies were in the planning stages of hosting their second USHA National Collegiate Handball Tournament. Published on pages 62 and 63 of the December 2001 issue of the USHA's *Handball* were the entry forms and information about the next tournament:

COLLEGIATE HANDBALL

2002 USHA National Collegiate Championships

Feb. 21-24 at Texas A&M University, College Station, Texas

Site: Rec Center, Texas A&M campus. Phone: 979-845-7826 or 979-458-2652. Fax: 979-845-0838. E-mail: L-Lowy@HLKN.tamu.edu.

Eligibility: See official USHA collegiate rules. Verification of full-time student status from university registrar or admissions office must accompany entry form. Eye protection is mandatory.

Entry fee: $40 singles, $50 doubles. Non-USHA members may join at the tournament ($10).

Mail entry to: Coach Lowy, Texas A&M University, Rec Center #241, College Station, Texas 77843-4250. Make checks payable to Texas A&M Handball.

Deadline: Friday, Feb. 8. Must arrive by Wednesday, Feb. 20, as play will begin at 8 a.m. Thursday, Feb. 21.

Awards: T-shirts to all participants. Trophies to semifinalists and finalists in all divisions. First- and second-place trophies in team competition.

Lodging: Hilton Hotel, 801 University Drive East, College Station, Texas 77840. Phone: 979-693-7500 or 800-225-5466. Fax: 979-260-1931. E-mail: www.hilton.com. Reservation deadline is Thursday, Jan. 31. Single and double room rate is $79. Triple and quad room rate is $84. Rate includes full breakfast in the Plaza Cafe. Rates also are available at the Best Western Chimney Inn for $79 for one to four people (Best Western is one block from Hilton and you get the Hilton's breakfast buffet). Phone: 800-528-234. E-mail: www.bestwestern.com. Shuttle will be provided from airport to hotel and from Rec Center to Hilton. Mention the National Collegiate Handball Championships when making reservations.

Airlines: American and Continental serve College Station. Houston is 90 miles away and Dallas is 180.

Seeding: Coaches will make the draw at 3 p.m. Wednesday, Feb. 20, at the Rec Center. Players meeting will be at 7 p.m. at the Rec Center.

Format: Women will play five-division drop-down format. Men will play seven-division drop-down format.

Play begins: 8 a.m. Thursday, Feb. 21.

Division: ☐ Men ☐ Women

My usual division of play is: ☐ Open ☐ A ☐ B ☐ C ☐ Novice

Name: _____ School: _____

Campus address: _____

City/state/zip: _____

Campus phone: _____ E-mail: _____

Permanent address: _____

City/state/zip: _____

(Include verification of full-time student status) *See Scholarship Opportunities on pgs. 67 & 71

Waiver and release: The undersigned, in consideration of this entry being accepted, hereby assumes all responsibility for any and all risk of damage or injury that may occur or arise from participation in the above event. The undersigned specifically releases and discharges Texas A&M University, the Texas A&M Rec Center, the USHA, their agents, representatives, successors or assigns for any or all injuries which may arise from participation.

Signature: _____ Date: _____

COLLEGIATE HANDBALL

Intercollegiate rules

Rule I: Matriculation

A. Participation is permitted in any collegiate handball contest provided the player is a bona fide matriculated student at an accredited university or college (not a business or trade school, etc.), and is regularly enrolled, doing full-time work as defined by the regulations of the institution at which he or she is enrolled.

B. Eligibility of participants shall by verified by letter, with school seal affixed, from the office of the dean of admissions or registrar before the tournament.

Rule II: Participation

A. Participation in collegiate handball will be limited to four national collegiate tournaments over a period of five consecutive college years. This rule is intended to allow full-time undergraduates, part-time seniors and full-time graduate students to play in four national collegiate tournaments within five years from the time they played in their first such tournament as an undergraduate. Exception to this rule must be appealed to the national collegiate commissioner. (The intent of this rule is to encourage participation of new handball players at the collegiate level; it is not for veteran players who may have returned to graduate school.)

B. In the event of a student's regular attendance being interrupted by military service in any of the armed forces, the period of eligibility shall be five years exclusive of time in military service, except the years in which, during the player's military service, he or she may have represented an educational institution.

C. Freshmen are eligible for varsity competition in handball.

D. Transfer students or graduates from a junior college may continue handball competition without complying with the one-year residence rule. Total years of competition shall not exceed four.

E. Senior students requiring less than a full-time academic curriculum to graduate will be allowed to participate.

Rule III: Tournament play

A. Players may participate in only one singles event.

B. Members of a doubles team must be from the same institution.

C. Players are permitted to participate in both singles and doubles.

D. Players entered in both singles and doubles competition are eligible to compete in a contenders bracket if they are eliminated in both divisions in an early round. Players may compete in only one contenders event.

Rule IV: Scoring

A. Each school represented at the national tournament will be awarded points based on the achievements of its players. There is no limit to the number of participants from any school, but a maximum of six men and six women scorers will count toward the men's. women's and combined championships.

Players entering both singles and doubles can earn points in only one event. The determinant in awarding points to players competing in both singles and doubles will be the event in which most points are won, i.e., combined singles points or doubles points.

Special note

The tournament host shall have the option to shorten the matches by using a best two-out-of-three to 15 points and 11-point tiebreaker for first two rounds of play.

As with any collegiate competition there are rules to be enforced and followed.

For the 2002 National Collegiate Handball Tournament these are the rules governing eligibility and participation. The rules are established, maintained, reviewed yearly and changed when necessary, by the USHA National Collegiate Handball Commissioners. As the host, Texas A&M is required to ensure these rules are observed and there are no violations.

Additionally, each entry must be checked against past performance/performances to have the entrants in the proper seeding within each division-male or female.

With the home field advantage, the Aggie Men were able to secure their first team championship victory in the National Collegiate Handball Tournament. The men's team would follow that with their second team victory in 2003. See the coverage of these victories under the team 2000-2009 chapter.

While Shumate was making her history at the top level, another Aggie, Sal SantaAna, began to make his presence felt among the men's professional ranks. After qualifying for some of the pro tournaments through pro qualifiers, SantaAna was able to gain ranking high enough to be listed among the top professionals. This meant no pro qualifiers, but it also meant he would be seeded against the best players of the pro ranks. At the pro stop in early March 2003 in Concord, California, SantaAna was defeated in the first round by Vince Munoz, ranked number two, and then moved into the consolation bracket. There he defeated Sean Lenning, ranked number 12, who currently is the winningest Open doubles player in the history of USHA handball (since 1953), and then, Anton Wilson, ranked number nine, in the semifinals. In the finals he was defeated by Marcos Chavez. The consolation win moved Chavez to eight in the pro rankings. Chavez was in 5th place in all time doubles wins with 13. Lenning's total was 16 doubles wins. The rankings listed were after the Concord pro stop. SantaAna was ranked number16.

At the next pro tournament, held in Anchorage, Alaska, SantaAna was defeated in the first round by the number-four seed, John Bike. This moved SantaAna into the consolation bracket where he defeated number 11 ranked Dan Armijo in the first match. In the semifinals, he defeated number 14 ranked Chris Tico. In the finals, he earned the consolation crown by defeating number 2 ranked Walter O'Conner.

Going into 2005-2006, Coach Lowy and the Aggies team knew they had a lot of work to do. In addition to making an improved showing at the National Collegiate Handball Tournament, the Aggies were the host team this year. The following information was printed on page 65 in the February 2006 issue of the USHA's *Handball*:

COLLEGIATE HANDBALL

Team spirit makes the collegiates a don't-miss tournament.

Accept the challenge: Enter '06 collegiates

By Ian Kelly
Collegiate development coordinator

For most of us, college is a time to leave home to network and hone our social skills. For others, it means attending classes to obtain a diploma that will lead to success in life. For a talented few, it is an opportunity to join a sports team to compete and represent the school.

And for the elite, college has students who partake in all three. These are the players on college handball teams. These men and women stand out from the crowd and play a vintage sport centuries old, a sport they know doesn't get the hype it should.

These are the players who are devoted and driven to represent their colleges. These are the players who bleed their schools' colors and live to compete. These are the players who will participate in the 2006 USHA National Collegiate Championships.

Do you have the spirit to represent your school at the best collegiate tournament in the nation? Do you want to have fun and compete with the finest handball players of your age?

If so, come to the 2006 collegiates hosted by Texas A&M in College Station. With more than 200 college players, you will have the chance to compete among friends and rivals for prestigious awards and pride.

Some 42 colleges participated in the 2005 championships, and the USHA hopes to see at least five new colleges playing in 2006. There is no team too small or too large to compete at the championships, and that is why we would like to see you and your friends participate and enjoy the biggest collegiate event of the year.

Hurry! Deadline is Feb. 8! Be sure to have all your paperwork for being a USHA member and the official verification of full-time or graduating senior status from the registrar or admissions office with the official school seal accompanying the entry form.

Code of Conduct for all players

1. Players shall refrain from possessing or using drugs (except for medical purposes) while traveling, competing, socializing and/or using host facilities.
2. Players shall refrain from consuming alcohol while traveling, competing or spectating.
3. Players shall refrain from excessive arguing with referees, tournament officials, coaches or other players.
4. Players shall treat other players with respect.
5. Players shall adhere to the rules of the game as stated in the USHA rulebook.
6. Players shall adhere to the rules and regulations of the host facility and hotels.
7. Players shall demonstrate good citizenship and good sportsmanship and shall exemplify the spirit of handball at all times.

Code of Conduct for all parents

1. Parents shall support players, coaches, tournament officials and referees in a positive manner.
2. Parents shall adhere to the rules and regulations of the host facility and hotels.
3. Parents shall refrain from arguing with players, coaches, other parents, tournament officials or referees.
4. Parents shall demonstrate good sportsmanship and exemplify the spirit of handball.

Code of Conduct for all coaches

1. Coaches shall support players in a positive manner.
2. Coaches shall refrain from using alcohol, tobacco or drugs while coaching.
3. Coaches shall adhere to the rules and regulations of the host facility and hotels.
4. Coaches shall refrain from arguing with players, other coaches, parents, tournament officials or referees.
5. Coaches shall adhere to the rules of the game as stated in the USHA rulebook.
6. Coaches shall treat participants, spectators and officials with fairness and respect.
7. Coaches shall ensure, as much as possible, safety of each player.
8. Coaches shall model good sportsmanship and exemplify the spirit of handball.

Violation of the Code of Conduct may result in:
■ Ejection from the game or match.
■ Ejection from the tournament.
■ Forfeiture of any individual or team awards.
■ Ejection from the tournament if ejected from the tournament hotel(s).
■ Forfeiture of all games or matches won and possible team elimination from current and future USHA-sponsored or -endorsed events.

The tournament director and/or USHA representative shall make decisions regarding violations. For collegiate events, the USHA Collegiate Disciplinary Committee shall make decisions regarding violations. Please be sure you cooperate with this important USHA initiative.

As in the past, the Aggies had to ensure compliance with the rules and verify all of the player qualifications. Following is the entry form that was used for each player:

2006 USHA National Collegiate Championships
Feb. 22-26 at Texas A&M University, College Station, Texas
(All players must provide official verification of full-time student status in order to play)

Eligibility: Must be a full-time college student and current USHA member, or part-time if a documented graduating senior (see official USHA collegiate rules on facing page). Official verification of full-time or graduating senior status from the registrar or admissions office with the official school seal must accompany entry form. Class schedule slips are not valid. Contact Dr. Mike Steele at steelem@pacificu.edu or call 503-352-2806 for eligibility questions.

Site: Texas A&M Rec Center, College Station, Texas. Phone: 979-458-2652.

Entry fee: $50 per player for singles, $60 if also playing doubles. USHA membership of $10 may be paid at the tournament. Membership is required.

Mail entry to: Make entry fee check payable to Texas A&M Handball. Make membership check payable to USHA. Mail entry fee, entry form and verification letter to Texas A&M University, Student Recreation Center #241, College Station, TX 77843-4250, Attn: Coach Lance Lowy.

Deadline: Feb. 8. Deadline will be adhered to strictly. Entries received after Feb. 8 will be returned unopened.

Rules: USHA rules apply. Eyeguards are mandatory.

Awards: To all singles, doubles and team finalists.

Lodging: • Homewood Suites, 950 University Drive East, College Station, TX 77840. Phone: 979-846-0400. Fax: 979-846-0700. E-mail: jodyl@intermtn.biz. Web site:www.collegestation.homewoodsuites.com. One king bed and one queen fold-out couch with cooking area (sleeps four), $89.
• Hawthorne Suites, 1010 University Drive East, College Station TX 77840. Phone: 979-695-9500. Fax: 979-695-9501. E-mail: tx376sales@aol.com. Web site: www.choicehotels.com. Two queen beds and one queen fold-out couch (sleeps six), $75.
Both hotels offer complimentary breakfast and provide airport shuttles. Shuttles between these hotels and the Rec Center will be provided. Mention the USHA National Collegiates to receive these rates.

Directions: Take University Dr. exit off Hwy. 6. Hotels will be on left behind McAlister's Deli as you drive to campus.

Information: Contact Coach Lowy at L-Lowy@hlkn.tamu.edu or 979-458-2652.

Seeding: Preliminary seeding will take place Feb. 8. Seeding meeting will take place at 2 p.m. Feb. 22 at the Rec Center. Coaches only; no players will be allowed in this meeting. Player representatives of their schools are not considered coaches. Independent players or players without coaches should contact their regional commissioners with seeding information.

Doubles: There will be a limit of 16 teams in each division: open, B and women's. Each school may enter one team in open, one in B and one in women's. Multiple teams from the same school in the same division will be accepted if fewer than 16 schools are entered. If there is an open or A player on a team, the team must play open doubles. B doubles is for B or lower division players.

Play begins: 4 p.m. Wednesday, Feb. 22.

Name: _____ School: _____ Phone: _____

Campus address: _____ E-mail address: _____

Permanent address: _____

Partner: _____ (schools with more than one team on a space-available basis)

I want to enter: [ ] Singles [ ] Open doubles [ ] B doubles [ ] Women's doubles.
Seeding information: I played in this event last year and finished in the [ ] open, [ ] A, [ ] B [ ] C, [ ] Intermediate, [ ] Challengers, [ ] Contenders, [ ] Novice, [ ] Consolation. Further, I finished in the [ ] round of 32, [ ] round of 16, [ ] quarterfinals, [ ] semifinals, [ ] finals. This is my first collegiate tournament [ ]. List tournaments that you have played this year, with division and result [attach extra sheet if necessary]:

Waiver and release: The undersigned, in consideration of this entry being accepted, hereby assumes all responsibility for any and all risk of damage or injury that may occur or arise from participation in this event. The undersigned specifically releases and discharges Texas A&M University, the USHA, their agents, representatives or assigns for any and all injuries that may arise from participation. My signature below also verifies that I will subscribe to all the provisions of the USHA Code of Conduct for this tournament. (Code of Conduct on Page 67)

Signature: _____ Date: _____

66 FEBRUARY 2006

This event was the largest National Collegiate Handball Championship tournament in the history of USHA. A total of 310 handball players played in the tournament-209 men and 101 women. Of the 63 colleges and universities that had handball programs, 37 sent handball players to A&M. There were 11 colleges and universities from Ireland for a total of 48 at the A&M tournament. Obviously, there was a lot of planning and coordination to handle all of the challenges that are always present in an event of this size. But the Aggies did it with class and professionalism. Considering that each of the 310 players were guaranteed a minimum of three games, and many played more, the magnitude of this tournament using the drop-down format, which all felt got the correct level of each player playing against those of nearly equal skill level, was mind boggling. As one coach said, "I hope Coach Lowy has fully trained all of us in the system before he retires." As was written in the April 2006 issue of the USHA's *Handball,* "Texas A&M did a splendid job of hosting the event Feb. 23-26 in College Station."

Results of tournaments other than the Aggieland Classic and the USHA National Collegiates are not a part of this history; however, the 2007 USHA Masters Singles/George Lee Invitational had such a successful Aggie field that it is worthwhile being a part of this story.

In the Open field, two brothers, Marshall and Dutch Lowy, squared off for the prize money to go to the champion and second place. In this match, Marshall came out on top 21-13, 21-4.

Marshall (left) and Dutch with their Open Championship and 2nd place plaques

Dylan Van Brunt (right) with his A Championship plaque

(*Handball*, April 2007, page 21)

Aggie Dylan Van Brunt won the A division championship by defeating Rich Tomaselli 8-21, 21-17, 11-2. Josh Smith, another Aggie, won the B division by defeating Duane Constantino 21-17, 21-14. In the 100-Plus doubles championship Ozzie Burke and Charlie Bokelman won that division by defeating Bob Frisch and Frank Swehosky 21-7, 21-2.

And, in the Masters singles part of the tournament, Aggie Wayne Neumann proved victorious in the 65 Plus division. Vern Roberts takes us through the matches on the way to Neumann's victory reported on page 25 of the April 2007 issue of the USHA's *Handball*:

> Wayne Neumann won his first national title in what he described as a "perfect storm". Everything fell into place just when he was on the ropes.
>
> Not too many people can say they lost the first game of their last three matches and still won the tournament. But that's exactly what Neumann survived in the 65-plus.
>
> Neumann took a quarterfinal tiebreaker over Dennis Moser, won by default after losing the first to Harry Scott in the semis and then prevailed in a three-game final over Mike Driscoll.
>
> Of course, there's an old adage about preparation and luck, and Neumann was primed to make his breaks. As a city planner in Missouri City, Texas, he was recently the high-point recipient in the workout logs. That's no small feat when you're 65.
>
> "I feel your body is like a machine that needs oil every day," Neumann said. "A machine is going to freeze up. I feel like I've got the momentum, so I can't stop now."

Neumann hitting a shot in the finals

(*Handball*, April 2007, page 25)

His regimen consists of handball games three days a week and on-court practice three days a week. Top that off with weights three times a week and three bike workouts and you've got on oiled (and tired) machine.

Against Moser and then Driscoll, Neumann could feel the momentum turning his way as the match progressed. Even though he held

a comfortable 16-6 lead in the final only to lose the first game, Neumann

had the recent match with Moser to recall.

"I just told myself to keep going and not give up on any shots," Neumann said. "In both matches, the adrenaline kept coming. I went for every ball. I felt strong at the end."

Neumann has played in national events occasionally since 1983, but work and family took priority.

"My mom always said to develop good habits, and over time I've excelled at handball because I've kept at it," he said. "Work extra hard and eventually you succeed."

In the semifinals, there was some hard-working handball when Driscoll outhustled the scrambling Vince San Angelo. The length of each rally may have taken a toll on Driscoll, eligible for the 70s next year. Neumann knew he was fortunate that Scott's injury had given him the semifinal win. After taking the first game 21-9, Scott pulled a groin muscle and had to stop.

Neumann also knew he had a great opportunity as it's his first year in the 65s and Ernie Virgili hadn't entered.

"I played Ernie in Houston (in 2005) and lost," Neumann said. "That guy's a machine."

Maybe people who see Neumann play will start saying the same thing about him.

With the retirement of Lowy from Texas A&M and no one who played handball teaching the Kinesiology handball course, the end results were beginning to show in the number of players on the Aggie handball team and the fall off of the team's competitiveness at the National Collegiate Handball Tournament. This result was particular obvious with only three Aggie women participating in the 2009 nationals.

The term Kinesiology became the descriptive curricula for the Physical Education (PE) courses that thousands of Aggies were familiar. The change had been discussed by the A&M Health and Physical Education Department for some time but had never made a move for change. Kinesiology is more descriptive of the courses offered. The State of Texas passed a law in the early 1990's that stated no department in any college or university in the state could list Physical Education as a course more than 6 times in its curriculum. As a result, Kinesiology replaced the previous use of Physical Education in most college and university curricula. The use of the term "Kinesiology" began at Texas A&M with the 1992-93 Undergraduate Catalog.

Having participated in handball essentially all of his life, winning many tournaments at different levels, being an assistant coach of the Aggie team since 2002, then as the head coach beginning in December 2007, Ozzie Burke was accorded another significant honor from the United States Handball Association by being named a USHA "ACE" in 2010. This honor was that he, along with help from Kayla Jones, Beth Rowley and Houston Handball, pulled off a very successful National Collegiate Handball Tournament amidst the split between USHA and the World Professional Handball group and did so having to drive, plan, supervise and coordinate at a facility 2½ hours from home.

In the national Collegiate Commissioners meeting between the 2015 and 2016 National Collegiate Handball Tournament, the decision was made to change the rules for naming All-American handball players. The talented players coming to the collegiate tournament from Ireland really were not American players although many had been named All-American based on their finish at the annual tournament. The Commissioners felt that All-Americans should be players from American colleges and universities. The rule change for the 2016 National Collegiate Handball Tournament and each succeeding year thereafter would honor the top four "American" players in the Open field-two men and two women.

It would be appropriate to mention those who taught the handball classes beginning in the 1920s; however, that is not possible. The Texas A&M yearly catalogs list the faculty and staff each year. The problem in identifying those who taught handball is that the faculty is listed by Department and College and not the specific subjects taught. I do know that Herman Segrest, the handball club sponsor when the author was a student here, taught handball classes. Others known to have taught the subject are Robert Merski, Bob Fennessey, Emil Mamaliga, Eric Hunter, Dennis Corrington, Mike Thornton, Seay, Kayla Jones, Kara Edwards and the author. One name is missing from this list and for a very specific reason. No one who has ever taught handball at A&M, or possibly anywhere else, can match or even come close to having taught handball to the unbelievable number of students Lance Lowy taught. By adding the numbers by year for the fall, spring and most summer sessions for 29 years the total is over 26,000 students taught by one person. He alone, with the teaching of handball classes and coaching of the A&M handball team, is responsible for a large portion of the success of handball at Texas A&M.

The year 1999-2000 can be viewed as a year that began a decline in the number of students potentially exposed to the game of handball. What had been for years on end four required semesters of Kinesiology(Physical Education), was now one semester of Health and Fitness and three semesters of physical exercise in some sport. The same requirement held for the following year. The following is found on page 18 of the 2001-2002 Undergraduate Catalog:

> As the ancient scholars knew and as modern research has confirmed, the development of the body as well as the mind is an integral part of the educational process. Kinesiology requirements are to be fulfilled by completing KINE 198 (previously listed as KINE 199) Health and Fitness and any other "ONE" (author's emphasis) KINE 199 course. KINE 199 used to fill University Core Curriculum requirements must be taken S/U. Transfer students with fewer than 2 hours of Kinesiology credit must meet the KINE 198 requirement either by transfer of credit or by taking the course at Texas A&M.

It soon became apparent that those who make curricula decisions no longer believed in the adage that a part of the educational process should be development of a sound body. The requirement for all undergraduate students to take KINE 198 and 1 hour of KINE 199 would continue through the 2013-2014 year. Afterward, the requirement was eliminated except for those with a major of Kinesiology.

By the 2017-18 academic year the impact of those decisions on handball was enormous. Only two Aggies were available for the 2018 National Collegiate Handball Tournament and handball was being taught by non-handball players only one semester per year. And, there were only five regular handball players at Texas A&M. They were Charles Bokelman, Ozzie Burke, Jack Gressett, Kayla Jones and Don Johnson. All, except Kayla, were well past the spring of their lives and as we looked around and ponder the future of handball at Texas A&M, there simply wasn't any sign of a revival and the possibility of handball at A&M becoming ancient history was very real.

To further illustrate how the decision to no longer require one hour of Kinesiology 199 impacted enrollment consider that there were only 4,155 students enrolled in Kinesiology 199 courses during the fall of 2019. That is basically 6 percent of the 69,425 students enrolled. In the spring semester of 2020, there were only 4,257 students enrolled in Kinesiology 199. The spring 2020 enrollment of 64,961 was very close to 6.5 percent of the students enrolled. Kinesiology 199-handball is not a course that students have a familiarity from high school. Golf, dancing, weight training and many other physical activities offered are more familiar from earlier years, so those courses are much easier to fill. Enrollment in the handball classes is key to having a highly competitive handball team and is the reality Coach Lowy and those before him enjoyed as the Texas A&M handball team coach/sponsors. Most young people of today want instant gratification so the enticement to enroll in handball classes by offering $300 to each who finishes with a passing grade has not proven an effective way to recruit. The $300 is applied to the next semester's fees which means the student will never touch, feel or see the money. For most, the $300 is not an incentive to enroll in Kinesiology 199-handball.

We are all familiar with hundreds of movies where the main character/characters reach the lowest point where survival, be it romance, life, ideas, countries, individuals, all rely on a miracle or happening for a happy ending. For Texas A&M handball, the script seen in movies is following the same path. A life-long proponent, enthusiast and player of handball, Doug Randolph, knew of the program's plight. Doug had been to Texas A&M and played in the Aggieland Classic many times, had met and made many friends through handball and thought he could help with reviving handball. Doug made a decision that would be welcomed. All he had to do was to find the process to make it happen. That process is covered in Chapter 14-Revival.

CHAPTER 2
Handball Courts

From the very beginning of the game of hitting a ball with the hands, there had to be a place to play. The size of the area or even the consistency of the "ball" that was used to play the game is not known. However, as the game of "handball" evolved from its beginning, and the beginning is not accurately known, the first known record of a ball rebounding to be hit by an opponent was recorded in the Town Statutes of Galway, Ireland. In 1527, the statutes forbade the hitting of a ball against any of the walls of the buildings in the town.

Through the years, as the game progressed, one wall, then three walls and eventually four walls became the accepted court for the game of handball. Originally some of the courts were much larger than the standard courts of today. The author has played on a one wall court, a 30x60 foot court and of course, the 20x40 foot standard court of today. Each type of court requires a different strategy with the larger court being more a game of endurance rather than the very fast game on the 20x40 foot court.

Most experts on the game of handball generally agree that the Irish made handball popular here in the United States. Handball was becoming more and more popular and was one of the favorite games of our 16th President, Abraham Lincoln. It has been recorded that when some Illinois politicians sought to tell Lincoln they wanted to nominate him for the Presidency, he was on the handball court in the alley near his office.

The handball that Lincoln used

(Internet, Abraham Lincoln and handball)

Lincoln is shown playing his game of "Fives" in the alley behind his law Office. This is the cover of the February 1971 *Ace* Magazine.

As the game spread throughout the US, the size of the four-wall court officially became 20x20x40 feet. In 1925, when handball was approved to be one of the intramural sports at Texas A&M, there were no four-wall courts available. According to Carl Landis, professor and Head of the Health and Physical Education Department from 1943 to 1979, now deceased, handball was played on a one-wall court located near the site of the now replaced Grove and the Wofford Cain athletic dormitory. One-wall handball would not accommodate the full intramural program of handball matches that Mr. Penberthy, the newly hired Director of Intramurals, envisioned. It is not officially recorded but it is likely that he had a conversation with Mr. James Sullivan, Athletic Business Manager, about building indoor courts.

Mr. James Sullivan was offered the position of Athletic Business Manager in June 1919. Even though the athletic department was $17,000 in debt, which was an unbelievable amount during those years, James Sullivan accepted the position. He worked miracles to get the athletic department out of debt and then started upgrading the athletic facilities. He added additional bleachers to Kyle Field and then started building a new gymnasium. The dedication ceremony for the new gym was reported in *The Battalion* of 18 February 1925. The article was found in Cushing Archives of Texas A&M University. The story follows:

(1932 *Longhorn*, page 279)

New Memorial Gymnasium

Simple dignity and impressiveness marked the formal dedication of the new Memorial Gymnasium last Monday evening preceding the basketball game with Texas University. The new gymnasium, probably the finest in the southwest, was decorated with flags and bunting, and the crowd which gathered for the ceremony and game filled the gymnasium to capacity. The numerous old "T" men of A. & M. who had come back to A. & M. to attend the reunion of "T" men here were present in masse, adding to the occasion the famous "Aggie" spirit accumulated the past three decades.

The dedicatory exercises were opened with "America," sung by the audience led by Rev. W. H. Matthews. Rev. S. M. Bird offered a prayer extolling those men of A. & M. who sacrificed their lives in the World War and dedicating the "Memorial Gymnasium" to the furtherance of the principles for which they fought. In the main address of the evening,

President W. B. Bissell praised the "T" men who have helped develop the athletic traditions of A. & M. to their present high standard of true sportsmanship. He described the new structure as a building set apart for clean sportsmanship and the athletics, and christened it the "Memorial Gymnasium" in honor of the soldier dead of the college who played "the real game to a finish."

Dean Chas. E. Friley recounted those events of the past year which resulted directly in the erection of the building. Describing the organization of the Department of Physical Education, he detailed the importance of its work in supervising intra-mural sports and giving courses in athletic coaching. He then officially presented the Memorial Gymnasium to the student body and athletic teams of the College. Following his address, the ceremony was closed with "The Star-Spangled Banner," rendered by the A. and M. Band.

NOTE: The "T" men referred to in the article are those who have earned athletic letters in sports during their student years at A.&M.

Needing indoor handball courts, Sullivan built two four-wall courts inside Memorial Gymnasium. The courts were finished in 1926 and intramural handball moved from the outdoor one-wall courts to the newly constructed four-wall courts. The dimensions of the new courts are not known but they were new, inside, and handball quickly became one of the most popular intramural sports.

A story dated 9 July 1926 in *The Eagle* describes how Sullivan was able to add the handball courts:

New equipment being added to the gymnasium building is a feature of its renovation. At the time of the erection two years ago the north wing of the building was left uncompleted. This section is now being converted into a small gym floor which is to contain two handball courts, and other accessories needed in the physical education work required of the army of freshmen who will enter next September. In addition to the handball courts, the gym will be provided with punching bags, parallel bars, horses and other equipment. Dressing rooms, shower rooms, and offices of the building have been repainted.

(Cushing Archives, Texas A&M University)

It did not take long for the handball courts to be placed in full use. The handball classes and the intramural program made full use of the courts during the normal academic day so any student wanting to practice his game usually did so in the evening hours. It was obvious by the 1927-28 school year that more courts were needed. Mr. Sullivan felt very strongly that more courts should be provided. Since it was so far into town (Bryan), more facilities would help provide the cadets with entertainment aside from the academic day/week. Mr. Sullivan went to work and by August 1929 new handball courts, along with some other athletic facilities, were ready for use. The new building became known as the "Little Gym" and the handball courts were where the author learned to play and spent many great hours of fun, competition and camaraderie while a student. It is the place where Ozzie Burke and thousands of others learned to enjoy the game of handball. It is the place where late one September evening when Phil Collins, then ranked #4 in the world of handball and an airman at Bryan Air Force Base, knocked on the door and asked if he could play with the only two handball players at the courts. Little did Jim Mathis and I know what an enormous impact that simple knock on the door would have.

The Eagle reported Wednesday 7 August 1929 on the completion of the "Little Gym":

"Fish" Athletes At A&M Given New Building

New wood and steel education building to supplement the facilities of the Memorial Gymnasium at the A. & M. College of Texas is now in readiness for the influx of the students expected with the opening of the college year in the fall. The supplementary structure was found necessary by reason of the increasing number of freshmen from year to year, physical training being a compulsory course for the "fish".

This addition to the physical education facilities of the college contains five regulation sized handball courts, a 50x70 foot basketball court, and wrestling and tumbling rooms. The building itself is 70x100 feet.

The new building makes space available for 250 additional lockers for freshmen in the Memorial Gymnasium where physical education classes have been held in the past. Approximately 1,000 lockers were in use last year. One of the handball courts in the gymnasium was released for additional lockers and the other for a wrestling room.

(Cushing Archives of Texas A&M University)

The writer was not familiar with "regulation" sized handball courts as these were not regulation size. However, that did not matter to the thousands who played in the "Little Gym." Handball would quickly become one of the most popular individual participant sports on the campus as the classes, intramural and individual handball moved from the two courts in Memorial Gymnasium.

Many, if not all of those reading this history will not recall or have ever heard of "Memorial Gymnasium" on the Texas A&M campus. An automobile accident in the spring of 1939 would result in a name change.

In a story printed in *The Battalion* Thursday, 22 May 1941 and found in Cushing Archives of Texas A&M University, Dub Oxford writes:

The DeWare Field House as it is now called was originally known as Memorial Gymnasium, but by an act of the Board of Directors on November 29, 1939 the name was changed to DeWare Field House and that is what it is known by today.

Charles DeWare, Sr. was a student at Texas A&M in 1906, '07, '08, '09, and '10. He played football and baseball and was the captain of the football team in 1908 and captain of the baseball team in 1909.

On the gridiron field, DeWare distinguished himself by the superb playing of the position of an end. And, in fact, Jinx Tucker, a prominent Waco sports writer, still includes DeWare senior as an end on the all-time Southwest Conference team.

At the time of his death, which occurred on 6 April 1938, he was living in Brenham and had never tired of supporting the Aggies. In the 28th meeting of the Brenham Chamber of Commerce a resolution was passed to ask Texas A&M to name one of the newly constructed dorms (currently the Corps of Cadets dorms) on the A&M campus as the Charles A. DeWare dorm. Instead, the Board of Directors chose to rename Memorial Gymnasium as the Charles A. DeWare Field House to serve as a permanent reminder of the great athletic contribution he made to Texas A&M.

After World War II, as A&M made the transition to once again provide the youth of Texas and the nation with a quality education in the agricultural and mechanical disciplines, the number of students continued increasing at a rapid rate, once again creating the need for new facilities. The "Little Gym" handball courts were no exception and the need for more courts was reported in *The Battalion,* dated 3 March 1957:

> Handball is by far the most popular individual participant sport on the A&M campus. Records show that 115 six-man teams and from 100 to 150 individuals participate in the intramural team and open handball action alone, much less the hundreds of others who play the game on their own.

> A&M has five handball courts-three doubles and a pair of singles. At the most, 16 men can play at one time, and rarely can you drop by the "Little Gym" and not find Aggies waiting to get on a court. In fact, intramurals tie up the meager facilities for the entire second semester, outside of the Physical Education Department classes.

> The five courts are located in the grey, frame building west of Downs Natatorium. The building has been here since before 1920-and looks it. The doubles courts are 22 feet wide, 12 feet high and 28 feet long, with the singles courts two feet narrower. The walls are nothing more than plain boards, the ventilation is nil and the lighting is very poor.

> Regulation handball courts call for dimensions of 20 by 20 by 40 feet with hardwood floors, plaster walls, good lighting and proper ventilation (if you've ever smelled a court, you'll know why). A&M's fall so short of regulation as to be ridiculous. They are cold in the winter and absolutely unbearable in the summer.

> A&M needs at least 15 good, regulation courts to even meet the demand. It's obvious that a new building just for handball courts is out of the question, we already have a place to put in new courts-DeWare Field House. The main structure of DeWare is still in good shape, and will be for some time to come. The seats could be ripped out and the old basketball floor partitioned off into regulation courts. The situation is desperate and something must be done. Whether or not it will is yet to be seen.

> (Cushing Archives of Texas A&M University)

Even though many recognized the great need for more handball courts, other priorities would be addressed before plans for new courts were made known. Over four-and-a-half years after the need was published in *The Battalion,* another story was released 15 November 1961 informing the students of Texas A&M when they would get the much-needed handball courts:

New Handball Courts Planned for DeWare

The recent razing of the old Little Gym building does not mean the end of handball activity on the campus, Howard Badgett, manager of the Office of Physical Plant, has announced.

The Little Gym, which housed the college's handball courts, was torn down to make room for the new outdoor, Olympic-type swimming pool now under construction just west of the P. J. Downs Natatorium.

Badgett said an area in DeWare Field House has been set aside for construction of 14 handball courts. Construction bids will be opened Nov. 17, and work is expected to start shortly after Dec. 1.

Architect plans show the courts to be built on a new "floor" in DeWare, to be supported by a steel framework, 25 feet above the existing basketball court. Four courts will be situated on each side, over the bleacher area. Six more will occupy the area above the present basketball court.

The courts are to be official size and mechanically air conditioned with ducts in the walls to allow air ventilation.

The courts would serve the physical education program, intramurals and off-hour play just as the others did, according to Carl E. Tishler, head of the Department of Health and Physical Education.

Tishler added that the new courts will enable the department to increase the size of its classes and get more students into the handball course.

Many students used the old courts as a means of getting exercise later in the evenings and during the day. The new courts will mean that more students can take advantage of the facilities.

(Cushing Archives of Texas A&M University)

Obviously, for all involved in handball-whether through teaching, intramurals or just individual play-excitement prevailed when the new courts were opened for use. As time would tell, these courts fell far short of "good handball courts". I played weekly for a number of years on these courts, so fully understand the shortcomings; however, these were the best courts available at the university and the exercise, enjoyment of competition and the shared camaraderie far exceeded the wish for better handball courts. With the passage of time, it did become obvious that the university should consider new and better courts. Ozzie Burke related his feelings and that of many others to Gary Sherer, a sports writer for the *The Battalion*, and he published the shortcomings in the following article on 30 May 1968:

Handball at A&M

Saying that Ozzie Burke is not enthusiastic about handball is like saying that Randy Matson doesn't want to win an Olympic Gold Medal.

The junior Industrial Arts major is the president of the Texas A&M Handball Club that includes 50 members made up of students and faculty.

Burke, who hails from Bryan, has been playing handball since high school and his reputation precedes him around DeWare Fieldhouse.

We talked recently to Ozzie about the handball situation at A&M. It should be noted that he and Dan Kennerly helped to put Texas A&M in the national handball spotlight about three weeks ago when the pair won the National Intercollegiate Doubles Championship at St. Louis.

"It's a shame people can't get to see us play," Ozzie related when we discussed further in the handball facilities at DeWare. There are several courts in the fieldhouse but only two are equipped with places where several people can observe the action.

Even these courts aren't adequate, as a wire mesh covers the opening and you get the same view as if you were looking through a catcher's mask. The club members are unhappy about this, but Ozzie says the real problem is the courts themselves.

"In order to keep your game in shape, the courts should be of plaster," Ozzie pointed out. DeWare's courts are all wood and the club has been after the Physical Education Department to make renovations but they have met with little success.

A comparison can be made with Texas' facilities which Ozzie observed are close to the best college courts in the nation. They, like A&M, are a state-supported school, but they have much better facilities. We would surmise from this, that some serious thought should be given to improve the handball courts here.

The Aggie Club financed the team at the St. Louis tournament but with that exception, the club has received little financial help from the university. Possibly more effort on the part of those responsible and some of those changes might become a reality. Is there enough enthusiasm for those changes? Just talk to Ozzie Burke, and you'll get your answer.

(Cushing Archives of Texas A&M University)

NOTE: Ozzie Burke grew up in College Station on a small farm just south of Texas A&M and not in Bryan as indicated in the article.

After reading the article in *The Battalion*, Carl Landis wrote Ozzie Burke the following letter:

TEXAS A&M UNIVERSITY

COLLEGE OF LIBERAL ARTS

COLLEGE STATION, TEXAS 77843

Department of
HEALTH AND PHYSICAL EDUCATION

May 30, 1968

Mr. Ozzie Burke
P. O. Box 373
College Station, Texas

Dear Ozzie:

Congratulations on your recent achievement of winning the National
Colligiate Doubles Championship in St. Louis. Your victory over
the University of Texas team in the final round 21-4, was quite
an accomplishment!

You will be glad to know that I have requested certain renovations
in some of the courts to include refinishing, plastering the front
wall, and improving the area over the door.

Again congratulations.

                                        Sincerely yours,

                                        C. W. Landiss
                                        Head of Department

CWL:rjf

Having played in the courts many times and also in checking with Ozzie Burke, the recommended changes never occurred. It is likely other budgetary items were given a higher priority.

During the 1970s, it became apparent to the Texas A&M Athletic Department that the seating capacity of Kyle Field needed to be increased. The Athletic Department believed it could raise the funds through a fund-raising campaign; however, it was very concerned about raising enough funds to start the project any time within the near future.

With the increasing student population, demand on the DeWare handball courts grew tremendously. Racquetball and handball were extremely popular and, with women joining and becoming part of the A&M handball club, the need to expand court availability became obvious to Coach Lance Lowy and the Health and Physical Education Department. All of this also resulted in a need to increase staff and office space. Clearly, the Department had outgrown its space within the old G. Rollie White Coliseum.

The Departments of Athletics, and Health and Physical Education, with a need to increase capacity, came up with a plan to increase space by eliminating the rifle range under East Kyle seating. The rifle range was, at the time, being used on a limited basis. By using that space for the handball courts and office space for the Department of Health and Physical Education, it became apparent to the Athletic Department that the University could assist in providing the funding for the expansion of Kyle Field. The plan would be a win-win situation for both. With plans finalized and funds committed, construction began in 1979 and in 1980, Texas A&M opened 14 new handball courts that were known as the East Kyle courts. Of course, the new office space for the Health and Physical Education Department and additional seating in Kyle Field also became a reality.

The new 93,000 square-foot sports and recreation center was renamed the Read Building in 1985. The renaming was in honor of Thomas A. Read, who, with his wife Joan, funded scholarships for almost 100 students each year. Thomas Read did not graduate from Texas A&M but had a deep admiration of the Corps of Cadets and the university in the early 1950s.

As happened many times previously in the history of Texas A&M, the increased student population placed increased demands on the handball courts at A&M. In addition, it was becoming clear that the old courts in DeWare were becoming unsafe for continued use. Dennis Corrington, Director of Recreational Sports, and his staff began planning for a state-of-the-art facility. They called their ideas, expressed on page one in the annual Department of Recreation Sports calendar of 1993-94, as:

The Building of a Dream

The Recreational Sports Building and Natatorium Project challenged us with an opportunity to provide the best possible setting for education, recreation, and sports competition for a student body that deserves nothing but the best.

The process started in January, 1987, when a referendum was initiated to create a funding source through a recreational sports fee. After garnering support from students, administrators and legislatures the design process began.

The process consisted of gathering ideas from literally hundreds of people through surveys, and meetings with participants, instructors and coaches. In gathering those ideas, it was hoped to determine the best in design, equipment, and materials. The Department conducted several open forums to solicit input from anyone who had an interest or expertise in the field.

An example of the massive information gathering was the design charette. Twenty-five architects and engineers from the Houston firm of Marmon Mok, a dozen architects and engineers from Facilities Planning, the staff and faculty from the Rec. Sports Advisory Committee, along with students shared ideas about the building. The charrette (*a meeting*) was two days for input, discussion, presentations, sketching, discussion, more sketching and more presentations. The outcome of this meeting and the many that followed can be witnessed between now and the projected occupancy of January, 1995.

On March 25, 1993, the ground breaking ceremony was held complete with sunshine, sports whistles, flashpots, and a crowd of over 200. Many were on hand to witness the beginning of what Dr. Mobley called, "a facility dedicated exclusively to the students". NOTE: Dr. Mobley was then the President of Texas A&M.

So, as we anxiously await the grand opening of this structure, we invite you to watch the dreams of many Aggies come to life.

Many thanks and congratulations to all of the Aggies who helped make the Student Recreation Center become a reality.

Handball coach Lance Lowy supervised the design and construction of the 12 new handball courts. He was very aware, as were many of those who played in the previous courts, that from time-to-time humidity built up on the walls and would cause the handball to "skip". Lowy was very particular to ensure that the heating and cooling system in the new courts kept the courts free from moisture developing on the walls. In the hundreds of games the author has played in the new handball courts, he has never experienced a ball skipping off the walls. Balls sometimes skip on the floor but that is caused from sweat having dropped on the floor and not the result of a design flaw.

Coach Lowy was unable to sell the idea of a central glass court where several spectators could view the action from seats surrounding three glass sides. Of course, that plan would have a solid-not a glass-wall to hit the ball against. All of the courts have a glass backwall and two of the courts have a side glass wall. The courts were highly praised by those who played in, coached, or attended the National Collegiate Handball Tournament soon after the courts were opened.

The Texas A&M University Recreation Sports Center
(Courtesy Rick Hall)

The $36.4-million structure is a premier facility among university recreation and fitness complexes. The building is 286,000 square feet, roughly the size of five football fields and contains 14 handball courts. It also contains a quarter-mile four-lane indoor track, a natatorium that seats 2,500 with a 50-meter diving well with one- and three-meter springboards and competitive platforms, basketball courts, a soccer court, rock climbing wall, many different machines and areas for weight and exercise training and includes the offices for all of the Recreation Sports faculty and staff.

Handball Court 1, Recreation Center
(Author's Collection)

Currently, there are no plans to add additional handball courts, although the idea has surfaced to add some one-wall courts at some location on campus to allow play during times when the indoor courts are unavailable.

(*Handball*, November 1982, page 64)

Only a very few of those of us still playing handball today will be able to relate to this cartoon. Those who played in the Auxiliary Gym (Little Gym) and DeWare handball courts will remember the washing and drying of handball gloves on a regular basis. Technology, efficient heating and cooling, and advanced construction techniques have eliminated, for the most part, what we had to put up with in days gone by. Yes, the handball courts of today are much improved; however, for those who play the game, the passion has not changed. For the author, and others still in the game, it's "still there."

CHAPTER 3
Intramural Directors

One of the elements of a military organization is physical fitness. From the very first day of A&M's opening in October 1876, one of the mantras of the school was a strong military presence and training to prepare the young men/cadets as well developed, both physically and mentally, future citizens of the state and nation. Within a short time of A&M's beginning, athletic competition was developing between the various cadet outfits. Then, leagues were formed to further that competition for their physical well-being and by 1900 the leagues were the primary recruiting source for varsity athletic teams. Baseball, football and track were the early sports. Basketball would follow in 1913 and by 1925 golf, tennis, wrestling and cross country had been added.

With the increased student population and the increasing athletic competition, scheduling, officiating and supervision were being overwhelmed. To address this increasing problem the then Director of Physical Training and Intramural Sports recommended the formation of a group for the purpose of supervising and administering intramural sports. Approval was obtained on 7 October 1912 for the formation of the Company Athletic Council. The purpose of the Council was to administer the intramural sports program. The Council would be composed of the College Athletic Director as the Chair and each Battalion would provide a cadet officer. This Council oversaw the rules for competition, academic eligibility (cadets must pass at least 14 hours each week), settled disputes and ruled on other issues that came before the Board. This new idea of having cadets (students) be a part of the supervision and administration of the intramural sports program met with immediate success in its first year and started a system that is still in effect today, 110 years later. From a historical standpoint, the first Chair of the newly formed Company Athletic Council could be listed as the first Director of Intramural Sports at Texas A&M. Some could argue that the first Director would have been years earlier when the company leagues were started. A quote from a 1925 ledger in Cushing Memorial Library referring to intramural program records states: "The intramural program as we know it today was begun by H. H. House in 1923." House left A&M for a position at Washington State, which left an opening for a new hire. Others will argue that the new hire replacing House, Mr. Walter Lawrence "Penny" Penberthy, should be listed as the first Director. Most of the past and current staff of the Department of Recreational Sports consider Penny the "father of intramural sports at A&M." The formation of the Company Athletic Council in 1912 was a positive step in the evolvement over the years into the intramural program of today. The first Director with the sole responsibility to run the intramural sports program would come later.

The first Chair of the Company Athletic Council was Charles B. Moran who continued during the 1913-14 year. In 1915 C. C. Lucid was the Chair and W. L. Driver took over in 1916 and would hold that position for six years. It cannot be determined who held the Chair of the Company Athletic Council after W. L. Driver; however, it is likely that H. H. House replaced Driver.

As the College continued to grow in student population, the need for a better organized program of intramural athletics was recognized. The following course of action and result was reported on page 284 of the 1926 *Longhorn*:

Along with the growth of intramural athletics came the necessity for a better and more comprehensive organization in the administration of intramural activities. The Athletic Council in March, 1925, appointed a committee to draw up a constitution and by-laws to govern intramural athletics. This constitution and by-laws were submitted to and approved by the Athletic Council in May, 1925.

The Intramural Board is the governing body of the Intramural Athletic Association and conducts all of the activities and business incident to this organization. The Board consists of: the director of intramurals, chairman of the board; professor of physical education; one member of the faculty, appointed by the Athletic Council; Senior Manager of Intramural Athletics and one member of the senior class to act as Secretary of the Board.

The Intramural Board determines the activities that shall be conducted and makes all the necessary rules governing the various sports; rules on all protests; drafts all schedules; decides upon eligibility of all players and such other matters that would logically come before the Board for consideration.

The purpose of intramural athletics is to give every student the opportunity to participate in some form of competitive athletics, therefore, it is the aim of the Board to promote as many different forms of competition as facilities, time and money will permit.

Leagues are formed in cross-country, basketball, football, and playground ball; tournaments are held in tennis, handball, wrestling, boxing, gymnastics, swimming, etc. By conducting a variety of sports and games it is hoped that each student may find something that specially interests him and that his interest will then lead him to try his skill in some new activity in which he is a novice. In this way, a single interest may be the means of developing many interests which will do much towards helping the individual student to find some activity that is beneficial and in which he can participate enjoyably and with healthful profit.

With the approval of the new Intramural Board, the need for the appropriate individual to chair the program and move it forward became a necessity. It is not known how many applied for the position but one certain fact soon became evident. The newly hired Director of Intramurals was Walter Lawrence Penberthy, a new graduate out of Ohio State University. His hire, over time, would prove invaluable to the intramural program and to Texas A&M.

The following write-up and photo, found on page 296 of the 1928 *Longhorn*, reveals Penny's first year as the Director of Intramurals:

Last year there came to A. and M., as Director of Intramural Athletics, a very capable young man from the University of Ohio. Fresh from the university, with plenty of vim, vigor, hopes and ambitions, Mr. Penberthy was just what our Intramural Athletics needed to arouse it from its lethargy.

He wasted no time, but began immediately to put his new ideas into practice. As a result, the intramural program for the past year was the most successful in the history of the college.

Walter L. "Penny" Penberthy

The average person would have been satisfied, but not "Penny". With the beginning of the new school year, he had many new sports to introduce to the students, each with wonderful success. At present the Intramural Athletic Department embraces almost every conceivable sport.

Truly, Mr. Penberthy is doing a wonderful work and we wish him all the success in the world.

It is interesting to note that the students gave Mr. Penberthy his "nickname" during his first year in the job. It would stay with him the rest of his life.

Penberthy was hired with a title of Assistant Professor assigned to the Physical Education Department. And, of course, he was hired to be the director of intramural sports. It did not take long for him to earn the title of Associate Professor which happened in 1928-29 and, in 1930, he was promoted to full Professor. In 1930-31, a new course requirement was listed in the Undergraduate Bulletin-Physical Education 101 and 102. It cannot be verified, but it is likely that Penberthy was involved in that decision and may have, in fact, recommended the additional courses. He served on the Academic Council in the late '30s and early '40s.

Penberthy continued to build the Intramural program to what has been acclaimed as the largest intramural program in the world. The following quote was found in *The Battalion* dated 3 October 1941: "Facilities for this program include 27 basketball courts, 10 softball diamonds, five football fields, 15 volleyball courts, 10 tennis courts, five handball courts, a swimming pool and a tumbling room."

Handball benefitted greatly from Penberthy's intramural vision. He established the handball team concept where each unit would provide a team to compete in separate leagues and eventually for the college handball championship. Thousands of Aggies experienced the great game of handball under his program. By the late 1930s and before World War II, 1,500-plus cadets were involved yearly playing for the various teams to win the handball championship.

During World War II, Penberthy was placed in charge of the college physical conditioning program to ready the Aggies to be physically fit when called or volunteered for active military duty in support of the war effort. With the college going to three 16-week semesters each year, beginning 1 June 1942 for the purpose of earlier graduation, the intramural program took a backseat. Yes, the intramural program continued under the direction of Penberthy; however, he had assistants handle the day-to-day planning and supervision of the program. In the 1944 *Longhorn* mention is made that he was still head of the department, but Nicky Ponthieux was heading the intramural program with Penberthy running the physical exercise program. Penberthy's primary mission during that period was to keep the physical conditioning program on a pace for all cadets to be in "perfect" physical condition when leaving the college for their or their country's purpose.

When the war ended Penberthy relinquished the responsibility for the intramural program and continued as Professor and Head, Department of Physical Education. In 1947 he accepted the position of Dean of Men and continued in that position until 1956 when he was named Head of the Department of Student Activities. In 1960-61 he returned to the Department of Physical Education as Professor and remained there until his retirement on 31 August 1966.

Penberthy's ability to organize, coordinate, supervise, provide guidance to students and teach made him popular with students and with his co-workers. There can be little doubt that Mr. Walter Lawrence Penberthy left his legacy at this university as only a few others have done.

At the end of World War II, a young man, who had been responsible for physical training for the US Navy during the war, came back to A&M and accepted the position of Director of Intramurals. The new Director of Intramurals for 1946-47 was Carlton G. "Spike" White,'35. It is not known if White left A&M after graduation in 1935 and then came back in 1939; however, it is known that he was working in intramurals as an assistant to Penberthy in 1939 and would continue in that position until he left as an Ensign for duty in the Navy. The 1943 *Longhorn* states the following: "Spike" White, one of the most popular assistants, has gone into the Navy physical fitness program as an Ensign. He will be greatly missed by all of us."

Carlton G. "Spike" White
(Author's collection)

White held the position of Director of Intramurals for one year and then moved to another position at A&M.

Following Spike White as Director of Intramurals was an Aggie football legend, Mr. Fowler B. "Barney" Welch '45. It was during Welch's leadership in intramurals that the Aggie handball team was created for the purpose of competition against teams from other colleges and universities. It cannot be verified that Welch formed the first A&M handball team but, having the experience of varsity competition at the college/university level, it is likely he had some, if not all, of the input to make the A&M team a reality. Neither can it be verified when Welch started playing handball but he became one of the better and most competitive handball players at A&M and remained so for many years.

Over the years of Welch's time as Intramural Director there were many accolades written in the *Aggieland* yearbooks. The write-up (includes photo to the left) on page 265, of the 1953 *Aggieland*, expresses the student's relationship with Welch.

Fowler "Barney" Welch
(Author's collection)

It reads: "Barney needs no introduction to any Aggie. His face is as familiar as the next-door neighbor at home. He is always thought of as the man who is always ready to help with both advice or work. Barney is the guiding spirit behind the intramural program at A&M. He was its chief architect from its lowest ebb after WWII up to its present position as one of the largest and most comprehensive student athletic programs in existence. To every Aggie he is the symbol of fair play, good sportsmanship and worthwhile accomplishment".

One of Welch's early problems was running an intramural program at the Bryan Air Field Annex, where the Corps freshmen lived, in addition to the program on campus. He was ably assisted with the freshmen program by Nicky Ponthieux, who had supervised the intramural program for Penberthy during the war years. Welch managed the two-campus intramural program just as easily as he had avoided tacklers on the gridiron-no problem.

Beginning in 1947-48, Welch was the guiding light and spirit of the intramural program until he left A&M and entered into private business in 1961 as an agent for Mercantile National Insurance; however, he remained in the Bryan/College Station area and focused primarily on providing insurance needs to graduating seniors.

Dr. Charles McCandless
(Author's Collection)

When Welch retired, there was a young Aggie, Charles (Chuck) Emory McCandless '56, ready to take his place. McCandless was hired as an Assistant Professor of Physical Education in 1961 and also named Intramural Director. McCandless received his Bachelor of Science degree from A&M in 1956 and his Master's of Education in 1958. Though working for A&M, he continued his education with North Texas State and earned his Education Doctorate in 1966.

McCandless worked for Barney Welch for two years as Student Administrative Assistant and when Welch decided to step away from the position of Intramural Director, he recommended that A&M hire McCandless. McCandless has always said how grateful he was to have had the experience of working with Welch and how much he meant to him. During McCandless's time as Intramural Director, the program advanced with the help of student managers including senior manager Donald (Buck) Henderson '62, who became a life-long friend. McCandless left intramurals to pursue a career in teaching and administration at A&M. He held several different positions until he left A&M as Associate Provost. He left to be Executive Vice President at Iowa State University.

When Chuck McCandless decided to pursue another career path in 1964, he was replaced as Intramural Director by Gerald Gordon Stephens. Stephens graduated with a Bachelor of Science degree from McMurray College in 1962. He was hired by A&M as an Instructor in Physical Education with the additional job title of Intramural Director. No intramural information is available during his tenure as Intramural Director.

Gerald Stephens was replaced as Intramural Director in 1965 when Texas A&M hired Raymond Lee Fletcher as an Instructor in Health and Physical Education. Fletcher earned his bachelor's degree in 1959 and his master's in 1963, both from Sam Houston State Teachers College. Fletcher remained the Intramural Director until 1971 when he was replaced by Les Palmer.

Leslie (Les) Lloyd Palmer received his bachelor's degree from Texas A&M (Agricultural and Mechanical College of Texas at that time) in 1948. As a junior, he was an intramural manager and then in his senior year was named the chief of intramural officials. Palmer stayed at A&M and received his Master's of Education in 1951. He was hired at A&M and continued teaching in the Department of Health and Physical Education for a lifetime of service. Having been a significant

Les Palmer
(Author's collection)

part of the intramural program during his undergraduate years he accepted the position of Intramural Director when Fletcher vacated the position. Palmer continued the large, smooth running intramural program just as those who served before him.

In 1973, Texas A&M hired Dennis Arthur Corrington as an Instructor in Health and Physical Education but also to the position of Intramural Director, sports club programs and manager of the recreational facilities. Corrington earned his bachelor's degree from Morningside College in Sioux City, Iowa. He was not a native Texan; however, he adopted Texas as his home and wasted no time in getting to know Aggie traditions and culture. Corrington faced a problem other Intramural Directors had not; however, Les Palmer was in the early stages of dealing with this new problem. The new problem, and it was a problem not in the sense of not wanted, but the burgeoning population of women attending A&M created a need for intramurals and sport club activities readily acceptable to them. Just as Penberthy dealt with creating an intramural program that would fit the male students (cadets) in his early years, Corrington was now faced with creating an intramural program and activities for the women at A&M. The blueprint was there, established through years and years of experience providing sporting activities for male students. The first couple of years, it was trial and error, but it did not take long to establish an equal program for the women. It then became apparent that co-recreational activities could be established within the intramural program to add another dimension. Corrington provided activities the students wanted. He was such an innovator that he would have set up tiddlywinks tournaments if there had been enough student interest.

Dennis Corringto
(Author's collection)

From the beginning of the Penberthy era until 1993, the Director of Intramurals reported to, or through, the Department of Health and Physical Education. As the student population and activities increased, it became apparent that those hired to be lecturers in Health and Physical Education simply did not have the time available to teach and adequately perform their responsibilities within the department headed by Corrington. He requested and received approval to be placed under the supervision of the Division of Student Affairs. He also was successful in changing the name of the department to Department of Recreational Sports. Within two years after the change, personnel in recreational sports no longer taught classes for the Department of Health and Physical Education.

As had been done during the WWII years when Penberthy was placed in charge of the physical exercise training, Corrington, though still in charge of the intramural program, designated others within the department to program and supervise the conduct of the intramural program. The first to be placed in this position of responsibility was Rick Hall who served 1979-84. He was followed by Eric Hunter-1984-85, Tom Reber-1985-94, James Welford-1994-98, Mike Waldron-1998-2004, James Welford-2004-06, Drew McMillen-2006-12, Jerrod Jackson-2012-18 and Nick Heiar-2018-current. The author is very familiar with all and can attest to their professionalism in carrying out the assigned duties. Over time, all earned extensive time with programming and conducting intramural activities and helped to continue the smooth-running intramural program that is the best in the nation, and if not, among the best. The department in earlier years had focused primarily on intramural sports; however, under the leadership of Corrington, was now multi-dimensional catering to all aspects of recreation. Also, under his leadership, came the completion of the Texas A&M Recreation Center in 1995. Corrington left his mark that will not be forgotten. Chuck McCandless said it best: "In all of my years in administration I never saw a better match than Dennis Corrington and intramural athletics at Texas A&M."

Rick Hall
(Author's Collection)

When Corrington retired in 2018, the normally difficult choice for a replacement was easily found within the department. Many of Corrington's staff had years of experience working within the well-established and highly successful program. Richard (Rick) Lee Hall, a graduate of Virginia Polytechnic Institute and State University, earned the nod to continue as department head. He received his bachelor's degree in 1975 and his master's in 1976 and then moved to Texas A&M in 1979 as a lecturer in Health and Physical Education and to work for Corrington in intramurals. It is fully expected that Hall will continue the overall excellence of recreational sports.

CHAPTER 4
Intramural Handball

Handball at Texas A&M became an intramural and recreational sport in 1925. The following page (270) found in the 1926 *Longhorn* explains the beginning:

Note that handball was one of the new sports that would become a part of the intramural sports program. In the beginning, there would not be handball leagues, but the game would be played by holding tournaments. Obviously, for the cadets to learn the game, classes had to be established.

The thousands who have enjoyed the game at A&M owe a debt of gratitude to whomever on the committee appointed by the Athletic Board in January 1925, knew about the game of handball. In a cursory check of where the student population hailed from, it was found, as expected, that the majority came from Texas and most out of state students came from the surrounding states of New Mexico, Oklahoma, Arkansas and Louisiana. Students claiming a home elsewhere did exist but the numbers were insignificant. So, at this point in time, it is very likely that no A&M student had ever heard of the game of handball. That would change in the fall of 1925. Since there were no handball courts in any of the buildings, an area would have to be designated for classes and play. The introduction to handball at this point would have to be the one-wall game and played outside. Carl Landis, Professor of Physical Education, 1943-79 and Head at his retirement, told Dennis Corrington (See the chapter on Intramural Directors.) that the first courts were outside.

Classes and play would not be outside for long, thanks to James Sullivan for coming up with the plan to establish two courts inside Memorial Gymnasium and soon to follow, the Little Gym courts where the author learned to play the game. (SEE the Chapter: Handball Courts.)

It is not known who won the first, or even the second handball title, or the format used; however, the intramural tennis format of one singles player and one doubles team from each company was so successful that the same format would be used in handball competition. The first team handball champion found was E Battery, Field Artillery during the 1929-30 school year. E Battery would repeat as champions in 1930-31. J. M. Mitchell of B Battery, Field Artillery won the singles championship in 1931-32. F. E. Haltom and R. E. Porter of E Battery, Field Artillery won the doubles championship. During the year 1932-33 the record for the winning team is not available.

The "tennis format" would not be in use for long. From the intramural records found in the Texas A&M Recreation Center the following rules for handball were in effect for the year 1931-32.

Handball

The handball team shall consist of six men arranged in three sets of doubles.

Each captain will report to the scorer his men properly paired and no changes will be allowed except that new men may be substituted at any time, but a man removed from a team may not play again until the next contest.

Captains or Managers will toss a coin for the right to place their respective sets of doubles. The winner of the toss will decide how his pairs will compete with his opponents.

A contest consists in winning two out of three matches from an opposing team. A team whose sets of doubles are victorious in two out of three matches, wins the contest. A match will consist of two out of three games of 21 points each.

Leagues will be formed in this sport and eliminations will be held to determine the college championship team.

Official Handball Rules will govern all contests in this sport. A set of these rules will be posted in each court.

A doubles and a singles tournament will also be held in this sport to determine the college champions. In these tournaments each company will be represented by its best individual player in the singles tournament and its best doubles team in the doubles tournament.

For 1933-34, the Field Artillery units were still at the top of the heap. B Battery, Field Artillery won the championship by defeating E Battery, Field Artillery in the championship match. Members of the winning team were Herbert Y. Cartwright, Jr, William B. Cochran, Herbert W. Hartung, Johnny M. Mitchell, C. E. "Ed" Reichardt, Harry C. Stefani, S. J. Tremonte and C. S. York. The handball season consisted of team play among 25 different Corps units divided into five separate leagues. After the league champions were determined, an elimination series among the five team champions was held, and with the winning teams continuing until there were two teams left. The two teams then played for the college championship. A total of 205 cadets participated in league handball play.

In 1934-35, the Field Artillery units were still on top of the A&M intramural handball program. That year F Battery, Field Artillery won the championship and D Battery, Field Artillery came in second. Handball was quickly becoming one of the most popular sports of the intramural program. During tournament play, there were 29 teams entered. These teams were divided into six different leagues. The handball competition had 61 matches (there were also some forfeits) among the 222 cadets who played in the handball league. Battery F cadets who contributed to the championship season were W. L. Eads, Felix A. Hunter, M. A. Lagley, Henry M. Long, Clyde T. Norman, Roland H. Prove, Warren D. Sorrells and William L. Thomasson.

1935 Intramural Handball Champions
Individual names not listed
(1935 *Longhorn*, page 288)

In 1935-36, F Battery, Field Artillery repeated as champions. B Battery, Field Artillery came in second. The cadets who helped contribute to the championship season were Felix A. Hunter, Henry M. Long, W. S. Miller, J. A. Nelson, Malford C. Schraub, C. A. Smith, William L. Thomasson and Lloyd D. Upshaw. F Battery won the championship by winning every match played in its league and then the elimination series. There were 32 teams divided into six leagues. A total of 346 handball players participated in the season.

1936 Intramural Handball Champions
Individual names not listed
(1936 Longhorn, p. 313)

As the 1936-37 school year began, the question to be answered for the Field Artillery units was, "Who will win the handball title this year?" E Battery, Field Artillery ended up in the winner's circle after all matches were completed. Cadets who played for E Battery were Edwin P. Arneson, Jack W. Burk, Robert G. Cameron, Jr., Daniel A. Foote, Garrett F. Melton, James F. Roark, Emanuel H. Schultis (manager),

1937 Intramural Handball Champions
Individual names not listed
(1937 *Longhorn*, page 335)

Clinton W. Uhr and Lloyd M. Walls. D Battery was the runner-up and one of the 29 teams that were divided into five separate leagues. A total of 254 cadets played during the league handball season.

1938 Intramural Senior Handball Champions
Individual names not listed

(1938 *Longhorn*, page 368)

Since the beginning of handball play in intramurals, the championship had always come down to the Field Artillery. The 1937-38 year would not bring a change. E Battery, Field Artillery repeated with another team handball title; however, the champions did not have an undefeated season. D Battery, Coast Artillery tied E Battery in league play but E Battery advanced based on some extra points earned during league play. Thirty-nine teams were divided into seven leagues for the season's play. A total of 289 cadets participated in the season. The cadets who played for E Battery were Edwin P. Arneson, Jr., Jack W. Burk, Daniel A. Foote, H. G. Howard, Jr., R. V. Johnson, James F. Roark, (manager), Clinton W. Uhr and Lloyd M. Walls.

For the 1938-39 year, the leagues were changed from Senior to Class A, which would be the advanced player leagues and Class B, which would be the leagues for beginners and for headquarters and staff organizations that did not have the numbers to compete with the standard units. Typically, the freshmen in any outfit would not have had any handball experience so rarely, except for exceptional athletes, had the opportunity to play in the league. Another of the problems was the fact that between the league play and handball classes there simply was no time to get a court for practice and the learning experience so necessary to develop the off-hand and strategy needed to become a good handball player. To provide more opportunity to the new cadets to learn and play handball, the league for beginners was formed.

The league changes had no effect on determining the winner and E Battery, Field Artillery won the Class A handball championship again. Members of the team were Jack Burk, Charles Dwyer, Daniel Foote, John Gibson, H. G. Howard, Jr., Ralph Parker, Lloyd Walls, Gus Worthington and Clinton Uhr. Obviously, the seniors on the team had a great run during their time as members of the Corps. It cannot be determined the part Robert Rhea had in winning the championship; however, he was available for the team photo.

1939 Intramural Class A Handball Champions
FRONT ROW: Ralph W. Parker, John O. Gibson, Jr., Lloyd Walls, John P. Howard
BACK ROW: Robert M. Rhea, Gustave T. Worthington, Charles F. Dwyer, Jr., Jack Burk

(1939 Longhorn, page 383)

Coming in second in the Class A League was the team from 2nd Headquarters, Field Artillery. A total of 399 students played on the 41 teams that made up the seven leagues of Class A handball. By looking at the numbers it is readily apparent why a second league was formed. A total of 539 students played from the 40 teams that made up the eight leagues of Class B handball competition. A Company, Chemical Warfare Service won the title with A Company, Infantry coming in second. Members of the winning team were Sam Arisco, William Burch, Jr., James Clutter, George Coffey, B. E. Massey (manager), Edward McAdam, Edward Overbeck, Scott Stubbs, William Swain and Kenneth Terrell.

I am sure that the Field Artillery's dominance in intramural handball felt like it would continue into the next century, but time has a way of replacing champions. In 1939-40, a new intramural handball champion emerged as C Battery, Coast Artillery came out on top as the Class A handball champion. Members of C Battery's team were Allen W. Burgess, Berry F. Davis, Jr., Willis G. Kellogg, Cornelius B. Marsh, Jr., William D. McMahon, James E. Melancon and Thomas F. Sharp, Jr.. E Battery, Field Artillery made a great run but couldn't overcome C Battery and ended up as runner-up. Fifty-four (54) teams divided into nine leagues and 582 participants made scheduling a major issue. In addition, 52 teams divided into 10 leagues with 671 handball players from the Class B Leagues added serious coordination problems. At the time, there were only five courts available on campus and all were located in the Little Gym. However, this would prepare the intramural staff for larger numbers during the next two years.

The 1939-40 intramural handball champion team in Class B was B Battery, Coast Artillery. A Company, Chemical Warfare Service was the runner-up. The winning members from B Battery were John T. Cox, Jr., E. C. Dooley, J. C. Dunn, R. B. Gillette, Henry C. King, Jr., Paul B. Langdale, (manager), L. J. Maher, John R. Mullins, Maurice J. Nethery, Jr. and Earl L. Voskamp.

In 1940-41, the Field Artillery Regiment was back in the championship handball circle again after one year. B Battery, Field Artillery had a banner year as they won both the Class A and Class B handball titles.

The runner-up in Class A competition was G Company, Infantry. There were 57 teams in the 11 different leagues of Class A handball with 697 cadets participating. In the Class B competition, E Battery, Field Artillery was the runner-up. Class B intramural handball had 52 teams in the 10 separate leagues with 738 cadets participating. That is a total of 1,435 cadets playing handball in league competition. It is probable that a number of other cadets played from time to time and were not part of their outfit's team. Class B members of the B Battery team were Dalton P. Albert, Tom A. Carlile, Carl L. King, Arthur J. LeBlanc, Garvis C. Marsh, Donald W. McIntyre, Richard H. Phillips, Jr., Arthur D. Schwarz, Jr., Jack W. Tynes, and Wilfred W. Walton.

C Battery, Coast Artillery
1940 Class A Intramural Handball Champions
FRONT ROW: Willis G. Kellogg, William H. Reber, Jr., Thomas F. Sharp, Jr., William D. McMahon
BACK ROW: James E. Melancon, Cornelius B. Marsh, Jr., Berry Davis, Jr., Allen W. Burgess
(1940 *Longhorn*, page 403)

B Battery, Coast Artillery
1940 Class B Handball Champions
IN THE PHOTO: Maurice J. Nethery, Jr., Henry C. King. Jr., Paul B. Langdale, Earl L. Voskamp, John T Cox, Jr.
(1941 *Longhorn*, page 432)

B Battery, Field Artillery
1941 Class A Intramural Handball Champions
FRONT ROW: George F. Bentinck, John A. Kenagy, Isaac T. Houston, Jr., Wilbert S. Shea, Ellis S. Marks
BACK ROW: J. H. Maher, Joe D. Stokes, Jr., Carroll W. Cooper
(1941 *Longhorn*, page 425)

B Battery, Field Artillery
1941 Class B Intramural Handball Champions
IN THE PHOTO: Arthur D. Swartz, Jr., Garvis C. Marsh, Donald W. McIntyre, Willfred W. Walton
(1942 *Longhorn*, page 445)

One of the author's great friends, George G. Harris, Sr., '41, spoke of his time playing handball and the enjoyment he benefited from the game. Obviously, he was there and played during the height of handball popularity at Texas A&M. Harris always coordinated and made arrangements for the Corps parade in downtown Houston when the Aggies played Rice University in football.

E Battery, Field Artillery
1942 Class A Intramural Handball
Champions
FRONT ROW: Lee W. Rogers, Donald W.
Simmons, Charles E. Lehman, Charles
L. Crowder
NOTE: One name was missing -
Crowder at far right is the only
positive identification
BACK ROW: William C. Donnell, Charles
M. Taylor, Louis O. Schaper
TEAM MEMBERS NOT IN PHOTO: Dr.
Robert L. Brown, Joseph C. Maroney
(1942 *Longhorn*, page 439)

In 1941-42, E Battery, Field Artillery earned the title as the Class A champion handball team. A Company, Chemical Warfare Service was the runner-up. D Battery, Field Artillery was the Class B team champion with E Battery, Field Artillery as the runner-up. Members of D Battery, Field Artillery were Herbert M. Cree, Jr., Vance G. Denton, James J. Hill, Rufus J. Lackland, W. R. Lloyd, William S. McLeod, Jr., Oscar Neunhoffer, John B. Payne, Clifford V. Slagle, and E. W. Stebbins.

Never before or since have there been so many Aggies playing handball. A total of 1,796 participated in the team competition. With that number, the winning teams in both Class A and B were an elite group. In the Class A competition, there were 62 teams divided into 12 different leagues with 854 cadets playing. In Class B, there were 62 teams divided into 12 different leagues with 942 cadets playing. There can be no doubt that the number playing in the handball team competition would have soon exceeded 2,000 had not events occurred that brought this country into World War II.

As a consequence of World War II and its impact on Texas A&M and its cadets, the academic year was divided into 3 semesters per year. Mr. Penberthy adjusted the intramural sports program to accommodate the new trimester system. Greater emphasis was put on physical fitness as opposed to learning new intramural sports. Even though the emphasis was on physical fitness, the same 15 intramural sports were still being played. Obviously, with the fewer number of cadets the number of leagues dropped in comparison to the total student population. Handball was still being played and the named champion for 1942-43 was still within the Field Artillery. E Battery, Field Artillery repeated as the champion. A Company, Chemical Warfare Service was the runner-up. Members of the winning team were John H. Bradley, Jr., Gordon E. Brin, Charles L. Crowder, Glen W. Hudson Jr., Charles E. Lehman, Joseph C.

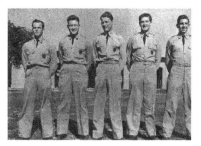

D Battery, Field Artillery
1941-42 Class B Intramural Champions
IN THE PHOTO: James J. Hill, Vance
G. Denton, W. R. Lloyd, William S.
McLeod, Jr., E. W. Stebbins
(1943 *Longhorn*, page 383)

Maroney, C. W. Pittard, and Donald W. Simmons. There were 784 cadets playing for the 64 teams divided into 13 leagues. The Class B competition was discontinued. The 1942-43 handball league competition was played during the first trimester of the school year and would be the last of the team handball until the war ended.

With cadets leaving for the war and to better prepare the students for active military service, organized physical activity for military service became the emphasis and intramural competition secondary. At some point during the summer or fall of 1943, the College introduced a five hour per week Physical Education program. The new program required each student, unless he was physical unfit, to take four hours of organized physical education and to participate in a minimum of one intramural game per week. The physical education classes were divided into regular physical training groups and swimming groups.

With A&M in full scale preparation mode for the war it is likely that very little handball was being played until the war's end. After the peace treaty had been signed, with America getting back into daily life without the total support of the war effort and the constant bombardment of war news, A&M started looking forward to the future and returning back to the daily routine of academia. As the Department of Intramurals discovered very quickly, there would be a need to open intramurals to returning veterans. Handball again would very quickly become a popular activity. The Field Artillery owned the handball championships from the time intramural handball competition began. B Battery, Field Artillery would pick up where the Artillery units left off in the fall of 1942 by winning the Class B (freshman) team championship in the fall of 1946. Members of the winning team were Thomas O. Galbreath, John C. Henderson, Malcolm McGregor, Floyd H. Patterson, Jr., George M. Rogers, and Malcolm Williams. C Company, Infantry was runner-up. There were 27 teams playing, divided into five separate leagues. The number of participants was not recorded.

With a large number of veterans in campus dorms, it was quickly realized that a new league was needed. In the spring of 1947, Dorm 17 became the first non-Corps team champion. Mitchell Hall was runner-up. There were eight dorm teams participating in the new league. The number of participants was not recorded.

Also added to the intramural handball program was the Open handball singles and doubles tournaments. The winner of the singles and doubles tournament was George E. Tubb. Edwin J. Stanley earned the doubles championship with Tubb.

The Corps champions for the spring of 1947 was not a Field Artillery Battery but C Company, Infantry. Not only was this a "changing of the guard" from Artillery to Infantry at the top, but the Infantry dominated the elimination series with A Company, C Company, D Company and G Company, all making it to the quarterfinals. There were 28 teams divided into five separate leagues which indicates that handball was still very much in demand. Unfortunately, when intramural play resumed on a more regular basis the total of individuals participating was not recorded.

With the renaming and separation of the United States Air Force from the Army in 1947, the Air Force Reserve Officers Training Corps (ROTC) was established at Texas A&M and units within the Corps reflected that change. The first year, two units, Squadrons A and B, Air Corps became active participants with all the other Corps units. The records reflect that A Squadron lost all 5 of its handball matches and B Squadron lost 4 of its 5 matches. With time and experience those respective records would improve.

Dorm 17
1947 Civilian Dorm Intramural Handball Champions
FRONT ROW: Charles E. Walker, George P. Cavitt, Hal B. Carrington
BACK ROW: George E. Tubb, John F. Zummo, George C. Walker, III
(1947 *Longhorn*, page 280)

1947 Open Singles Champion-George Tubb (right)
1947 Doubles Champions-George Tubb and Edwin Stanley
(1947 *Longhorn*, page 281)

C Company, Infantry
1947 Class A Intramural Handball Champions
FRONT ROW: Floyd W. Grona, John P. McConnell, Thomason C. Eklund, James E. Kunkel
BACK ROW: Tommy R. Splittgerber, Victor G. Klaushopf, Victor H. Schulze
(1947 *Longhorn*, page 279)

The Open singles and doubles tournaments of 1946 were popular enough to initiate the tournaments on an annual basis. Both tournaments were offered during the fall of 1947. It is not known how many

entered the Open singles tournament; however, the records only list those who reached the quarterfinals. Of those, Burke and Scheumach reached the finals match. The singles champion was Scheumach. In the Open doubles competition, 64 players entered the competition. This was also played during the fall semester. The winners of the Open doubles tournament were Scheumach and Connally.

Fall 1948 Open Doubles Champions
Scheumach and Connally
(1948 *Longhorn*, page 279)

NOTE: Throughout the book individual first, middle initial and last names are given only when positive identification can be confirmed.

C Company, Infantry added another title by winning the Military League intramural handball team championship. The runner-up team was Company A, Composite. There were 22 teams entered and those were divided into four separate leagues. As has been the norm after the war and resumption of intramural play, participants were not recorded.

In the Class A League, the winner was Dorm 16. The runner-up was Dorm 14. There were 10 teams in this league and those were divided into three separate leagues for play.

A total of 30 players participated in league play.

C Company, Infantry
1948 Military League Intramural Champions
FRONT ROW: William L. Mackey, Richard L. Kunkel, William A. Barber, Jr.
BACK ROW: Tommy R. Splittgerber, Victor G. Klaushopf, Victor H. Schulze
(1948 *Longhorn*, page 279)

Dorm 16
1948 Class A Intramural Handball
Champions
FRONT ROW: Charles E. Washington, Lloyd W. Smith, Dr. Erwin R. Soyars, Jr., J. D. Carroll
BACK ROW: Preston K. Cook, Dr. Stewart J. McConnell, Dr. Varley F. Young
NOT IN PHOTO: Jack M. Balderas, Jr.
(1948 *Longhorn*, page 279)

In the 1948-49 year, freshmen handball champions were not listed and it cannot be verified if there was an opportunity for freshmen to play as a team; however, in the 1949 *Aggieland*, yes *Aggieland*, (the name of the yearbook was changed from *Longhorn* to *Aggieland*) mention was made that there were four leagues of team play in intramurals-Corps, Annex (freshmen), Non-Corps (dorm veterans) and Clubs. Yes, the freshmen were living at the Annex which was located at the old Bryan Air Base and current location of the Rellis campus. It is not probable that the freshmen participated in handball in any way since there were no handball courts located at the Annex. Also, during that time very few cadets and probably no freshmen had automobiles.

There are no records available for handball league play for 1948-49. The only record to be found is in the *Aggieland.* Below are the team champion photos of the Corps and Non-Corps Leagues:

A Company, Infantry
1949 Corps Intramural Handball
Champions
FRONT ROW: Gerald R. MacManus, Sam Pate, James E. Sauls
BACK ROW: Frank Simpson, Danny James, Art Gorman
(1949 *Aggieland,* page 266)

Walton Hall
1949 Non-Corps Intramural Handball
Champions
FRONT R`OW: Burt Layne, P. R. Connelly, William C. Miller
BACK ROW: C. L. Roberts, Jack M. Balderas, Jr.
(1949 *Aggieland,* page 266)

1949 Open Handball
Champions
Singles: Jewell McDowell (right)
Doubles: Jewell McDowell, Burt Layne
(1949 *Aggieland,* page 268)

It is years between Jewell McDowell '52 and All-Americans Brad Alesi '02 and Sal SantaAna '94, but McDowell was probably at the same level as those two. McDowell was a two-time All Southwest Conference Basketball Player and in a handball match between A&M and the University of Texas, McDowell dominated their best player 21-6, 21-4. He also dominated the Open handball tournaments at A&M during his time as a student. During the late 1940s and 1950s varsity coaches encouraged their varsity athletes to participate in handball to help with their hand-eye coordination and physical fitness. During that time period, varsity sports were not a year-long activity as many of them are today.

In the fall of 1948, fifty-one handball players entered the Open singles tournament and 64 individuals entered the doubles competition.

Jewell McDowell won the fall 1949 (1950 *Aggieland*) intramural handball Open singles championship. The Open doubles champions were Jack M. Balderas, Jr. and P. A. Scheumach. Their photos are not available for this year. Entries in the singles tournament was 80 with 52 participating in doubles.

The only team handball played was in the Military League. A Company, Athletics won the championship over 43 other teams. Squadron E, Air Force was the runner-up. The 44 teams were divided into eight separate leagues. A total of 300 cadets played for their respective outfits.

1950 Corps Intramural Champions
Max Greiner, Carl Molberg, John Centilli, Richard Frey, Dick Gardemal
NOT IN PHOTO: Patrick Diffie
(1950 *Aggieland,* page 456)

As the new school year (1950-51) opened and the entrants for the singles and doubles began to stack up, it was apparent there would be new singles and doubles champions. From a total of 64 players, Arthur F. Clevenger came out the champion with Bo Hoskins as the runner-up. In the doubles tournament, the team of Bill Bristow and Bo Hoskins won over 22 other teams. The runner-up team was Roy Nance and Jack Wood.

1951 Open Intramural Handball Champions
Singles-Frank Clevenger (left)
Doubles-Bo Hoskins, Bill Bristow
(1951 *Aggieland*, p. 465)

A ASA
1951 Corps Intramural Handball Champions
FRONT ROW: Skippy Johnson, Jewell McDowell
Bo Hoskins, Jack Wood
BACK ROW: Hub Horton, Fred Sommers, Bert Gorrod
(1951 *Aggieland*, p. 464)

1951-52 Open Intramural Handball Champions
Singles-Jack Wood
Doubles-Don Fisher, John Vittrup
(1952 *Aggieland* page 289)

In the Military Class A League, A Company, Army Security Agency won the championship over 40 other teams. A Company, Athletics was the runner-up. The teams were divided into seven leagues with 328 cadets playing. The freshmen were no longer housed at the Bryan Air Force Base complex, so again, the freshmen of the Corps were able to play in a separate league which was designated as Military Class B. Company 5 won the Class B championship and the runner-up was Company 2. Over the years the unit (outfit) designations were changed from time to time based on many factors. There were 120 cadets playing for the 12 separate teams which were divided into three separate leagues. There were no photos of the Class B champions; however, the individuals on the winning team were recorded for historical purposes. The individuals making up the Company 5 team were Bennie Gallagher, Damian Golla, Bobby Poteet, Davis Richmond, Buck Roberts and Bill Utsman.

The world's largest intramural program was the claim before World War II, and the pace of the program had not changed. Barney Welch just kept everything going smoothly and the Aggies kept participating.

The fall 1951 Open intramural handball singles champion was Jack Wood. He won the title over 49 other players. Harry Keibler was the runner-up. In the doubles competition, the champions were Don Fisher and John Vittrup. There were 66 total entrants in the doubles competition. The runner-up doubles team was Ralph Dresser and Rodney East. The Military Class A League champion was A Company, Athletics. The runner-up team was E Battery, Field Artillery. There were 41 teams divided into seven separate leagues with a participation of 330 cadets. The team winner of the Military Class B League was Squadron 15. The runner-up was Company 9. A total of 16 teams divided into four leagues played in the Class B League. The total number of participants was not recorded. Again, there was no Non-Corps League.

Squadron 15
1952 Freshman Intramural Handball Champions
FRONT ROW: James B. Johnson, Key Kolb, Jr.,
Phil Orr, Jack Hendrick
BACK ROW: Carl O. Moore, Jim Mathis, Lawrie King
(1952 *Aggieland*, page 292)

A Athletics
1952 Corps Intramural Handball Champions
James Self, Don Garrett, Ralph Cox, Jaro Netardus
NOT IN PHOTO: Dick Gardemal, Elo Nohavitza,
John Centilli
(1952 *Aggieland*, page 290)

NOTE: The author has noted that the records of the handball intramural competition are not as complete as during the 1930s and early 1940s. What is being reported in this book is based on the available records. Obviously, from a historical standpoint, accuracy and completeness is of utmost importance.

For the fall of 1952, Harry Keibler took the Open handball championship by defeating Lawrence Laskoskie in the final match. A total of 56 players competed for the Open championship. In the Open doubles championship, the winners were John Centilli and Houser by winning the final match over Barclay and Field. A total of 76 handball players competed for the Open doubles championship.

Squadron 10 won the Military Class A League championship by defeating Squadron 4. A total of 28 teams were divided into five separate leagues. The total number of participants was not recorded.

Squadron 10
1953 Corps Intramural Handball Champions
Charles Little, Larry Hoffman,
Charlie Johnson, Ralph Cox, John Centilli
(!953 *Aggieland*, page 268)

1952 Open Handball Champion
Harry Keibler
(1953 *Aggieland*, page 270)

Going into the 1953-54 year the questions to be answered were: "Who will rise to the top in the Open championships and who can keep Squadron 10 from another team championship?" The answer for the team championship was that Squadron 10, with many of the same players back, would win another championship. There were 29 teams playing for the Class A Military team championship and those teams were divided into five separate leagues. The number of handball players participating was not recorded. Apparently, there were no Non-Military or Class B Military Leagues during the year. Company A, Ordnance was the runner-up team.

John Centilli won the Open singles title by defeating Dave Korry in the final match. The author and Jim Mathis each won their way to the quarterfinals where Centilli defeated Johnson and Korry defeated Mathis. A total of 56 handball players entered the singles competition.

In doubles competition, John Centilli earned a win to "slam" with both the Open singles and doubles titles. Teaming with Centilli in doubles was Doug Scott. Centilli and Scott defeated the team of Glen Rice and Dave Korry to win that crown. There were 28 players in the doubles competition.

As the year 1954-55 unfolded, it was well known that the Air Force had a considerable number of good handball players and would be hard to beat in the team championships. As the season unfolded and the finals were finished, Squadron 1 sat on top with the intramural handball championship crown. A Battery, Anti-Aircraft Artillery was the runner-up. A total of 45 teams divided into nine separate leagues made up the Class A intramural handball play. In Class B intramural handball competition, A Company, Ordnance came out on top with Squadron 5 as the runner-up. As in Class A, the total number of teams in Class B was 45 divided into nine separate leagues. The total number of handball players participating in the competition was not provided; however, a minimum number would be at least 450 with five players on each of the 90 teams, but the total number was probably closer to 500.

In the Open singles play Jim Mathis came out on top with Don Johnson as the runner-up. The two teamed up to take the Open doubles championship with Don Dittmar and Glen Langford as the runner-up team. A total of 85 participated in the singles play while 78 entered the doubles competition.

Squadron 10
1953-54 Corps Intramural Handball Champions
FRONT ROW: Bob Carpenter, Doug Scott, Tom Skrabanek, Ken Norton
BACK ROW: Larry Hoffman, Gary Leslie, Howell Patterson, Jr.
(1954 *Aggieland*, page 333)

1953-54 Intramural Handball Doubles Champions
John Centilli, Doug Scott
(1954 *Aggieland*, page 333)

Squadron 1
1955 Class A Corps Intramural Handball Champions
IN THE PHOTO: Irving Ramsower, II, John Dillard, III, Glen Rice, David Korry, Jerry Ash
(1955 *Aggieland*, page 138)

Open and National Collegiate
Doubles
Handball Champions
Don "Johnny" Johnson, Jim Mathis
(1955 *Aggieland,* page 138)

A Ordnance
1955 Freshmen Intramural Handball Champions
FRONT ROW: Newton Harris, III, Peter Schaar, Donald Wood, Arthur Tofte
BACK ROW: William Singleton, Charles Batson, Richard Lott, Jr., Donald Duzan
(1955 *Aggieland,* page 141)

The intramural office settled on a consistent classification for the team championships. Class A would be used to designate upper-class Corps competition. Class B would be used to designate Corps freshmen competition and Class C would be used to designate the civilian dorm competition. Class D was used for club competition; however, it would not likely occur in intramural handball since there were not that many club members in each of the clubs who competed on the handball courts. The exception would be the handball club, but most of those individuals participated with their own outfit/dorm team. However, all individuals at the college (not yet designated as a university) were invited to participate in the annual Open handball tournament which was under the supervision of the Director of Intramurals.

Squadron 1 continued their supremacy in Class A intramural handball for the 1955-56 year by defeating Squadron 11 in the final match. A total of 49 teams divided into nine separate leagues with 392 cadets playing in` the league. In Class B action, B Company, Infantry came out with the championship. In the final match they defeated B Battery, Field Artillery. A total of 48 teams divided into 12 separate leagues and 384 cadets played for the Class B championship. In Class C action Leggett Hall won that championship by defeating all comers in the four matches they played. Milner Hall was runner-up with three wins and one loss. Obviously, the loss was to Leggett Hall. A total of five teams participated in Class C League play.

Squadron 1
1956 Class A Intramural Handball Champions
FRONT ROW: Glen Rice, Donald Turbeville, John Dillard, III
BACK ROW: Allen Lee, Irving Ramsower, II, Bob Carpenter
NOT IN PHOTO: Dave Korry
(1956 *Aggieland*, page 375)

B Infantry
1956 Class B Intramural Handball Champions
FRONT ROW: Wiley Sonnier, John Speedie, Jr., Charles Hind
BACK ROW: Henry Everts, Jr., James McKnight, Clyde Tew
(1956 *Aggieland*, page 380)

Leggett Hall
1956 Class C Intramural Handball Champions
Gard, Skidmore, Anton Brucks, Halenor
(1956 *Aggieland*, page 381)

Gary Leslie of A Battery, Anti-Aircraft Artillery defeated Johnson from Hart Hall to win the 1955-56 Open singles handball championship. Participation in the singles tournament was down to 30 players this year. A total of 58 players participated in the doubles tournament. Gary Leslie teamed with Howell Patterson, Jr. to take the doubles crown by defeating Ashburn and McCandless.

The Air Force dominance of the Class A competition ended in 1956-57 when A Company, Ordnance won the championship by defeating the wearer of the crown for the past two years, Squadron 1, in the championship match. There were 50 teams divided into 10 leagues with 350 cadets playing. Squadron 1 still was very competitive; however, and ended their season as runner-up. A Company, Ordnance could not "slam", but the freshmen team of A Company, Ordnance was the runner-up in Class B competition. Squadron 16 became the title holder in Class B by defeating 48 other teams, which were divided into 12 separate leagues. The Class B competition had 390 cadets playing for their individual outfits. There are no records indicating Class C competition.

In the 1956-57 Open singles competition, no one could overcome the game of John Dillard, III. Dillard slammed by teaming with Carl Carpenter to also take the Open doubles title. Gary Staley of Squadron 22 was runner-up to Dillard in singles. Carpenter and Dillard from Squadron 1 defeated Ashburn from Hart Hall and Brady (team/dorm affiliation unknown) in the doubles final. Thirty-two handball players competed in the singles competition and 64 in doubles.

Squadron 11 met the challenges of 44 other intramural handball teams to remain unbeaten in league and the elimination series to earn the Class A championship for 1957-58. A Company, Quartermaster was runner-up. The 45 teams were divided into nine separate leagues. A total of 360 cadets took part in league play.

A Ordnance
1956-57 Class A Intramural Handball Champions
FRONT ROW: William Hitt, Daniel Stalmach, Edward Brod, James Bayley
BACK ROW: Richard Lott, Jr., Charles Batson, Frederic Golding, George Truesdale
(1957 *Aggieland*, page 390)

Squadron 16
1957 Class B Intramural Handball Champions
James Midkiff, Greg Hartness, Richard Bailey, Doyce Nance, Charles Miller
(1957 Aggieland, p. 391)

Open Handball Champions
Doubles: Carl Carpenter (left)
Singles, Doubles: John Dillard, III
(1957 *Aggieland*, page 395)

Squadron 11
1958 Class A Intramural Handball Champions
FRONT ROW: Jerry Pitts, Ray Laird, Thomas Wallace
BACK ROW: Don Linenberger, H. Adonn Slone, Jerry Corbin

(1958 *Aggieland*, page 388)

Squadron 17
1959 Class A Intramural Handball Champions
FRONT ROW: Thomas Wallace, John Parks,
O'Gene Barkemeyer, Gerald Griffith
BACK ROW: James Pate, William Frost, Bob Reeh

(1959 *Aggieland*, page 95)

A Infantry
1959 Class B Intramural Handball Champions
FRONT ROW: Dave Gabriel, Marion Walton, Jr.,
Donald Gardner, Donley Brothers
BACK ROW: David Lewis, Patrick McGaughey
NOT IN PHOTO: Winston Welch

(1959 *Aggieland*, page 95)

In the Class B League, the champion team was Squadron 10. A Company, Infantry was the runner-up. A total of 44 teams divided into 11 leagues made up the competition in this league. A photo was not available of the winning team. The following cadets made up the Squadron 10 team: Bernie Berman, Gary Billings, Henry Fitzhugh, Henry Holubec, Richard Ward and Willis Ward. Three hundred eight cadets played in the Class B League.

There is no record of Class C intramural handball for 1957-58.

John Dillard, III, repeated as the Open singles champion. He teamed with Lee to take the Open doubles championship. A total of 33 entrants competed in the singles competition while 48 took part in doubles.

In 1958-59, it was Squadron 17 surviving the gauntlet of 50 other Corps outfits to take the Class A intramural handball championship. For the second year in a row, A Company, Quartermaster was the runner-up. The 51 units of Class A handball were divided into nine separate leagues. A total of 310 cadets played in the League. In Class B intramural handball, A Company, Infantry won the championship. A Company, Quartermaster was the runner-up team. The 49 teams of Class B were divided into 10 separate leagues to determine the championship, with 400 freshmen cadets participating. In Class C competition, Bizzell Hall came out on top by being undefeated. Law Hall came in second. There were 45 students competing in the five separate dorm teams. Members of the Bizzell Hall team were: Cal and Walt Bayley, Larry Clark, Jim Conway, Fred Golding and David Wight. There was no photo available of the winning team.

The 1958-59 Open singles champion was John Hunt. Hunt had to survive 46 others wanting to be named the champion, including David Glickman, who was the runner-up. Seventy signed up to play in the Open doubles tournament. Samuel McKenney and Clyde Tew rose to the top to claim the championship. Bob Reeh and Thomas Wallace were the runner-up team.

Reading this history some may question why every unit of the Corps of Cadets, both the upperclassmen (there were no women in the Corps during these years) and the freshmen, were so involved in handball while those not in the Corps had difficulty in establishing a league among the non-Corps dorms. Anyone delving into the history of the Corps at Texas A&M would find that the competitive spirit in athletics,

1959 Open Intramural Handball Doubles Champions
Clyde Tew, Samuel McKenney
(1959 *Aggieland*, page 95)

marching, military appearance in both the uniforms and living quarters, and academics has always been a large part of the Corps from the very beginning of the university-formerly college. The competition still exists to this day for the many annual awards given near the end of the school year. Intramural competition was regarded in earlier years as being very much a part of the physical development of the individual cadet, and handball was and still is one of the best physical conditioning sports available.

Readers may also question why photos of intramural handball winners who were not in the Corps are not as available as those featuring cadets. To take photos of Corps members was simple. Commanders in the chain of command within the Corps routinely require cadets requested to be present for certain tasks to be at the designated place at the time specified. This type of leadership/followership did not exist in the non-Corps dorms which meant, of course, individuals may or may not be available. The author also believes that the Class A champions are shown annually due to the fact that the *Aggieland* editor was almost always a senior from the Corps of Cadets and members of the Class A team are well known to and may be good friends with the editor.

Squadron 12 was the unit that rose to the top and earned the Class A championship in 1959-60. Company A-1 was the runner-up team, not A Company, Infantry. This was the year that the Office of the Commandant changed the designation of all the Army ROTC units. The reason for the change was to reflect the new changes in the Army ROTC program. Army ROTC at Texas A&M no longer taught military subjects relating to the various branches of the Army, but changed to a general military curriculum for all cadets taking Army ROTC courses. Under this new program the senior cadets who sought commissions in the Army made their branch choice during their senior year in the Corps.

A total of 37 teams divided into seven leagues participated in the Class A handball program. A total of 350 cadets played for their respective teams. In the Class B intramural leagues,

Squadron 12
1960 Class A Intramural Handball Champions
FRONT ROW: Thomas Wallace, O'Gene Barkemeyer, James Schlotzhauer, Thomas Fields
BACK ROW: Bob Reeh, Gerald Griffith, William Frost, James Pate
NOT IN PHOTO: Don Coker
(1960 *Aggieland,* page 242)

the underclassmen of the Class A champions won as the Squadron 12 Class B team came through with that championship. Squadron 14 was the runner-up team. All 37 teams of Class A handball play entered a team in the Class B league. The 37 teams were divided into nine separate leagues with 270 cadets playing for their respective teams. Members of the Class B team champion, Squadron 12, were James Drake, Rodney Goodman, James Leach, William Reisser, Joe Salinas, and Perry Wilcox, Jr. In the Class C competition Hart Hall emerged as the champion among the four teams competing. The runner-up team was Bizzell Hall. A total of 30 handball players competed for their respective teams.

In the Open singles competition, Gary Staley earned the championship over the 25 other competitors. Staley also won the Open doubles championship by teaming with Ed Merritt. Merritt was the runner-up in Open singles competition so the two obviously were tough competition as a team. A total of 36 handball players participated in the singles tournament and 36 were also in the doubles competition.

Company A-1 used its experience and handball skills learned as runner-up in 1959-60 to win the Class A championship in 1960-61. Runner-up in the Class A League was Company E-2. There were 38 teams competing for the championship and that involved 840 handball players. The Company A-1 Class B team obviously learned from the Class A team as they took the championship. Freshmen cadets on the Class B team were: Calvin Chlapek, John Fredricks, Kenneth Matocha, Billy Mulligan, Percy Smith and Thomas Tracy. The runner-up to Company A-1 in Class B was Squadron 3. One hundred forty-eight (148) cadets played for the 37 teams in the Class B League. Milner Hall took the championship in Class C competition. Puryear Hall was the runner-up team among the nine teams in the Class C League.

For the second consecutive year, Gary Staley and Ed Merritt battled it out for the Open singles championship. The results were the same as the previous year with Gary Staley taking the crown. A total of 38 handball players participated in the singles tournament. Thirty players teamed up for the Open doubles crown with the team of Merritt/Staley leading the way. The competition ended at the quarterfinals level with no play beyond that point. The records do not indicate why the competition ended at this point in the tournament.

There are no available records of intramural handball at the Recreation Center or in the '62 Aggieland for the 1961-62 year. The reason there are no records cannot be determined; however, a change in the Director of Intramurals may have impacted the record keeping process.

Hart Hall
1960 Class C Intramural Handball Champions
Gary Staley, Frederick Davidson, Robert Stein, Maskal
NOT IN PHOTO: Tommy Flood, Ed Merritt, Tuck
(1960 *Aggieland*, page 242)

Company A-1
1961 Class C Intramural Handball Champions
FRONT ROW: Dale Gabriel, Paul King, Warren Nichols, Tommy Nelson
BACK ROW: Gordon Hudson, Marion Walton, Jr., Dave Lorms, Harrell Brown
(1961 *Aggieland*, page 265)

Milner Hall
FRONT ROW: H. C. Stoever, Clyde Bayley, Jr. Dave Koehler
BACK ROW: Bill Hedrick, Eudoro Galindo, Jr., R. A. Jordan
NOT IN THE PHOTO: Garza, Martin
(1961 *Aggieland*, page 267)

In 1962-63 the Class A team champion was Company F-3. Members of the team were Christian, Hardeman, Benjamin Jackson, McCulloch, Pedigo, and James Riggs. NOTE: The author could find no verification of the first names of four members of the team. Also, the four team members listed as part of the championship team of F-3 were not in the unit photo under the Corps section of the *Aggieland*. Adding to the difficulty of positively identifying the four is the fact that a Third Brigade was formed in the Corps and Company F-3 was in its first year as a new unit. The runner-up team in the Class A League was Squadron 15. A total of 39 teams and 334 cadets participated in the Class A League. In Class B action, Company F-1 came out on top. The runner-up team was Squadron 6. Participating in the Class B League were 228 cadets among the 38 teams. From the seven teams that made up the Class C League, the Vet (veterans) students come out on top. The runner-up team was Puryear Hall.

Company F-1
1963 Class B Intramural Handball
Champions
FRONT ROW: Jim Douglas, Mac Thornhill
BACK ROW: Coy Mitchell, Bailey Holman
NOT IN PHOTO: Bill Lyon, Charles Hoffer

(1963 *Aggieland*, page 245)

Vet Students
1963 Class C Intramural Handball
Champions
FRONT ROW: Powell Charlton, Ray Allen
BACK ROW: Bob Lowe, Howard Hayes, Ken
Herpst, Ed Merritt

(1963 *Aggieland*, page 248)

In the Open singles championship Ed Merritt was the champion after having to experience Gary Staley besting him in the finals the past two years. Merritt won in the finals over Altman by the convincing score of 21-12, 21-9. Thirty handball players participated in the Open singles competition. In Open doubles play Merritt teamed with Ernest Reesing to take that championship. The runner-up team were brothers Ozzie and Stoney Burke. Eighteen (18) players played in the doubles competition.

The 1963-64 school year would be a major landmark in A&M's history. This educational institution was no longer to be known as the Agricultural and Mechanical College of Texas but would for all of the world's population become known as Texas A&M University. It was decided to keep the A and the M, and the result is that the University would no longer be the Agricultural and Mechanical University but simply known as Texas A&M. As for intramural handball, Company G-2 won the Class A championship. The runner-up team was Company C-3. The Class A competition consisted of 40 teams divided into seven separate leagues.

In Class B competition, Company A-1 came out on top with the crown. The runner-up team was Squadron 1. A total of 40 teams was divided into seven separate leagues to make up the Class B competi-

Company G-2
1964 Class A Intramural Handball Champions
FRONT ROW: Jerry Vick, Malcolm Basham, Thomas Wagner
BACK ROW: Robert Mitchell, William Crain, James Beamer, Thomas Rodriquez, Jr.
(1964 *Aggieland*, page 245)

Company A-1
1964 Class B Intramural Handball Champions
FRONT ROW: Franklyn Supercinski, Robert Lackland, Sydney Jones, D. M. Parks
BACK ROW: Harold Schade, Kim Keisling, Garza, Robert Grove
(1964 *Aggieland*, page 245)

Company C-3
1965 Class A Intramural Handball Champions
Oscar Pena, Joe DePasqual, Stephen Heartwell, William Davis, Jack Wilson, Thomas Fine, III
(!965 *Aggieland*, page 126)

tion. The Vets came out with the championship among the 11 teams divided into two separate leagues that made up the Class C handball competition. Members of the winning team were Howard Hayes, Paul Lillard, Ed Merritt, Allan Ray, Ernest Reesing and Howard Whitford. Puryear Hall was the runner-up team.

The results of Open singles and Open doubles competition are not available for 1963-64 and are not found in recorded history until the year 1974. Without question these tournaments were held annually under the intramural program; however, the purpose/reason for non-availability of the name/names of the winner/winners cannot be determined.

Company C-3 won the 1964-65 Class A intramural team title over 40 other teams that were divided into 7 separate leagues. The runner-up team was Squadron 3. In Class B action, Company D-3 earned the crown while Squadron 13 was runner-up. Playing for the championship team were Terrance Herzik, Dan Kennerly, Bill Kinder, Kenneth Mattoon, John Van Winkle and Fred Ward. A total of 39 teams participated in the seven separate leagues. The Class C League had great growth in its competition. Twenty teams divided into four separate leagues made for an interesting handball year in Class C. The winning team was from Hart Hall. There were two teams entered from Hart Hall with the number-one team earning the crown. Hart Hall number-two was in the quarterfinals of the elimination series where they were defeated by Law Hall. Law Hall couldn't overcome the athleticism and skill of the number-one Hart Hall team, so had to settle as the runner-up team.

Company D-2 earned the intramural Class A team championship of 1965-66 by eliminating all challengers on the way to the final elimination series match where they defeated the runner-up team, Company A-1. Members of the champs were Bill Goode, Trey Helmcamp, Steve Hightower, Perry Kinder, Dan Kennerly, Ken Mattoon and Tommy Ward. No photos were available of any handball winners this year. A total of 30 teams divided into six

separate leagues made up the Class A League. In Class B competition, Squadron 10 earned the championship by defeating Squadron 8 in the final match. Members of the champs were Mike Birdsong, Randy Bubb, Paul Burns, Jim Christian, Dick Dubois, Larry Stewart, Bud Welch and Dennis Wilson. A total of 30 teams divided into five leagues comprised the Class B League. In Class C competition there were 14 teams divided into three separate leagues. Dorm 13 came out as the winning team after defeating Pan Am in the final match of the elimination series. Members of the Dorm 13 team were Hector Diaz, Milton Henri and Gary Scharver.

Company A-1 came up a little short in '65-66 but won the Class A championship in 1966-67. The runner-up team was Company E-2. A total of 32 teams divided into eight separate leagues made up the competition. In Class B competition, there were 31 teams divided into six leagues. Winning the championship was Squadron 11, who defeated Company G-1 in the final match. Members of the Squadron 11 team were Bill Corey, Tom Emshoff, Ron Jackson, Richard McKenney, Paige Moore, Jerry Richerson and Randy Spangle. Based on the number of team entries during the past two years, the author is reasonably certain that a Class C League existed; however, there are no records available for verification.

Company A-1 repeated as the intramural Class A champion team for the 1967-68 year. Company E-2 had to be satisfied with the runner-up spot for a second consecutive year. There was no available record of the members of the Company A-1 championship team; however, it is likely that some of the players on the championship team of the previous year were still on the team in '67-68. A total of 32 teams divided into six separate leagues comprised the competition in Class A play. In Class B competition, Company B-2 earned the championship by defeating Squadron 2 in the elimination series final match. A total of 32 teams divided into six separate leagues comprised the competition in Class B play. In Class C action, a team named LSA won the championship by defeating Dorm 21 in the final match. A total of 20 teams, divided into five separated leagues, comprised Class C play.

Squadron 12 earned the championship crown in the intramural Class A league for the 1968-69 year. Company G-1 was the runner-up team. A total of 30 teams, divided into six leagues, made up the Class A competition. In Class B, Squadron 1 earned the right to wear the crown by defeating Company E-2 in the final match. There were also 30 teams, divided into 6

Hart Hall #1
1965 Class C Intramural Handball Champions
Roger Dittmar, Robert Paulson, Joseph Wellborn, Ryan, Diaz, Ford
NOT IN THE PHOTO: Doyle Beavers, James Gibbs
(1965 *Aggieland*, page 128)

Company A-1
1967 Intramural Handball Champion
FRONT ROW: Riley Rhorer, Kim Keisling, Gregory Peyrefitte
BACK ROW: Robert Lackland, Noel Adams, Jr., Harlan Berger, Stephen Hodgkins
(1967 *Aggieland*, page 457)

Company B-2
1968 Class B Intramural Champions
FRONT ROW: Thomas Althaus, Michael Reese, Terry Hogwood, Walter Thornton
BACK ROW: Michael Christiani, Larry Hubbell
(1968 *Aggieland*, page 472)

leagues, to comprise the freshmen competition. In Class C action, the 24 teams were divided into four leagues. Winning the championship was Schumacher Hall. Law Hall was the runner-up team.

Team LSA
1968 Class C Intramural Champions
LEFT TO RIGHT: Barry Smedberg, Dorian David,
Michael Mattern, Michael Deika

(1968 *Aggieland*, page 472)

Squadron 12
1969 Class A Intramural Handball Champions
FRONT ROW: Ken Hess, Ken Donaho
BACK ROW: Gary Burt, David Frost, Melton Fehrle
NOT IN THE PHOTO: Bubba Craighead

(1969 *Aggieland*, page 251)

Squadron 1
1969 Class B Intramural Handball Champions
Kirby Babb, George "Cupe" Adams,
John Brady, David Romine
NOT IN THE PHOTO: Paul Haase,
Terry Stewart

(1969 *Aggieland*, page 251)

Schumacher Hall
1969 Class C Intramural Handball Champions
FRONT ROW: Charles Church, Bill Hagland, Henry Abel
BACK ROW: George Beeler, Jr., Ron Snider, Juan Medina
NOT IN THE PHOTO: Purcell

(1969 *Aggieland*, page 251)

In 1969-70 a new Intramural Director stepped into the shoes that had been notably occupied in past years. As happens many times, changes were made. The method of keeping records was changed from a system used since 1933-34. The only records available during this Intramural Director's time is found in the *Aggieland*. Those records follow as recorded in the photos:

NOTE: The Class C Intramural Champions were not shown in the *Aggieland*. The author firmly believes that the League existed.

Three Intramural handball champion teams were published in the *Aggieland* for the 1970-71 year.

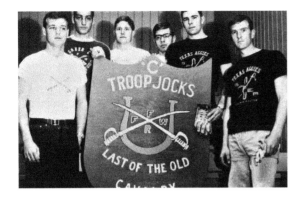

Company C-1
1969-70 Class A Intramural Champions
FRONT ROW: Larry Ferguson, Russel Hawkins
BACK ROW: Douglas Huebner, Dan Colbert, Jerry Wheaton, Paul Irke

(1970 *Aggieland*, page 158)

Squadron 3
1970 Class B Intramural Handball Champions
FRONT ROW: Dan Gear, Lewis Nunely,
Jim Green, BACK ROW: Robert Lee, Keith
Shackleford, David Godwin

(1970 *Aggieland*, page 158)

Squadron 2
1971 Class A Intramural Handball Champions
FRONT ROW: Doug Davis, Paul Nauschutz, John Jackson
BACK ROW: John McNevin, Tim Booker

(1971 *Aggieland*, page 147)

Company E-1
1971 Class B Intramural Handball Champions
FRONT ROW: Craig Ezell, Allen Broesche
BACK ROW: Ted Paup, Ron Asto

(1971 *Aggieland*, page 144)

Davis-Gary Hall
1971 Class C Intramural Handball
Champions
David Ammons, David Donaldson, Randy
Ross Andre Piazzo

(1971 Aggieland, page 147)

Company G
1971-72 Class A intramural
Handball Champions
FRONT ROW: J. D. Richmond, Buddy
King
BACK ROW: Donnie Byrd, Wade
Smith, Pete Starks

1972 Aggieland, page 142)

"Saints"
1972 Class D Intramural Champion
FRONT ROW: John Wilson, Charles
Clark, Stewart Carpenter
BACK ROW: Joe Tillerson, Darrell
Denman, James Willbeck

(1972 Aggieland, page 142)

Law Hall
1971-72-Class C Intramural Handball
Champions
Ralph Alonzo, Ruben Gonzalez, Terry
Earley, Wade Habshey, Dennis Grafa, Steve
Logsdon

(1972 Aggieland, page 143)

For the first time the *Aggieland* published the Class D Intramural handball team champion. The Class D league in all sports had been available since early in the years of Barney Welch's reign as the Director of Intramurals; however, a league and team championship could not be established unless there was more than one team available in any sport. The Class D league involved those Aggies who were not housed in a dorm. For 1972, the Class D intramural champion was a team named "Saints".

For 1973 there were no team photos. Squadron 3 won the Class A intramural handball championship. The team members were Lewis Nunley, Danny Gear, Gary Buis, Jim Green, Scott Eberhart and Mark Nilius. The Class C intramural handball champion was Law Hall. The team members were Ruben Gonzalez, Joel Pena, Steve Logsdon, Terry Earley, Dennis Grafa and Karl Von Rosenberg.

For 1973 a new league designation surfaced. The Class X intramural handball champion team members were Roland Borey, Steve Keng, Dave Kinison, Robert Lengefeld, Dick Madden, Max Rodgers, Gary Sheffield, James Shepard and Johnny Vernor. The author believes the new designation of Class X simply replaced the designation Class D.

As the saying goes "Times are changing". With women being admitted to the university in increasing numbers, fraternities and sororities became an option, and with an ever-increasing enrollment, intramural sports saw an increase in the number of leagues offered. This would impact what is shown in the intramural portion of the *Aggieland*. Which champions should have photos shown in the *Aggieland* became a question increasingly difficult to solve, so the *Aggieland* began reporting the champions with no individual or team photos.

In 1974, Company D-1 earned the title as the men's team champion. Team members were Craig Ezell, Alex Korzenewski, Patrick Ivey, Terry Royder, Frederick Martin and Allen Broesche. The champion team in Class A action was Company C-2. Hart Hall won the Class C team championship. The individual singles title went to Dennis Corrington. Jeff Bronson and Bernard Shapiro won the doubles title. A total of 433 handball players participated in the team competition. The Open handball singles tournament had 38 entrants while the doubles tournament had 74.

The year of 1973-74 was the end of team championships for handball. Henceforth, all handball tournaments would be singles and doubles tournaments. The first intramural singles and doubles tournaments in the intramural program began this year as evidenced by the singles and doubles champions listed above. The author checked with Dennis Corrington to get an understanding of why intramural team play in handball was discontinued. This was essentially the beginning of his many years as Intramural/Recreational Sports Director and he was unable to recall what prompted the decision for change.

As the university has grown and changed over the years so did intramural sports. As the era of team competition in handball was ending, the following rules for eligibility and competition in intramural sports were provided. They have been essentially unchanged for many years, and should remain in effect- with the flexibility for change to compensate as time and situations dictate:

An example of the recognition award Intramural winners received for their championship. This certificate was received by Frederick "Rusty" Martin. When the author was a student at A&M, intramural winners received a small pendant to be worn on a key chain with the cadet uniform.

(Courtesy Rusty Martin)

RULES AND REGULATIONS

ARTICLE I. ORGANIZATION ELIGIBILITY

Section I. Group Eligibility—A group is eligible to participate in the intramural program if:
    A. Its membership is not denied to anyone on the basis of race, nationality, religion, or sex; and
    B. Is not under disciplinary penalty prohibiting participation.

Section II. Military Division
    A. This division shall consist of teams organized from ROTC units as designated by the Commandant's Office.
    B. Members of teams in this division shall be upper classmen in the Corps of Cadets.
    C. Combined ROTC units are subject to the approval of the Director of Intramurals.

Section III. Fish Division
    A. This division shall consist of teams organized from ROTC units as designated by the Commandant's office.
    B. Members of teams in this division shall be freshmen in the Corps of Cadets.
    C. Combined ROTC units are subject to the approval of the Director of Intramurals.

Section IV. Civilian Dorm Division
    A. This division shall consist of teams organized from residents of university operated men's residence halls.
    B. Members of teams in this division shall compete for the dormitory in which they reside.

Section V. Independent Division
    A. This division shall consist of teams organized from independent (off-campus) men.
    B. Men living in university operated housing, wishing to compete in this division shall furnish the Intramural Office a release form signed by his team manager.

Section VI. Recreation Division
    A. This division shall consist of teams or individuals organized from university students, faculty, or staff:
    B. Second and third teams organized from the military, fish, and civilian dorm divisions shall compete in this division.

Section VII. Women's Division
    A. This division shall consist of teams organized from university women students, faculty, and staff.
    B. Women living in university operated dormitories shall compete for the dorm in which they reside.
    C. Off-Campus women shall not compete for a dorm team.

Section VIII. Co-Rec Division
    A. This division shall consist of teams organized from university students, faculty, and staff.

CHAPTER 5
Individual Intramural Handball

In the year of transition, 1973-74, from the team championships which had been used since handball was introduced beginning with the new intramural programs approved in 1925, both team and individual tournaments were held. Dennis Corrington won the singles championship by defeating 37 other entrants. Jeff Bronson and Bernard Shapiro won the doubles championship by defeating 72 other handball players.

In team competition during previous years, opportunities existed for several team titles. Initially, the beginning of individual tournament play resulted in only a singles and doubles title. The opportunity to participate in different skill level tournaments would follow. As time progressed, with more women playing, co-rec team play and a continuing interest in the game of handball, any university student or faculty/staff could choose a tournament to match their level of play.

In 1975, Jack Gressett won the intramural Open singles title. The Open tournament was open to all university students, staff and faculty. Kley Hughes from Company M-1 earned the Corps Championship and Tim Billingsley won the Fish title. Paige Cokinos from Moore Hall came out on top in the Civilian Championship. In the doubles competition, Jack Gressett and Jeff Bronson were the All-University Champions. Kley Hughes and Thomas Culberson from Company M-1 won the Corps title. Tim Billingsley and Charlie Knarr from Squadron 4 won the Fish title while the winners of the Civilian division were Dennis Grafa and Van Kelly from Law Hall. There were 359 handball players who competed in the singles tournaments. For the Doubles tournaments, 520 played for those titles. This would be the last year for the doubles tournament to be played in the fall and the singles in the spring. Henceforth, the singles would be played in the fall semester and the doubles during the spring. That rotation continued until 1994-95 when both singles and doubles was played in the fall and again in the spring.

E. D. Glover won the Faculty-Staff singles tournament in the fall of 1975. The men's independent champion was Wayne Neumann. Tim Billingsley of Squadron 4 earned another handball title by taking the Corps championship. The Fish champion was David Rutledge from Company B-1 while Dennis Dickinson from Dunn Hall took the Civilian title. In the doubles competition Jeff Bronson and Wayne Neumann won the Faculty-Staff championship. The men's independent champions were Cody Birdwell and Jack Gressett. Tim Billingsley teamed up with Charlie Knarr to take the Corps championship. Chuck Brown and Richard Schrader of Company K-1 won the Fish doubles title while Edwin Bigon and Tommy Bruns of Moore Hall did the same in the Civilian tournament. The handball singles tournaments brought out 208 handball players to vie for the division championships. In doubles, there were 352 to answer the call for tournament play.

For the first time in more than 50 years of intramural handball at Texas A&M, the opportunity for women to participate in an intramural handball tournament came in the fall semester of 1976. Jeannie Buckles earned the championship title to become the first woman to win a singles handball tournament in intramural handball at Texas A&M. Jeff Bronson added another handball title to his burgeoning handball mastery by taking the fall 1976 men's independent singles title. In other Class A action, Tim Billingsley from Squadron 4 won the Corps championship while Ken Madison of Squadron 9 won the Fish title. In the men's dorm division, Edwin Bigon of Moore Hall came out as the winner. In Class B singles, the winner of the men's independent tournament was Steve Thomas. The Corps champion was Jim Huff of Company A-1 and the men's dorm champion was Bob Martin of Hart Hall. In Class C singles, the Corps champion was Terry Stanislav of Squadron 9 while the men's dorm champion was Rick Williams of Schumacher Hall. In the doubles competition, Jeff Bronson teamed with Don Johnson to take the men's independent championship. In other Class A doubles action, Brent Ramage and Joe Taylor from Squadron 6 won the Corps championship while Bob Dimmick and Mark Previty of Company F-2 won the Fish crown. The men's dorm champions were Tom Bozeman and Stu Walker of Hart Hall. In the Class B division, the men's independent winners were Charlie Deyble and Richard Shutt. The Corps champions were Bus Gonzales and Kent Riper of Company K-1, while the men's dorm champions were Alan Dishoughn and Kirk Hall of Law Hall. In Class C doubles, the winners of the men's independent tournament were Larry Glomski and Mike Murphy. A total of 236 handball players participated in the singles handball tournaments. In the doubles competition there were 230 to vie for their respective championships.

Nothing had changed when the fall 1977 intramural singles handball tournament results were finalized for the Class A men's independent championship. No one had been able to edge Jeff Bronson out, so he added another championship to his resume. A personal note here as the author can attest to the difficulty in winning a match from Bronson. A single game, yes, but a match was never easy. In the Corps, Tim Billingsley from Squadron 4 was a repeat winner while Bill Breffeith from Company F-2 won the Fish title. The men's dorm champion was Daryl Taraba from Aston Hall. In the Class B division, the men's independent winner was Carl Shafer. The Corps champion was Kurt Jentsch from Company D-2 while Ron Bottoms from Squadron 10 won the Fish title. The men's dorm champion was Kirk Hall from Aston Hall. In the Class C division, the men's independent winner was Steven Worley. The Corps winner was Mike Baringer from Company K-1 and the men's dorm winner was Bill Schlafer from Davis-Gary Hall. In the doubles competition, the winners of the men's Independent title were Rick Copeland and Lance Lowy. The Corps champions were Tim Billingsley and Mike De La Cruz from Squadron 4. The Corps Fish champions were Gerardo Garcia and Jim Lawson from Company D-1. The men's dorm winners were Greg Buchanan and Daryl Taraba from Aston Hall. Competing for the titles in the singles competition were 250 handball players while the doubles drew 312.

The number of handball players participating in the fall 1978 singles tournaments was 284. The spring 1979 handball doubles tournaments brought out 239 handball players. A doubles team consists of 2 players so the number 239 would likely be 238 or 240; however, if one player played with more than one doubles team in separate tournaments 239 could be correct. The winning Class A men's independent champions were Dennis Corrington and Mike Werner. Winning the Class A Corps championship was Tommy Albright and Dan Urban of Company D-2. The Corps Fish championship team was Richard Harrison and Keith Nelson from Company K-I. The men's dorm champions, Greg Buchannan and Darryl Taraba, were from Aston Hall. In Class B competition, the men's independent doubles team champions were Phil Naughton and Bill Schlafer. The Corps champions were Gary Nesloney and Eric Neilson of Squadron 7, while the Fish champions were Gary Branch and James Salmons of Company K-2. The men's dorm champions were Jeff Johnson and Phil Tibbs of Crocker Hall. In the Class C tournament, the men's independent champions were Jimmy and Ricky Seawright. From the Corps, the winners were Tim Conrow and Tom Langford of Company K-1. The men's dorm champions were Terry Easterwood and Bill Yablon. The Class A women's champions were Lani Jacobs and Susan Oakleaf. Coming all the way from West Hartford, Connecticut, Oakleaf wasted no time in getting her name in the A&M handball record book. This would be her first of many championships while a student at Texas A&M. The women's Class B champions were Tammy Carlisle and Phyllis Golden.

NOTE: In the following years, open or independent title designations also carry the title of All-University Champion. The Fish champion will always be from the Corps of Cadets and the men's Residence Hall champion will include all dorms on campus except the Corps of Cadets dorms.

In the handball tournaments of 1979-80, there would be some repeat champions. Jeff Bronson won the men's independent title in Class A and Dan Urban of Company F-1 won the Corps title. John Welch of Dunn Hall won the men's dorm title. The women's independent tournament champion was Sue Oakleaf. Coke Smith won the Class B men's independent championship. The Class B Corps champion was Doug McGowan from Company E-2 and the Fish champion was Jeff Davison of Squadron 2. In the Class C men's tournament, Gary Alke came out on top and in the women's Class C, Gus Archer was the champion. In intramural handball doubles, the All-University champions were Jeff Bronson and Mike Moore. The All-University co-rec handball doubles champions were Beth Rowley and Ricky Seawright. In Class A, the men's intramural handball doubles Corps champions were Dan Urban and Tommy Albright of Company F-1. In Class B doubles competition, the men's independent champions were Terry Kirkland and Mark Patterson. The Corps champions were Richard Harrison and Tim Conrow of Company K-1 while Jeff Davison and Kevin Smith of Squadron 2 earned the Fish title. The men's dorm champions were John Welch and Kyle House of Dunn Hall. In Class C men's doubles competition, Steve Folk and Tom Shults came out on top. The number of participants in the singles tournaments was 244. The number of players in the doubles tournaments was recorded as 111. The number could have been either 110 or 112 since a team in doubles competition involves two people: however, 111 is possible if one person participated on more than one doubles team.

The 1980-81 All-University champion in Intramural men's handball singles was Jeff Bronson while Susan Oakleaf added another All-University Class A title to her resume. Richard Harrison of Company K-1 added another Corps championship to his resume. The Fish champion was Jeff Crofton of Company B-2. John Welch of Dunn Hall added another Class A men's dorm title to his list. Tim Feickert won the Class B men's independent championship and Beth Warinner won the women's title. Kimberly Holtz of Squadron 14 won the women's dorm championship. The Corps men's champion was John McAdams of Company D-1. In Class C, Mike Seawright earned the title. In the doubles competition, Jeff Bronson and Mike Moore repeated as the All-University champs. The Class A co-rec intramural handball doubles champions were Beth Rowley and Coke Smith. Richard Harrison and Eddie Garza of Company K-1 won the Corps doubles championship. In Class B doubles competition, the men's champions were Matt Pokryfki and Raymond Walkup. The women's champions were Hilary Huffard and Jill MacAluso. For the co-rec championship, Terri Miller and Scott Elkins earned the title. Greg Powell and Mark Thurman of Crocker won the men's dorm title and Patrice Owens with Kelly Wells as a partner from Mosher Hall did the same for the women's dorm title. Danny Coolidge and Paul Pylate of Squadron 2 won the Corps championship. In Class C doubles competition, the women's title went to Laura Crout and Carol Caboda. The co-rec doubles champions were Kristi Solderman and Chris Duncan. It was a great year for intramural handball. There were 188 entered in the singles competition and 248 in doubles. There was no doubt that this increasing number of participants was the ready acceptance and enjoyment that the women at the university were experiencing. Women were increasingly being accepted into the world of sports, once dominated only by males. The singles tournaments were held during the fall semester and the doubles were held during the spring semester.

For the school year 1981-82, Jeff Bronson continued as the All-University champion in Class A singles; however, this year a new category was added as Faculty/Staff/Graduate. This was the title Jeff won and was regarded as the All-University champion. Coke Smith won the Class A men's independent title. Jeff Davison won the Corps championship. Ray Trimmer won the men's Class B independent title, while Barbara DiSioudi of Neeley Hall earned the Class B women's dorm title. Bill Moore earned the men's dorm title and Dan Coolidge of Squadron 2 won the Corps title. In intramural handball doubles, the Class A men's championship went to Matt Pokryfki and Coke Smith. In women's competition, Hilary Huffard and Ariela Vader won the title. Sue Oakleaf and Matt Pokryfki won the co-rec doubles intramural handball title. In Class B doubles competition, Pete Marchbanks and Butch Reinke won the men's competition, and Hilary Huffard with Bill McMullen were the victors in co-rec doubles competition. The normal rotation of the handball tournaments-with the fall being devoted to singles and the spring to doubles-continued. Participation numbers for the singles tournaments were down from recent years to 114 and also in doubles at 128.

For the school year 1982-83, the Class A intramural handball singles champion was Eric Hunter for the men and Kay Kern was the champion in the women's competition. In Class B intramural handball singles, the men's champion was Steven Taliaferro, and Corine Sasser won the title for the women. The Corps champion was Tim Tollette, while Brent Bertrand of Schumacher Hall earned the men's dorm title. In the Class A doubles competition, Coke Smith and Matt Pokryfki continued to prove they were a great doubles handball team and once again came away with the championship crown. For the women's doubles competition, Corine Sasser and Caroline Henning were the All-University handball doubles champions. In Class B doubles competition, the co-rec doubles champions were Corine Sasser and Ricky Van while the men's independent champions were Bill McMullen and Jamie Taylor. David Allen and David Utsey of Hart Hall earned the men's dorm doubles title. In Class C doubles, Kevin Canales and Chris Ingram earned the top crown. A total of 124 players competed for the singles titles and 90 participated in the doubles tournaments.

In 1983-84 Class A intramural handball singles, Bobby Winans played his way to the top in men's independent competition. In the women's competition, Corine Van duplicated the effort. The men's dorm champion was Brent Bertrand of Schumacher Hall, while Caroline Henning from Clements Hall won the women's dorm title. In Class B action, Larry Wisdom won the men's independent championship while Mark Smith of Walton Hall won the men's dorm championship. In Class C, the men's independent winner was Dave Eggers and Scott Sedberry was the winner of the men's dorm competition. Ninety-four turned out for the singles competition while 68 entered the doubles.

Coke Smith won another intramural handball championship as he captured the 1984-85 Class A men's singles title. Julie Werner was making her name known as the best women's handball player on campus by capturing the women's Class A intramural handball singles championship. Randy Pullen won the championship in Class B men's singles and, in Class C, the winner in the men's competition was Randy Armstrong while Dawn Bell won the Class C title in the women's tournament. I regret not being able to provide the winner's names in doubles competition, but will give the winning team names. In Class A doubles of the women's dorm tournament, the top team was the Neeley Knockouts. In Class B doubles, the co-rec champions were the Whalers and for the men's dorm, the Davis-Gary Sheepherders came out on top. In the men's All-University doubles competition, the LPC Keelers were the champions and for the women's All-University doubles team, the Briggs Brigands team came out with the crown.

For school year 1985-86, Bobby Winans won another Class A intramural handball singles championship in the men's independent tournament. In Class A of the men's dorm tournament, Paul Brozovic, representing Moore Hall, won the title. In Class B, the men's dorm champ was Walt Weeks of Crocker Hall; the men's independent champion was Dennis Hernandez; and the women's independent champion was Krista Gregory. In Class A intramural handball doubles competition, the Smalley twins, Gloria and

Wendy, proved to be the top team in the women's independent tournament. In the men's independent tournament, Todd Bryan and Jerry Ordonez proved to be the best team. The Class B champions in the co-rec tournament were Terri Riha and Bernard Zee. The men's dorm champions were Branch Ward and Paul Porcard representing Moore Hall. In Class C men's independent, the winners were Anthony Moore and Steve Wolfe. There were 131 handball players who played in the singles competition and 56 participated in the doubles tournaments.

In Class A intramural singles handball, the 1986-87 men's champion from the men's independent tournament was Coke Smith, adding another title to his resume. From the men's dorm tournament, John Reyes of Moses Hall came out as the victor. Gloria Smalley added another title to her resume by winning the championship in the women's independent tournament. In the men's Class B independent tournament, Thomas Moelmurry was the winner while Jose Hernandez from McInnis Hall took the men's dorm title. The women's dorm champion was Mary Bradshaw of Gainer Hall. Madison (no first name listed) of Moses Hall was the champion of the men's dorm tournament in Class C singles. The men's dorm Class C champion was Tom Swaldi. In the doubles competition, the men's Class A independent champions were Todd Bryan and Jerry Ordonez, and in the women's independent tournament, Gloria and Wendy Smalley added another championship to their title collection. In Class B competition, the co-rec champions were repeat winners Terri Riba and Bernard Zee, while Branch Ward and Paul Porcard were repeat winners from Moore Hall in the men's dorm tournament. In the Class C doubles competition, the men's dorm tournament saw Anthony Moore and Steve Wolfe come out on top. The handball singles were played during the fall semester and the doubles competition was held in the spring semester.

Going into the intramural handball competition for the 1987-88 year the question was probably, "Will there be any repeat champions as there were during the previous year?" As the results of the competition began to come in, the answer would soon reveal no repeat winners, although Todd Bryan won the intramural singles title in Class A men's independent tournament. He won in doubles the previous year. The Class A men's dorm title winner in Class A was Matthew Montelongo. Francis Woodcock won the championship in the women's independent tournament. In Class B singles of the men's dorm tournament, the winner was Wayne Crouch from Hart Hall. The men's champion of the Class B independent tournament was Fran McCann. Bonnie Hoekstra mirrored McCann's win in women's independent Class B singles. The men's dorm winner in Class C was Robert White, and Mauricio Freyre was the All-University champion. In doubles competition, the Class A co-rec champions were Amy Ripley and Dennis Hernandez. The Class A men's doubles champions were Aaron Cooper and Trey Delamoriniere. The Class B men's championship team was composed of Rouel Rothenberger and Anthony MacAluso while Bart Bartkowiak and Walter Postula teamed up to take the Class C crown. There were 61 handball players who participated in the singles tournaments and 18 who played in the doubles contests.

It is always interesting to see the names of those who rise to the top in intramural handball. Success at the USHA National Collegiate Handball Tournament doesn't necessarily mean the same winners in intramurals. Many times, those who achieved All-American status, or at least finished in the top 16 nationally, didn't play in the intramural tournaments. Most would rather play others among the team for greater competition. An intramural title at that point in their handball career would have little significance. It is those among the team who are gaining experience, and are future handball stars, that gain the most from the intramural tournaments. A good case in point are the winners of the intramural handball tournaments in 1988-89. Some new winners will go on to become familiar names on the Aggie handball team.

The 1988-89 men's Open singles champion was Eddy Johnson. For the women, Kim King came away with the top title. The Class A men's Residence Hall champion was Rouel Rothenberger of Moses

Hall. Diane Purinton was the Class A women's champion while Stephen Naftanel won the crown in the men's independent tournament. Vernon Hegwood won the Class B singles title and in Class C, Chris Uren won the men's independent tournament. Anna Gonzalez won the women's Class C title. Mark Harman came away with the men's Class C Residence Hall title. In intramural doubles competition, Chris and Mike Miller won the Open championship. Ruben and Miguel Perez teamed up to win the Class A doubles championship. In Class C, the men's independent winners were Michael Sawyer and Ronnie Bryant, while the men's Residence Hall title went to Michael Myers and Fritz Maletzschy. The Intramural Department changed the name of the men's dorm tournament to the men's Residence Hall tournament, which corresponded with the name used within Student Services. The singles tournament was held during the fall semester and the doubles tournament was held during the spring semester. The total participants in the singles tournaments were 58 players and in the doubles tournaments there were 22. The number of participants in the intramural handball tournaments is not a good indication of the usage of the handball courts. During the year from June 1988-May 1989, the courts in the Read building were used 54,560 times while the courts in DeWare were used 14,635 times. The distinction between handball and racquetball was not kept separate but usage is all-inclusive.

Beginning a new decade of handball, Kim King added a second women's intramural Open championship title to her handball resume. The1989-90 Class A men's independent champion was Chris Miller; the men's Residence Hall champion was James Frazer; the women's independent champion was Betsy Boswell; and the men's Open or All-University champion was Chris Phythian. In Class B, Chris Uren added the men's independent title to his Class C title of 1988. David Ortiz won the Class C men's independent title. Reagan Rothenberger was the winner of the Class C men's Residence Hall tournament. In the doubles competition, the Open women's team champions were Kim King and Anna Gonzalez while the men's Open champions were John Tomme and Chris Miller. Chong Hsin Liu teamed with Lilian Tan to win the co-rec Open doubles title. The Class A co-rec champions were Tim Chang and Ming Liu; the men's independent champions were Kyle Cooper and Allan Farrow; and the women's independent champions were Jan Moss and Mollie Huber. In the Class B competition, the co-rec champions were Matt Jackson and Betsy Boswell while the team of Greg Damron and Ron Farace teamed up to win the men's independent tournament. The singles tournaments were during the fall semester and the doubles tournaments were held in the spring. According to the Recreational Sports historical record only 19 players participated in the singles tournaments. There were 24 players who competed in the doubles competition.

In 1990-91, Vernon Hegwood displayed the handball skills he had developed since he first started playing the game. He was now the intramural handball Open singles champion. The Class A men's independent champion was Shane Rothenberger and the same title went to Audrea Stork in the women's independent tournament. In Class B competition, the All-University men's champion was John Walls, while Casey Clark reigned supreme in the men's independent competition. Tammy Reyes was the women's independent champion. Colin Errington was the champion of the men's Residence Hall handball competition. In Class C competition, Tim Karger took both the men's independent and men's All-University titles. Noel Keen was the winner of the men's Residence Hall competition. The men's Open doubles champions were Aaron Cooper and John Walls; the women's Open doubles champions were Betsy Boswell and Sharon Baylor while Matt Jackson and Betsy Boswell took the Open doubles co-rec crown. In the Class A doubles competition, Steven Meyers and Eric Fields took both the men's All-University and men's Residence Hall titles while the co-rec champions of the previous year, Tim Chang and Ming Liu, repeated. In Class B doubles, the men's independent champions were James Howard and Casey Clark while Tim Chang and Hsin Liu took the co-rec title. In Class C doubles competition, Matt

Jackson and Daniel Johnson won both the men's All-University and men's Residence Hall titles and, in the men's independent tournament, Jeff and Tom Walsh come out winners. The intramural singles tournaments were held in the fall semester and the doubles tournaments were held during the spring semester. A total of 38 played in the singles tournaments while 37 participated in the doubles competition. The number of 37 participants in the doubles competition is suspect since a doubles team requires two players.

For the 1991-92 year, there was no Open bracket in the handball tournaments. In Class A singles, the men's All-University champion was John Tomme. Betsy Boswell added to her title collection by winning the women's All-University crown. The Class A men's Residence Hall champion was Matt Jackson. In Class B singles competition, the men's All-University champion was Chad Lienau. Teri Slusarek was the women's All-University champion in Class B singles. Jeff Walsh won the men's Residence Hall crown. In Class C competition, Amy Hyatt took the women's All-University crown while Gaius Roemer won the All-University crown. Chris Brown won the men's independent tournament. In Class A doubles competition, the Aggie handball stars began to shine. Three of the four winners in Class A doubles would go on to become All-Americans. John Tomme did not become an All-American but he teamed up with Sal SantaAna to take the doubles titles in the All-University bracket. Betsy Boswell and Sharon Baylor duplicated the win in the women's competition. The co-rec title winners were Betsy Boswell and Chris Uren. In Class B competition, the men's Residence Hall winners were Thomas Trask and Mike Thompson while Mark Ritter and Tammy Ray won the co-rec title. Jeff and Tom Walsh teamed up to win the men's independent crown while Yvonne Chu and Hsin Wang earned the women's independent crown. In Class C competition, the co-rec doubles winners were Tiffany Precht and Tommy Grace. Fifty-two handball players entered the singles competition and 40 participated in the doubles tournaments.

Names that are familiar to the Aggie handball team were prevalent during the 1992-93 intramural handball competition. In Class A singles, the men's independent champion was Sal SantaAna, while Betsy Boswell won the women's independent championship. Shane Rothenberger was the winner of the men's Residence Hall tournament. In Class B, the men's independent champion was Jeff Jeffers while Tamara Moore won the women's independent title. Scott Korth was the men's Residence Hall winner. In Class C competition, Mark Ritter won the men's independent title and S. McAlister won the men's Residence Hall competition. In the doubles competition, the Class A men's independent champions were Shane Rothenberger and Colin Errington while the co-rec winners were Kelly LeWallen and Colin Errington. In Class B, the men's independent champions were Mark Ritter and Josh Ely while Otto Orr and Michael Condra won the men's Residence Hall title. A total of 43 handball players participated in the singles tournaments and 34 participated in the doubles play.

Probably the best ever male Aggie handball player, Sal SantaAna, added another intramural title as he won the 1993-94 Class A men's All-University title. Tiffany Precht showed how much she had improved over the past year by taking the women's All-University title. The Class A men's Residence Hall title went to Keith Gerhart and Michelle Alton won the women's Residence Hall title. In Class B competition, Tom Walsh won the men's All-University title. Joanne Langlinais won the women's All-University title. David Hutchison won the Class B men's Residence Hall title. In Class C, the All-University champion was Bryan Holmes, while Beth Oliver won the title in women's competition. The men's Residence Hall winner was Jason Ward. In Class A women's independent doubles, Beth Oliver and Cassandra Tijerina won the crown. In Class B doubles, the men's independent champions were David Hutchison and Matt Miller. Julie Young and Steven Soto won the co-rec doubles title, and in Class C doubles, the winners of the women's independent title were Ida Koll and Sarah Adams. There were 60 entrants in the handball singles tournaments, which was played in the fall semester. The doubles competition was held during the spring semester. A total of 62 entered those tournaments. A handball singles tournament was held in both summer sessions of 1994. Winners of the tournaments held during the summer sessions were not listed.

During the fall 1994 intramural handball competition, another best ever Aggie handball player began the game as a freshman and won at the Class B level. Priscilla Kojin won the women's independent singles championship during the fall semester soon after she started playing the game. She would quickly establish herself as a future star. The Class A men's independent singles championship went to Eric Fields. In Class B singles play, Joel Petershagen won the men's All-University title and David Hutchison was the men's independent tournament champion. The men's Residence Hall winner was Jason Bryant. In Class C, Scott Layh won the All-University championship while the men's Residence Hall title went to Eric Wojcik.

In the spring 1995 intramural competition, the Class A winner of the men's All-University and men's independent titles was Jeff Walsh. Cassandra Tijerina won the same two titles in the women's tournaments. In Class B competition, Ryan Isenberg won both the All-University and men's independent titles. In class C, the All-University and men's independent champion was Paul Kerlin while M. Haight took the Residence Hall title. There was no listing in women's Class B or C. The All-University and men's independent doubles champions was won by Jeff Jones and Jeff Jeffers. The Class A All-University and women's independent doubles champions were Tiffany Precht and Cassandra Tijerina. The co-rec champions were Jeff Walsh and Cassandra Tijerina. There was no listing for doubles competition in Class B. In Class C, E. McClellan and M. Croft came away with the champions title. There were 48 doubles teams and 54 singles players that participated in the tournaments.

The fall 1995 intramural men's singles champion in Class A was Eric Fields, and Priscilla Kojin reigned supreme in the women's competition. In Class B, the All-University title for the men was Ivan Berrios. Angela Chavez won the women's title. In the men's independent championship, Jason Bryant took the honors. The men's Residence Hall champion was Daniel Chen while Angela Chavez earned the title for the women's Residence Hall. In Class C, Will McClendon came away with the All-University title; Jeremy Hubble won the men's independent title; and Eric McClellan earned the men's Residence Hall title. In the doubles competition, Eric Fields and Jeff Walsh won in Class A All-University and men's independent titles. Larry Prewitt and Juan Gonzales won the Class B All-University and men's independent titles, and Kevin Weir and Tony Cisneros were the winners in Class C.

The winner of the spring 1996 intramural Class A All-University men's singles title was Andrew Bailey. Ricky Reynolds won the same title in Class B. The Class B men's Residence Hall champion was E. McClellan. The Class C All-University champion was Mike Madigan. The women's All-University champion was Deborah Quinn. In doubles competition, there were no entrants in Class A. Andy Bailey and Steven Soto earned the Class B men's All-University title. In Class C doubles, E. McClellan and Matthew Croft earned the All-University title. The total number of participants in the 1995-96 handball tournaments was not recorded.

The intramural handball competition for 1996-97 may or may not have had as many entries as in previous years; however, when there are 600-700 students enrolled in handball classes it is unlikely that interest in tournament competition had waned. Even so, the only winners the author could find were the winners of the fall men's independent tournaments where Ben Barbour earned the title in Class A, Tony Cisneros in Class B and Joel Cervantes in Class C. For the spring, no doubles competition was recorded, but the Class A singles men's independent champion was Don Bond. Ryan West was the women's independent champion. According to the 1996-97 calendar, handball singles and doubles were scheduled for the fall, spring, and both summer sessions of 1997.

Handball singles and doubles were scheduled for the fall, spring, and both summer sessions for the 1997-98 year. There is no record available of the tournaments held or the winners.

In the fall semester of 1998, five handball players participated in the intramural handball tournament. In the spring of 1999, there were three participants in the handball tournament. The Department of Recreational Sports no longer kept a record of annual champions in intramural competition.

Handball singles and doubles were scheduled for the fall and spring semesters of the 1999-2000 year. For the fall semester, five handball players participated in the tournament. The spring semester had an increase in the number of participants to 24. Again, no record of the winners was kept. With five participants in the fall semester, the tournament would have been for a singles tournament. Without listed winners there is no possible way to determine whether the spring tournament was a singles or doubles event.

Handball singles and doubles were scheduled for the fall and spring semesters of 2000-01. Twenty-three handball players took part in the fall intramural handball tournament. In the spring, only seven handball players participated in the handball tournament. No winners were listed.

Handball singles and doubles were scheduled for the fall and spring semesters of 2001-02. Did anyone play in the tournaments? Unfortunately, no records were kept so that question will never be answered. When was the last year for intramural handball to be offered? Again, there is no answer.

Can handball become a regular intramural sport as it has been for many of the past years? The author has asked this question to the current Director of the Recreation Center and the current Intramural Director and the answer is yes. The current Intramural Sports Director has set up and run handball tournaments before coming to Texas A&M, so offering and holding intramural handball tournaments is not an issue. The answer lies with the Texas A&M student body and whether or not someone, or a group, can spark enough interest in handball to make a handball tournament, singles and/or doubles, a worthwhile intramural venture.

CHAPTER 6
A&M Handball Teams 1947-1959

Beginning very early in the history of Texas A&M, athletic competition was a valued aspect of the overall development of its students. In the 1890s, team sports at the varsity level were developed for competition with other teams within the state. Football and baseball were the first teams organized for intercollegiate competition. A track team would soon follow. Basketball was introduced in 1909 but little interest was shown. Basketball became a varsity sport in 1913. Other teams (clubs as they were called at the time) were formed in the early 1900s and by 1925 tennis, golf, cross country and polo teams competed outside the University. Handball was introduced in 1925 at the intramural level, but no team competed beyond that level. Without question, the interest and skill level was available at the college. Without a coach/ sponsor and the probable hindrance of transportation and limited competition at other colleges/universities, handball at the intercollegiate level did not exist for Aggies. Evidence of the interest in handball was that by the 1934-35 school year, 29 teams made up of five handball players each entered the intramural handball championship. The teams were divided into six leagues and there were 61 matches played to determine the championship team. To win a match the team had to win three points out of a possible five. Obviously, the level of interest in handball was very high.

Barney Welch, one of the great backs in A&M football, was hired to the position of Intramural Director for the 1947-48 school year. Already acclaimed in the early 1940s as the most extensive intramural program in the world, it is believed that Barney thought he could add to the athletic development and skill level of the students by adding college teams (club sports) for intercollegiate competition. One can only speculate the vision that Barney had when club sport activities were added to the already massive intramural program. Did he even remotely have the concept that the handball team would historically become a force in collegiate competition? At that time, there was no method for determining national collegiate handball champions. That would not be long in coming. And he would not have thought that women would represent the university (then college) at the championship level. However, as with all successful ventures, there had to be a starting point.

Barney's expanded vision enabled the first University handball team to come together in 1947-48. Bill Rippetoe, a Physical Education major, was a senior on the first team. There is no record of others on the team though it was very likely that juniors Victor M. Currie, Jr., David T. Gentry and Billy E. Watson were also on the team. Whether or not the team traveled to compete outside the University cannot be ascertained. It is likely that the team existed for the purpose of promoting handball and competition among the better players at the University. If there was a team sponsor, it likely would have been Herman Segrest who was a sponsor for the team for a number of years.

The 1948-49 team was sponsored by Herman Segrest of the Physical Education department. The team competitive record cannot be found. The team was made up of seniors Victor M. Currie, Jr., David T. Gentry and Billy E. Watson. Without question, Jewell McDowell, an All Southwest Conference Basketball player his junior and senior years, would have been on the team. He won the Open division handball title in both singles and doubles. Most likely his doubles partner, L. A. Layne was on the team. It is also likely that Jack M. Balderas, Jr. was also on the team.

The only available record of a handball team for the 1949-50 school year is found by checking the listing of activities by seniors in the *Aggieland*. Jack M. Balderas, Jr. listed handball team as one of his activities. It is probable that some of the members of the 1948-49 handball team (not the seniors) were on the 1949-50 handball team. No records can be found of the competitive results of handball intercollegiate matches for 1950. Herman Segrest is thought to have been the sponsor. Again, there is no doubt that Jewell McDowell would have been the main cog on the handball team. He was the Open singles and doubles handball intramural champion for the second year in a row. It is likely that his doubles partner, P. A. Scheumack, was also on the team.

Mr. Bob Kendler, a Chicago businessman, organized the United States Handball Association for the purpose of conducting championship handball tournaments at the national level to include the collegiate level. These championships would expand worldwide in the future. It is very likely that the 1951 handball team would have been very competitive at the national collegiate level and possibly national champions but at that time no handball intercollegiate championship tournament existed. That would not happen until 1953. The 1951 team went to Austin to take on the University of Texas Longhorns and came away with a 3-1 victory. Jewell McDowell downed the top Longhorn star by the scores of 21-6, 21-4. Longhorn Harris beat Aggie Wood and Balderas (A&M) beat Hampton (UT). In doubles, McDowell and Balderas beat Cobb and Harris. Mr. Herman Segrest was the team sponsor. He does not appear in the following team photo which is from the 1951 *Aggieland*, page 464:

Known members of the 1951 Handball Club are Jack M. Balderas, Jr.; John Centilli, Dick Gardemal, William Groff, Hub Horton, Bo Hoskins, Jerry Houser, Jewell McDowell, Fred Sommers and Jack Wood. The other members of the team shown in the above photo are not listed in the *Aggieland*

The Handball Team of 1952 participated in several matches in the Southwest. Results of their matches are not available but it is known they were very competitive. Practice time and coaching was limited, but it is likely they performed at a high level in every tournament.

Herman Segrest continued to sponsor the handball team. The competitive record for the1953 handball team is not available.

The handball team continued to grow under the sponsorship of Herman Segrest. The team travelled to a few handball matches and continued to be very competitive. The only available record for team competition was with the Longhorns. John Centilli, president of the club, Don Johnson, Larry Laskoskie, Dickie O'Connor and Phil Randol made the trip to Austin. A significant passenger on the trip was Phil Collins, ranked number five in the US at that time and stationed with the Air Force at Bryan Air Force Base. Phil gave an exhibition match on the handball courts at the University of Texas campus.

1952 Handball Club
FRONT ROW: Herman Segrest, Jack Wood, Bernard Lemmons
BACK ROW: Kenneth Lewi, Don Garrett
NOT IN PHOTO: Team member,
Ralph C. Dresser
(1952 *Aggieland*, page 284)

Early in the 1954 fall semester two members of the 1954-55 team (Jim Mathis and Don Johnson) were playing late one night when they heard a knock on the door. Upon opening the door, Phil Collins graciously asked if he could play. It should be obvious Mathis and Johnson were no match for the highly ranked Collins. After the game Collins asked to join them again and did so from time to time throughout the semester. Later in the semester he suggested that A&M send a team to the National Collegiate Handball Tournament to be held that year at the YMCA courts in Chicago. Arrangements were made and the team travelled over the holidays between the fall and spring semesters. At that time a team consisted of four players. The team that went to Chicago was Don Grant as the number 1 singles, Paul Meiners as the number 2 singles and Jim Mathis and Don Johnson as the doubles team. Mathis and Johnson chose to go as a doubles team since both had been playing against Collins and his partner-also from Bryan Air force Base-during much of the fall semester and surprisingly winning one game from Phil and his partner.

1953 Handball Club
FRONT ROW: J. L. Boring, Paul Meiners, Phil Randol, H. J. Keibler, J. D. Centilli
BACK ROW: D. Smith, B. Hunt, D. Tabb, C. R. Johnson.
NOT IN PHOTO: Team members Don L. Garrett and Richard C. Hartwig
(1953 *Aggieland*, page 268)

1954 Handball Club
FRONT ROW: J. Johnson, L. Laskoskie, I. Greenhaw, Bubba Hunt
SECOND ROW: D. Korry, P. Randol, G. Rice, D. Scott, D. O'Connor, J. Centilli, J. L. Maxwell
BACK ROW: L. Hoffman, M. Dhig, J. Mathis, P. Guimarin, F. Cox, J. Lonquist, C. Hargan, Herman Segrest (Sponsor)
NOT IN PHOTO: Team member Charles D. Shreve
(1954 *Aggieland*, page 339)

The following was reported on pages 16-18 and 28, volume five, number one, February 1955 edition of *ACE* magazine. At that time, *Ace* was the name of the official magazine of the newly formed United States Handball Association.

> Intercollegiate handball competition on a national scale came of age with the second annual tournament sponsored by the United States Handball Association at the town Club of Chicago Dec. 27 through 30.
>
> The field was almost double that of the first national intercollegiate held last March in Evanston. The second meet has 38 players from 17 colleges as compared to 21 entrants from ten schools in the inaugural event.
>
> Southpaw Mal Dorman, a 37-year-old medical student at the University of Pennsylvania, won the no. 1 singles championship with Don Milazzo of Detroit University capturing no. 2 singles honors. The doubles competition, conducted on a round-robin basis, went to the Texas A. and M. duo of Don ("*Johnny*") Johnson and Jim Mathis, who had six consecutive victories. Detroit was second in doubles, losing only to Texas A. and M.
>
> Detroit won the team title with 11 points, split between their six in doubles and five in singles. The University of Illinois at Chicago was second with nine, followed by Texas A. and M. with eight and Ohio State and Washington University of St. Louis with three each. Other schools participating included Illinois of Champaign, Northwestern, Notre Dame, De Paul, Loras of Dubuque, Ia., Purdue, Pennsylvania, University of Chicago, Joliet Junior College, George Williams College of Chicago, Boston University, and Vanderbilt. A four-man entry was necessary to qualify for the team title.
>
> Ohio State's doubles players, Ed Kawachika and Yoshi Oyakawa, are from Hawaii and both are varsity swimmers. Yoshi, in fact, is world record holder in the 100-yard and the 100-meter backstroke, having broken Adolph Kiefer's marks. Both lads from Hawaii showed remarkable dexterity on the court and observers remarked that with a little more experience, both could easily become topflight performers.
>
> Johnson and Mathis, who carried away doubles for Texas A. and M., made a great showing despite the fact that they lacked experience on a full-sized court. They drove from College Station, Tex., and swept to six straight victories, a top achievement when the caliber of the contestants is considered. Their most important win, of course, was over Detroit's pair, Joe DeGroot and John Dunnigan. The Aggies won in straight games but by only a single point in each, 21-20.

The other three team members and I will always remember how cold it was on the way to Chicago. Travel to Chicago was in Johnson's 1950 Plymouth which had a heater; however, the heat available was not sufficient to totally overcome the cold. We expected to see snow over much of the area beginning in Missouri, but we were pleasantly surprised to find clear roads and good travel conditions even into the city of Chicago. We did see some snow along the side of the road within 50 miles of Chicago but no hindrance to travel. We were all glad to finally experience warmth as we arrived at our destination. I know Jim and I will never forget the handball doubles finals which we won by the scores of 21-20. The team was very appreciative of the help we received from our sponsor, Herman Segrest, and of course the one who made it all possible, Phil Collins. Without Collin's mentorship and guidance, A&M's first National Handball Intercollegiate Champions would have come years later.

Don "Johnny" Johnson and Jim Mathis receiving the National Intercollegiate
Handball Doubles championship trophy from Bob Kendler

(*Ace*, February 1955, page 18)

1955 Handball Club
FRONT ROW: Herman Segrest (Sponsor),
Don "Johnny" Johnson (President), Lawrence
Laskowskie, Gary Leslie, Glen Rice, John Dillard
BACK ROW: Jim Mathis, Don Grant, Charlie
Johnson, Paul Meiners
NOT IN PHOTO: Paul Guimarin, Charles
Horgan, David Korry, J. R. Riley, Albert
Schlichter

(1955 *Aggieland*, page 129)

This letter was awarded to Don Johnson as a member
of the handball team. The star signifies president of the
club/team. The two stripes indicate the number of years
on the handball team. At this time all members of any
varsity or recreation club received letters to indicate
that activity. Members of the Corps of Cadets wore their
letters on white sweaters and were considered a part of
the military uniform. Of course, there were regulations
when the sweater was not authorized.

(Author's Collection)

Interest in membership to the handball club continued in the 1955-56 school year; however, no records of competition or photos of the team are available. Team members were Billy R. Bates, who was also a regular on the A&M fast pitch softball team, Glenn D. Buell, Fred R. Cox, Bill J. Graham, Donald L. Grant, David E. Korry, Ernest O. Reesing, Jr., Glen E. Rice, Albert G. Schlichter, Clarence A. Tubbs, Jr., Dr. Ruede M. Wheeler, and Robert W. Young. Dr. Wheeler remembers that the team had a handball ladder and anyone below a listed name could challenge anyone above and move up the ladder by winning the challenged match. The ladder would be new for this school year since it had not been used by Herman Segrest during the years he was sponsor. The handball ladder was most likely introduced by Major Conoley. Dr. Wheeler remembers only two people he played that school year. One was Jack Pardee, the great Aggie fullback, who later played football professionally. Dr. Wheeler played him three times, winning each time. Pardee was not an accomplished handball player at the college level but had a great love for the game. Dr. Wheeler also played Major Conoley many times. Maj. Conoley was to become the coach for the 1956-57 team. After Dr. Wheeler finished Dental School, he began to play racquetball because there were no handball players available in his local area. He later built his own court for competition.

The fact that Major Conoley, an Air Force major with an assignment as an Associate Professor of Air Science, became the coach of the handball team for the 1956-57 school year is indication that Segrest was no longer available, or had other assignments limiting his available time for the handball team. It is known that Segrest was conferred his Masters of Education Degree at A&M in the spring of 1955 and continued as faculty through the year 1963-64. Since Major Conoley was enrolled in graduate studies with the Education Department and an excellent handball player, he probably was given the assignment to coach the handball team as part of his graduate program. President of the club/team was John A.

1957 Handball Club
FRONT ROW: Charles Saxe, Daniel Stalmach, John Dillard III, Ragsdale
BACK ROW: Major Conoley (Sponsor), Grady Kane, Fred Huttanus, Irving Ramsower
NOT IN PHOTO: Dr. Lavon N. Anderson, Samuel L. Smith

(1957 *Aggieland*, page 385)

Dillard, III. The vice president was Charles S. Saxe and the secretary-treasurer was Fred L. Huttanus. No record is available of the team's competition with other handball teams.

Dr. Lavon Anderson remembers playing Maj. Conoley. He challenged Maj. Conoley who was on the handball ladder. Maj. Conoley was older than Dr. Anderson's other handball playing friends and did not appear to be in good physical condition. As so many young handball players have discovered over the years, physical appearance can be deceiving. Jim Mathis and I discovered that the night we met Phil Collins. After being thoroughly defeated by Maj. Conoley, Dr. Anderson said something to the effect "I was hardly in the game".

Even though handball remained a popular intramural sport there is no record of a club or team beginning with the school year 1957-58 and continuing through the 1959-60 school year. Billy Rogers and Irving Ramseur listed their activities in the 1958 yearbook as being on the handball team. There is no record of a handball club/team for 1958 and it is possible their listing is from being a member in a previous year or years. It is also a possibility they were listing their participation in intramurals as a member of their team. From the earliest yearbooks and through 1972, all seniors, veterinary and fifth-year architecture students listed their academic major, hometown, scholarships, awards received and any activities in which they participated. Of course, there were some seniors who did not have their picture taken and some who may not have listed all of their activities.

CHAPTER 7
A&M Handball Teams 1960-1969

In the 1961 yearbook, Gary E. Staley listed that he was the president of the handball club. Robert J. Brown listed that he was a member of the handball club. Based on the listing of these two, it is probable the club continued after Major Conoley was no longer the coach. It is a guess that the handball ladder established in 1956-57 was continued and, if your name was on the ladder, you were considered a member of the club. To have a president of the club meant there most likely was a club sponsor to ensure compliance with college policies.

No seniors listed being a member of the handball club/team for the 1961-62 school year. It is assumed that the team was active but no record has been made of its existence.

The following quote is from page 239 of the 1963 *Aggieland*. "A&M's newly-revived handball team took second place at the annual SWC Handball Tournament in Houston this year. Ed Merritt won the Class A singles for A&M and Jerry Levy turned in what Merritt called a 'real fine performance' to take the Class B singles award."

The page in the *Aggieland* used the term *SWC* which would indicate the Southwest Conference of which A&M was a member. The SWC was a part of the NCAA. The NCAA did not and has never put on a handball tournament. It is believed the article referred to the Southwest handball tournament that the USHA sanctioned.

1963 Handball Club

FRONT ROW: William Altman (Pres/Treasurer), Herbert Johns, Pete Hickman, Lynn Hardeman,
Ed Merritt, (Capt.) Peising
BACK ROW: C. E. Evans (Sponsor), Jerome Levy, Jr., Ray Allen, Robert F. Lowe, Ernest Reesing, P. Willcox
NOT IN PHOTO: Joe A. DePasqual, Hector Diaz, Thomas M. Fine, III, William E. Harwood, Jr.
(1963 Aggieland, page 239)

C. E. Evans was listed as the sponsor of the handball team for the 1963-64 school year. There is no record available of the competition the team faced during the year. After the "revival" of the team during the past year, it is probable the team met with much of the same success as the 1962-63 team.

1964 Handball Club
FRONT ROW: Pete Hickman, Ed Merritt, Bill Altman, Ben Jackson, Dave Engle
BACK ROW: C.E. Evans (Sponsor), Jim Mackfee, Bill Gibbs, Joe DePasqual, Hector Diaz, Jerry Levy
NOT IN PHOTO: William Ray Allen, George Behrendt, Thomas M. Fine,III, Howard Maxwell, Jr., Robert. T. Fergeson, Ted Sparling
(1964 *Aggieland*, page 243)

Joe DePasqual, Class of 1965, reported that the A&M team played Rice, which had a very active handball club, several times during the 1963, '64, and '65 years. The Aggies were successful in winning each time the teams met whether it was in Houston or at A&M. *The Battalion*, fall of 1964, reported "The A&M handball team took eight singles and five doubles matches to beat the Rice University handball team here Saturday to win its second match of the year over the Owls. Rice won three singles tilts and one doubles match in the competition. In a side match, Barney Welch, A&M's former intramural director, defeated Rice's coach, Bob Bland, two straight games. Wearing the Maroon and White were Bill Altman, John Hedrick, Ed Merritt, Jerry Levy, Ben Jackson, Pete Hickman, Hector Diaz, Dave Engle, Bill Gibbs, Joe De Pasqual, Howard Whitford, Robert Treadwell, Powell Charlton and Paul Lillard." (Cushing Archives)

In February 1965, *The Battalion* reported "The A&M Handball Team won 17 out of 19 matches to defeat the Rice Owls Saturday in DeWare Field House. In a separate match, club advisor Gene Evans defeated the Rice team coach Paul Pfeiffer. Playing for the Aggies were George Behrendt, Bill Altman, Dave Engle, Hector Diaz, Bob Paulson, Joe DePasqual, Lou Stout and Jim McAfee. The team will travel to Houston Friday to compete in the Southwest Invitational Collegiate Tournament." (Cushing Archives)

The University of Texas opened a state-of-the-art handball facility in Gregory Gym in 1964, the facility had 12 courts plus a central, three-sided glass walled court with surround seating. In the planning of the current A&M Recreation Center, the A&M handball coach, Lance Lowy, recommended a similar handball facility for A&M. That recommendation was not approved. Pete Tyson, the UT coach, had a great handball program and hosted the A&M team several times. The A&M team traveled there more than once for instruction and to pair off against his players. Pete was very good at evenly matching his players against the Aggies for the competition as opposed to winning the day.

Prior to the National Collegiate Handball Tournament of 1965, which was held on the University of Texas handball courts, the team participated in the Southwest Handball Tournament, held in Houston. Results of the tournament competition are not available. The National Collegiate Handball Tournament was held in late March. This tournament was the high point of the year for the A&M handball team even though they did not advance very far. The team did bring home a couple of trophies, but the record what the trophies represented is not available. The good coaching some of the schools had was very evident to the Aggies.

1965 Handball Team at the National Collegiate Tournament

Joe DePasqual, Bill Altman, Dave Engle, Hector Diaz, Bob Paulson, George Behrendt

(Courtesy Joe DePasqual)

1965 Handball Club

FRONT ROW: Hector Diaz, Joe DePasqual, Tommy Fitz, Bill Altman

BACK ROW: C. E. Evans (Sponsor), Lou Stout, Robert Paulson

NOT IN PHOTO: George Behrendt, Thomas M. Fine, III, Stephen Hartwell, Alex Treadway, Ted Sparling

(1965 *Aggieland*, page 121)

A photo of the 1966 team is not available. Team members were Jack Patrick Blake, Hector Diaz, (secretary-treasurer), Glynn Robert Donaho, and Ted Ray Sparling. All were in their last year at A&M so it is likely there were underclassmen on the team.

Not having a photo in the *Aggieland* would indicate a transition of sponsors for the club. While there is no record, it is likely the team participated in the Southwest Handball tournament and other matches with club/college/university teams. It is also likely that the handball ladder started in 1956 was still in existence.

The 1966-67 school year would bring renewed energy to the club. Stan Lowy, who grew up in the Bronx playing one-wall handball in a very competitive environment, moved to Texas A&M with the Department of Aerospace Engineering and became a member of the handball club. Though he may not have been officially designated the sponsor he took a leadership role and moved the club in a positive direction. Also arriving was a new freshman Ozzie Burke and his brother Cyril, who grew up on a 19-acre farm just south of the campus. Ozzie was a regular at the courts while in high school and was an experienced player as a freshman.

1967 Handball Club
FRONT ROW: Hector Diaz, Ozzie Burke,
Robert Holcomb, Stan Lowy, Cyril Burke
BACK ROW: William Sturmer, John Shiffert,
Dr. Thomas Kozik, Jack Blake
NOT IN PHOTO: Kenneth Alan Clayton,
Jimmy A. McAfee

(1967 *Aggieland*, page 461)

The 1967-68 school year would be another National Collegiate Handball Doubles Championship year for the handball team. *Ace* Magazine, in 1968, reported the following account of the championship:

> The Texas A&M team of Ozzie Burke and Dan Kennerly won the doubles bracket, beating the University of Texas team of Love and Squires, 21-17, 14-21, 21-3.

Reporting the championship by Mary Jane Graham in the *Young Teen Power* magazine, Vol. 5, No. 2, April, May, June 1970, page 3, and featuring Ozzie Burke, the story follows:

> "Think we'll make it, Ozzie?"

> Ozzie Burke gasped for air during the 10-minute break. With his doubles partner, Dan Kennerly, he had just finished two grueling games in May 1968 in the finals of the national intercollegiate handball tournament in St. Louis.

> "We've got to, Dan," he puffed. "This last game will decide the championship!"

> "Let's change our strategy," Ozzie Burke replied, wiping the sweat from his face. "Here's what we'll do...."

> The two Aggies from Texas A&M had been hook serving and were driving the ball hard against their University of Texas opponents. Now between games they were making some vital decisions.

> "Maybe we should soften our serves and lob them along the walls to their weak hands," suggested Ozzie. "Hey, that's a great idea! Let's hope it works."

> Ozzie and Dan had advanced from the Houston regional to St. Louis to join twelve other schools in the battle for the championship. After winning three matches they faced the University of Texas duo in the finals.

> The Aggie strategy paid off, as Dan and Ozzie breezed to a victory.

> "Our opponents just fell apart," recalls Ozzie.

The victory was a climax to a big handball year for Ozzie, a Christian person whom *Young Teen Power* contacted later for this story: (Courtesy Ozzie Burke)

"The aspects of handball really challenge me," Ozzie says, "A good player has to be quick, ambidextrous and strong in the legs and upper body."

Ozzie enjoys the mental aspects of handball as well as the physical. "The strategy involved makes the game fascinating," he says. "You warm up with an opponent and watch for weaknesses. You experiment with your serves, maybe a hard, spinning serve is best or a lob serve or a Z serve. I like to move the ball around a lot. I won't go for broke from deep court, but you have to play offensively and take the good shots when they open up."

1968 Team at the National Tournament
FRONT ROW: Ozzie Burke, Dan Kennerly (Doubles)
BACK ROW: Tommy Patrick, Cyril Burke (Singles)

(1968 *Aggieland*, page 463)

Congratulatory message from Barney Welch who played many handball games with Ozzie

(Courtesy Ozzie Burke)

With the success of the team in Saint Louis and a National Collegiate Doubles Handball Championship to cherish, the Aggies would always remember this as a great trip with no problems. Wrong! When remembering this event, the four will always remember and talk of the cold night they spent in Missouri. Dianna Burke writes as told by Ozzie. For the story see Chapter 15 under Ozzie Burke personal.

The victory was a climax to a big handball year for Ozzie, a Christian person whom *Young Teen Power* contacted later for this story: (Courtesy Ozzie Burke)

Ozzie was featured on the 17 May, 1970 cover of *Young Teen Power* magazine.
A portion of the featured article is found on page 94.

This was the last year that USHA used a regional tournament for qualification to go to the National Intercollegiate Tournament. Thereafter, all teams and individuals had to attend other tournaments as singles to get in tournament shape for the Nationals. It still remains so at this writing.

The 1968-69 school year was not as successful for the handball team as the previous year. The four-man team representing A&M at the National Collegiate Handball Tournament, held in Austin, was Cyril Burke, Ozzie Burke, Hector Diaz and Tom Patrick. Ozzie and Tom competed as the doubles team with Cyril and Hector playing as singles. The Aggies could not meet the challenges to come away with a team championship or as individuals.

1968 Handball Club

FRONT ROW: Cyril Burke, Ozzie Burke, Stan Lowy, Dr. Jeff Bronson, Hector Diaz
BACK ROW: Gregory Peyrefitte, Jack Blake, Dan Kennerly, William Sturmer, Dr. Tom Kozik
NOT IN PHOTO: Isaac J. Benson, Donovan R. Cumbie, Gerald R. Gantt, Stephen C. Hightower, Jimmie C. Johnson

(1968 *Aggieland,* page 463)

Officers
President..Ozzie Burke
Vice-President.......................................Cyril Burke
Secretary-Treasurer................................Dan Kennerly
Advisor..Stan Lowy

1969 Handball Club

FRONT ROW: Ozzie Burke, Eric Oshlo, Milton Thompson, Stanley Moczygemba, Patrick Scott, Dr. Jeff Bronson, Robert Le Greca
BACK ROW: Cyril Burke, Tommy Patrick, Rodney Dennison, Wes Rogers, Mike Kearney, Bill Hoermann, Don Scherrer
NOT IN PHOTO: Gary Hornback, Stan Lowy, Francis McKenna, Harold Welch, III

(1969 *Aggieland,* page 247)

Officers of the 1969 Handball Club
President..Ozzie Burke
Vice-President.......................................Tommy Patrick
Secretary-Treasurer................................Eric Oshlo
Advisor..Stan Lowy

CHAPTER 8
A&M Handball Teams 1970-1979

The 1969-70 handball team that went to the National Collegiate Handball Tournament, held at the Lake Forest courts in Chicago, Illinois, was composed of Cyril and Ozzie Burke, Hector Diaz and a fourth player who cannot be identified. Cyril and Ozzie advanced to the semifinals in doubles and lost in a very close match to the doubles team from Miami Dade Junior College. Cyril and Ozzie won the match between the other semi-final team to finish in 3rd place. The two singles players did not fare well in their competition.

There is no photo available of the 1970 handball club. Members of the club were: Dr. Jeff Bronson, Cyril and Ozzie Burke, Hector Diaz, Richard L. Goss, Russell C. Hawkins, Gary D. Hornback, Stan Lowy, and Sherman M. McKean. The sponsor was Dr. Homer Tolsen.

The only record of competition beyond the confines of the A&M handball courts for the 1970-71 school year was Ozzie Burke, who traveled alone by air to the University of Tennessee in Knoxville for the National Collegiate Tournament (SEE next page for entry form). In the first round of A singles, he defeated Roger Madsen of Washington State University 21-19, 21-13. In the quarterfinals, John Paveletz of John Baruch College (City of New York) defeated Ozzie 21-14, 21-15. Although the results were not provided in the April 1971 edition of the USHA's *Ace* magazine, Ozzie does remember placing 5th in the A singles competition. That would be the end of four memorable years for Ozzie as a member of the A&M handball team.

Members of the club were: Dr. Jeff Bronson, Ozzie Burke (president), Michael C. Kearney, Stan Lowy and Sherman M. McKean. A photo of the team is not available. Obviously, there were more members of the team, but without verifiable records no one else can be listed.

As in some previous years, there is very little information about the activities of the handball team during the 1971-72 school year. A photo in the *Aggieland* does provide some information.

1972 Handball Club
FRONT ROW: Stan H. Lowy (Co-Faculty Advisor), Dr. Jeff Bronson (Co-Faculty Advisor)
BACK ROW: Gary W. Sheffield, Roger A. Duelm, R. Max Rodgers
NOT IN PHOTO: Gary G. Drake, Guadalupe Morales
Officers of the 1972 Handball Club
Roger Duelm.....................President
Gary Sheffield.....................Vice-President
Max Rodgers.........................Secretary
(1972 *Aggieland*, page 133)

This would be the National Collegiate entry form that Ozzie Burke completed to compete in the 1971 tournament. Of note is the composition of the team. The four-person team remained the same from the tournament's beginning in 1953 until the 1980s when the team composition would change to include women, increase the number of team members, and change the scoring to determine team championships. It is also interesting to note the cost for a room.

USHA NATIONAL INTERCOLLEGIATES
at University of Tennessee, Knoxville
March 4-7, 1971

DEADLINE FOR ENTRIES: March 2, 1971

ELIGIBILITY: Open to all full-time undergraduate students. Participants must be members of USHA. $2 for 1971; $5 for 1971-73 (includes subscription to ACE magazine). If not current member player may sign up at tournament site. Players may enter one event only.

ENTRY FEE: None.

TROPHIES: First four places in each event.

EXPENSES: All participants are responsible for their own expenses. Winners of division college tournaments get partial travel allowances from USHA.

OFFICIAL BALL: Spalding ACE.

All participants will be guaranteed two matches.

A school may enter one or more players.
Individual players can enter, and vie for the individual awards.
Team consists of an A singles; a B singles, and doubles.

There will be a meeting of all partcipants on Thursday, March 4, 5 p.m., at the New Physical Education Bldg., 1914 Holt ave. Tournament play will begin at 7p.m., March 4.

Send entries to: Ben A. Plotnicki, tournament chairman; School of Health, Physical Education and Recreation, University of Tennessee, Knoxville, TN 37916. Office (UT) Phone: 974-5111. Home (Lenoir City): 986-8375.

Please enter _____ in the 1971 National USHA Intercollegiates.
                    college

Please enter _____   Team:
                  as individual.

A Singles ( )
                                                A Singles
B Singles ( )
                                                B Singles
Doubles ( )

With _____

HOUSING: SHERATON CAMPUS INN — TOURNAMENT HEADQUARTERS — (Three Blocks from Tournament Site. 1706 Cumberland Avenue; Phone 524-4681; Mr. Sherbakoff, Mgr.

UNIVERSITY INN — (Five Blocks from Tournament Site) — 17th Clinch Avenue; Phone 546-5974; Mr. Warren, Mgr.

KNOXVILLE Y.M.C.A. — (One Mile from Tournament Site); 605 Clinch Avenue; Phone 524-7493.

SUGGESTED RESTAURANTS — Sheraton Campus

Inn; University Inn; Byerley's Cafeteria (Located on White Avenue, Five Blocks from Tournament Site).

RATES: — Single: 10.00; Two to Rm.: $12.00 (Double Bed); Three to Rm.: $16.00 (Twin Doubles); Four to Rm.: $18.00 (Twin Double).

RATES: Single: $10.50; Rm. with 2 Double Beds, 2 Persons: $12.00; Each additional perhon per room: $3.00.

RATES: Per Person: $4.00 First Night; $3.00 Each additional night. (Bath down hall); $2.00 Refundable Key Deposit.

(*Ace*, February 1971, page 69)

There is no record for the 1973 handball team. It is assumed that Stan Lowy and Dr. Jeff Bronson continued as Co-Faculty Advisors.

In 1974, three Aggies, Charles Bokelman, Jeff Carter and Jack Gressett, traveled to the University of Colorado, Boulder to compete in the National Collegiate Handball Tournament. Jeff Carter played in the B singles division winning his first match against Ed Thieme of the University of Colorado 21-17, 21-10.

In his second match, he was defeated by Ed Boland of the University of Montana 21-15, 21-10. Boland continued and eventually won 3rd.

1974 Handball Club
FRONT ROW: Dr. Jeff Bronson (Co-Faculty Advisor), Robert Almon,
Stan Lowy (Co-Faculty Advisor), Lewis W. Zingery
BACK ROW: Dr. Glenn Williams, Marion J. Gressett (President), Mike Richter
NOT IN PHOTO: Charles Bokelman, Jeff Carter
(1974 *Aggieland*, page 397)

Charles Bokelman and Jack Gressett entered the doubles competition. In the first round, they were defeated by Joe Miller/Terry Jackson of Memphis State University 21-13, 21-10. This first round loss dropped them into the Consolation bracket of doubles competition. There is no record of their progression to the Consolation finals. In the final match of the Consolation doubles championship Charles Bokelman/Jack Gressett were defeated by Bill Peoples/Tom Ryan of the University of Montana.

Though women could take handball in Kinesiology, none had joined the handball club before the 1974-75 school year. The 1975 handball club opened a new door for A&M women to handball competition outside the university; however, the USHA National Collegiate Handball Tournament remained closed to women. On 9 April 1945, *The Battalion* reported that the A&M team participated in the Texas State YMCA championship held in Victoria. The team competed in the C bracket which can be assumed to be the college bracket. The Aggies finished in second place with John Arizpe finishing second as an individual and Kley Hughes finishing third. The following week the team went to San Antonio to participate in the Alamo handball tournament. Jack Gressett and Todd Worrell placed second in B doubles. John Arizpe played in B singles and did not place. Other teams at the tournament were from San Antonio, Dallas, Waco, Houston and Odessa. The team participated in the National Collegiate Tournament hosted by the University of Texas. Two members of the team representing the Aggies in Austin were Jack Gressett and Wayne Neuman. Cody Birdwell travelled with the team as an alternate. The team did not place.

The 1975 Handball Club
FRONT ROW: Charlotte Griffin, Linda Mihalko, Stan Lowy (Club Advisor), Linda Kuntz, Dorothy Morrogh
BACK ROW: Wayne E. Neuman, Arthur J. Leuterman, B. J. King, Pam Minneman, Mary J. Peppler,
Cody Birdwell, Sharon Riggs, Marion J. Gressett, Shannon Birdwell
IN THE PHOTO BUT NOT MEMBERS OF THE TEAM: Arthur J. Leuterman, Shannon Birdwell
NOT IN PHOTO: Charles Bokelman, (President)
(1975 *Aggieland*, page 481)

Charles Bokelman would remain president of the club until 1992. No one made an issue of electing or appointing someone else to the position. As coach of the A&M handball team, Lance Lowy handled all of the administrative, logistical and funding issues of team tournament entry, team roster and team travel without consulting with any member of the handball club.

Membership of the handball club cannot be confirmed for the years 1976-1979. It is probable that Cody Birdwell, Linda Kuntz, Linda Mihalko, Pam Minneman, and Dorothy Morrogh continued their membership with the 1976 handball club. Using the same analogy, it is likely that Linda Kuntz, Linda Mihalko, Pam Minneman and Dorothy Morrogh continued to be members of the handball club in 1977. Pam Minneman and Dorothy Morrogh likely continued to be members in 1978. Newcomers to the club in 1978 (not confirmed) were: Jerry Kirkland, Benjie Nelson, Mark Patterson and Bill Schlafer All four were members of the 1979 handball club with probable newcomers Richard Harrison, Jill MacAluso, John Welch and Bill Moore. Glorian "Peanut" Motal joined the club late in the fall of '79 while taking handball as a Physical Education class. It is also probable that the non-student annual members of the club continued as members throughout this time period.

In late 1976, the pro tour began using the 11-point "tiebreaker" instead of the 21-point third game. The "tiebreaker" proved to be more exciting and was a fitting end to a hard-fought match. It kept the suspense of the 3rd game high through all 11 points. Other tournaments at all levels soon followed the same "tie- breaker" format and today the 21-point match deciding the third game is distant history.

CHAPTER 9
A&M Handball Teams 1980-1989

**NOTE: All handball players listed in this Chapter are from Texas
A&M unless a player's college or university is listed.**

For the first time since the National Collegiate Handball Tournament was created, in 1980 the USHA offered the opportunity for women to compete at the national level. Texas A&M women were ready to make their impact on the national scene. One woman especially, Susan (Sue) G. Oakleaf, made her entrance immediately at the championship level.

Steve Sisney reported on 16 April 1980 in *The Battalion* under the heading "Oakleaf Seeks Handball Titles," an indication of the level that she had attained:

> Fresh off a first-place finish at the Texas A&M University Handball Tournament, junior Sue Oakleaf continues sweeping her way toward the National Open Handball championships in June with one victory after another.

> Named the national champion at the National Intercollegiate Handball Tournament at the University of California in Irvine in March, Oakleaf has captured five tournament titles this year.

> This was the first year women have competed at the National Intercollegiate Championships. Oakleaf is also the Southwest Divisional Champion and a two-time state champion.

> "Her technique is the best of any girl I have ever seen," said head handball coach Lance Lowy about Oakleaf's game.

> No less impressive is the fact that Oakleaf is the first person from Texas A&M ever to take a national championship since Ozzie Burke and Dan Kennerly took the National Intercollegiate Doubles Championship in 1969.

> The San Antonio city tournament this weekend will be the next stop for Oakleaf. She is currently the defending champion at the tournament.

> Oakleaf isn't the only talented player on the Aggie handball team as witnessed by the fact that teammates Gloria Motal and Jill MacAluso, at the national tournament, finished third and won Consolation.

> Both Oakleaf and Motal will go to the National Open Championship in Tucson, Ariz. in June. The tournament will draw the top players in the nation.

Lowy feels, "that with the University talent, and interest, A&M has to be considered to have one of the top five handball programs in the country."

Lake Forest College in Chicago is the perennial national power, closely followed by the University of Texas. Lake Forest is the only college that awards handball scholarships.

"We're building right now," Lowy said. "We should be at the level of UT in one to two years."

Due to the demand for court space, the Aggie handball squad does not get to practice as often as it wishes.

The situation is such that with the amount of people wanting to play, and with the number of courts available, "things could be better," said Lowy. (Cushing Archives)

NOTE: *The Battalion* incorrectly reported the year of Burke and Kennerly's Intercollegiate Handball Doubles Championship as 1969. The correct year is 1968.

On 17 March the results of the 1980 National Collegiate Handball Tournament were reported in *The Battalion* in the following story:

> In the recent National Intercollegiate Handball Tournament held in Irvine, California, February 29-March 2, Texas A&M sent four players. Sue Oakleaf won the National Women's Open Singles Championship, while Glorian Motal took 3rd place and Jill MacAluso won the Consolation bracket. Sue has been the Texas State Women's Singles Champion the past two years while Glorian and Jill were both semi-finalists this year.
>
> Our fourth player, John Welch, made it to the quarter-finals in the national tournament in a very tough "C" division. John is the Southwest Intercollegiate "C" division singles champion for 1980.
>
> The results of the national tournament and other recent Texas tournaments reflect the enthusiasm and talent in handball that is present at Texas A&M. We plan to have over forty players participating in the upcoming Southwest Divisional Handball Tournament in Austin, March 21-23. (Cushing Archives)

In the preliminary round of the women's singles of the National Intercollegiate Handball Tournament, Jill MacAluso defeated Gambera of the University of California 21-10, 21-7. In the quarterfinals, Sue Oakleaf defeated Sears of Southwest Texas 21-2, 21-4; Glorian Motal defeated Kallo of the University of California 21-20, 21-16 and Meyer of the University of Texas defeated Jill MacAluso 21-19, 21-7. In the semifinals, Sue Oakleaf defeated Rubin of the University of Texas 21-11, 21-9 and Meyer of the University of Texas defeated Glorian Motal 21-16, 14-21, 11-3. In the finals, Sue Oakleaf defeated Meyer 21-16, 21-18.

As happens so many times there are always stories of adversity that students have to handle. One of those times happened to the Aggie team on the way to the national tournament. Peanut Motal tells the story:

> Sue (Oakleaf) convinced me to go to collegiate nationals. A funny (scary) story ensued. We were poor college students and thus tried to make this the cheapest flight possible. There were 3 women and 1 man. We drove to Houston to get a red eye to Los Angeles.

When we got there at 2AM, we were to drop off our fellow male handball player at USC, where he was going to stay with a friend. Back then, there were no cell phones. It was the guy's responsibility to guide us to USC. We drove close to there and then the neighborhoods started to get worse and worse. Finally, we stopped at a phone booth and the USC student asked us where we were. We looked at the street signs and were at the corner of Executioner and another street. Immediately the USC student said, "Get the hell out of there." It appears we were in the heart of Watts, one of the worst neighborhoods of LA at 2AM. Needless to say, we escaped and everything went well after that.

During the 1980-81 school year, A&M's handball team continued to prove it was one of the top collegiate programs in the nation. The following report by *The Battalion* of 13 March 1981 under the heading of "Handball Team Finishes Third" was an indication of the level of play by the team:

> The Texas A&M University handball team finished third in the national championship last weekend in Boulder, Colorado.
>
> Aggie junior Sue Oakleaf dominated a field of 23 women from across the nation Saturday and Sunday to win her second consecutive national intercollegiate championship. Jill MacAluso and Beth Rowley also contributed important team points by advancing to the quarterfinals.
>
> The men on the handball team were: John Welch, Tim Feickert, Richard Harrison, Matt Pokryfki, Bill Moore and Raymond Walkup. Feickert lost to the eventual champion, Kevin Novak from Memphis State, in the quarterfinals.
>
> Harrison and Moore also lost close matches in the quarterfinals. Welch, Pokryfki and Walkup all performed well in the consolation bracket.
>
> Lance Lowy, coach of the handball team, expressed satisfaction and optimism because of the team results. The experience gained, Lowy said, will help all the players.
>
> The University of Texas and Lake Forest College of Chicago tied for first in the team standings while Memphis State took second. Texas A&M beat out such handball powers as the University of Cincinnati, California-Berkeley and Montana for third place.
>
> The Handball Club will send 40 to 50 players to Austin March 27-29 for the Southwest Divisional Handball Tournament. The tournament will draw top players from Texas, Oklahoma, Arkansas and Louisiana. (Cushing Archives)

With the beginning of the 1981-82 school year, optimism was high throughout the handball club membership. During the last four years, the membership had quadrupled under the leadership of Coach Lowy. The membership totaled 125 at the start of the spring semester and Coach Lowy had to make a tough decision: who to take to the National Collegiate Tournament? Through competition within the club, he chose 12 handball players to go. Results of the showing at the national tournament was reported in *The Battalion* 22 March 1982 under the heading of "A&M Handball Club Third in National Tourney":

> The Texas A&M handball club placed third in the National Intercollegiate Handball Tournament held March 5, 6 and 7 in Memphis, Tennessee.

The 23-team competition was won by Lake Forest College for the second straight year. Second place was taken by last year's second place team-The University of Texas. The host team, Memphis State, placed fourth.

The team was headed by Sue Oakleaf, a two-time winner, who placed second after losing in the finals of the women's open Division. Beth Rowley added points to the team's total by winning the consolation bracket of the women's open Division.

Raymond Walkup, finished third in the C division, Bill Moore and Jeff Davison placed in the quarterfinals. Coach Lowy said, "All of the team members played well to help A&M finish third."

(Cushing Archives)

Though this was a finish in 3rd place nationally it was an indication that the handball program was one of the tops in the nation. Considering there were no scholarships and no recruiting of players who played before attending college, it was a remarkable achievement.

One of the sad memories for the 1982 team was Hilary Huffard, a promising young player who had made enough progress to make the team trip to Memphis. Huffard did not live long enough to play in a national collegiate tournament or to get her Aggie ring. She lost her battle for life to leukemia.

The 1982 National Collegiate Handball Tournament used a different scoring system than had been used since the collegiates were started in 1953. Previously, the team consisted of A singles, B singles and a doubles team - all men. The new rules required a handball team of six players with at least one being a woman. Players could also participate in singles and doubles. The new format proved to be very successful.

In 1980, Lowy predicted the A&M handball team would be on a level with the University of Texas in one to two years. The A&M team would prove him right in 1983. The following article was reported on 14 February 1983 in *The Battalion* under the heading "TAMU Handball Club #One in Southwest Region" would confirm the Aggie level of play:

On February 5 and 6, the Texas A&M Handball Club went to Austin to play in the Southwest Regional Collegiate Handball Tournament against ten other teams from Texas and Oklahoma. In the regional tournament points are awarded to a team for each individual entrant's match that he/she wins. Eighty-five individual entrants competed for the Southwest Championship. The final team outcome was:

1st Place	TEXAS A&M UNIVERSITY	36 points
2nd Place	University of Texas	26 points
3rd Place	North Texas State	10 points
4th Place	UT—San Antonio	6 points

Highlights of the championship tournament would include:

Brenda Crim	Winner	Women's A division
Jeff Davison	Winner	Men's B division
Cliff McInnis	Winner	Men's C division

Other players who did well: Matt Pokryfki and Coke Smith were Semi-Finalists in men's A division. Bobby Winans and Dean Talbot were Semi-Finalists in men's B division.

This was the first time that the Ags have beaten Texas in regional handball competition. The TAMU handball Club will compete for the National Championship in Chicago on March 4, 5 and 6.

For 1983, the collegiate handball committee ushered in a new composition of the handball team. A team was now composed of 6 team members. One of the 6 must be a woman. If a team had 6 men on the team only the points from the 5 high men would be counted for the team championship. (Cushing Archives)

The Aggies would continue their 1983 mastery over the University of Texas at the National Collegiate Tournament held in Chicago, but would not be able to climb another step up the ladder to the national championship. The Aggies ended up in third place with 17 points. This was their third year in a row to place third at the National Collegiate Tournament. Lake Forest won the championship with 25 points followed by Memphis State University with 21 points. The University of Texas was in sixth place with four-and-a-half-points.

Aggies scoring points were Matt Pokryfki with two points in B singles, Jeff Davison with five points in C singles, Brent Bertrand with two points in C singles, Susan Oakleaf with three points in women's A singles and Brenda Crim with two points in women's A singles. Competing for Texas A&M but earning no points were Caroline Henning, Coke Smith and Dean Talbot.

Lance Lowy wrote about the women's singles at the tournament and the article was published in the May 1983 issue of the USHA's *Handball,* page 18. NOTE: The following is only that part of the article that pertains to Sue Oakleaf.

> The women's Division of the 1983 Collegiate Handball Tournament in Chicago began with a field of seventeen entrants. It was apparent from the outset that this was going to be a two-women race between Allison Roberts of Memphis State and Sue "Smokeleaf" Oakleaf of Texas A&M.
>
> The domination of these two women in collegiate handball was obvious as each moved through the quarterfinals and semifinals with no problem. This is not to detract from some other fine handball being played by the rest of the field. Karen Trotter of Pacific displayed fine talent in defeating Caroline Henning of Texas A&M, while Brenda Crim, also of Texas A&M, turned the tables on Pacific's Julie Driscoll.
>
> The top two seeds then showed the gallery their stuff in the semis. Allison blew Brenda off the court and Sue, surprisingly, had no trouble whatsoever with Marie Martineau, from Cegep Lidiolou, Canada. This set the stage with the best two women players in collegiate handball history. Sue had won back-to-back intercollegiate women's titles until last year in Memphis, when Allison entered the picture and promptly won her first title over Sue. Allison won by beating Sue 21-13, 21-17. Brenda Crim won thir3rd place in Women's A Division and Caroline Henning won 3rd place in Women's B Division.

Reporting the C singles competition on page 21 of the May 1983 issue of the USHA's *Handball* magazine with a heading of "Aggie Jeff Davison Routs the Field," the writer stated:

Texas A&M has been at the top of the collegiate heap in women's handball for the four years of women's competition thanks to Coach Lance Lowy's dedication and Sue Oakleaf's example. Because women's handball was relatively new, Lance's crew was able to compete with the traditional powerhouses who were just embarking on their women's programs at the same time.

Now Jeff Davison has proved that the Aggies are making gains in the men's Divisions, as well, by winning the C singles for the Aggies first collegiate men's title since 1954 when Don ("*Johnny*") Johnson and Jim Mathis took the doubles for Texas A&M.

Davison took the C singles without any difficulty and will surely be a strong contender in the B singles next year when he's forced to move up. The Aggies were assured of a men's title when Bobby Winans of Texas A&M defeated Joe Cecin of the US Military Academy in their semifinal bout.

Meanwhile, Davison was destroying teammate Brent Bertrand in their semifinal. Thus, three of the four semifinalists were members of the Texas A&M squad and will help catapult their men's program to the same level of respect that their women's squad has been enjoying.

This year it was all Davison as he allowed an average of under seven points per game throughout his weekend march to the title. Teammate Bobby Winans did tally the most points against Davison, but the 21-11, 21-7 final score was hardly close.

NOTE: The above article is incorrect by stating this was the first title since Don "Johnny" Johnson and Jim Mathis won the doubles title in 1954. Ozzie Burke and Dan Kennerly won the doubles title in 1968.

Tom Easterling reported the results of the 37th George Lee Invitational in the May 1983 issue of the USHA's *Handball* magazine, pages 47 and 48. Following is how the Aggies fared:

In the C singles, it was the day of the Aggies. Two Texas A&M students met in the finals. In two close games unseeded Brent Bertrand defeated fellow Aggie Bobby Williams, 21-17, 21-16. In the Women's Division, Sue Oakleaf showed why she is the class of Texas by beating improved Lee Ann Fuson, 21-16, 21-9.

The 1983 Texas A&M Handball Team at Nationals
FRONT ROW: Dean Talbot
SECOND ROW: Caroline Henning, Brenda Crim, Coach Lance Lowy, Bobby Winans, Sue Oakleaf
BACK ROW: Coke Smith, Jeff Davison, Matt Pokryfki, Brent Bertrand
(Cushing Archives)

As the 1983-84 year unfolded there was continued optimism that the Aggies would place higher than third in the National Collegiate Handball Tournament. New faces started their handball learning experience and the "old" hands wanted to keep improving. There was excitement and a desire to be on the team and have the opportunity to go to a totally different handball environment. The national tournament would be held at the Air Force Academy in Colorado Springs. The altitude of the facility would be a challenge to all coming from an area less than a thousand feet above sea level. The altitude at the Academy is approximately 7,000 feet above sea level.

Consistent with the altitude, the Aggies placed the highest any Aggie handball team had ever finished in national collegiate competition. The team earned 18½ points for second place. That was only two-and-a-half points behind perennial powerhouse Lake Forest. With scholarships provided to its handball team, Lake Forest is able to always recruit players who have had high school experience and are excellent players when they arrive on campus. That fact, when compared to the Aggies who have no scholarships and who must rely on the talent coming through the pipeline of Physical Education (Kinesiology) classes, is an indication of the dedication and hard work the Aggies put in to achieve their lofty status. It is obvious that much of the credit has to go to Coach Lowy.

Reporting on the women's singles, the following write-up was in the USHA's *Handball*, May-June 1984, page 46.

> Now a junior at Xavier University in Cincinnati, Allison Roberts dominated the Women's singles for the third straight year. Roberts allowed her opponents an average of just three points per game. In the finals, Allison faced her toughest foe, Julie Werner of Texas A&M, but Julie was obviously over matched, 21-2, 21-5.
>
> The semifinals pitted the talent and experience of Roberts against the determination of Renee deLassus, also of Texas A&M. Renee had defeated Lucy Glenn of the University of Texas and former Canadian champ in the quarterfinals, 21-14, 21-9. Allison rolled to the 21-4, 21-3 win by consistently hitting the bottom board. deLassus promises a tougher match next year.
>
> In the other semifinal, Werner handled Sandy Nichols of Lake Forest College, 21-8, 21-9, keeping
>
> constant pressure on Nichols by controlling front court.
>
> The Women's A and B Divisions were determined by having the opening-round losers going into the B Division and winners progressing to the A Division. Third place in women's A went to deLassus, who overcame a rocky start to come back and win in the tiebreaker. Glenn won the women's A Consolation over Julie Driscoll of Pacific. Kay Kern of Texas A&M won the Women's C Division over Susan Paik of Pacific. Caroline Henning of Texas A&M won the Women's B Consolation over Cathie Griffin of Lake Forest.

Twenty players were entered in men's B division singles. The Aggies' Matt Pokryfki won his matches leading up to the semifinals. The semifinal results were reported in the USHA's *Handball*, May-June 1984, page 46, follows:

> The cream rose to the top in the semis as Lake Forest's Tim Zender gave Shapiro, University of Arizona, his toughest challenge and Matt Pokryfki of Texas A&M met

another University of Arizona student, John Baldauf. Shapiro took it to Zender in the first for the 21-10 win. However, Zender led most of the second game only to have Shapiro squeak past him, 21-20. In the other semifinal, Pokryfki had the Aggies behind him in full force. Pokryfki's flat kills mixed with pin-point passes and diving gets were too much for Baldauf, 21-9, 21-15.

In the final, Shapiro displayed the consistent serve-and-shoot game that got him to the final and stayed with him for the final. He handily won the first, 21-12. Pokryfki fought to stay close in the second game up to the middle, but Shapiro's tempo took its toll as he pulled away, 21-11. Both finalists played their hearts out over the weekend for themselves and their teammates.

The men's C division singles featured a field of 45 players, which may have been the largest collegiate entry ever in a specific bracket. It is not known how many Aggies were entered in the C division field, but two made some important wins. Following is a report from the USHA's *Handball*, May-June 1984, page 47.

In the other semifinal, James Shine of Memphis State and Brent Bertrand of Texas A&M battled to the wire. Shine started fast and grabbed a large lead in the first game, winning 21-8. Bertrand put together a great game in the second, nipping Shine at the end, 21-18. The tiebreaker between the evenly matched players with similar styles was a battle of wills and guts. Shine made the crucial shots in the tie breaker to squeak it out, 11-8, as the altitude was taking its toll on both players.

Freund grabbed third place over Bertrand while David Key of the University of Texas won the C Consolation over Kevin McIntosh of Texas A&M in the final.

A tournament committee met each year to review and make changes to the rules and procedures to be followed at the National Collegiate Tournament. Lance Lowy, coach for the Aggies, had been a member of the committee for a number of years, but it was not until 1982 that he was given the right by the committee to be a voting member. He served as chair of the committee 1983-85. This year, the committee agreed to allow players playing in both singles and doubles to play in the Consolation bracket if eliminated in an early round. The committee also made the decision to eliminate the term *consolation* and change the bracket to *contender*. There was no change to the point structure of the bracket. The only change was the name.

Upon returning home, the best Aggie team ever to go to the National Collegiate Tournament received its share of congratulations and media coverage. Karen Wallace wrote the following story for *The Battalion* on 27 March 1984.

The Texas A&M handball team brought home a second-place trophy from the 1984 United States Handball Association's National Collegiate Tournament held in Colorado Springs, Colorado.

"We came in second in the nation out of an 18-team field," said Lance Lowy, coach of the team.

"Lake Forest, from Chicago, Illinois, won the tournament, but A&M gave them a run for their money," Lowy said.

"Lake Forest gives scholarships for handball so they are an automatic powerhouse," Lowy said. "We had a great chance to beat them, but we came out a little short."

The tournament was broken down into men's and women's A, B, and C Divisions.

Lowy said that Matt Pokryfki, the top player on the team, played a major part in the team's success. Pokryfki, a senior on the team, placed second in Division B.

Pokryfki said everybody had a hand in bringing home the team's second place title. "It felt good to place second because for the last three years we've placed third," Pokryfki said. "It wasn't just me; it was everybody."

Another place holder is Brent Bertrand, who placed fourth in Division C for the second year in a row. "Bertrand is twice as good as he was last year and he still placed fourth," Lowy said, "That shows you how fast the quality of playing changes."

Lowy, who has won various tournaments himself, said it was the women on the team that really pulled them through.

"We would have the best women's team in the country if we had a separate women's team," he said. Lowy said the men and women are combined to one team for the "team camaraderie."

"My girls are all champions," Lowy said. He said the best part of the tournament was the bond created among the team members.

"There was a great feeling of togetherness." Lowy said. "The players who lost in the first rounds went berserk cheering in the stands. The value of the whole thing was to go up there and do the best we can. Some got beat, but it was a great learning experience."

Lowy said the handball team consists of 30 members chosen from his handball classes. "Each person deserves recognition for their contribution to the team," he said.

(Cushing Archives)

1984 Handball team at the National Collegiate Handball Tournament
held at the Air Force Academy in Colorado Springs, Colorado

(Cushing Archives)

Team 2nd place Trophy

(Author's Collection)

Members of the team making the trip to Colorado Springs were Les Lehrmann, Danny Coolidge, Randy Pullen, Bobby Winans, Mark Smith, Larry Wisdom, Gary Mueck, Raymond Walkup, Kevin McIntosh, Alan Padfield, Matt Pokryfki, Mike Frieda, Tim Sutton, Todd Bryan, Keith Martin, Brent Bertrand, Cliff McInnis, Trey Taylor, Kevin Cokinos, Julie Werner, Caroline Henning, Kay Kern, Rene deLassus, Paige Healy and Cissy Burns.

Leaving the record-setting 1984 Aggie handball team to history, Coach Lowy entered the 1985 season with great optimism. He had some key players returning and saw improvement in the overall team. His long sought national team championship at the national collegiate level was finally realized in Austin as the University of Texas hosted the 1985 National Collegiate Handball Championship Tournament. Tournament results of the A&M team's competition was reported by Cindy Gay in *The Battalion* on 7 March 1985 under the headline "Aggie Handball Team Wins Nationals".

> Handball coach Lance Lowy loves walking into his office this week.
>
> Embracing the front corner of his desk is the national championship trophy which his Texas A&M Handball Team triumphantly carried home this past weekend.
>
> Forty-five players traveled to the University of Texas campus in Austin to compete against 14 other teams in the National Collegiate Handball Tournament.
>
> For the first time ever, the Texas A&M men's and women's teams came out on top.
>
> "It was a big surprise because Lake Forest College of Chicago has won the tournament for nine years in a row," Lowy said.
>
> Accumulating a total of 26 points the Aggie handball team finished with a comfortable four-point edge over Memphis State University.
>
> "We clenched the national championship on Saturday night," Lowy said. "It was unbelievable, because that never happens."
>
> A&M's Julie Werner now reigns as the individual national champion in women's handball, with her first-place finish in Class A. Renee deLassus clinched third place for the Aggies in that category.
>
> "In the women's, we just wiped them out." Lowy said. "The support they gave to each other pulled out some wins for us."
>
> The only Aggie to compete in men's Class B, Bobby Winans reached the quarter-finals. David Allen, Randy Pullen and Tim Sutton boosted A&M's point total to winning second, third and fourth places respectively in the men's Class C.
>
> A&M's Dave Utsey, Mark Smith and Larry Wisdom were Class C quarter-finalists.
>
> "We just pounded through with depth," Lowy said.
>
> Unlike the teams who roped in the "hot-shot junior players" from high school, Lowy said all the A&M players were introduced to handball at college. A&M's Winans said he began playing his freshman year.
>
> After capturing second place in the tournament last year, Wemer said the pressure intensified for her to win the national championship this time around.

Drawing from the 150 members of the Texas A&M Handball Club, a flexible number of players compete in tournaments throughout the school year, including two Aggieland Classics.

Winans said he expected the teamwork exhibited in the past weeks to pay off at Nationals.

"I figured we'd win this year as a team," he said

Lowy added, "Camaraderie was what the whole thing was all about."

(Cushing Archives)

A great strength of the Aggie team was the women handballers. A&M entered 16 women in the tournament and, as the national championship trophy was carried back to Aggieland, all could be thankful that the USHA opened the tournament to women in 1980. In such a short time, the Aggies have won three women's handball singles titles and had been finalists in singles the other three years.

In the women's singles play of the preliminary round, Peggy O'Neill of Lake Forest College defeated Kim Denman (no score given); Evy Grace of the University of Texas defeated Brenda Machac 21-4, 21-1 and Liz Kalina defeated Mary Lou Baker of the University of Texas 19-21, 21-12, 11-9. In first round action, Julie Werner defeated Angie Hutchinson of the University of Texas 21-2, 21-1; Cynthia Lanier of the University of Texas defeated Deb Oaks 15-21, 21-17, 11-8; Terri Fabris of Pacific University defeated Missy Sheffield 21-15, 21-1; Angie Lim of the University of Texas defeated Ginny Stover 21-1, 21-2; Paula Chabal of the University of Texas defeated Dawn Bell 21-13, 21-15; Gina Ross of Lake Forest College defeated Suzy Fisk 21-2, 21-15; Cissy Burns defeated Liz Kalina 21-2, 21-5; Lolita Velez of Pacific University defeated Sylvia Andrews 21-6, 21-16; Maria Rogers of the University of Texas defeated Julie Hutchinson 21-2, 21-1; Cathy Griffin of Lake Forest College defeated Teresa Letson 21-0, 21-7; Selena Solis of the University of Texas defeated Caryn Stallings 21-15, 21-18; Rebecca Braly defeated Aubrey Gaines of Lake Forest College 21-16, 21-16 and Renee deLassus defeated Debbie Herr of Pacific University 21-3, 21-1.

In the second round, Julie Werner defeated Cynthia Lanier of the University of Texas 21-4, 21-4; Cissy Burns defeated Lolita Velez of Pacific University 21-8, 21-10 and Renee deLassus defeated Rebecca Braly 21-4, 21-2. In the quarterfinals, Julie Werner defeated Angie Lim of the University of Texas 21-5, 21-1; Julie Driscoll of Pacific University defeated Cissy Burns 21-5, 21-7 and Renee deLassus defeated Cathy Griffin of Lake Forest College 21-3, 21-8. In the semifinals, Julie Werner defeated Susan Paik of Pacific University 21-9, 21-13 and Julie Driscoll of Pacific University defeated Renee deLassus 21-9, 21-10. Julie Werner easily won the national championship by defeating Julie Driscoll 21-7, 21-11.

The scores and winners of the other women's divisions were not available.

Mike Steele, coach of Pacific University, wrote the following and was reported on pages 20 and 21 of the May-June 1985 issue of the USHA's *Handball:*

The Queen is Dead! Long Live the Queen, Texas A&M's Julie Werner

Or so it seemed as the women began their play at the University of Texas. The absence of Allison Roberts, three-time champ but not in school and ineligible for a fourth straight, brought many hopefuls wishing to ascend to the throne of women's collegiate champion.

It promised to be a wide-open race, but Julie Werner of Texas A&M gained the No. 1 seed and successfully defended that ranking against a host of veterans and newcomers, defeating Julie Driscoll of Pacific University in the final, 21-7, 21-11.

The competition got stiffer as the first two rounds were completed in the largest Women's collegiate event to date. First-round losers became the Women's C entrants. Second-round losers became the Women's B entrants. Third-round losers became the Women's A Contenders entrants. All the women got plenty of play.

Once there were only Women's A entrants remaining, 16 women still had hopes claiming the vacant throne. However, Werner used an aggressive shooting game, complimented by her front-court mobility to sift through the field. In the round of 16, Werner defeated Cynthia Lanier of the University of Texas 21-4, 21-4. In the quarters, Werner bombed Angie Lim of the University of Texas 21-5, 21-1.

Coach Lowy with Julie Werner, 1985 National Collegiate Handball Tournament Women's Champion

(Courtesy Lance Lowy)

In the semifinals, Werner met Susan Paik of Pacific University, a three-time veteran of national collegiate play. Paik came on strong in the second game, but remained just a little short of forcing a tie-breaker, 21-0, 21-18. In the final, it was Julie against Julie Driscoll. Driscoll's patient defensive game plan wasn't up to the task of containing the offense of Werner. Werner became the new champ on the glass exhibition court, 21-9, 21-10.

What emerged in this division was a hard-fought contest between the two emerging powers of women's college handball-Texas A&M and Pacific University. The Aggies entered 16 women while Pacific sent five. Both teams were left with four players each after the A singles cut-off, and two each in the semifinals. The excitement was intense as both teams had hopes for their own players to face each other in the final. The semis became even more intense as the Aggies needed a win to stay on top of the team point total.

The field of forty women at this year's nationals was the largest in collegiate history. It was obvious that they are benefiting from the excellent coaching as a well-balanced and competitive field was the result. All handball players will soon be enjoying the numbers of competent women players adding their spark to our great game.

NOTE: The scores in the article do not match, in all cases, the scores given in a report of the women's play. In either case Werner clearly won the championship with ease.

Basking in the glory of the 1985 championship season, the Aggie team received the accolades a champion deserves. A story in the 1 November 1985 University newspaper, *The Battalion*, the writer describes the action, mentality, and background of the members in the Aggie handball club. The headline was "Handball team No. 1 in nation":

The 1985 National Collegiate Handball Champion Team
FRONT ROW: Coach Lance Lowy with the National Championship Team Trophy

PHOTO INCLUDES: Alan Padfield, Mark Smith, Mike Miller, Eddy Johnson, Rick Orr, David Utsey, Dave Allen, Jerry Ordonez, Randy Pullen, Tim Sutton, Larry Wisdom, Mike Frieda, Bobby Winans, Caryn Stallings, Suzy Fisk, Missy Sheffield, Krista Gregory, Caroline Henning, Kay Kern, Dawn Bell, Julie Hutchinson, Robert Rausch, Mike Forbes, Dennis Hernandez, Julie Werner, Renee DeLassus, Todd Bryan, Paul Brozovic, and Gary Mueck.

(Cushing Archives)

There are those who say that to have a winning team, any kind of winning team at all, it's gotta cost money. But the handball club has proven that dictum simply isn't true. Without an expensive recruiting effort, splashy uniforms or heavily publicized games, the Texas A&M club won the national championship in Austin last year.

"Our main competition was Lake Forest in Chicago, who won the championship nine years in a row before us," Coach Lance Lowy says, "and Memphis State has a pretty good team, too, but they give scholarships to their players."

A&M has no scholarships or recruiting for the handball team. There's no Cain Hall or BMW's for the best of them. Most stumbled on to it by accident but all play because they love it. Tim Sutton, club president, says almost no one on the team had played handball before coming to A&M.

The banner representing Texas A&M's first National Collegiate Handball Team Championship

(Author's Collection)

"I hadn't even heard of the game 'til I got here, probably like a lot of other people," he says. "I had wanted to play racquetball (for P.E.) but it was filled and handball was next door."

Sutton, who also went to nationals last year, says he took the class and took to handball. He stuck with it because it's challenging and competitive.

"It's something to keep me in shape," he says, "something to help keep the Hamburger Helper off."

Sutton says A&M was able to take 45 players to the national tournament last year because it was so close to home, and this might have contributed to their success because of the way winners are picked. Tournaments are generally divided into three divisions: A, B and C.

"The only people who play in A are people who have played for quite a few years or on the professional circuit," he says.

Players in B and C are progressively less experienced. The tournaments are scored by with a win in C counting as one point, in B as two points and in A as three points. Women get one point for each win.

When the dust clears and all the matches end, the scores of the top six players from each club are added together and called a team, and the winner is found.

"We had so many people in the Austin tournament and that made room for a lot of points to be won." Sutton says. "We made up the majority of the finalists in the men's C division and then we had the women's first and third place winners."

This in no way detracts from their accomplishment, however, because the A&M team had threatened to take the title from Lake Forest several times in recent years. Three years ago, Lowy says, the A&M team came in third in nationals and last year they moved up to second. Although he says he thinks the team will retain the title next year, it's really unpredictable until he sees where the best high school players go to school.

"To be honest, I thought we'd win it two years ago in Colorado Springs," he says. "Last year I didn't think we'd win it and we did."

Competing in the tournament in Berkeley next year, as individual or team champs, will be more difficult because of the pressure to do a repeat performance, says Julie Werner, the women's national champion and a senior marketing major at A&M.

"The pressure's on us to win the title this year," she says. "Because we're not the underdog anymore, we're the one everyone wants to beat."

Although she'd never played handball before playing at A&M either, at least Werner had heard of it because her father played in the Navy. Like Sutton, she played her first handball match because racquetball was such a popular and rapidly filled P.E. class. She took her first class in the spring of her freshman year and has taken it every semester since.

Lowy encourages people to take his class after the requirements are filled. Although certain courts are reserved each night for team practice, Lowy says he prefers team members to be in his classes so he knows they're playing regularly.

"The more you play," he says, "the better you're going to get. I like to get them in classes so I can be as critical with them as I can, if you know what I mean."

Sutton says the rules for handball are just like the rules for racquetball. Both are played in square, bare rooms, using four walls, a ball and goggles—an inexpensive sport if there ever was one.

What makes them different, he says, is that handball requires that players use both hands because one isn't taken up by a racquet. It also takes good hand eye coordination, quickness, agility and stamina.

It's also a sport not plagued by injury.

"You can break a few blood vessels," Werner says, "or turn your ankle and stuff like that. I've got a lot of bruises—mainly it's from a lot of falling down and running into walls." Players also suffer from swollen or bruised hands and ice down their shoulders or arms after a big tournament because of the extensive use of arm and shoulder muscles during the game, Sutton says.

"It's just something your hand has to get accustomed to," he says. "You get aches in your arms and shoulder and elbow kind of like a baseball pitcher."

Sutton says handball is traditionally a male sport because it is very physical, but more women are signing up to play. Werner says more women are beginning to realize it's a sport they can play.

"They use a different kind of ball for the women called a family ball that's a little bit softer," she says. "It's not as hard as with the harder ball but it's still really challenging."

Werner says about 20 women regularly participate in the club and about 40 women from all over the country competed in the nationals last year.

The handball club has over 100 members. It participated in regular tournaments against the University of Texas, Lowy's alma mater, and anyone in the club is free to go. The club attends mainly open tournaments which pit the young against the old, holding only to the divisions of A, B and C in fact the only times the club participates as a formal team is at the regionals in February and the March National.

The club sponsors its own tournament the weekend before Dead Week—Dec. 6-8 this year. The tournament is open to anyone who wants to play and had nearly 180 participants last year. Players compete in the C, B-Plus or C, Sutton says.

(Cushing Archives)

With the Aggies on top of the collegiate handball world, interest in handball at A&M continued. Handball classes (P. E.) were full and the club continued to have over 100 members. Obviously, Coach Lowy and the club were looking to repeat as the collegiate champions. Of course, the Aggies were now the target and the other top college handball teams were working hard to knock the Aggies from the top of the hill. At the 1986 National Collegiate Handball Tournament held at the University of California-Berkeley, the Aggies found out how hard it was to repeat especially when there were no scholarships at A&M to be awarded for handball. Memphis State, which had handball scholarships, replaced the Aggies as National Collegiate Handball Champions. The Aggies did not go away easily. Memphis State won with 21½ points to the Aggies 20. The University of Texas had returned to be one of the top collegiate handball powers but finished behind the Aggies with 19 points. Lake Forest, the perennial powerhouse in collegiate handball, slipped to 5th place with 11½ points.

To compete for the National Collegiate Handball Championship, the Aggies had to rely on strong performances in the men's division B and C, and a strong performance from the women in the women's division. The Aggies rarely had a player in men's division A which awards more points than the B and C divisions. Some of the division A players compete in handball's pro circuit.

In B singles, John Utsey lost in the first round 21-8, 21-13 to Shawn Massey of Memphis State and Tim Sutton lost 21-11, 21-12 to Jerry Carillo from the University of Arizona. These results meant there would be no points earned in the men's Class A and B.

Coach Lance Lowy reported C singles action in the following paragraph of the June 1986 issue of the USHA's *Handball*, page 9:

The C singles featured 49 players representing 15 schools with fatigue and upsets ruling the event. Number 1 seed Larry Silver of Memphis State went down to defeat in a round of 16 tie breaker to Robert Landy of Texas. Meanwhile, the surprise of the tournament, University of Montana's Kent Barr was advancing with ease, defeating Texas A&M's Garrett Smith, 21-11, 21-11.

In the quarter finals, Barr ended Landy's upset spree, 21-7, 21-11. In one of the best matches of the tournament, A&M's Todd Bryan out-dueled Memphis State's Kevin Fitzgerald, 20-21, 21-14, 11-4. Completing the semifinal matchups, Pacific's Richard Jones topped A&M's John Mark Smith, 21-10, 21-6 and A&M's Larry Wisdom squeaked past teammate Gary Mueck, 13-21, 21-8, 11-7.

In their third match of the day, Barr grabbed two quick games over Jones, 21-8, 21-5, while Bryan held off a tired Wisdom, 21-13, 21-16.

In the final, Barr shot effectively in the first game, earning an easy 21-2 win. Bryan slowed the pace in the second game to stay close, but didn't have enough firepower to match Barr, losing, 21-15. Wisdom grabbed third place over Jones, while Glen Gaddy of the University of Texas won the contenders event over University of California's Deron Van Hoff, 21-12, 21-15.

The coverage in the USHA magazine of the women's competition did not provide detail on how the Aggies performed. Coach Lowy was able to go back into his memory for that year and provided the following: Julie Werner did not survive her semifinals match to make it into the championship. She won a playoff for third. Rene delassus and Dawn Bell both were eliminated in the quarterfinals and Deb Oaks won women's B division. Missy Sheffield advanced to the semifinals in women's B division.

For the first time that I can determine, an Aggie played in the Graduate men's singles. Graduate singles do not count toward a team championship but provides the opportunity for a graduate student from any college or university to compete in the National Collegiate Handball Tournament. Women's graduate singles was added to the 1985 National Collegiate Tournament. In the men's Graduate singles finals, Bobby Winans lost to

The 1986 Handball Team at the National Collegiate Handball Tournament at the University of California-Berkeley
PHOTO INCLUDES: Mike Forbes, Missy Sheffield, Dawn Bell, Garrett Smith, Mike Miller, Rene DeLassus, Bobby Winans, David Utsey, Julie Werner, John Reysa, Gary Mueck, Todd Bryan, Debbie Oaks, Caryn Stallings, Larry Wisdom, Mark Smith and Coach Lance Lowy
NOT IN PHOTO, BUT ON THE TEAM AND MAKING THE TRIP: Tim Sutton and Eddy Johnson
(Courtesy Lance Lowy)

Carl Libis of Arizona State University 21-1, 21-4. Bobby competed in the national tournament the three previous years as an undergraduate and was an important contributor to the team's success.

After seeing Memphis State squeak by to win the national title in 1986, the Aggies looked to recharge for the future. Having lost some very talented players, the Aggies spent 1987 looking toward the top and gaining experience for another championship at a future date. This is not to say the Aggies were not a good handball team, they were, and proved so by finishing third in the men's team standings and second in the women's team competition. The 1987 tournament was held in Memphis, Tennessee.

In the men's competition, A&M had no player who could compete at the A or B singles level. All Aggie competitors were in C singles competition. Representing the Aggies were: Larry Wisdom, Dennis Hernandez, Lance Mobley, Tom Kohler, Mike Miller, John Reysa, Chris Miller, Mike Walls, Jerry Ordonez, Aaron Cooper, Garrett Smith, John Wyatt, Eddy Johnson, Mike Forbes, Jay Wigginton, Burt LeJeune, Dan Watts and Matt Montelongo.

In the first round of men's C Singles competition, the following Aggies received a bye: Larry Wisdom, John Reysa and Mike Forbes. The results of Aggies who played in the first round were Dennis Hernandez defeated C. Brown of the University of Texas 21-6, 21-6; M. Hosford of the University of Texas defeated Lance Mobley 21-14, 21-9; Tom Kohler defeated S. Mayer of the University of California-Berkeley 21-18, 16-21, 11-0; Mike Miller defeated A. Burton of Pacific University 21-1, 21-0; Chris Miller defeated S. Melnar of the University of Texas 21-10, 21-10; Mike Walls defeated G. Garcia of the University of Texas 19-21, 21-9, 11-7; Jerry Ordonez defeated A. Antaramian of the University of California-Berkeley 21-4, 21-0; Aaron Cooper defeated J. Biehl of Chabot College (Hayward, California) 19-21, 21-19, 11-10; Garrett Smith defeated B. Fitzgerald of Memphis State University 21-1, 21-3; John Wyatt defeated A. Flores of Chabot College 17-21, 21-13, 11-7; Eddy Johnson defeated B. Flahire of Lake Forest College 13-21, 21-19, 11-5; P. Trevino of Lake Forest College defeated Jay Wigginton (score not given); Burt LeJeune defeated R. Smith of the US Air Force Academy 21-18, 21-2; B. Cooper of the University of Texas defeated Dan Watts 21-20, 15-21, 11-5 and Matt Montelongo defeated E. Torres of the University of Texas 21-13, 21-18.

In the second round of men's C singles, Larry Wisdom defeated C. Crespi of Lake Forest College 21-11, 21-18; Dennis Hernandez defeated D. Van Hoff of the University of California-Berkeley 21-18, 21-18; D. Sheidt of Pacific University defeated Tom Kohler 21-11, 21-16; D. Gibson of Chabot College defeated Mike Miller 9-21, 21-12, 11-5; John Reysa defeated Chris Miller 21-3, 21-16; K. Hill of Memphis State University defeated Mike Walls 21-4, 21-7; M. Hogan of the University of Illinois defeated Jerry Ordonez 21-13, 21-15; Garrett Smith defeated Aaron Cooper 21-13, 21-14; K. Crespi of Memphis State University defeated John Wyatt 21-8, 20-21, 11-2; S. Yeang (college/university unknown) defeated Eddy Johnson 21-6, 21-9; Mike Forbes defeated P. Trevino of Lake Forest College 21-11, 21-0; C. Biersborn of Lake Forest College defeated Burt LeJeune 21-2, 21-14 and L. Wachholz of the University of Montana defeated Matt Montelongo 21-7, 21-12.

In the third round of men's C singles, S. Brown of the University of Texas defeated Larry Wisdom 9-21, 21-13, 11-8; S. Walleck of Lake Forest College defeated Dennis Hernandez 21-6, 21-7; K. Hill of Memphis State University defeated John Reysa 21-11, 21-4; M. Hogan of the University of Illinois defeated Garrett Smith 21-11, 21-8 and Mike Forbes defeated C. Biersborn of Lake Forest College 21-7, 21-19. In the quarterfinals, Mike Forbes defeated L. Wachholz of the University of Montana 8-21, 21-15, 11-5. In the semifinals, K. Crespi of Memphis State University defeated Mike Forbes 18-21, 21-20, 11-2.

In the preliminary round of doubles competition, Dennis Hernandez and Dan Watts of A&M defeated A. Antaramian and Steve Mayer from the University of California-Berkeley 21-4, 21-17. Now playing against some of the players from the A's and B's, the Aggies found the doubles competition much tougher. In the first round of doubles, Mark Polgrabia and Kevin Hill of Memphis State University defeated Mike Miller and Larry Wisdom 21-8, 21-1; Kevin Fitzgerald and Kevin Stanfield of Memphis State University defeated Mike Forbes and Garrett Smith 21-6, 21-6 and Ken Crespi and Pat Conway of Memphis State University defeated Burt LeJeune and John Reysa 21-18, 21-1.

The format of the women's division was different from the men's division. In the women's division all competitors started in the Open. First round losers dropped down to B. Second round losers in the Open became those in women's A. First round losers in B would make up the C division. This assured all 33 women competing in women's singles to play a minimum of three contests. This "drop-down" format was developed by A&M Coach, Lance Lowy.

Representing A&M in the women's singles were Bonnie Hoekstra, Anna Griffin, Julie Hutchinson, Wendy Smalley, Gloria Smalley, Dawn Bell, Lisa Smith, Tracy Johnson, Susan Owens, Caryn Stallings, Dawn Crane, Krista Gregory, Missy Sheffield, Tanya Brackeen and Melissa Falconer.

In the preliminary round of women's singles, Caroline Jansing of Lake Forest College defeated Bonnie Hoekstra 21-5, 21-3. In the first round, Anna Griffin defeated Kathy Nielson of the University of Texas 21-8, 21-19; Julie Hutchinson defeated Caroline Guip of Lake Forest College (no score given); Wendy Smalley defeated Peggy O'Neill of Lake Forest College (no score given); Gloria Smalley defeated Paula Piepho of Lake Forest College 21-4, 21-5; Dawn Bell defeated Kim Cooling of Memphis State University 21-5, 21-4; Evy Grace of the University of Texas defeated Lisa Smith 21-3, 21-2; Gina Ross of Lake Forest College defeated Tracy Johnson 21-11, 21-5; Laquita Herndon of the University of Texas defeated Susan Owens 21-5, 21-9; Caryn Stallings defeated Daphne Honma of Pacific University 21-6, 21-16; Mary Hutchinson of the University of Texas defeated Dawn Crane 21-10, 21-6; Janet Burke of Memphis State University defeated Krista Gregory 21-11, 20-21, 11-0; Missy Sheffield defeated Rose Wong of the University of California-Berkeley 21-4, 21-6; Tanya Brackeen defeated Cathy Blassingame of Memphis State University 21-15, 21-16 and Noel Adorno of the University of Texas defeated Melissa Falconer (no score given).

In the second round, Carrie Cooke of American River College (North Highlands, California) defeated Anna Griffin 21-0, 21-8; Wendy Smalley defeated Julie Hutchinson 21-12, 21-6; Gloria Smalley defeated Mischea McMcory of Memphis State University 21-16, injury default; Evy Grace of the University of Texas defeated Dawn Bell 21-0, 21-14; Mary Hutchinson of the University of Texas defeated Caryn Stallings (no score given); Missy Sheffield defeated Janet Burke of Memphis State University 21-20, 21-16 and Noel Adorno of the University of Texas defeated Tanya Brackeen 21-3, 21-7.

In the quarterfinals, Carrie Cooke of American River College defeated Wendy Smalley 21-2, 21-6; Gloria Smalley defeated Evy Grace of the University of Texas 21-20, 21-10 and Noel Adorno of the University of Texas defeated Missy Sheffield 21-8, 21-4. In the semifinals, Cooke defeated Gloria Smalley (scores not available) eliminating the last Aggie in the Open.

In A division, two Aggies who knew each other's game through and through held one of the most thrilling matches of the tournament. Anna Griffin defeated Julie Hutchinson 21-13, 11-21, 11-10. A match just doesn't get closer than that. Dawn Bell defeated Mischea McCrory of Memphis State University 21-7, 21-17. Gina Ross of Lake Forest Chicago defeated Caryn Stallings 21-4, 21-10. Janet Burke of Memphis State University defeated Tanya Brackeen 21-18, 21-17. Of the 5 Aggies in the A division, two continued to the semifinals.

It would have been better if the two Aggies had been matched against the other two players but it was not to be. Anna Griffin defeated Dawn Bell (no score available) and Ross defeated Burke. In the finals of A division, Ross defeated Anna Griffin 21-10, 21-6.

In the first round of B division, Kathy Neilson of the University of Texas defeated Bonnie Hoekstra (no score available); Kim Cooling of Memphis State University defeated Lisa Smith 21-18, 21-16 and Tracy Johnson defeated Peggy O'Neill of Lake Forest College 21-14, 21-13. In the semifinals, Daphne Honma of Pacific defeated Tracy Johnson 21-17, 21-2.

In the women's C division quarterfinals, Susan Owens defeated Bonnie Hoekstra (no score available); Paula Piepho of Lake Forest College defeated Lisa Smith 21-11, 21-9 and Dawn Crane defeated Peggy O'Neill of Lake Forest College 21-11, 21-11. In the semifinals, Piepho defeated Susan Owens 21-2, 21-0 and Dawn Crane defeated Cathy Blassingame of Memphis State University 21-1, 21-3. In the finals, Crane was outscored by Piepho 21-8, 21-8.

For the first time, women's doubles became a part of the National Collegiate Tournament. In the first round, Piepho and Jansing of Lake Forest College defeated Krista Gregory and Tracy Johnson 21-14, 21-13; Dawn Bell and Caryn Stallings defeated Cooling and Blassingame of Memphis State University 21-2, 21-3; Gloria and Wendy Smalley received a bye; Burke and McCrory of Memphis State University defeated Missy Sheffield and Tanya Brackeen 21-18, 16-21, 11-6 while Herndon and Grace of the University of Texas squeaked by Anna Griffin and Julie Hutchinson 12-21, 21-5, 11-10.

In the quarterfinals, Dawn Bell and Caryn Stallings defeated Beinhauer and Honma of the University of Texas (no score available) and Gloria and Wendy Smalley defeated Burke and McCrory of Memphis State University 21-5, 21-14. In the semifinals, Adorno and Mary Hutchinson defeated Dawn Bell and Caryn Stallings (no score available) and Herndon and Grace of the University of Texas defeated Gloria and Wendy Smalley 21-14, 21-15. With both Aggie women's doubles teams being eliminated, there would be no doubles championship this year.

Women' 2nd place trophy

(Author's Collection)

With this tournament also came All-American recognition to all who finished semifinalists in singles and finalists in doubles. Gloria Smalley received the All-American designation to become the first Aggie, male or female, to receive this honor.

The National Collegiate Handball Tournament was initiated and developed by the United States Handball Association and continues to be under that sponsorship. However, the oversight, rules, eligibility, sight selection and production of the tournament is the responsibility of the committee of six Commissioners, all who represent a college or university. Most, if not all, are the coaches of the teams that participate in the tournament. The Commissioners are selected by the coaches. All coaches may sit at the annual meeting but only the Commissioners vote and make decisions. Being a Commissioner is an honor and selection is based on knowledge of the game of handball, the college/university environment and success as a coach. It is an acknowledgement of respect from the other coaches. Shown below are the six Commissioners for the 1987 year. Each will continue as Commissioner until personal initiated separation or no longer associated with their respective college or university. Photo is from the USHA's *Handball*, June 1987, page 21.

Mike Steele (Pacific University), Pete Tyson (The University of Texas), Larry Aguiar (Chabot University), Charlie Mazzone (Memphis State University), Mike Dau (Lake Forest College), Lance Lowy (Texas A&M University)

In the history of handball there have been many accidents that altered the eyesight of players hit in the eye with a handball. Dr. Lavon Anderson of College Station was one of the players who was hit and had his eyesight altered from the ball's impact. To avoid possible eye injury during the National Collegiate Handball Tournament or any other USHA collegiate sanctioned tournament, the committee passed a requirement that all players are required to wear a "properly worn" eye guard. The term "properly worn" was added to prevent players from wearing eye guards as headbands, necklaces or another adornment. The rule was passed during the 1987 summer meeting of the Commissioners and required in all subsequent tournaments beginning with the 1988 National Collegiate Handball Tournament. Additionally, the Commissioners recommended that all eye guards have polycarbonate lenses. That ruled out open eye guards that experts have proven did not properly protect the eyes.

Another important issue settled in the meeting was the assigning of points to certain levels of play. Previously, players in the A (Open) divisions were awarded the same number of points for a win as a player in a lower division. It was strongly felt that players in the A (Open) divisions should be awarded a larger point total for a win than those in lower divisions. The point total for wins in the A division would be awarded 40 points, for wins in the B division 25 points and 14 points for wins in the C division.

In recent years there has been no available record of the Aggie handball team members' participation in tournaments other than the National Collegiate Tournament and the Aggieland Classic. Basically, individuals enter other tournaments as individuals and not as a team. All other tournament experience is helpful to each participating as an individual and also very helpful to the coach to help determine how individuals should be seeded at the National Collegiate Tournament. Individual seeding at the national tournament became much more involved with the 1988 collegiate tournament. The collegiate committee adopted the drop-down format for the men. The drop-down format, developed by Lance Lowy, was used the previous year for the women's competition and was very popular. With this format a new scoring system was devised which gave more points to those in the higher brackets than even the champions of some lower brackets. Some on the committee were still upset that Texas A&M won the 1985 national team championship with sheer numbers while having no one in the A division. One of the great advantages of the drop-down format is the guarantee that every player at the tournament will play a minimum of three matches. With the old format some players would be eliminated in the first match and then would be finished for the tournament.

In the 1988 preliminary round of the men's A division singles, Jay Wigginton defeated Angelo Gonzalez of Penn State and Tom Kohler defeated Scott Parker of Chabot College. All other Aggie men received a bye to the first round. In first round play, John Bike of the University of Texas defeated Jay Wigginton 21-10, 21-2; Curt Heiting of Memphis State University defeated Aaron Cooper 21-6, 21-17; Chris Tico of Lake Forest College defeated Wayne Crouch 21-7, 21-14; Ken Crespi of Memphis State University defeated Jerry Ordonez 21-10, 21-16; Luke Friendshuh of St. Cloud Technical College defeated Charles Johnson 21-10, 21-8; Robert Landy of the University of Texas defeated Chris Miller 16-21, 21-8, 11-1; Mike Hogan of the University of Illinois defeated Dennis Hernandez 21-13, 21-9; Kevin Hill of Memphis State University defeated Matt Montelongo 21-14, 21-6; Bob Haddon of Lake Forest College defeated Danny Watts 21-11, 21-7; Todd Bryan defeated Spencer Wood of Southwest Missouri State University 21-7, 21-9; Michael Forbes defeated Gilbert Garcia of the University of Texas 21-9, 21-10 and Garrett Smith defeated Steve Kearney of Penn State University 21-7, 21-10.

In second round action, Todd Bryan defeated Chris Panczyk of the University of Illinois 7-21, 21-20, 11-8. Kevin Fitzgerald of Memphis State University defeated Michael Forbes 21-15, 21-19 and Jeff Cottam of Memphis State University defeated Garrett Smith 21-14, 21-5. As the last remaining Aggie in A division, Bryan was not successful in his third-round action, losing 21-10, 21-14 to Larry Haskell of Lake Forest College.

Detailed scoring in the other divisions was not reported. In the C division action, the eventual champion, Scott Mittman of the University of Texas, defeated Wayne Crouch and Jerry Ordonez to reach the finals. In the Contenders division, Jay Wigginton was defeated by Alex Gonzalez of Austin Community College in a squeaker 21-15, 12-21, 11-9.

The A&M men did not participate in the doubles competition.

In first round action for the Aggie women, Anna Griffin defeated Annette Crespi of Schoolcraft 21-1, 21-2; Wendy Smalley defeated Sharon Bramer of Southwest Missouri State University (no score available); Gloria Smalley received a bye; Kim King defeated Caroline Jansing of Lake Forest College 21-17, 21-10; Julie Hutchinson defeated Angie Angelici of Memphis State 21-6, 21-6; Dawn Crane defeated Mishea McCrory of Memphis State 21-10, 21-11 and Francis Woodcock defeated Janet Burke of Memphis State 18-21, 21-18, 11-8. Krista Gregory and Lisa Smith dropped down to the C division.

In second round action, Wendy Smalley defeated Anna Griffin 21-19, 21-5; Gloria Smalley defeated Kathy Neilson of the University of Texas 21-7, 21-20; Jennifer Roberts of Memphis State defeated Kim King 21-1, 21-9; Lucie Marcoux of Laval defeated Julie Hutchinson 21-4, 21-1; Angie Hutchinson of the University of Texas defeated Dawn Crane 21-8, 21-4 and Gina Ross of Lake Forest College defeated Francis Woodcock 21-15, 21-11. Anna Griffin, Kim King, Julie Hutchinson, Dawn Crane and Francis Woodcock dropped to the B division.

In the quarterfinals, Carrie Cooke, 1987 Women's National Champion, of California State-Northridge defeated Wendy Smalley 21-9, 21-9; and Jennifer Roberts of Memphis State defeated Gloria Smalley 21-14, 21-4.

The Aggies' Francis Woodcock rolled through a strong B singles field dominated mostly by players from Lake Forest and the University of Texas. She wasn't challenged until the finals where she won in a tiebreaker over Kathy Nielsen of the University of Texas 20-21, 21-17, 11-3.

A surprised Anna Griffin received the Sportsman Trophy for women. Mike Steele, 1988 Collegiate Commissioner, said Anna always seemed to have an encouraging word for everyone she met, yet was genuinely surprised when she received her award for the women.

1988 Handball Team at the National Gollegiate Tournament in Chicago
PHOTO INCLUDES: Gloria Smalley, Wendy Smalley, Kim King, Julie Hutchinson, Anna Griffin, Dawn Crane, Francis Woodcock, Todd Bryan, Mike Forbes, Wayne Crouch, Jerry Ordonez, Garrett Smith, Matt Montelongo, Aaron Cooper, Danny Watts, Jay Wigginton, Krista Gregory, Dennis Hernandez, Chris Miller, Mark Rhodes, Ricky Cole, Tom Kohler, Diane Purinton and Coach Lance Lowy

(Cushing Archives, Texas A&M University)

The top Aggie handball story of the 1988 National Collegiate Tournament was the women's team and their National Women's Team Championship. The Aggies won easily by the total score of 131 to 71. Lake Forest College finished second.

As the date of the 1989 National Collegiate Handball Tournament approached, there was not a lot of administrative planning since the tournament would be held in Austin. Once again, the Aggie spirits were high for another championship. Coach Lowy knew he would have a competitive women's team and had hopes for the men to do well. The men's field included 124 men from 22 schools. With the drop-down format, which all agreed was a positive improvement over past formats, 124 men readied themselves for the preliminary and first round play. The drop-down format assured each competitor that they would play a minimum of three matches.

No scores are available for the Aggie men's singles. No Aggies made it to the round of 16 in the A division. The B division featured 32 players. In B division action, Aggies Phillip Vick, Ricky Cole, Mark Rhodes, Steve Naftanel, Tom Kohler, Stan Minter and Lyn McDonald were defeated before making the semifinals. Wayne Crouch was the only Aggie to make it to the semifinals of the B division. In the semifinals, Scott McDowell of UCLA outlasted Crouch in a draining 3-game match. The tough match against Crouch would prove to be too much for McDowell to win in the finals.

No scores of the Aggies competing in the C division are available. The records for each game in each of the divisions was not reported; however, the final point total for the men's competition was enough for the Aggie men to be third in the nation with 148 points. That point total was only 15 points behind second place Lake Forest College and well in front of the University of Texas at 93 points.

The banner representing the women's National Collegiate Team Championship
(Author's Collection)

As in the men's team, there was almost no reporting of the action for the women at the tournament. In the women's B division, Diane Purinton in her first year of being at the national tournament, played her way to the finals. In the finals against Caroline Jansing of Lake Forest College, Diane won the first game with Jansing winning the second. Diane would not have enough left to win, losing in the tiebreaker 11-3. Gloria and Wendy Smalley made it to the finals in doubles competition where they lost to Lake Forest's Jennifer Roberts and Caroline Jansing 21-19, 21-17.

The women's team easily won the national championship with a point total of 164. The closest team was Lake Forest with 94 points. With the men and women's combined total points of 312 it clearly was another national championship for the Aggies. Lake Forest finished a distant 2nd with 257 total team points.

A more complete report of who played in which division was provided by *The Eagle*, on 9 March 1989 and is found in Cushing Archives at Texas A&M University. Earning points in the men's A division were: Chris Miller, Danny Watts, Aaron Cooper and Matthew Montelongo. In the men's B division, Jay Wigginton was a quarterfinalist and, as reported above, Wayne Crouch was a semifinalist. In the

Diane Purinton
(*Handball*, June 1989, page 39)

men's C division, Chris Phythian was a semifinalist. In the women's A bracket, Gloria Smalley, Wendy Smalley and Lisa Smith were quarterfinalists and Kim King was a semifinalist. As reported above, Diane Purinton was a finalist in the women's B division and the Smalley sisters were second in doubles.

Banners and trophies representing the most successful handball teams in Texas A&M history to this date.
(Author's Collection)

CHAPTER 10
The A&M Handball Teams 1990-1999

**NOTE: All handball players listed in this Chapter are from Texas
A&M unless a player's college or university is listed.**

With many players from the 1989 championship team returning, optimism for another championship year was high throughout the school year as the team readied for the National Collegiate Handball Tournament to be hosted by Pacific University in Portland, Oregon. A total of 126 players from 26 schools competed for the 1990 National Collegiate Handball Championships.

The first round (men and women) of any National Collegiate Handball Tournament, with the current format, features all of the players either receiving a bye, playing to stay in the top division or dropping down to another category. As mentioned previously, this assures each player the opportunity for three matches and is generally agreed by most if not all of the coaches to be a fair method of determining the national champions.

In first round action, the following Aggies received a bye to continue to the round of 64: Vern Hegwood, Chris Miller and Dan Watts. Results of Aggies not receiving a bye were as follows: John Tomme defeated Mike Clark of Reed 15-0, 15-3; Mark Rhodes defeated David Hicks of the US Military Academy 15-1, 15-2; Lyn McDonald defeated Dan Peterson of Reed 15-3, 15-7; Kevin Hobbs defeated Pete Martenson of Reed 15-2, 15-2; Matt Brown defeated Chad Gerondale of Pacific University 15-0, 15-4 and Steve Naftanel defeated David Tamburn of the US Military Academy 15-0,15-10. NOTE: In first round action, the games only went to 15 points. Obviously based on the scores there was no point in extending the matches. This saved a lot of time in running the tournament. In reviewing all of the first round scores, only two matches went to three games. This indicates that the seeding process was done as accurately as possible.

In the round of 64, Vern Hegwood defeated Steve Sharpe of Pacific University 21-9, 6-21, 11-5; Chris Watkins of Victor Valley College defeated John Tomme 21-4, 21-3; Chris Miller defeated Jason Sutton of the US Air Force Academy 21-3, 21-9; Mike Totall of North Carolina Bible College defeated Mark Rhodes 21-4, 21-5; Carlos Guiterrez of San Diego Community College defeated Lyn McDonald 21-5, 21-6; Dan Watts defeated Bill Blevins of Pacific University 21-3, 21-4; Steve Roberts of University of Utah defeated Kevin Hobbs 21-5, 21-5; David McGrath of San Diego Community College defeated Matt Brown 21-14, 21-16 and Chase Tessman of the University of Utah defeated Steve Naftanel 21-5, 21-5. Those winning in the round of 64 remained in the A singles division. John Tomme, Mark Rhodes, Lyn McDonald, Kevin Hobbs and Steve Naftanel moved down to the B division.

In the round of 32 of the A singles division, Jeff Cottam of Memphis State University, who would repeat as the National Singles Handball Champion, defeated Vern Hegwood 21-9, 21-3; Chris Watkins of

Victor Valley College defeated Chris Miller 21-10, 21-6 and Chris Jennings of Memphis State University defeated Dan Watts 21-6, 21-5. No Aggie made the round of 16 in the men's A singles division.

In the B singles division, Steve Naftanel was defeated in the quarterfinals 21-6, 21-6 by Carl Huether of the University of Cincinnati. Mark Rhodes was defeated in the semifinals 21-6, 21-15 by Mike Lee of Portland State. No other scores of the Aggies competing in the B division were reported.

There were no Aggie men participating in the C or in the Contender's divisions. Also, the Aggies decided not to participate in the doubles competition.

In the women's singles, it was evident that the depth and domination of the Texas A&M team would prevail for the title, but the skill and experience of Jennifer Roberts of Lake Forest College would prevent total domination by the Aggies. In first round action of 32, Anna Gonzalez defeated Malia Meyer of Pacific University 15-2, 15-0; Sharon Baylor defeated Sara Richardson of Southwest Missouri State University 15-3, 15-2; Mollie Huber defeated Kari Steinbock of Pacific University 15-3, 15-2; Wendy Smalley defeated Joni Black of Penn State University 15-0, 15-0; Gloria Smalley defeated Holly Stein of the US Military Academy 15-0, 15-0; Audrea Stork defeated Darci Reeves of Pacific University 15-9, 15-3 and Kim King defeated Cheryl Pudlowski of Southwest Missouri State University 15-0, 15-3. As with the men's competition, the first round games were complete at point 15.

In the round of 16, it was inevitable that Aggies would be competing against their own teammates. Sharon Baylor defeated Anna Gonzalez 21-8, 21-4; Mollie Huber defeated Annette Hatfield of Pacific University 21-0, 21-0; Wendy Smalley defeated Jennifer Giese of Lake Forest College 21-7, 21-6; Gloria Smalley defeated Audrea Stork 21-9, 21-5 and Kim King defeated Lara Puffer of Pacific University 21-1, 21-3.

In the quarterfinals, 5 of the 8 players were Aggies. Jennifer Roberts of Lake Forest College defeated Sharon Baylor 21-6, 21-6; Wendy Smalley defeated teammate Mollie Huber 21-6, 21-1; Gloria Smalley defeated Linda Davis of Pacific University 21-2, 21-3 and Kim King defeated Kelly O'Brien of Lake Forest College 21-3, 21-1.

Three of the four players in the semifinals were Aggies. Jennifer Roberts of Lake Forest College defeated Wendy Smalley 21-11, 21-18 and Gloria Smalley defeated Kim King 17-21, 21-10, 11-5. The women's singles final was played to a packed house. The first game was close until midway when Roberts changed strategy and kept Gloria Smalley in the back court. Roberts dominated from that point on in the match. The final scores were 21-11, 21-6.

At the left is Gloria Smalley and Coach Lowy. Gloria and her sister Wendy made a great contribution to the A&M handball program and helped the women's team become a dominant force in the national collegiate handball scene. Both were missed going into the 1991 season.

(*Handball*, June 1990, page 12)

In the photo to the right Audrea shows her winning smile right after capturing the women's B division National Collegiate Handball Championship.

(*Handball*, June 1990, page 12)

Audrea Stork dropped down to B division when she was defeated in the second match of A division. Matched with 8 others players in the B division, Audrea showed she was ready for the challenge by defeating Noe Makua of Pacific University 21-18, 21- 0 and Lara Puffer of Pacific University 21-1, 21-0. In the finals against Jennifer Giese of Lake Forest Chicago, she was in complete control. Stork moved Giese around the court throughout the match and controlled the play with a powerful Z-serve to the left, winning 21-11, 21-13.

Texas A&M had no women in the C or in the Contender's division. This was a great indication of the strength of the team.

In doubles competition, Gloria and Wendy Smalley were the only Aggie team to enter. In the first round, the Smalley's defeated the team of Lakeisha Frieson and Holly Stein of the US Military Academy 21-0, 21-1. In the semifinals, the Smalley's defeated Katherine Baldwin and Jennifer Giese of Lake Forest College 21-16, 21-12. This set up the highly anticipated match between Gloria and Wendy Smalley and Kelly O'Brien and Jennifer Roberts of Lake Forest College for the doubles championship. The Smalley's controlled the match by taking the first game 21-15. In the second game, the Lake Forest team changed their strategy. Roberts, the women's singles champion, started taking all of the serves by the Smalley's and O'Brien started serving a lob to the left. The strategy worked and the Lake Forest team won the match and the women's National Collegiate Handball Doubles Championship by taking the second game 21-14 and the tiebreaker 11-7.

As reported by Lance Lowy in the USHA's *Handball*, June 1990, page 13:

> This match seemed to encompass all the good things in the current collegiate format: rivalries, enthusiasm, intensity, desire to win, and when it was all over the sportsmanship showed through when all four players shook hands and bowed to the crowd's applause.

In the men's competition, the Aggies totaled 129 points to finish third and the Aggie women totaled 178 points to clearly show team dominance over the second place women's team from Lake Forest, which totaled 100 points. With the strong showing of the Aggie women added to the third place total of the men's competition, the combined total of 307 easily outdistanced second place Lake Forest's 268 total points for the Combined Team Championship.

The 1990 A&M Women's National Collegiate Handball Champions at Portland, Oregon.
NOTE: The Combined Championship Trophy is also in the photo
FRONT ROW: Audrea Stork, Kim King, Anna Gonzalez
BACK ROW: Molly Huber, Wendy Smalley, Coach Lance Lowy, Gloria Smalley, Sharon Baylor
(Courtesy Lance Lowy)

It was a great honor to have the 1990 National Handball Champion Aggie team photo on the cover of the June 1990 issue of the USHA's *Handball* magazine. It should also be remembered that the number of championships the Aggies have won helped to earn that distinction.

Handball

June 1990 $3.00

The Official Voice of the United States Handball Association

Warming Up, Stretching and Cooling Down
Chapel Hill, Spokane and Houston Pro Stops
National Collegiates and Masters Doubles
One-Wall Fantasy Match: Durso vs. Sandler
Eliminating Errors, Ceiling Shot and Practice Instructional

Membership USHA Drive

Texas A&M Collegiate Champs
Cottam Leads MSU Men

PHOTO INCLUDES: Vern Hegwood, Chris Miller, Dan Watts, John Tomme, Mark Rhodes, Lyn McDonald, Kevin Hobbs, Matt Brown, Steve Naftanel, Aaron Cooper, Moly Huber, Gloria and Wendy Smalley, Sharon Baylor, Audrea Stork, Kim King, Anna Gonzalez and Coach Lance Lowy

(*Handball*, June 1990, Cover)

Banners and Trophies from the 1990 Texas A&M Handball Championship Season (Author's Collection)

Beginning the 1991 handball season the question would be, "Can we make it three in a row for the Combined Team National Collegiate Handball Championship?" For the women's team the question would be, "Can we make it four in a row?" All team members were looking forward to the National Collegiate Tournament to be hosted by Cincinnati University February 28-March 3.

A total of 130 handball players representing 28 different schools began play on the first day. In the men's preliminary singles round, the Aggies had three entries. Vince Hegwood defeated Chris Meyers of Southwest Missouri State 15-13, 15-2; Ricky Cole defeated Matt Watzek of Cincinnati University15-3, 15-0 and Mark Scheffler defeated Bruce Aaron of Pacific University 10-15, 15-6, 11-3. All of the other Aggies received a bye into the round of 64.

In the round of 64, Shane Rothenberger defeated Jason Sutton of the US Air Force Academy 15-5, 15-2; Salvador SantaAna defeated Neal Pason of the US Military Academy 15-2, 15-2; Scott McDowell of UCLA defeated Vince Hegwood 15-12, 15-5; Ricky Cole defeated Jim Hudson of Southwest Missouri State 14-15, 15-5, 11-7; Vern Hegwood defeated Mike Bell of Southwest Missouri State 15-5, 9-15, 11-2; Brian Carr defeated Dan Alexander of Southwest Missouri State 15-8, 15-1; Kevin Hobbs defeated Jim Allen of the Cincinnati University 15-1, 15-1; Aaron Cooper defeated Dave Clark of Cincinnati University 15-2, 15-5; Mark Rhodes defeated Greg Voisin of Los Positas 15-7, 15-7; Steve Naftanel defeated Kieran Smith of the US Air Force Academy 15-5, 13-15, 11-6; Chris Uren defeated Todd Sturt of Cincinnati University 15-7, 15-5 and Dave Weinhaus of the University of Texas squeaked by John Tomme 15-5, 8-15, 11-10.

In the round of 32, Jeff Cottam, three time National Collegiate Champion of Memphis State, defeated Shane Rothenberger 21-6, 21-4; Salvador SantaAna defeated Scott McDowell of UCLA 21-7, 21-3; Chris Tico of Lake Forest College defeated Ricky Cole 21-5, 21-1; Bryan Lee of Portland defeated Vern Hegwood 21-13, 14-21,11-5; Eric Plummer of the University of Montana defeated Brian Carr 21-7, 19-21, 11-7; Matt Hiber of Memphis State defeated Kevin Hobbs 21-3, 21-3; Aaron Cooper defeated Jason Adams of Southwest Missouri State 21-4, 21-13; Mark Hammond of Lake Forest College defeated Mark Rhodes 21-9, 21-10; Curt Heiting of Memphis State University defeated Steve Naftanel 21-7, 21-8 and John Libby of the University of Nevada in Reno defeated Chris Uren 21-6, 21-6.

In the round of 16, Salvador SantaAna defeated Chris Tico of Lake Forest College 21-6, 21-10 and Matt Hiber of Memphis State defeated Aaron Cooper 21-4, 21-13.

In the quarterfinals, Jeff Cottam of Memphis State defeated Salvador SantaAna 21-6, 21-12. Santa Ana was the last Aggie to be eliminated from the A division First Flight. A new division was created for the players who failed to advance past the round of 32. This was called the Second Flight A singles. Aggies in this division were Rickey Cole who lost to Mike Totall of North Central Bible College 21-12, 21-12. Rob

Gaither of the University of Arizona defeated Vern Hegwood in a semifinal match 6-21, 21-6,11-9. No other scores of the Aggies in this division were reported.

The only reported score in B division was Greg Voisin of Las Positas defeating John Tomme 21-11, 21-15 on his way to the finals. Voisin lost a close match in the finals to Bear Dylla of the University of Texas.

The Aggies had no players in the C or in the Contender's divisions and the Aggies did not enter a team in the doubles championship.

The men's team finished with 159 points which was good for 2nd behind Memphis State's 176 and well in front of the University of Texas at 109 points.

In the women's singles preliminary round, Katherine Baldwin of Lake Forest College defeated Laura Gross 15-12, 6-15, 11-8; Tammy Reyes defeated Rhonda Hembree of Southwest Missouri State 15-3, 15-2; Katie Hutcheson defeated Charla Cuttie of Pacific University 15, 5, 15-8 and Leigh Ann Williams defeated Jennifer Giese of Lake Forest College 15-9, 6-15, 11-6.

In the round of 16, Betsy Boswell defeated Debbie Deal of the University of Texas 15-1, 15-2; Tammy Reyes defeated Noe Makua of Pacific University 15-9, 15-8; Kelly O'Brien of Lake Forest College defeated Katie Hutcheson 15-4, 15-2; Audrea Stork defeated Kari Steinbock of Pacific University 15-4, 15-3; Heather O'Bryan of Southwest Missouri State defeated Leigh Ann Williams 15-4, 15-4 and Sharon Baylor defeated Michelle Twitt of Southwest Missouri State 15-3, 15-4.

The 1991 Aggie Men's Team at Cincinnati University
PHOTO INCLUDES: Aaron Cooper, Steve Naftanel, Mark Rhodes, John Tomme, Mark Scheffler, Shane Rothenberger Vern Hegwood, Vince Hegwood, Kevin Hobbs, Chris Uren, Sal SantaAna, Brian Carr, Ricky Cole and Coach Lance Lowy
(Courtesy Lance Lowy)

In the quarterfinals, Betsy Boswell defeated Tammy Reyes 21-12, 21-10; Audrea Stork defeated Kelly O'Brien of Lake Forest College 21-11, 21-9 and Sharon Baylor defeated Heather O'Bryan 21-2, 21-16.

The semifinals had a repeat of the 1990 semifinals with three Aggies and the reigning women's National Collegiate Handball Singles Champion, Jennifer Roberts of Lake Forest College. Jennifer Roberts defeated Betsy Boswell 21-6, 21-3 and Sharon Baylor defeated Audrea Stork 21-4, 21-15. In the finals, Jennifer Roberts repeated as the champion by easily defeating Sharon Baylor 21-1, 21-9.

Tommy Burnett reported the action in B division in the USHA's *Handball*, June 1991, page 35:

> Noe Makua of Pacific barely missed receiving a special birthday present when she failed to return a shot in the deep left corner to give Katie Hutcheson an 11-10 victory in the women's B singles. Makua, who turned 22 on the final day of the tournament, forced a third game with a 21-10 win in the second game after dropping the first, 21-15.
>
> Hutcheson of Texas A&M was in her first collegiate tournament and executed well. Coupling power and good court coverage, Hutcheson earned the first game, while Makua turned on the big serve for the second game win. But Hutcheson maintained her tremendous retrieving pace through the tiebreaker to emerge victorious.

Hutcheson had her hands full in every match. Katie defeated Steinbock (Pacific University) in her first round, 21-14, 21-14, and then needed an 11-6 tiebreaker to turn back Leigh Ann Williams in the semis. Makua advanced to the final with a semifinal win over Baldwin.

In the June 1991 issue on page 36 of the USHA's *Handball*, Mike Steele reports the action in the C division:

> Lake Forest College and Texas A&M students met in another final as Jennifer Geise of Lake Forest and Laura Gross of Texas A&M provided cheering opportunities galore in the scintillating three-game match. Geise, a finalist in last year's women's B, edged Gross, a recent tennis convert, 18-21, 21-20, 11-6.
>
> Gross, who has played handball for just five months, played a steady, disciplined game featuring a high toss and bounce (from tennis?) on her serve. Laura's court coverage kept the more experienced Geise guessing throughout the match and forced Jennifer into errors that allowed Gross back into the first two games after large leads had been mounted. Geise settled down in the tiebreaker, holding onto an early lead for the win.

There were no other scores provided in C division and there were no Aggies in the Contender's division. The Aggie women entered two doubles teams in the competition. In first round action, Tammy Reyes and Audrea Stork defeated Charla Cuttie and Kari Steinbock of Pacific University 15-9, 15-4 while Sharon Baylor and Betsy Boswell defeated Karen Hendrix and Breanna Johnson of Pacific University 15-4, 15-5. In the semifinals, Jennifer Roberts and Kelly O'Brien of Lake Forest College defeated Tammy Reyes and Audrea Stork 21-7, 21-7. Sharon Baylor and Betsy Boswell defeated Darcy Reeves and Noe Makua of Pacific University 21-6, 21-5. In the finals, Baylor and Boswell could not stay with Roberts and O'Brien and were defeated 21-16, 21-12. According to the report of doubles play, Baylor and Boswell provided the best competition than any Lake Forest doubles team had faced in recent years.

The A&M women repeated as the Women's National Collegiate Handball Team Champions with a team score of 164 which easily outdistanced Lake Forest's total of 108. Lake Forest edged out Southwest Missouri 108 to 107.

Tim Stanfield, staff writer for *The Eagle* of Bryan, wrote the following article which was reported in the 6 April 1991 newspaper that can be found at Cushing Archives at Texas A&M University:

> For the fourth consecutive year, the Texas A&M women's handball team finished first it the National Collegiate Handball Tournament.
>
> A&M coach Lance Lowy's women's team won its latest title February 28-March 3 in Cincinnati.
>
> Team members included All-Americans Sharon Baylor and Betsy Boswell, while Audrea Stork and Tammy Reyes finished as quarterfinalists in the women's Open division. Katie Hutcheson won the women's B division, while Leigh Ann Williams was a semifinalist and Laura Gross won second place in the women's C division.
>
> The A&M men's team finished second in the national tournament behind Memphis State. Its members included Sal SantaAna, Aaron Cooper, Vern and Vince Hegwood, Chris Uren, Ricky Cole, Kevin Hobbs, Steve Naftanel, Mark Rhodes, Shane Rothenberger, Brian Carr, John Tomme and Mike Scheffler completed the men's team.

The combined men's and women's team won the third straight national title as they easily outdistanced the rest of the 30-team field.

As reported by Tim Stanfield the combined total easily outdistanced the field. The Aggie combined team total was 323. The nearest competitor, which was Southwest Missouri State, had a combined team total of 212.

Banners from the Texas A&M Handball
Team Championship Season
(Author's Collection)

1991 Aggie National Champion Handball Team

PHOTO INCLUDES: Sharon Baylor, Betsy Boswell, Laura Gross, Katie Hutcheson, Tammy Reyes, Audrea Stork, Leigh Ann Williams, Brian Carr, Ricky Cole, Aaron Cooper, Vern Hegwood, Vince Hegwood, Kevin Hobbs, Steve Naftanel, Mark Rhodes, Shane Rothenberger, Sal SantaAna, Mark Scheffler, John Tomme, Chris Uren and Coach Lance Lowy

(*Handball*, June 1991, page 32)

Going into the 1992 handball season the Aggies were confident of continued success even with the knowledge that Southwest Missouri State, which had a comparatively short life in national handball collegiate competition, was a newcomer to be reckoned with. All members of the team looked forward to travelling to Chicago where the National Collegiate Handball Tournament would be hosted by Lake Forest College February 19-23.

In preparation for the National Collegiate Handball Tournament, several of the Aggies entered the Southwest Collegiate Handball Tournament, held in Austin 31 January-2 February. A&M won all eight divisions offered in the tournament. There were four men's and four women's events. In the men's events Sal SantaAna won the men's Open division, Vern Hegwood won the B division, Casey Clark won the C division and Scott Cooner won the Contenders division. In the women's events, Sharon Baylor won the women's Open division, Katie Hutcheson won the B division, Anna Gonzalez won the C division and Jennifer Bellomy won the Contenders division.

After winning all 8 division championships at the Southwest Collegiate Handball Tournament in Austin, the Aggies headed to Chicago fully confident in extending their dominance in the Women's and in the Combined Team Championships at the National Collegiate Handball Tournament.

In the men's division, the new five-division format would be used. This new format replaced the previous format of four divisions. In the first round John Tomme received a bye; Matt Jackson defeated Mike Greco of the US Military Academy 15-6, 15-1; Vern Hegwood received a bye; Shane Rothenberger received a bye; Darin Booth of the US Air Force Academy defeated Dusty Davis 15-11, 15-6; Eric Fields received a bye; Ricky Cole received a bye; Casey Clark defeated Jason Vranes of the US Military Academy 15-2, 15-12; Sal SantaAna received a bye; Jeff Swoboda received a bye; Chris Uren received a bye; Chip Abernathy defeated Chris Rosetta of Pacific University 15-13, 15-5; Colin Errington defeated Chris Prevo of the US Military Academy 15-9, 15-1; Emmet Myatt defeated Brian Symonds of the US Military Academy 15-??, 15-6; John Reider defeated Brian Ivie of the US Military Academy 15-1, 15-4 and Tim Poskey received a bye.

In the round of 64, John Tomme defeated Kieran Smith of the US Air Force Academy 15-7, 15-13; Brian Johnson defeated Matt Jackson 15-9, 15-6; Chris Meyer of Southwest Missouri State defeated Vern Hegwood 15-13, 15-11; Shane Rothenberger defeated William Lynch of Santa Clara 15-9, 13-15, 11-1; Les Seago of Memphis State University defeated Erick Fields 14-15, 15-12, 11-10; Ricky Cole defeated Jeff Biehl of Las Positas 15-10, 15-9; Robert Gaither of the University of Arizona defeated Casey Clark 15-10, 15-3; Sal SantaAna defeated Herb Heagh-Avritt of Pacific University 15-1, 15-0; Brian Lescinskas defeated Jeff Swoboda 15-7, 15-11; Chris Uren defeated Dax Taylor of Southwest Missouri State 15-7, 15-10; Mark Hammond of Lake Forest College defeated Chip Abernathy 15-0, 15-4; Mike Bell of Southwest Missouri State defeated Colin Errington 15-7, 15-4; Joe Paterna of Lake Forest College defeated Richard Myatt 15-10, 15-8; Don Cottam of Memphis State University defeated John Reider 15-2, 15-8 and Tim Poskey defeated Jason Sutton of the US Air Force Academy 12-15, 15-12, 11-8.

In the round of 32, Matt Hiber of Memphis State University defeated John Tomme 21-3, 21-5; Eric Plummer of the University of Montana defeated Shane Rothenberger 21-13, 21-10; Robert Gaither of the University of Arizona defeated Ricky Cole 21-20, 21-2; Sal SantaAna defeated Jon Bates of the University of Texas 21-9, 21-1; Andrew Schad of the US Air Force Academy defeated Chris Uren 21-16, 21-10 and Chris Jennings defeated Tim Poskey 21-3, 21-1.

The only Aggie to move on to the round of 16 was Sal SantaAna who then defeated Robert Gaither of the University of Arizona 21-2, 21-6. In the quarterfinals, Norm Dunne of Santa Clara defeated Sal SantaAna 21-6, 21-19.

In the men's B division, the only scores given were from the semifinals through the finals. Ricky Cole was the only Aggie to reach the semifinals. In the semifinals, he was pitted against Don Cottam of Memphis State University who won 21-17, 21-4.

In C division action, the following was reported by Mike Rice and Andrew Schad in the June 1992 issue of the USHA's *Handball*, page 31:

> The C division was extremely competitive this year. In the semifinals, Bill Lynch of Santa Clara met a feisty Jeff Cardinal of Las Positas. Lynch shot well during the first game and won it 21-17. In the second game, Lynch took an early lead, but Cardinal fought back, bringing the game even at 19. But Lynch held off the comeback and won the game 21-19.

The other semifinal pitted Jason Sutton of the Air Force Academy against Vern Hegwood of Texas A&M. Hegwood looked to be in complete control of the match when he won the first game 21-12. However, Sutton came out firing in the second game and won a close one, 21-20. This set the stage for probably one of the best finishes of the tournament. In the tiebreaker, Hegwood took a 9-3 lead and was on the verge of putting Sutton away, However, Sutton fought back with incredible digs and great shots. Sutton ran off seven points and took the lead 10-9. They exchanged serves several times at 10-10 before Hegwood finally put the game away to bring this sensational match to an end.

The final pitted the similar styles of Hegwood and Lynch. Both relied on their steady, consistent play throughout the tournament. In this match, Hegwood's consistency wore Lynch down and forced him to make uncharacteristic errors. Hegwood capitalized on Lynch's lapses and won the first game 21-11. Hegwood was in a groove, and even an extra-long period between games due to team pictures failed to disrupt him, as he easily won the second game 21-8, to cap a steady tournament performance.

Dusty Davis made the finals in the Contenders division. This division was filled with new players. Dusty was a beginner who switched from racquetball to handball to get a better workout. He enjoyed the competition at the National Collegiate Tournament and definitely planned to continue with handball. In the finals, the match went to a tiebreaker with Dan Kneeshaw, a scholarship athlete from Southwest Missouri State, winning the match 11-2.

There were no Aggies in the Novice division, which was the newly added fifth division of the men's singles competition.

The Texas A&M men's Team finished the tournament with 420 points which was good for 2nd place. Memphis State won the men's title again with a total of 539 points, which was a comfortable margin over the Aggies. Lake Forest was close behind the Aggies in third place with 411 points.

In the women's division, the Aggies may have had the most dominating performance seen since the women started playing in 1980. In first round action, Sharon Baylor defeated Amy Bunton of Southwest Missouri State 15-3, 15-1; Kim Harris defeated Patricia Carter of Southwest Missouri State 15-2, 15-3; Cassie Tijerina defeated Brenda Johnson of Pacific University 15-4, 15-8; Terry SantaAna defeated Kari Steinbock of Pacific University 15-8, 15-5; Audrea Stork defeated Sharon Hill of Southwest Missouri State 15-1, 15-2; Anna Gonzalez defeated Angie Smithwick of Southwest Missouri State 15-10, 15-12; Teri Slusarek defeated

The 1992 A&M Men's Team at the National Collegiate Handball Tournament in Chicago

PHOTO INCLUDES: Sal SantaAna, Ricky Cole, Shane Rothenberger, John Tomme, Chris Uren, Tim Poskey, Vern Hegwood, Casey Clark, Richard E. Myatt, Eric Fields, Jeff Swoboda, Colin Errington, Chip Abernathy, Dusty Davis, John Reider, Matt Jackson and Coach Lance Lowy

(Courtesy Lance Lowy)

Charla Cuttie of Pacific University 15-3, 15-8; Katie Hutcheson defeated Cynthia Gillum of Southwest Missouri State 15-6, 15-1 and Betsy Boswell defeated Kendra Scott of San Diego State (score not listed). All Aggies participating moved on to the round of 16.

In the round of 16, Sharon Baylor defeated Beth Adrian of Southwest Missouri State 21-2, 21-10; Kim Harris defeated Cassie Tijerina 21-16, 21-10; Terry SantaAna defeated Julie Flattre of Southwest Missouri State 21-16, 21-7; Audrea Stork defeated Anna Gonzalez 21-16, 21-7; Heather O'Bryan of Southwest Missouri State defeated Teri Slusarek 21-3, 21-6; Katie Hutcheson defeated Katherine Baldwin of Lake Forest College 21-15, 21-15 and Betsy Boswell defeated Melanie Wright of Southwest Missouri State 21-3, 21-10.

In the quarterfinals, Sharon Baylor defeated Jennifer Giese of Lake Forest College 21-3, 21-9; Kim Harris defeated Terry SantaAna 13-21, 21-11, 11-10; Heather O'Bryan of Southwest Missouri State defeated Audrea Stork 21-12, 21-7 and Betsy Boswell defeated Katie Hutcheson 21-9, 21-11.

Coach Lance Lowy described the action of the four women remaining in the Open division in the USHA's *Handball* issue of June 1992, found on pages 32 and 33:

> The unique format of the National Collegiate Tournament dictated that only the top four women in the nation would be classified as Open players. As the draw unfurled, top-seed Sharon Baylor of Texas A&M defeated a much-improved Jen Giese of Lake Forest College to earn a berth in the Open. Second-seeded Betsy Boswell of Texas A&M dispatched teammate Katie Hutcheson to secure her spot. Southwest Missouri State's Heather O'Bryan beat Texas A&M's Audrea Stork in a tough match to also make the top four. Two more Texas A&M women, Kim Harris and Terry SantaAna fought it out with Harris winning the final spot in a tiebreaker.
>
> This set the stage for the semifinals as each of these four women had earned All-American status at this point. The first match between teammates Baylor and Harris had Baylor setting a very fast driving pace that proved too much for Harris. Serving very well, Baylor would get the setup she wanted, draw Harris in then pass her. Harris put up a valiant fight but went straight to the oxygen following the match. The match between Boswell and O'Bryan featured two contrasting styles and was played to a packed gallery. Boswell is very quick and usually dominates in the front court. O'Bryan is a more controlled and consistent player. As it turned out, O'Bryan's well-placed passes and coolness under pressure won the Open semifinal for her.
>
> The final pitted the two top collegiate women players for 1992. They had dispatched all their opponents without losing a game. The anticipation of a great match started early as the crowd packed the viewing area well before the contestants even warmed up. The actual play in the first game was tainted by nerves on both sides, but O'Bryan was able to control the tempo and win, 21-15. In between games, the partisan Aggie crowd performed cheers and were their usual enthusiastic selves. The Southwest Missouri contingent also turned it up and this created the atmosphere that is unique at the National Collegiate Tournament. This is the only tournament where individuals play for their team and their school and the enthusiasm is like being at a football or baseball game. O'Bryan jumped out to a 7-0 lead in the second game before Baylor seemed to relax and get herself together. The score remained close until 14-14 when Baylor got her second wind and O'Bryan seemed to tire. Baylor won the second game 21-14 to set up a third. It was nip and tuck until 4-4 when Baylor got pumped again. Although O'Bryan gave a great performance and played very well, Baylor's strength and tenacity won this match and the women's Open national championship, 11-4.

All of the scores were not reported in the B division singles, but Bill Wright reported on the play in the USHA's *Handball* issue of June 1992, page 33:

> This year's B singles final was a rematch of the 1990 B final: Jennifer Giese of Lake Forest College vs. Audrea Stork of Texas A&M. Having played each other before when a title was on the line, they showed respect for each other's game. Both players were cautious before going for the kill. They maintained good defensive positioning on the court, resulting in many long rallies with incredible retrievals of put away attempts.
>
> In the first game, Giese mixed her serves well, jumping out to a 10-2 lead. Stork, a powerful side-winding southpaw, used a Z-serve to the left to climb back into the game at 10-7. But Giese's steady play and sound mechanical strokes prevailed 21-11.
>
> The second game looked like a carbon copy of the first. Giese led 12-4 before Stork once again battled back with the Z-serve to the left to pull within one at 12-11. Giese called a timeout to stem the tide. She quickly got back the serve and used a Z-serve of her own to put five quick points on the board. At that point it looked like Giese would avenge her '90 loss to Stork, but the lefty showed there was no quit in her. Stork powered her way to an 18-16 lead. Giese used her second timeout to psyche herself up. Jennifer let loose with a power game of her own to go ahead 20-18, Stork came right back to make it 20-19, but Giese gained her revenge with an ace serve to the southpaw's strength to capture the '92 B title.
>
> Texas A&M had three semifinalists in this division. Terry SantaAna lost to Giese 21-11, 21-17, while Katie Hutcheson lost to teammate Stork 21-12, 21-14.

In the C division of women's singles, Noe Makua defeated Anna Gonzalez 21-11, 21-11 while Beth Adrian of Southwest Missouri State defeated Teri Slusarek 17-21, 21-20, 11-1 and then defeated Cassie Tijerina 21-13, 21-12. Makua won the match for the C division title over Adrian 21-1, 21-5.

The Aggies had no players in the Contenders or Novice division. This is a direct reflection on the strength throughout of the Aggie women's team.

To further show the strength of the Aggies, Sharon Baylor and Betsy Boswell won the women's National Collegiate Tournament Doubles Championship. In first round action, Sharon Baylor and Betsy Boswell defeated Shirley Norris and Karen Hendrix of Pacific University 21-6, 21-0; Kim Harris and Terry SantaAna defeated Jennifer Giese and Katherine Baldwin of Lake Forest College 21-16, 10-21, 11-10 and Audrea Stork and Katie Hutcheson defeated Kari Steinbock and Brea Johnson of Pacific University 21-18, 21-10. In the semifinals, Sharon Baylor and Betsy Boswell defeated Kim Harris and Terry SantaAna 21-8, 21-18; Heather O'Bryan and Beth Adrian of Lake Forest College defeated Audrea Stork and Katie Hutcheson 21-3, 21-17. Adrian injured her shoulder in a singles match and was unable to continue. Sharon Baylor and Betsy Boswell were the champions.

Coach Lance Lowy congratulates Sharon Baylor and Betsy Boswell for winning the 1992 National Collegiate Handball Tournament Doubles Championship. This was the first handball doubles championship for the Aggie women's Team.

(*Handball*, June 1992, page 32)

1992 Texas A&M National Collegiate Handball Combined Team Champion

PHOTO INCLUDES: Sal SantaAna, Terry SantaAna, Sharon Baylor, Chris Uren, Jeff Swoboda, Betsy Boswell, Emmett Myatt, John Tomme, Anna Gonzalez, Chip Abernathy, Audrea Stork, Kim Harris, Dusty Davis, Cassie Tijerina, Tim Poskey, Teri Slusarek, Eric Fields, Ricky Cole, Katie Hutcheson, Shane Rothenberger, John Reider, Colin Errington, Vern Hegwood, Matt Jackson, Casey Clark and Coach Lance Lowy

(*Handball*, June 1992, page 28)

The Aggie women won the women's team title with 504 points, almost doubling the point total of 288 by Southwest Missouri State University. The 504 points added to the men's team total easily enabled the Aggies to claim the Combined Team Championship. The Aggie's total combined points of 924 was far ahead of the second place team, Southwest Missouri State University. The point total for Southwest Missouri was 620. This may be the most dominating team ever to play in the National Collegiate Handball Tournament.

Banner and Trophies Representing the 1992 Texas A&M Handball Championship Team

(Author's Collection)

Vern Hegwood shooting during his championship match against Bill Lynch. Hegwood won the C division championship match 21-11, 21-8.

(*Handball*, June 1992, page 31)

Sharon Baylor showing her kill shot form during her 11-4 tiebreaker finals victory to win the National Singles Champion title of the women's Open division and also the match win that secured the women's National Team Championship for Texas A&M. With championship titles at stake, it was understandable for Sharon to be nervous as she dropped the first game 15-21 and fell behind 0-7 to begin the second game. Sharon finally relaxed and played her game. Sharon's tenacity, strength and endurance won the match.

(*Handball*, June 1992, page 32)

The Aggies began the 1993 season with a big target on their backs after being the dominant team for the last four years. The season also began with a number of the past stars graduated, especially from the women's team. Returning, though, for the men, was Sal SantaAna who continued to improve to become one of the best Aggie men to play the game. All looked forward to the National Collegiate Handball Tournament which would be hosted by the University of Texas in Austin February 25-28.

The collegiate tournament just kept getting larger and larger. Representing 21 colleges and universities were 128 men and 38 women for the first day of play. In the men's first round of singles, Mike Bell of Southwest Missouri State defeated Brett Altman 15-0, 15-2; Brian Johnson of Lake Forest College defeated Jeffrey Townsend 15-1, 15-3; Frank Szatkowski of Loyola defeated James Machac 15-0, 15-2; Dustin Davis defeated Sean Blair-Turner of the University of Texas 15-6, 15-0; Matthew Jackson defeated Mark Dostal (college/university not listed) 15-0, 15-2; Tim Poskey defeated Rick Elma of Cincinnati University 15-1, 15-7; Jeff Coble defeated (first name not listed) Pason of the US Military Academy 15-4, 15-6; Jeff Swoboda defeated James Cauthen of the University of Texas (scores not listed); Chris Meyer of Southwest Missouri State defeated Kevin Richardson 15-2, 15-4; Jeff Walsh defeated Michael Blazes of the US Air Force Academy 15-5, 15-1; Dave McGrath of Memphis State University defeated Nathaniel Wilganowski 15-2, 15-1; Shane Rothenberger defeated Joseph Soto (both Aggies) 15-0,15-4; Steven Lindemuth of the US Air Force Academy defeated Jason Ayers 15-14, 11-15, 11-8; Colin Errington defeated Mike Perun of the University of Texas 15-0, 11-15, 11-6; Greg Tomyasan of the University of Texas defeated Chad Branum 15-7 15-7; Jeffrey Jones defeated Charles Schwalbe of the University of Texas 15-3, 15-4; Carl Huether of Cincinnati University defeated Gary Hickman 15-2, 15-0; Richard Myatt defeated David York of Southwest Missouri State 15-10, 15-9; Stephen Wagstaff of the University of California-Davis defeated Corey McCutchan 15-2, 15-0; Scott Cooner defeated Adam Berliner of the University of Texas 15-6, 15-4; Noel Keen defeated Eric Ritter of the US Air Force Academy 15-3,

15-7; Brian Shumate of the University of Texas-Dallas defeated Chris Richards 15-1, 15-2; Eric Fields defeated David Salisbury of the US Air Force Academy 15-0, 15-2; Mark Elma of Cincinnati University defeated Ryan Isenberg 15-11, 15-9; Steve Dobrash of Memphis State University defeated John Doolittle 15-2, 15-0; Damian Crowson of Pacific University defeated Ben Keating 15-0, 15-3; Mike Rice of the US Air Force Academy defeated Warren Ferguson 15-4, 15-1; Kieran Smith of the US Air Force Academy defeated John Blevins 15-3, 15-7; Scott Korth defeated (first name not given) Halferty of the US Military Academy 15-13, 15-6; Don Cottam of Memphis State University defeated Jose Castro 15-0, 15-0; Jeffrey Jeffers defeated Greg Dillon of Pacific University 15-3, 15-2; Jason Sutton of the US Air Force Academy defeated Ricky Reynolds 15-2, 15-4 and Sal SantaAna defeated (no first name listed) Greco of the US Military Academy (no score listed).

In the round of 64, Frank Szatkowski of Loyola defeated Dustin Davis 15-3, 15-4; Omar SantaAna of the University of Texas-El Paso defeated Matthew Jackson 15-5, 15-3; Les Seago of Memphis State University defeated Tim Poskey 15-12, 15-8; Mike Totall of North Central Bible College defeated Jeff Coble 15-0, 15-5; Jeff Swoboda defeated Jess Smith of Pacific University 15-9, 15-4; Chris Meyer of Southwest Missouri State defeated Jeff Walsh 12-15, 15-5, 11-6; Shane Rothenberger defeated Steven Lindemuth of the US Air Force Academy 15-8, 15-4; Matt Lauderdale of the University of Texas defeated Colin Errington 15-7, 15-12; Jeffrey Jones defeated Ray Clayton of Portland Community College 15-10, 15-3; Carl Huether of Cincinnati University defeated Richard Myatt 15-3, 15-1; Steve Johnson of Lake Forest College defeated Scott Cooner 15-1, 15-1; Mark Beverly of Memphis State University defeated Noel Keen 15-0, 15-1; Eric Fields defeated Brian Shumate of the University of Texas-Dallas 15-4, 14-15, 11-9; Joe Paterna of Lake Forest College defeated Scott Korth 15-6, 15-5; Jason Sutton of the US Air Force Academy defeated Jeffrey Jeffers 15-11, 15-2 and Sal SantaAna defeated Jason Schroeder of the University of Texas 15-3, 15-2.

In the round of 32, Mike Totall of North Central Bible College defeated Jeff Swoboda 21-8, 21-12; Shane Rothenberger defeated Brian Lescinskas of Lake Forest College 21-7, 20-21, 11-1; Andrew Schad of the US Air Force Academy defeated Jeffrey Jones 21-6, 21-3; Tommy Little of Southwest Missouri State defeated Eric Fields 21-4, 21-7 and Sal SantaAna defeated Troy Peterson of Portland Community College 21-10, 21-13.

With the round of 16, the Open division was established. The Aggies had two in the Open division, Shane Rothenberger and Sal SantaAna. James Komsthoeft of Lake Forest College defeated Shane Rothenberger 21-4, 21-10 and Sal SantaAna defeated Don Cottam of Memphis State University 21-11, 21-13. In the quarterfinals, Sal SantaAna defeated Steve Dobrash of Memphis State 21-11, 21-13. In the finals, SantaAna came up a little short as Chris Jennings took the first game 21-18. In the second game, Jennings showed consistency and experience to win the game 21-5. Jennings, a senior, finished his collegiate career, but SantaAna would have one more opportunity to compete for the National Collegiate Handball Open Singles title. With his 2nd place finish SantaAna became the first male Aggie All-American.

In the B division, Jeff Swoboda was defeated 21-11, 21-16 by Chris Meyer of Southwest Missouri State University. No other scores of Aggie players in the B division are available.

In the C division quarterfinals, Colin Errington defeated Jeff Walsh (both Aggies) 21-7, 12-21, 11-6 and Brian Shumate of the

Salvador SantaAna
(*Handball*, June 1993, page 35)

University of Texas-Dallas defeated Richard Myatt 21-4, 21-3. In the semifinals, Mike Rice of the US Air Force Academy defeated Colin Errington 21-7, 7-21,11-8.

The Aggies had two players, Ryan Isenberg and Corey McCutchan, in the Contenders division. Unfortunately, both were paired in the first round. Isenberg outlasted McCutchan 21-17, 11-21, 11-6. In the semifinals, James Swansinger of Las Positas College defeated Isenberg 21-7, 21-2.

In the Novice division, Jeff Townsend defeated Rick Elma of Cincinnati University 21-17, 15-21, 11-5 and Warren Ferguson defeated Jose Castro (both Aggies) 21-15, 21-13. In the semifinals, Chris Pouley of Gonzaga defeated Jeff Townsend and Warren Ferguson defeated David Salisbury of the US Air Force Academy (no scores listed). In the finals, Chris Pouley of Gonzaga defeated Warren Ferguson 14-21, 21-13, 11-8.

No Aggies participated in doubles at the National Collegiate Handball Tournament.

Even though Sal SantaAna earned All-American status in the tournament as the first Aggie male to achieve that honor, the team overall had a lot of inexperienced players. As a result, the Aggie men came in fourth in the team standings with 428 points. Southwest Missouri State University men's team was just ahead at 435 points and the US Air Force Academy was in fifth place with 381 points. Memphis State University continued its string of men's team championships with 501 points.

As with the men's Team, the women had a lot of new players. Gone were the All-Americans Sharon Baylor, Betsy Boswell and Kim Harris. In the women's preliminary round, Bryna Dye of the University of Texas defeated Joan McDowell 15-2, 15-5 and Dayna Moore of the University of Texas defeated Georgann Kidd 15-9, 15-6.

In the round of 32, Kari Steinbock of Pacific University defeated Kelly LeWallen 15-13, 15-8; Anna Gonzalez defeated Sharon Hill of Southwest Missouri State 15-1, 15-5; Julie Flattre of Southwest Missouri State defeated Joann Langlinais 15-4, 15-1; Becky Pinkard defeated Julie Berra of Southwest Missouri State 15-4, 15-2; Michelle Alton defeated Shirley Norris of Pacific University 15-11, 13-15, 11-1; Cassie Tijerina defeated Rhonda Knezek of the University of Texas 15-3, 15-5; Tiffany Precht defeated Amy Bunton of Southwest Missouri State 15-2, 15-6 and Karen Hendrix of Pacific University defeated Joanne Jackson (no score listed).

In the round of 16, Amy Wellinger of Southwest Missouri State defeated Anna Gonzalez 15-11, 8-15, 11-5; Julie Flattre of Southwest Missouri State defeated Becky Pinkard 15-13, 15-1; Lisa Drewen of the University of Texas defeated Michelle Alton 15-6, 15-2; Cassie Tijerina defeated Celeste Colvin of the US Air Force Academy 6-15, 15-6, 11-0 and Angie Smithwick of Southwest Missouri State defeated Tiffany Precht 15-9, 15-5.

One Aggie, Cassie Tijerina, made it to the quarterfinals of the women's Open division. Cassie was defeated in a squeaker by Jeni Burnett of Southwest Missouri State 1-21, 21-9, 11-10. Unlike the past few years, the Aggies did not pick up many points in the Open division.

In the first round of the women's B division, Anna Gonzalez defeated Kari Steinbock of Pacific University 21-7, 21-15; Becky Pinkard defeated Michelle Alton (both Aggies) 15-21, 21-11, 11-10 and Karen Hendrix of Pacific University defeated Tiffany Precht by injury default. In the semifinals, Anna Gonzalez defeated Becky Pinkard (no score listed) and in the finals Karen Hendrix defeated Anna Gonzalez 21-4, 21-17.

In the first round of the women's C division, Kelly LeWallen defeated Sharon Hill of Southwest Missouri State 21-9, 21-6. In the semifinals, Kelly LeWallen defeated Shirley Norris of Pacific University (no score listed). In the finals, Rachell Hall of the University of Texas defeated Kelly LeWallen 21-14, 8-21, 11-4.

In the first round of the Contenders division, Jennifer Gallagher of the University of Texas defeated Joann Langlinais 21-4, 21-5 and Joanne Jackson defeated Amy Bunton of the University of Texas 5-21, 21-12, 11-3. In the semifinals, Heather Meherry of Pacific University defeated Joanne Jackson 21-8, 21-3.

In the Novice division, Georgann Kidd came in second and Joan McDowell came in fourth.

With the lack of top players and a new group of women, the Aggie dominance in the women's team championship came to an end. With a total of 424 points, the team came in second behind Southwest Missouri State University's 504 points. Finishing third, and not far behind the Aggies, was the University of Texas team with 392 points.

The combined Aggie team, though not the champions, were still a very strong power in the national collegiate handball picture. The Aggies combined team total of 856 was a comfortable lead ahead of third place the University of Texas' 691 points. Southwest Missouri State University became the new combined team champion with a total of 939 points.

A new 1993-1994 handball season began with anticipation of a return to the National Collegiate Handball Tournament which would be held in Portland, Oregon. The Aggies wanted to add another chapter to their impressive handball record. Sal SantaAna, a finalist in men's Open division singles this past year, was ready to lead the Aggies to another championship.

As the first round unfolded Aggie Sal SantaAna, the tournament's number 1 seed, received a bye. Scott Korth defeated James Hall of the US Military Academy; Matt Jackson defeated Bill Hopper of Portland State; Jeff Swoboda and Jeff Jones received byes; Jon King of Pacific University defeated Ricky Reynolds 21-16, 21-12; John Blevins defeated Jerry Sentell of the US Military Academy; Eric Fields received a bye; Casey Clark defeated Steve Barb of Cincinnati University (no score given) and Ben Keating defeated Mark Elma of Cincinnati University to complete the top division. In the bottom division, Chris Pouley of Gonzaga University defeated Ryan Isenberg; Jeff Walsh defeated Alton Rossman of Pacific University; Jeff Jeffers defeated Pat Hessler of Pacific University; Scott Cooner defeated Anthony Randall of the US Military Academy; Tim Poskey defeated Blair Anessi of Pacific University and Shane Rothenberger received a bye. Other than those already stated, there were several matches where no score was available.

In the second round, SantaAna defeated David Salisbury of US Air Force Academy 21-1, 21-1; Shane Conneely of Lake Forest College defeated Scott Korth 21-10, 21-9; Tommy Little of Southwest Missouri State defeated Matt Jackson 21-9, 21-10; Jeff Swoboda defeated Bryan Molitor of Pacific University (no score given); Jeff Jones defeated Jon King of Pacific University 15-21, 21-3, 11-4; Frank Szatkowski of Loyola University defeated John Blevins 21-4, 21-5; Eric Fields defeated Phil Redden of Lake Forest College 21-5, 21-6; Casey Clark defeated Jess Smith of Pacific University 21-12, 21-19; Tyler Hamel of Southwest Missouri State defeated Ben Keating 21-0, 21-4; Justin Blakenbush of Montana Tech defeated Jeff Walsh (no score given); Brian Shumate of Southwest Missouri State defeated Jeff Jeffers 21-18, 21-6; Steve Dobrash of Memphis State University defeated Scott Cooner 21-5, 21-1; Bear Meiring of Memphis State University defeated Tim Poskey 21-4, 21-6 and Shane Rothenberger defeated Chris Powers of Pacific University 21-10, 21-10.

In the third round, SantaAna defeated Steve Lindemuth of US Air Force Academy 21-4, 21-4; Tommy Little of Southwest Missouri State defeated Jeff Swoboda 21-9, 21-7; Frank Szatkowski defeated Jeff Jones 21-5, 21-5; Chris Meyer of Southwest Missouri State defeated Eric Fields (no score given) and Bear Meiring of Memphis State University defeated Shane Rothenberger (no score given).

In the fourth round, SantaAna defeated Shane Conneely of Lake Forest College 21-11, 21-11. In the quarterfinals, SantaAna defeated Frank Szatkowski of Loyola University 21-10, 21-13. In the semifinals, SantaAna defeated Tyler Hamel of Southwest Missouri State 21-4, 21-14. To help understand the level of competition at this point in the tournament, Hamel was the current singles handball champion from

Canada. It did not get any easier as SantaAna faced David Chapman in the final match for the collegiate handball singles championship. Chapman was the teenage phenomenon who had already won on the professional handball tour in both singles and doubles. A freshman from Southwest Missouri State, Chapman won 21-2, 21-5.

The following results are for the Aggies who were defeated in the third round and dropped down into the B division. Mark Beverly of Memphis State University defeated Jeff Swoboda 21-8, 21-5; Jaret Treber of Western Washington University defeated Casey Clark (no score given); Thomas Polzin of Western Washington University defeated Eric Fields 14-21, 21-10, 11-4 and Shane Rothenberger defeated Jeff Jones 21-14, 21-14. In the quarterfinals, Nick Dobrash of Memphis State University defeated Shane Rothenberger 21-15, 21-10.

The Official Voice of the United States Handball Association $4.00

National Masters Singles
Detroit and Houston Pro Stops
World and National Championships Updates
USHA Certified Referees
Eliminating Errors and Concentration Strategy

Chapman Wins Collegiate
Singles and Doubles

SantaAna Upsets Hamel -- Southwest Missouri State Wins Combined Title

The win of Sal SantaAnna over Tyler Hammel, current singles handball champion in Canada, earned the honor of being featured on the cover of the USHA's *Handball* Magazine

The results in men's C division singles, which is made up of players who were defeated in the second round and dropped down, were: Les Seago of Memphis State University defeated Scott Korth 21-15, 7-21, 11-9; Matt Jackson defeated Bryan Molitor of Pacific University 21-6, 21-2; John Blevins defeated Jon King of Pacific University; Jeff Jeffers defeated Phil Redden of Lake Forest College 21-10, 21-4; Jess Smith of Pacific University defeated Ben Keating 21-8, 21-1; Jeff Walsh defeated Chris Pouley of Gonzaga 21-6, 21-16; Jason Schroeder of the University of Texas defeated Scott Cooner and Tim Poskey defeated Chris Power of Pacific University. No scores were available for some of the matches.

In the second round of C division, Matt Jackson defeated Tyron Thompson of the University of Oregon 21-6, 21-9; Jeff Jeffers defeated Chris Pape of Cincinnati University 21-18, 21-10; Jeff Walsh defeated Nick Molnar of Memphis State University (no score given); Tim Poskey defeated Ravi Kurakulusuriya of Pacific University 21-9, 21-15 and Ryan Conlon of Harper Junior College defeated John Blevins 21-6, 17-21, 11-5.

In the quarterfinals, Les Seago of Memphis State University defeated Matt Jackson 21-19, 21-10; Jess Smith of Pacific University defeated Jeff Jeffers 21-10, 21-7; Scott Olsen of Western Washington University defeated Jeff Walsh 15-21, 21-20, 11-5 and Ryan Conlon of Harper Junior College defeated Tim Poskey 16-21, 21-20, 11-7. All Aggies were eliminated at this point in the C division.

In the Contenders division, which consisted of players who lost in the first round, Ricky Reynolds defeated Jerry Sentell of the US Military Academy 21-18, 21-12 and Alton Rossman of Pacific University defeated Ryan Isenberg 21-16, 21-8. Ricky Reynolds then defeated Bryan Molitor of Pacific University (no score given) and Neal McKeever of the University of Oregon 21-12, 21-20. In the semifinals, Damian Crowson of Pacific University defeated Ricky Reynolds 21-7, 21-10.

In the Novice division, which consisted of those who lost the first two matches, Lance Lowy reported the action on page 32 in the June 1994 issue of the USHA's *Handball*:

> Bill Hopper, who transferred from Pacific to nearby Portland State, overcame a shaky start in the tournament, and a loss to a former Pacific teammate, Brian Molitor, to defeat a gutsy, courageous player from Texas A&M, Ryan Isenberg, in a great Novice final, 21-19, 15-21, 11-10. Anyone who saw Isenberg in the tournament saw a player who had amazing retrieving and shot recovery abilities. He simply made very few hand errors over the four-day event. So, the question was whether anyone else could be patient enough and have enough offensive skills to overcome Isenberg's staggering ability to run and retrieve shots, who needed to ignore an injured shoulder and sore elbow.

> Hopper, blessed with a great name for a handball player, had enough speed and offense to neutralize Isenberg for the win, but not without some long rallies and great gets by both players in the tiebreaker. Bill Hopper won the match but no one thinks of Ryan Isenberg as a loser. He personifies what's great about the game of handball.

To reach the finals, Ryan defeated Daniel Currier of Pacific University, Shane Connell of Pacific University, Todd Lyles of Southwest Missouri State University 21-2, 21-1 and Pat Hessler of Pacific University 19-21, 21-20, 11-5.

In the first two rounds of action in the women's singles, Becky Pinkard defeated Manuella Proksch of Southwest Missouri State University 21-7, 21-0; Celeste Colvin of US Air Force Academy defeated Jill Emerson 21-4, 21-7; Georgann Kidd defeated Rachel Hall of the University of Texas (no score given); Jamie Rupple defeated Shirley Norris of Pacific University (no score given); Cassie Tijerina defeated Cory Dodge of Southwest Missouri State University 21-3, 21-0; Michelle Alton defeated Stacy Lindeman of

Southwest Missouri State University 21-5, 21-12; Angi Smithwick of Southwest Missouri State University defeated Beth Oliver 21-9, 21-9; Amy Wellinger (college/university not listed) defeated Joanne Jackson 21-12, 21-9; Tiffany Precht defeated Stephanie Crawford of Pacific University (no score given) and Kim McKinney defeated Mary Coleman of Southwest Missouri State University 21-14, 21-2.

In the third round, Celeste Colvin of US Air Force Academy defeated Becky Pinkard 21-14, 21-20; Georgann Kidd defeated Julie Flattre of Southwest Missouri State University 21-0, 21-12; Lisa Drewen of the University of Texas defeated Jamie Rupple 21-10, 21-8; Michelle Alton defeated Angi Smithwick of Southwest Missouri State University 20-21, 21-6, 11-7; Tiffany Precht defeated Amy Wellinger of Southwest Missouri State University (no score given) and Jeni Burnett of Southwest Missouri State University defeated Kim McKinney 21-15, 21-15.

In the quarterfinals, Lisa Drewen of the University of Texas defeated Georgann Kidd 21-6, 20-21, 11-2; Cassie Tijerina defeated Michelle Alton 21-2, 21-0; Jeni Burnett of Southwest Missouri State University defeated Tiffany Precht 21-19, 21-10 and in the semifinals, Cassie Tijerina defeated Jeni Burnett of Southwest Missouri State University 21-12, 21-7.

In the June 1994 issue of the USHA's *Handball*, page 30, Tommy Burnett, Coach of the Southwest Missouri State University handball team, reported the action in the final round to determine the National Collegiate Women's Handball Champion:

> Texas A&M's Cassie Tijerina returned this year pounds lighter and her concentration keener. She dispensed Heather Meharry of Lane Community College in the qualifier, 21-4, 21-4 and teammate Michelle Alton in the quarterfinals. Then, flirting with fate, Tijerina was again matched up with SMSU's Burnett, this time in the semifinals. However, she was not to be denied, as Burnett failed to solve her strong left hand serve, falling 21-12, 21-7.

> Tijerina's mission was quickly jeopardized in the final, as Adrian combined her beautiful ceiling, shooting and passing game into a 21-11 victory. During the second game, Adrian jumped out to a comfortable lead, 12-5. Possibly anticipating her impending doubles final Adrian dropped her concentration and Tijerina rekindled her mission rallying to 15-16. Trading points during the next few rallies, apprehension gripped Beth's coaches as Cassie tied the game at 20-20. However, Adrian never seemed to panic as she boldly shot the left front corner from 35 feet to regain the serve. Her next serve was all cannon and although Tijerina made a gallant attempt to return it, it ended Tijerina's comeback bid and clinched Adrian's return to the crown.

In women's B division, Texas A&M dominated as Tommy Burnett reported in the June 1994 issue of the USHA's *Handball*, pages 32, 33:

> Tiffany Precht and Georgann Kidd of Texas A&M found themselves on familiar turf playing each other. Tiffany had survived a tough match with another teammate, Michelle Alton, finally winning, 17-21, 21-7, 11-6. Kidd defeated a much-improved Celeste Colvin from the Air Force Academy 21-15, 21-16.

> The first game of the final provided a lot of opportunity for the Aggie teammates who were watching to alternate their encouragement and cheering for both players. Precht, with her great smile and winning personality just never seems to give up. Kidd, an up-and-coming player with a determined style, makes up for a lack of experience with a

competitive spirit. Trailing 4-11, Kidd began to chop away at Precht's lead until 16-18 when Tiffany finally pulled away and scored three straight points.

The second game was all Precht as a tired Kidd succumbed 21-2. A proud Coach Lowy collected 228 points toward his eventual women's title.

Chatten Hayes, center, congratulates women's B finalists Georgann Kidd and Tiffany Precht (right)

(*Handball*, June 1994, page 33)

In women' doubles, only one A&M team entered. Tiffany Precht and Cassie Tijerina teamed up to challenge for the doubles championship. In the first round, they defeated Angie Keller and Mary Coleman of Southwest Missouri State University 21-0, 21-0. In the semifinals, they defeated Angie Smithwick and Amy Wellinger of Southwest Missouri State University 21-6, 21-5. The finals would not be so easy.

In the June 1994 issue of the USHA's *Handball* magazine, page 33, Tommy Burnett reported the doubles final match as follows:

> For the past three years, the women's crown has been on a rollercoaster between SMSU and Texas A&M, with Pacific and Texas providing strong threats. This year was no different.
>
> Beth Adrian and Jeni Burnett of SMSU provide a good doubles balance. Beth with her beautiful mechanics and power serves; Jeni with her coolness and retrieving ability.
>
> Cassie Tijerina and Tiffany Precht also have strong balance. Cassie, a lefty, has a booming serve and a deceptive court awareness. Tiffany has a long reach and an uncanny ability to return difficult shots.
>
> The semifinals saw Adrian and Burnett jump out early to a 12-4 lead. Although Tijerina/ Precht rallied, the rhythm remained with the SMSU squad as they prevailed 21-18.
>
> The second game started off the same, with Adrian/Burnett providing an effective combo and settled into a comfortable 14-8 lead. After a timeout, the A&M duo came roaring back with a vengeance. Precht refused to miss and Tijerina kept hitting pinpoint pass shots that seemed to evaporate in the back corners, giving them a 21-18 victory.
>
> As the crowd grew, each rally became a prelude to loud cheering and applause. But the tiebreaker that was to close the 1994 Collegiates on a rising crescendo was not to be. Victory came swift without drama as the SMSU duo played near perfect doubles, blanking the A&M pair 11-0.

In the first round of the women's C division, Becky Pinkard defeated Angie Keller of Southwest Missouri State University 21-6, 21-4; Julie Flattre of Southwest Missouri State University defeated Jamie

Rupple and Kim McKinney defeated Amy Wellinger of Southwest Missouri State University. No scores were given for the last two listed matches. In the semifinals, Julie Flattre of Southwest Missouri State University defeated Becky Pinkard and Angi Smithwick defeated Kim McKinney which eliminated the Aggies from further competition in the C division.

In the women's Contenders division, Jill Emerson defeated Manuella Proksch of Southwest Missouri State University 21-0, 21-14; Beth Oliver defeated Stacy Lindemann of Southwest Missouri State University 21-16, 21-11 and Joanne Jackson defeated Stephanie Crawford of Pacific University 21-15, 21-9. In the quarterfinals, Jill Emerson defeated Lora Andrews of Pacific University 21-13, 21-19; Sharon Hill of Southwest Missouri University defeated Beth Oliver 21-6, 21-1 and Mary Coleman of Southwest Missouri State University defeated Joanne Jackson 21-17, 21-9. In the semifinals, Sharon Hill of Southwest Missouri State University defeated Jill Emerson 21-5, 18-21, 11-5. The Aggies were now eliminated from further competition in the Contenders division.

There were no Aggies in the women's Novice division.

Even though the doubles match ended without a championship for Cassie (right) and Tiffany, it did earn each All-American honors. Coach Lance Lowy is in the photo at the left with his two stars.

(*Handball*, June 1994, page 30)

The 1994 Texas A&M Women's National Collegiate Handball Championship Team
PHOTO INCLUDES: Becky Pinkard, Jill Emerson, Georgann Kidd, Jamie Rupple, Cassie Tijerina, Michelle Alton, Beth Oliver, Joanne Jackson Tiffany Precht, Kim McKinney and Coach Lance Lowy
(*Handball*, June 1994, page 33)

Once again, the Aggies proved they were a national power in collegiate handball. The Aggie men's team finished third with 424 points. This was well in advance of fourth place Lake Forest College with 308 points. Memphis State University finished in second place with 487 points. The Aggie women added another National Collegiate Handball Championship to the trophy case. A&M scored 428 points which was a comfortable but not commanding lead over Southwest Missouri State University with 404 points.

Southwest Missouri State University was the Combined Team Champion with 902 points, easily ahead of Texas A&M's point total of 852. A&M finished in second place well ahead of Memphis State University's 487

The National Championship Banner representing the Aggie women's title

(Author's Collection)

Going into the 1995 season, Coach Lowy knew the mountain he had to climb to return to the top of the National Collegiate Handball Combined Team Championship. With David Chapman, already a professional handball player, and Tyler Hamel, the Canadian handball champion, both returning to Southwest Missouri State and with other up and coming handball players, it was a daunting task. Coach Lowy had been there before so he was not without experience or without some stars of his own. All of the Aggies were looking forward to another great showing at the National Collegiate Handball Tournament to be held on the home courts of Southwest Missouri State University.

For the first time in many years, the USHA's *Handball* magazine did not report the game results. After the first rounds were completed, the Aggies had three players in the Open singles division. They were Eric Fields, Jeff Jones and Jeff Jeffers. David Chapman and Tyler Hamel, both from Southwest Missouri State University, played for the championship. As expected, David Chapman won the Open Championship.

In the men's B division, two Aggies won their way into the finals to battle for the championship. Lance Lowy reported the action in the USHA's *Handball* magazine of June 1955, page 31:

The men's B division was made up of players who lost in the round of 32 in a tournament that began with 105 players. All 16 players in B were talented and accomplished players to have made it to the round of 32. Geoff Smyth of Las Positas opened with a hard fought two-game win over Casey Clark of Texas A&M. Chris Pape of Cincinnati followed with a two-game victory over Danny Maupin of Southwest Missouri State. Noel Keen of Texas A&M beat Rob Powers of Pacific and Greg Tomasyan of Texas defeated freshman Joel Petershagen of Texas A&M. In the bottom half of the division, Bill Bartlett of SMSU was beaten by Chris Johnson of Texas. Jason Schroeder of Texas turned back a determined effort by Brad Warthman from Ohio St. In one of the best matches of the tournament, Jason Stolley of Texas matched dig for dig and retrieve for retrieve with Richard Lynch of SMSU before winning 11-8 in a two-hour match. Jeff Walsh of Texas A&M outlasted a very formidable Adam Berliner of Texas, 11-2, in a two-handed shoot-out.

In the quarters, Pape played patiently and shot the ball if Smyth gave him a shot, to win, 11-4. Keen played like a man possessed, digging, chasing, killing and rekilling to beat Tomasyan in two games. Teammates, Johnson and Schroeder, played a spirited and competitive match with Schroeder prevailing, 11-6. Walsh continued his winning ways over Stolley, 11-3, but something was becoming more and more apparent. Walsh was shooting everything with both hands, he was getting to everything and he wasn't wearing down.

The semifinals featured two very well-played matches, but the outcomes did not seem to be in doubt. Keen built leads in both games against Pape only to see them disappear. However, his diving and determined style pulled him through to win, 21-18, in both games. Pape deserves a lot of credit for his heart and talent because Keen was everywhere. Walsh, on the other hand, was a relaxed shooting machine, hitting reverse, low, power serves that gave him the set ups he wanted. Schroeder also fought hard and had a great tournament but Walsh was rolling.

The final was a battle from the coin toss. Actually, it started the night before because these two Texas A&M teammates were staying in the same room at the Park Inn. The shooting, the diving, the spirit and will of these two players went down to the wire in the first game as Walsh pulled it out, 21-20. The second game was even at nine when Walsh shifted to another gear and methodically pulled away to win, 21-9. The players in this division deserved the admiration and applause they received for showing the talent and guts it takes to win or lose gracefully at the National level. Congratulations to you all.

B division finalists Jeff Walsh (left) and Noel Keen (right)

(*Handball*, June 1995, page 31)

On page 32 of the June 1995 issue of the USHA's *Handball*, Ralph Weil reported the action concerning the men's C division:

> Scott Korth is a senior from Texas A&M. Scott has maintained a B average in Mechanical Engineering. He has been playing since his freshman year when Lance Lowy taught him in the handball class. In addition to handball, Scott participates in intramural basketball, baseball and football. He likes the game because it is physically and mentally challenging. The program at Texas A&M has 120 women and 250 men enrolled in handball classes.
>
> The semifinal against James Swansiger from Las Positas College went all Scott's way when James made a few errors and his fist shot failed him. Scott said his serve was effective and he was able to control the front court. The final score was 21-9, 21-7.
>
> Pat Hessler is a senior in Biology/Chemistry at Pacific University and plans a career in Physical Therapy. Pat has played handball for a year and has an extensive sports background having played offensive guard on the varsity football team and third base on the varsity baseball team. He likes handball because it is a great workout, and makes him think and concentrate. Handball gives Pat stress relief from his studies.
>
> In the first game, Andy Bailey from Texas A&M killed everything and Pat had trouble playing the ball so he conserved his energy for the next game. In the second game, Bailey had the lead so Coach Mike Steele had Pat change his game plan to hit power shots to Bailey's left and to kill the returns. In the tiebreaker, Bailey lost his composure and showed signs of tiredness. The scores were 11-21, 21-20, 11-6.
>
> In the final, Scott Korth cornered a tired Pat Hessler early with a run-and-gun style that seemed to nullify Hessler's great retrieves. Korth won the final in the C division, 21-12, 21-14.

In the men's Contenders division, the US Military Academy, Texas A&M and Southwest Missouri State University dominated the quarterfinals; however, none of the Aggies made it to the finals.

In the men's Novice division, A&M had another winner. Bill Sharton reported the final match in the June 1995 issue of the USHA's *Handball* magazine, page 33:

> Joshua Ely, a junior representing Texas A&M, captured the men's Novice division at the 1995 United States Handball Association (USHA) National Collegiate Handball Championships with a 21-17, 21-10 victory over Chris Shaff of the University of Utah.
>
> In game one of this title contest, the lead changed hands three times and the score was knotted on six different occasions. Neither player was able to rattle off more than three points in a row in this evenly matched game until late in the contest.
>
> After Ely mounted a 14-9 lead midway through game one, Shaff came back with eight straight points to gain a 17-14 advantage. However, this would prove to be the last hoorah for Shaff as Ely responded with seven straight points of his own to register the 21-17 win. Ely's last two points of the game featured a left wall passing shot and left corner reverse kill shot.
>
> In game two, Elly picked up where he left off and quickly jumped out to a 10-0 lead before Shaff managed to get on the board.
>
> Shaff was able to narrow the margin to five points (15-10) during the middle stages of the game, but Ely would not allow him to get any closer. Ely tallied the next six points in unanswered fashion for a 21-10 win and the title.
>
> Following the match, Ely said he had played handball off and on for about three years and this was his first trip to the Collegiate Nationals. "I had never played any sport before I started playing handball," said Ely. "This experience will definitely be a motivator to keep me playing."

In the women's competition, the Aggies had two players, Cassie Tijerina and Priscilla Kojin, among the eight who made up the Open singles division. First, the eventual champion, Jessica Gawley of Regina University in Canada, defeated Priscilla Kojin 21-8, 21-11. Cassie Tijerina defeated Celeste Colvin of US Air Force Academy 21-0, 21-4. In the semifinals, Jessica Gawley defeated Cassie Tijerina 21-2, 21-5.

Coach Lance Lowy reported the action in the women's B division on page 34 of the June 1995 issue of the USHA's *Handball*:

> The top eight collegiate women in the nation made up the women's Open division, with the women who lost to the top eight comprising the B. The quarterfinals featured two tiebreaker wins and two two-game affairs. Things opened up with Stephanie Crawford of Pacific beating Kim McKinney of Texas A&M 11-3. Mary Dean Coleman of SMSU won a hard-fought battle over Joanne Jackson of Texas A&M, also 11-3. Heather Meharry of SMSU won over Shirley Holstad of Pacific in two games. Holstad deserves special merit here, not only for her style and talent in a handball court, but for her sportsmanship and pleasant demeanor on and off the court. In the last quarterfinal match, Tiffany Precht displayed her consistent, patient style to beat Angie Keller of SMSU in two games.

In the best women's B match of the tournament, Crawford unleashed the power and court coverage that she is capable of and turned back a very determined Coleman in two close games, 19 and 17. In the other semifinal, Precht was all business as she got to everything and forced Meharry into mistakes while winning in two games.

The final had the potential to be an exciting match contrasting Crawford's power and Precht's control. However, this did not materialize as Precht jumped out to big leads in both games and with inspired and experienced play took Crawford out of her game. Precht cruised to her B championship in two games.

B finalists Stephanie Crawford and Tiffany Precht are congratulated by Eric Fields. Tiffany is to Eric's left. Eric of Texas A&M was one of the top 16.

(*Handball,* June 1995, page 34)

The men's (left) and women's runner-up trophies

(Author's Collection)

Holly Ridings and Stacey Tuttle were the only Aggies in the women's C division. No scores were given for any of their matches but neither made it to the finals. There were no Aggies entered in the women's Novice or Contenders divisions. Anja Dabelic made it to the semifinals in the Contenders division where she was defeated by Sharon Hill of Southwest Missouri State University 21-5, 21-5.

In women's doubles, two Aggies-Cassie Tijerina and Tiffany Precht, played and won their way to the final match. In the semifinal match, the two defeated Alissa Donaldson and Angie Keller of Southwest Missouri State University 21-1, 21-5. The team of Tijerina and Precht were unable to overcome the skill and experience of Jeni Burnett Hopkins and Beth Korsi of Southwest Missouri State University ending up on the short end of the match 21-16, 21-7.

The 1995 A&M women's 2nd Place Doubles Team Tiffany Precht (left) and Cassie Tijerina

(*Handball,* June 1995, page 35)

It was another good year for the Aggie handball team but not enough to overcome a strong Southwest Missouri State University team. The Aggie men's team was second in the nation with 476 points which was not far behind the total of 549 for first. The women's team also was second in the nation totaling 448 points to 492 for first. The Aggie Combined team score of 924 was far ahead of the University of Texas third place with 665 points but well behind the total of 1041 of the national champion Southwest Missouri State University team.

An additional highlight of the tournament was the selection of Eric Fields as one of the two sportsmanship award recipients from the 155 handball players representing 20 colleges and universities.

The 1995 A&M Team at Southwest Missouri State University

PHOTO INCLUDES: Eric Fields, Jeff Jeffers, Noel Keen, Casey Clark, Joel Petershagen, Jeff Walsh, Scott Korth, Andy Bailey, Joshua Ely, Cassie Tijerina, Priscilla Kojin, Kim McKinney, Joanne Jackson, Tiffany Precht, Holly Ridings, Stacey Tuttle, Steven Soto, Jeff Jones, Bryan Holmes, Andrew Lellis and Coach Lance Lowy

(*Handball*, June 1995, page 1)

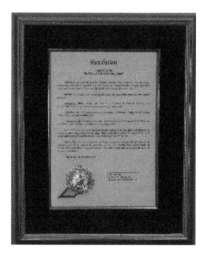

The Texas A&M Board of Regents recognized the many years of excellence displayed by the handball team and specifically the Honors earned in 1995.

(Author's Collection)

Priscilla Kojin receives Sportsmanship Award

The first Marty Decatur sportsmanship award was awarded to Priscilla Kojin at the First Annual Hall of Fame tournament in Tucson in March. A trophy with her name on it will be displayed in the Hall of Fame building. Besides being awarded in memory of Marty, the award is also in memory of Hilary Huffard.

When I received the brochure advertising the Handball Hall of Fame Champions Video and the grand opening of the Hall of Fame building, Hilary's name was identified as a player who lost the game to leukemia. I sent the brochure to Hilary's parents, Philip and Edith, knowing they would be proud that the USHA is active in the fight against Leukemia and that Hilary has remained in our thoughts. Edith wanted to donate an award in memory of Hilary for this tournament. Having played handball with, and a very close friend to Hilary at Texas A&M, I knew a "good sportsmanship" would be most appropriate. Offering to referee any needed matches and filling the Gatorade containers when empty were only a few items that made Priscilla worthy of such an honor. Priscilla has, so much like Hilary possessed, a way of meeting people and feeling comfortable immediately. She knew everyone at the tournament by the end of the weekend in Tucson. "Whenever I am around handball, I am on cloud nine," Priscilla said. Those aspiring to receive the sportsmanship award and/or to just "having fun" at tournaments could learn from her.

Priscilla, 20, is from Sao Paulo, Brazil. She graduated from high school in Decem-

ber, 1992. After attending college for a year in Brazil, she transferred to Texas A&M in the Spring of '94 to pursue a marketing degree. Having played "team handball" since she was a child, she was excited to see "handball" offered as a physical education course. She couldn't wait to teach the American college kids how to play her game. In for a rude awakening her first day of handball class, she has adapted well to her new sport. Only in her third semester of handball, her future is very bright. She made it to the round of 16 at the recent Classic and to the quarterfinals at the Collegiate Nationals. Look for her name a lot in the future.

Beth Rowley presents the Marty Decatur Sportsmanship Award to Priscilla Kojin.

Even the stressed-out Editor noticed Priscilla's positive presence at the tournament.

Handball 25

The Marty Decatur Sportsmanship Award is presented in honor of the Hall of Fame player and is given each year at the USHA Handball Hall of Fame tournament. It is given to a person who embodies "The Spirit of Handball", which is Respect, Fairness, Self-Discipline and Camaraderie. Marty Decatur is considered one of the best doubles players in the history of the game. As a doubles partner, he won eight four-wall, six three-wall and four one-wall titles. In singles he won five three-wall titles. At his Hall of Fame induction, he said of his doubles titles, "I simply played a role with a better player." A great display of true sportsmanship.

Reporting the story about the first awarded Marty Decatur Sportsmanship Award was Beth Rowley. Her story was published in the June 1995 issue of the USHA's *Handball*, page 25. Of special note was her reference to her friend Hilary Huffard. (SEE: Aggie handball team of 1982 in Chapter 9, Team 1980-1989.)

As the 1995-96 year began in Aggieland the handball team was looking forward to the 1996 National Collegiate Handball Tournament to be hosted by the University of Cincinnati and once again to prove the team was a national power in collegiate handball.

At the 1996 National Collegiate Handball Tournament it was evident this would be another record year. With 159 handball players it was the largest number of entries ever and exceeded the 1995 tournament entry of 155. Also, a new record for women were the 50 who were ready to play.

Jeff Walsh was the only Aggie in the men's Open singles. With David Chapman and Tyler Hamel returning for Southwest Missouri State University there was not much chance for Jeff to reach the finals. Jeff, being in the top 16, did earn some points for the Aggie team.

In men's B singles division, Bryan Holmes defeated Matt Seviert of Pacific University 15-21, 21-19, 11-6; Scott Korth defeated teammate Jeff Jones 21-8, 21-18 and Casey Mayo of Bowling Green University defeated Shawn Cummings 21-9, 21-10. In the quarterfinals, Jai Ragoo of Lake Forest College defeated Bryan Holmes 21-9, 19-21, 11-6 and Casey Mayo of Bowling Green University defeated Scott Korth 21-9, 21-9.

Coverage of the men's play at the National Collegiate Handball Tournament by the USHA's *Handball* magazine was very limited. There were no Aggies mentioned in the coverage of the men's C and Contenders divisions and only one Aggie, last name of Edwards, was listed in the men's Novice division. He was defeated by Danny Ellis of Southwest Missouri State University (no score given). The Aggie men's team totaled 399 points, which was enough for third, but well behind Lake Forest College's 510 points and the Southwest Missouri State University team which totaled 542 points.

In the women's Open division, no scores were given in the round of 64; however, the winners and those defeated were listed for each match. Stacey Tuttle defeated Ginger Jordan of Cincinnati University; Jennifer Pelton of Southwest Missouri State University defeated Nikki Nelson; Julie Young defeated Melissa Macklin of Pacific University; Holly Ridings received a bye; Kelly Seaman defeated Ronnie Barragan of the University of Texas; Priscilla Kojin received a bye; Kim McKinney received a bye; Jen Powis defeated Niama Connely of Lake Forest College and Lisa Setchfield defeated Colleen Reardon of Pacific University.

In the round of 32, Stacey Tuttle defeated Joanne Weinbrecht of Pacific University 21-16, 21-13; Cori Dodge of Southwest Missouri State University defeated Julie Young 13-21, 21-17, 11-5; Holly Ridings defeated Rachel Taylor of Pacific University 21-11, 21-11; Jeni Hopkins of Southwest Missouri State University defeated Kelly Seaman 21-2, 21-4; Priscilla Kojin defeated Ashley Rankin of Southwest Missouri State University 21-2, 21-1; Kim McKinney defeated Lauren Hall of the University of Texas 21-8, 21-5; Jen Powis defeated Amie Riggan of Pacific University 21-8, 21-8 and Alissa Donaldson of Southwest Missouri State University defeated Lisa Setchfield 21-2, 21-3.

In the round of 16, the number 1 seed Jessica Gawley of Regina University in Canada defeated Stacey Tuttle 21-4, 21-5; Holly Ridings defeated Jeni Hopkins of Southwest Missouri State University 21-14, 21-19; Priscilla Kojin defeated Maggie Grelle of Southwest Missouri State University 21-7, 21-2; Sasha Gawley of University of Regina in Canada defeated Kim McKinney 21-3, 21-4 and Alissa Donaldson of Southwest Missouri State University defeated Jen Powis 21-5, 21-8.

In the quarterfinals, Stephanie Crawford of Pacific University defeated Holly Ridings 21-14, 21-17 and Priscilla Kojin defeated Sasha Gawley of Regina University in Canada 21-16, 21-10. In the semifinals, Priscilla Kojin defeated Alissa Donaldson of Southwest Missouri State University 21-5, 21-9. In the finals for the women's National Collegiate Handball Championship, the more tournament experienced Jessica Gawley from Regina University in Canada maintained her composure against the very talented Priscilla Kojin and was able to come away with a win 21-12, 21-11.

Priscilla Kojin displaying
her Aggie Spirit

(*Handball*, June 1996, page 26)

Priscilla Kojin and Holly Ridings
showing their 2nd place plaques
in women's Open Doubles

(*Handball*, June 1996, page 24)

Coach Lowy reported the action in women's B division in the June 1996 issue of the USHA's *Handball*, page 24:

> The women's division began with the largest draw ever in the National Collegiate Handball Tournament with 50 competitors. When the draw was whittled down to the top 16 women in the country, the women's Open and B were determined. The top eight went to the Open, while the losers continued in the B. This was a very talented group.
>
> The top half of the draw had the graceful Tanya Dietzler of Lake Forest College, facing the powerful Stacey Tuttle of Texas A&M. It was nip and tuck all the way with Tuttle winning the first game 21-12, before Dietzler won the next two 21-7, 11-8. In a battle between Southwest Missouri State teammates, Jeni Hopkins bested Cori Dodge 21-9, 21-10. In the bottom half of the draw, Kim McKinney of Texas A&M won a grueling, well played match against Maggie Grelle of SMSU 21-12, 5-21, 11-2. Jen Powis of Texas A&M played some of her best handball defeating Molly Hedgpeth of SMSU, 21-6, 21-6.
>
> In the semifinals, Dietzler displayed poise and conditioning as she defeated an understandably tired Hopkins 21-15, 21-19. Powis and McKinney were in the midst of a tiebreaker shoot-out when an ankle injury forced McKinney to default. An important observation at this point is both finalists were in the women's C last year and to make it to the top 16 and the B final is quite an accomplishment.
>
> The first game of the final was all Dietzler as she controlled the tempo and won 21-9. At this point, Powis' intensity increased as she won the second game 21-12. The fair play and enthusiasm stood out in the tiebreaker, as Powis surprised the gallery and the referee as she called a wrist ball on herself on match point, then won anyway 11-7. Congratulations to all these women. Their hard work and dedication really show.

Jen Powis displaying
her B division
women's Singles
National Handball
Championship
Plaque

(*Handball*, June 1996,
page 24)

Texas A&M had no women in the C division.

In the preliminary round of the women's Contenders division, Nikki Nelson defeated Michal Chandler of Texas University 21-11, 17-21, 11-10. In the round of 16, Colleen Reardon of Pacific University defeated Nikki Nelson 21-14, 21-7. No other Aggies were in the Contenders division.

USHA 1996 National Collegiate Handball Tournament Sportsmanship Award winners: Pacific's Stephanie Crawford, Texas A&M's Holly Ridings, center, and SMSU's Richard Lynch.

(*Handball,* June 1996, page 27)

Being defeated in the match in the round of 16 of the Contenders division, Nikki Nelson dropped down to the women's Novice division. In the Novice division, Nikki was defeated by Rhonda Korsi of Southwest Missouri State University 21-6, 21-11.

The team results were not what was envisioned at the beginning of the tournament; however, the Aggies once again proved that they were a power in collegiate handball. The Aggie men's team totaled 399 points, well behind Lake Forest College with 510 points and Southwest Missouri State with 542 points. The women came so close to another national championship but ended up in second with 449 points just behind Southwest Missouri State with 456 points. The Aggie combined team total of 848 was comfortably in front of third place Lake Forest with 747 points but not close to first place Southwest Missouri State's 998 points.

Excitement abounded among the handball family at Texas A&M as the 1996-97 school year began. For the first time A&M would host the National Collegiate Handball Tournament. As is the Aggie culture, the Aggies put on a great show. Tommy Burnett, handball coach for Southwest Missouri State University and the current Collegiate Handball Committee Chair, wrote in the June 1997 issue of the USHA's *Handball*, page 11:

> The highlight of this year's tournament was Texas A&M's $23 million Student Recreation Center. Congratulations to Coach Lance Lowy and his Aggie squad for hosting an outstanding event. The TAMU facility staff was very hospitable and accommodating as well. It was a truly fabulous handball venue for the USHA National Collegiates. Thanks to Lance and Texas A&M University.

As play began in the men's Open division, the Aggies found themselves in unfamiliar surroundings. There were no Aggies in the Open division. As happened in 1995 and 1996, there was no record of the men's division match play results. In the men's B division, it was reported that Casey Mayo of Bowling Green University defeated Bryan Holmes on his way to the finals. In the lower half of the division, Adam Berliner of the University of Texas defeated Shawn Cummings to reach the finals. Casey Mayo won the B division championship with a 11-9 win in the tiebreaker.

In the men's C division, there was more information reported in the June 1997 copy of the USHA's *Handball* on page 15, Coach Lowy described the action:

> The semantics of men's C at the National Collegiate tournament is misleading, because not one of these players play at this level in their local or state tournaments. It is, simply, the nature of the five-division drop-down format that labels this division as C. Make no mistake, there are no C players here you would want to play.

The tournament started with 134 men, so the 32 players that comprised the C division won in the round of 128 and then lost in the round of 64.

The list of players who competed in this division from all over the country, but who didn't make the semifinals: Ping Yeh from Texas, Steve Newman from SMSU, Ernie Oar from Pacific, Rene Palomarez from Texas, Alton Rossman from Pacific, Dennis Caldwell from Pacific, Tony Cisneros from Texas A&M, Joshua Ho from Penn State, Rob Sandler from Texas, Kevin Wier from Texas A&M, Brett Frost from SMSU and John Beattie from Cincinnati. These are all fine players who will only get better. Look for these names in future tournaments because there is a lot of talent here.

The semifinals were comprised of four Texas A&M players who have varied styles and personalities. In the first semifinal match, Sophomore Jason Green played Freshman Ike Haines. Green is a guy with a great sense of humor and a burning will to win. Haines is more relaxed, but his drive to win is second to none. The many matches it took to reach this point in the tournament seemed to calm Green down as he patiently waited for his opportunities and took advantage of them. Shooting the ball better than he had all weekend, Green finally wore Haines down to win in two games.

The other semifinal was even more of a contrast in styles. Junior Joel Petershagen is a very cool customer who seems to come out of the woodwork at tournament times. Freshman Mike Cox is in a court every time I turn around. Petershagen began controlling the tempo in both games, but bent under the pressure that Cox put on.

Cox and Green put on quite a show in the final until Green found his niche and decided to start shooting every opportunity. Green beat Cox 21-5, 21-6. Many of the matches in this division could have gone either way. The players and coaches deserve credit for the talent and sportsmanship shown during and after play.

After all of the matches had been played the A&M men's handball team totaled 392 points, which was well behind the second place Lake Forest handball team with a total of 479 points. A&M's team was well ahead of the fourth place team from the University of Texas with a total of 315 points.

The A&M women's handball team had a rising star in Priscilla Kojin. Though all of the results from the women's matches were not available, Lance Lowy reported the dominance of Priscilla in her matches. This was published in the USHA's *Handball* on pages 12 and 13 of the June 1997 issue:

> Out of 60 women who entered the National Collegiate tournament, the top eight filled out the women's Open division. Obviously, these are very elite players who have worked very hard. In the quarterfinals, top-seeded Priscilla Kojin of Texas A&M defeated a game Sabrina Zamora of Lake Forest College 21-4, 21-9. Alissa Donaldson of Southwest Missouri State won over a very talented player from Queens College in Belfast, Ireland, Brid McCorry, 21-11, 21-15. Freshman Amber Rounseville of SMSU defeated teammate Maggie Grelle 21-10, 21-10, but Grelle had already achieved the upset of the tournament by defeating Stephanie Crawford of Pacific 21-11, 21-10. Rounding out the quarters, another fine player from Belfast, Elizabeth Campbell, defeated a solid player from LFC, Tanya Lozaro 21-12, 21-13.

The semifinals provided some of the best handball of the week. Kojin showed why she is rising through the ranks of the top women in the world as she defeated Campbell in two games—and Campbell played very well! Donaldson kept playing her steady, make-very-few-mistakes-type of game going and beat up-and-coming Amber Rounseville in a tiebreaker 11-4.

In my many years coaching collegiate handball and having had numerous Women's National Champions, what I saw in the final was history in the making. Those of us fortunate enough to have seen Jeff Cottam from Memphis, John Bike from Texas and, of course, David Chapman from SMSU, realized that those players were unbeatable at the college stage of their careers. In the past year, Kojin has defeated the likes of Alison Roberts, LeaAnn Martin, and Beth Rowley. Kojin left absolutely no doubt who the best player in Collegiate women's handball in 1997 was as she demolished all opponents, including a 21-5,

21-1 win over Donaldson. Kojin displayed the abilities to shoot flat, to pass at will, to control the whole court and, you know what, she plays like that in Tuesday evening pick-up games. Congratulations to you all, but, in particular, to C-Kool. You earned it.

In the women's doubles action, Tommy Burnett, coach of the Southwest Missouri State University handball team, can describe the doubles action better than I can write, so I am leaning on his following report, published in the USHA's *Handball*, June 1997, pages 13 and 14, to describe some exciting doubles play:

Doubles at Collegiates typically carry no points for teams. They are basically for fun and the entries have grown steadily over the last few years. This year, 17 teams entered and there were plenty of hot matches to watch.

Top seeds Alissa Donaldson and Amber Rounesville (SMSU) faced the University of Texas team of Nicole Gutierrez and Jennifer Chang, Maggie Grelle and Courtney Murdock of SMSU, and survived a 20-21, 21-19, 11-4 match against Alisha Boggs and Sabrina Zamora of Lake Forest College to get a shot at the women's doubles championship.

Second seeded Priscilla Kojin and Stacey Tuttle (TAMU) danced through two SMSU teams, Debbie Gibson/Chrissy Schatz and Mandy Rounseville/Jessica McDonnell, before defeating Tanya Lozaro and Tanya Dietzler (LFC), 21-13, 21-11 in the semis. Kojin, her sights on "slam," had already won the Open singles. Her much improved mechanics and power had created a cakewalk through the singles division. She had yet to be challenged. Her partner, Stacey Tuttle, is a strong player who gives 110 percent.

Senior Donaldson and freshman Rounseville had met each other in the singles semis and then Donaldson was defeated in the final by Kojin. They were ready to even the score: Donaldson with her patient control game and Rounseville with her cool head and snakebite killshots.

The readiness of the SMSU squad was evident in the first game. After trailing 3-1, Donaldson and Rounseville stirred up a mix of offensive and defensive strategy that kept Kojin and Tuttle out of position and second-guessing their own strategy, finally winning, 21-14.

Enter Kojin. Priscilla turned up the heat in game two, virtually retrieving the ball all over the 800 square feet of court one, with Stacey filling in the gaps. Twenty minutes later, the TAMU squad capped a 21-12 victory.

Kojin entered the tiebreaker fatigued, yet determined. Tuttle was fresh and confident. Donaldson was focused; Rounseville was full of energy and ready to rumble. The tiebreaker was one of those games you hope a tiebreaker will be—two teams battling for every point and refusing to be denied victory. During the first part of this game, the TAMU squad controlled the pace and were ahead, 6-4. After a time-out, the SMSU pair inched back into control, up 8-7. The next few points were grueling exhibitions of multiple side-outs with an occasional point being scored: first with Donaldson and Rounseville up 10-8, and then Kojin and Tuttle holding strong to tie it at 10-10. With SMSU serving, Rounseville went for a backwall kill that skipped a cat hair short of the front wall. On the first serve by the Aggies, Donaldson's ceiling return fell short and Kojin and Tuttle collected the women's doubles crown, making Kojin a double Open division winner.

What was not recorded above was that Charlie Bokelman, who was serving as coach of the Aggie doubles team, called for a time-out with the score in the tiebreaker tied at 10-10 and the SMSU pair having the serve. Knowing that both of the SMSU pair would be serving to Tuttle, Bokelman told Tuttle the type return she should hit. The first serve after the time-out, Tuttle did exactly what Bokelman said and rolled the ball out. It was with the second serve that Tuttle successfully returned and the later ensuing shot by Rounseville, as described by Burnett above, that skipped short of the front wall and giving the Aggies the opportunity to serve the winner.

It is unfortunate that all of the play has not been kept but it is known that Ashley Kuehn reached the semifinal in the women's C division. Nikki Nelson reached the semifinal in the women's Contenders division and Jennifer Bailey came in second in the Novice division.

The total points for the women's team were 368, which placed them third behind the team from Lake Forest College. Lake Forest's total was 426 which was a comfortable margin over the Aggies. With the points from the Aggie men, the total combined team points were 760 and they enjoyed a third place finish on their home court.

Another highlight of the tournament was the announcement that Priscilla Kojin was named a recipient of the John Sabo, Sr. Scholarship. The USHA chose Priscilla and James Bardwell, from Penn State University, to be the recipients of the first ever "handball scholarships" based upon their academic performance, academic promise, and commitment to the sport of handball. Each received $1000 made possible by contributors to the College Scholarship Fund. (*Handball*, June 1997, p. 17)

The following members of the A&M handball team who participated in the National Collegiate Handball Tournament were: Andy Bailey, Jennifer Bailey, Troy Baker, Benjamin Barbour, Corey Barker, Kevin Chance, Tony Cisneros, Mike Cox, Shawn Cummings, Kindal Dubose, Jorge Garcia, Ray Garza, Howard Graff, Jason Green, John Haines, Scott Hearon, Bryan Holmes, David Huryeh, Keith Kasprzak, Priscilla Kojin, Ashley Kuehn, Jason Langridge, Wesley Larkin, Maria LaRoe, Benjamin Levine, Kim McKinney, Matt Miller, Nikki Nelson, Joel Petershagen, Daniel Rodriguez, Kelly Seaman, Kim Singleton, Jeff Tomblin, Stacey Tuttle, Ryan West, Kevin Wier, John Witherspoon, Brad Wallner, Karla Wray and Eric Zimmerman. Except as reported above no scores, opponents, or match results were available.

1997 Handball Team

PHOTO INCLUDES: Ben Barbour, Priscilla Kojin, Stacey Tuttle, Bryan Holmes, Kevin Wier, Tony Cisneros, Nathan McCoy, Brad Wallner, Andy Bailey, Karla Wray, Nikki Nelson and Coach Lance Lowy

(*Handball,* June 1997, page 5)

There was excitement among the handball team at A&M as the new 1997-98 school year began. Coach Lowy knew he had the top women's collegiate handball player in the world and her National Collegiate Doubles Championship partner, Stacey Tuttle, returning for their last year. He also knew that Southwest Missouri State University had David Chapman, three years Open Collegiate Handball Singles Champion and USHA's number one ranked pro, returning for his last year plus a women's team that had some upcoming players with great potential. It would not be easy to get to the top again, but there was always hope. For the 1998 National Collegiate Handball Tournament, to be hosted by the University of California-Berkeley, there would be a change from the five divisions format to seven divisions. In addition to the Open, B, C, Contenders and Novice divisions of recent years, the divisions of A and Challenger was added. The new divisions were added to accommodate the larger group of players. As the entries for the 1998 National Collegiate Handball Tournament were being counted, 198 players, the most ever, would be playing their hearts out for individual, team and their respective colleges and universities honors. This total included 18 Irish players representing six colleges. The increasing number of Irish players at the tournament resulted in the Collegiate Commissioners renaming the annual tournament. Beginning in 1999, the tournament would be known as the USHA International Collegiate Championships.

Before play began it had to be determined which players would be in the round of 64. Out of that round would come the players in each of the A, B and C divisions. From the 64 players, with the drop-down format, there would be 16 players in each division. Of course, the seeding would be very important since this was primarily where the team points were earned.

In the round of 64, Jason Green defeated J. Duran of San Jose State University 17-21, 21-16, 11-5; Jason Jones of Texas A&M Corpus Christi defeated Tony Cisneros 21-12, 21-13; Ben Barbour defeated J. Leutkenhaus of Southwest Missouri State University 21-13, 21-3; Dan Navarro of the University of Texas defeated Brad Wallner 21-12, 21-16; Bryan Holmes defeated Ernie Oar of Pacific University 21-7, 21-20; Jay Springer of Southwest Missouri State University defeated Kevin Wier 21-13, 21-14 and Mike Cox defeated A. Rossman of Pacific University 21-10, 21-7.

In the round of 32, Joe Hagen of Lake Forest College defeated Jason Green 21-7, 21-10; Mike Bargman of Lake Forest College defeated Ben Barbour 21-15, 21-7; Dane Szatkowski of Lake Forest College defeated Bryan Holmes 21-9, 21-16 and Chris Rusing of Western Washington University defeated Mike Cox 21-14, 21-7. All of the Aggies who started in the round of 64 had now been defeated, so no one would advance to the final 16 of the Open division.

Making up the 16 players in the A division were those who won in the round of 64 but were defeated in the round of 32. Jason Jones of Texas A&M Corpus Christi defeated Jason Green 21-14, 11-21, 11-3; Ben Barbour defeated Dan Navarro of the University of Texas 21-2, 21-12; Mark O'Leary of Lake Forest College defeated Bryan Holmes 21-12, 21-13 and Jamie Simon of Southwest Missouri State University defeated Mike Cox 21-5, 21-6.

Advancing to the quarterfinals, Ben Barbour defeated Mark O'Leary of Lake Forest College 21-8, 21-8. In the semifinals, Ben Barbour defeated Jamie Simon of Southwest Missouri State College 21-14, 21-18. Ben could not find enough game to defeat Kevin Pettus of Southwest Missouri State University in the finals. The final score was Pettus winning 21-5, 21-5.

Those who were defeated in the first round of 64 moved into the round of 32 to determine who would remain in the B division and who would drop down to the round of 16 in C division. In the round of 32, Tony Cisneros defeated M. Steele of Pacific University 21-18, 12-21, 11-1 and Kevin Wier defeated K. Aemissegger (college or university unknown) 21-15, 21-13. In the round of 16, J. Duran of San Jose State University defeated Tony Cisneros 21-10, 21-9 and Keith Vassal of Lake Forest College defeated Kevin Wier (no scores given).

The men's C division was made up of 32 players, 16 who dropped down from the original 64 and 16 not in the original 64. In the round of 32, Ben Levine defeated J. Leutkenhaus 11-21, 21-13, 11-8 and Mark Hill defeated K. Aemissegger (college or university unknown) 21-16, 21-20. In the round of 16, Ernie Oar of Pacific University defeated Ben Levine 21-2, 21-9 and Mark Hill defeated Vasalis of the University of Texas 21-5, injury default. In the quarterfinals, Mark Hill defeated C. McCormick of Oregon State University 15-21, 21-20, 11-3. In the semifinals, Hill was not able to overcome the relentless power game and great court coverage of Ernie Oar of Pacific University. He was on the short end of the 21-14, 21-6 battle.

The men's Contender division began with 64 players none of whom were in the Open division. In the round of 64, Taylor defeated Haywood of the US Military Academy 10-21, 21-12, 11-9; Ryan Miller defeated Worobec of Southwest Missouri State University 6-21, 21-18, 11-4; Troy Baker defeated Earwood of Southwest Missouri State University 21-2, 21-4; Ben Levine defeated King of Los Positas Junior College 21-13, 21-0 and Mark Hill defeated Sweigert of the US Military Academy 21-4, 21-1. In the round of 32, Taylor defeated Ha of University of California-Berkeley 21-4, 21-4; Miller defeated Vinert of the University of Texas 21-0, 21-3; Coombe of the US Military Academy defeated Baker (no score given), Spagnoli of Cincinnati University defeated Mark Hill (no score given) and Widener of Cincinnati University defeated Levine (no score given). In the round of 16, Taylor defeated Cheng of the University of Texas by default and Coombe of the US Military Academy defeated Miller 21-16, 21-18. In the quarterfinals, Martinez of Los Positas Junior College defeated Taylor 21-3, 21-1.

There were no Aggies entered in the men's Challengers or Novice divisions.

As the women's play began, the Aggies were confident that their own Priscilla Kojin would win her third Open title. In the round of 32, Priscilla Kojin defeated Carol Salinas of the University of Texas 21-1, 21-2; Erika Sove of University of California Santa Barbara defeated Nicole Nelson 21-3, 21-3; Robin Collins of Southwest Missouri State University defeated Karla Wray 21-5, 21-5; Jennifer Powis defeated Cortni Sedgwick of Southwest Missouri State University 21-19, 21-13; Mandy Rounseville of Southwest

Missouri State University defeated Ryan West 21-5, 21-2; Stacey Tuttle defeated Melisa Macklin of Pacific University 21-8, 21-6 and Amber Rounseville of Southwest Missouri State University defeated Janna Althaus 21-3, 21-4.

In the round of 16, Priscilla Kojin defeated Paula Pennington of Southwest Missouri State University 21-3, 21-4; Mandy Rounseville defeated Jennifer Powis 21-8, 21-1 and Brigid McCrory of Queens College in Belfast, Ireland defeated Stacey Tuttle (no score given). Priscilla Kojin was the lone Aggie remaining in the Open singles. Coach Lance Lowy described the Open division action that can be found on page 19 of the April 1998 issue of the USHA's *Handball*:

> The best eight female collegiate players in the nation composed the women's Open division. All eight had won two matches to get to this prestigious division, and in the final the best of the best was on display as Priscilla Kojin of Texas A&M beat Amber Rounseville of Southwest Missouri State for her third Open crown. The final consisted of four distinct runs, two by each player. In the first game, Rounseville jumped to a 5-0 lead, exposing Kojin's nerves with cameras rolling everywhere. But Kojin settled down with perfect kills and timely passes, zooming to an 18-5 lead and eventual 21-9 win.
>
> The second game opened with Kojin continuing her aggressive play and power serving to a big 19-13 lead. At that point, Rounseville turned it up and began killing the ball, cutting the deficit to 19-16. Kojin, however, closed out the match with steady defense and opportunistic offense.

Priscilla Kojin showing the athleticism that propelled her to the second National Collegiate Handball Open Singles Championship. Amber Rounseville appears to be in doubt as to where to go.

(*Handball*, April 1998, page 19)

Based on the number of women entered in the tournament, a new division (A) was added. In the past, the Open and A division were basically one and the same. It cannot be confirmed whether the A division was added this year or in 1997. The results of the women's tournament matches were not reported in 1997. In the women's A division, featuring those who won in the round of 32 but failed to win in the round of 16, the play started with the quarterfinals. Jennifer Powis defeated Megan Haug of Pacific University 21-7, 21-9 and Stacey Tuttle defeated Margie Hill of Pacific University 21-6, 21-19. In the semifinals, Jennifer Powis defeated Stacey Tuttle 21-9, 19-21, 11-7. As happened in the women's Open division, the A singles final pitted an Aggie, Jennifer Powis, against Robin Collins of Southwest Missouri State University. Richard Lynch describes the play in the finals on page 20 of the April 1998 issue of the USHA's *Handball*:

> The eight-women A division came down to one in a series of finals pitting players representing Texas A&M and Southwest Missouri State. This time, SMSU came out on top as Robin Collins defeated Jennifer Powis in a tiebreaker.
>
> The first game lived up to the crowd's expectations. Collins led 20-16, but Powis showed her determination in mounting a comeback to win 21-20.

The second game was equally as exciting, but this time Collins prevailed 21-17., forcing a tiebreaker. And like the preceding two games, the third was very entertaining. Collins pulled away to win 11-3.

In the women's B division, 16 players, those who dropped down from a first-round loss, vied for the championship. In the round of 16, Nicole Nelson defeated Brenda Godsey of Southwest Missouri State University 21-8, 21-14; Karla Wray defeated Tamra Kay of Southwest Missouri State University 10-21, 21-12, 11-6; Cortni Sedgwick of Southwest Missouri State University defeated Ryan West 21-9, 21-14 and Debbie Gibson of Southwest Missouri State University defeated Janna Althaus 21-10, 21-9. In the quarterfinals, Nicole Nelson defeated Carol Salinas of the University of Texas 21-4, 21-12 and Anna Youngerman of Lake Forest College defeated Karla Wray 21-14, 12-21, 11-10. In the finals, Cortni Sedgewick of Southwest Missouri State University defeated Nikki (Nicole) Nelson 21-3, 21-9.

Ryan West was the lone Aggie playing in the women's C division. She won her first match (quarterfinals) defeating Brenda Godsey of Southwest Missouri State University 21-14, 17-21, 11-10. A tired Ryan West could not muster enough energy to win the semifinals. Tamra Kay of Southwest Missouri State University defeated her 21-18, 21-4.

The top 32 women handball players in the collegiate ranks played in the Open, A, B, and C divisions. Other women at the tournament played for the fun and experience and began in the Contenders division. No Aggies competed in the preliminary round. In the round of 16, Kelly King of Lake Forest College defeated Carolyn McCrary 21-16, 21-7. Carolyn would now drop down into the Challengers division.

In the quarterfinals of the Challengers division, Carolyn McCrary defeated Mie Iwasaki of Pacific University 21-16, 21-9 and in the semifinals, Carolyn McCrary defeated Jennifer Chang of the University of Texas 21-14, 21-15. Coach Lance Lowy described the Challenger division finals on page 21 of the April 1998 issue of the USHA's *Handball:*

> The women's Challengers was a new addition in the seven-Division drop-down format used for the first time. This Division was made up of first and second round losers in the C and Contenders. Once these players lost their first match, they had to win their second match to get into the Challengers.
>
> It was apparent in the final that Carolyn McCrary's preparation and hard work was going to pay off. The Texas A&M player controlled the tempo, varying her serves and moving Pacific's Ruth Ann Heim around the court. All the good rallies seemed to end with McCrary winning and she took the championship with a solid 21-11, 21-8 victory.

There were no Aggies entered in the women's Novice division.

There was only one Aggie team entered in the Women's Handball Doubles Championship. However, the good news was that the team was the reigning doubles champions, Priscilla Kojin and Stacey Tuttle. Lance Lowy described the play on page 22 in the April 1998 issue of the USHA's *Handball:*

> History repeated in the women's doubles as reigning champions Priscilla Kojin and Stacey Tuttle of Texas A&M defended their crown. This time they took down the Rounseville sisters, Amber and Mandy, of Southwest Missouri State 21-17, 21-8.
>
> The first game had all the ingredients of great doubles—teamwork, digging, shooting, covering, hustling and emotion. Kojin and Tuttle built an early edge but then had to

hold on to win. The second game was not as dramatic as the champs called on their experience to win easily.

Stacey Tuttle making a right corner kill in the women's doubles final

(*Handball*, April 1998, page 22)

In semifinals, Kojin and Tuttle had little difficulty winning over Maggie Grelle and Robin Collins of SMSU 21-5, 21-11. However, the other semi presented a real battle. Long rallies and great hustle characterized the Rounsevilles' 21-20, 11-21,11-6 triumph over Sabrina Zamora and Tanya Lazaro of Lake Forest.

The eleven team division featured a thrilling preliminary match when four SMSU players locked up. After splitting two games, Brenda Godsey and D'Lynn Robinson edged Debbie Gibson and Tamra Kay 11-10. This gave them the right to face Kojin and Tuttle, who coasted 21-4, 21-3.

At the tournament, the men's team placed third with 601 points well ahead of the fourth-place team, University College of Dublin with 477 points. Southwest Missouri had a comfortable lead in second place with 690 points.

The Aggie women's team placed second with 624 points. Southwest Missouri State University was the champion with a comfortable total of 720 points. The third-place team was Lake Forest College with 573 points.

In the combined team standings, the Aggies were in third place with 1,225 total points. That total was well ahead of the University of Pacific's 1,001 points, but Lake Forest College ended with a comfortable lead over the Aggies with 1,323 total points.

As the 1998-99 school year emerged Coach Lowy would be without his handball star, Priscilla Kojin, who had moved on to a career beyond college. Lowy had been there before and now had to develop the new handball players to continue the strong handball tradition at Texas A&M. With newcomer Brad Alesi, Lowy knew that he had a star in the making. Lake Forest College, in the western suburbs of Chicago, hosted the newly named USHA International Collegiate Handball Tournament.

In the men's Open singles first round (round of 64), Brad Wallner defeated Matt Steele of Pacific University 21-16, 21-10; Brad Alesi defeated Rafael Martinez of University of California 21-10, 21-10; Mike Bargman of Lake Forest College defeated Mark Hill 21-8, 21-15; Tony Cisneros defeated Kevin Price of Mesa State College 14-21, 21-19, 11-8; Ben Barbour defeated Keith Parker of Southwest Missouri State University 21-16, 21-10; Joe Hagen of Lake Forest College defeated Richard Reynosa 21-7, 21-8; Brandon Cuaresma of Southwest Missouri State University defeated Jeremy Doege 21-11, 21-16; Mike Munson of Lake Forest College defeated Nathan Rucker (no score given) and Jason Green defeated Craig Prather of US Air Force Academy 21-14, 21-8.

In the round of 32, Ricky McCann of University of Ulster, Ireland defeated Brad Wallner 21-8, 21-10; Brad Alesi defeated Shane Dormer of University of Dublin, Ireland 21-19, 21-12; Jai Ragoo of Lake Forest College defeated Tony Cisneros 21-16, 21-17; Ben Barbour defeated Jay Sprenger of Southwest Missouri State University 10-21, 21-18, 11-2 and Jamie Simon of Southwest Missouri State University defeated Jason Green 21-12, 19-21, 11-3.

In the round of 16, Brad Alesi defeated Mike Bargman of Lake Forest College 21-10, 21-17 and Jai Ragoo of Lake Forest College defeated Ben Barbour 21-16, 16-21, 11-10. In the quarterfinals, Anton Wilson, a professional handball player, defeated Brad Alesi 17-21, 21-14, 11-10.

The men's A singles featured those who were defeated in the round of 32 of the Open singles. Jeff Werstein of Lake Forest College defeated Brad Wallner 21-17, 21-14; Tony Cisneros defeated Jay Sprenger of Southwest Missouri State University 21-17, 17-21, 11-3 and Jason Green defeated Chris Talley of Southwest Missouri State University 21-11, 21-15. Moving into the quarterfinals, Bill Mehilos of Lake Forest College defeated Tony Cisneros 21-5, 21-17 and Larry Neves of Fresno City College defeated Jason Green 21-12, 21-5. At this point no Aggies remained in the A division singles.

Moving to the men's B singles were those who were defeated in the first round of 64 of the Open singles division. Mark Hill defeated John Nolan of University of Galway, Ireland 21-8, 20-21, 11-7; Richard Reynosa defeated Brett Frost of Southwest Missouri State University 12-21, 21-9, 11-0; Jacob Kunkle of US Air Force Academy defeated Jeremy Doege 21-19, 21-16 and Padraic Gaffney of Dublin Institute of Technology, Ireland defeated Nathan Rucker 21-11, 21-8. In the round of 16, Jeff Cheng of University of California defeated Mark Hill 21-14, 21-14 and Ho (no name or college/university listed) defeated Richard Reynosa 21-7, 21-20. No Aggies advanced to the quarterfinals.

The only Aggies entered in the men's Open doubles competition was the team of Brad Wallner and Tony Cisneros. In the round of 32, they defeated Nick Vilelle and Tom Marks of Southwest Missouri State University 21-19, 21-15. In the round of 16, they defeated the team of Craig Prather and Jake Kunkle of US Air Force Academy 21-10, 21-14, and in the quarterfinals, Mike Munson and Jai Ragoo of Lake Forest College defeated Wallner and Cisneros 21-7, 21-6.

Men's C singles began with those players not in the top 64 of the Open division. All Aggies received a bye in the first round and advanced to the round of 64. In the round of 64, Chad Lucas defeated Joe DeFilippo of US Military Academy 21-7, 21-11; Morris Libson defeated Mark McNamara of US Military Academy 21-11, 21-20; Ben Levine defeated Lawrence Aguiar of Las Positas College 21-14, 21-11; Danny Knapp defeated Nicholas Vilelle of Southwest Missouri State University 21-17, 21-8; Ryan Miller defeated Randy James of Las Positas College 21-14, 21-10 and Wesley Larkin defeated Andy Gonzalez of San Jose State University 21-10, 21-18.

In the round of 32, Chad Lucas defeated Allan Hall of the University of Texas 21-3, 21-7; Morris Libson defeated Michael Corley of University of Galway, Ireland 21-10, 21-7; Ben Levine defeated Tom Marks of Southwest Missouri State University (no score given); Danny Knapp defeated Arne Gibbs of US Military Academy (no score given); Ali Ranganian of Las Positas College defeated Ryan Miller 21-16, 21-9 and Wesley Larkin defeated Michael Haywood of US Military Academy 21-20, 21-15.

At this point of the men's C singles, those advancing from the round of 32 were joined by the round of 32 losers in men's B singles division. In the combined round of 32 in men's C singles, Chad Lucas defeated Jason James of the University of Texas 21-2, 21-6; Zach Kinzer of Pacific University defeated Morris Libson 21-10, 21-10; Craig Prather of US Air Force Academy defeated Ben Levine 21-7, 21-8; David Tormey of University of Galway, Ireland defeated Danny Knapp 21-8, 21-5; Nathan Rucker defeated Mark Kanpetch of the University of Texas 21-13, 21-10; Morris Martin of University of Galway, Ireland defeated Wesley Larkin (no score given) and Jeremy Doege defeated Calvin Lee of California University 21-2, 21-5.

In the round of 16, Rafael Martinez of California University defeated Chad Lucas 21-12, 21-20; Troy Frandson of Southwest Missouri State University defeated Nathan Rucker 21-16, 21-16 and Michael McClean of Dublin Institute of Technology, Ireland defeated Jeremy Doege 20-21, 21-6, 11-6. No Aggies remained in men's C division singles.

There were no Aggies defeated in the first round or in the round of 64 of C division matches, so there were no Aggies entered in the Challengers division.

Those defeated in the round of 32 of C division dropped down to the Contenders division. Ryan Miller was the only Aggie in the Contenders division, and he left his mark. Greg Stinson reported the action under the heading of "Love of Speed, Power Evident for Miller" in the April 1999 issue of the USHA's *Handball*, page 15:

> In his free time, Ryan Miller builds racing cars. The junior from Texas A&M loves "speed and power," and reflects this in the way he plays handball.
>
> Miller powered his way to the Contenders championship, capturing the title by defeating Tom Marks from Southwest Missouri State 21-7, 21-6. Marks, a football player for SMSU, began playing handball this year for cross-training and to stay in shape during the off-season. This was only his third tournament.
>
> Both players stayed even in the opening stages of the first game, but then Miller raced to a nine-point lead, scoring four points off aces. Marks was unable to recover and Miller's devastating back-wall kills sealed the victory.
>
> Marks exhibited his own power in the second game but was unable to build a lead. Miller's quickness and endurance, developed on the soccer field, allowed him to survive most of Marks' attempts to pass or kill. After two eight-point runs, Miller closed out the second game and the championship.
>
> Both finalists had difficult roads to the championship match. Marks defeated Neil McDermott from Galway, Ireland, in the quarterfinals. In Marks' semifinal match, he needed a tiebreaker to defeat Daniel Lucero of San Jose State.
>
> Miller went to war against two players from the US Military Academy to advance to the final. He defeated Arne Gibbs, a junior at USMA with two years in handball, in the quarters.
>
> Miller was almost eliminated in the semis by Mike Haywood, also a junior at USMA. Haywood was able to get a glove on every one of Miller's shots, and led by as much as 10 points in both games. But Haywood could not close out either game, which allowed Miller to come back in heart-stopping fashion from a 20-15 deficit in the first and a 19-9 deficit in the second.

Ryan Miller did whatever it took to take the Contenders championship. Here he is shown making a diving retrieve.

(*Handball*, April 1999, page 15)

There were no Aggie men participants in the Novice singles division.

For the first time, coaches voted to add another doubles championship. This was for the players who lost in the first round of the Open division. The new doubles division was an exhibition this year and did not count toward team points. No Aggies participated in the doubles exhibition matches.

Gone from the women's team were stars of the past and a new group was anxious to test their skill with the nation's best collegiate handball players. In the women's Open singles first round, Sandi Bruner defeated Kara Hodges of Pacific University 21-6, 21-10; Christina Matthews defeated Karyn Buckmaster of Pacific University 21-6, 21-16; Karla Wray defeated Megan Mirczak of US Military Academy 21-8, 21-6; Lisa Barker defeated Kim Pompa of Lake Forest College 21-7, 21-13; Wendi Dunkel of Pacific University defeated Kindal Dubose 21-16, 21-14; Janna Althaus defeated Shasta Vargas of Pacific University 21-7, 21-7; Elise Fillingham defeated Danielle Gamache of Pacific University 21-8, 18-21, 11-2 and Ryan West received a bye.

In the round of 32, Mary Gerke of Lake Forest College defeated Sandi Bruner 21-8, 21-7; Lenora Coyle of Dublin Institute of Technology, Ireland defeated Christina Matthews 21-8, 21-6; Megan Haug of Pacific University defeated Karla Wray 21-11, 21-10; Claire Heneghan of University of Galway, Ireland defeated Lisa Barker 21-6, 21-6; Ryan West defeated Niamh Conneely of Lake Forest College 21-12, 19-21, 11-5; Janna Althaus defeated Kathy Collins of Southwest Missouri State University 21-10, 16-21, 11-10 and Sabrina Zamora of Lake Forest College defeated Elise Fillingham 21-10, 21-6.

In the round of 16, Kelly Collins of Southwest Missouri State University defeated Ryan West 21-6, 21-6 and Sabrina Zamora of Lake Forest College defeated Janna Althaus 21-10, 21-2.

None of the Aggie women wanted to enter the doubles division.

In women's B division singles, which featured those who dropped down from the round of 16 in the women's Open division, Kelly Collins of Southwest Missouri State University defeated Ryan West 21-15, 21-19 and Megan Haug of Pacific University defeated Janna Althaus 21-12, 21-8.

In women's C division, which featured those who dropped down from the round of 32 in the women's Open division, Sandi Bruner defeated Stephanie Ballard of US Air Force Academy 21-3, 21-2; Deidre Shores of Southwest Missouri State University defeated Christina Matthews 21-11, 21-9; Karla Wray defeated Theresa Gomez of Fresno City College 21-3, 21-16; Christina Diebel of US Air Force Academy defeated Lisa Barker 21-19, 21-8 and Kathy Collins defeated Elise Fillingham 21-6, 21-3. In the quarterfinals, Sandi Bruner defeated Deidre Shores of Southwest Missouri State University 14-21, 21-18, 11-9 and Erica Murriella of Fresno City College defeated Karla Wray 21-6, 17-21, 11-7. In the semifinals, Erica Murriella of Fresno City College defeated Sandi Bruner 21-3, 21-3.

In women's Contenders division, which featured those who dropped down from the first round of the women's Open division singles, Kindal Dubose defeated Shasta Vargas of Pacific University 21-7, 21-5. In the quarterfinals, Kindal Dubose was defeated by the eventual champion Kelly King of Lake Forest College 21-14, 20-21, 11-8.

There were no Aggies in the Novice division.

Once again, the Aggies proved a power in Collegiate handball. The Aggie men finished with 659 points edging out Southwest Missouri State University's 657 points to end up in second behind Lake Forest College with 774 points. The Aggie women were not as strong this year but still came in third with 566 total points behind the 605 points of the Lake Forest College women's team. The combined points for the Aggie team totaled 1,225, which placed them well ahead of the fourth place total of 830 points earned by the Pacific University women's team. Lake Forest College combined team total of 1,379 points was a comfortable margin ahead of the Aggies' third place finish.

The men's runner-up plaque from the National Collegiate Handball Tournament

(Author's Collection)

CHAPTER 11
A&M Handball Teams 2000-2009

**NOTE: All handball players listed in this Chapter are from Texas
A&M unless the player's college or university is listed.**

As the 21st century began, the question was: can the Aggies continue the handball success of past years? Coach Lowy knew the challenge to get to the top was always there, but remaining there was fragile. However, Lowy knew he had some future stars at A&M and was anxious to begin. The upcoming National Collegiate Handball Tournament would be held at Southwest Missouri State University in Springfield, Missouri. It should be noted that the Collegiate Commissioners recommended on 30 and 31 July 1999, in a meeting at Lake Forest College between coaches and members of the USHA board, that the word "International" be dismissed and the annual collegiate handball tournament be known as the National Collegiate Handball Tournament. The suggestion was approved.

The men's 2000 Open singles opened with the round of 64. Vincent Letteri of Harvard University defeated Jeremy Doege 21-7, 21-12; Keith Vassall of Lake Forest College defeated Chad Lucas 21-16, 21-16; Silas Goldman of Southwest Missouri State University defeated Ryan Miller 21-7, 21-0; Jeron Powell defeated Ryan Johnson of Southwest Missouri State University 21-14, 21-14; Jay Sprenger of Southwest Missouri State University defeated Danny Knapp 21-18, 21-5; Zach Lowy defeated Kiel Peck of Pacific University 21-14, 21-7; Richard Reynosa defeated Marcos Florez of the University of Texas 21-7, 21-13; Ross Burke defeated Brandon Simpson of the University of Texas 21-9, 21-6; Keith Parker of Southwest Missouri State University defeated Nathan Rucker 21-15, 11-21, 11-4; Morris Libson defeated Rafael Martinez of the University of California-Berkeley 21-9, 21-16 and Brad Alesi defeated Derek Fritze of the University of Minnesota 21-5, 21-6.

In the round of 32, Mark O'Leary of Lake Forest College defeated Jeron Powell 21-8, 21-8; Nate Podrid of Lake Forest College defeated Zach Lowy 21-7, 21-13; Mike Bargman of Lake Forest College defeated Richard Reynosa 21-3, 21-1; Ross Burke defeated Eamon O'Leary of Lake Forest College 21-13, 21-17; Miles Paine of the University of California-Irvine defeated Morris Libson 11-21, 21-14, 11-5 and Brad Alesi defeated Chris Talley of the University of Nebraska 21-9, 21-6.

In the round of 16, Kevin Pettus of Southwest Missouri State University, who had qualified once for the pro tour, defeated Ross Burke 21-12, 21-7 and Brad Alesi defeated Padraig Gaffney of Dublin Institute of Technology, Ireland 21-8, 21-6.

Lance Lowy described the action in the quarter and semi-final matches as reported in the April 2000 issue of the USHA's *Handball*, page 4:

The men's Open Division at the USHA National Collegiate Tournament showcased the best our game has to offer at this level. The championship match pitted the top Irish and the top American college players today.

The quarterfinals went pretty much by the book as Brady whipped much-improved Mark O'Leary of Lake Forest 21-4, 21-6, Bargman stopped teammate and doubles partner Mike Munson 21-13, 21-17, Pettus got the best of UC-Irvine's Miles Paine 21-16, 21-11 and Alesi beat former Illinois junior rival Bill Mehilos of LFC, the current 19-and-under national juniors' champion, 21-13, 21-8.

In the semis, Brady defeated Mike Bargman of Lake Forest College in a well-played match. The difference was that Brady executed his game plan better and advanced to the final with a 21-12, 21-9 win.

On the other side of the bracket, Alesi tangled with Kevin Pettus of Southwest Missouri State. This match was a war.

It was nip-and-tuck in the first game until Alesi built a lead at 15-11 with low power serves to the right and flat kills with both hands. It seemed every rally lasted a couple of minutes until an opportunity presented itself and Alesi took advantage, winning the first grueling game 21-17. Everyone knew it was going to be a fight when Alesi got the 21st point and Pettus screamed, "Good, let's play a tiebreaker!"

Pettus, who has qualified once for the pro tour, slowed the pace in the second game with an effective lob serve that affected Alesi's game. The result was a 21-18 Pettus victory. The tie-breaker was blood (literally) and gut check. At a 7-7 tie, Alesi made a run to 10, but was stopped by Pettus on a clean pass to the left. After a Pettus error, Alesi won the match with a rollout in the right corner, and both warriors walked off the court to a standing ovation.

In the finals top-seeded Paul Brady of Dublin Institute of Technology simply had more in the tank emotionally, as every furious rally lasted until an opportunity presented itself. Unbelievable hustle and gets were the norm as Brady and his challenger, sophomore Brad Alesi of Texas A&M, went at it.

Brad Alesi showing the form that propelled him into the Championship match of the men's Open singles

(*Handball*, April 2000, page 3)

These tremendously gifted athletes put on a show the fans won't soon forget, with Brady prevailing on this day 21-17, 21-15.

In the men's A singles, which included players who dropped down from the Open singles after they were defeated in the round of 32, Michael Hausman of Harvard University defeated Jeron Powell 21-20, 21-11; Zach Lowy defeated Leo Arensberg of Lake Forest College 21-17, 20-21, 11-5; Eamon O'Leary of Lake Forest College defeated Richard Reynosa 21-13, 21-13 and Morris Libson defeated Keith Parker of Southwest Missouri State University 21-9, 21-12.

In the quarterfinals, Joe Duran of San Jose State University defeated Zach Lowy 21-2, 21-14 and Morris Libson defeated Eamon O'Leary of Lake Forest College 21-14, 21-6. In the semifinals, Morris Libson defeated Nick Brown of Lake Forest College 20-21, 21-8, 11-8.

Lance Lowy described the action of the championship match of the men's A division singles as reported on page 12 of the April 2000 issue of the USHA's *Handball*. The heading of the article was a play on words: "Libson Makes His Opponent Pay the Price."

> The final of the men's A division, consisting of players who won their first round and lost their second, was one of the best matches of the tournament.
>
> Morris Libson of Texas A&M came out serving and shooting and took the first game 21-10 over Kevin Price of Mesa State College. But in a distinct turnaround, Price forced the action and beat Libson in the second game 21-9.
>
> The tiebreaker was filled with drama as Price shot his way to a 9-2 lead. Then it appeared that a light went on in Libson's head as he inched his way back into the game.
>
> Price became conservative with his lead, choosing to fist everything to the ceiling rather than go on the offensive. Libson, on the other hand, was looking to shoot everything. If Price fisted to the ceiling and it came off the back wall, Libson flattened it. If Price missed the ceiling; Libson shot it.
>
> With no timeouts left, Price could only watch as Libson reeled off nine straight points to seal the victory 11-9.
>
> Libson was then mobbed by his Texas A&M teammates, who poured into the court.

In the men's B division, consisting of players who were defeated in the first round of 64 of the men's Open singles, Jeremy Doege defeated Alex May of the University of Illinois 21-15, 21-20; Val Rodriquez of the University of Texas defeated Ryan Miller 21-10, 21-19; Chad Lucas defeated Lawrence Aguiar of Los Positas Junior College 21-10, 21-8; Danny Knapp defeated Steve Chen of the University of California-Berkeley 21-13, 21-15 and Nathan Rucker defeated Oleg Daurov of Pacific University 21-15, 21-11.

In the round of 16, Jeremy Doege defeated Joe Luetkenhaus of Southwest Missouri State University 21-17, 21-10; Chad Lucas defeated Chad McCormick of Oregon State University 21-8, 21-3; Danny Knapp defeated Josh Lee of the University of Texas 21-15, 21-18 and Rafael Martinez of the University of California-Berkeley defeated Nathan Rucker 21-18, 21-20.

As play continued in the men's B division, Burns Macdonald described the action as reported in the April 2000 issue of the USHA's *Handball*, page 13:

> In the men's B singles, 32 slots were shared by 12 universities. By the semifinals three of five Texas A&M entrants had survived, as had one of four from Cal-Berkeley.
>
> Texas A&M teammates Jeremy Doege and Danny Knapp battled in one semifinal. Doege won a close first game 21-19 and then picked up the pace to win the match 21-8.
>
> In the other semi, Rafael Martinez of Cal-Berkeley played Chad Lucas, the last of the TAMU trio. Lucas' strong kill shot was a big factor in the first game but Martinez won 21-16 using an excellent power serve to the left-handed Lucas's off hand. The second game was dominated by Martinez 21-10 as he gained confidence in his very effective kill shots.

In the B final Doege lost a close first game to Martinez 21-17. The second game was a different matter when he was able to keep Martinez mostly on the defensive, winning 21-10.

The tiebreaker was Doege's 11-4, as a tiring Martinez's kills were just not low enough.

Doege's strong, steady game earned him the title of champion in a field of remarkably good B players.

In the men's C division singles round of 64, Wes Larkin defeated Dan Lucero of San Jose State University 21-14, 21-14; Bill Phillips received a bye and Jarrett Roberts defeated Jason Hurja of Western Washington University 21-17, 21-10. In the round of 32, Wes Larkin defeated Chris Burke of Pacific University 21-7, 21-10; Bill Phillips defeated Manuel Moreno of San Jose State University 21-18, 21-14 and Jarrett Roberts defeated Brian DeLucchi of Los Positas Junior College 21-14, 21-3.

At this point the round of 32, winners were joined by the losers in the round of 32 from the men's B singles division. Wes Larkin defeated Bryce Grady of the University of Minnesota 21-13, 21-11; Ryan Miller defeated Abe Cuddeback of the US Air Force Academy 21-10, 21-20; Bill Phillips defeated Dustin Kochis 21-8, 21-11 and Jason Stuwe of Pacific University defeated Jarrett Roberts 21-19, 21-18.

In the round of 16, Alex May of the University of Illinois defeated Wes Larkin 21-6, 21-9; Ryan Miller defeated Scott Heuston of Pacific University 21-16, 21-14 and Bill Phillips defeated Jason Stuwe of Pacific University 21-8, 21-8. In the quarterfinals, Ryan Miller defeated John Page of the US Air Force Academy 21-17, 17-21, 11-8 and Bill Phillips defeated Edgar Marquez of San Jose State University 21-16, 21-16. In the semifinals, Alex May of the University of Illinois defeated Ryan Miller 21-6, 21-7 and Bill Phillips defeated Brandon Simpson of the University of Texas 12-21, 21-11, 11-1.

This set up the championship match between Alex May of the University of Illinois and Bill Phillips. Larry Aguiar described the action as reported in the April 2000 issue of the USHA's *Handball*, pages 13 and 14:

> May survived the strong 32 player C division. He was also one of the few players without a coach to turn to for particulars on playing weaknesses of opponents. May did it all on his own and capped his weekend with a huge 21-4, 21-2 victory over Bill Phillips of Texas A&M.
>
> May used mainly a power serve, but he has developed a good ceiling shot selection on defense, too. All of May's shots commanded a good deal of power, as was obvious to Phillips. Phillips has been playing for two years and learned the game from Coach Lance Lowy of Texas A&M.
>
> Phillips started playing handball to keep in shape for basketball and found that it only took one more player to get a great workout, not like basketball, where you need a few guys to really compete and play a good game. And Lowy also makes it lots of fun to play.
>
> "Coach Lowy is the man," said Phillips.
>
> Phillips dominated his earlier matches until he found May in the finals.
>
> "Alex handled me like I had been handling all of my opponents." said Phillips. "I gave him a very good game, but his power just kept me off balance and forced many hand errors. He played very well and I certainly need more court time and practice to beat him."
>
> In May's five C matches, no opponent scored in double figures.

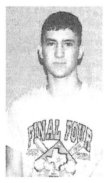

Morris Libson   Jeremy Doege   Bill Phillips
A Singles   B Singles   C Singles
Champion   Champion   2nd

(Three photos from the USHA's *Handball*, April 2000, Libson page 12, Doege page 13, Phillips page 14.)

There were no Aggie men in the Contenders, Challengers, or Novice divisions. Also, the Aggie men did not participate in the Open or B doubles division competition.

As the women's Open singles play began, A&M had only one entrant in the first round. Megan Head was defeated by Carmen McClelland of Southwest Missouri State University and would drop down to the Contenders singles division.

In the round of 32, Christina Matthews defeated Terri Lynch of Southwest Missouri State University 21-9, 21-8; Kelly King of Lake Forest College defeated Jennifer Minarcik 21-8, 21-3; Karla Wray defeated Jessie Wachter of Pacific University 21-7, 21-5 and Ryan West defeated Kelly Smith of Southwest Missouri State University 21-1, 21-4.

In the round of 16, Erika Sove of Lake Forest College defeated Christina Matthews 21-9, 21-4; Robin Collins of Southwest Missouri State University defeated Karla Wray 21-11, 21-14 and Ryan West defeated Amy Sove of Lake Forest College 21-3, 21-7. In the quarterfinals, Sabrina Zamora of Lake Forest College defeated Ryan West 21-2, 21-8. At this point no Aggie women remained in Open singles.

In the women's B singles were those who dropped down from the Open round of 16. In the quarter-finals, Kelly King of Lake Forest College defeated Christina Matthews and Karla Wray defeated Rebecca Brown of Southwest Missouri State University (no scores were given in the quarterfinals). In the semi-finals, Karla Wray defeated Amy Sove of Lake Forest College 21-13, 21-13 to set up the championship match between Wray and Mary Gerke of Lake Forest College.

The championship match was reported in the April 2000 issue of the USHA's *Handball*, page 9. The report was written by Mike Dau and Mary Gerke:

> Two seniors competing in their final national collegiates put on an outstanding exhibition of handball in the women's B final. Neither Mary Gerke of Lake Forest nor Karla Wray of Texas A&M had trouble advancing to the final. They saved the fireworks for the championship match.
>
> Wray overcame a large deficit in the first game to win a squeaker 21-19. But Gerke regained lost momentum and rallied for a convincing 21-10 win in game 2.
>
> In the tiebreaker, Gerke jumped to a 5-0 lead, most of those points resulting from an excellent three-wall serve. Wray did bounce back with several touch serves of her own,

closing the gap to 5-4. When Gerke regained the serve, she ran off three quick points to make it 8-4 and after several exchanges closed out the match 11-6.

In the semifinals, after some players had already played three previous matches, Wray defeated Amy Sove of Lake Forest 21-13, 21-13 in a very long and physically exhausting match. Both women played extremely well, but serves and scrappy defense were what brought Wray to the finals, Gerke caught a break and advanced on forfeit.

In the women's C singles division, featuring those who dropped down from the round of 32 in the Open division, Jennifer Minarcik defeated Carmen McClelland of Southwest Missouri State University 21-9, 21-6. In the quarterfinals, Jennifer Minarcik defeated Terri Lynch of Southwest Missouri State University 21-14, 21-18 and in the semifinals, Angels Lightner of Pacific University defeated Jennifer Minarcik 21-14, 21-18.

Megan Head was defeated in the first round of the women's Open division, so dropped down into the Contenders division where she was defeated by Elizabeth Rini of the US Air Force Academy 21-10, 21-1. This loss dropped her into the Novice division where she defeated Emily Vinson of the US Air Force Academy 21-1, 21-7. This set up the championship match between Head and Susan Doyle of Pacific University. Mike Steele described the individuals and action under an article headed "Finalists Outstanding Players and Outstanding Individuals". The following write-up was in the April 2000 issue of the USHA's *Handball*, page 11:

> The finalists in the women's Novice division came from very different colleges: Texas A&M, a huge school, and tiny Pacific University, with barely 1,000 undergrads.
>
> But A&M's Megan Head and Pacific's Susan Doyle shared many more factors in their lives than those things separating them. Both have played soccer, both were juniors in college, and both were in their first collegiate tournament.
>
> More to the point, however, is the fact that these two players represent the best in the college game for what they have done with their lives and gifts.
>
> Head, an education major, hails from Dallas, where she was a founding member of the Young Variety Clubs of North Texas. This organization is deeply involved with many charity functions for underprivileged children, such as building a playground at an orphanage in Dallas, sponsoring a gala Christmas party for 1,100 wide-eyed youngsters, adopting a family for sharing the Christmas holidays and developing a home for abused children.
>
> Doyle, a social work major, spent Pacific's three-week winter break doing service learning at the Navajo reservation at the Four Corners area of northeast Arizona, specifically working with children at the Lukachukai Boarding School. She also chopped wood for needy Navajo elders and was welcomed into the Navajo nation in several of their ceremonies.
>
> If you ever wonder about the state of the game of handball, meeting and getting to know two such wonderful young

Karla Wray
2nd
Women's B Singles

(Handball, April 2000, page 9)

Megan Head
2nd
Women's Novice Singles

(Handball, April 2000, page 11)

players, who have already made major contributions to the world they live in, will renew your faith in the future of the game and those who will carry it.

On the court, Doyle won the novice class over Head 21-6, 21-4. Doyle used a variety of well-placed serves, operated efficiently with back-wall shots and sustained quality shots in the rallies.

To reach the novice finals, both players defeated competitors from Air Force, Doyle defeated Danielle Willard 21-8, 21-2 and Head stopped Emily Vinson 21-1, 21-7. Both showed good court coverage and serving skills in these wins.

The men's team finished in third just being nosed out by Southwest Missouri State University's 700 points to A&M's 699. The women's team also earned third with a total of 500 points which was well behind Lake Forest College's 716 points. The combined team total points were 1,199 points and earned a third place finish.

One of the highlights of the tournament was the awarding of the sportsmanship awards. It was a thrill for the Aggies to hear the name of Ryan West called as the women's winner.

Bob Hickman, President of the USHA, presents the sportsmanship awards at the USHA National Collegiate Tournament to Jermaine Ervin of Hardin-Simmons and Ryan West of Texas A&M.

(*Handball*, April 2000, page 2)

The 2000 Aggie Handball team

Team Members are Christina Matthews, Jennifer Minarcik, Karla Wray, Ryan West, Megan Head, Jeremy Doege, Chad Lucas, Ryan Miller, Jeron Powell, Danny Knapp, Zach Lowy, Richard Reynosa, Ross Burke, Nathan Rucker, Morris Libson, Wes Larkin, Bill Phillips, Jarrett Roberts, Brad Alesi, and Coach Lance Lowy

(*Handball*, April 2000, page 13)

As the 2000-01 school year started, Coach Lowy had reason to be optimistic. He had a star handball player in Brad Alesi and now his sister Lynn, who had won many junior titles, had enrolled at A&M and joined the team. As the time for the National Collegiate Tournament neared all were looking forward to playing in the courts at the University of Minnesota.

In the men's Open singles round of 64, Brad Alesi defeated Pedro Villa of the University of California-Berkeley 21-10, 21-7; Richard Reynosa defeated Christian Knapp of the University of Nebraska 12-21, 21-13, 11-4; Morris Libson defeated Roger Hill of Hardin-Simmons 21-12, 21-8; Jay Sprenger of Southwest Missouri State University defeated Greg Harkey 21-8, 21-8; Juan Zavala defeated Nick Brown of the University of Minnesota 21-6, 21-6; Chad Lucas defeated Brian Johnson of the University of Minnesota 21-10, 21-1; Brian Ault of the University of Southern California defeated Danny Knapp 21-14, 21-7; Jeremy Doege defeated Kiel Peck of Pacific University 21-7, 21-6; Jeron Powell defeated Jacob Knapp of the University of Nebraska 21-11, 21-10 and Zach Lowy defeated Matt Dean of Southwestern University 21-1, 21-8.

In the round of 32, Brad Alesi defeated Oliver Conway of National University of Ireland-Galway 21-13, 21-1; David Munson of Lake Forest College defeated Richard Reynosa 21-8, 21-5; Morris Libson defeated Xabi Laduche of the University of California-Berkeley 21-15, 21-6; Matt Steele of Pacific University defeated Juan Zavala 21-2, 21-17; Mark O'Leary of Lake Forest College defeated Chad Lucas 21-9, 21-1; Mike Munson of Lake Forest College defeated Jeremy Doege 21-7, 21-6; Padraig Gaffney of Dublin Institute of Technology, Ireland defeated Jeron Powell 21-17, 21-6 and Shane Vigen of Lake Forest College defeated Zach Lowy 21-4, 21-8.

In the round of 16, Brad Alesi defeated Jordan Fromstein of Lake Forest College 21-9, 21-11 and David Munson of Lake Forest College defeated Morris Libson 21-4, 21-4. In the quarter finals, Brad Alesi defeated David Munson of Lake Forest College 14-21, 21-20, 11-6 and in the semifinals, Brad Alesi defeated Dessie Keegan of Dublin Institute of Technology, Ireland 14-21, 21-5,11-0. Coach Lance Lowy described the story of the finals which was reported on page 5 of the April 2001issue of the USHA's *Handball*:

> Defending champion Paul Brady could not make the trip from Ireland, so the men's Open title was up for grabs. And Eoin Kennedy of Dublin City University looked as sharp as ever, keeping the crown on the other side of the Atlantic by routing Brad Alesi of Texas A&M 21-7, 21-4 in the final.
>
> The final was somewhat anticlimactic as Alesi's right shoulder bothered him. Kennedy, being the veteran he is, exploited Alesi's weaknesses.
>
> While the match should not demean how well Alesi played all weekend, Kennedy played with confidence and poise and is a champion in every sense of the word.
>
> "Brad's very good," said Kennedy after winning his first collegiate championship. "I could tell he was pumped up and ready to play. In the second game he started favoring his right shoulder and I knew he was not 100 percent; I just played my game."
>
> Indeed, Alesi's right shoulder was hurting. He even started serving with his left hand in the second game. "I haven't played with my right hand in nine months," said Alesi. "This weekend was the first time I used my right and I played a lot of handball this weekend. Next year is my senior year and I'll be in shape and ready to play."

In the men's A, composed of those who were defeated in the round of 32 in the men's Open division, Richard Reynosa defeated Xabi Laduche of the University of California-Berkeley 21-14, 21-6; Chad Lucas defeated Juan Zavala 21-4, 21-9; Jeremy Doege defeated Bergan Hugos of the US Air Force Academy 21-14, 21-12; Eamon O'Leary of Lake Forest College defeated Jeron Powell 21-4, 21-15 and Zach Lowy defeated Chad McCormick of Oregon State University 21-8, 20-21, 11-4.

In the quarterfinals, Oliver Conway of National University of Ireland-Galway, defeated Richard Reynosa 21-18, 11-21, 11-6; Chad Lucas defeated Rafael Martinez of the University of California-Berkeley 21-2, 21-7; Jeremy Doege defeated Dave McAndrew of Dublin City University, Ireland 21-13, 21-9 and Zach Lowy defeated Eamon O'Leary of Lake Forest College 21-18, 21-19. Coach Lance Lowy described the road to the championship of the men's A division on page 9 of the April 2001 issue of the USHA's *Handball*:

> Nothing was easy for Oliver Conway, but he persevered and captured the men's A championship by winning four very tight matches.
>
> Conway, representing NUI Galway in Ireland, opened with a close 21-20, 21-19 victory over hard-working Richard Reynosa of Texas A&M. Then Conway got the best of another A&M player, Chad Lucas, in a 21-20, 21-18 semifinal war.
>
> By now used to nail-biters, Conway faced yet another Texas A&M standout in Jeremy Doege for the championship. Conway overcame an early Doege push in which the senior won 21-18 in the first game. But Conway got hot and cut down on his mistakes in the second game and dominated 21-5.
>
> The tiebreaker was two different situations. Doege was up 7-2, but then Conway methodically came back and, point by point, knotted it up. Conway did not make any more errors and shot the ball well to win 11-8.

In the men's B division were those players eliminated by first round losses in the round of 64 of the men's Open division, and who won in the round of 32 to determine who would continue in the B division and who would drop down into the C division. In the round of 32, Danny Knapp defeated Pedro Villa of the University of California-Berkeley 21-7, 21-9 and Richard Berger of Oregon State University defeated Greg Harkey 21-14, 21-15. In the round of 16, Danny Knapp defeated Alex May of the University of Illinois 17-21, 21-20, 11-3. In the quarterfinals, Pat Nolan of Limerick University, Ireland defeated Danny Knapp 21-8, 13-21, 11-3.

All of those men at the National Collegiate Handball Tournament not in the top 64 began their play in the men's C division. The first round of play was to determine which players would continue in the C's round of 64. In the first round, Jarrett Roberts defeated Matt Walsh of Southwest Missouri State University 21-5, 21-7; Chris Moeller of the US Air Force Academy defeated Josh Cuttill 21-3, 21-9; Chad O'Neal defeated Bryce Grady of the University of Minnesota 21-12, 21-15; Lance Hoffman defeated Kevin Flynn of the University of California-Berkeley 21-2, 21-3; Colin Corcoran defeated Dave Hunn of Western Washington University 21-6, 21-1; Jon Fox defeated Connor McGinty of Dublin Institute of Technology, Ireland 21-7, 21-11; Lance Hoffman defeated Derrick Tiveron of Lake Forest College 21-13, 21-7; Jarrett Roberts defeated (no first name listed) Krueger of the University of California-Berkeley 21-8, 21-10; (no first name listed) Cole of the University of Texas defeated Chad O'Neal 21-10, 21-3 and Lee Nichols defeated Ray Burzie of the University of Illinois 21-18, 21-12. NOTE: There were so many entries that some had to play twice before reaching the round of 64.

In the round of 64, C division, Jon Fox defeated Erich Neupert of Pacific University 21-4, 21-7; Jarrett Roberts defeated Dan Seaver of Pacific University 21-8, 21-11; Chad O'Neal defeated John Root of Lake Forest College 21-7, 21-14; Lance Hoffman defeated (first name not given) Gomes of Los Positas College 21-10, 21-8; Colin Corcoran defeated Liam Tuffy of Dublin City University, Ireland 21-5, 21-2 and Lee Nichols defeated Lucas Hanson of Western Washington University 21-5. 21-9.

In the round of 32, Jon Fox defeated Pedro Villa of the University of California-Berkeley 21-14, 21-15; Greg Harkey defeated (first name not listed) Henry of Dublin City University, Ireland 21-14, 21-10; Paul Dunphy defeated Jarrett Roberts 21-6, 21-1; (first name not listed) Aguirre of Lake Forest College defeated Colin Corcoran 21-14, 21-14 and Lee Nichols defeated Peter Davern of National University of Ireland-Galway 21-15, 17-21, injury default. NOTE: Aguirre of Lake Forest College could not be traced so it could not be determined how he earned this place in the round of 32. He was not a drop-down from the round of 64 in the men's Open singles and was not listed anywhere in any round leading up to the round of 32, C division. Obviously, with so many players vying for the championship in men's C division, it was difficult to accurately report all results.

In the round of 16, Nick Villelle of Southwest Missouri State University defeated Jon Fox 21-13, 16-21, 11-6; Derek Fritze defeated Greg Harkey 21-17, 21-18 and Lee Nichols defeated (first name not listed) Congdon of the US Air Force Academy 21-19, 21-20. In the quarterfinals, Lee Nichols was defeated by Dustin Kochis of Pacific University 21-18, 21-20.

There were no Aggies playing in the men's Contenders division.

In the first round of the men's Challenger division, Josh Cuttill defeated J. D. Foy of the US Air Force Academy 21-14, 21-14. In the second round, Josh Cuttill defeated Angelo Belard of the University of California-Berkeley 21-4, 21-10. In the round of 32, Darrin McArdle of Dublin Institute of Technology, Ireland defeated Josh Cuttill 21-10, 21-15. There were no other Aggies in the men's Challenger division.

There were no Aggies playing in the men's Novice division.

The Aggies typically did not enter the men's doubles; however, this year four Aggies decided to play doubles in addition to their singles matches. The A&M teams of Jeremy Doege/Richard Reynosa and Morris Libson/Danny Knapp received a bye during the first round. In the round of 32, Jeremy Doege/ Richard Reynosa defeated Travis Kulwicki/Christian or Jacob Knapp (Knapp's first name was not given) of the University of Nebraska 21-16, 21-17 and Morris Libson/Danny Knapp defeated Gerard and Darrin McArdle of Dublin Institute of Technology, Ireland 21-6, 21-3. In the round of 16, Mark O'Leary/ Keith Vassall of Lake Forest College defeated Jeremy Doege/Richard Reynosa 21-10, 21-12 and Morris Libson/Danny Knapp defeated Peter Davern/(first name not listed) McDermott of National University of Ireland-Galway 21-10, 21-15. In the quarterfinals, Mark O'Leary/Keith Vassall of Lake Forest College defeated Morris Libson/Danny Knapp 21-8, 21-11.

In the first round of the women's Open singles, Joy Fell of Pacific University defeated Heather Henry 21-3, 21-17; Jennifer Fernandez defeated Beth Heim of Southwest Missouri State University 21-2, 21-10; Dara Crain defeated Kim Callaway of Pacific University 21-17, 21-5; Sarah Roberts of Lake Forest College defeated Jennifer Minarcik 21-20, 21-10; Lacy Harkey defeated Terri Guajardo of Hardin-Simmons University 21-3, 21-1; Meagan McDuff defeated Angie King of Hardin-Simmons University 21-10, 21-14; Christina Matthews defeated Jodi Lovell of Hardin-Simmons University 21-1, 21-1; Carrie Lucas defeated Bridgett Lovell of the University of Texas 21-11, 21-11; Kirsten Bode defeated Jodi Reisig of Southwestern University (no score listed) and Lynn Alesi received a bye.

In the round of 32, Samantha England of Lake Forest College defeated Jennifer Fernandez 21-1, 21-3; Erika Sove of Lake Forest College defeated Dara Crain 21-1, 21-3; Leslie Boyle of Lake Forest College defeated Lacy Harkey 21-9, 12-21, 11-5; Kelly Collins of Southwest Missouri State University defeated Meagan McDuff 21-7, 21-3; Christina Matthews defeated Olivia Durr of the University of Texas 21-4, 21-7; Kathy Collins of Southwest Missouri State University defeated Carrie Lucas (no score listed); Amy Sove of Lake Forest College defeated Kirsten Bode 21-2, 21-4 and Lynn Alesi defeated Angela Lum of the University of California-Berkley 21-2, 21-0.

In the round of 16, Kathy Collins of Southwest Missouri State University defeated Christina Matthews, injury default, and Lynn Alesi defeated Kristen Bowerly of Pacific University 21-1, 21-1. In the quarter-finals, Lynn Alesi defeated Emily McPherson of the University of Nebraska 21-8, 21-4. In the semifinals, Lynn Alesi defeated Fiona Healy of Dublin Institute of Technology, Ireland 21-4, 21-4.

As written by Chris Talley and reported on page 6 of the April 2001issue of the USHA's *Handball*, the women's Open singles final match outcome was as expected:

> Megan Mehilos entered the intercollegiate championships as the top seed, then promptly earned it. In fact, she received the top seed as a freshman, which not even David Chapman was given in his first year.
>
> The Lake Forest player faced another freshman, Lynn Alesi of Texas A&M, in the final. Mehilos used her powerful serves and percentage handball to defeat Alesi 21-13, 21-8, by keeping Alesi on defense and staying in control of center court.
>
> The final began at a slow pace. The two Illinois natives went back and forth for the first few points. Mehilos started to pull away midway through the game. Alesi made several attempts at a comeback, but Mehilos pulled away and finished the first game with a pass shot down the left side.
>
> The second game started the same way. It was all Mehilos. She placed her shots like a pro, passing when Alesi started covering the front, killing when Alesi was in the back.
>
> Playing a great game against a great opponent, Mehjilos ended the match to win the championship and prove that she deserved the No. 1 seed.

Christina Matthews was the lone Aggie handball player to drop down into the women's A division. Katee Wolf of the University of Nebraska won the match by injury default. For the official record; Matthews was in the A division; however, her injury happened while she was playing in the women's Open.

In the round of 16, women's B singles, Dara Crain defeated Sarah Roberts of Lake Forest College 21-12, 21-8; Meagan McDuff defeated Rebecca Haschle of the University of Texas 21-12, 21-2; Megan Gibson of Lake Forest College defeated Lacy Harkey 21-8, 21-6; Carrie Lucas defeated Olivia Durr of the University of Texas 21-8, 21-4 and Kirsten Bode defeated Zoilla Murillo of Lake Forest College 21-1, 21-2.

In the quarterfinals, women's B singles division, Meagan McDuff defeated Dara Crain 21-17, 21-12; Megan Gibson of Lake Forest College defeated Carrie Lucas 21-6, 21-10 and Kirsten Bode defeated Page Applegate of Southwest Missouri State University 21-3, 21-13. In the semifinals, Meagan McDuff defeated Fallen Onkels of Western Washington University 21-20, 21-16 and Megan Gibson of Lake Forest College defeated Kirsten Bode 21-12, 18-21, 11-7.

Mark Carpenter described the action of the women's final in B singles division and was reported on page 13 of the April 2001 issue of the USHA's *Handball*:

> If you're playing on Sunday at the collegiates, you're a finalist and one of the rare 20 people yet to be eliminated. This was the case for Meagan McDuff of Texas A&M and Megan Gibson of Lake Forest, who made it to the women's B singles final.
>
> But in that final, it was all Gibson, just as the tourney seemed to be all Lake Forest. Gibson's hard returns and serves were too much for McDuff, who fell 21-1, 21-9.

When McDuff looked at the draw before the semis, she was looking forward to an all-Texas A&M final. However, first she had to beat Fallon Onkels of Western Washington. McDuff was able to overcome Onkels' speed and agility as she won two tight games 21-20, 21-16.

Gibson's road to the final was smoother at least until the semis. There she faced tough Kirsten Bode of Texas A&M. They split two games before Gibson spoiled McDuff's plan for an all-A&M final 11-7.

In the first round of the women's C division, Heather Henry defeated Beth Heim of Southwest Missouri State University 21-11, 21-8 and Jennifer Minarcik defeated Kim Callaway of Pacific University 21-7, 21-14. In the round of 16, Carol Chang of the University of California-Berkeley defeated Heather Henry 21-9, 8-21, 11-7 and Jennifer Minarcik defeated Jodi Reisig of Southwestern University 21-8, 21-6. In the quarterfinals, Jennifer Minarcik defeated Carol Chang of the University of California-Berkeley 21-3, 21-13. In the semifinals, Jennifer Minarcik defeated Angie King of Hardin-Simmons University 18-21, 21-13, 11-2. Mark Carpenter described the action of the women's final in B singles division on page 13 of the April 2001 issue of the USHA's *Handball*:

> The women's C championship match turned out to be one of the closest finals as Kim Hall of Hardin-Simmons squared off with Jennifer Minarcik of Texas A&M, winner of the sportsmanship award.
>
> Minarcik took the first game easily 21-2. But Hall stormed back 21-9 in game 2.
>
> In the tiebreaker, both women were hitting the ball hard and utilized their athletic prowess to the max. Hall had the upper hand in the tiebreaker, winning a close one 11-9.

In the first round of the women's Contenders division, Jodi Reisig of Pacific University defeated Heather Henry 21-10, 21-13. Heather was the only Aggie playing in this division.

Only one Aggie team entered the women's Open doubles division. In the first round, Lynn Alesi/Christina Matthews defeated Andrea Berry/Jodi Reisig of Southwestern University 21-3, 21-2. In the quarterfinals, Lynn Alesi/Christina Matthews defeated Kathy and Kelly Collins of Southwest Missouri State University (score was not listed). In the semifinals, Lynn Alesi/Christina Matthews were defeated by the eventual champions Megan Mehilos/Amy Sove of Lake Forest College and, as in the quarterfinals, no score was listed.

The men's team, the women's team and the combined team came very close to winning it all but the total points of each were just short of Lake Forest's total. The A&M men's team earned 709 points, just behind the 769 of Lake Forest. The women's team totaled 608 points to the 720 for Lake Forest. The combined team points for the Aggies totaled 1,317. The Aggies second place in all teams was well ahead of third place Southwest Missouri State in each of the team points. Southwest Missouri State men's team total was 497, the women's team total was 473 and the combined team was 970.

Sportsmanship award winners
Roger Hill of Hardin-Simmons,
USHA board member Tom Sove,
Jennifer Minarcik of Texas A&M
and Xabi Laduche of Cal-Berkeley

(*Handball* April 2001, page 5)

The 2001 Texas A&M Handball team

PHOTO INCLUDES: Brad Alesi, Richard Reynosa, Morris Libson, Greg Harkey, Juan Zavala. Chad Lucas,
Danny Knapp, Jeremy Doege, Jeron Powell, Zach Lowy, Heather Henry, Jennifer Fernandez, Dara Crain, Jennifer Minarcik,
Lacy Harkey, Meagan McDuff, Christina Matthews, Carrie Lucas, Kirsten Bode, Lynn Alesi, Jarrett Roberts, Josh Cuttill, Chad
O'Neal, Lance Hoffman, Colin Corcoran, Lee Nichols and Coach Lance Lowy

(Courtesy Lance Lowy)

2001 National Collegiate
Handball Championship
Combined Team and Men's
Runner-up Plaques

(Author's Collection)

The start of school year 2001-02 would be an exciting time for A&M handball. Not only did the team have two returning All-Americans in Brad and Lynn Alesi, but for the second time, A&M would host the 2002 National Collegiate Handball Tournament.

The coordination and effort that goes into hosting a successful national collegiate handball tournament is a massive project and creates the opportunity to showcase the best of the hosting college or university. Texas A&M Department of Recreational Sports and the handball club spared no details in providing all that was needed for the 2002 National Collegiate Handball Tournament.

Texas A&M welcome banner to the 220 handball entrants and their coaches.

(*Handball*, April 2002, page 2)

As a testimonial to the success of hosting the tournament by Texas A&M, USHA president Bob Hickman wrote an article about the collegiate handball game that was published in April 2002 in the USHA's *Handball*, pages 2 and 3. Following are some selected quotes from the article:

> Name our largest tournament. The four-wall nationals, of course! Name our second-largest four-wall event. Most players would hesitate answering this one. Perhaps our Masters doubles, junior nationals or Hall of Fame.
>
> Ask anyone closely involved and they'll quickly respond. "The USHA National Collegiate Championships." This event has quietly grown from 50 or so entries many years ago to about 100 entries ten years ago. Today it boasts well over 200 of our college youths engaging in singles and doubles, with team standings. This event could easily grow to more than 300 in the next few years. Our best kept secret is going public!
>
> This year at Texas A&M there were 220 participants representing 32 colleges and universities, including four from Ireland. And 25 of these qualified as a team, with at least three players and an official coach. Nine of the teams' coaches are Commissioners and full voting members of the collegiate committee. These nine have shown longevity, with at least three successive years of participation.
>
> What is it about this tournament that makes it so unique, so interesting? I've decided the answer lies in three aspects: the players, the format and the coaches.
>
> The format of the tournament is also unique. The brain child of Texas A&M coach Lance Lowy, the event uses a multi-drop-down format that allows any player of any skill level to play several competitive matches.
>
> Athletes play for their own victory and also for team scores. The scoring is complicated, but basically the more advanced into the tournament brackets the players get, the more points they score. Team scoring is limited to the top six players to negate a team winning by sheer numbers. Galleries are filled with players from one school cheering loudly for their comrade, countered by those cheers from the other school. The atmosphere is loud, electric, and full of good, old-fashioned fun!
>
> Final team standings are as coveted as an individual victory, At the banquet, rival schools sing their college songs, playfully taunt opposing teams and proudly stand for

their photos as their team is announced as winner or runner-up. The pride on the faces of those players deemed All-Americans radiates throughout the room.

The coaches represent the final aspect of what this event is all about. They work their tails off coaching, raising money, organizing the teams and organizing the tournament. At the pre-tournament seeding meeting, they lobby for their players, scrapping for the best position in the draw. Some have described it as organized mayhem.

They follow matches closely helping their proteges where they can, offering their pride in victory and solace in defeat. They do all of this for the joy of winning and more important, for the joy of being part of a young person's growth and development. They do all this for no money. They do it for the love of the game!

In the photo are the coaches of the teams represented at the 2002 National Collegiate Handball Tournament. They are Larry Aguiar, commissioner, Las Positas; Tommy Burnett, commissioner, Southwest Missouri State; Mike Dau, commissioner, Lake Forest; Greg Stinson, US Military Academy; Lance Lowy, commissioner, Texas A&M; Bill Scharton, commissioner, Air Force Academy; Mike Steele, commissioner, Pacific; Ray Leidich, Oregon State; Warren Simpson, Hardin-Simmons; Pete Tyson, commissioner, Texas; Mike Shaughnessy and Steve Sayers, Cincinnati; Burns Macdonald, commissioner, California-Berkeley; Jeff Cardinal, commissioner, San Jose State; Mike Hiber, Minnesota; Padraig Gaffney, Dublin Institute of Technology; Fred Olsen, Western Washington; Eugene McCormick, Southwestern University; Patrick Devereux, University College of Dublin; John Nolan, National University of Ireland, Galway; Eugene Donaghy, Queens College-Belfast; Marvin Ballwit, Linfield College; Leo Simpson and A. J. Arem, Kentucky; Art Padilla, North Carolina State.

(Handball, April 2002, page 5)

As play began in the round of 64 of the Open singles, Brad Alesi defeated Mike Hejna of Lake Forest College 21-0, 21-1; Barry Durham of Southwest Missouri State University defeated Lee Nichols 21-8, 21-7; Emmett Peixoto of Southwest Missouri State University defeated Chad O'Neal 21-14, 21-8; Juan Zavala defeated Dustin Kochis of Pacific University 21-15, 21-3; Zach Lowy defeated Ben Moore of Pacific University 21-3, 21-1; Raphael Marinez of the University of California-Berkeley defeated Colin Corcoran 21-15, 21-18; David Munson of Lake Forest College defeated Greg Harkey 21-8, 21-3; Ross Burke defeated Robin Lindsay of the University of California-Davis 21-10, 21-0 and Richard Reynosa defeated Kevin Tauer of the University of Minnesota 21-8, 21-1.

In the round of 32, Brad Alesi defeated Kevin Downes of the Dublin Institute of Technology, Ireland 21-3, 21-0; Emmett Peixoto of Southwest Missouri State University defeated Juan Zavala 21-6, 21-8; Ference Dominguez of Lake Forest College defeated Zach Lowy 20-21, 21-6, 11-7; Ross Burke defeated Chad McCormick of Oregon State University 21-7, 21-0 and Richard Berger of Oregon State University defeated Richard Reynosa 21-16, 21-13.

In the round of 16, Brad Alesi defeated Barry Durham of Southwest Missouri State University 21-16, 21-11 and Matt Steele of Pacific University defeated Ross Burke 10-21, 21-20, 11-1.

In the quarterfinals, Brad Alesi defeated Pat Flanagan of Southwest Missouri State University 21-3, 21-11. In the semifinals, Brad Alesi defeated Emmett Peixoto of Southwest Missouri State University 21-14, 21-19. In the finals, Dessie Keegan of the Dublin Institute of Technology, Ireland defeated Brad Alesi 21-6, 21-7.

In the men's A division round of 16, Zach Lowy defeated Juan Zavala 21-8, 21-7 and Richard Reynosa defeated Calvin Lee of the University of California-Berkeley 21-10, 21-13. In the quarterfinals, Zach Lowy defeated Raphael Martinez of the University of California-Berkeley 21-15, 21-4 and Richard Reynosa defeated Zach Gault of Colorado State University 21-5, 21-12.

In the semifinals, Jesse Harris of Mendecino Junior College defeated Zach Lowy 21-14, 21-7 and Michael McClean of Letterkenny Institute of Technology, Ireland defeated Richard Reynosa 19-21, 21-17, 11-10. As was written in the USHA's

Brad Alesi (left) in the finals against Dessie Keegan
(*Handball*, April 2002, page 6)

Handball magazine, "McClean escaped 11-10 over a determined Richard Reynosa of A&M."

In the men's B division round of 32, Lee Nichols defeated Saul Benitez of Southwestern University 20-21, 21-20, 11-3; Chad O'Neal defeated Dustin Kochis of Pacific University 21-8, 21-1; Colin Corcoran defeated Garrett Silveira of Lake Forest College 21-20, 21-13 and Greg Harkey defeated Neil Larson of Southwestern University 21-11, 21-9.

In the round of 16, Kiel Peck of Pacific University defeated Lee Nichols 21-17, 8-21, 11-10; Chad O'Neal defeated Adam Coronado of the University of California-Davis 21-9, 21-9 and Colin Corcoran defeated Greg Harkey 21-20, 21-11.

Just as happened in the round of 16 when an Aggie eliminated another Aggie, the same unfortunately happened in the quarterfinals when Chad O'Neal defeated Colin Corcoran 21-19, 21-20. It simply cannot get much closer than that. In the semifinals, Chad O'Neal defeated Matt Dean of Southwestern University 21-5, 21-18.

Tommy Burnett reported the action in the men's B division and was published in the April 2002 issue of the USHA's *Handball*, page 18:

> The men's B division develops after the second round of drop-downs and will usually consist of players who were seeded from 33rd through 49th in the top-64 draw.
>
> Chad O'Neal of Texas A&M was one such player. An earlier oversight caused him to be added as the 48th seed instead of the mid-30s, where he more likely belonged. But one benefit of the drop-down format is that it allows a mistakenly seeded player the opportunity to prove his skills and still remain competitive.
>
> O'Neal defeated Adam Coronado of California-Davis in the round of 16 by a surprisingly large margin, winning both games 21-9. Next up was teammate Colin Corcoran. The fact that Corcoran and O'Neal play each other on a regular basis was evident as both seemed to anticipate each other's shots with precision. Although O'Neal eventually won 21-19, 21-20, Corcoran provided a strong opponent early in this Division.

O'Neal next faced Southwestern University's Matt Dean, the tournament coaches' pick for the men's sportsmanship trophy. Dean's start was spotty, as he scored only five points in Game 1. However, he regrouped in the second game and came close to forcing a tiebreaker, scoring 18 points.

Next for O'Neal was Alex Martinez of Lake Forest in the final. Martinez had escaped a barnburner tiebreaker in the quarters against the Air Force Academy's Bergen Hugos in which he prevailed 21-13, 20-21, 11-4. He next encountered doubles-weary Nick Velelle of Southwest Missouri State, finishing him off 21-6, 21-11.

The final was well balanced with the talent of these two young men. O'Neal won the first game, a long, hard-fought affair, by the score of 21-20. Martinez came back in the second game when O'Neal succumbed to his one-wall style 21-13. The tiebreaker, however, found O'Neal ready to keep Martinez in the backcourt, which resulted in an 11-0 blitz for O'Neal.

Chad O'Neal goes for the shot against Martinez in the B division final.

(*Handball*, April 2002, page 10)

In the first round of the men's C, Mike Landry defeated Josh Cuttill 15-14, 15-13; Derek Henry defeated Daniel Aiderman of Las Positas College 15-1, 15-1; Grant Potter defeated Dermott Reynolds of the Dublin Institute of Technology, Ireland 15-11, 15-9; Jonathan Ragsdale defeated Kyle Lahde of the University of Kentucky 15-8, 15-4; Chris Werner defeated Kevin Flynn of the University of California-Berkeley 15-2, 15-7 and Aaron Burcham defeated Jon Sarno of the University of Texas 15-8, 15-12. NOTE: Due to the large number of participants, all games of the first-round matches were played to 15 points rather than the normal 21 points, with the exception of the top rated 64 men who played their first round matches to 21-point games. For the remainder of the matches, the game total resumed to the normal 21 points.

In the round of 64 of the men's C, Nicholas Wood of Oregon State University defeated Mike Landry 21-11, 21-4; Derek Henry defeated Chris Alger of Southwest Missouri State University 21-7, 21-17; Lawrence Aguilar of Las Positas College defeated Grant Potter 21-3, 21-17; Alex Mints of the University of California-Berkeley defeated Jonathan Ragsdale 21-0, 21-4; Ryan Collier defeated Steve Mendoz of the University of Texas 21-11, 8-21, 11-2; John Mark Davidson defeated Scott Muelberger of the University of Texas 21-10, 21-6; Chris Kubinski of the University of Texas defeated Chris Werner 16-21, 21-6, 11-8; Reif Chron defeated Josh Nowak of Southwestern University 21-5, 21-0; Aaron Burcham defeated Adam Pomerleau of St. John's University 21-6, 21-13 and Lance Hoffman defeated Patrick Aguiar 21-11, 21-15.

In the round of 32 of the men's C, Derek Henry defeated Shaun Frazier of Western Washington University 21-14, 21-18; Alex Mints of the University of California-Berkeley defeated Ryan Collier 21-10, 21-11; Brent Camp of Hardin-Simmons University defeated John Mark Davidson 4-21, 21-19, 11-6; Reif Chron defeated Misha Zitser of the Massachusetts Institute of Technology 21-14, 21-15 and Lance Hoffman defeated Aaron Burcham 21-9, 21-10. NOTE: At this point of the tournament the men's C division was formed.

In the round of 32 of the men's C division, Lance Hoffman defeated Mike Sheehan of Lake Forest College 21-17, 21-20; Derrick Fritz of the University of Minnesota defeated Derek Henry 21-2, 21-7 and Reif Chron defeated Grant Wheeler of Southwest Missouri State University 21-16, 21-10.

In the round of 16 of the men's C division, Lance Hoffman defeated Dustin Kochis of Pacific University 13-21, 21-20, 11-8 and Reif Chron defeated Steve Vasquez of the University of Minnesota 21-16, 21-13.

In the quarterfinals, Lance Hoffman defeated Neal Larson of Southwestern University 4-21, 21-19, 11-7 and Lawrence Aguiar of Las Positas College defeated Reif Chron 21-18, 21-16. In the semifinals, Sandesh Sadalge of Stony Brook University defeated Lance Hoffman 21-9, 21-5.

In the first round of the Contenders division, Chris Werner defeated Duong Hang of the University of California-Berkeley 8-21, 21-19, 11-7; Mike Landry defeated Justin Dunlap of the University of California-Berkeley 21-18, 21-9 and Grant Potter won by default but Potter's opponent was not listed.

In the round of 32, Christian Gomez of San Jose State University defeated Chris Werner 21-2, 21-19; Mike Landry defeated Mark Enriquez of the Air Force Academy 21-14, 21-13 and Grant Potter defeated Eoghan Collins of the Dublin Institute of Technology, Ireland 21-7, 21-13.

In the round of 16 of the men's Contenders division, Mike Landry defeated Steve Mendoza of the University of Texas 21-14, 21-19 and Grant Potter defeated Noah Levinson of the University of California-Berkeley 21-11, 21-9.

In the quarterfinals, Christian Gomez of San Jose State University defeated Mike Landry 21-18, 21-6 and Grant Potter defeated Ryan Klein of the University of Kentucky 21-7, 21-18. In the semifinals, Patrick Aguiar of Las Positas College defeated Grant Potter 21-8, 21-16.

In the round of 16 of the men's Challenger division, Ryan Collier defeated Shaun Frazier of Western Washington University 21-10, 21-15; Chris Kubinski of the University of Texas defeated John Mark Davidson 17-21, 21-15, 11-7 and Misha Zitser of the Massachusetts Institute of Technology defeated Aaron Burcham 21-6, 21-5.

In the quarterfinals, Ryan Collier defeated John Root of Lake Forest College 21-17, 14-21, 11-4. In the semi-finals, Ryan Collier defeated Nicholas Wood of Oregon State University 21-7, 21-18. In the finals, Matt Zehnder of Western Washington University defeated Ryan Collier 21-1 21-7.

The Aggies had no entrants in the men's Novice division and chose not to participate in the doubles matches.

The first round of the women's Open singles of the National Collegiate Handball Tournament would determine who would continue to round 32 of the

The first men's National Collegiate Handball team champions from Texas A&M

FROM LEFT TO RIGHT: Zach Lowy, Aaron Burcham, Lee Nichols, Lance Hoffman, Ross Burke, Colin Corcoran, Brad Alesi, Chad O'Neal, Juan Zavala, Richard Reynosa

(*Handball*, April 2002, page 5)

Open division and who would drop down to another division. As play began, Sheree Fell of Pacific University defeated Katie Wielbacher 21-5, 21-1; Courtnee Gordon defeated Natalie Gamboa of the University of Texas 21-1, 21-1; Katie East defeated Amanda LaRue of Hardin-Simmons University 21-4, 21-10; Meagan McDuff defeated Lia Chowdbury of the University of Texas 21-0, 21-2; Carrie Lucas defeated Arian Story of Southwestern University 21-2, 21-0; Jennifer Minarcik defeated Jean Kasamoto of Pacific University 21-14, 21-18; Olivia Durr of the University of Texas defeated Veronika Libson 21-7, 21-4 and Dara Crain defeated Leslie Landers of the University of Texas 21-0, 21-0.

In the round of 32 of the women's Open singles, Page Applegate of Southwestern Missouri State University defeated Courtnee Gordon 21-4, 21-4; Leslie Boyle of Lake Forest College defeated Katie East 21-2, 21-0; Meagan McDuff defeated Terri Quajardo of Hardin-Simmons University 21-1, 21-1; Carrie Lucas defeated Beth Heim of Southwest Missouri State University 21-2, 21-4; Fiona Healy of the Dublin Institute of Technology, Ireland defeated Jennifer Minarcik (score not given); Amy Sove of Lake Forest College defeated Olivia Durr 21-2, 21-5; Sarah Roberts of Lake Forest College defeated Dara Crain 21-18, 21-2 and Lynn Alesi (bye in the first round) defeated Jennifer Phipps of the University of Texas 21-2, 21-1.

Lynn Alesi showing her All-American form in the women's Open singles finals

(*Handball*, April 2002, page 4)

In the round of 16, Leslie Boyle of Lake Forest College defeated Meagan McDuff 21-9, 21-11; Alexis Cloutier of the University of Winnipeg, Canada defeated Carrie Lucas 21-11, 21-5 and Lynn Alesi defeated Sarah Roberts of Lake Forest College 21-3, 21-0. At this point in the competition, the women's Open division was formed and consisted of the top eight collegiate women handball players.

In the quarterfinals, Lynn Alesi defeated Megan Gibson of Lake Forest College 21-5, 21-4. In the semifinals, Lynn Alesi defeated Fiona Healy of the Dublin Institute of Technology, Ireland 21-3, 21-13 and in the finals, Lynn Alesi was defeated by Megan Mehilos of Lake Forest College 21-8, 21-20.

In the first round of the women's A division championship, Meagan McDuff defeated Carrie Lucas 21-14, 21-13. In the semifinals, Meagan McDuff defeated Danielle White of Lake Forest College 21-10, 11-21, 11-6. The final match was described by Mike Steele and was reported on page 16 of the April 2002 issue of the USHA's *Handball* magazine:

Texas A&M's Meagan McDuff held off Lake Forest's Sarah Roberts to capture the women's A championship on her home court.

McDuff, a lanky athlete from Houston majoring in marketing in her senior year, took a while to settle into her accustomed game, allowing Roberts to win a tough first game 21-15.

McDuff took command in the second game, letting her height and ability to cover large areas of the court give her the advantage on most shots. With a solid service game, she kept steady pressure on Roberts and took the victory in convincing fashion 21-4.

The Aggie sustained her momentum in the tiebreaker for an 11-2 win, showing excellent skills in all phases of the game. With her championship, McDuff looks forward to her graduation, marriage and studies in photography.

In the round of 16 in the women's B division, Courtnee Gordon defeated Fallon Onkels of Western Washington University 21-5, 21-11; Terri Quajardo of Hardin-Simmons University defeated Katie East 21-9, 21-16; Joy Fell of Pacific University defeated Jennifer Minarcik 21-10, 21-6 and Dara Crain defeated Jennifer Phipps of the University of Texas 21-7, 21-5.

In the quarterfinals, Courtnee Gordon defeated Emma Hopkins of Southwest Missouri State University 21-15, 21-3 and Dara Crain defeated Angie King of Hardin-Simmons University 21-17, 17-21, 11-3. In the semifinals, Courtnee Gordon defeated Kim Hall of Hardin-Simmons University 21-10, 21-1 and Joy Fell of Western Washington University defeated Dara Crain 21-15, 17-21, 11-5.

Meagan McDuff (left) with her trophy and Sarah Roberts after their championship match

(*Handball*, April 2002, page 16)

Mike Steele described the B division finals as reported on page 17 of the April 2002 issue of the USHA's *Handball*:

> Pacific University's Joy Fell and Texas A&M's Courtnee Gordon, both juniors, staged a great contest to decide the championship of the women's B Division.
>
> Fell, a business major from Astoria, Oregon showed little rust from her handball layoff while studying in Granada, Spain, last autumn.
>
> Gordon, a Management Information Systems major from Houston, showcased a highly cerebral command of The Perfect Game to complement her considerable athletic skills.
>
> Fell won a grueling first game 21-16 in which neither player could take command and pile up a big lead. Gordon played a steady game, warming to the task, while Fell displayed flashes of tremendous power and speedy foot work.
>
> Gordon's steadiness took over in the second game for a 21-10 victory. Using precise serves and well-placed rally shots, Gordon piled up points in bunches and frustrated Fell.
>
> Both women played great handball in the tiebreaker, but Fell seemed re-energized after Gordon's second game triumph. The Pacific player's shots cracked around the court with authority as she kept the taller Gordon behind her as often as possible.
>
> At the midway point of the tiebreaker, Gordon's power serves into the low left rear corner posed a real threat, but Fell geared up again and pulled away for an 11-6 victory and the B title.

Courtnee Gordon during the finals of the women's B division championship

(*Handball*, April 2002, page 4)

In the round of 16 of the women's Challengers division, Katie Marsten of Pacific University defeated Veronika Libson 21-3, 21-10.

In the first round of the women's Contenders division, Kara Hodges of Pacific University defeated Veronika Libson 21-8, 21-19.

There were no Aggies entered in the women's doubles competition.

When all the matches were completed and the scores finalized, the men's team had accomplished something that they had never done and that was to capture the first men's National Collegiate

Handball Team Championship. The margin of victory over Lake Forest College was A&M 688 points to Lake Forest's 646. The Lake Forest women's team earned the team championship with 756 points. Texas A&M women's team earned a second place finish with 636 points which was comfortably in front of third place Southwest Missouri State's 544 points. The combined team total was Lake Forest first with 1,402 points, A&M second with 1,324 points and Southwest Missouri State with 1,144 points.

Banner representing the first Men's National Team Championship
(Author's Collection)

Fresh from the first men's team National Collegiate Handball Championship, the Aggies were looking forward to having another great year in handball and repeating the success of past years. The 2003 National Collegiate Handball Tournament was to be hosted by Mike Steele of Pacific University and held in Portland, Oregon.

As the first round of play began in the men's Open singles competition, 64 handball players were anxious to get started. In the round of 64, the Aggies' Jeron Powell defeated Steven Mendoza of the University of Texas 14-21, 21-2, 11-4; Ross Burke defeated Neil Larson of Southwestern University (no score given); Chad O'Neal defeated Travis Hoover of San Jose State University 21-13, 13-21, 11-4; Juan Zavala defeated Saul Benitez of Southwestern University 21-1, 21-11; David Munson of Lake Forest College defeated Grant Potter 21-1, 21-3; Jeff Hurst of the University of Texas defeated Lee Nichols 11-21, 21-8, 11-8 and Zach Lowy defeated Derek Fritze of the University of Minnesota 21-2, 21-3.

In the round of 32, Zach Gault of Colorado State University defeated Jeron Powell 2-21, 21-9, 11-8; Ross Burke defeated Neil Larson of Southwestern University 21-4, 21-3; Oliver Conway of National University of Ireland, Galway defeated Chad O'Neal 21-9, 21-13; Ricardo Diaz of Cabrillo College defeated Juan Zavala 21-2, 21-3 and Adrian Kelly of Waterford Institute of Technology, Ireland defeated Zach Lowy 21-2, 21-10.

In the round of 16, Oliver Conway of National University of Ireland, Galway defeated Ross Burke 21-12, 21-9. With the loss of Burke, there were no Aggies to advance beyond the round of 16 in the Open singles competition.

Aggies defeated in round of 32 of the Open division dropped down into the A division. Brian Ault of the University of Southern California defeated Jeron Powell 21-15, 21-13; Juan Zavala defeated Paul Fitzpatrick of the Dublin Institute of Technology, Ireland 21-20, 21-17; Zach Lowy defeated Jeff Hurst of the University of Texas 21-10, 21-18 and Ryan Daly of Queen's University of Belfast, Ireland defeated Chad O'Neal 21-11, 21-11. In the quarterfinals, Juan Zavala defeated Pat Nolan of the University of Limerick, Ireland 21-6, 21-15 and Neil McDermott of the National University of Ireland, Galway defeated Zach Lowy 20-21, 21-17, 11-6. Brian Ault of the University of California defeated Juan Zavala 21-12, 21-9 in the semifinals to end the Aggie hopes of a title in the A division.

The Aggies who were defeated in the round of 64 of the Open division dropped down into the B division. In the first round of competition, Derrick Tiveron of Lake Forest College defeated Grant Potter 21-5, 21-10. Lee Nichols defeated Mike Sheehan of Lake Forest College 21-9, 21-12. These were the only Aggies in the B division. Lee Nichols defeated Derin McArdie of Dublin Institute of Technology, Ireland 21-6, 21-13 to move into the quarterfinals. David Tormey of the National University of Ireland, Galway defeated Lee Nichols 21-10, 12-21, 11-2 to eliminate the only remaining Aggie in B division.

In the first round of C division, Mike Landry defeated Ben Smith of Western Washington University 21-12, 21-12; Brendan Fleming of the National University of Ireland, Galway defeated Clint Alexander 21-10, 21-9; Randy Key defeated Reed Fisher of The University of Tennessee-Chattanooga 21-10, 21-11; Mikey Cruse of Hardin Simmons University defeated Chris Annis 21-10, 21-7; Clay Walker defeated Grant Weathers of Las Positas College 21-2, 21-0; Joey Moctezuma defeated Igor Gladkov of Pacific University 21-5, 21-5; Nathan Postillion of the University of Arizona defeated Matt Hill 21-9, 21-13 and Mike Gibson defeated Nick Henry of the University of California-Berkeley 21-6, 21-4. In the next round of play, Mike Landry won his match by default; Alex Ng of University of California-Berkeley defeated Grant Potter 21-18, 16-21, 11-5; Derek Meiring of Lake Forest College defeated Matt Hill 21-11, 21-16 and Mike Scott of Southwest Missouri State College defeated Joey Moctezuma 21-4, 21-15. Randy Key, Clay Walker and Mike Gibson won their first match; however, they were not listed in the results of the next round of play. Mike Landry is the only Aggie who advanced to the round of 16 where he was defeated by Brendan Fleming of the National University of Ireland, Galway 3-21, 21-10, 11-9.

Another division was added this year in men's competition and was named the Intermediate division. The three Aggies not listed in C division after their first-round win played in this division. Randy Key defeated Drew Adams of the University of Minnesota 17-21, 21-16, 11-5; Clay Walker defeated Mark Estrada of Hardin Simmons University 12-21, 21-6, 11-3 and Mike Gibson was defeated by Howie Angelo of Cabrillo College 21-12, 20-21, 11-4. In the quarterfinals, Randy Key defeated Clay Walker 21-9, 21-13. In the semifinals, Antonio Villalobos of San Jose State University defeated Randy Key 17-21, 21-18, 11-5.

There were no Aggies playing in the Contenders division; however, three Aggies were in the Challengers division. Clint Alexander defeated Bruce Brown of the University of Minnesota (no score given); Chris Annis defeated Nathan Frost of the National University of Ireland, Galway 21-6, 14-21, 11-3 and Matt Hill defeated Nick Henry of the University of California-Berkeley 21-10, 21-14. In the round of 16, Matt Berzins of the University of Arizona defeated Clint Alexander 10-21, 21-3, 11-3 and Reed Fisher the University of Tennessee-Chattanooga defeated Chris Annis 21-8, 21-8.

No Aggies competed in the Novice division.

None of the Aggie men competed in doubles.

The 2003 National Collegiate Men's Championship Team

PHOTO OF TEAM MEMBERS: Clint Alexander, Chris Annis, Ross Burke, Mike Gibson, Matt Hill, Randy Key, Mike Landry, Zach Lowy, Joey Moctezuma, Lee Nichols, Chad O'Neal, Grant Potter, Jeron Powell, Clay Walker, Juan Zavala and Coach Lance Lowy.

(Handball, April 2003, page 8)

In the women's Open singles, Joy Fell of Pacific University defeated Courtnee Gordon 21-0, 21-8; Christina Matthews defeated Michelle White of Lake Forest College 21-14, 6-21, 11-7; Carrie Lucas defeated Beth Heim of Southwest Missouri State College 10-21, 21-5, 11-3; Courtney Peixoto of the University of Arizona defeated Wendy Ridings 21-2, 21-2 and Lynn Alesi defeated Christina Granado of Southwestern University 21-0, 21-0. In the round of 16, Page Applegate of Southwest Missouri State University defeated Christina Matthews 21-3, 21-10; Courtney Peixoto of the University of Arizona defeated Carrie Lucas 21-10, 21-1 and Lynn Alesi defeated Kristen Bowerly of Pacific University 21-3, 21-2. In the quarterfinals, Lynn Alesi defeated Sarah Roberts of Lake Forest College 21-1, 21-0. In the semifinals, Alesi defeated Samantha England of Lake Forest College 21-10, 21-17. This set up the final match with Megan Mehilos who had won the last two women's Open titles. The final match was described by Mike Steele and reported in the USHA's *Handball*, April 2003 issue, page 7:

> Megan Mehilos of Lake Forest won her third consecutive women's Open collegiate championship with a thrilling 21-9, 12-21, 11-10 victory over Texas A&M's Lynn Alesi. It also marked the third straight year that Alesi had fallen in the final.
>
> Mehilos added to her accolades by also winning her third consecutive women's open doubles championship, this time with Amy Sove.
>
> Both singles finalists shot well, forced errors and played tough in the hard grind of the match that could have gone either way. In fact, it almost did go another way, with Alesi serving at match point.
>
> Rallying from a 9-6 deficit, Alesi served at 10-9. On the ensuing rally and in close quarters with Alesi, Mehilos skipped in a kill attempt that was replayed due to a call of "contact".
>
> Mehilos regained the serve and hit two great serves for the win, leaving Alesi to wonder what might have been. With one more year remaining in her eligibility, Alesi will be trying to garner the elusive title.
>
> Both players showed great class all through the tournament.

In the women's A division, Danielle White of Lake Forest College defeated Carrie Lucas 21-17, 21-15 and Christina Matthews defeated Cathy Jasan of Southwest Missouri State University 21-12, 17-21, 11-10. In the semifinals, Kristen Bowerly of Pacific University defeated Christina Matthews 21-6, 20-21, 11-10.

In the women's B division, Tina Apolinaria of Cabillo College defeated Deanna Johnson 21-2, 21-4; Kendall Caran defeated Avelina Kuahaulua of Pacific University (no score given); Lauren Greico of the University of Texas defeated Joy Orr 21-8, 21-4; Wendy Wheeler defeated Amanda Smith of Miami University-Ohio (no score given); Debbie Abbott of Western Washington University defeated Veronika Libson 21-8, 21-10 and Jessica Taylor defeated Stephanie Castro of Cabrillo College 21-1, 21-4. In the round of 32, Courtnee Gordon defeated Tina Apolinaria of Cabrillo College 21-2, 21-6; Angela Lum of the University of California-Berkeley defeated Kendall Caran 21-3, 21-3; Lauren Greico of the University of Texas defeated Wendy Ridings 21-6, 21-11; Molly Regan of the University of Texas defeated Wendy Wheeler 21-4, 21-11 and Angie King of Hardin Simmons University defeated Jessica Taylor 21-8, 21-2. In the round of 16, Courtnee Gordon defeated Shannon Vandike of Southwest Missouri State University 21-1, 21-4 and was the only Aggie still playing in the B division. In the quarterfinals, Gordon defeated

Jodi Reisig of Southwestern University 21-1, 21-4 and in the semifinals, Gordon could not keep up with Jessie Wachter of Pacific University losing 21-3, 21-9.

The Aggies had seven women in the C division. In the preliminary round, Deanna Johnson defeated Heather Yoder of Southwestern University 21-0, 21-5; Joy Orr defeated Brooke Boggs of the University of Texas 21-1, 21-6 and Veronika Libson defeated Robin Thompson of Southwestern University 21-8, 14-21, 11-10. In the first-round action, Deanna Johnson defeated Dorothy Cassidy of Dublin Institute of Technology, Ireland 21-1, 21-16; Christy Cooper of the University of Texas defeated Joy Orr 5-21, 21-18, 11-10; Becka Boggs of Western Washington defeated Veronika Libson 21-17, 21-2 and Jessica Taylor defeated Nadia Fazel 21-8, 1-21, 11-0. In the round of 16, Kendall Caran defeated Christy Cooper of the University of Texas 21-16, 21-13; Deanna Johnson defeated Bonnie Levitt of the University of California-Berkeley 21-0, 21-6; Wendy Ridings defeated Brina Chang of Pacific University 21-14, 21-8; Becka Briggs of Western Washington University defeated Wendy Wheeler 21-10, 21-0 and Andrea Fisher of Capella University defeated Jessica Taylor 21-5, 21-4. In the quarterfinals, Tina Apolinaria of Cabrillo College defeated Kendall Caran 21-8, 21-16 and Wendy Ridings defeated Deanna Johnson 21-18, 21-11. In the semifinals, Wendy Ridings defeated Tina Apolinaria of Cabrillo College 21-11, 21-6 to advance to the finals. Two Texans, Wendy Ridings from A&M and Amy Martin of the University of Texas, battled it out for the championship. Ridings gave her all in the first game and won 21-16 but had nothing left for the second game with Martin winning 21-1 and then in the tiebreaker 11-2.

There were no Aggies entered in the Intermediate or Challengers.

The team of Lynn Alesi and Christina Matthews were the only Aggies entered in the doubles competition. They received a bye in the first round and then in the quarterfinals, defeated Cathy Jasan and Shannon Vandike of Southwest Missouri State University 21-4, 21-1. In the semifinals, Alesi and Matthews defeated Samantha England and Megan Gibson of Lake Forest College 21-1, 21-17. In the finals, Alesi and Matthews were defeated by Megan Mehilos and Amy Sove of Lake Forest College 21-9, 21-7.

Lynn Alesi and Christina Matthews with their doubles trophies and their All-American smiles

(Courtesy Christina Luther)

The 2003 Aggie Handball Team at the National Handball Tournament
PHOTO INCLUDES: Chris Annis, Lynn Alesi, Clint Alexander, Ross Burke, Kendall Caran, Mike Gibson, Courtnee Gordon, Matt Hill, Deanna Johnson, Mike Landry, Veronika Libson, Zach Lowy, Carrie Lucas, Randy Key, Christina Matthews, Joey Moctezuma, Lee Nichols, Chad O'Neal, Joy Orr, Grant Potter, Jeron Powell, Wendy Ridings, Jessica Taylor, Clay Walker, Wendy Wheeler, Juan Zavala and Coach Lance Lowy.

(*Handball*, April 2003, page 8)

When all of the scores were tallied the Aggies had edged the Dublin Institute of Technology, Ireland 1,003 to 985, to win another men's team title. The women's total was at 952, good for third place in the women's division. They pushed Southwest Missouri State University for second place but came out short of the 970 points of SMSU. Pacific University was a distant fourth with 856 points. In the combined team

total the Aggies were in second place with 1,955 points to first place Lake Forest College with 2,070 points.

The Committee for the National Collegiate Handball Tournament established a new ranking system for this tournament and subsequent national tournaments. With so many new schools and entrants, it was felt there should be a Division I combined team total made up of the schools who would have at least one male at the C division level or at least one female at the B division level. Any school, no matter the number of entrants, with no player at either level would be classified as a Division II school for combined team purposes. This made it possible for a school that likely would never be able to compete for the combined team championship to have a chance for a national team handball championship even though the championship would not be at the highest level of play. A great example, made possible by the new ruling for the Division II schools, was when Hardin Simmons University went home with a combined team national championship trophy in handball.

Banner representing the second men's National Handball Team Championship
(Author's Collection)

With 2003-2004 school year underway, Coach Lowy was trying to figure how he could win another championship. With the Irish edging closer every year, the championships would be harder to earn. However, the Aggies had been there before and looked forward to another great year in handball. And, with the upcoming National tournament being held in Springfield, Missouri, at the home of the Southwest Missouri State University team, the home field advantage would be with them.

In the round of 64 of the Open, Ross Burke opened up with a win over Matt Hill, another Aggie, 21-0, 21-1; Jeff Kastner of Pacific University defeated Mike Gibson 21-5, 21-7; Pat Flanagan of Southwest Missouri State University defeated Jeff Terrill 21-2, 21-9; Adam Bernhard of the University of Texas defeated Mike Barranco 21-4, 21-10; Dutch Lowy defeated Garrett Silveira of Lake Forest College 21-17,

21-13 and Emmett Peixoto of Cabrillo College defeated Randy Key 21-4, 21-4. In the round of 32, Jesse Harris of Mendocino Community College defeated Ross Burke 21-4, 21-11 and Rich Berger of Columbia University defeated Dutch Lowy 21-17, 21-13. Burke and Lowy were the only two Aggies to advance to the round of 32, and with their loss the Aggies had no one left in the Open competition. Aggies losing in the round of 64 would drop down to divisions B and C. Burke and Lowy would drop down to the A division.

In the round of 16 of the A division, Ross Burke defeated Larry Watson of Southwest Missouri State University 21-5, 21-11 and Dutch Lowy defeated Jeff Hurst of the University of Texas 21-7, 21-5. Moving into the quarterfinals, Burke defeated Brian Ault of the University of Southern California 21-18, 17-21, 11-9 and Lowy defeated George Watson of Southwest Missouri State University 21-9, 21-5. In the semifinals, Barry Durham of Southwest Missouri State University defeated Ross Burke 21-10, 21-6 while Lowy defeated Zach Gault of

Dutch Lowy (upper left) waiting to return a shot in the finals of A
(*Handball*, April 2004, page 9)

Colorado State University 17-21, 21-11, 11-1. Lowy was unable to overcome the game of Durham in the finals. The score of the winner was 21-16, 21-13.

In the B division, Matt Hill defeated Matt Brunkow of Pacific University 21-12, 21-14; Mike Scott of Southwest Missouri State University defeated Mike Gibson 4-21, 21-12, 11-8; Tyler Stevens of Lake Forest College defeated Jeff Terrill 21-11, 21-2; Arturo Herrera of Lake Forest College defeated Mike Barranco 21-13, 21-8 and David Tormey of National University of Ireland, Galway defeated Randy Key 21-8, 21-17. After Niall McGrath of Sligo Institute of Technology, Ireland defeated Matt Hill 21-20, 21-3 in the round of 16, no Aggies remained in competition for that title.

In the C division round of 32, Gregory Carr of Southwest Missouri State University defeated Randy Key 21-20, 21-19; Hap Potter defeated Chris Alger of Southwest Missouri State University 21-14, 21-15; Matt Berzins of the University of Arizona defeated Josh Haverland 21-7, 21-12; Mike Gibson defeated Ryan Klein of the University of Kentucky 21-12, 20-21, 11-4; Matt Schilz of the University of Arizona defeated Jeff Terrill 21-12, 17-21, 11-9; Jason Headings of Miami University of Ohio defeated Mike Barranco 21-14, 13-21, 11-7 and Garrett Silveira of Lake Forest College defeated Clint Doege 21-15, 21-16. In the round of 16, Hap Potter defeated Ben Johnson of the University of Nebraska 5-21, 21-13, 11-9 and Matt Berzins of the University of Arizona defeated Mike Gibson 21-17, 21-6. In the quarter-finals, Hap Potter defeated Luis Diaz of Evergreen Valley College 21-7, 21-12. In the semifinals, Matt Berzins of the University of Arizona defeated Hap Potter 21-14, 21-13 to end Aggie hopes of a championship in this division.

In the preliminary round of the Intermediate, Ian Kelly of the University of Arizona defeated Clint Alexander 21-18, 1-21, 11-7; Hap Potter defeated Steven Harben of Southwestern University 21-8, 21-5; Ryan Klein of the University of Kentucky defeated Jake Brown 21-9, 21-2; Eric Lippert defeated J. B. McLandrich of the University of Kentucky 21-19, 21-18; Josh Haverland defeated Tom Cinquini of Pacific University 21-16, 21-6; Scott Muehlberger of the University of Texas defeated Josh Smith 18-21, 21-14, 11-9 and Clint Doege defeated Sean Steele of Pacific University (no score given). In the round of 32, Hap Potter defeated Austin Myers of the University of Texas 21-15, 21-17; Gustavo Gonzalez of the University of California-Berkeley defeated Eric Lippert 21-20, 21-18; Josh Haverland defeated Chad Schatz of Southwest Missouri State University 21-11, 20-21, 11-2 and Clint Doege defeated Scott Muehlberger of the University of Texas 21-13, 21-8. With the drop-down format, those winning in the round of 32 (Potter, Haverland and Doege), would move up to C division. Lippert would stay in the Intermediate division and play in the round of 16, where he was defeated by Ryan McReynolds of the University of California-Berkeley (no score given).

The Aggies in the Challengers division were those defeated in the preliminary round of the Intermediate division. To begin play in this division, Clint Alexander defeated Chris Prater of Lake Forest College 21-18, 21-13; Jake Brown defeated Chris May of the University of Minnesota 21-20, 21-4 and Josh Smith defeated Sean Steele of Pacific University 21-11, 21-13. In the round of 16, Clint Alexander defeated Sam Horwich-Scholefield of the University of California-Berkeley 21-5, 21-16; Mike Anderson of the University of Miami-Ohio defeated Jake Brown 21-18, 21-9 and Josh Smith defeated Chris Brizendine of Southwest Missouri State University 21-9, 21-13. In the quarterfinals, Clint Alexander defeated Jeremy Memming of the University of Nebraska 21-14, 21-14 and Matt Hinderman of the University of Oklahoma defeated Josh Smith 2-21, 21-14, 11-6. In the semifinals, John Sarno of the University of Texas defeated Clint Alexander 21-10, 21-12 eliminating the last Aggie from this division.

In the Contenders division, Cain Kohutek defeated Bohl of the University of Minnesota 21-3, 21-6 and Donoghue of the University of Miami-Ohio defeated Nicholas Dimitri 21-2, 21-8. In the round of 32, Cordero of San Jose State University defeated Cain Kohutek 19-21, 21-20, 11-7. After his defeat in the first round, Nicholas Dimitri would drop down to the Consolation bracket of the Contenders division. There he defeated Flynn of the University of California-Berkeley and then in the round of 16, he defeated Wheeler of Fort Scott Community College 21-5, 21-3. In the quarterfinals, Morales of Hardin Simmons University defeated Dimitri. After the round of 32 loss suffered by Cain Kohutek, he dropped down to the Novice division. There he defeated Williamson of Fort Scott Community College 21-6, 21-0. After Dimitri was defeated in the Consolation bracket of the Contenders division, he was moved into the Novice division with Kohutek. In the round of 32, he was defeated by Perez of the University of Minnesota 21-11, 21-10. Kohutek then defeated Hunter of Western Washington University. In the quarterfinals, he defeated Prater of Lake Forest College 21-15, 21-16. In the semifinals, he defeated Ramirez of the University of California-Berkeley 21-14, 21-5. Kohutek was unable to keep his winning streak alive in the finals where he was defeated by Middleton of the University of Kentucky 21-3, 11-21, 11-8. NOTE: First names of those in the Contenders and Novices were not given. The scores were reported here when available.

Ross Burke and Dutch Lowy entered the doubles competition and won their first match against Jeff Kastner and Matt Brunkow of Pacific University 16-21, 21-4, 11-2. In the quarterfinals, they were defeated by Luis Diaz and Ricardo Diaz of Evergreen Valley College 21-4, 21-11.

As the women got underway in the Open division, Jessica Taylor was matched against the number 1 seed and the Open champion for the past three years, Megan Mehilos of Lake Forest College. Mehilos defeated Jessica 21-1, 21-0; Carrie Lucas defeated Robin Thompson of Southwestern University 21-18, 21-3; Danielle White of Lake Forest College defeated Kendall Caran 21-2, 21-3; Michelle White of Lake Forest College defeated Wendy Wheeler 21-10, 18-21, 11-4; Samantha England of Lake Forest College defeated Veronika Libson 21-1, 21-1; Sarah Roberts of Lake Forest College defeated Joy Orr 21-2, 21-4 and Lynn Alesi defeated Diane Luttrell of Southwest Missouri State University 21-2, 21-2. In the round of 16, Carrie Lucas defeated Danielle White of Lake Forest College 1-21, 21-10, 11-5 and Lynn Alesi defeated Becca Briggs of Western Washington University 21-2, 21-3. In the quarterfinals, Megan Mehilos of Lake Forest College defeated Carrie Lucas 21-2, 21-0 and Lynn Alesi defeated Jayme Davis of Southwest Missouri State University 21-7, 21-6. In the semifinals, Lynn Alesi was defeated by Courtney Peixoto of the University of Arizona 2-21, 21-18, 11-0. This was the last match of Alesi's handball career at A&M.

The women's A division was made up of those who lost in the second match of the Open division. There were no Aggies in this division.

In the women's B division, all of the Aggies who were defeated in the opening round of the Open received a bye in the preliminary round. Michelle Melton was not seeded in the Open but was seeded high enough to play in B where she was defeated in the preliminary round by Julie York of Miami University-Ohio 21-14, 21-9. In the round of 32, Jessica Taylor defeated Allison Hendley of Southwestern University 21-8, 21-5; Kendall Caran defeated Edie Kowalkowski of the University of Minnesota 21-3, 21-16; Wendy Wheeler defeated Mollie Tilleson of the University of Minnesota 21-6, 21-9; Veronika Libson defeated Cindy Matsubara of Pacific University 21-1, 21-3 and Joy Orr defeated Sara Mayfield of Southwestern University 21-6, 21-9. In the round of 16, Katie Stack of Southwest Missouri State University defeated Jessica Taylor 21-16, 21-10; Kendall Caran defeated Robin Thompson of Southwestern University 16-21, 21-17, 11-8; Wendy Wheeler defeated Sharron Jecmenek of the University of Texas 21-13, 21-11; Tina Apolinario of Cabrillo College defeated Veronika Libson 21-9, 21-7 and Joy Orr defeated Tina Koludrovic of Lake Forest College 13-21, 21-17, 11-5. In the quarterfinals, Katie Stack of Southwest Missouri State University defeated Kendall Caran 21-12, 21-20; Wendy Wheeler defeated Tina Apolinario of Cabrillo College 11-21, 21-14, 11-5 and Shannon Van Dike of Southwest Missouri State University defeated Joy Orr 21-13, 21-16. In the semifinals, Wendy Wheeler defeated Katie Stack of Southwest Missouri State

University 21-11, 21-5 to reach the championship match. Coach Lowy described the finals action which was reported on page 13 of the April 2004 issue of the USHA's *Handball*:

> Wendy Wheeler of Texas A&M lost her first match of the tournament and dropped down to the women's B. Then she never lost again.

> The women's B final took on added excitement because the winner of that match decided the winner of the women's team championship. Andrea Thurmond of Southwest Missouri State gave an outstanding effort and left it all on the court, but Wheeler's coolness under pressure and experience won her the championship 21-17, 21-18 and clinched the women's title for Lake Forest.

Wendy Wheeler (right) displaying her winning smile after her championship performance.

(*Handball*, April 2004, page 13)

This match did indeed decide the women's team championship. The Lake Forest College women walked away with the championship with a total of 1,057 points and Southwest Missouri State had to settle for second with 1,056 points. The Aggie women finished in third place with 981 points. In the words of Coach Lowy, "This was one of the few times that Lake Forest heartily cheered for the Aggies."

Women in the C division were those who were defeated in the round of 32 of B division. All Aggies in B advanced with wins to the round of 16, so there were no Aggies in this division. Also, there were no Aggies entered in the Challengers or Contenders. In the Intermediate, Michelle Melton, was the lone Aggie entrant. She made her presence known. Coach Lowy describes her play which was reported on page 15 of the April 2004 issue of the USHA's *Handball*:

> The women's Intermediate was composed of relatively new players to the collegiate tournament, but many will be heard from in the near future.

> First and foremost was freshman Michelle Melton of Texas A&M, who stormed through the tournament without losing a game.

> The final was a preview of matches to follow in the years to come as Melton and Lisa Jeziorney of Lake Forest displayed their talent. Melton won this one in two games, 21-1, 21-12, and look for these two again in the future.

Michell Melton (left) displaying her championship trophy

(*Handball*, April 2004, p. 15)

> Melton's semifinal victim was Stacy Rittmueller of Arizona in two close games, 21-15, 21-19.

In the first round, Melton defeated Summer Mathis of the University of Texas 21-1, 21-0. In the round of 16, Melton defeated Priya Kewada of Southwestern University 21-10, 21-2. In the quarterfinals, Melton defeated Kathy Castagnos 21-0, 21-3 to reach the semifinals. Play in the semifinals was reported by Coach Lowy above.

The women did not participate in the doubles competition.

The Aggies were not at the top of the handball world but still came away with some firsts. In the men's team competition, the men earned 872 points to rank fourth behind Lake Forest's 957 points and ahead of the University of Texas with their 828 points. The Aggie women earned 981 points to rank third behind Southwest Missouri State with 1,056 points, but well ahead of Pacific University with 693 points. The combined team total was 1,853 points and good for third place. Lake Forest was in second place with 2,014 points and the University of Texas in fourth with 1,457 points.

Beginning the fall semester of 2004-2005 Coach Lowy knew he would be without four-year star Lynn Alesi, but as always, hoped to develop new talent that would be competitive at the national collegiate level. As always, the players were excited to travel to the University of Minnesota for the year's national tournament.

As the men's Open began play, Damien Martin of Sligo Institute of Technology, Ireland defeated Clint Doege 21-0, 21-0; Matt Schitz of the University of Arizona defeated Matthew Hill 12-21, 21-0, 11-3; Adam Bernhard of the University of Texas defeated Josh Haverland 21-4, 21-2; Larry Watson of Southwest Missouri State University defeated Mike Barranco 21-9, 13-21, 11-9; Arturo Herrera of Lake Forest College defeated Hap Potter 21-6, 21-5 and Dylan Van Brunt defeated Jacob Kavkewitz of the University of Tennessee 21-7, 21-1. In the round of 32, Luis Diaz of Evergreen Valley College defeated Dylan Van Brunt 21-14, 21-7. Each of the Aggies defeated in the first round would drop down to B division while Van Brunt would drop down to A division. In the first round of play in A division, Dylan Van Brunt was defeated by Derek Meiring of Lake Forest College 21-8, 11-21, 11-10. This defeat eliminated all Aggies in the top two divisions.

In the first round of play in B division, Dan McNabney of Lake Forest College defeated Clint Doege 21-9, 21-11; Matthew Hill defeated Hong Qu of the University of California-Berkeley 11-21, 21-14, 11-1; Dara O'Gara of Dublin Institute of Technology, Ireland defeated Josh Haverland 21-5, 21-13; Mike Barranco defeated James Clerkin of University College-Dublin, Ireland 21-4, 21-9 and Jon Kreyer of Miami University-Ohio defeated Hap Potter 21-5, 21-12. Aggies defeated in first round action dropped down to C division. In the round of 16, Matthew Hill defeated Nicolas Wood of Oregon State University 21-12, 16-21, 11-2 and Mike Barranco defeated Danny Knapp of the University of Nebraska 21-6, 21-13. In the quarterfinals, Donny Little of Fort Scott Community College defeated Matthew Hill 21-18, 21-6 and Joe Walch of the University of Texas defeated Mike Barranco 21-12, 21-20 to eliminate the Aggies from B division.

In the first round of C division play, Daniel Meek of the University of Texas defeated Clint Doege 21-9, 21-5; Josh Smith defeated Hong Qu of the University of California-Berkeley 21-19, 21-15; Ben Johnson of the University of Nebraska defeated Jake Brown 21-11, 20-21, 11-1; Josh Haverland defeated Ryan McReynolds of the University of California-Berkeley 21-8, 21-18 and Eugene O'Reilly of Dublin City University, Ireland defeated Jason Adams 21-7, 21-12. In the round of 16, Eugene O'Reilly defeated Josh Haverland 21-7, 21-18 to eliminate the Aggies' chances of victory in C division.

In the first round of the Intermediate division, Cain Kohutek defeated Patrick Dedrick of Pacific University 21-3, 21-0; Rob Farrelly of the National College of Art/Design, Ireland defeated Eric Winkler 21-4, 21-11; Matt Martin of Southwest Missouri State University defeated Russell Carby 21-12, 21-6; Jason Adams defeated Josh Middleton of the University of Kentucky 21-1, 21-1; Ryan McReynolds of the University of California-Berkeley defeated Grant Rybak 21-11, 21-12; Clint Martin defeated Billy Stanton of Southwestern University 21-10, 21-4; Josh Smith defeated Billy Gates of Pacific University 21-1, 21-5; Jake Brown defeated Mike Hinderman of the University of Oklahoma 11-21, 21-14, 11-5 and Brandon Jumonville defeated Ben Azevedo of the University of California-Berkeley 21-14, 21-4. At the end of the first round those defeated dropped down to the Challengers division. In the second round,

Zach Buchanan of Colorado State University defeated Cain Kohutek 21-11, 21-1; Jason Adams defeated Isaac Laughlin of Miami University-Ohio 21-14, 21-8; J. D. McLandrich of the University of Kentucky defeated Clint Martin 21-6, 21-8; Josh Smith defeated Liam Donohgue of Miami University-Ohio 21-9, 21-5 and Jake Brown defeated Brandon Jumonville 21-2, 21-7. After the second round, winners would move up into the C division and those defeated would continue in the Intermediate division. In the round of 16, Zach Arem of the University of Kentucky defeated Cain Kohutek 21-8, 9-21, 11-9; Clint Martin defeated Victor Pacheco of Lake Forest College 21-11, 21-7 and Brandon Jumonville defeated Liam Donohgue of Miami University-Ohio 21-11, 8-21, 11-7. In the quarterfinals, Clint Martin defeated Ken Gannon of University College Dublin, Ireland 21-17, 18-21, 11-6 and Joe Muck of the University of Texas defeated Brandon Jumonville 19-21, 21-8, 11-7. In the semifinals, Muck defeated Martin 21-14, 21-12 to eliminate Aggies from further competition in this division.

In the first round of the Challengers division, Eric Winkler defeated Nick Smith of the University of Kentucky 21-8, 7-21, 11-5; Dermot Reynolds of Dublin Institute of Technology, Ireland defeated Russell Carby 21-13, 21-14 and Grant Rybak defeated Doug Swenson of the University of Minnesota 21-5, 7-21, 11-2. In the round of 16, Eric Winkler defeated Dermot Reynolds of Dublin Institute of Technology, Ireland 21-16, 21-20 and Grant Rybak defeated Calvin Key of Hardin Simmons University 21-8, 21-18. In the quarterfinals, Grant Rybak won the first game 21-20 over his friend Eric Winkler. At this point, Winkler had to drop out due to injury. In the semifinals, Matt Hinderman of the University of Oklahoma defeated Grant Rybak 21-4, 21-6.

In the Contenders-Novice-Consolation preliminary matches, Miguel Garza defeated Andrew Wooline of the University of Florida 21-7, 21-2; Brian Cullum defeated Eric Lieberman of Miami University-Ohio 21-11, 21-12 and Nikolas Libson defeated Marty Andrade of the University of Minnesota 21-11, 21-5. In the second round, Miguel Garza defeated Michael Dolan of Southwest Missouri State University 21-3, 21-0; Brian Cullum defeated Joe Van Thomme of the University of Minnesota 21-6, 21-12 and Nikolas Libson defeated Ryan Moore of Pacific University 21-4, 21-5. Winners of this round moved into the Contenders division.

In the first round of the Contenders division, Tony Giononni of the University of Florida defeated Russell Carby 21-18, 21-9; Brian Cullum defeated Nick Smith of the University of Kentucky 21-14, 21-17; Josh Middleton of the University of Kentucky defeated Miguel Garza 21-10, 21-12 and Nickolas Libson defeated Marvin Romero of the University of Florida 21-12, 21-5. In the round of 16, Tony Giononni of the University of Florida defeated Brian Cullum 21-17, 21-20 and Nickolas Libson defeated Jeremy Tvirdik of the University of Minnesota 21-11, 21-0. In the quarterfinals, Billy Stanton of Southwestern University defeated Libson 21-15, 21-14.

There were no Aggies who dropped down to the Novice or Consolation divisions.

There were no Aggie entrants in the men's Open doubles or the men's B doubles competition.

Playing in the first round of the women's Open division, Danielle White of Lake Forest College defeated Kendall Caran 21-6, 21-6; Alethia Mendez of Stonybrook University defeated Kelly Arunski 21-2, 21-0; Carly Stickles of Lake Forest College defeated Veronika Libson 21-8, 21-0 and Michelle Cochrane defeated Michelle White of Lake Forest College 3-21, 21-9, 11-2. In the round of 16, Jean Kasamoto of Pacific University defeated Michelle Cochrane 21-3, 21-10.

Michelle Cochrane provided one of the tournament's upsets when she defeated 10th seeded Michelle White in the first match of the women's Open division, but could not keep the same pace in the second game so dropped down to the A division, where she defeated Lauren Ritter of Southwest Missouri State University in the quarterfinals 21-10, 21-20. She defeated Andrea Thurmond of Southwest Missouri State

University 21-4, 21-14 in the semifinals. In the finals, Emer Coyle of the Dublin Institute of Technology, Ireland defeated Cochrane 21-4, 21-8.

Michelle Cochrane (left)
with her second-place trophy
(*Handball*, April 2005, page 13)

In the first round of women's B-C-Intermediate preliminary matches, Pam Early defeated Dania Lopez of the University of Texas 8-21, 21-9, 11-1; Kadee McLaughlin of Pacific University defeated Heather Sablatura 21-16, 21-6 and Jessica Kelley defeated Melissa Goebel of the University of Minnesota 21-2, 21-11. First round winners Early and Kelley would move up to B division. In the round of 16, Melissa Goebel of the University of Minnesota defeated Heather Sablatura 21-1, 21-10 and this would drop her down to the Challenger division.

In the first round of B play, Kendall Caran defeated Kim Lanser of Lake Forest College 21-4, 21-9; Sarah Mayfield of Southwestern University defeated Pam Early 21-11, 12-21, 11-1; Kelly Arunski defeated Tracie Hayashi of Pacific University 21-3, 21-7; Veronika Libson defeated Rachel Goold of Hardin Simmons University 21-3, 21-10 and Shannon Vandike of Southwest Missouri State University defeated Jessica Kelly 21-1, 21-3. In the round of 16, Kendall Caran defeated Stephanie Castro of San Jose State University 21-12, 21-6; Diane Luttrell of Southwest Missouri State University defeated Kelly Arunski 9-21, 21-17, 11-8 and Mary Masalkis of Southwest Missouri State University defeated Veronika Libson 21-1, 21-20. In the quarterfinals, Cindy Matsubara of Pacific University defeated Kendall Caran 7-21, 21-3, 11-6.

Jessica Kelley shows
of her second-place
trophy
(*Handball*, April 2005,
page 13)

In the first round of play in the women's C division, Lindsay Ross of Lake Forest College defeated Pam Early 21-7, 21-11 and Jessica Kelley defeated Kristi Kotenberg of the University of Minnesota 21-2, 21-10. In the quarterfinals, Jessica Kelley defeated Niamh Egan of the Dublin Institute of Technology, Ireland 21-16, 21-9. In the semifinals, Kelley defeated Clare Longfellow of Lake Forest College 21-3, 21-8. Kelley gave it a great try in the finals, but came up just short in the second game to lose the match 21-5, 21-20 to Tina Apolinario of the University of Arizona.

Heather Sablutura defeated Sarah Frankhauser of Hardin Simmons University 21-18, 21-17 in the quarterfinals of the Challengers division. In the semifinals, Priya Kewada of Southwestern University defeated Sablutura 21-9, 19-21, 11-6.

There were no Aggies in the Contenders division and no Aggies entered in doubles competition.

As a team, the Aggies were not at the normal competitive level as in past years. The men's team finished in sixth place with 833 points just behind the University of Texas with 838 points. The women's team did better and finished in third place with 875 points behind Southwest Missouri's 956 points. The combined team total was 1,708 points, good enough for third place behind Southwest Missouri's 1,838 points.

One of the most positive awards to be earned by an Aggie at this tournament was the Sportsmanship Award. Veronika Libson earned this award by setting the example in the following areas:

1) No trash talking (yet heated rivalries exist).

2) No showboating, high-fiving or dancing after points (yet many, naturally, expressed emotions and applause for good play was evident towards all competitors).

3)   No bragging or whining (competitors shake hands win or lose).

4)   No ESPN bad-behaviors highlights (no antics, only competition and character).

> Libson is affectionately referred to as the "house mom" for all she does to help her coaches and team. She is one of the friendliest persons around, always talking to someone. She plays hard and never complains or brags, win or lose.

The above written statement on page 15 of the April 2005 issue of the USHA's *Handball* perfectly describes why she was one of four, out of more than 300 handball players at the tournament, to be named for this prestigious award.

As the 2005-06 school year began, plans were made to host the National Collegiate Handball Tournament at A&M. Also, Coach Lowy was planning to have a more competitive team than in 2005 since many of the players were returning and would improve over the school year.

In the first round of play in the men's Open Division, Dutch Lowy defeated Arturo Herrera of Lake Forest College 21-13, 21-2; Marshall Lowy defeated Steve Buchanan of Butte Community College 21-7, 21-2; Rikki O'Gara of the National University of Ireland, Galway defeated Dylan Van Brunt 21-14, 21-20 and Brian Carroll of Dublin Institute of Technology, Ireland defeated Matt Hill 21-3, 21-4. In the round of 16, Dutch Lowy defeated George Watson of Missouri State University 21-14, 21-14 and Marshall Lowy was defeated by Eddie Morales of Missouri State University 21-19, 21-8. NOTE; Southwest Missouri State University officially changed its name to Missouri State University. In the quarterfinals, Jonathan Iglesias defeated Dutch Lowy 21-14, 12-21, 11-9.

Veronika Libson (second from left) displays her award plaque.
(*Handball*, April 2005, page 15)

In the quarterfinals of the 9-16 playoffs, Marshall Lowy defeated Ivan Ruiz of Lake Forest College 10-21, 21-20, 11-4. In the semifinals of the 9-16 playoffs, Marshall Lowy defeated Paul Moran of Dublin Institute of Technology, Ireland 21-13, 21-13 and in the finals, Patrick Finnegan of University College Dublin, Ireland defeated Marshall Lowy 21-19, 21-2 which would earn Lowy a 10th place finish.

In the preliminary round of A division (winners to A-B, losers to B-C), Dara O'Gara of Dublin Institute of Technology, Ireland defeated Jake Brown 7-21, 21-3, 11-6 and Naill Gordon of

Aggie welcome sign at the tournament
(*Handball*, April 2006, page 3)

Dublin Institute of Technology defeated Jason Adams 21-13, 21-8. In the first round of A division (losers to B), Dylan Van Brunt defeated Dara O'Gara of Dublin Institute of Technology, Ireland 21-6, 21-15 and Rob Farrelly of The National College of Art/Design, Ireland defeated Matt Hill 21-10, 9-21, 11-4. In the round of 16, Mike Mehilos of Lake Forest College defeated Dylan Van Brunt 21-20, 21-13.

In the preliminary round of B (winners to B-C, losers to C-Intermediates), Zach Arem of the University of Florida defeated Chris Patton 21-3, 21-5; Grant Rybak defeated Thein Kieu of the University of

Nebraska 21-9, 21-8; Clint Martin defeated Phillip Russell of the University of Texas 21-0, 21-10; Robert Burda of Lake Forest College defeated Matt Acker 21-8, 21-9; Cain Kohutek defeated Eric Mueller of the University of Florida 21-3, 21-3 and Brandon Jumonville defeated Morgan Stevens of the University of Florida 21-8, 21-7. In the first round (Winners to B, losers to C), Wes Myers of the University of Texas defeated Grant Rybak 11-21, 21-3, 11-3; Tommy McGrath of the Dublin Institute of Technology defeated Cain Kohutek 1-21, 21-3, 11-2; Jake Brown defeated Colin Melody of Trinity College of Dublin, Ireland 21-11, 21-9; Mike Hinderman of the University of Oklahoma defeated Jason Adams 9-21, 21-12, 11-9 and Brandon Jumonville defeated Matthew Hunter of Western Washington University 21-11, 21-12. In the round of 32, Raul Felix of Pima Community College defeated Brandon Jumonville 21-12, 21-4; Kevin Jarvis of Lake Forest College defeated Jake Brown 21-17, 21-17; Donny Little of Fort Scott Community College defeated Clint Martin 21-8, 21-4 and Matt Hill defeated Brendan Waite of the University of Nebraska 21-1, 8-21, 11-4. In the round of 16, Dan McNabney of Rochester University defeated Matt Hill 21-7, 21-11.

In the preliminary round of C division (winners to C-Intermediate, losers to Intermediate-Challengers), Michael Morgan of Fort Scott Community College defeated Miguel Garza 21-10, 21-12. In the first round of C division (winners to C, losers to Intermediate), Dan Enders of Miami University-Ohio defeated Chris Patton 10-21, 21-10, 11-0 and Matt Acker defeated Paul Hayes of University College-Dublin, Ireland 21-10, 21-11. In the round of 32, Grant Rybak defeated Dustin Brittian of Western Washington University (no score given); Matt Acker defeated Robert Burda of Lake Forest College 21-7, 21-14; Cain Kohutek defeated Colin Kambak of Pacific University 21-10, 21-16 and Jason Adams defeated Morgan Stevens of the University of Florida 21-13, 21-16. In the round of 16, Tim Kappes of the University of Minnesota defeated Grant Rybak 21-3, 21-13; Brian Campbell of the University of Texas defeated Matt Acker 21-18, 21-9; Cain Kohutek defeated James Zender of Lake Forest College 21-11, 21-4 and Dustin Sanderson of Hardin Simmons University defeated Jason Adams 21-8, 15-21, 11-3. In the quarterfinals, James Dominguez of the University of Florida defeated Cain Kohutek 21-17, 21-7.

In the preliminary round of the Intermediates (winners to Intermediate-Challengers, losers to Challengers-Contenders), Andrew Woolwine of the University of Florida defeated Chris Campbell 21-0, 21-7; Trey Kohutek defeated Shane Hayes of the National University of Ireland, Galway 11-21, 21-13, 11-6 and David Cargill defeated Sean Bryan of the University of Minnesota 21-0, 21-6. In the first round (winners to Intermediate, losers to Challengers), Trey Kohutek defeated Joe Gallagher of Rathmines College, Ireland 13-21, 21-2, 11-7; David Cargill defeated Kevin Coker of Emporia State University 21-0, 21-3 and Miguel Garza defeated Dathan Jones of Hardin Simmons University. In the round of 32, Thien Kieu of the University of Nebraska defeated David Cargill 21-12, 21-10; Tankut Can of the University of California-Berkeley defeated Trey Kohutek 21-15, 21-13 and Miguel Garza defeated B. J. Reynolds of Hardin Simmons University 21-5, 21-12. In the round of 16, Casey Bowman of Fort Scott Community College defeated Miguel Garza 21-10, 21-12.

In the first round of the Challengers division (winners to Challengers, losers to Contenders), Chase Turner of Hardin Simmons University defeated Chris Campbell 21-9, 21-7. There were no other Aggies entered in the Challengers division.

In the first round of the Contenders division, B. J. Reynolds of Hardin Simmons University defeated Chris Campbell 21-3, 21-4.

No Aggies participated in the Novice, Open doubles or B doubles competition.

In the round of 16 of the women's Open division (losers to A-B), Eimear Ni Fhalluin of the University College-Dublin, Ireland defeated Kelly Arunski 21-2, 21-0.

In the preliminary round of the women's A division (winners to A-B, losers to B-C), Sarah Corley of Sligo Institute of Technology, Ireland defeated Pam Early 21-2, 21-0 and Jessica Kelley defeated Angie Miller of Missouri State University 21-7, 21-6. In the round of 16 (losers to B), Jessica Kelley defeated Katie Mackoul of Missouri State University 21-10, 21-10 and Kelly Arunski defeated Sarah Corley of Sligo Institute of Technology, Ireland 21-1, 21-12. In the quarterfinals, Jessica Kelley defeated Lisa Jeziomy of Lake Forest College 19-21, 21-4, 11-10 and Kelly Arunski defeated Katie Stack of Missouri State University 12-21, 21-15, 11-4. In the semifinals, Lauren Ritter of Missouri State University defeated Jessica Kelley 21-4, 21-8 and Cindy Matsubara of Pacific University defeated Kelley Arunski 21-12, 21-10 to end the Aggies' hopes of a championship in this division.

In the preliminary round of B (winners to B-C, losers to C-Intermediate), Ember Strand of Hardin Simmons University defeated Jessica Olivares 21-0, 21-5; Ashley Gregg defeated Danica Applegate of the University of Arkansas 21-8, 21-12; Lindsay Liles of the University of Texas defeated Sarah Wood 21-13, 21-7 and Amanda Collier defeated Katie Robinson of the University of Minnesota 21-17, 21-18. In the first round (losers to C), Niam Egan of Queen's University-Belfast, Ireland defeated Ashley Gregg 10-21, 21-4, 11-5; Pam Early defeated Melissa Goebel of the University of Minnesota 21-3, 21-11 and Angie Miller of Missouri State University defeated Amanda Collier 21-7, 8-21, 11-7. In the round of 16, Diane Luttrell of Missouri State University defeated Pam Early 17-21, 21-12, 11-8.

In the preliminary round of C division (winners to C-Intermediate, losers to Intermediate-Challengers), Ashley Ochs defeated Lindsay Costly of Pacific University 21-3, 21-5. In the first round (winners to C, losers to Intermediate) Jill Winger of Pacific University defeated Jessica Olivares 12-21, 21-10, 11-2; Emily Frank of the University of Florida defeated Sarah Wood 21-10, 21-3 and Katie Robinson of the University of Minnesota defeated Ashley Ochs 21-4, 21-5.

There were no Aggies in the preliminary and first rounds of the Intermediate division. In the round of 16, Sarah Wood defeated Becca Neal of Hardin Simmons University 21-5, 21-17 and Stacy Sueoka of Pacific University defeated Ashley Ochs 21-11, 11-21, 11-6. In the quarterfinals, Sarah Wood defeated Karine Hoffman of the University of Florida 21-9, 16-21, 11-6. In the semifinals, Stacy Sueoka of Pacific University defeated Sarah Wood 21-17, 21-12.

There were no Aggies entered in the Challengers, Contenders, Novice or women's doubles.

For the tournament, the Aggie men finished in fourth place behind the University College-Dublin, Ireland. The Aggies totaled 948 points and UC-D totaled 961. The Aggie women's team finished in third place with a total of 855 points behind Lake Forest's 929 points. For the combined team total, the Aggies finished in third place with a total of 1,803 points. Lake Forest was in second place with 2,009 points.

For the second year in a row, the Aggies had one of the four Sportsmanship Award winners. Kelley took on extra duties during the tournament and her contributions were reported on page 5 of the April 2006 issue of the USHA's *Handball*:

Jessica Kelley, second from left
(*Handball*, April 2006, page 5)

Jessica Kelley is an upper-level player who took it upon herself, in conjunction with some friends and her coach's blessing, to take pictures of the tournament participants and transfer them onto CD-ROMs for every tournament attendee. The photos were shown in a slide show on the big screen preceding the awards banquet.

In addition, Kelley played quality handball throughout the tournament around her picture-taking duties. And her extra efforts will ensure that all participants can relive the memorable experience of the tournament.

Another positive award for the Aggies at the tournament was Dutch Lowy receiving the Sabo Scholarship. The scholarships, $1,000 each, are awarded based on participation in USHA events, a good academic record and financial need. Lowy is the second Aggie to receive the scholarship. In the first year

Dutch Lowy (second from the left) with his Sabo Scholarship award

(*Handball*, April 2006, page 2)

of its existence, Priscilla Kojin-Shumate was named a recipient.

As the 2006-2007 school year commenced, the team was glad that the work and rewards of holding a national tournament was history. Now they could totally concentrate on getting ready for the next National Collegiate Handball Tournament and anticipating a trip to Los Angeles, site of the next tournament.

In the first round of the men's Open division (losers drop down to A-B), Dutch Lowy defeated Abraham Montijo of Pima Community College 18-21, 21-11, 11-1; Billy O'Donnell of Queens College, Ireland defeated Josh Smith 21-12, 21-1 and Marshall Lowy defeated Daniel Perez of Pima Community College 21-17, 21-4. In the round of 16 (losers drop down to 9-16 playoff), Suhn Lee of Lake Forest College defeated Dutch Lowy 21-2, 11-21, 11-9 and Ger Coonan of the University of Limerick, Ireland defeated Marshall Lowy 21-13, 21-16. In the quarterfinals of the 9-16 playoff of the men's Open division, Billy O'Donnell of Queens College, Ireland defeated Dutch Lowy 21-6, 21-10 and Marshall Lowy defeated Chris Doolin of Sligo Institute of Technology, Ireland 21-12, 21-13. In the semifinals, Marshall Lowy defeated John Horgan of University College-Dublin, Ireland 21-6, 21-17. In the final match, Billy O'Donnell of Queens College, Ireland defeated Marshall Lowy 19-21, 21-10, 11-1. Marshall Lowy earned 10th place in the National Collegiate Handball Men's Open division.

In the first round of the men's A division (losers drop to B-C, winners to A-B), Zach Arem of the University of Florida defeated Jason Adams 21-16, 21-18 and Aidan Devine of Queens University-Belfast, Ireland defeated Matt Acker 21-9, 21-16. In the first round of A-B (winners to A, losers to B), Adam Loomis of Missouri State University defeated Josh Smith 21-20, 21-16 to eliminate the only Aggie in A division.

In the first round of the men's B (losers drop to C-Intermediates, winners to B-C), Fausto Castro of the College of the Desert defeated Trey Kubacak 21-15, 21-14; David Cargill defeated Steve Marken of Dublin City University, Ireland 21-8, 21-18; Tom Dearing of Missouri State University defeated Chris Patton 21-5, 21-20; Dustin Delay defeated Tankut Can of the University of California-Berkeley 21-19, 21-9; Ryan Elliot of Niagara University defeated Jonathan Norman 21-8, 21-14 and Gary Lee of Stony Brook University defeated Miguel Garza 21-16, 21-2. In the first round of men's B-C (losers drop to C, winners to B), Tom Doerning of Missouri State University defeated Jason Adams 21-13, 21-20; Brett Asato of Pacific University defeated David Cargill 21-10, 21-12; Bryan Campbell of the University of Texas defeated Dustin Delay 21-15, 21-14 and Brian Connolly of Lake Forest College defeated Matt

Acker 19-21, 21-5, 11-1. In the first round of B division, Brian Sides of Missouri State University defeated Josh Smith 16-21, 21-18, 11-5.

In the first round of men's C division (losers to Intermediate-Challengers, winners to C-Intermediate), Nicolas Paine of the University of Texas defeated Wyatt Lautzenheiser 20-21, 21-9, 11-10. In the first round of men's C-Intermediate (losers to Intermediate, winners to C), Trey Kubacak defeated Asa Reynolds of Lake Forest College 21-11, 16-21, 11-10; Lee Fabiatos of Lake Forest College defeated Chris Patton 14-21, 21-18, 11-10; Daniel Hagelberg of Southwestern University defeated Jonathan Norman 21-17, 21-20 and Nicolas Paine of the University of Texas defeated Miguel Garza 21-18, 21-7. In the first round of men's C, David Cargill defeated Shane Hayes of the National University of Ireland, Galway 21-5, 21-14; Chris Gavigan of Sligo Institute of Technology, Ireland defeated Jason Adams 21-7, 21-8; Dustin Delay defeated Michael Morgan of Pensacola Junior College 20-21, 21-14, 11-9; Matt Acker defeated Joe Frankenfield of the University of Miami-Ohio 21-9, 21-15 and Gary Lee of Stoney Brook University defeated Trey Kubacak 21-13, 21-17. In the round of 16, David Cargill defeated Chris Gavigan of Sligo Institute of Technology 21-11, 21-7; Dustin Delay defeated Jimmy Kite of Lake Forest College 21-7, 21-17 and Matt Acker defeated Brendan Waite of the University of Nebraska 21-16, 21-6. In the quarterfinals, Dustin Delay defeated David Cargill 21-11, injury default, and Matt Acker defeated Matt Martin of Missouri State University 21-19, 21-19. In the semifinals, Conor O'Riardan of the University of Limerick, Ireland defeated Dustin Delay 15-21, 21-12, 11-8 and Matt Acker defeated Lee Fabiatos of Lake Forest College 21-14, 21-9. Coach Lowy described the action in the final match as reported on page 10 of the April 2007 issue of the USHA's *Handball*:

> The men's C final boiled down to two players from different countries with different styles but a common will to win.
>
> Matt Acker, a sophomore from Texas A&M, beat Conor O'Riardan from the University of Limerick in Ireland for the championship.
>
> O'Riardan's teammate, Ger Coonan, said the University of Limerick has only a 60-foot by 30-foot court, though the university intends to build two 40-by-20 courts by 2009. As a result, O'Riardan travels an hour each way to practice three times a week.
>
> So, the final pitted players of different backgrounds, different practice habits and different lifestyles but possessing a common goal.
>
> Both well-conditioned athletes played seven matches in three days to make the final. Acker outlasted O'Riardan in the final by scores of 21-17, 21-14.

Matt Acker (right) with his championship trophy

(*Handball*, April 2007, page 10)

In the first round of the men's Intermediate-Challenger play (Loser to Challengers, winners to Intermediate), John Stoller of the University of California-Berkeley defeated Justin Crockett 17-21, 21-20, 11-5 and Wyatt Lautzenheiser defeated Matt Levine of Pacific University 21-5, 21-6. In the first round of men's Intermediate-Challengers-Contenders (losers to Challengers-Contenders, winners to Intermediate), Justin Crockett defeated Chris Schulhoff of the University of Miami-Ohio 21-5, 21-8 and Mike Carpenter of Lake Forest College defeated Joel Rice 21-6, 21-8. In the first round of the Intermediate division, Asa Reynolds of Lake Forest College defeated Wyatt Lautzenheiser 21-14, 19-21, 11-4; Chris Patton defeated Casey Merscher of Pacific University 21-8, 21-2; Chad Reeves of Colorado School of Mines defeated Jonathan Norman 21-5, 21-8 and Miguel Garza defeated Kushal Modi of Lake Forest College 21-5, 21-14. In the round of 16, Chris Patton defeated Mike Carpenter of Lake Forest College 21-7, 21-10 and Miguel Garza defeated Juan Carreon of Southwestern University 21-16, 21-11. In the quarterfinals, Chris Patton defeated John Yi of Southwestern University 21-11, 21-17 and Miguel Garza defeated Matt Rossheim of the University of Florida 21-12, 21-11. In the semifinals, Chris Patton defeated Asa Reynolds of Lake Forest College 21-10, 21-6 and Chad Reeves of Colorado School of Mines defeated Miguel Garza 21-18, 21-12. The match for the Intermediate championship between Patton and Reeves was reported by Coach Lowy on page 11 of the April 2007 issue of the USHA's *Handball*:

Chris Patton (left) with his Intermediate championship trophy

(*Handball*, April 2007, page 11)

The men's Intermediate division featured two relative newcomers to the Collegiates. Chris Patton of Texas A&M played last year but went three-and-out. With relentless practice habits and a deep desire to win, Patton approached this year's tournament with a vengeance.

Enter Chad Reeves from the Colorado School of Mines. Playing seven matches in three days is not for the faint of heart or the unconditioned ball player. Playing at elevation seemed to have helped Reeves prepare tremendously. He ran through the field with relative ease, playing just one tiebreaker.

Patton was on a mission. He sliced up the field and beat Reeves 21-10, 21-15.

There were no Aggies in the first round of the men's Challengers-Contenders-Novice play (winners would drop down to Challengers-Contenders and losers would drop down to Contenders-Novice). In the first round of the Challengers-Contenders (winners to Challengers, losers to Contenders), Michael Deal of the Colorado School of Mines defeated Joel Rice 21-14, 17-21, 11-9. In the first round of play in the Challengers division, Justin Crockett received a bye. In the round of 16, Barrett Gates of the University of Texas defeated Crockett 9-21, 21-18, 11-8 to eliminate the Aggies from the Challenger division.

In the round of 16 of the Contenders division, Joel Rice defeated Andrew Backovski of the University of Miami-Ohio 21-2, 21-2. In the quarterfinals, Rice defeated Frankie Diaz of Los Positas College 20-21, 21-10, 11-7. In the semifinals, Eric Hinojosa of the University of Texas defeated Joel Rice 21-12, 17-21, 11-8.

There were no Aggie men entered in the Novice, Open doubles or B doubles.

In the round of 16 of the women's Open-A/B (winners to Open, losers to A-B), Kelly Arunski defeated Katie Machoul of Missouri State University 21-19, 21-8. In the quarterfinals, Eimear Ni Fhalluin of University College-Dublin, Ireland defeated Kelly Arunski 21-3, 21-0. This moved Arunski to the fifth-eighth semifinals where Catriona Casey of the National University of Ireland, Galway defeated Kelly Arunski 21-14, 15-21, 11-5.

In the first round of the women's A-B-C play (winners to A-B, losers to B-C), Lindsay Ross of Lake Forest College defeated Jessica Gray 21-16, 15-21, 11-7 and Zoe Kind of the University of Miami-Ohio defeated Pam Early 21-18, 18-21, 11-7.

In the first round of women's B-C-Intermediate (winners to B-C, losers to C-Intermediate), Stacey Sueoka of Pacific University defeated Alice Cole by default; Alex Charron of Lake Forest College defeated

Kayla Jones 21-6, 7-21, 11-4; Lisa Ault of the University of Southern California defeated Sarah Wood 17-21, 21-20, 11-4 and Ashley Gregg defeated Mandy Harvey of Western Washington University 19-21, 21-3, 11-1. In women's B-C (winners to B, losers to C), Jessica Gray defeated Lisa Ault of the University of Southern California 21-5, 21-5; Pam Early defeated Elizabeth Mitchell of Western Washington University 21-19, 21-10 and Ashley Gregg defeated Kim Braden of Lake Forest College 21-12, 21-5. In the first round of women's B, Ashley Gregg defeated Diane Lutrell of Missouri State University 21-6, 20-21, 11-7; Pam Early defeated Wenifer Liu of Pacific University 21-2, 21-7; and Jessica Gray defeated Afrk Naughton of Dublin Institute of Technology, Ireland 21-12, 21-15. In the quarterfinals, Sarah Corley of Sligo Institute of Technology, Ireland defeated Ashley Gregg 21-9, 21-6; Pam Early defeated Laura Berettini of Missouri State University 21-17, 21-16 and Jessica Gray defeated Brittany Babida of the University of Texas 21-20, 21-11. In the semifinals, Pam Early defeated Sarah Corley of Sligo Institute of Technology, Ireland 21-18, 21-15 and Lisa Falvey of the University of Limerick, Ireland defeated Jessica Gray 21-0, 21-9. In the final match for the championship, Falvey defeated Early 21-3, 21-3.

Pam Early (right) shows her second place trophy

(*Handball*, April 2007, page 16)

In the women's C-Intermediate-Challengers play (winners to C-Intermediate, losers to Intermediate-Challengers), Carmen Littleford defeated Fiona Egan of Dublin Institute of Technology, Ireland 21-4, 21-14; Colleen Beach of the University of Florida defeated Sally Kenworthy 9-21, 21-16, 11-9; Lindsey Costley of Pacific University defeated Hope Pond 21-11, 21-14 and Amy Conine of the University of Texas defeated Jennifer Johnson 21-8, 2-21, 11-7. In the women's C-Intermediate (winners to C, losers to C-Intermediate), Carmen Littleford defeated Tracey Eimen of Southwestern University 21-9, 21-6; Sarah Wood defeated Celia Goetz of the University of California-Berkeley 21-2, 21-1 and Kayla Jones defeated Colleen Beach of the University of Florida 21-18, 21-2. In the round 16 in the women's C division, Sarah Wood defeated Alicia Stoll of the University of Texas 21-3, 21-19; Elizabeth Mitchell of Western Washington University defeated Kayla Jones 21-7, 21-7 and Laura Keaver of Dublin Institute of Technology, Ireland defeated Carmen Littleford 21-11, 21-7. In the quarterfinals, Elizabeth Mitchell of Western Washington University defeated Sarah Wood 21-5, 20-21, 11-6.

In the first round of the women's Intermediate-Challengers play (winners to Intermediate, losers to Challengers), Sarah Messick of the University of Minnesota defeated Sally Kenworthy 21-13, 16-21, 11-2; Jennifer Penny of the University of Texas defeated Hope Pond 21-2, 21-13 and Jennifer Johnson defeated Emily Rund of the University of Minnesota 21-16, 21-4. In the first round of the women's Intermediate division, Colleen Beach of the University of Florida defeated Jennifer Johnson 11-21, 21-0, 11-3.

In the first round of the women's Challengers division, Sally Kenworthy defeated Sabra Abernathy of the University of Minnesota 21-5, 21-6. In the quarterfinals, Sally Kenworthy defeated Marisa Kanoe Bartel of Pacific University 21-0, 21-9 and Hope Pond defeated Emily Rund of the University of Minnesota 21-15, 21-19. In the semifinals, Sally Kenworthy defeated Erica Balasko of the University of Minnesota 21-6, 21-10 and Hope Pond defeated Sara Matsumoto of Pacific University 21-0, 14-21, 11-0. Coach Lowy described the championship match of the Challengers division as reported on page 18 of the April 2007 issue of the USHA's *Handball*:

> The final of the women's Challengers pitted two Texas A&M freshmen. Sally Kenworthy dropped into this after losing a 11-9 tiebreaker to Intermediate finalist Colleen Beach of

Florida. Hope Pond won her way into the final with a powerful right hand that surprised many opponents because of her small frame.

The two practice together every week. In this final, Kenworthy beat Pond 21-5, 21-7.

Sally Kenworthy (left) with her championship trophy and Hope Pond with her second-place trophy

(*Handball,* April 2007, page 18)

Though the Aggies were not at the level of past years they still were one of the teams that many were trying to emulate. The men's team finished in fifth place with 895 points which was not far behind Pima Community College with 959 points. The women's team finished in third place with 900 points well in front of the University of Texas with 691 points. The women's total points, well in front of the fourth place team (University of Texas), raised the combined team into a third place. The combined team total of 1,795 points was comfortably ahead of the Dublin Institute of Technology, Ireland with 1,626 points. Second place Missouri State University, with 2,028 points, finished comfortably ahead of the Aggies. Lake Forest finished just ahead of Missouri State with 2,040 points

NOTE: Alice Cole was a promising first year player on the team who became sick at the tournament and had to forfeit her first match to Stacey Sueoka of Pacific University. See first round play of the B-C-Intermediate division above. Alice's father, an M. D., ordered a prescription for her and had her return home. She recovered and was listed as a member of the Class of 2010. She did not continue to play with the Aggie handball team.

The USHA Collegiate Tournament committee departed from the practices of the past and only awarded two (usually four awards) Sportsmanship Awards this year. However, one of those recognized for their overall character and sportsmanship was an Aggie, Matt Acker. This was the third year in a row for an Aggie to be recognized with this prestigious award. Considering that each year there are 300 plus college students participating in the National Collegiate Handball Tournament, for an Aggie to be named to this award three consecutive years attests to the quality of students representing Texas A&M.

The Texas A&M Handball Team at the 2007 National Collegiate Handball Tournament
FRONT ROW: Dutch Lowy, Carmen Littleford, Hope Pond, Jessica Gray, Kayla Jones
SINGLE BEHIND FRONT ROW: Jennifer Johnson
SECOND ROW: Sally Kenworthy, Sarah Wood, Ashley Gregg, Pam Early
THIRD ROW: Chris Campbell, Chris Patton, Coach Ozzie Burke, Kelly Arunski, Jason Adams, Matt Acker, Wyatt Lautzenheiser, Dustin Delay
BACK ROW: Coach Charles Bokelman, Trey Kubacak, Marshall Lowy, David Cargill, Joel Rice, Josh Smith, Miguel Garza, Justin Crockett, Jonathan Norman

(Courtesy Lance Lowy)

As the 2007-2008 school year kicked off, the Aggie handball team started looking forward to the next National Collegiate Handball Tournament to be hosted by Missouri State University. Coach Lance Lowy announced his retirement to Ozzie Burke on 22 December 2007. Since Coach Lowy's sons would be participating in their last National Collegiate Handball Tournament, he asked to represent the team at the Nationals. Coach Burke agreed to the arrangement.

As play began in the men's Open A-B (winners to Open, losers to A-B), Dutch Lowy defeated David Brainard of Missouri State University 21-15, 18-21, 11-7 and Marshall Lowy defeated John Horgan of the University of California-Davis 21-11, 21-2. In the round of 16, Suhn Lee of Lake Forest College defeated Dutch Lowy 21-9, 21-12 and Aaron Garner of Pacific University defeated Marshall Lowy 21-5, 21-7. In the men's ninth-place playoff of the Open, Daragh Daly of Ulster-Jordantown, Ireland defeated Dutch Lowy 21-9, 21-16 and Marshall Lowy defeated Ollie Cassidy of Limerick University, Ireland by default. In the semifinals, Daragh Daly of Ulster-Jordantown, Ireland defeated Marshall Lowy 12-21, 21-19, 11-6.

In the men's A-B-C play (winners to A, losers to B-C), Guillermo Pallares of the University of Texas defeated Matt Acker 21-6, 21-19 and Dylan Van Brunt defeated Danny Pry of the University of Texas 21-10, 21-11. In the round of 32 of the men's A division (losers to B), Abraham Montijo of Pima Community College defeated Dylan Van Brunt 21-9, 21-7.

In the men's B-C-Intermediate play (winners to B, losers to C-Intermediate), David Smith of Dublin City University, Ireland defeated Trey Kubacak 21-9, 21-12; Chris Patton defeated Chad Sanderson of Hardin Simmons University 21-6, 21-3; Joel Rice defeated Eric Perrott of the University of Florida 21-7, 21-8; Dustin Delay defeated Michael Beach of the University of Florida 21-15, 21-2 and Darragh Ruane of the University of California-Davis defeated David Cargill 21-15, 21-10. In men's B-C (winners to B, losers to C), Sean McCorry of Ulster-Jordanstown, Ireland defeated Matt Acker 21-15, 9-21, 11-5; Alex Carpenter of the University of Texas-Permian Basin defeated Chris Patton 21-7, 21-5; Tommy McGrath of Dublin Institute of Technology, Ireland defeated Joel Rice 21-8, 21-12 and Dustin Daly defeated Minh Nguyen of the University of Nebraska 21-13, 16-21, 11-2. In the B division round of 32, Shane Heraty of Dublin Institute of Technology defeated Dustin Daly 21-11, 21-17 and Dylan Van Brunt defeated Joey Urbani of Lake Forest College 21-3, 21-12. In the round of 16, Dylan Van Brunt defeated Brian Burke of Inver Hills Community College 21-12, 21-13. In the quarterfinals, Will Hutchinson of the University of Minnesota defeated Van Brunt 21-9, 21-3.

There were no Aggies in the first round of the men's C-Intermediate-Challengers (winners to C-Intermediate, losers to Challengers). In the first round of the men's C-Intermediate (winners to C, Losers to Intermediate), Trey Kubacak defeated Ross Toungate of the University of Texas 21-5, 21-12 and David Cargill defeated Juan Carreon of Southwestern University 21-12, 21-3. In the round of 32 in the men's C, David Cargill defeated Daragh O'Gara of Dublin Institute of Technology, Ireland 21-13, 21-16; Matt Acker defeated Ciaran O'Sullivan of Dublin City University, Ireland 21-9, 21-4; Chris Patton defeated Michael Deal of Colorado School of Mines 21-19, 21-6; Joel Rice defeated Brandon Glaze of Minnesota State-Mankato 18-21, 21-20, 11-5 and Alex Barbag of the University of Florida defeated Trey Kubacak 21-20, 13-21, 11-7. In the round of 16, Cathal Walsh of Dublin City University, Ireland defeated David Cargill 21-10, 21-17; Matt Acker defeated Dan Dilworth of Texas State University 21-13, 21-14; Chris Patton defeated Matt Martin of Missouri State University 21-19, 20-21, 11-1 and Chris Gavigan of Sligo Institute of Technology, Ireland defeated Joel Rice 11-21, 21-20, 11-2. In the quarterfinals, Matt Acker defeated Chris Patton 9-21, 21-19, 11-7. In the semifinals, Matt Acker defeated Minh Nguyen of the University of Nebraska 21-15, 9-21, 11-2. Coach Burke provided the write-up of the championship match and was reported on page 10 of the April 2008 issue of the USHA's *Handball*:

> Matt Acker of Texas A&M repeated as the men's C champion by rolling over David Smith of Dublin City University 21-11, 21-13.

> Acker started in A-B-C and lost to Guillermo Pallares of the University of Texas 21-6, 21-19, so he was forced down to B-C.

Trying to regroup, he was sent down to the C division, this time by Sean McCorry of the University of Ulster-Jordanstown 21-12, 9-21, 11-5.

That'll test your determination to face five more grueling matches for team points in the division you won last year!

But Acker kept his spirits up. He started by walking through Ciaran O'Sullivan of Dublin City University 21-9, 21-4 in the first round.

Matt Acker (left) with his championship plaque

(*Handball*, April 2008, page 10)

Then Acker got the best of Dan Dilworth of Texas State 21-13, 21-14 in the round of 16. But he struggled to beat teammate Chris Patton 9-21, 21-19, 11-7 in the quarterfinals before outlasting Minh Nguyen of Nebraska 21-15, 9-21, 11-2 in the semifinals.

That propelled Acker to his old territory in the final, where he disposed of Smith with a solid all-around effort for his second consecutive C title.

What a tribute to your love of the sport, putting pride aside to perform for the team and having the conditioning to play seven tournament matches in four days.

In the first round of the men's Intermediate-Challengers-Contenders (winners to Intermediate-Challengers, losers to Challengers-Contenders), Asa Reynolds of Lake Forest College defeated Josh Gavin 21-1, 21-1; Mike Carpenter of Lake Forest College defeated Tim Grothe 21-4, 21-11; Daniel Connevey defeated Paul Demby of the University of Florida 21-13, 21-4 and Kushai Modi of Lake Forest College defeated Steve Bremer 21-0, 21-1. In the first round of the men's Intermediate-Challengers (winners to Intermediate, losers to Challengers), Nathan McCartin of the National University of Ireland, Galway defeated Daniel Connevey 21-18, 21-17. Loss of this match eliminated all Aggies from the Intermediate division.

In the first round of the men's Challengers-Contenders-Novice (winners to Challengers-Contenders, losers to Novice), Nick Miller defeated Andy Judd of the University of Minnesota 21-12, 19-21, 11-9 and Stephen Wood defeated Evan Townsend of Fort Scott Community College 21-4, 21-4. In the first round of the men's Challengers-Contenders (winners to Challenges, losers to Contenders), Dakota Hall of Fort Scott Community College defeated Josh Gavin 15-21, 21-12, 11-4; Nick Miller defeated Mark Schrock of the University of Miami-Ohio by default; Pat Jarvis of Lake Forest College defeated Tim Grothe 21-5, 21-2; Stephen Wood defeated Aiden Melia of Dublin Institute of Technology, Ireland 21-11, 21-1 and Lee Moyers of Pacific University defeated Steve Bremer 21-12, 14-21, 11-5. In the round of 32 of the men's Challengers division, Stephen Wood defeated Kevin Coker of Pittsburg State University 21-18, 19-21, 11-4; Dan Perez of San Jose State University defeated Daniel Connevey 21-16, 21-12 and Paul Ratterree of Hardin Simmons University defeated Nick Miller 21-6, 18-21, 11-5. In the round of 16, Stephen Wood defeated Reese Moriyami of Pacific University 21-11, 21-19. In the quarterfinals, Wood was defeated by Tom Cirone of Lake Forest College 21-4, 21-1.

In the first round of the men's Contenders division, Zachary Profant of the University of California defeated Tim Grothe 19-21, 21-13, 11-3 and Steve Bremer defeated Alex Eschenbach of the University of Texas 21-4, 21-9. In the round of 16, Josh Gavin defeated Antriksh Mithal 21-13, 21-19 and Steve Bremer defeated Trevor Cole of the University of Florida 21-11, 21-2. In the quarterfinals, Josh Gavin defeated

Matt Novak of the University of Minnesota 20-21, 21-9, 11-10 and Steve Bremer defeated Tim Smith of San Jose State University 21-12, 21-11. In the semifinals, Josh Gavin defeated Zachary Profant of the University of California 11-21, 21-19, 11-5 and Eamon Briggs of Southwestern University defeated Steve Bremer 21-11, 21-14. Gene McCormick described the action in the final and was reported on page 13 of the April issue of the USHA's *Handball*:

Josh Gavin (right) with his second place plaque

(*Handball*, April 2008, page 13)

> This year's men's Contenders championship match had a little bit of everything for the players and fans. In the first game, Eamon Briggs of Southwestern University got off to a fast start with great wraparound serves that kept his opponent, Josh Gavin of Texas A&M, in the back court and on the defensive. But Gavin came storming back to win the opener 21-15.
>
> In the second game, Gavin got his Z-serve working and also made some great kill shots. The game was his for the taking, but with both players tired, Briggs had a little extra at the end, winning 21-19. That forced the match to a tie-breaker, where Briggs, a bit fresher, grabbed the title with an 11-4 victory.

There were no Aggies in the Novice or Consolation divisions.

As the round of 16 began for the women's Open title there were no Aggie women ranked to compete in this division.

In the first round of the women's A-B-C (winners to A-B, losers to B-C), Jessica Gray defeated Kim Braden of Lake Forest College 21-16, 21-4; Ashley Gregg defeated Leah Betcher of the University of Minnesota 21-3, 21-15 and Pam Early defeated Sarah Messick of the University of Minnesota 21-11, 21-5. In the women's A division, Jessica Gray defeated Andrea Thurmond of Missouri State University 21-8, 21-11; Bailey Chandler of Missouri State University defeated Ashley Gregg 21-11, 21-6 and Lauren Ritter of Missouri State University defeated Pam Early 17-21, 21-14, 11-10. In the quarterfinals, Jessica Gray defeated Angie Miller of Missouri State University 21-18, 21-13. In the semifinals, Karen Lawlor of Limerick University, Ireland defeated Jessica Gray 21-3, 21-17.

In the first round of the women's B-C-Intermediate (winners to B-C, losers to C-Intermediate), Kayla Jones defeated Jessica Long of Missouri State University 21-7, 21-14 and Sally Kenworthy defeated Lindsey Wuenker of the University of Florida 21-9, 21-8. In the first round of the women's B-C (winners to B, losers to C), Kayla Jones defeated Melissa Goebel of the University of Minnesota 21-6, 21-16 and Sally Kenworthy defeated Sarah Messick of the University of Minnesota. In the round of 16 of the women's B division, Andrea Thurmond of Missouri State University defeated Sally Kenworthy 21-20, 21-17; Laura Berettini of Missouri State University defeated Kayla Jones 21-11, 21-13; Ashley Gregg defeated Brittany Babida of the University of Texas 13-21, 21-19, 11-0 and Pam Early defeated Kim Braden of Lake Forest College 21-15, 21-1. In the quarterfinals, Amanda Harvey of Western Washington University defeated Ashley Gregg 21-2, 21-3 and Catriona Casey of National University of Ireland, Galway defeated Pam Early 21-9, 21-9.

There were no Aggies playing in the women's C division.

In the women's Intermediate-Challengers play (winners to Intermediate, losers to Challengers), Dawn Rackel defeated Crystal Pihl of Pittsburgh State University 21-7, 21-2 and Angie Burrer defeated

Jennifer Huntsman of Southwestern University 21-13, 21-3. In the first round of women's Intermediate-Challengers (winners to Intermediate, losers to Challengers), Sarah Abernathy of the University of Minnesota defeated Dawn Rackel 16-21, 21-11, 11-7 and Angie Burrer defeated Katie Long of Missouri State University 21-11, 21-9. In the round of 16 of the women's Intermediate division, Rachel Gibbons of Southwestern University defeated Angie Burrer 21-10, 21-8.

In the round of 16 of the women's Challengers division, Dawn Rackel could not meet the challenge of Joanne Logan of University College of Dublin, Ireland and was defeated 21-4, 21-8.

No Aggie women were entered in the women's Contenders, Novice or doubles.

The Aggie men's team improved over the previous year's final standings to third place. Their 931 points were just ahead of the fourth place team of Pima Community College's 905 points. The Aggie women's team again placed third with 865 points which was a comfortable margin over the fourth place team of the Dublin Institute of Technology, Ireland's 739 points. The combined team total of 1,796 points was good enough for third place. It was a great learning experience for A&M's first year head coach, Ozzie Burke.

As the 2008-2009 school year emerged the Aggies knew there was work to be done just to stay at the competitive level of the past few years. All began looking forward to the work ahead and going to the University of Minnesota for the next National Collegiate Handball Tournament.

As play began in the opening matches in the round of 32 of the men's Open-A-B (losers to A-B), David Brainard of Missouri State University defeated Dustin Van Brunt 21-6, 21-1 to eliminate the only Aggie in the top 32 from the Open division.

In the first round of the A-B-C play (winners to A-B, losers to B-C), Darragh Ruane of the University College-Dublin, Ireland defeated Philip Russell 21-9, 21-11; Joel Rice defeated Seamus Casserley of Dublin Institute of Technology, Ireland 21-6, 21-6; Victor Espinosa of Pima Community College defeated Chris Patton 11-21, 21-9, 11-4; Brian Quigley of the National University of Dublin, Galway defeated Dustin Delay 21-10, 21-12 and Matt Acker defeated Michael Cain of the University of Miami-Ohio 21-7, 21-3. In the round of 32 of the A-B play (winners to A, losers to B), Dustin Van Brunt defeated Paddy Sherry of the University of Ulster-Jordanstown, Ireland 21-19, 21-20; Nick Tovar of Pima Community College defeated Joel Rice 21-8, 21-5 and Evan Brown defeated Matt Acker 21-11, 21-10. In the A division round of 16, Dustin Van Brunt defeated James Zender of Lake Forest College 21-18, 21-8. In the quarterfinals, Nick Tovar of Pima Community College defeated Dustin Van Brunt 18-21, 21-13, 11-3.

In the first round of the B-C-Intermediate play (winners to B-C, losers to C-Intermediate), Mathias Langhorst of the University of Minnesota-Duluth defeated Stephen Wood 21-5, 21-6. In the first round of the B-C play (winners to B, losers to C), Dustin Delay defeated Jesse Fleck of the University of Minnesota 21-1, 21-1 and Chris Patton defeated Casey Merscher of Pacific University 21-1, 21-2. In the round of 32 of B division, Joel Rice defeated Dylan Raintree of the University of California 21-7, 21-6; Darragh Ruane of the University College - Dublin, Ireland defeated Dustin Delay 14-21, 21-19, 11-2; Phillip Russell defeated Brian Connolly of Lake Forest College 12-21, 21-11, 11-4; Chris Patton defeated Joey Urbani of Lake Forest College 17-21, 21-12, 11-4 and Matt Acker defeated Chad Bolin of Missouri State University 21-5, 21-8. In the round of 16, David Smith of Dublin City University, Ireland defeated Joel Rice 21-8, 13-21, 11-4; Michael Donnelly of Queen's University-Belfast, Ireland defeated Phillip Russell 16-21, 21-17, 11-7; Chris Patton defeated Wes Myers of the University of Texas 21-10, 21-10 and Michael Wu of the University of California defeated Matt Acker 21-10, 21-7. In the quarterfinals, Michael Wu of the University of California defeated Chris Patton 21-20, 21-13.

In the first round of the C-Intermediate-Challengers play (winners to C-Intermediate, losers to Intermediate-Challengers), Nick Miller defeated Dakota Hall of Fort Scott Community College 21-13,

8-21, 11-7; Matt Levine of Pacific University defeated Tim Grothe 21-6, 21-8 and Steve Bremer defeated Mark Austin of Missouri State University 21-13, 21-10. In the first round of the C-Intermediate play (winners to C, losers to Intermediate), Steve Wood defeated Alan Noonan of the University College-Dublin, Ireland 8-21, 21-12, 11-2; Nick Miller defeated Rick Aouad of the University of Texas 21-6, 21-5 and Steve Bremer defeated Jeff Van Boovan of Missouri State University 21-12, 21-13. In the round of 32 of C division, Matt Whitaker of Missouri State University defeated Nick Miller 21-7, 21-13; Steve Bremer defeated Jesse Fleck of the University of Minnesota 6-21, 21-9, 11-9 and Dan Sterrett of Lake Forest College defeated Stephen Wood 21-14, 21-10. In the round of 16, Casey Merscher of Pacific University defeated Steve Bremer 21-1, 21-1.

In the first round of the Intermediate-Challengers-Contenders play (winners to Intermediate-Challengers, losers to Challengers-Contenders), Danny Williams of Pacific University defeated Logan Vincent 21-4, 4-21, 11-4 and Drew Warren defeated Devon Tally of Fort Scott Community College 21-8, 21-13. In the first round of Intermediate-Challengers (winners to Intermediate, losers to Challengers), Michael Petefish of the University of Florida defeated Tim Grothe 21-11, 21-3 and Drew Warren defeated Chris Yard of Minnesota State University-Mankato 21-10, 21-6. In the Intermediate division round of 32, Darren O'Neil of the National University of Ireland, Galway defeated Drew Warren 21-18, 21-2.

In the first round of the Challengers-Contenders-Novice play (winners to Challengers-Contenders, losers to Contenders-Novice), Brady Adams of Utah State University defeated Matt Chase 21-2, 21-6 and Alex Mok of Stonybrook University defeated Jared Biermann 11-21, 21-1, 11-3. In the first round of the Challengers-Contenders play (winners to Challengers, losers to Contenders), James Flaherty of Stony Brook University defeated Logan Vincent 21-7, 21-5. In the Challengers division round of 32, Jack Olsen of Utah State University defeated Tim Grothe 21-4, 21-11.

In the first round of the Contenders-Novice play (winners to Contenders, losers to Novice), Jared Beirmann defeated Josh Salway of Minnesota State University-Mankato 14-21, 21-11, 11-1. In the Contenders division round of 32, Logan Vincent defeated Kyle Moodie of Pittsburg State University 21-4, 21-14 and Jared Biermann defeated Jarrett Spitzner of Colorado School of Mines 21-14, 21-12. In the round of 16, Bryan Lucero of Stony Brook University defeated Logan Vincent 21-11, 21-10 and Travis Hoover of San Jose State University defeated Jared Beirmann 21-9, 21-18.

There were no Aggies entered in the Novice division.

Dustin Van Brunt and Phillip Russell decided to enter the Open doubles competition and were defeated in the first round 21-3, 21-2 by Ciaran Burke and Brian Quigley of the National University of Ireland, Galway.

In B Doubles competition, Drew Warren and Tim Grothe met the same fate as Van Brunt/Russell had in the Open Doubles competition. David Lozano and Winston Pool of Southwestern University defeated Warren/Grothe 21-6, 21-4. Having the Aggies compete in doubles was a change from the Lowy coached teams where Aggies only competed if there was a chance for a high finish. Doubles at the tournament does not count for points toward the team competition. When Coach Burke played and won the Collegiate Doubles Championship in 1968 the doubles team was half of the handball team of four and could not play in the singles competition. Likewise, the two singles players could not opt to play in the Doubles competition. Currently, knowing that the Aggie team would not be competing for the team championship, Coach Burke wanted the players to have as much fun as possible and also gain additional experience through the Doubles competition.

In the first round of the women's Open play (losers to A-B), Maria Dugas of Lake Forest College defeated Jessica Gray 21-2, 21-4 and Katie Costello of the Dublin Institute of Technology, Ireland defeated Sally Kenworthy 10-21, 21-6, 11-1. Obviously, this eliminated all the Aggie women from the Open division.

In the round of 16 of the A-B play (winners to A, losers to B), Jessica Gray defeated Danielle Daskalakis of Stony Brook University 21-12, 21-5 and Alex Charron of Lake Forest College defeated Sally Kenworthy 21-2, 21-8. In the quarterfinals, Jessica Gray defeated Ashley Moler of the University of Iowa 3-21, 21-14, 11-5. In the semifinals, Jessica Gray was defeated by Missy Miller of Western Washington University 21-11, 9-21, 11-10. It does not get any closer than that.

In the first round of the B-C-Intermediate play (winners to B-C, losers to C-Intermediate), Amanda McKay of Missouri State University defeated Krystin Deason 21-3, 21-3. In the round of 16 of B division, Sally Kenworthy defeated Amanda McKay of Missouri State University 21-8, 21-5. In the quarterfinals, Sally Kenworthy defeated Laura Keaver of the Dublin Institute of Technology, Ireland 21-2, 21-2. In the semifinals, Lara Berrettini of Missouri State University defeated Sally Kenworthy 21-15, 21-16.

In the first round of the C-Intermediate play (winners to C, losers to Intermediate), Krystin Deason defeated Maureen Kumar of the University of Texas 21-10, 21-11. In the round of 16 of C division, Viri Del Bosque of Lake Forest College defeated Krystin Deason 21-15, 9-21, 11-5.

There were no Aggie women entered in the Intermediate, Challengers, Contenders or doubles competition.

The Aggie men's team finished in third place with 893 points which was just ahead of the University of Texas with 850 points. With only three women on the women's team the Aggies did not have the opportunity to earn a lot of points but did finish in seventh place with 449 points. The combined team score of 1,342 points was good enough for sixth place.

CHAPTER 12
A&M Handball Teams 2010-2022

NOTE: All hand ball players listed in this Chapter are from Texas A&M unless the player's college or university is listed.

The National Collegiate Handball Tournament became a contentious event in 2010. Texas A&M, under an earlier agreement with the College Commissioners, was scheduled to host the tournament. Lance Lowy, retired A&M faculty and handball coach, a member of the World Players of Handball (WPH), strongly felt that under his guidance (he had done this before) and, under the umbrella of the WPH, that Texas A&M would put on a great National Collegiate Handball Tournament. Ozzie Burke, the A&M handball coach, had already made a commitment to the USHA, the organization that started the tournament in 1953 and continued sponsorship of the tournament over the previous 56 years. Typically, it had been the responsibility of the coach of the host team to plan, supervise and ensure a great tournament experience for all visiting players and teams to include the hosting team's own handball players. Caught between the two entities, the Director and Staff of the A&M Recreation Center did not feel comfortable hosting the tournament. It cannot be accurately determined who officially cancelled the handball tournament scheduled to be held on the A&M handball courts; however, when that decision was made Coach Burke had to cancel all of the hotel reservations and other plans made in conjunction with the tournament. Coach Burke, still wanting to host the tournament, started making plans for another site.

When problems surface, good leaders solve the problem. Two articles in the April 2010 issue of the USHA's *Handball* magazine help explain how the problem was solved and why it is very important to work together for a mutual goal. The article, written by the USHA staff and found on page 20, follows:

Houston, we have no problem: Tourney thrives

When the USHA National Collegiate Championships lost the Texas A&M rec center as the site for this year's event, the Texas players were put in a bind, as they had planned on having a low-cost travel year.

Besides that, the TAMU Handball Club still wanted to host. But finding a facility with adequate courts to host the collegiate is extremely difficult. Just a few sites have enough courts in one building.

As soon as this predicament popped up, the Houston Downtown YMCA was the site where all attention turned. Disappointed by the split in organizations, the Houston Handball Club and Chuck Reeve were deliberate in giving us their answer, hoping a single tournament could still be salvaged.

When that option disappeared, Reeve and the Houston club got behind the collegiates-and got behind it in a big way. In addition to helping obtain the facility, Reeve and Derek Lucas had all the hours of play covered as well as the morning food, all-day fruit, Gatorade and other snacks.

It wasn't Houston's tournament, but it sure felt like it. Many, many thanks go out to Reeve, Lucas and the Houston Handball Club for providing a great venue, great hospitality and a great spot for the Texas collegiate players to stay close to home.

Hosting a tournament three hours from home is less than optimal, but coach Ozzie Burke and TAMU Handball Club president Kayla Jones pulled it off. They made several scouting trips to help organize the food-one of the most important ingredients in a college event.

When a band was mentioned as a possibility, Burke and Beth Rowley stepped up to help with the cost.

Manpower is key in organizing the draw, and the USHA staff was most fortunate to have Tom and Cass Sove and Gary Cruz on hand to handle the brunt of the work. The tournament ran very smoothly and on time, and much of that thanks goes to the players and their teams for stepping up and refereeing as required or need.

As Cruz noted: "The kids are great."

The following article was from Mike Dau, Lake Forest College handball coach, who added his insight into the problem and was reported on the same page, same magazine issue, as the article above:

A perspective on the Collegiate

At the 2010 USHA National Collegiate Championships, hosted by Texas A&M at the Houston Downtown YMCA, the main topic of discussion was the state of college handball confronted with two separate tournaments.

There was unanimous agreement among coaches and the USHA staff that one college tournament best served the interests of our young players. The question evolved as to what to do about it.

Over the last 58 years, the USHA has had a deep involvement in the structure and maintenance of the tournament. Historically, a collegiate committee, made up of the participating coaches, submitted a wide range of recommendations to the USHA board. The issues have included budgeting, eliminating the team concept, player eligibility, elimination of doubles, professional participation and beyond. Some of these issues have met with approval by the board, others have not.

For the last several years, the concept of autonomy has become a critical issue for some of the college coaches, who had a sense of losing control of the tournament to the USHA. However, at the 2002 summer coaches meeting, a request was unanimously approved by all the coaches in attendance that the USHA appoint a national collegiate tournament manager. At its next meeting, the board approved the resolution. It ultimately relieved the host coach from tournament management responsibility. Installing player information into a computer took much of the contentiousness out of seeding. In the last three tournaments, seeding meetings have become somewhat obsolete, with draw sheets e-mailed to coaches the weekend before the event.

I mention all of this because of the confusion over the term "autonomy" as it relates to the different opinions. What autonomous responsibilities does one group seek that another group fails to seek?

Is it budget, with one group wanting more control over the money, while the other group doesn't want additional financial responsibility?

Does one group want tournament management back in the hands of the host coach, while the other group is satisfied with the current arrangement?

Is one group offended by board disapproval of certain resolutions, while the other group is satisfied with its decision?

It's common knowledge that some very strong-minded people have butted heads over these issues. But should personality conflicts hinder what is best for the game? The USHA has successfully run a national junior tournament and a national collegiate tournament for more than 50 years. Two separate junior tournaments and two separate collegiate events are clearly not in the best interests of the young people involved in our game.

It's time to try to resolve the differences. If an agreement cannot be reached, the growth of handball might be at stake.

It should be noted that the split between the World Players of Handball (WPH) and the USHA reached an agreement and the USHA maintained control of the National Collegiate Handball Tournament. It is generally known that Fred Lewis, a professional handball player with many national championships and WPH President, is given much of the credit for the two factions obtaining closure on their issues. Closure was reached at the January meeting of the Boards of the USHA and WPH. The official resolution reached was printed on page 3 of the April 2011 issue of the USHA's *Handball* magazine and states as listed below:

Official USHA and WPH resolution

WHEREAS the WPH and USHA seek to promote the growth of the sport of handball, and

WHEREAS the two organizations and their members and supporters show a deep love for the game of handball:

BE IT RESOLVED: that the two handball organizations, the USHA as the national governing body of handball, and the WPH, the World Players of Handball foundation, agree to cooperate to support the innovative promotion, exposure, and development of professional handball, including such means as filming and webcasting. The USHA and WPH also agree to work collaboratively on amateur promotion and development.

The two groups shall work together to achieve a common goal-the growth and development of handball at all levels.

In the article by Mike Dau, mention was made of computer use to seed the players at the national tournament. Previous to computer use, the seeding process normally became heated and took a long time for resolution. It is very understandable that coaches wanted to avoid their players playing a professional or one of the previous Open winners of the tournament as long as possible. Avoidance of the more talented players was a big issue and rightfully so since the more victories in the more skilled divisions meant more points toward a possible team championship.

Despite the split, many teams decided to come to the USHA sponsored tournament hosted by Texas A&M and held in Houston. Obviously, most teams had already budgeted for the trip to Texas so going to Houston rather than College Station did not significantly alter their trip. Since the Aggies hosted the event, and that is where the Aggie team played, only results from that tournament are reported. Some of the usual college/university teams played in a national tournament hosted by the WPH.

In the round of 32 in the men's Open-A-B-C (losers to B-C), Billy O'Donnell of Queens College, Ireland defeated Drew Warren 21-8, 21-0; Joe Welch of the University of Washington defeated Stephen Wood 21-6, 21-1 and Dustin Van Brunt defeated Kevin Cui of the University of Texas 21-5, 21-3. In the round of 16 (winners to Open, losers to A), Dustin Van Brunt defeated Joey Urbani of Lake Forest College 21-2, 21-19. In the quarterfinals, Suhn Lee of Lake Forest College defeated Van Brunt 21-6, 21-9.

There were no Aggies entered in the A division.

In the first round in the B-C-Intermediate-Challengers play (winners to B-C, losers to Intermediate-Challengers), Alex Lin of Stony Brook University defeated James Warren 21-8, 21-6; Lane Patterson defeated Andrew Backovsky of Miami University-Ohio 21-10, 21-7 and Alex Eschenbach of the University of Texas defeated Nick Miller 21-4, 10-21, 11-10. In the round of 32 play (winners to B, losers to C), Drew Warren defeated Alex Lin of Stony Brook University 21-8, 21-14 and Stephen Wood defeated Lee Moyers of Pacific University 21-14, 21-6. In the B division round of 16, Drew Warren defeated Peter Gerde of the University of North Dakota 21-9, 21-9 and Josh Bateman of Pacific University defeated Stephen Wood 21-14, 21-20. In the quarterfinals, Simon Hanover of Michigan State University defeated Warren 21-13, 21-19.

In the round of 16 of C division, Dan Schonhardt of Minnesota State University-Mankato defeated Lane Patterson (score not given). Patterson was the lone Aggie entered in C division.

In the first round of play in Intermediate-Challengers-Contenders-Novice (losers to Novice-Consolation), Jared Biermann defeated Kevin Reilly of Western Washington University 21-20, 21-11. In the second round of play (winners to Intermediate-Challengers, losers to Contenders), Justin Novak of Lake Forest College defeated Austin Acosta 21-3, 21-4. In the round of 32 (losers to Challengers), James Warren defeated Justin Novak of Lake Forest College 21-16, 21-14 and Nick Miller defeated Anthony Guarrancia of Michigan State University 21-15, 21-20. In the round of 16 of the Intermediate division, James Warren defeated Jonathan Johnson of the University of Texas-San Antonio 21-8, 21-6 and Nick Miller defeated Jared Komo of Pacific University 21-4, 21-10. In the quarterfinals, Travis Otwell of the University of Texas defeated Drew Warren 21-15, 18-21, 11-7 and Lucas Wesley of the University of Texas defeated Nick Miller 21-8, 8-21, 11-5.

There were no Aggies entered in the Challengers division.

In the round of 16 play in Contenders-Novice-Consolation (losers to Consolation), Austin Acosta defeated Brady Maddox of Lone Star College by default and Thomas O'Rourke of Colorado School of Mines defeated Jared Beirmann 21-13, 4-21, 11-9. In the quarterfinals, Austin Acosta was defeated by Collin Weigel of Pacific University 21-10, 21-9.

There were no Aggies entered in the Novice division.

In the first round of the Consolation division Jared Beirmann defeated Samuel Arriola of Pacific University 21-8, 21-11. In the semifinals Marco Montes of the University of Texas defeated Beirmann 21-7, 21-15.

In the first round of the men's Open doubles competition, Dustin Van Brunt and Stephen Wood defeated Ty Tindell and Kolson Lucas of the University of Texas 21-1, 21-3. In the semifinals, Suhn Lee and Nikolai Nahorniak of Lake Forest College defeated Dustin Van Brunt and Stephen Wood 21-4, 21-7.

In the first round of the men's B doubles competition, Nick Miller and Lane Patterson defeated Stephen Copeland and Matt Kamas of Southwestern University 21-0, 21-3. In the round of 16, Dan Schonhardt and Matt Novak of Minnesota State University-Mankato defeated Drew Warren and James Warren 17-21, 21-12, 11-1 and James Flaherty and Chris Falciano of Stony Brook University defeated Nick Miller and Lane Patterson 21-6, 21-16.

In the first round of the women's Open-A-B-C-Intermediate-Challengers competition (winners to Open-A-B-C, losers to Intermediate-Challengers), Dawn Rackel defeated Alissa Crawford of Michigan State University 21-7, 21-15. In the round of 32 of the Open-A-B-C competitions (winners to Open-A, losers to B-C), Bianca Greene of Lake Forest College defeated Dawn Rackel 21-0, 21-7; Angie Burrer defeated Viri Del Bosque of Lake Forest College 20-21, 21-19, 11-10; Krystin Deason defeated Elizabeth Sherman of Pacific University 21-8, 21-15 and Kayla Jones defeated Ashleigh Benz of the University of Illinois 21-9, 21-7. In the round of 16 of the women's Open division, Sarah Brusig of Lake Forest College defeated Angie Burrer 21-8, 21-5; Danielle Daskalakis of Stony Brook University defeated Krystin Deason 21-1, 21-12 and Andrea Sabato of the University of Alaska-Anchorage defeated Kayla Jones 21-5, 21-20.

In the quarterfinals of the women's A division, Kayla Jones defeated Annaliese Szutenbach of Lake Forest College 21-3, 20-21, 11-0; Krystin Deason defeated Bianca Greene of Lake Forest College 13-21, 21-14, 11-7 and Angie Burrer defeated Amalia Desardi of Lake Forest College 21-16, 21-15. In the semifinals, Kayla Jones defeated Krystin Deason 21-12, 9-21, 11-6 and Maureen Kumar of the University of Texas defeated Angie Burrer 21-9, 21-7. Coach Burke described Kayla's way to victory and was reported on page 18, April 2010 issue of the USHA's *Handball*:

Kayla Jones of Texas A&M convincingly won the women's A championship by breezing past Maureen Kumar of Texas 21-9, 21-9 in the final.

But in advancing from the Intermediate in 2009 to runner-up in the A in one year, Kumar proved she will be one to watch.

Jones won her initial round in the Open against Ashleigh Benz of Illinois 21-9, 21-7 before Andrea Sabato of Alaska-Anchorage defeated her 21-5, 21-10.

A determined Jones defeated Anneliese Szutenbach of Lake Forest 21-3, 20-21, 11-0 in the opening round of the A, then edged teammate Krystin Deason in a strategically played semifinal 21-12, 9-21, 11-6.

Accommodating her final opponent Kumar's request to play a day early, Jones rolled to the championship anyhow.

Kayla Jones with her championship trophy
(*Handball*, April 2010, page 18)

In the first round of women's competition in B-C (winners to B, losers to C), Dawn Rackel defeated Katherine Quiram of Minnesota State University-Mankato 21-8, 21-4. In the quarterfinals of B Division, Tracey Kaplan of the University of Texas defeated Dawn Rackel 21-8, 21-2 to eliminate the only Aggie in B division.

There were no Aggie women entered in the C, Intermediate, or Challengers divisions.

In the first round of women's Open doubles, Nicole Moser and Bianca Greene of Lake Forest College defeated Krystin Deason and Kayla Jones 21-9, 21-20.

In the first round of women's B doubles, Dawn Rackel and Angie Burrer defeated Ashleigh Benz and Robin Eastwood of the University of Illinois 21-8, 21-1. In the semifinals, Elizabeth Sherman and Jenny Novak of Pacific University defeated Dawn Rackel and Angie Burrer 21-15, 21-14.

In the men's team competition, Lake Forest was a clear winner but the competition for the next four spots was very, very close. Texas A&M men's team finished in fifth place but only 27 points behind the second place team, Pacific University with 843 points. That is the difference of only one or two wins. The men's 816 points combined with the women's 672 points gave the Aggies a combined total of 1,468 points which was good enough for third place. The women's team total of 672 points was significantly behind the women of Lake Forest but enough to be the second place team in the tournament. A&M's women were just ahead of third place Pacific University with 656 points.

Kayla Jones and Krysten Deason with coach
Ozzie Burke showing the team's runner-up trophy

(*Handball*, April 2010, page 18)

There is always an awards presentation banquet at each tournament. Here we see Coach OzzieBurke and wife, Diana, enjoying the band which they helped in paying the expenses.

(*Handball*, April 2010, page 5)

With the knowledge that there will be only one tournament for the National Collegiate Handball Championships, the Aggies began their 2010-2011 preparation for the trip to Arizona State University, site of the next National Collegiate Handball Tournament.

As the pairings were made, there were now three different divisions for the men to be assigned. For the most talented, assignment to Division I was made. Talented and experienced players not ranked high enough for Division I were assigned to Division II. The rest of the field were assigned to Division III.

As play began for the men's Division I Open-A-B play-in, (NOTE: new term *Play-In* are the preliminary rounds used to determine in which division the competitor will ultimately compete) Dustin Van Brunt was defeated by Alfredo Herrera of Pacific University 21-16, 21-12. He then moved to the Open-A-B-2 play-in, and in that competition, Van Brunt was defeated by Riley Kloss of Lake Forest College 21-20, 21-12 eliminating him from the Open and A divisions.

In the first round of the men's B singles, Conor O'Gormen of Dublin City University, Ireland defeated Dustin Van Brunt 21-8, 21-10. This eliminated the lone Aggie from the top three divisions.

In the C-Intermediate-Challengers play-in, Lane Patterson defeated Cathal Reynolds of University of College-Cork, Ireland 21-4, 21-11. In the C-Intermediate play-in, Lane Patterson defeated Michael Wilbanks of Missouri State University 19-21, 21-18, 11-3. In the first round of C division, Paddy Sherry of the University of Ulster-Jordanstown, Ireland defeated Lane Patterson 21-17, 21-19.

In the first round of Division II A-B-C (winners to A-B, losers to C), Rafael Mascarro of San Jose State University defeated Austin Acosta 21-4, 21-4. In the first round of the B-C-1 play-in, Ben Olsen of Minneapolis Community and Technical College defeated Jared Beirmann 21-6, 21-4. In the B-C play-in, Eric Doyle of Western Washington University defeated Austin Acosta 21-9, 21-3. In the C-Intermediate-Challengers play-in, Eric Essenwein of the University of Florida defeated Clayton Mansfield 21-3, 21-6. In the C-Intermediate play-in, Eric Essenwein defeated Barrett Martin of Missouri State University 19-21, 21-4, 11-5.

In the first round of C Division II, Kevin Lammi of the University of Minnesota defeated Austin Acosta 21-2, 21-1.

In the first round of Division II Intermediate matches, Peter Li of Stony Brook University defeated Jared Biermann 21-10, 21-6.

In the first round of Division II Intermediate-Challengers-Contenders (winners to Intermediate-Challengers, losers to Challengers-Contenders), Steven Zhu of Stony Brook University defeated Ben Knighton 21-9, 21-5. In the Challengers-Contenders play-in (winners to Challengers, losers to Contenders), James Thurlow of the Colorado School of Mines defeated Ben Knighton 21-3, 21-8. In the quarterfinals of Division II Challengers, Jonathan Larson of Utah State University defeated Clayton Mansfield 21-9, 21-2.

In the first round of Division III A-B-C (winners to A-B, losers to B-C), Ryan Sparks of Colorado School of Mines defeated John Preble 21-2, 21-8. In the first round of Division III B-C-Intermediate play-in (winners to B-C, losers to C-Intermediate), Mark Quinn of Dublin Institute of Technology, Ireland defeated Christian Quintero 21-9, 21-11. In the Division III B-C play-In (winners to B, losers to C), Matthew Pringle of Michigan State University defeated John Preble 21-2, 21-2. In the first round of Division III C, Kendy Wu of Stony Brook University defeated John Preble 21-13, 21-4. In the first round of Division III C-Intermediate-Challengers (winners to C-Intermediate, losers to Intermediate-Challengers), Andrew Munguina of Utah State University defeated Zachary Smith 21-10, 18-21, 11-9. In the Division III Intermediate, John Derbish of the University of Florida defeated Christian Quintero 21-14, 21-6. In Division III Challengers, Brad Jernberg of Minnesota State University-Mankato defeated Zachary Smith 21-12, 21-5.

In first round of men's Open doubles, Lane Patterson and Will Van Brunt defeated Sean McCorry and Paddy Sherry of University of Ulster-Jordanstown, Ireland 21-8, 7-21, 11-9. In the quarterfinals, Scottie Moler and Jonathan Hingey of Missouri State University defeated Lane Patterson and Will Van Brunt 21-6, 21-4.

In the first round of men's B doubles, John Preble and Clayton Mansfield were defeated 21-2, 21-0. The opponent was not listed. Also, in the first round, Joseph Boo and Steven Zhu of Stony Brook University defeated Jared Beirmann and Austin Acosta 21-2, 21-5. This ended the doubles play for the men on the Aggie team.

In the first round of women's play in the Open-A-B competition, Shauna Hilley defeated Kayla Jones 21-0, 21-3. In the first round of play in Open-A-B-C division play-in, Krystin Deason defeated Katherine Orveez of the University of Florida 21-3, 21-8. In the Open-A-B play-in, Stephanie Miller of the University of Florida defeated Krystin Deason 21-15, 21-2 and Stephanie Coleman of Tallaght Institute of Technology-Dublin, Ireland defeated Kayla Jones 21-4, 21-4. This placed both Deason and Jones in B division.

In the first round of women's B singles, Cheryl Chen of Stony Brook University defeated Krystin Deason 11-21, 21-9, 11-0 and Kayla Jones defeated Emma Swanson of Lake Forest College 21-19, 21-10. In the quarterfinals, Addison Rogers of Western Washington University defeated Kayla Jones 17-21, 21-19, 11-10.

In women's Open doubles, Kayla Jones and Krystin Deason defeated Elizabeth Sherman and Jenny Novak of Pacific University 21-9, 21-1 in the preliminary round. In the first round, Amanda McKay and Madeline Brown of Missouri State University defeated Jones and Deason 21-16, 21-12.

For reasons unknown all of the match results were not reported for men or women at this National Collegiate Handball Tournament. If more Aggie women participated in the tournament the results were not given. The Aggie women's team earned a score of 694 points to rank 10th at the tournament. That is a lot of points earned for just two participating women. The Aggie men's team earned 1,461 points to rank seventh. The combined team total of 2,155 points was enough to place the combined team in seventh place.

Going into the 2011-12 year, the best women's player and the only one capable of playing at the Open or A division level from the previous year's team had moved on. Dustin Van Brunt, the best men's player on the Aggie team, returned, as well as some others with some experience. However, Coach Burke had to look for replacements as the new school year began. Plans to attend the 2012 National Collegiate Handball Tournament to be hosted by Missouri State University were put on hold as the search for new players became the number one priority. Gone were the great times during Coach Lowy's years when PE (Physical Education), now Kinesiology, was required for four semesters. So, the challenge to find handball players for the Aggie team was the top priority.

As tournament time approached there was some talent on the men's team and their spirits were high as they left for the annual trip to the National Collegiate Handball Tournament. As in the past year, all of the match results were not reported in the May 2012 issue of the USHA's *Handball* magazine so the only Aggie matches listed here will be those in print. It is apparent from the reporting of tournament match results that all of the preliminary rounds of the men's singles competition were not printed. The preliminary rounds were played on Wednesday and Thursday and were used to confirm preliminary seeding and to finalize play in each division. Once the preliminary rounds were finished, the individual division play and points earned for the team championships would begin. Divisions would now be made up of no more than 16 players, but could be less. All division play began on Friday and the championship finals were on Sunday.

In the round of 16 of the men's A Division I, Dustin Van Brunt defeated Julian Armendariz of Missouri State University 21-9, 21-4. In the quarterfinals, Eric Matiasek of Lake Forest College defeated Dustin Van Brunt 21-12, 21-16.

In the round of 16 of the men's B Division I, Justin Novak of Lake Forest College defeated Andrew Warren 21-10, 21-16.

In the round of 16 of the men's C I, Tyler Bettenhausen of the University of Illinois defeated Will Van Brunt 21-5, 21-0 and Andrew Christiansen of the University of Minnesota defeated Brandon Bush 21-17, 21-10.

In the round of 16 of the Intermediate I, Frankie Weinberg of Missouri State University defeated John Preble 21-9, 20-21, 11-10 and Steven Zhu of Stony Brook University defeated Michael Walker 21-8, 21-10.

In the round of 16 of the men's C II, Clayton Mansfield defeated Joshua Poncedeleon of Lake Forest College 21-5, 10-21, 11-0. In the quarterfinals, Peter Johnson of the University of Texas defeated Clayton Mansfield 21-15, 21-11.

In the round of 16 of the men's Challengers II, Jordan Wong of Pacific University defeated Greg Speer 21-7, 21-9 and Zachary Smith defeated Trenton Edwards of Minnesota State University-Mankato 21-0, 21-0. In the quarterfinals, Zachary Smith defeated Marko Mitkoski of Michigan State University 21-17, 10-21, 11-1. In the semifinals, Joel Carlson of Pacific University defeated Smith 21-4, 21-15.

The Aggies had no team to play in Open doubles competition. In the B doubles preliminary round, Clayton Mansfield and John Preble defeated Jerad Michels and Joseph Schnelgelberger of Minnesota State University-Mankato 21-20, 21-19; Will Van Brunt and Michael Walker defeated Stanley Wu and Georo Zhou of Syracuse University 21-2, 21-1 and Babalola Ajisafe and John Chan of Stony Brook University-New Paltz defeated Austin Acosta and Zachary Smith 21-3, 21-5. In the round of 16, Paul Dodson and Frankie Weinberg of Missouri State University defeated Clayton Mansfield and John Preble 21-8, 21-13; Andrew Warren and Brandon Bush defeated Derek Eggbert and Josh Hoflock of Minnesota State University-Mankato 21-6, 21-14, and Will Van Brunt and Michael Walker defeated Kevin Lo and Lawrence Li of Stony Brook University 18-21, 21-19, 11-7. In the quarterfinals, Jon Johnson and Nick Paine of the University of Texas defeated Brandon Bush and Andrew Warren 21-16, 20-21, 11-10 and Gavin Brown and Aaron Cochrane of Pacific University defeated Will Van Brunt and Michael Walker 21-5, 21-14.

The Aggie men's team did well with 1,974 points which was good for third and comfortably ahead of the fourth place team, Stony Brook University with 1,834 points. Missouri State finished comfortably ahead of the Aggies with 2,196 points. With no women making the trip for the Aggies, the combined team total was the same as the men's total and was overall in 12th place of 38 college/university teams.

After a high finish at the 2012 Nationals, Coach Burke knew it would be tough to get up there again, but he would have Will Van Brunt back for another season. He would also be looking for some women to comprise a team since there were none at the last national tournament. Aggies were always optimistic about the upcoming season, no matter the sport, so the recruiting, practice and planning for the team was put into place for the trip to Arizona State for the nationals.

Arriving for the 2013 tournament with excitement, the Aggies started playing and when the preliminary rounds were finished, no Aggies had qualified for the Open and A divisions. In the first round of B Division I, Isaac Garcia of the University of California-Santa Cruz defeated Brandon Bush 21-18, 21-13 and Eric Lee of Brooklyn College defeated Will Van Brunt 21-2, 21-13 to eliminate the Aggies from the top three divisions. The Aggies had no one playing in C Division I.

In Division II, the Aggies were represented in B by David Bood, who was defeated in the first round by Tom Werner of Minnesota State University-Mankato 21-8, 21-18. In the first round of C Division II, Kenny Laing of Stony Brook University defeated Matt Garza 21-10, 21-13. In the first round of Intermediate Division II, Weston Bond of Angelo State University defeated Daniel Ehrhardt 21-18, 13-21, 11-7.

In Division III, the Aggies were represented in A by Enrique Clarke, who defeated Holden Smith of the University of Texas in the first round of a two-game match 21-15, 21-4. In the semifinals, Clarke was defeated by the eventual champion, Andres Godinez of Northern Arizona University, 17-21, 21-13, 11-10.

In men's B doubles, Will VanBrunt and Brandon Bush earned a bye for first round play. In the round of 16, Will VanBrunt and Brandon Bush defeated Chris Patterman and Nathan Stables of the University of Illinois 21-7, 21-9. In the quarterfinals, Joel Barber and Scott Clawson of Colorado School of Mines defeated VanBrunt and Bush 20-21, 21-9, 11-8.

The Aggies had no women entered in the Open or A divisions.

In the women's Division I B, Ashley Burney defeated Shannon Strand of Minnesota State University-Mankato 21-9, 21-6. In the quarterfinals, Katie Van Cardo defeated Burney 21-11, 21-2.

In the first round of the women's Division II A, Chandler Peterson of Michigan State University defeated Brooke Kuehler 21-15, 21-5.

In the first round of the women's Division II C, Samantha Goldau of San Jose State University defeated Hope Voegele 21-4, 21-0.

The Aggie women did not enter the doubles competition.

The Aggie men totaled 1,273 points which placed them at number 12 of 36 colleges/universities. The Aggie women totaled 618 points which placed them at number 16 of 29 colleges/universities. The combined team total of 1,891 points was enough to place the Aggies in 13th place out of a total of 42 colleges/universities represented at the tournament. NOTE: Although the USHA announced the total points as a team total, all colleges/universities did not have the requisite number of players to make up an official team.

2013 Aggie handball team at Nationals
KNEELING: Brandon Bush
MIDDLE ROW: Brooke Kuehler, Matt Garza, Hope Voegele, Ashley Burney
BACK ROW: David Bood, Will Van Brunt, Enrique Clarke, Daniel Ehrhardt, Coach Ozzie Burke
(Courtesy Ozzie Burke)

As the team readied for the 2014 USHA National Collegiates, excitement was there because the team would be going to North Carolina State University and this would be the first time in 15 years that the Collegiates had been held east of the Mississippi. The Aggies had no one who was ranked high enough to be in Division I, but that did not matter to the players. They wanted to do well and have the experience that came with the tournament. Another reason for the excitement was they would see Martin Mulkerrins, who had won the last two men's national collegiate singles titles and who was an exchange student at Texas A&M during the fall semester. Also, for the women, they would see Catriona Casey (Ireland) play, who had so completely dominated the last two women's national collegiate singles that many considered her the most complete player to have ever played in the tournament. To win the Collegiates as a freshman by only having given up 13 points in four matches (eight games) and then as a sophomore giving up 14 in four matches was domination at an unbelievable level.

The Aggies only had one player in Division II. In the round of 16 of Division II C, David Bood defeated Jacob Norton of North Carolina State University 9-21, 21-11, 11-2. In the quarterfinals, David

Bood defeated Justin Roney of Pacific University 9-21, 21-13, 11-1. In the semifinals, Geoffrey Atkinson defeated Bood 21-7, 21-13.

In the first round of Division III A play, Marcous Phillips of the University of Illinois defeated Marshall Strain 21-17, 21-15. In the first round of Division III B, Tyler Isenhart defeated Tyler Edwards of Minnesota State University-Mankato 21-4, 21-5. In the quarterfinals, Tyler Isenhart defeated Brendan King of the University of Washington 21-16, 21-10. In the semifinals, Isenhart defeated Tyler Woodward of the University of West Florida 21-5, 21-10. In the finals, Isenhart came up just short of the championship title by the score of 21-17, 8-21, 11-7. Jared Iserman of the University of West Florida won the title.

Tyler Isenhart (right) earned runner-up honors in Division III B
(*Handball*, May 2014, page 17)

In the first round of Division III C, Michael Henrietta defeated Kyle Leuenberger of the Colorado School of Mines 21-20, 13-21, 11-1. Coach Burke reported the results of Henrietta's remaining matches to earn the championship. The story was reported on Page 17 of the May 2014 issue of the USHA's *Handball*:

> Michael Henrietta of Texas A&M defeated Pom Reagor of Angelo State 21-6, 21-5 to win the Division III C title.
>
> In the quarterfinals Henrietta bested Journey Perry of Western Florida 21-6, 21-8. In his toughest match, he defeated Yonas Berhe of Western Washington 21-20, 21-5 in the semifinals.
>
> Henrietta showed great promise in adjusting his strategy based on his opponent's skill set and to rally consistently, even in his seventh match in five days.

Michael Henrietta
(*Handball*, May 2014, page 17)

In the first round of B doubles competition, Mark Quinn and Neil McEnaney of Dublin Institute of Technology, Ireland defeated Marshall Strain and Michael Henrietta 21-9, 21-12 and William Yuan and Jimmy Ji of Stoney Brook University defeated Andrew Miller and Tyler Isenhart 21-3, 21-5.

In the round of 16 of women's Division I B competition, Ashley Burney defeated Elisabeth Casarez of Minnesota State University-Mankato 21-4, 21-2. In the quarterfinals, Ashley Burney defeated Marina Alessi of Lake Forest College 21-18, 21-10. In the semifinals, Elissa Borromeo of the University of Texas defeated Burney 21-7, 18-21, 11-6.

The Aggies had no one who could qualify the team for Division I. In Division II, the men totaled 745 points to finish ninth and the women with 352 points to finish 16th. The combined total of 1,097 placed them in ninth in Division II.

As the 2014-2015 school year was ready to start, Coach Burke was hopeful that the returning players and those yet to be recruited would have a better showing than in the past few years. Little did he or the team know that it would be a special year. Of course, as the year progressed and the plans firmed up for the trip to Pacific University, hosts for the 2015 National Collegiate Handball Tournament, the excitement built.

Checking into the internet under 2015 USHA National Collegiate Handball Tournament, the following story was revealed:

63rd USHA National Collegiate Handball Championships
hosted by Pacific University of Portland, OR, February 18-22, 2015

NOTE: All photos this page courtesy Ozzie Burke

Playing in Division II classification *(mostly players who learned handball in college)* Texas A&M (TAMU) Handball took top combined team honors outscoring rivaling DII teams from University of Western Florida (UWF), University of Illinois (UI), Angelo State University (ANSU), Michigan State University (MSU) and Utah State University (USU). Overall, thirty-one Universities were in attendance.

Up to the top six players by gender (who win at least one of six potential matches) earn combined team points as per USHA's competitive bracket scale. University combined scores were: TAMU 3,468, ANSU 2,592, MSU 2,436, UI 2,412, USU 2,092 & UWF 2,076.

TAMU women's team point earners were: Macie Morris 340, Emily Seyl 332, Anne Marie Zuilhof 324, Sarah Lehman 324 and Kayla Leal 308.

TAMU men's team point earners were: Marshall Strain 312, Jordan Lyle 308, Robert Siddall 308, Ryan Siddall 304, David Bood 304 and Kevin Lackey 304.

Competing in USHA's competitive bracket system, "one of the keys to a strong team is a deep bench," says Coach Ozzie Burke '71. "Unlike other sports, bench players in handball compete just as much as point earners, gaining valuable experience for next year, but just at a lower *player in development* skill level position as per the spot they earn on TAMU's practice *Challenge Ladder*."

The 64th Collegiates will be held at University of Minnesota in Minneapolis, MN February 2016. TAMU Handball's goal is to take 12 women and 20 men players.

We have some recruiting/training to do and we need supporters to help raise the necessary funds for the trip.

Macie Morris (in maroon to the left) of Seymour, Texas, lost her 1st preliminary match in a tiebreaker against Jeanne Munk of Utah State University (an eventual finalist in the DI-B competitive bracket). Determined, Macie breezed past Kerry Lee of Pacific University 21-4, 21-4 in her second preliminary match to settle into the DI-C competitive bracket of 16 players. Lamenting of her 15th seed position, thirteen-year Coach Ozzie assured Macie "seeding really doesn't matter... it's your performance that's everything!"

(Courtesy Ozzie Burke)

So, Macie stayed focused, first taking on and beating Geena May of University of Texas (UT) 21-6, 21-3 in the round of 16. Then she defeated Ellen Culver of UT 21-11, 21-8 in the quarters and another UT player, Hannah Lerner 21-8, 21-15 in the semis. The next day after a 7:15am practice, Macie faced her toughest opponent in DI-C Lindsey Boelter of Utah State in the finals who had edged Macie's teammate Emily Seyl in her semi-final match, 11-6 in a tough tie- breaker.

With a barrage of Z, diamond and a few runner serves down the right coupled with well-placed rally ending pass shots down the left side, Macie breezed to a 21-7 first game win. But Lindsey was not to be deterred! In the second game she mixed up her serves with more power and better angles pulling away for a win, holding Macie to a momentum changing 15 points. Tension mounted! In the tiebreaker, Macie had first served and not only grabbed the lead early, but poured on unrelenting service pressure and precise rally shots to win going away 11-0. Congratulations to a gal with a competitive heart as big as Texas!

Bill Foran (in green to the right)

(Courtesy Ozzie Burke)

From 4A (at the time) football powerhouse Highland Park High School in Dallas, Texas, Bill Foran, former quarterback signee then a redshirt at Purdue who transferred to Princeton and played quarterback and ran sprints on the track team, lost a close one in his first preliminary match to Adrian Anderson of Minnesota State Mankato 19-21, 15-21. The 2nd preliminary match proved even tougher against Andy Graves of Utah State University giving Bill an 0-2 start after scoring only 8 and 12 in a two-game match loss while suffering an injury of his hamstring at the knee attachment on his right leg. A comeback was the only road forward now. But Bill's legendary high school football coach, Randy Allen, (Coach Ozzie's pre-marriage roommate) had prepared Bill to be mentally tough to deal with comebacks.

With a healthy mix of determination and post and pre-match therapy by the tournament trainers, Bill faced a must win scenario in the round of 16 against Ty Edwards, also of Minnesota State Mankato, and win he did: 21-6, 21-3. His quarter-final opponent, Brendan King of University of Washington, gave Bill a tough first game before faltering two points short at 19, then taking it on the chin getting just 9 points in the second game. On to the semis where Bill faced a very evenly matched opponent in Jon Vargas of

Lake Forest College of Illinois. Bill took the first game 21-5, lost 7-21 and won an 11-5 tiebreaker.

PICTURED: Jordan Lyle, Marshall Strain, Bill Foran, Macie Morris & Will Jones

(Courtesy Ozzie Burke)

Getting up for an 8am final after five matches is an experience few players' relish. But Bill pushed hard and won the first game facing Steven Roy of Missouri State 21-13. The second and third games took their toll on an injured leg and exhausted handballer letting Bill down 16-21 and 5-21. His spirit was willing but his body was injured at tournament end. A hearty congrats was voiced by all to this young Marine!

(Coverage of the 63rd National Collegiate Handball Tournament by Ozzie Burke)

TAMU team individual awards were a surprise addition at the USHA Saturday night banquet when Coach Ozzie presented the Leadership Award to Marshall Strain, Club President. In turn, Marshall presented the Heart Award to Bill Foran, the Master Recruiter Award to Will Jones, and the FastTrack to Excellence Awards went to Macie Morris and Jordan Lyle. Congratulations to all teammates and award winners for a great Nationals!

Although all of the scores from all the men's and women's matches were not available, the following is a more complete report of the competition after the preliminary matches.

In the round of 16 of the men's Division II A singles, Marshall Strain defeated Peter Johnson of the University of Texas 21-14, 21-8; Stefan Lemak of Pacific University defeated David Bood 14-21, 21-14, 11-10; John Thompson of the University of Minnesota defeated Kevin Lackey 21-11, 21-16; Robert Siddall defeated Steven Armes of Pacific University 21-17, 21-5; Jordan Lyle defeated Darren Miller of the University of Illinois 16-21, 21-15, 11-2 and William Yuan of Stony Brook University defeated Ryan Siddall 21-17, 21-5. In the quarterfinals, Marshall Strain defeated Tye Macon of the University of Texas 21-16, 21-13; Bai Xin Lin of Stony Brook University defeated Robert Siddall 21-13, 21-6 and William Yuan of Stony Brook University defeated Jordan Lyle 21-13, 21-18. In the semifinals, John Thompson of the University of Minnesota defeated Marshall Strain 21-7, 21-10.

In the round of 16 of the men's Division II C singles, Brett Mahnke defeated Xavier Higa of Lake Forest College 10-21, 21-6, 11-1 and Erik Medhurst of the University of Illinois defeated William Jones 21-9, 21-9. In the quarterfinals, Danny Kwok of Stony Brook University defeated Brett Mahnke 21-13, 21-10.

In the round of 16 of the men's Division II Intermediate singles, Mark Munson defeated Scott Clark of Stony Brook University-New Paltz 21-2, 21-4 and Nathaniel Curran of the University of California defeated Ryan Foley 21-7, 21-15. In the quarterfinals, Mark Munson defeated Carter Kounovsky of Lake Forest College 21-14, 21-5. In the semifinals, Ryan Boxer of Missouri State University defeated Mark Munson 18-21, 21-12, 11-3.

In the round of 16 of the men's Division III A singles, Collins Bronsnon of the University of Texas defeated Chris Hitch 21-20, 6-21, 11-8; Jon Vargas of Lake Forest College defeated Colin Croteau 21-6, 21-11 and Bill Foran defeated Tyler Edwards of the University of Minnesota-Mankato 21-6, 21-3.

In the quarterfinals, Bill Foran defeated Brendan King of the University of Washington 21-19, 21-9. In the semifinals, Bill Foran defeated Jon Vargas of Lake Forest College 5-21, 21-7, 11-5. As reported above Foran was not able to overcome his injury to win the championship.

The only Aggies entered in the B doubles competition were Marshall Strain and Jordan Lyle. They won the first round against Andy Graves and Bodey Hancock of Utah State University 21-15, 21-19. In the round of 16, Marshall Strain and Jordan Lyle defeated John Thompson and Ted Spencer of the University of Minnesota 21-19, 21-20. In the quarterfinals, Michael Mathis and Jared Iserman of the University of West Florida defeated Marshall Strain and Jordan Lyle 21-12, 21-3.

In the round of 16 in the women's Division I B singles, Lindsey Boelter of Utah State University defeated Anne Marie Zuilhof 21-6, 21-6; Emily Seyl defeated Tara Tough of the University of Texas 21-14, 21-4; Hannah Lerner of the University of Texas defeated Sarah Lehman 10-21, 21-8, 11-2 and Macie Morris defeated Geena May of the University of Texas 21-6, 21-3. In the quarterfinals, Emily Seyl defeated Linnette Jessop of Pacific University 21-4, 21-18 and Macie Morris defeated Ellen Culver of the University of Texas 21-11, 21-8. In the semifinals, Lindsey Boelter of Utah State University defeated Emily Seyl 21-13, 20-21, 11-6 and Macie Morris defeated Hannah Lerner of the University of Texas 21-8, 21-15. In the finals, as reported in the story above, Morris defeated Boelter 21-7, 15-21, 11-0 to become the champion.

In the first round of the women's Division II A singles, Kayla Leal defeated Breauna Gabriel of Angelo State University 21-3, 21-6. In the quarterfinals, Kylie Martin of Pacific University defeated Kayla Leal 21-3, 21-18. In the first round of the women's Division II B singles, Tesia Wright of Pacific University defeated Christina Hoffpauir 11-21, 21-7, 21-0.

In the quarterfinals of the women's B doubles competition, Macie Morris and Kayla Leal defeated Nikki Theobold and Laurie Hiebert of the University of Minnesota-Mankato 21-9, 21-5. In the semifinals, Teresa Wright and Julia Naumes defeated Macie Morris and Kayla Teal 12-21, 21-13, 11-7.

As reported above both the men's and women's teams placed second in their respective divisions. The men's team total of 1,840 points was only 40 points behind first place Stony Brook University. The women's team total of 1,628 points was only 24 points behind first place Angelo State. The combined team total of 3,468 points was far enough ahead of second place Angelo State's 2,592 points that the Aggies knew they had won the combined championship well before the last matches were played.

2015 Texas A&M handball team at the Collegiate National Tournament
FRONT ROW: Coach Ozzie Burke, Ryan Siddall, Marshall Strain, Tyler Isenhart, Brett Mahnke, Chris Hitch
SECOND ROW: Colin Croteau, Anne Marie Zuilhof, Christina Hoffpauir, Sarah Lehman, Emily Seyl, Kayla Leal, Macie Morris, Robert Siddall
BACK ROW: Jordan Lyle, David Bood, Ryan Foley, Mark Munson, Will Jones, Kevin Lackey, Bill Foran
(Courtesy Ozzie Burke)

As has happened many times in the past the College Commissioners changed the division designations for the 2016 Nationals. Gone were the Division I, II and III categories. The new divisions would continue with both the men and women's Open but the other divisions would be A and B for the men and A for the women. For the combined team score, the divisions would be Open and A. Coaches and players were looking forward to the new format and attending the collegiates at the University of Minnesota handball courts. It only took one year for the Commissioners to realize they needed to add a C division for the men and a B division for the women. Also, in determining what division a player might compete, the computer rank ordered all players. For example, M33-48 would indicate rank order among the men competitors who would begin play within that group and then based on success or failure, be placed in a final grouping for competitive play. For the women, W33-48 would indicate the same.

In addition, the National Collegiate Commissioners made the decision to change the rules for naming All-American handball players. The talented players coming to the Collegiate tournament from Ireland really were not American players although many had been named All-American based on their finish at the annual tournament. The Commissioners felt that All-Americans should be players from American colleges and universities. The rule change for the 2016 National Collegiate Handball Tournament and each succeeding year thereafter would honor the top four "American" players in the Open field. This change assured that eight American handball players-four men and four women-would receive All-American honors each year.

In the 2016 Wednesday preliminary matches, the highest ranked Aggies in the men's singles play were placed in the M33-48 group where Angel Marquez of Pacific University defeated Will Van Brunt 21-13, 21-8 and Jordan Lyle defeated Alan Armstrong of Queens University-Belfast, Ireland 21-12, 21-13. In the group of M49-64, Adrian Anderson of Minnesota State University-Mankato defeated Mark Munson 21-6, 17-21, 11-3 and Marshall Strain defeated William Yuan of Stony Brook University 21-14, 21-7. In the M65-80 group, Nathan Riddle defeated Marcous Phillips of the University of Illinois 21-13, 21-4 and Bill Foran defeated Alex Grochowski of the University of West Florida 21-15, 21-16. In the M81-96 group, Chris Hitch defeated Mike Desgrottes of the University of West Florida 21-6, 21-2; Ryan Foley defeated Kosta Lecos of Michigan State University 21-20, 21-12 and Mike Henrietta defeated Blake Sanacos of the Colorado School of Mines 21-14, 21-11. In the M113-128 group, Michael Garcia of Angelo State University defeated Adam LaMasters 21-12, 18-21, 11-4.

In the men's Thursday preliminary matches of the MA1/A2 group, Matt Vollink of Missouri State University defeated Jordan Lyle 21-14, 17-21, 11-9. In the MA2/A3 group, John Hurley of the University of Limerick, Ireland defeated Will Van Brunt 21-15, 21-8 and Alex Birge of Missouri State University defeated Marshall Strain 21-19, 21-10. In the A3/B1 group, Bai Xin Lin of Stony Brook University defeated Mark Munson 21-12, 21-11, Bill Foran defeated Marcus Haslam of Utah State University 21-11, 21-8 and Nathan Riddle defeated Jackson Turrentine of Missouri State University 21-12, 21-19. In the MB1/B2 group, James Tobin of the University College-Dublin, Ireland defeated Chris Hitch 21-4, 20-21, 11-3; Ryan Foley defeated Ben Carson of the University of Minnesota 21-16, 21-11 and Benjamin VanArsdale of the University of Illinois defeated Mike Henrietta 21-12, 21-3. In the MC1/C2 group, Alex Sadegholvad of Stony Brook University defeated Adam LaMasters 21-8, 21-15.

The Aggie men had no entrants in the Open or A1 divisions, but in the round of 16 of division A2, Jordan Lyle defeated Carter Kounovsky of Lake Forest College 21-14, 21-15. In the quarterfinals, the eventual champ, Darren Carter of the National University of Ireland, Galway, defeated Jordan Lyle 21-4, 21-19. In the round of 16 of division A3, Will Van Brunt defeated William Yaun of Stony Brook University 21-6, 21-9; Ryan Boyer of Missouri State University defeated Nathan Riddle 21-3, 21-15; Lee Sugarek of the University of Texas defeated Bill Foran 21-8, 21-5 and Marshall Strain defeated Taylor McQueary of

Missouri State University 21-0, 21-4. In the quarterfinals, Alan Armstrong of Queens University-Belfast, Ireland defeated Will Van Brunt 21-13, 17-21, 11-2 and Marshall Strain defeated John Thompson of the University of Minnesota 21-9, 21-18. In the semifinals, Bai Xin Lin of Stony Brook University defeated Marshall Strain 21-19, 21-11.

In the round of 16 in B-1, Jon Vargas of Lake Forest College defeated Ryan Foley 15-21, 21-13, 11-0 and Mark Munson defeated Benjamin VanArsdale of the University of Illinois 2-14, 21-19. In the quarterfinals, Mark Munson defeated Jackson Turrentine of Missouri State University 21-8, 21-3. In the semifinals, Mark Munson defeated Travis Massengill of the University of Texas 21-7, 21-8. Munson won the championship in B-1 singles. The complete report and the meaning of his victory in the finals is reported below. In the round of 16 in B-2 singles, Chris Hitch defeated Sean McNeill of the University of Illinois 21-16, 21-19 and Derek Ng of Stony Brook University defeated Mike Henrietta 21-9, 21-11. In the quarterfinals, Spencer Siu of Stony Brook University defeated Chris Hitch 21-12, 21-15.

The Aggies had no one entered in the Open doubles competition. In the quarterfinals of the A doubles competition, Will Van Brunt and Marshall Strain defeated Jimmy Alden and Matt Menendez of Missouri State University 21-13, 21-6. In the semifinals, Jimmy Ji and William Yuan of Stony Brook University defeated Will Van Brunt and Marshall Strain 21-14, 21-12. In the round of 16 in the B doubles competition, Nathan Riddle and Bill Foran defeated Kyle Dickens and Cody Ramirez of Pacific University 21-11, 21-3. In the quarterfinals, Nathan Riddle and Bill Foran defeated Andrew Bales and Blake Sanders of the Colorado School of Mines 11-21, 21-9, 11-9. In the semifinals, John Cruz and Kenny Ta of Stony Brook University defeated Nathan Riddle and Bill Foran 21-8, 21-8.

In the round of 16 of the women's Open division, Leslie Amminson of Memorial University of Newfoundland, Canada defeated Katie Nieswiadomy 21-8, 21-3. This loss moved Katie to the 9-16 bracket of the Open division. In the quarterfinals, Katie Nieswiadomy defeated Shona Ruane of the National University of Ireland, Galway 21-5, 17-21, 11-10. In the semifinals, Katie Nieswiadomy defeated Jessica Edwards of Michigan State University 21-20, 21-15. Katie won the 9-16 bracket of the Open division. Her road to victory is reported in the article below.

In the round of 16 of the women's A1 competition, Kate Moran of Waterford Institute of Technology, Ireland defeated Sarah Lehman 21-10, 21-4 and Macie Morris defeated Teresa Wright of Pacific University 21-8, 21-12. In the quarterfinals, Kyra Vidas of Lake Forest College defeated Macie Morris 21-18, 19-21, 11-6. In the round of 16 of the women's A2 competition, Corinna Mendez of Angelo State University defeated Emily Seyl 9-21, 21-7, 11-6.

In the round of 16 of the women's B1 competition, Laurie Hiebert of Michigan State University defeated Kayla Leal 21-11, 21-15. In the first round of the women's B2 competition, Lily Shehadi of Lake Forest College defeated Cassi Urbanowski 21-17, 21-17.

In the quarterfinals of the women's A doubles competition, Katie Nieswiadomy and Sarah Lehman defeated Siomha Ni Chonchubhair and Roisin Meehan of Trinity College of Dublin, Ireland 21-0, 21-1 and Macie Morris and Kayla Leal defeated Caylen Vinson and Gretchen Gregory of Missouri State University 21-12, 21-20. In the semifinals, Nieswiadomy and Lehman defeated Becca Brown and Karissa Komo of Pacific University 21-17, 21-9 and Teresa Wright and Julia Naumes of Pacific University defeated Morris and Leal 13-21, 21-15, 11-10. Nieswiadomy and Lehman won the championship and is reported in the article below.

The women's team scored 1,423 points to finish in fifth place of the women's Open. The men's team won the men's division A championship with 1,976 points, a mere eight points ahead of second place Stony Brook University. The combined team total was 3,399 points which placed the Aggies in seventh place.

The following report published on the internet provides the success of the Aggies at the tournament:

2016 Collegiates
64th USHA National Collegiate Handball Championships February 24-28, 2016
University of Minnesota in Minneapolis, MN

(Coverage of the 2016 National Collegiate Handball Tournament below, except "A&M's Burke is Coach of Year", by Ozzie Burke)

TAMU men's handball team took top honors in division A *(players who learn the game in college)* nudging Stoney Brook University, New York on the last day of the tournament.

If a men's team title for TAMU handball was to be won, it would be on the broad shoulders of leftie Mark Munson to win his final match in division B1 facing rival Ben Browder of University of Texas. Mark played confident and steady with a smart mix of good serves followed by kills, pass shots and solid defense winning the men's individual National B1 Title, worth 320 team points, by defeating Browder 21-10, 21-14, thus securing the men's team division A championship over Stoney Brook. Other teams rounding out division A were University of Illinois, University of Minnesota and Pacific University.

Top six team point earners for TAMU handball were Jordan Lyle at 348, Marshall Strain at 336, Will Van Brunt at 328, Bill Foran at 324, Nathan Riddle at 324 and Mark Munson at 320.

TAMU Handball men's team 2016
L-R: Bill Foran, Chris Hitch, Michael Henrietta, Ryan Foley, Will Van Brunt, Coach Ozzie Burke '71, Nathan Riddle, Mark Munson, Jordan Lyle, Adam LaMasters & Marshall Strain.

USHA 2016 Collegiate men's B1 Champ
Mark Munson

(All photos this page and next courtesy Ozzie Burke)

TAMU Handball Women's Singles Results

Katie Nieswiadomy of Texas A&M University doggedly wins the Women's 9-16 championship Bracket defeating Natasha Coughlan of University of Limerick in the finals 15-21, 21-15, 11-5...her eighth handball match in five days. Court sense, from years of racquetball tournament play, teamed well with Katie's confidence under pressure for her first Nationals ninth place finish in women's Open singles. Impressive!

Texas A&M women's 2016 team
L-R: Cassi Urbanowski, Emily Seyl, Kayla Leal, Coach Ozzie Burke '71,
Macie Morris, Sarah Lehman, Katie Nieswiadomy

Developing a wider variety of serves and increasing her rally ending skill set will be the key to Katie's future handball success.

TAMU Handball Women's Doubles Results

Katie Nieswiadomy and Sarah Lehman of Texas A&M University decisively win the Women's A Doubles Championship Bracket defeating Teresa Wright and Julia Naumes of Pacific University in the finals 21-5, 21-11.

Coming off her Women's 9-16 Championship Bracket win earlier Sunday morning, Katie found A Doubles with Sarah a much easier challenge with good teamwork and consistent play from the pair.

Earlier, doubles wins in the round of eight against Roisin Meehan and Ni Choichubhair (TDC), then in the semi's vs. Becca Brown and Karissa Komo of (PU) preceded the championship match vs. Wright and Naumes (PU). Congrats!

2016 USHA Collegiate 9-16 women's champ

Champs Katie Niesmiadomy and Sarah Lehman

(Courtesy Ozzie Burke)

Following the success of 2015-2016, the accolades continued. Coach Ozzie Burke was named the Collegiate Coach of the Year. In making the announcement to the handball world, USHA ran the following article in the May 2016 issue of the *USHA's Handball,* page 6.

A&M's Burke is Coach of Year

(*Handball,* May 2016, page 6)

We all know how difficult it is to start a handball program, but in many ways reviving a collegiate program is equally challenging.

We unfortunately have seen collegiate programs disappear. Transitions between coaches are a challenge, and the programs often have a difficult time being sustained.

Only a few years ago, the Texas A&M team's size dropped from 15 or more players to fewer than 10. What was once a Division I contender had dropped to D3 and was struggling.

But the USHA's 2016 Coach of the Year, Ozzie Burke, began a rebuilding process. The Aggies' team size has returned to 15-plus players, including more women.

In 2015, those efforts were rewarded with a Division 2 title. In 2016, the school found itself competing in the Open (equivalent of DI) for women and repeated as champions in the A group (equivalent of D2).

For that we have Ozzie Burke to thank.

With team championships of the past two years, the Aggies were full of hope and excitement as they traveled to Arizona State for the 2017 National Collegiate Handball Tournament.

In the Wednesday preliminary matches of the M145-160 group, Ryan Noborikawa of Pacific University defeated Luis Flores 21-0, 21-2; in the M113-128 group, Wyatt Vidmar of the Colorado School of Mines defeated Adam LaMasters 21-8, 21-14; in the M97-112 group, Chris Hitch defeated Jose Hernandez of the University of California 21-19, 18-21, 11-4; in the 81-96 group, Alan Moore of Western Florida University defeated Wilson Tao 21-0, 21-1 and Erik Gilman defeated Dakota Cornelius of Arizona State University 21-7, 21-10; in the 49-64 group, Jacob Garcia defeated Dillon Timboe of Arizona State University 21-5, 21-20; in the 33-48 group, Jordan Lyle defeated Adrian Anderson of Michigan State University 21-6, 17-21, 11-6 and Max Roberts of Lake Forest College defeated Marshall Strain 21-13, 21-10.

In the Thursday preliminary matches of the MC3/C4X group, Manuel Santana of Utah State University defeated Luis Flores 21-6, 21-4; in the MC1/C2 group, Zack Zimmerman of Minnesota State University-Mankato defeated Adam LaMasters 21-11, 21-11; in the MB2/B3 group, Trevor Bachman of the Colorado School of Mines defeated Wilson Tao 21-10, 21-18 and Chris Hitch defeated Logan Benson of Angelo State University 21-13, 21-5; in the MB1/B2 group, Xavier Higa of Lake Forest College defeated Erik Gilman 21-9, 21-9; in the MA2/A3 group, Alejandro Almada of the University of Texas defeated Jacob Garcia 21-13, 21-8; Garrett Bacon of Missouri State University defeated Marshall Strain 21-15, 13-21, 11-5 and David Schiller of Hamline University defeated Jordan Lyle 21-13, 21-11.

In the round of 16 in the men's C4 division, Luis Flores received a bye. In the quarterfinals, Nate Gruber of Arizona State University defeated Luis Flores 21-2, 21-15. In the round of 16 in the men's C2 division, Alex Kraski of Minnesota State University-Mankato defeated Adam LaMasters 21-20, 21-10.

In the round of 16 in the men's B3 division, Matt Craig of the Colorado School of Mines defeated Wilson Tao 21-8, 21-15. In the round of 16 in the men's B2 division, Derek Doyle of Arizona State University defeated Erik Gilman 13-21, 21-1, 11-8 and Chris Hitch defeated Daniel Cucarola of the Colorado School of Mines 21-3, 21-20. In the quarterfinals, Chris Hitch defeated Dakota Cornelius of Arizona State University 21-4, 19-21, 11-6. In the semifinals, Ricardo Sanchez of the University of Texas-El Paso defeated Hitch 21-10, 21-5.

In the round of 16 in the men's A3 division, Michael Mathis of the University of West Florida defeated Jacob Garcia by default and Ryan Beyer of Missouri State University defeated Marshall Strain 11-21, 21-12, 11-3. In the round of 16 in the men's A2 division, John Hurley of the University of Limerick, Ireland defeated Jordan Lyle 21-18, 13-21, 11-10.

In the women's W33-48 group, Marilyn Delgado defeated Ashley Gilliam of the University of West Florida 21-9, 21-7. In the W1-16 group, Katie Nieswiadomy defeated Angelo Snow of Angelo State University 21-3, 21-5.

In the women's WA1/A2 group, Marilyn Delgado defeated Kendra Kaupa of Michigan State University 21-13, 21-8. In the round of 16 in the WA1 division, Marilyn Delgado defeated Caylen Vinson of Missouri State University 8-21, 21-13, 11-10. In the quarterfinals, Marilyn Delgado defeated Ellen Culver of the University of Texas 21-18, 21-2. In the semifinals, Marilyn Delgado defeated Angelo Snow of Angelo State University 18-21, 21-17, 11-8 and in the finals, Lindsey Boelter of Utah State University defeated Delgado 21-5, 21-20.

In the women's Open division, Katie Nieswiadomy defeated Corinna Mendez of Angelo State University 21-13, 21-11. Then Clodagh Nash of the University College-Dublin, Ireland defeated Nieswiadomy 21-4, 21-11.

None of the Aggie men or women participated in the doubles competition.

In the team competition the men totaled 1,432 points which earned them seventh place. The women, only two, totaled 764 points and placed 12th. The combined team total was 2,196 points and that placed the team in 10th place.

The most positive outcome of the tournament was the play of Katie Nieswiadomy. She earned All-American honors and was the top American woman player at the tournament. The other three women All-Americans were defeated in the round of 16 of the Open division. Katie was defeated in the quarterfinals.

As the 2017-2018 school year began Coach Burke knew he had a serious problem. Gone were almost all of the team that participated in the National Collegiate Handball Tournament the previous year. However, as coaches know, you must carry on with what you have to work with. By tournament time, there were only two Aggies going to the National Tournament.

As tournament play began, Michael Guillen was in the M97-112 group. In his first match, he defeated Noah Peterman of the University of Illinois 13-21, 21-19, 11-9. Chris Hitch had been flighted in the M33-48 group. Jian Cheng Hu of Stony Brook University defeated Chris Hitch 21-1, 21-6. In Thursday's preliminary matches, Michael Guillen was in the MB2/3 group and was defeated by Calvin Liu of the University of Texas 21-6, 21-15. Chris Hitch was in the MA2/A3 group and he defeated Spencer Straw of Sinclair Community College 21-8, 21-9.

As a result of the preliminary matches, Michael Guillen was in the MB3 division. In the round of 16, Michael Guillen defeated Tyler Borst of Missouri State University 21-4, 21-4. In the quarterfinals, Mark McDonald of Queens University-Belfast, Ireland defeated Guillen 21-5, 11-21, 11-5. Chris Hitch was in the MA2 division and in the round of 16, he was defeated by Oran Kiernan Dublin City University, Ireland 21-12, 16-21, 11-4.

The two Aggies earned a total of 612 points and that placed them at 14th place in the men's competition.

After the 2017-2018 season, any new student showing any interest in handball would be a welcome sight. Thanks to Doug Randolph's endowment (SEE: Chapter titled *Revival*) the enthusiasm generated among the few regulars at the handball courts was akin to the phoenix of ancient Greek folklore rising to new life. With the new members of the handball team, along with the only returning handball player, Michael Guillen, excitement filled the air as the team readied to go to the 2019 National Collegiate Tournament hosted by the University of Minnesota. Long-time coach, Ozzie Burke, was not able to travel with the team due to health issues. Charlie Bokelman volunteered to accompany the team and handle all the administrative, coaching and miscellaneous duties associated with the tournament. Charlie was an excellent choice based on his vast tournament experience and the individual without peer on the handball courts in the Bryan/College Station area. He had been to the Collegiates before and is one of the Aggies all-time great handball players. Priscilla (Kojin) Shumate claims him to have been her coach and the reason she was so successful at the game.

In Wednesday's preliminary men's matches of the M113-144 group, Marcus Shanaa defeated Victor Kolcan of the University of Illinois 21-0, 21-1; Alan Boone defeated Ben Fields of the University of Illinois 21-10, 21-15; Jacob Knostman received a bye; and Blake Bellomy defeated Edgar Juarez-Lopez of Hamline University 21-1, 21-0. In the M113-128 group, Marcus Shanaa defeated Peter Callahan of Pacific University 21-15, 21-11; Marshall Fabricant of the University of West Florida defeated Alan Boone 21-10, 21-19 (played Thursday morning); Jacob Knostman defeated Jesse Huang of the University of Texas 21-4, 21-8 and Blake Bellomy defeated Joe Jones of the University of Illinois 21-13, 21-7. In the M97-112 group, Logan Call defeated Brenden Hoehn of Hamline University 21-16, 17-21, 11-7. In the M65-80 group, Sam Matenaer of the University of Minnesota defeated Michael Guillen 21-14, 21-19.

In Thursday's preliminary matches of the MC1-/C2X group, Peter Callahan defeated Alan Boone 21-9, 21-18. In the MC1/C2 group, Alan Boone defeated Jesse Huang of the University of Texas 21-9, 21-13. In the B3/C1 group, Marcus Shanaa defeated Matt Bundy of the University of Minnesota 21-4, 21-2; Jacob Knostman defeated Henry Yeary of the University of Illinois 21-2, 21-6 and Colton Grindal of the University of Texas defeated Blake Bellomy 21-6, 21-4. In the MB2/B3 group, Kyle Schmidt of the University of Minnesota defeated Logan Call 21-5, 13-21, 11-5. In the MB1/B2 group, Benjamin Kleineschay of North Hennepin Community College defeated Michael Guillen 21-17, 21-18.

In the round of 16 in the MC2 division, Alan Boone received a bye. In the quarterfinals, Jordan Turnquest of the Colorado School of Mines defeated Alan Boone 21-8, 10-21, 11-4. In the round of 16 of the MC1 division, Blake Bellomy defeated Kevin Tran of the University of Minnesota 21-1, 21-1. In the quarterfinals, Peter Callahan of Pacific University defeated Blake Bellomy 21-8, 21-4.

In the round of 16 of the MB3 division, Jacob Knostman defeated Ryan Erwin of the University of Texas 21-17, 17-21, 11-0; Logan Call defeated Colton Grindal of the University of Texas 8-21, 21-16, 11-6 and Marcus Shanaa defeated Andrew Unick of Minnesota State University-Mankato 21-14, 11-21, 11-5. In the quarterfinals, Eric Vickers of the University of California defeated Jacob Knostman 21-9, 21-19; Logan Call defeated Ryan Holdsworth of the University of California-Berkeley 21-20, 21-11 and Marcus Shanaa defeated David Frances of Arizona State University who had to default. In the semifinals, Eric Vickers defeated Logan Call 21-16, 21-9 and Zack Saros of Pacific University defeated Marcus Shanaa 21-15, 21-13. In the round of 16 of the MB2 division, Michael Guillen defeated Ben Thompson of the University of Minnesota 19-21, 21-8, 11-6. In the quarterfinals, Michael Guillen defeated Oran Chak of Stony Brook University 21-8, 21-20. In the semifinals, Zander Andreasen of Utah State University defeated Guillen 21-8, 14-21, 11-9.

The Aggies had two women participating in the tournament, both first time players. In Wednesday's preliminary round of the 49-80 group, Julie Sandkamp of Michigan State University defeated Lauren Waters 21-15, 21-7 and Bethany Butler defeated Kenzie Boldt of the University of Minnesota 21-12, 21-3.

In Thursday's preliminary round of WB1/B2X, Bethany Butler defeated Hannah Ramsey of Pacific University 21-5, 21-4 and Lauren Waters defeated Maty Lagdon of Michigan State University 21-12, 21-11. In WB1/B2, Bethany Butler defeated Julia Brito of the University of Texas 21-12, 17-21, 11-9 and Lauren Waters defeated Gwen Caudle of the University of Texas 21-4, 21-0. This placed both Aggies in the WB1 division. In the first round of the WB1 division, Bethany Butler defeated Karla Ocampo Valle of San Francisco State University 21-6, 21-18 and Lauren Waters defeated Monica Redfern of Lake Forest College 11-21, 21-17, 11-5. In the quarterfinals, Bethany Butler defeated Emily Wichgers of Lake Forest College 15-21, 21-6, 11-3 and Lauren Waters defeated Julie Huestis of Pacific University 8-21, 21-15, 11-9. In the semifinals, Bethany Butler defeated Claire Hagstrom of Michigan State University 18-21, 21-17, 11-5 and Lauren Waters defeated Kin Kunitomo of Pacific University 21-16, 21-12. This advanced both Aggie women into the championship match. The final match was covered on page 21 of the May 2019 issue of the USHA's *Handball* magazine:

Waters takes thrilling all-Aggies B1 final

Lauren Waters held on to defeat teammate Bethany Butler 21-13, 3-21, 11-10 in an all-Texas A&M final for the women's B1 championship.

To see the round of 16 draw, no one could have predicted that two A&M teammates would meet in the final-except their coach, Ozzie Burke. It might have felt like a practice match for the two Aggies with much higher stakes as a national title was on the line.

"I knew if they met, it would be close," Burke says. "They squared off back in January, and that went to an 11-8 tie-breaker, but Bethany took that match."

Perhaps that memory fueled Waters to take the first game by playing solid, error-free handball. But Waters' momentum was torn away in Game 2 as Butler, a volleyball player in high school, utilized her athleticism and sense of urgency to score a blowout win.

In the tiebreaker, Waters solved Butler's serves to avoid a repeat of the second game collapse but still had to fend off match point before securing the 11-10 victory.

Lauren Waters (left) and Bethany Butler

First and Second in the women's B1 division of the 2019 National Collegiate Handball Tournament

(*Handball*, May 2019, page 21)

As the points began to add up, it became apparent the Aggies would do well considering all were newcomers except Michael Guillen. The men won the National title in the men's B division with 1,580 points. Colorado School of Mines was a distant second with 1,064 points. The men's total earned them ninth place of the 32 colleges and universities with men at the tournament. The women's total of 676 points placed them at number 12 of the 21 colleges and universities with women at the tournament. The combined team total of 2,256 points earned the team 10th place among all of the colleges and universities represented at the tournament.

Texas A&M handball team at the 2019 National Collegiate
Handball Tournament
FRONT ROW, LEFT TO RIGHT: Lauren Waters, Brittany Butler
MIDDLE ROW, LEFT TO RIGHT: Michael Guillen, Alan Boone,
Jacob Knostman
BACK ROW, LEFT TO RIGHT: Logan Call, Blake Bellomy,
Marcus Shanaa

(Courtesy Lauren Waters)

Logan Call (third from left) with his Spirit of Handball
Award

Following is the published narrative of the Spirit of Handball Award from the May 2019 issue of the
USHA's *Handball*, with the above photo and article found on page 10:

> Collegiate handball mixes the passion of the game with school pride and loyalty.
> Individual and team championships are won and lost each year, yet players demonstrate
> the best examples of sportsmanship and fair play.
>
> Playing hard and doing one's best is encouraged, but not at the expense of the Spirit of
> Handball-which refers to the respect, fairness, self-discipline and camaraderie required
> in our sport.
>
> Because players not only adhere to these guidelines but go above and beyond expec-
> tations with their actions and attitudes, the USHA is recognizing four outstanding
> individuals with the Spirit of Handball Award. For this recognition, coaches and peers
> evaluate and recommend the men and women who go above and beyond the code.

Logan Call (Texas A&M)

> Call served as team captain and took a last-minute lead role when coach Ozzie Burke
> couldn't make the trip. While some 18-year-olds might seem overwhelmed by traveling
> and leading a handball team across the country, Call took the helm and flourished. At
> the start of each match, he would go out of his way to greet his opponents and make it a
> point to form a connection. From all accounts, Call was a true gentleman on the court
> and a pleasure to compete against. Off the court, he stepped up numerous times as his
> team's representative and was a true goodwill ambassador for his school.

With all of the men on the team returning, hope for a greatly improved team was high. On the women's
team Lauren Waters was the only returning team member. Recruiting during the year helped increase

the number of members, both men and women, on the Aggie team. An increased excitement was also felt since the 2020 National Collegiate Handball Tournament would be held at the University of Texas handball courts and that meant some familiarity with the courts and easier travel arrangements.

As the Wednesday preliminary rounds began in the M113-128 group Samson Tellam defeated Nolan Levy of the University of Illinois 21-7, 21-4. In the M97-112 group Adam Cearley defeated Nathan Roden of the University of Illinois 21-19, 21-19. In the M81-96 group, Timothy Mei of Stony Brook University defeated Michael Guillen 21-14, 21-18 and Logan Call defeated Barry Greene of the University of Limerick, Ireland 21-1, 21-3. In the M65-80 group, Ricardo Sanchez of the University of Texas-El Paso defeated Marcus Shanaa 21-4, 21-5 and Jacob Knostman defeated Thomas Klapperich of Minnesota State University-Mankato 21-8, 21-12.

In the Thursday preliminary round of MB3/C1, Samson Tellam defeated Jimmy Diadone of Missouri State University 21-14, 21-9. In the MB2/B3 group, Brandon Sanchez of Lake Forest College defeated Michael Guillen 21-17, 7-21, 11-7 and Tyler Armer of Missouri State University defeated Adam Cearley 21-5, 17-21, 11-5. In the MB1/B2 group, Marcus Shanaa defeated Spencer Louis of the University of Texas 21-11, 21-11 and Dillon Savage of Pacific University defeated Logan Call 14-21, 21-11, 11-1. In the MA3/B1 group, Jacob Knostman defeated Jean Hession of the National University of Ireland-Galway 21-14, 21-15.

As the matches began on Friday in the round of 16 in the MB3 division, Samson Tellam defeated Barry Greene of the University of Limerick-Ireland 21-7, 21-4; Adam Cearley defeated Ryan Holdsworth of the University of California-Berkeley 21-14, 21-8 and Michael Guillen defeated Nathan Rhoden of the University of Illinois 21-13, 21-4. In the round of 16 in the MB2 division, Logan Call defeated Peter Callahan of Pacific University 21-2, 21-6. In the round of 16 in the MB1 division, Isiah Hong of City University of New York-Brooklyn College defeated Marcus Shanaa 21-3, 21-10. In the round of 16 in the MA3 division, Jong Woo Han of Stony Brook University defeated Jacob Knostman 21-14, 21-9. In the quarterfinals of the MB3 division, Jacob Granley of the Colorado School of Mines defeated Samson Tellam 21-9, 21-14; James Lin of Stony Brook University defeated Adam Cearley 21-8, 21-7 and Michael Guillen defeated Simon Fields of Pacific University 21-20, 21-17. In the quarterfinals of the MB2 division, Logan Call defeated Scott Nelson of Missouri State University 21-17, 12-21, 11-5. In semifinal action of the MB3 division, Michael Guillen defeated Pratybush Vyas of Stony Brook University 21-1, 21-20,

and in the MB2 division, Andrew Unick of Minnesota State University-Mankato defeated Logan Call 20-21, 21-6, 11-10. In the finals of the MB3 division, Michael Guillen could not cope with the offensive fire power of Jacob Granley of the Colorado School of Mines and was defeated 21-9, 21-6.

In the round of 16 in the men's B doubles competition, Landon Le and Jordan Turnquest of the Colorado School of Mines defeated Adam Cearley and Samson Tellam 21-20, 21-12, and Marcus Shanaa and Logan Call defeated Doug Van Arsdale and Julian Nava of Ohio State University 21-11, 21-3. In the quarterfinals, Marcus Shanaa and Logan Call defeated Clinton Hemphill and Daniel Galuska of the Colorado School of Mines 21-3, 21-5. In the semifinals of the doubles competition, Shanaa and Call defeated Timothy Mei and Shih Bin Tsao of

(Courtesy of Lauren Waters)

Stony Brook University 21-20, 12-21, 11-6. This set the stage for the final championship match against the doubles team of Landon Le and Jordan Turnquest of the Colorado School of Mines who defeated Aggies Cearley and Tellam in the round of 16. In a closer match than the score indicated, Shanaa and Call were defeated by the score of 21-17, 21-17.

Following is the report of B doubles play found on page 13 of the May 2020 issue of the USHA's *Handball*:

> If one were to take 10 minutes to watch the B doubles final, it would be obvious why handball is The Perfect Game. All four players-Landon Le and Jordan Turnquest from Colorado School of Mines and Marcus Shanaa and Logan Call from Texas A&M-were super competitive and giving 100% on every point. Questionable calls were taken in stride, pro or con. A lot of friendly bantering, fist bumps and great sportsmanship was evident throughout the match from both teams.

> TAMU had powerful, fast serves that threw CSM off balance, with several aces mixed in. But Le/Turnquest have played doubles for a little over a year, and although not textbook, they certainly had a rhythm that led them to victory.

Only two women represented Texas A&M at the tournament, Lauren Waters and Briley Buchanan, and they would both earn championship medals.

In the Wednesday preliminary matches of the W49-80 group, Briana Pena Venezuela of Pima Community College defeated Briley Buchanan 21-3, 21-3. In the W33-48 group, Lauren Waters defeated Hannah Ramsey of Pacific University 21-9, 21-11. In Thursday's preliminary matches, Briley Buchanan defeated Cora Rose Gleeson of the University of Limerick-Ireland 8-21, 21-1, 11-0. In the WA1/A2 group Paige Taylor of Missouri State University defeated Lauren Waters 15-21, 21-16, 11-5.

After the preliminary matches, Briley Buchanan was in the WB2 division where she was defeated by Clarissa Marquez of the University of California-Berkeley 21-3, 7-21, 11-8. Lauren Waters was in the WA2 division and in the round of 16, she defeated Kili Kunitomo of Pacific University 21-2, 21-6. In the quarterfinals, Lauren Waters defeated Nicole Walker of Missouri State University 21-2, 21-7. In the semifinals, Lauren Waters defeated Monica Redfern of Lake Forest College 21-2, 21-4 to advance to the finals for the second year in a row. The finals proved to be a greater challenge, but only in the first game, where she defeated Skyler Collison of Missouri State University 21-16. The second game and final for the championship proved much easier, as Waters established her dominance early and moved on to the final score of 21-8 and the title of the A2 division.

The following story was reported on page 16 of the May 2020 issue of the USHA's *Handball*:

> Playing her eighth match in five days, Lauren Waters of Texas A&M handily won the women's A2 championship. She defeated Skyler Collison of Missouri State in the final 21-16, 21-8, then slammed with first-year teammate Briley Buchanan in the B doubles.

> After winning the B1 championship the previous year, Waters focused on additional skill development and court sense by emphasizing consistent practices and tournament attendance. She teamed this with confidence under pressure to post convincing wins in the A2 bracket against Kili Kunitomo of Pacific, Nicole Walker of Missouri State and Monica Redfern of Lake Forest on the journey to the final.

> For Waters, winning is a good balance of the sword-and-shield strategy of developing a few basic, consistent serves and offensive skills with her dominant right hand to go with complementary defensive skills with her left hand.

When coupled with serving to her opponent's weakness, patient shot selection within her skill set in volleys and physical stamina, Waters can be proud of the winning combination she has created.

It will be interesting to watch her continued development after she graduates in May.

The two Aggie women wanted to enter the doubles competition. Since Briley had only been playing handball for 4 weeks, they entered the women's B division doubles. In the first round, Briley Buchanan and Lauren Waters defeated Carli Feist and Kili Kunitomo of Pacific University 21-8, 20-21, 11- 2 which would prove to be their toughest match. In the semifinals, Buchanan and Waters defeated Claire Hagstrom and Paige Kennedy of Minnesota State University-Mankato 21-7, 21-14. In the last match of her handball career in the National Collegiate Handball Tournament as a representative of Texas A&M, Lauren Waters was feeling the total physical effort expended in the seven previous handball matches. The tiredness reflected in her face as she would look up to her parents, who supported her with their presence at all of her matches, as if to say, "I won't let you, Briley or Texas A&M down." However, somehow, she would find the energy and the discipline to end the match against Alexis Anderson and Molly Hlebichuk of Minnesota State University-Mankato with a score of 21-7, 21-7. In the history of the National Collegiate Handball Tournaments only a comparatively few players have "slammed"-won both a singles and doubles title in the same year. Lauren Waters is now in that elite group.

Lauren Waters and Briley Buchanan (right) with their Doubles championship medals

Lauren Waters with her Singles championship medal

(Both photos courtesy Lauren Waters)

Thanks to his total dedication, self-discipline and hard work, Jacob Knostman was able to move up into the prestigious A division. As a result of his being in the A division, the team would be competing for the men's team championship of that division. The men's team earned a fourth place finish with a total of 1,732 points. That total was not that far behind first place Arizona State University's 1,836 points. With only two women participating for the Aggies there was no team score. The requirement to compete for a team title is to have a minimum of three of the same gender. The maximum number that can be counted from a team is six of the same gender.

2020 Texas A&M Handball Team at the National Collegiate Handball Tournament
FRONT ROW, LEFT TO RIGHT: Lauren Waters, Michael Guillen, Jacob Knostman
BACK ROW, LEFT TO RIGHT: Marcus Shanaa, Logan Call, Samson Tellam, Adam Cearley, Briley Buchanan
(Courtesy Lauren Waters)

Members of the A&M Handball Club for 2019-20 were: Charlie Bokelman, Ozzie Burke, Logan Call, Adam Cearley, Britt Dickens, Laurel Gray, Jack Gressett, Michael Guillen, Alex Hagood, Don Johnson, Kayla Jones, Jacob Knostman, Dino Pucci, Marcus Shanaa, Samson Tellam and Lauren Waters.

Returning from the National Collegiate Handball tournament the members of the team and handball club resumed their normal routine. No one realized the devasting blow to handball at A&M and world-wide that was just ahead.

Prior to spring break (mid-March), the author told his Kinesiology/handball students "Have a great spring break. I will see you in a couple of weeks." The COVID-19 pandemic hit Texas A&M full force during the break. All classes of the spring semester were finished online. Obviously, the Aggie handball club suffered the same calamity.

When the fall 2020 semester began, Texas A&M made the announcement that handball singles could be played using protective masks and would be played for 15 minutes, and then playing partners must be changed. So went the handball classes. No cutthroat or doubles could be played. The handball club did not actively resume its activities, although Logan Call and Marcus Shanaa, continuing members of the Aggie handball team and club, attempted to play. Being allowed to play for only 15 minutes and no other members available to switch courts, was totally unsatisfactory. Rules for playing handball in the spring of 2021 were not changed. Of course, similar rules of handball play existed at other colleges and universities. The USHA wisely cancelled the 2021 Collegiates which were scheduled to be hosted by Missouri State University.

It was a joyous occasion when the A&M president announced that all classes would resume in the normal manner beginning with the fall 2021 semester. Many things had changed for the A&M handball club during the hiatus of 2020 and 2021. Ozzie Burke stepped down as the handball coach. Jack Gressett accepted the position and responsibility as head coach. Don Johnson agreed to continue as assistant coach. The only returning student member of the previous handball club was Logan Call. Jason Buley, who had started playing handball in high school, was the only other student member of the club, and so it went throughout the fall semester. The coach and assistant coach announced practice times; however, with only two student members, the club was not functional. Call and Buley would meet frequently from time to time to play, but not enough for either of them to improve their handball skills.

At some point, Call announced to Buley that he would not continue with the club for the spring semester. So, as the 2022 spring semester began, Buley was the lone student member of the A&M handball team. During the first week of the spring semester, William Henry, IV, came to the normally scheduled time for the handball club to meet and said he wanted to be in the club. Now the coaches, Gressett and Johnson, had two members on the A&M handball team.

The first scheduled Kinesiology 199/handball class of the 2022 spring semester, taught by Don Johnson, met on 18 January. After the initial introduction, the class was given a handball to hit. Going from court to court to help the students, it was evident that two women were very athletic. Johnson asked the two, Rebekah Hailey and Faith Kucera, if they would like to become members of the handball team. They accepted. Now the club would have four members on the team. One week later, 25 January, the author asked four of the men in the class if they wanted to be members of the club. Of the four, Andrew Applewhite, Phillip Barrett and Hayden Gee accepted. One week later a friend of Gee's, Ethan Fritzsche, came to practice and said he wanted to learn the game of handball. There were other friends who came and played with the team; however, the others were not available to attend the collegiates.

On 22 February 2022, the A&M handball team left the confines of Aggieland to attend the National Collegiate Handball Tournament hosted by Missouri State University in Springfield, Missouri. Jason Buley, the only experienced handball player on the A&M team, had conflicts and could not make the trip. With one player who had taken handball in the fall, William Henry, IV, five players with one month and four days of handball play, one player with three weeks play, and two coaches, the team was on the way with expectations of fun, camaraderie and a great learning experience.

During the preliminary rounds of the men's competition, Ethan Fritzsche kept winning and earned his way into the MB1 group where he was defeated in the round of 16 by Brendan Coggins of Lake Forest College 21-13, 21-5. Andrew Applewhite, Phillip Barrett and Hayden Gee earned their way into the MB2 group. In the round of 16, Andrew Applewhite defeated Ian Joshi of The University of Texas 21-10, 9-21, 11-5; Phillip Barrett defeated Luis Bailon of Missouri State University 21-0, 21-4 and Cameron Cavanaugh of Angelo State University defeated Hayden Gee 21-8, 21-6. In the quarterfinals, Andrew Applewhite defeated Anthony Justice of Angelo State University 21-9, 21-16 and Phillip Barrett defeated McTzviel Oyerinde of the University of Texas 21-8, 21-12. In the semifinals, Evan Downing of Pacific University defeated Andrew Applewhite 21-4, 21-7 and Phillip Barrett defeated Cameron Cavanaugh of Angelo State University 21-8, 21-20. In the finals, Phillip Barrett lost his first game to Evan Downing of Pacific University 21-15. Phillip Barrett came back strong in the second game to win 21-8. Barrett continued his strong play into the tiebreaker and won 11-2 to become the national champion of the MB2 group. William Henry, IV, was placed in the MB3 group where he received a bye in the round of 16 and in the quarterfinals. In the semifinals, Henry defeated Trey Lopez of Angelo State University 21-0, 21-13. In the finals, Henry was matched against another player from Angelo State University, Jacob O'dell, who won the first game 21-15. During the first game, O'dell made the discovery that Henry had difficulty returning a soft diamond serve. O'dell never strayed from that serve during the entirety of the second game and won the MB3 championship 21-2.

During the preliminary rounds of the women's competition, Rebekah Hailey and Faith Kucera played their way into the WA2 group. Fate, some would say luck, is always present during pairings within any group. Rebekah Hailey, known by the A&M coaches, was one of the better handball players in the WA2 group; however, her first match, round of 16, was against Jasmine Chen of Stony Brook University who won her way to the championship of the WA2 group. Jasmine Chen defeated Rebekah Hailey 21-5, 21-15.

In the round of 16, Faith Kucera defeated Krithika Ravishankar of the University of Texas 21-9, 21-4. In the quarterfinals, Faith Kucera defeated Rachael Fisher of Utah State University 21-14, 19-21, 11-0. In the semifinals, Faith Kucera was defeated by Dixie Dowell of Missouri State University 21-4, 21-2.

The total points earned by the Aggies were: men 1,456 and women 696. The combined team total was 2,152 points. These point totals were not known as the team settled in for the annual banquet. Earlier in the day, Andrew Applewhite had been named to the committee for selection of the sportsmanship awards. At some point, Applewhite volunteered or was named one of two handball players to make the award announcements. When the time came for the announcements, Applewhite left our table without giving any indication of what he was about to do. We, coaches and team members, followed his progress as he weaved his way through the maze of tables and then up the steps to the stage. All seated at the A&M table were totally surprised when Applewhite announced the runner-up team in women's division A to be Texas A&M. Another surprise followed when Applewhite announced the runner-up team in men's division B to be Texas A&M. The author of this book and assistant coach of the Texas A&M handball team jumped with exhilaration along with the other Aggies seated at the table when Applewhite announced loudly, "The winner of the Division A Combined Team National Collegiate Handball Championship is Texas A&M." High fives, handshakes and hugs were shared around the table. Both A&M coaches were still not convinced the final result to be accurate and asked the next day that the results be verified. Verification proved the combined team championship by Texas A&M to be correct.

Trophies from the 2022 national collegiates.

(Author's collection)

Texas A&M handball team at the 2022 National Collegiate Handball Championships

LEFT TO RIGHT: William Henry, IV, Andrew Applewhite, Hayden Gee, Ethan Fritzsche, Don Johnson, Jack Gressett, Phillip Barrett, Faith Kucera, Rebekah Hailey

(Courtesy Hayden Gee)

CHAPTER 13
Aggieland Classic

The Aggieland Classic was initiated by Lance Lowy soon after he was placed in charge of the handball program at A&M. Lowy knew that, to develop a handball team that would be competitive on a national collegiate level, the team would have to participate in tournaments. Playing in class and playing each other from time to time in the confines of your own courts would never develop the skill level and tournament experience needed to be competitive at the national level. He came up with a plan and got approval to initiate a tournament that would not be limited to Aggies but would be open to all who wanted to participate at the different levels of play. In coming up with a name for the tournament, he settled on the name "Aggieland Classic". From the first day no one has ever wanted to change the name.

Lowy also envisioned that if the tournament was successful and grew in size that enough money could be made to help pay for the Aggie handball team to travel to the National Collegiate Handball Tournament. Another benefit of the tournament would be to assist in determining who could rise to the top in a competitive atmosphere and in turn represent A&M at away tournaments. In the beginning, he could not envision this tournament, one to be held in the fall and one to be held in the spring, becoming one of the most successful and largest handball tournaments anywhere.

Records were kept of each individual tournament but all were not saved as recorded history. What follows are the results of the tournaments that were recorded and reported in a medium that could be considered historical.

In the 1980 February-March issue of the USHA's *Handball*, page 39, Lance Lowy reported the results of the fall 1979 tournament. This was the third annual tournament and the first known results of play:

> Jeff Bronson won the Open singles of the third annual Texas A&M University handball tournament held October 19, 20, 21 in College Station, Texas. Bronson defeated Jack Gressett in the finals, 21-10, 21-8.
>
> In the Open doubles, Dennis Corrington and Lance Lowy defeated Phil Baranowski and Dick Edwards in the finals, 21-11, 21-17 for the title.
>
> B singles saw Eddie Martin defeat David Van Brunt for the championship 21-19, 4-21,11-10. In C singles, Jerry Dubose topped David Sladic for the title, 21-18, 18-21, 11-10.
>
> Sue Oakleaf won the women's singles by defeating Lani Jacobs, 21-6, 21-6.
>
> The tournament was a great success and reflects our dynamic handball program here at the University.

The 1980 spring Aggieland Classic saw Jack Gressett get revenge for the fall defeat by Jeff Bronson. In the spring tournament, Gressett beat Bronson in the Open singles finals 21-13, 12-21, 11-4. Gressett and

Ozzie Burke won the doubles championship by defeating Lance Lowy and Rick Copeland 21-15, 21-18 in the finals. David Van Brunt defeated Mark Patterson to win B singles. David Sladic defeated Ace Feickert to win C singles. Sue Oakleaf repeated as women's singles champ, defeating Jill MacAluso 21-8, 21-17.

The 1981 spring Aggieland Classic was played on April 24, 25 and 26 in the East Kyle handball courts. Steve Smith won the A singles division by defeating Ozzie Burke in the finals 21-11, 18-21, 11-8. Richard Harrison won A singles Consolation by defeating Eddie Martin from Houston 16-21, 21-9, 11-3. Eric Hunter won the B singles division by defeating Matt Pokryfki in the finals 21-15, 9-21, 11-6. Charley Pardue defeated Brent Bertrand 21-6, 10-21, 11-4 in the B Consolation finals. Two time national collegiate and state women's champion, Sue Oakleaf, entered the men's C singles division and easily won by defeating Greg Estes 21-9, 21-11. Hilary Huffard won the women's A singles division by defeating Jill MacAluso 21-16, 21-12 in the finals. Raylene Teel defeated Ariela Olivas 21-4, 21-20 to win the A Consolation. Janet Sweeney defeated Linda Bryan 21-13, 21-13 to win the women's B singles division. Kelly Graham won the women's B Consolation. In doubles, Jack Gressett and Lance Lowy defeated Jeff Bronson and Mike Moore 21-4, 18-21, 11-1 to win the championship.

The Aggieland Classic continued to become more popular with each passing tournament. In the sixth annual tournament, there were 168 entrants. The defending A singles champ, Steve Smith, defeated Ozzie Burke 21-14, 21-6 to retain his title. The A singles Consolation champ was Dennis Corrington who defeated Bob Davidson in the finals 9-21, 21-8, 11-5. Carol Henning defeated Brenda Crim in a hard fought final 21-19, 19-21, 11-5 to win the women's A division championship. In the women's A Consolation final, Kirsten Brekken defeated Marilyn Schindler 21-8, 21-16 for the title. In the men's B division finals, Mark Buckner from Austin defeated Brent Bertrand 20-21, 21-18, 11-9. Dave Utsey defeated Dave Washington 21-12, 21-7 to win the B Consolation title. Julie Werner won the women's B singles title by defeating Rene deLassus. The final score was not available. In the women's B Consolation final, Cathy Caylor defeated Heather McWilliams 21-15, 21-14 for the title. In the men's C division, Ricky Van defeated Tim Sutton 21-3, 21-10 to win the title and in C Consolation final, Bill Kester defeated John Hirshhorn 21-17, 21-10 for the title. In men's doubles, Ozzie Burke and Jeff Bronson defeated Jack Gressett and Chuck Trees 21-9, 21-17 to win the title.

The seventh Aggieland Classic, held in December 1983, was the largest to date. There were 178 handball players signed up to vie for the different divisional championships. In the men's Open singles, Steve Smith was able to defend his title by defeating Jack Gressett 21-20, 21-12. The finals were not easy since Steve and Chuck Trees had defeated Ozzie Burke and Lance Lowy 15-21, 21-9, 11-8 in a long, grueling Open doubles match 90 minutes earlier. These two victories earned Steve his first handball slam. In the Open Consolation bracket, Butch Willey defeated Dick Edwards 21-7, 21-12. In the men's B-Plus division, Bill Moore defeated Brent Bertrand 21-19, 21-19 to win that title. In the men's B- Plus Consolation bracket, Raymond Walkup defeated Randy Pullen 21-13, 21-13 for that title. In the men's B singles division, Larry Wisdom defeated Tim Sutton 13-21, 21-8, 11-10. Both are roommates at A&M and on the handball team. In the men's B Consolation bracket, Clint Etie defeated Tom Crump 21-14, 21-20 for the title. In the men's C division, Todd Bryan defeated Jerry Ordonez 21-20, 21-19 for the title. In the men's C division Consolation bracket, Ken Allison defeated David Pursell 21-20, 21-18.

In the seventh Aggieland Classic, the USHA National Collegiate Handball format was used for the women's championships. This format guaranteed that each entrant would play at least three games. In the women's A division, Julie Werner squeezed by Renee deLassus. After splitting the first two games, Julie earned the necessary points to win 11-8 in the tiebreaker. The women's A Consolation bracket was won by Angela Gonzalez by defeating Cheryl Miller 21-15, 18-21, 11-8. In the women's B division, Kelley

Cayton defeated Cindy Yates 21-10, 21-11. Liz Kalina won the women's B Consolation title by defeating Shelley Davies 20-21, 21-10, 11-5.

The eighth spring Aggieland Classic was held April 26-28. Once again, the number of entrants pushed the staff to complete play in the time scheduled for the event. In the men's Open singles, Ozzie Burke upset the defending Champ, Steve Smith, 21-10, 19-21, 11-5 to win the championship. The other semifinalists were Jack Gressett and Eric Hunter. Jeff Bronson won the Open Contenders bracket by defeating David Van Brunt. In the B-Plus singles, Bobby Winans defeated David Utsey 21-15, 21-14 for the title. Dick Edwards won the B-Plus Contenders bracket by defeating Brent Bertrand. In B singles, Ray Torres defeated Donald Manning 21-9, 21-18. The B singles Contenders title went to Mike Rayburn by defeating Kevin Canales 7-21, 21-13, 11-5. Mike Forbes won the C singles division, appropriately called the "War of 64," over Greg Torbet 21-5, 21-6. Chris Smith won the C singles Contenders bracket by defeating Kelly Smith. Renee deLassus, one of the better women players on the handball team, chose to play in the men's C singles division rather than the women's Open. She was defeated in the semifinals by the eventual champion, Mike Forbes.

In the women's Open singles of the eighth spring Aggieland Classic, Beth Palmer won the championship title by defeating Evy Grace 21-3, 21-20. The other semifinalists were Caryn Stallings and Missy Sheffield. Julie Hutchinson defeated Suzy Fisk to win the Contenders division. In the women's B division, Cindy Yates won the title by defeating Ginny Stover. Christine Cooper and Laurie Copeland were the other semifinalists. Brenda Machac won the B Contenders division by defeating Sheryl Perkins. It should be noted that the term "consolation" was no longer used. The new term "contenders" would later prove of use in the drop-down format, which was in its development stage by Lance Lowy. The term was later introduced, along with the drop-down format, into the National Collegiate Handball Tournament.

The Open doubles competition was loaded with excitement. The number 1 seeded team of Lance Lowy and Ozzie Burke advanced to the finals by defeating Bobby Winans and Danny Coolidge, The number 2 seeded team of Steve Smith and Tim Sutton defeated Eric Hunter and Dennis Corrington to advance to the finals. The final was a long, grueling match that saw Lowy/Burke defeat Smith/Sutton 21-17, 20-21, 11-2 for the championship. Just as Steve Smith had done the previous tournament, Ozzie Burke completed the slam.

The ninth annual fall Aggieland Classic continued the development of Aggie handball players and was equally exciting as any before. Todd Bryan's report of the Classic's results was published in the USHA's *Handball,* June 1986, page 41:

> The 9th fall Aggieland Classic attracted 170 participants to the Texas A&M campus to compete in eight divisions hosted by the A&M handball Club.
>
> Steve Smith was at his best in winning the Open singles title. In the semis, Smith shot with devastating accuracy to defeat Brad Joiner. In the final, Smith uncorked his left hand to bomb a tired Dale Littwin, 21-12, 21-14. Littwin looked spent after edging Coke Smith in the semis in an 11-9 tiebreaker.
>
> Doug Akers and Jan Jernberg were too strong for the Open doubles field, including Coach Lance Lowy and Ozzie Burke in the final 21-15, 21-17. In the semis, Lowy had 10 aces to help his team defeat Fred Bacchus and Jack Gressett.
>
> Ray Torres won his third consecutive Aggieland title by copping the men's B-Plus Division. Torres defeated a gallant Clark Lehrmann in the semis, while Chico Sutton

defeated Joe Joiner. In the final, Torres had plenty left to defeat Sutton 21-12, 21-14. Dave Allen won the Contenders bracket final over Dave Utsey.

Gary Mueck earned the B singles title with a string of upsets. In the semis, Mueck bombed Mike Forbes 21-15, 21-12. In the final, Mueck edged Glenn Gaddy 18-21, 21-13, 11-2. Gaddy defeated Dody Smith in the semis. Mike Cerna won the Contenders final over Steve Barnett.

The competition was fierce in the first B doubles event offered in this event. Todd Bryan and Jerry Ordonez grabbed the title over Mike Forbes and Mike Frieda 21-17, 21-18.

Once again, the C singles drew the largest field with 64 battling it out for the title. But there were surprisingly few surprises as the Nos. 1 and 2 seeds advanced to the final, where Tim Rainbolt had too much for the tiring Matt Montelongo 21-10, 21-11. Semifinalists were Eddy Johnson and Daniel Watts. Chris Smith won the Contenders event.

The women's Open drew 32 entries with Evy Grace and Jo Beth Palmer advancing to the final with semifinal wins over Dawn Bell and Missy Sheffield, respectively. Palmer grabbed the title with a final win over Grace 21-12, 21-14. All-American soft-ball player Cindy Cooper won the Contenders bracket over Sylvia Andrews.

Wendy Smalley copped the competitive women's B singles with a semifinal win over Judy Ovimet and a final win over Tracy Johnson. Johnson escaped the semis with a narrow victory over Jo Beth Greebon. Rita Shea won the Contenders over Jill Irwin.

Special thanks are due Jim Pillans of Brazos Valley Beverages and Ron Crozier of KBTX for making this event a success.

The ninth annual spring Aggieland Classic was held the first weekend in May and proved to be more than your average tournament as 208 players competed. In the men's Open singles, Steve Smith earned the opportunity to test his game against the ninth ranked professional handball player, John Bike. Bike proved why he was a professional by defeating Steve in the finals 21-10, 21-16. Smith earned his chance at Bike by upsetting highly regarded Doug Akers in the semifinals 21-19, 11-21, 11-7. Coke Smith won the Open Contenders title. In B-Plus singles, Dave Utsey defeated Doug Randolph in the semifinals and Brent Bertrand defeated Rick Hobson to meet Utsey in the finals. Utsey won the title by defeating Hobson 21-18, 21-8. Donald Manning was victorious in the B-Plus Contenders bracket. In the men's B singles division, four Aggies made the semifinals. John Reysa upset the number 1 seed Mike Forbes, 21-11, 21-6 to reach the finals, while Mike Miller defeated Garrett Smith 18-21, 21-5, 11-10 for the chance to meet Reysa in the finals. Reysa proved his win over the number 1 seed was not luck by edging Miller in the finals 21-17, 21-20. Dave Tague won the B Contenders bracket by defeating Charlie Shea 21-11, 21-15. As in the previous Classic, the men's C singles was "a war of survival" with 64 competitors. Surviving all comers, Jerald Kopp defeated the number 1 seed, Branch Ward, 21-20, 21-16 for the title. Don Lewis defeated Mark Rothfield to win the C Contenders bracket.

The ninth annual spring Aggieland Classic had a large number of women competitors. Missy Sheffield reported on page 67 of the August 1986 issue of the USHA's *Handball*:

The women's field proved how popular handball is at Texas A&M as 45 competed. Gloria Smalley advanced to the finals of the women's A with a semifinal win over Dawn Bell, 21-17, 21-11, while Missy Sheffield ousted Carol Cutter, 21-9, 21-6. Smalley grabbed the title over Sheffield with an exciting final, 21-15, 21-16. Julie Hutchinson won the women's A Contenders event.

Smalley's twin sister, Wendy captured the women's B singles event. In the semis, Wendy defeated "Miss San Antonio," Melinda Fritz, while Donna Demott defeated Tracy Johnson, 21-10, 21-5. Wendy grabbed the B title over Demott in an exciting match, 21-11, 21-20. Kathy Wright won the B Contenders event.

The Open doubles created a lot of excitement. In the semifinals, John Bike and Ross Selvaggi outlasted Ozzie Burke and Lance Lowy, 14-21, 21-17, 11-2, and in the other bracket, Doug Akers and Jan Jernberg defeated Dale Littwin and Don Reed. Akers and Jernberg won the Open doubles. In B doubles, Glen Gaddy and Alan Reininger proved too strong for the rest of the field. In the semifinals, they downed Mike Forbes and John Reysa, while Les Lehrmann and Mark Smith outlasted Todd Bryan and Jerry Ordonez. Gaddy and Reininger won a skillfully played final over Lehrmann and Smith 21-16, 21-11.

The Aggieland Classic just kept getting larger and larger. The 1987 fall Classic, held December 4-6 had over 250 players. In the Open singles, two-time Texas state champ Larry LeCompte defeated Sam Edgell in one of the best matches during the tournament with 11-10 in the tiebreaker. To reach the finals, LeCompte defeated Jerry Garcia and Edgell defeated Scott Mittman. Coke Smith took the title in the Contenders bracket with a win over Stan Melnick. Coke teamed with Steve Smith to take the Open doubles title over Charlie Bokelman and Ozzie Burke in three games. In B Plus singles, Bob Davidson outlasted Pete Marchbanks 21-18, 21-18 to take the crown. To reach the finals, Davidson defeated Mike Miller 11-9 in a tiebreaker and Marchbanks defeated Jess Fulcher. In the B-Plus Contenders bracket, Eddy Johnson took the crown with a final win over John Reysa. Forty-eight players entered B singles. Kurt Altenburg, Aaron Cooper, Chris Miller and Jay Wigginton survived to the semifinals. Miller defeated Wigginton and Cooper defeated Altenburg to reach the finals. Miller came out on top to win the B singles crown. In the B singles Contenders bracket, Fran McCann defeated Tommy Lukens for the championship. As usual, the C division drew the largest number of players. For this tournament there were 76 players. Four A&M freshmen survived all of the matches to reach the semifinals; however, in the finals Keith Cook played more consistently than Steve Austin to win the championship. In the C Contenders bracket, Mark Roberson defeated Scott Janecka to win that crown.

In B doubles competition, Mike Forbes and Garrett Smith defeated Stan Melnick and Beth Rowley in the semifinals while Danny Watts and Matt Montelongo defeated Kurt Altenburg and John Spann to reach the finals. In the finals, Forbes and Smith earned the crown.

For the women's division of the 1987 Aggieland Classic Lance Lowy provided the information as reported on page 53 of the April 1988 issue of the USHA's *Handball*:

> In what must have been the largest Women's draw anywhere, ever, 48 women started out in the drop-down event. Collegiate All-American Noel Adorno advanced to the final with wins over Caryn Stallings and Gloria Smalley. Wendy Smalley, Gloria's twin sister, arrived at the final with wins over Dawn Bell and Angie Hutchinson. The finals showed how much Wendy has improved as she pushed Adorno to an 11-9 tiebreaker before falling.
>
> Lisa Smith won the women's A singles with a final win over Miss Texas A&M, Melinda Fritz, as Melinda rushed off to the Christmas parade after the final. Susan Owens and Jeanette Bonke were semifinalists.

Frances Woodcock advanced to the finals of the Contenders with one of the best wins of the weekend in her semifinal win over Kim King. In the final, Woodcock defeated Krista Gregory, who defeated Julie Hutchinson in the semis. Barbara Jacobs won the B Contenders with a final win over Teri West.

Adorno and Angie Hutchinson teamed to win the women's doubles event with a final win over Gloria and Wendy Smalley.

The 12th annual fall Aggieland Classic, held 2-4 December 1988, was the largest ever with 275 entries. In the Open singles, Larry LeCompte, three-time state champ and the number 1 seed, worked his way to the finals by defeating Lance Lowy 21-12, 21-19 and Jerry Garcia 21-15, 21-15. In the other bracket, Steve Smith worked his way to the finals by defeating Brent Bertrand 21-10, 21-14 and Sam Edgell 21-5, 8-21, 11-4. Smith was not to be denied this year as he controlled the finals with accurate passing shots and fly kills. LeCompte was not to be denied a championship in the Open doubles as he teamed with Doug Akers to win over Landon Curry and Manuel Raymond. Raymond won the Contenders title of the Open division by defeating Joe DeBella. In the very competitive B-Plus division, A&M's Aaron Cooper met University of Texas Brett Cooper in the finals. Aaron controlled the tempo and picked up the pace at the end of both games to win 21-16, 21-17. Brett Cooper teamed with Brian Carr to win the B doubles championship over Eric Ostrowidski and Gil Garcia. Ostrowidski and Garcia made a close match of the championship by forcing Cooper and Carr to win in a tiebreaker. Matt Montelongo won the Contenders title. The B division final featured the same two Aggies who competed for the C division title during the spring Classic. Mark Rhodes defeated Steve Naftanel in a tiebreaker by almost the identical scores of the spring Classic. John Wyatt won the Contenders title. With so many players, another division was added and for the first time, C-Plus was added. The new division featured 50 players competing for the title. At the end it was Jeff Redding defeating Ricky Cole for the title. David Edgell won the Contender's title by defeating Jeff Sandford. The C division singles featured 64 players. Tony Metoyer survived all of the challenges presented as he played all the way to the title without losing a game. In the final, he defeated Mike Mireless. Steve Schneider won the Contenders final over Lance Bertrand.

Lance Lowy reported the results of the women's play, published on page 52 of the April 1989 issue of the USHA's *Handball*:

> The women's event drew 37 entries and was played with the drop-down format. Kim King dominated the Open event defeating Mollie Huber and Dawn Crane. Diane Purinton edged Katie Hutcheson to win the Open Contenders title. Tami Wise earned the B singles title with wins over Barbara Jacobs and Melissa Audrius. Maria Contreras won the B Contenders title over Elizabeth Griffin. Jana Rehler won the C singles title over Allison Shield while Yvette Clark won the C Contenders title over Lisa Ernest.

The 1989 spring Aggieland Classic, held April 27-29, continued to be as large and popular as any held before. Aaron Cooper provided the report found on page 49 of the December 1989 issue of the USHA's *Handball*:

> The 12th Annual Spring Aggieland Classic was as good as any before it, with over 250 players competing on the Texas A&M campus, April 27-29. Sponsored by CC Creations (Bud Nelson), and covered by local television station KBTX, the tournament was a great success.

The always competitive Open division singles featured Coach Lance Lowy and defending champ Dr. Steve Smith in the final. Smith worked his way to the final with wins over Aaron Cooper of A&M and Scott Mittman from the University of Texas. Meanwhile, Lowy advanced with wins over Dale Littwin and University of Texas student Brett Cooper. In the final, Lowy's tenacious play wasn't enough to overcome Smith's shot selection. Brett Cooper beat Aaron Cooper for the Open Contenders title.

The Open doubles saw former collegiate champs John Bike and Ross Selvaggi win the title over Brett Cooper and Mittman. Cooper and Mittman survived a three-game semifinal over Littwin and Jan Jernberg.

In the Men's B-Plus division, A&M's Chris Miller met Dr. Roy Dimon in the final. The fiercely competitive Miller couldn't scrape his way past the consistent play of Dimon. Miller got to the final by defeating Eric Ostrowidzski in the semis, while Dimon edged Matt Montelongo in a heated match. Terry Cosby won the Contenders title over Mark Rhodes.

The men' B singles was filled with up-and-coming talent. In the final, A&M's Vern Hegwood won two close games over UT's Joe Ostrowidzski in a very fast paced match. Hegwood advanced to the final with a semifinal win over Ricky Cole, while Ostrowidzski defeated Jay Wigginton. Chuck Walker took the honors in the B Contenders.

The B doubles final was quite exciting with the Hegwood brothers teaming to defeat Montelongo and Daniel Watts.

The very popular men's C-Plus division was won by A&M's Joe Don Eilers, who outplayed Stu Soileau in the final. Jeff Sandford played very well to take top honors in the Contenders bracket.

The Men's C singles was by far the largest field in the tournament. Chris Uren and Kevin Hobbs worked their way through many players and matches to reach the final, where Uren overcame Hobbs' power to take the title. Hobbs defeated Bear Dylla in the semis, while Uren topped Julio Cano. The C Contenders was won by Devin Hammack.

The women's field was outstanding. The Open final featured sisters Gloria and Wendy Smalley, both of whom are A&M students. Wendy edged Gloria in a tough battle. A&M freshman Sharon Baylor won the B event with wins over Tracy Stoll and Mollie Huber. The C singles title was taken by Shawn Stratton, who defeated Tami Moore and Paige Ainsworth. The Contenders event was won by UT's Andra Palmer over Jill Graves.

The 13th annual spring Aggieland Classic featured over 250 entrants from all over the State of Texas and some from out-of-state. Steve Smith had become the man to beat in the men's Open division. Steve won his third straight Aggieland Classic Open title by defeating Dave Littwin 21-14, 21-16. Manuel Raymond defeated Jeff Bronson in the finals to take the Open Contenders title. In the B-Plus division Daniel Watts proved too tough for all and won the title by defeating Lyn McDonald in the final. Defending champ Roy Dimon finished third. Trey Rothenberger defeated Kevin Hobbs in the final to take the Contenders title. In the B division singles, Bear Dylla held off Beth Rowley to win the title with a final score of 21-16, 21-19. John Edgell won the B Contenders title by defeating David Ortiz. Omar SantaAna defeated the number 1 seed Danny Alexander to take the C-Plus title. Casey Clark defeated Jeff

McCoy in the finals of the C-Plus Contenders bracket to take the title. As usual, the C division singles was the largest division. Surviving all of the matches on the way to the finals, Steve Mayers outlasted Jerry Batek 21-18, 21-20 to win the title.

Chris Miller sent the results of the tournament to the USHA's *Handball* magazine and it was reported in the October 1990 issue, pages 49 and 50. Of the women's action, Miller writes:

> The women's Open featured a round-robin format for the strong field. Beth Rowley proved the best by mixing up kills and passes with her rocket right. The Smalley twins, nationally ranked in the Collegiates, didn't have their usual edge due to a long hiatus prior to the tournament. Still, they gave their all and Wendy won second place, while Gloria took fifth. Former Aggie Sue Sellars earned a respectable third place, while Kim King kept her opponents on their toes with her power but settled for fourth place.

> The Women's B final was one of the closest finals with the lengthy rallies taking their toll on both players. Sharon Baylor emerged the victor over Betsy Boswell, 21-16, 21-20. Anna Gonzalez ravaged the Contenders field with sharp passing shots.

> Melinda Fritz won the women's C singles over a struggling Leigh Ann Williams.

The doubles division saw Mark Rhodes and Steve Naftanel victorious over Daniel Watts and Tom Kohler to earn the title.

The 13th annual fall Aggieland Classic set a record of players to date with over 300 entries. Held 17-19 November 1989 on the A&M campus, Kevin Hobbs made a report of the tournament's success. His story is found on page 52 of the February 1990 issue of the USHA's *Handball*. His report follows:

> Sam Edgell powered his way to the Open final against Coach Lance Lowy. Edgell defeated Chris Miller and Manuel Raymond, while Lowy defeated Dave Parsons, Brett Cooper and Brian Elley. Edgell's speed and ability to rekill gave him the edge over Lowy in a well-played final. David Van Brunt won the Contenders final over Miller.

> In the Men's B-Plus event, Marvin Harris held off a determined surge by Sue (Oakleaf) Sellars to win the title. Both players advanced to the final with great wins in the semi-finals, as Harris defeated Steve Naftanel and Sellars beat Chris Phythian. Rick Cole defeated Vern Hegwood to win the Contenders event.

> After winning the C title last semester, A&M Sophomore Chris Uren moved up to the B division and still won, defeating Jeff Redding in the final. Uren advanced over Kyle Cooper and Ken Dulaney, while Redding beat Joe Don Eilers and Jaime Liebl. Kevin Faske won the Contenders title over Bart Bartkowiak.

> The Men's C-Plus final proved very exciting. Kevin "Kevinito" Hobbs defeated vastly improved John Reider in three games to post his first-ever tournament win. Reider defeated pro baseball player Rob Swain in the semis, while Hobbs beat Mike Scheffler. David Edgell beat George Chin to win the Contenders title.

> The men's C event was the largest event with 85 players. Shane Rothenberger and Matthew Lauderdale worked their way to the final. Rothenberger defeated Lauderdale for the second time in two weeks as the two also played in the Texas State Championships.

Rothenberger defeated Jon Redding in his semifinal while Lauderdale turned back Casey Clark. Matt Jackson won the Contenders title over Scott Whitsel.

The Women's Open featured two former Aggie greats, Sue Sellars and Beth Rowley. By edging nationally ranked Beth Rowley, Sellars added the Women's crown to her second-place finish in B-Plus. Kim King held off Sharon Baylor to win the Contenders title.

Baylor had a busy weekend as she also copped the women's B title with a final win over the relentless Mollie Huber in a great match. Baylor defeated Audrea Stork in the semis, while Huber beat Allison Arnold. Anna Griffin won the Contenders title in this 40-player field with a final win over Shawn Stratton.

Theresa Reineger won the Women's C title by defeating Kim Shelton in the final match. In the semis, Reineger beat Leigh Ann Williams while Shelton beat Debbie Deal. Yvette Clark beat Melissa Whitten to win the Contenders title.

The Open doubles title went to Landon Curry and James Moody by defeating David Edgell and Manuel Raymond in a tiebreaker. The all-Houston B Doubles final was won by Bob Webster and Ed O'Connell over Dave Parsons and Chris Phythian.

In the 14th year of the Aggieland Classic, the number of entrants annually could be expected to be near 275. For the 14th annual fall Aggieland Classic, there were 265 players. Players continued to come from all over the state and sometimes from other states. Familiar names from the local community of handball players continued to earn titles and add to the excitement. The tournament always featured rising stars of the A&M handball team who usually made their names known by winning lesser divisions titles than the Open singles. Such was not the case when a newcomer, Salvador SantaAna, defeated all those who came before him to win the Open singles title by defeating Manuel Raymond in the final 21-16, 21-12. This quickly established SantaAna as a star of the future and definitely cast his shadow upon the national collegiate handball scene. Brett Cooper won the Open Contenders title by defeating some familiar (to the A&M handball community) players, including Brian Carr, Jeff Bronson and Danny Watts. In the B-Plus division, Bear Dylla defeated Roy Dimon in the finals 21-17, 21-17. John Tomme won the Contenders bracket by edging Bob Davidson in a tiebreaker final 11-10. In the B division, Omar SantaAna hung tough and consistent to defeat John Walls for the title. Eric Schmidt defeated Scott Neill in the Contenders final for that title. In the C-Plus division, unseeded Mark Lane surprised all with his strong play to easily win that title. He won the title by defeating Tim Poskey in the final. Eric Fields won the Contenders title in the C-Plus bracket. From a field of 96 players in C division, Donovan Scott emerged with a title when he defeated Paul Hewitt in the final match. Brandon Roberts won the Contenders title.

Ozzie Burke and Larry LeCompte were unstoppable on the way to the crown in the Open doubles competition. They defeated Scott Mittman and Manuel Raymond in the finals for the title. The father/son team of Joe and Kevin Hobbs won the B doubles title by defeating Marvin Harris and Stan Lowy.

As with the men's Open, another key member of the Aggie handball team rose to the top in the women's Open division. Sharon Baylor, who would earn All- American designation during her career at A&M, won the round robin format of the women's Open. To win she had to defeat Jennifer Saunders, who was a former National Junior Champ. Mollie Huber placed third. Laura Gross won the women's B division as she defeated Debbie Deal in the final. Tonye Stallings defeated Corey Walters to win the

Contenders title. In the women's C division, 12-year-old Tim Sellars defeated Dawn Wuthrich for the title. Sarah Davidson defeated Jill Simmons to take the Contenders title.

Results of the 15th annual Aggieland Classic were reported on page 53 of the October1991 issue of the USHA's *Handball*:

> The 15th annual spring Aggieland Classic attracted a large turnout of 260 men and women from across Texas. The tournament also attracted the Colorado State Chairman, Jim Benson, who is also a well-respected Aggie.
>
> Steve Smith, a professor at A&M, won the Open singles with a final win over Salvadore SantaAna 21-15, 21-18. Steve Naftanel won the Open Contenders title after breezing through the small field.
>
> The Women's Open was dominated by Sharon Baylor as she cruised to her final win over Wendy Smalley 21-8, 21-6. Wendy was disappointed in her final match after she convincingly defeated Betsy Boswell in her semifinal.
>
> In the B-Plus division, a much-improved Kevin Hobbs overcame a scrappy Ricky Cole 20-21, 21-17, 11-6. The B-Plus Contenders title was captured by Ken Dulaney.
>
> Bart Hull defeated Ted Watson in the B division and the Contenders was won by John Bates. The women's B featured an evenly matched field but was eventually conquered by Lisa Smith. Terry SantaAna took second place and Mary McElheney captured the Contenders title.
>
> The C-Plus event was won by Noel King as he defeated John Portillo. Brandon Elizondo took home the Contenders title. The huge C division composed of over 70 players was narrowed down to Jackson Reese and Chris Rice. Reese walked away with the first-place trophy as Rice took second place and Brian Boone won the Contenders.
>
> A persistent Kim Harris was triumphant as she defeated Cassie Tijerina in the Women's C division. The Contenders was won by Dana Caraway.
>
> The Open doubles proved to be an exciting event as Salvadore SantaAna, along with his brother Omar, defeated the powerful team of Sam Edgell and Manuel Raymond. In the B doubles the brutal team of Phythian and Ruffner defeated the Bertrands in an excellent match of skill and showmanship. Finally, the Women's doubles final was captured by the All-American team of Betsy Boswell and Sharon Baylor, as they defeated Gloria and Wendy Smalley, who led the Aggies to national titles in previous years.

When it was thought it could become no bigger, the 1991 fall Aggieland Classic proved that wrong. Over 300 participants were on hand to play, December 6-8. In the men's Open singles, Steve Smith was named the champion when his opponent in the final, Sam Edgell, could not play. Edgell injured his knee during his semifinal match against Sal SantaAna. Edgell was able to finish his match against SantaAna, but could not continue in the finals. Smith defeated Larry LeCompte in their semifinal match. Manuel Raymond defeated Tom Smith to take the Open Contenders title. Brett Cooper and LeCompte took the Open doubles title in two games over Ozzie Burke and Charlie Bokleman.

Lance Lowy described the remainder of the tournament action which was reported on page 54 of the April 1992 issue of the USHA's *Handball*:

In a very competitive B-Plus Division Dr. Roy Dimon beat Shane Rothenberger, while Chris Uren beat John Tomme to set up the final. In one of the best matches of the tournament, Dimon eked out an 11-10 victory to earn the honor of playing Open from now on. Rothenberger and Tomme earned a win over Mark and Chris Faulk in the B Doubles final and it was nice to see their father, Jim, at the tournament. Colin Errington defeated Chad Lienau for the B-Plus Contenders crown. Mark Faulk won the men's B final over Greg Damron, after having defeated Andres Iglesias in the semis. John Whittle beat John Blevins to win the B Contenders trophy.

The Men's C-Plus event was won by teenage wonder, Shawn Smith, as he defeated Ben Keating in the semis, while Chris Faulk defeated Miles Freeman. Smith beat Faulk in two games to add to his growing number of titles. The C-Plus Contenders was won by Michael Williams over Brandon Perryman. The men's C Division had a record 121 players, all of whom had played three months or less. The semifinals boiled down to Jeff Coble defeating Jason Bryan, while Scott Cooner beat Scott Korth. Fittingly, the final went three games with Coble pulling out the win. Corey McCutchan won the grueling C Contenders Division.

The Women's B event featured a semifinal upset win by Kim Harris over Terry SantaAna while Katie Hutcheson won a tiebreaker over Dawn Wuthrich. Hutcheson was playing well as she beat Harris two games in the final. Twelve-year-old Zach Lowy won the Women's B Contenders title defeating Teri Slusarek. The Women's C semifinals had Leslie Busch defeating Traci Fambro, while Lisa Drewen beat Jennifer Bellomy. The All-University of Texas final saw Drewen beat Busch for the title. The scrappy Nikki Rudolph rebounded to win the C Contenders title.

NOTE: There is no record of the women's Open singles and no record of the women's doubles matches.

This was the largest tournament that A&M had ever hosted. To be successful, as this tournament was, required a lot of volunteer work by students and members of the A&M handball club. Adding to the effort by staff and students were sponsors Brazos Beverages and CC Creations. The local television station, KBTX, covered the event and added to the success of the tournament. The large number of entrants, tournament sponsors and others contributed to enable the Texas A&M handball team to travel to the National Collegiate Handball Tournament held in Chicago the following February.

With over 300 entries in the 15th annual spring Aggieland Classic, following over 300 in the fall, the tournament was entering a plateau where additional entries might have to be restricted. Even with the large number of entries, the staff and A&M handball team members insured that all would have a good time playing. Sal SantAnna won the men's Open singles, but his play to the final was not easy. He survived a tiebreaker win over Kevin Hobbs in the semifinal while Manny Raymond squeaked by Chris Uren 11-9, to earn his way into the final. In the men's Open Contenders bracket, Bear Dylla defeated a determined Ricky Cole to earn the title. The B-Plus division featured two of A&M's best in one semifinal when Shane Rothenberger prevailed over Mark Faulk to earn a chance to derail Ken Dulaney, who had beaten Shane in a recent Houston pro stop tournament. Dulaney earned his way to the final by defeating Eric Fields. Dulaney maintained his mastery over Rothenberger in a very close 11-7 tiebreaker for the title. Ted Watson defeated A&M junior Tim Poskey to win the B-Plus Contenders title. The B division had a very interesting competitor from Colorado. Jim Benson, the Colorado handball Commissioner, earned his way to the final by defeating Texas' Brandon Roberts in a semifinal match. Benson, in the best physical condition of his life, was looking for an opportunity to run a 10k or a triathlon to warmup prior to his fifth match of the weekend. Benson's great physical condition was not enough to overcome the talented Noel Keen in the finals. Keen had defeated Jeff Walsh in their semifinal match to earn his way to the title match. John Edgell won the B Contenders title by defeating John Reininger. There were 60 entrants in the C-Plus division. The top seed Scott Korth reached the semifinals. The other three semifinalists were Scott Cooner, Jason Bryan and Jeff Coble. It was very unusual for each of the four to be in the semifinals because the same four were in the semifinals of the C division during the fall Aggieland Classic. This time, it was Scott Korth who won out for the crown. Korth defeated Scott Cooner in the semifinal and in the other semifinal, Jeff Coble defeated Jason Bryan. Coble was not able to play well enough to win the title. Clarence Cone came from New Mexico to win the C-plus Contenders title by defeating Tom Carpenter. The C division was made up of players who have only been playing handball for one semester. There were 76 to start play in the division. On paper, basically all players were evenly matched so a draw was the way each player was placed in their respective bracket. The semifinals boiled down to two players from the University of Texas and two from Texas A&M. Aggie Brian Smaistria defeated Aggie Rick Cantu to advance to play Texas' Chris Johnson. Johnson prevailed against Greg Tomasyan in their semifinal. Smaistria defeated Johnson in two long games to win the C title. To watch these two play, it was hard to believe each had only been playing a short time. Alejandro Delgado defeated Tom Tristan to win the C Contenders division.

The August 1992 issue of the USHA's *Handball*, pages 55 and 56, carried the story of the Aggieland Classic. Following is the write-up of the play for the remainder of the tournament:

> In the Women's Open singles a round-robin format was used to accommodate the five players. Beth Rowley, the National Women's Commissioner and former Texas A&M star, emerged unbeaten, although Sharon Baylor, 1992 National Collegiate Champion, gave her a scare. Betsy Boswell, Collegiate All-American, and another former Texas A&M star, placed third, while Brenda Crim came in fourth.
>
> The Women's Open doubles title was claimed by Baylor and Cassie Tijerina over Boswell and Katie Hutcheson in a close match. The Women's B was claimed by Hutcheson over Tijerina, after they had defeated Zach Lowy and Terry SantaAna to reach the final. Yet another great former player from Texas A&M won the B Contenders, as Lisa Walls beat Tammy Moore in the final. The Women's C featured some future A&M stars as Sheri Hermesmeyer smoked the field. She defeated Stacey Barnes, Susie Deshazer, and Erica Bohde enroute to her win. Nydia Fernandez beat Natalie Flores to win the Women's C Contenders. Of special note is Dutch Lowy's fine performance in his first tournament at nine years old.
>
> In the best match of this tournament, and some said the best they'd ever seen, Sam Edgell and Raymond nosed out Coach Lowy and SantaAna, 11-10 to win the Open Doubles. It was great to have Brent Bertrand and Danny Coolidge back playing very competitively.
>
> The sneaky, but good, doubles team of Ed O'Connell and Bob Webster won the B Doubles title, defeating Fields and Uren, 11-10. O'Connell and Webster defeated Dylla and Roberts in one semifinal, while Fields and Uren beat the Houston pair of Von Eiff and Elledge in the other.

Through the hard work of Sal SantaAna, Chris Uren, Emmett Myatt and other Texas A&M Handball Team members, we have acquired additional sponsorship. Albertson's Supermarket, Deluxe Burger Bar, Golden Corral, Mazzio's, and Emiliano's all deserve special thanks. Our main supporter and sponsor, C. C. Creations and Bud Nelson, are also well appreciated.

The fall 1993 Aggieland Classic was the largest of all to date with over 330 entrants. Lance Lowy did a great job of capturing the tournament to include some interesting information. His complete report was filed with the USHA and was reported on pages 54 and 55 in the April 1994 issue of the USHA's *Handball*:

Texas A&M has become known as a place where large handball tournaments take place. Well, we just hosted the largest in our history with over 330 entrants. This event would not be possible without the many sponsors and individuals who made it happen. Jim Pillans of Brazos Beverages, representing Miller Lite, was our primary contributor for our fall tournament. Special thanks to Jim and his crew for putting on a great show. Bud Nelson of CC Creations always puts out the best tournament shirts available. Thanks also to some of the great restaurants and markets that contributed to our cause, Rosarita's, Outback and EZ Mart. Special thanks to Paula Opal in the Rec Sports Dept., and hats off to John Egbert and Dr. and Mrs. Royal Benson for contributing to our Collegiate Fund for travel to Portland for the National Collegiates.

Two–time Texas State Champion, Sal SantaAna, was not to be denied in the Men's Open final as he defeated Dr. Steve Smith. Brian Carr and Larry LeCompte were semifinal-ists in the Open Division. Eric Fields had a fine tournament and won his first Open Contenders title by beating Bear Dylla. Jon Flynt and Texas State B Champion John Egbert were semifinalists in the Division.

The Open doubles Division was a different story as Sal and brother Omar beat Carr and Brett Cooper in the semifinals, while Sam Edgell and Manny Raymond were beating Ozzie Burke and Charlie Bokelman. Sal and Omar are a very formidable team who play very well together, but so do Sam and Manny. Manny controlled the front court while Sam hustled and took charge in the back as they beat the SantaAna brothers in two close games.

In B singles, Casey Clark returned from a year off with renewed enthusiasm as he demolished the field with his two-handed punishing style. Clark beat David Edgell in a three-game final after he had beaten Tom Walsh in the semis. Rick Cantu was the other semifinalist. Big Mike Scheffler beat Zach Lowy in the semis and Ricky Reynolds in a three-gamer to earn the B Contenders title.

The C Plus division featured some of the most competitive matches of the weekend. Dr. Royal Benson bested veteran Clifford Cone in three games in one semifinal, and former Denver Bronco defensive back Kip Corrington defeated Chris Richards in the other. Benson beat Corrington in the final as Kip rushed to the hospital for the birth of his third child. David Huryeh beat Joseph Jones in another three-gamer to win the C-Plus Contenders Division.

The C Division started with 130 players. On Saturday afternoon, in their sixth match of the weekend, Jeff Goldfarb beat Shea Morgenroth 11-10 in the top semifinal. Not to be outdone, Bryan Holmes beat Rick Dervin 11-10 in the other. As if they had not played enough, Goldfarb finally defeated Holmes on Sunday, 21-20, 20-21, 11-10. Sincere congratulations to all these freshmen. This Division was played for the first time ever with the White Ace. After talking to the players, everyone agreed that the ball was easier on their hands over the weekend, but everything else still hurt as usual. Jesse Hernandez won the C Contenders over Mark Allen.

The Women's/Juniors Open title was taken by 13-year-old Burney, as he beat two former standout Aggies, Terry SantaAna in the semis, and Kim King in the final. Tiffany Precht beat Becky Pinkard to win the Women's/Juniors Open Contenders title.

Two Aggie sophomores battled it out in the Women's B singles final. Kim McKinney beat Georgann Kidd to win as Joann Langlinais and Heather Reed also had notable showings. Joanne Jackson won the Women's B Contenders title.

In the Women's C division, Jamie Rupple beat fellow freshman, Kelly Dyer in one semifinal and Jill Emerson beat Beth Oliver in the other. In a well-played match, Emerson came out on top in the final. Laura Hogue beat Maribel Flores to win the Contenders crown.

The Women's/Juniors Open doubles featured some of the weekend's most entertaining matches. In the final, King and 11-year-old Dutch Lowy won the first game and had a 20-16 lead in the second, only to see Cassie Tijerina and Oliver come back to win the second game and the tiebreaker.

When a tournament this size is over, my first thought is not when the next one is going to be. But, the first weekend in May, we'll do it again. Also, coming by the end of 1994, or early '95, our new $40 million Recreation Building will be completed, featuring 12 new handball courts.

Not only was this the largest Aggieland Classic ever held, but a record was set that can never be beaten anywhere as long as there are two games of handball to 21 and a third to 11 to complete a handball match. Jeff Goldfarb and Bryan Holmes scored 103 points in their match. Jeff scored 52 (21, 20, 11) and Bryan scored 51 (20, 21, 10). It was a record for most points scored in a match and for a handball match, that cannot be any closer. Just as Aggie Steve O'Neal set a record for the longest punt in National Football League history that can be tied but never beaten, these two players set the record for most points scored in a handball match that can be tied but never beaten.

Many may wonder how it is possible to hold a handball tournament to accommodate over 300 players during 3 days and guarantee that each player has, at the minimum, two matches. At the time, there were 26 handball courts available – 14 in the Read Building and 12 at the Recreation Center. Even with that number of courts, great organization and attention to keeping all matches on schedule were critical aspects of the tournament. The only other tournament that was near that large in number of handball players was the National Collegiate Handball Tournament; however, that tournament, with over 250 players, was never completed in three days and was never attempted.

It is unfortunate that the Aggieland Classic tournament records of the winners of their respective division are not available for the years after 1993. The author does remember the winners of the 140 Plus division doubles in the fall of 2014, spring of 2015, fall of 2015 and the mystery doubles of the spring of

2016. Ozzie Burke and Don Johnson teamed up and won the title each of those years. The author can also recall the doubles winners in the spring of 2019. Charlie Bokelman and Doug Randolph made a doubles team that easily won the title.

From the beginning of the first Aggieland Classic in the fall of 1978, the tournament had been held twice a year, normally in early December for the fall semester and typically sometime in April for the spring semester. That routine changed after the tournament held in April of 2017. In July of 2017, the handball club officers voted to re-align the handball club with Texas A&M Student Activities. The primary purpose of the realignment was to gain greater autonomy in decision-making for the club. The club had previously been aligned with the Texas A&M Recreation Center. The realignment did disrupt the cycle of the Aggieland Classic. Jim Garner, a longtime handball enthusiast, supporter and leader of the San Antonio Handball Group, also longtime friend of Coach Ozzie Burke, offered to hold the Aggieland Classic in San Antonio and they would pay for the use of the facilities. This was an offer that would provide the tournament play but also would help the A&M club make some much-needed money. The first Aggieland Classic held in San Antonio was in January 2018. That tournament was followed the following January of 2019. Both tournaments were a success and as normally happens with handball tournaments, a following of handball players began to take place, and each year calendars were marked for the date of specific tournaments. However, in this situation, when Jim Garner stepped down as the leader of the San Antonio Handball Group, the money that had been set aside for the Aggieland Classic was committed elsewhere.

In 2016, for the first time since the beginning of the Aggieland Classic, Texas A&M handball could not host the tournament at Texas A&M. Through the efforts of Coach Ozzie Burke and others of the A&M handball club, contact was made with the San Antonio Handball Association. The Association secured 5 courts at the Greater San Antonio YMCA for the tournament. The annual tournament continued to be held in San Antonio through early 2019. Izzy Garcia, Jim Garner, Vince Martinez, James Mazuca, Jennifer and Danny Schmitt, David Stringer, Jeff Swoboda and Jeff Wall were key to continuing to help keep a long-running tournament alive.

Arrangements were made with the Texas A&M Recreation Center to hold the Classic in April 2019. The numbers who participated were not large, but it did signal to the handball world that once again Texas A&M would be holding the Aggieland Classic during the spring semester. Of note, all members of the University of Texas handball team that were available to travel came to play.

The spring 2020 Aggieland Classic was scheduled to be played on April 3-4. Dates of the tournament had been announced and as the Aggie students on the handball team left for spring break, beginning at the end of the academic day on Friday March 6, most were eagerly anticipating their return after the break to ready their handball skills for the Classic. It was expected that the students would return a week later to resume scheduled classes; however, it became evident during the week that for the health and safety of faculty, staff and students, spring break would be extended three days. That time frame was very quickly changed when it was announced that the first A&M student and a faculty member had tested positive for the coronavirus. In the very rapidly changing situation, Texas A&M and the cities of Bryan/ College Station were very much a part of the worldwide pandemic. Texas A&M would finish all of its classes online, and of course, the Aggieland Classic was cancelled. After holding the Aggieland Classic for 82 very successful and memorable times, the 83rd Classic would have to be put on hold for another time.

CHAPTER 14
Revival

Douglas Randolph, a very successful businessman and lifelong handball proponent, made the decision to help Texas A&M renew its handball program. Having done the same for the University of Texas in 2014, he believed a gift of a million dollars would do much the same for A&M as it had done for Texas. The University of Texas had long been a power in collegiate handball under the leadership, teaching and coaching of Pete Tyson, but as happens so many times when such an individual retires, the program goes into a downward spiral. Randolph saw that his gift to the University of Texas helped raise the program to a very respectful handball program at the collegiate level. Could the same gift help Texas A&M? He made the decision to try.

Not knowing who at Texas A&M to contact and, since Randolph had played in the Aggieland Classic many times, he contacted a member of the Recreation Center about the possibility of a gift. At the time, Ozzie Burke had been the handball coach since 2008, so he obviously was the person the Recreation Center needed to contact. Burke had been friends with Randolph for some time and was thrilled about the proposal; however, Burke was not familiar with the workings of Texas A&M. Burke knew that the author had worked for the university for many years and that the he would likely know the appropriate contact for the gift. The author contacted the Texas A&M Foundation and informed them about the proposal and the specific purpose of the gift. The Foundation wasted no time in assigning the Development Officer for the College of Education and Human Development, Jody Ford, to contact Doug about the proposal.

Doug was contacted and a date set to meet with A&M officials in the College of Education and Human Development to work out the details of the gift and, of course at this time, Randolph was not committed to the gift unless he could establish and reach a contract agreement of the rules under which the gift could be used to help the Texas A&M handball program.

The date set for this very important meeting was Wednesday, 13 June 2018, to be held at the Physical Education Activity Program (PEAP) building. Doug, having formed 11 businesses, partnered in two and acquired one, all of which are still in business today, does not go into any venture without doing research and gaining knowledge prior to important meetings. Randolph contacted Burke and wanted to talk before the meeting on the 13th. Randolph, Burke, Charles Bokelman, Jack Gressett and the author met at College Station's Fish Daddy's the night of 12 June to discuss the workings of the university, the Texas A&M Foundation and the individuals who would be at the meeting the next day. Excitement filled the air, especially among the four meeting with Randolph and at the end of the dinner meeting, they were looking forward to a new day and its possibilities for A&M handball.

At the scheduled time the following met at PEAP to discuss Randolph's proposal: Doug Randolph; Jody Ford; Ozzie Burke; Don Johnson; Dr. Melinda Sheffield-Moore, Department Head of Health and Kinesiology; Frank Thomas, Division Chair of PEAP; Lorinda Cohen Gomez, Associate Division Chair of PEAP and Kayla Jones, Administrative Coordinator for the College of Health and Kinesiology. After introductions, Ford presented Randolph's proposal. Many questions and much discussion ended when a general agreement about the use of the gift was reached with Randolph. Basically, it was agreed that 70 percent of the income from the gift would be used for the teaching of handball and 30 percent would go to the A&M handball team to fund the team's participation in the annual USHA Collegiate Handball Championship Tournament.

Any endowment must earn income before it can be used for the intended purpose. To get the "new" program started Randolph agreed to provide a gift of $2,000 per semester to those who taught handball and a gift of $300 to each student completing the Kinesiology 199/handball course. With this agreement, all left the meeting with a renewed feeling that the A&M handball program would be able to continue with a much brighter future.

At one point during the meeting Frank Thomas said, "Excuse me while I check on some classes." Little did those in the meeting know that while out of the meeting Thomas had already started the wheels in motion to establish four Kinesiology 199/handball classes for the 2018 fall semester. All four classes "made" and Kayla Jones, Kara Edwards and Mike Thornton were the teachers. Each class was limited to 24 students and according to university policy, a class must have a minimum of 10 students to "make". A total of 82 students enrolled in handball and from those classes the 2019 and 2020 handball team had a new beginning.

During this time period, Randolph and Jody Ford would have many conversations on the development of the final gift agreement and on 30 November 2018, Doug Randolph made good his proposal when he gave a million dollar gift to the Texas A&M Foundation for the purpose of promoting handball at Texas A&M. Heather Gillin of the College of Education and Human Development wrote the following press release about the gift.

Randolph Foundation Supports Texas A&M Handball Through $1 Million Endowment

By Heather Gillin, Texas A&M University College of Education and Human Development

COLLEGE STATION, Dec. ?, 2018 — For avid handball player Doug Randolph, handball is not just a game. He credits handball with facilitating lifelong friendships and fitness.

On Nov. 30 Randolph gave $1 million to support the Texas A&M Handball team and the sport of handball in Physical Education Activity Programs in Health and Kinesiology, a department in the College of Education and Human Development. This gift will help generations of Aggies find their own fulfillment for years to come.

"If you play handball, not only will you take care of yourself, but you will surround yourself with people that will be great friends," Randolph said. "Friends who will be competitive and encourage you to stay strong and compete for the rest of your life."

Randolph, founder of the Randolph Foundation for Higher Education, has been playing handball since he was a freshman in college. He honored retired Brigadier General Donald "Don" Johnson '55 through the naming of this endowment, entitled BG Donald "Don" Johnson (RET) '55 Handball Excellence Endowment.

As an undergraduate, Johnson became the first national championship handball player at Texas A&M. He went on to serve as a coach and mentor to the Texas A&M Handball team.

Handball was one of the first sports in Texas A&M's intramural program that began in 1925. As the sport grew in popularity, the team boasted many nationally ranked teams and players, like national champion Ozzie Burke '71.

Burke, who went on to coach the handball team, is friends with Randolph through a mutual love for the sport. By early 2018, the handball program at Texas A&M was fading. Burke brought the state of Texas A&M Handball to the attention of Randolph, who felt moved to help.

Through his gift, the Physical Education Activity Program in the Department of Health and Kinesiology will fund faculty to teach kinesiology 199 handball courses and support the Texas A&M Handball team to travel and compete at regional and national tournaments.

Dr. Melinda Sheffield-Moore '87, department head of Health and Kinesiology, played handball as an undergraduate at Texas A&M. She credits the sport with providing her the opportunity for travel and personal growth.

"With this generous gift, we have the opportunity to share Texas A&M Handball with many students and hopefully allow them to form a lifetime bond with fellow students like I did," Sheffield-Moore said.

Texas A&M handball had gained a new life. With this "new" beginning, the foundation for continued classes had been established and the handball team was experiencing greater success after the low of 2018. For team results at the National Collegiate Handball Tournament, see the Chapter Team 2010-2022.

During the spring of 2019, the author was asked to consider teaching the Kinesiology 199/ handball course. I did not want to take the place of someone who was already teaching; however, Kara Edwards had made it known that she would not be back for the 2019 fall semester so I agreed to accept the teaching responsibility.

While all of this was happening, discussion among Ozzie Burke, Charles Bokelman, Jack Gressett and the author was about the future of the handball team and where should Texas A&M look to find a future coach for the A&M handball team. Ozzie Burke had developed serious health problems during 2018 and in early 2019, lost his right eye. After recovery to the extent he could come back to the handball courts, Burke informed the three of us that he would no longer be the head coach. The three of us did not fully accept that announcement and still looked to him as the primary coach; however, we each agreed to be assistants and to help coach as a committee of four.

Bokelman had been to a handball tournament and while at the tournament, talked to Martin Mulkerrins, one of the top handball players in the world. Mulkerrins told Bokelman he really would like to have the opportunity to return to A&M in the future. We all remembered the 2013 fall semester he spent at A&M as an exchange student, and at the time, was the USHA national collegiate singles handball champion. Each of us agreed that Mulkerrins would be the ideal person to be the handball team coach. Of the four, only the author had any familiarity with the workings of the university, so I made contact with Mulkerrins and asked him if he would be interested in coming back to A&M. His answer was a "Yes" but only with certain conditions for him to be able to continue to perform at the national and world handball tournaments.

During the 2019 fall semester, as I began my teaching responsibilities and helping with the handball team, it occurred to me that it would be good for all my handball class students and the team to have handball stars visit and to give a handball clinic. Approval was obtained to hold the clinic and my first choice was to bring Mulkerrins here and one of the former Aggie All-American women handball players. Mulkerrins would be in America during the fall for two handball tournaments. He could not make it to A&M after the tournament in Las Vegas, but in November there would be a tournament in Atlanta and he would make the time for a clinic. Ozzie Burke and I agreed to pay his extra expenses for the additional time and travel. It was all set. Now to get him an appropriate opponent. Burke remembered Adam Bernhard from Austin, one of the best players in Texas and a regular on the pro tour. Bernhard agreed to come over for the clinic.

I was not as fortunate in getting a commitment from one of the former female handball stars. My first choice, Holly Ridings, NASA Chief Flight Director, was not in the country on the day of the clinic and the others I contacted were not able to come.

Prior to the handball match with Bernhard, Mulkerrins gave a 15-minute presentation about handball and where he had been and what he had done. Then he played some with Logan Call and Marcus Shanaa. Spectators were wowed at the skill and ease with which Mulkerrins played the game. Anticipation was high as Bernhard and Mulkerrins warmed up for their match. During warmup, it was obvious that the crowd would see two players at the top of their game and among the best in the world. The match did not disappoint, even though Mulkerrins won with apparent ease.

Prior to his arrival at Texas A&M for the clinic, an interview had been arranged for him to talk with Frank Thomas, Head of the Physical Education Activity Program. During the interview, Mulkerrins expressed his desire to return to A&M, to have an impact and to lead a handball resurgence. After

Thomas discussed the possibility of Mulkerrins' hire with Dr. Melinda Sheffield-Moore, a decision was reached to work out details of hiring him. All parties agreed, conditions of employment established and it was expected that he would be at A&M during the fall 2020 semester. No one could have predicted the COVID-19 pandemic and the impact it would have, not only on the nation, but also in a delay in his expected return to Aggieland.

Randolph makes contribution to A&M handball program

By ROBERT CESSNA
robert.cessna@theeagle.com

If 70-year-old Lubbock businessman Doug Randolph has a rare bad day at the office, he heads to the handball courts to put a smile back on his face.

Randolph decided to share his passion for the sport he's enjoyed for five decades by giving $1 million endowments to both Texas A&M and the University of Texas. He believes along with keeping students in great physical shape, handball is a great stress reliever.

"If you come play handball, all of that just gets erased, and all the poison just comes out of your body," Randolph said. "And then you get to start with a clean slate, with a clear mind."

Randolph decided to get financially involved in promoting the sport when he noticed every time a college handball coach retired, it was followed by the program being retired.

"I saw that happening at the University of Texas, and I saw that happening here, with no classes," Randolph said.

Randolph, founder of the Randolph Foundation for Higher Education, set up an endowment at UT six years ago and in November gave $1 million in support of A&M's handball team as well as the sport as part of the Physical Education Activity Programs in Health and Kinesiology, a department in the College of Education and Human Development.

Student participation in handball classes at Texas

Eagle photo by Dave McDermand
Martin Muelkerrins, the world's second-ranked handball player, visited The Texas A&M Rec Center on Monday to play an exhibition match against Adam Bernhard, the top player in Austin.

the weekend and will play next in Phoenix, attended A&M for a semester in 2013 while studying animal and crop production at Dublin University.

"Being so close to the guys here, they asked me if I'd be interested to come across to do an exhibition match and maybe a clinic to generate a little interest for the team," Muelkerrins said. "They were very good to me, I had a great time, so it was an easy decision."

Muelkerrins started playing handball to improve his coordination for

champion in 1971, and retired Brigadier General Donald Johnson, whom Randolph honored by calling the endowment the BG Donald "Don" Johnson '55 Handball Excellence Endowment.

Johnson and Jim Mathis were the U.S. Collegiate doubles champions in 1954. After his military career, Johnson returned to A&M as coach and mentor of the handball team. Johnson retired in 2004 but has returned to teach a class this semester.

Randolph started playing

Prior to the warmup and play of handball, Robert Cessna, sportswriter for *The Eagle*, took that opportunity to talk with Mulkerrins. Cessna's report (above) was on page B3 of the Tuesday, 8 October 2019 paper. NOTE: The rest of the first column states that student participation has increased at A&M. The second column continues with Mulkerrins play in "hurling" which he claims is the fastest game on grass in the world. During the winter months, he took up handball to help his "hurling" play by improving his hand-eye coordination. The third column continues with Randolph's businesses and what he does. That is all covered more extensively in the Chapter on "Personals".

An interesting side note: This press release was read by someone at Lubbock Christian University and the name of Doug Randolph was identified as a former student. Randolph was contacted and an appointment for a visit was agreed by both parties. At the meeting, Randolph was addressed as a former student, yet he had never given back to Lubbock Christian; however, he had given a million dollars to each of Texas A&M and The University of Texas. The question was posed, "Why have you not given anything to Lubbock Christion?" Randolph's reply, "You don't have any handball courts." Obviously, Lubbock Christian University did not pass on the opportunity to have handball courts built as a gift from a former student. On this date, 18 May 2020, construction was started on three handball courts at Lubbock Christian University.

To help with the revival, the 1954 national collegiate doubles champions, Jim Mathis and Don Johnson, agreed to permanently endow a scholarship through the Texas A&M Foundation that would pay $1,000 each school year as long as a handball team existed at Texas A&M. The scholarship was established to recognize a handball team member who has made the greatest contribution in promoting handball at Texas A&M. This includes, but shall not be limited to, overall leadership (with or without holding a formal officer position), attendance at scheduled practices, recruitment, participation in handball tournaments, as well in other club activities.

Logan Call
2019-20 recipient of
Mathis/Johnson
Handball
Scholarship

(Courtesy Lauren Waters)

Marcus Shanaa
2020-21 recipient of
Mathis/Johnson
Handball Scholarship

(Courtesy Lauren Waters)

Logan Call was named the recipient of the scholarship for the fall of 2021 and Jason Buley was the scholarship recipient during the spring 2022 semester. William Henry, IV has been named the recipient for 2022-23.

As the wait for the possible arrival of Martin Mulkerrins as the next handball coach for the Aggie team, many other questions can only be answered as the future unfolds. In 2025, Texas A&M will celebrate 100 years of handball. Will the gift from Doug Randolph result in Texas A&M handball rising to the level at which the Aggie team is once again a national collegiate power? Will the students at Texas A&M fill the Kinesiology 199/ handball classes? Will there be any local residents to continue playing and supporting handball after Ozzie Burke, Charlie Bokelman, Jack Gressett, Don Johnson and a few others are no longer available to play handball? Will any of the current and recent handball players return to the local area to continue to play handball at the Recreation Center? Will handball continue as a great sport at Texas A&M? One thing is certain. Doug's gift has a clause that states the gift will not remain with the Texas A&M Foundation or Texas A&M should handball not be continued. If the income monies from the gift are not used for handball for a consecutive period of two years, the total of the million-dollar gift would be transferred to support the handball program at The University of Texas. What greater incentive-insurance if you will-could Doug have placed on his gift to see that handball is revived and continued at Texas A&M?

CHAPTER 15
Personal Stories

A part of the history of handball at Texas A&M has to be who has played here, the impact on the lives of those who have played here, and their handball stories and lifetime achievements. This portion of the history will be devoted to help personalize the character, camaraderie, fun and overall benefits experienced through the great game of handball at this great institution of higher learning.

It would be impossible to make contact with all who have played the game here in the A&M handball courts, so I have made an attempt to contact those who have been a part of the handball club/team, those who have achieved some level of success playing in the National Collegiate Handball Tournament, and some notable handball players who were here for at least a semester and played in the courts on a regular basis. Current addresses/contact information are not available for many and some have chosen not to respond to my request for information. The stories of those who have responded are here. Also included are those who live in the Bryan/College Station community and have played in the courts for a number of years. All are listed alphabetically rather than by level of achievement or importance, which would be extremely hard to establish, and in the end would be arguable by most of those whose names appear here.

Allen, Robert L. "Bob"-Bob Allen played for many years and was part of the group of handball players who would play during the lunch hour in the DeWare courts. He was and still is an investment advisor and has lived in Bryan for many years. He no longer plays handball, but is into shooting, golf and physical exercise through weight training.

Anderson, Lavon N. "Andy," PhD '57-Dr. Anderson earned his bachelor's, master's and PhD in Chemical Engineering at Texas A&M. After many years in industry, he returned to College Station and taught in the Chemical Engineering Department at A&M for one year before retiring.

As a student at A&M, he did not take a handball class but joined the club to learn the game he thoroughly enjoyed. As he said, he got all of his lessons in handball from other members of the club. One day while playing he was struck in the eye by a handball and that forever changed his focus in one eye. Even today, he still has distant vision in one eye and short vision in the other. He also stated he later tried racquetball, but didn't play the "sissy" (his word) game for long. Dr. Anderson is one of the many statistics demonstrating why the wearing of protective glasses is now a requirement for play of handball.

Barkemeyer, O'Gene W. "Gene," PE '60-The following letter (handwritten) was received from him:

Dear Mr. (Gen) Johnson;

I appreciate the opportunity to reflect upon the past, including handball.

I had never heard of handball until I took it as a PE requirement as a "Fish." I never knew a club existed. I only played intramural HB. As I recall, 8 or 10 of us began playing each other as Fish in Sq. 20. We forged a lifelong friendship, a spirit of winning, team work, resulting in Corps championships in 1959 and '60 (Sq. 17 and 12, respectively). We spent many hours, especially during cool and winter months, in the courts on weekends.

I have not played HB since, nor seen an indoor court during either USAF or civilian assignments. I've never had an interest in taking up racquetball.

Seven of us were USAF Lt.'s. Four of us last met in New Braunfels in '16. Three are deceased (Frost, Parks, Wallace).

O'Gene W. Barkemeyer, PE

Baylor, Sharon (SEE: Davis)

Birdwell, Cody W. '76-The following letter (print too small for inclusion) was received from Cody:

Hello Donald,

Your letter was timely. Enclosed is a newspaper clipping I gave to my mother back in the 70's that I had long forgotten about but which she returned to me a couple of months ago.

Dennis Corrington arrived at A&M while I was there and did a great job of building an intramural program. I served as a Director of intramurals at A&M Church of Christ and remember we (The Saints) won the football (the Corps and non-reg champions played the championship game at night on Kyle Field) and the basketball championship in the same year. I got to know Dennis by accepting a role in refereeing Intramural football.

Bob Davidson, who was a mentor to me and served as the college students' minister at A&M Church of Christ, was an avid and accomplished handball player. He introduced me to the sport and challenged me to work hard at improving my skillset. The handball courts were located at DeWare Field House, which also housed a basketball court, and indoor and outdoor pools. The operation and care for the facility was under the responsibility of Dennis Corrington. Dennis offered to me and my roommate the opportunity to reside in the front corner room of DeWare Field House if we would assume the responsibility to open and close the facility daily. I accepted and that was the catalyst to allow me to have unprecedented access to the handball courts and greatly improve my skill set in a relative short period of time. I lived there about two years. It was heaven for me at that time of life.

As far as tournaments went, I do remember that A&M fielded a team around 1975 that competed in a UIL Interscholastic (I think this is how it was designated) tournament conducted at the University of Texas campus. Five of us students went to represent

A&M. Jack Gressett and Wayne Neuman were part of the team that played. I don't recall the other two. I was the fifth and was the alternate in the event someone went down. I do not recall placing high enough for a trophy of recognition. I hope you can find Jack, Wayne or Jeff to gain insight they may have.

I do not recall much in the way of women participation in handball back then. I do not have a 1975 yearbook. The year books I do have in that era do not include the handball club. I think it was sponsored by a professor (Seemed old at the time with white hair and a mustache, if I recall) that I enjoyed playing with occasionally. He and Bob Davidson were remarkable for their age.

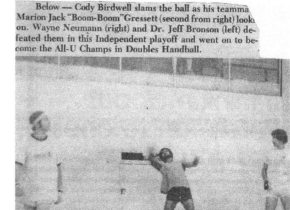

Below — Cody Birdwell slams the ball as his teamma Marion Jack "Boom-Boom" Gressett (second from right) look on. Wayne Neumann (right) and Dr. Jeff Bronson (left) defeated them in this Independent playoff and went on to become the All-U Champs in Doubles Handball.

I didn't play handball after I left college. There were no players to be found outside of campus. The general public was more interested in racquetball which I did play for a good season after school life.

I don't have much more to add but you are welcome to call me if you would like. Thanks so much and good luck!

(Photo Courtesy Cody Birdwell)

Cody Birdwell

Bokelman, Charles "Charlie"-Charlie was at A&M during the mid-1970s. He continued to play handball and never really had a long time period of inactivity away from the game. He was the A&M Club President during 1974-75 and continued serving in that capacity until 1991-92. During that time, he continued to learn the game strategically and all of the shots. He never hit a peak and leveled off. He has continued to improve his game and knowledge to this date. He was always there to give a hand in coaching young talent and helped many players through the years to become better. One of the best women handball players, and maybe the best ever to come through A&M, claims him as her mentor and coach. That player is none other than Priscilla Kojin, twice the national collegiate singles and doubles champion and later, after college, the best in the world. In a conversation with Bokelman, he said that Brian Shumate, Pricilla's husband, should also be given credit for helping develop her handball skills. And he also helped Bokelman with his game.

The author has played many handball games with Bokelman. The most enjoyable of those games was in doubles. He typically would put me on the left side and force me to take everything on the left and down the middle. That is until the game was on the line. He would never say anything but simply would just completely take over the game so we would get to 21 first.

Bokelman has won numerous handball tournaments in both singles and doubles over the years, helped coach the A&M handball team and is clearly the best in this area at determining what strategy to use in any match. His game was at such a level that no one in this area could provide enough competition for him to improve his game so he started going out of town to seek better competition for game improvement. He was at a level that he could definitely play at the national level in his age group. "Was" is a key word for the present. In 2020, he had an accident when he fell from a ladder. He cracked some vertebrae, fractured some ribs, punctured his lung and was knocked unconscious. In a fall of such magnitude, there are always other complications. He is now out of the hospital and has returned to the handball courts; however, a question that remains is his future in handball at the national level for his age group.

A testament to his character and how he played the game was the presentation of the Mrs. Maurice Grant Award at the 56th George Lee Tournament, Dallas, in the spring of 2002. The award is given to someone for exemplifying the true spirit of sportsmanship.

Bood, David D. '14-Bood started playing early during his education at A&M and was influenced to the game by his grandfather, David Korry '56, who was on the A&M team while a student at A&M. The author remembers David Korry very well and played him many times in the "Little Gym" handball courts. Korry was the number three player on the team in 1954-55; however, he was unable to go to the National Collegiate Tournament due to a conflict. Bood made sure he was able to go to the Collegiates for three years and realized the thrill of a combined team, Division II national championship during his last year at A&M.

One thing that Bood clearly remembers is that he was the only member of the team at practice many times when he started playing, and "commends his coach, Ozzie Burke, for not giving up on the team. The team grew each year I was a part of it and it is almost entirely due to the effort that Ozzie put in for the team."

Bronson, Jeff, PhD-Jeff is another of the local handball players with whom the author has had the honor of playing many games of handball. He was always a tough opponent and could strategize a game very quickly. He always kept very good records of his scores against individuals. Many times, he would remind his opponent of past scores. Through the years, he won many tournaments and played in many around the state. Following is his story that he provided for this book:

Jeff Bronson Handball History

I started playing at the beginning of the fall semester of 1955 and fell in love with the game. In the course of my Freshman year, my weight went from 185 to 150 pounds. As an under graduate, I did not play during the summers, but during my five years of graduate school, I played year-round. In fact, after four years in grad school, my research professor half-jokingly said that if I had not played so "god damned much handball" I would be finished now. I did finish and then spent one year in Switzerland as a post-doctoral fellow, during which time I had no access to handball. After that, I went to the University of Wisconsin in Madison for two years. I learned that the university did not have good courts so I very quickly went to the downtown YMCA and joined it because their courts were quite good. The only drawback was that the left wall was an outside wall and during the coldest winter days it would form an ice sheet, changing the bounce of the handball. The university opened some new courts shortly after I left (bad timing).

I started playing in away tournaments while at Wisconsin. I went to a couple of them in Milwaukee and played in the Madison city tournament

(Cushing Archives, Texas A&M University)

both years. The second year, I won the open singles and my partner and I won the open doubles. I also went to a regional YMCA tournament in Winona, Minnesota and finished second in the open. I also went to a tournament in Janesville, Wisconsin and won it. The local supporters expected their local hero to win it, so the first-place trophy was three times bigger than second place. I was very satisfied when I took home the bigger trophy.

After coming to Texas A&M in September 1967, I quickly became involved in the local play. I also missed the first day of work because I went to a tournament in Corpus Christi for Labor Day. I was asked why I missed my first day and I said it was a holiday (Labor Day) and they said 'not around here'. I started playing with the best players at A&M and continued to go to about half a dozen tournaments around Texas every year. I would normally play every day from Monday through Friday. We would play in DeWare field house which was not air-conditioned. We normally played from 4 pm until 6 pm, and in the summer, I would take about six totally soaked T-shirts home to wash. My favorite court was number 8, and continued to be even when we switched to the next two new buildings. At one point the competition sagged and for about six months I played twice a day on Monday through Friday. As the competition picked back up, I went back to my earlier schedule.

Just before turning 40, I went to the state tournament in Austin and won the Class B state championship. The next year I went back to the tournament, and as I walked into the gym, one of my victims from the previous year was already playing. When he saw me, he pointed up at me and said he was going to get me this time. I said there was no way since I was now 40 and playing in the Masters and he was not old enough. As the years progressed, I went to fewer out-of-town tournaments, but I always enjoyed them when I did.

I probably averaged five days per week for sixty years and as a result wore out my knees. I have recently had them both replaced and hope to get back on the court soon. Also, as the number of available handball players dwindled, I began to play racquetball fairly regularly. One time my handball opponent did not show up and one of my racquetball buddies was stood up. I said I would go get my racquet and we could play. I came back to the court and hit the ball three or four times and said I was ready. He said don't you want to warm up more? I rather facetiously said "I only need half of my body to play this." Then I proceeded to beat him.

Burke, O. T. "Ozzie," '71-Ozzie grew up just south of Texas A&M University. He is a gifted athlete and participated in high school sports. Somewhere along the way, he discovered the great game of handball. And, being close to the courts at Aggieland, he was ready to play at a high level when he entered college. When he started playing in the courts at A&M, he met Barney Welch, who was one of the best handball players in Aggieland. They became very good handball friends and a lot of the knowledge he gained was on the courts with Welch. Burke joined the handball club when he entered as a freshman and soon met his doubles partner, Dan Kennerly. Together, they won a National Collegiate Doubles title. Burke started providing leadership for the handball club when he joined the club, later serving as the president and mentor to the other players on the team.

Upon graduation, he remained in the local area and continued to enjoy the game of handball. Through the years he won many tournaments and was a mainstay among the local handball players. He started his coaching (not officially) during his years as a student. One of his pupils was Dr. Tommy Burnett who was inducted into the Missouri Sports Hall of Fame based on his coaching the Southwest Missouri State-now Missouri State University-handball team to several National Collegiate Handball Championships. That story will follow under Tommy Burnett. "Coach Ozzie" took the reins of the A&M handball team after Lance Lowy stepped down.

One of the author's fun times at handball was teaming as a 140 Plus age group doubles team with Burke. We were never beaten. We only played together at the annual Aggieland Classic. After the competition became zero, our last year together was against two of the other A&M club members.

Following is one of his handball stories:

The Missouri Cold Shoulder

Or

Four poor college students full of handball spirit headed to Collegiate Nationals

Written by Dianna Burke as told by Ozzie

To use a worn out slogan, "Times have changed". And for handball at Texas A & M, times have changed for the better.

Back in handball history, USHA guidelines invited only the best four (the top 2 singles players and best doubles team) from each school to Collegiate Nationals, not entire clubs. So, in 1968, here they are A&M's top four: Tom Patrick, Dan Kennerly, Cyril Burke, Ozzie's brother and Ozzie heading for Collegiate Nationals in St. Louis Missouri. With car packed full of 4 guys, all their gear for the entire tournament and $100 of spending money for gas and food, raised by then handball coach/advisor, Stan Lowy, they were on the road, with visions of handball splendor. $100 a half century ago was a hefty amount for Coach Lowy to raise, but not quite enough to cover lodging along the way. But no sweat!! Ozzie had been a counselor for a number of years at Kanakuk summer camps in Branson, Missouri, a good day's drive, and knew the school year facility care taker, Hillbilly Sam!

Ozzie had called ahead and asked Sam to open the camp for them to use one of the cabins as the night's lodging. Of course, he said "no sweat! Consider it done!!" So, they arrived, unloaded what they needed and headed into their "Hilton" for the night. Uh oh! None of the 4 guys considered the fact that screened in facilities during the summer had a different comfort value than when the same facilities were used in February. So, with no provisions for blankets, pillows, heaters, they were left to their own creative devices. No sweat!! They each covered with the mattresses of the uninhabited beds. Ah. And literally, NO SWEAT!! And who knows, maybe the raw facilities gave them a little more determination for Dan and Ozzie to win the Collegiate Nationals Open Doubles title for that year.

But that was then and this is now. Texas A&M is fortunate to be one of the few universities nationally that has an endowment which insures that handball classes will be taught into the future and foundational funds that will be endowed annually towards taking a men's and women's team to National Collegiates. All this thanks to the vision and generosity of Doug Randolph via The Randolph Foundation teamed with a cooperative spirit from Dr. Melinda Sheffield-Moore Department Head of Health & Kinesiology and Frank Thomas Chair Physical Education Activity Program. Texas A&M is also fortunate to have great facilities overseen by Director of Department of Recreational Sports Rick Hall and a group of experienced and dedicated volunteer coaches/fundraisers in Charles, Jack, Don, and Ozzie as well as Kayla who serves in the University required administrative roll for the Club. Kayla, Kara Edwards, Dr. Michael Thornton and Don Johnson have stepped up as instructors of handball classes. Whew! What a team.

In closing, observing from the gallery as a fan of the sport, you students have it made! NO SWEAT!!!!

Burke had some medical problems and lost an eye to surgery in early 2019. In March 2020, he began playing handball again as a doubles partner and was beginning to make real progress in being able to get back on the court. Unfortunately for all of us, the COVID-19 pandemic hit and there has been no handball played since that time.

After surgery, and after recovery, he made the statement that he was no longer the coach of the A&M handball team. However, that statement was not observed by those of us who was working with the team. During the summer of 2021, he stepped down from his position as coach of the Texas A&M handball team.

Burnett, Dr. Thomas H. "Tommy," '74 HPED-On the way back from Littleton, Vermont after celebrating the 100th birthday of my wife's friend, we decided to stop in Springfield, Missouri to interview Tommy. After finding his address through a receptionist at the Doubletree Hotel, we drove out to his ranch to find him at home.

Burnett wanted to talk football at the beginning. He was a football player at the University of Arkansas and in his words, was never a starter. He played many positions, and at 6' 2" and 215 lbs., and also the fastest man on the team, he was drafted by the Pittsburgh Steelers but ended up playing for the New York Jets where he was part of the team that won Super Bowl III in 1969.

After football, he decided to earn a doctorate and chose Texas A&M for his degree work. Still in his athletic prime and wanting to work out by shooting baskets at DeWare, he went there, and finding no one about, decided to look around. He saw some stairs and decided to investigate. At the top of the stairs, he found handball courts but had no idea what they were. Checking them out he found an "old" guy hitting a ball in one of the courts. He asked the "old" guy what he was doing. The "old" guy said he was playing handball, so Burnett asked for the ball and threw it against the wall a few times. Being a great athlete, Burnett thought that he might be able do what the "old" guy was doing.

The "old" guy told Burnett he had to use gloves to play the game. With the score 19-0 the "old" guy let Burnett have a point. Here in the story, the author asked him if that was why he always required his handball players to never shut out an opponent. He replied that was a part of the reason.

To Burnett it was simply incredible that someone as old as that person could completely dominate him in an athletic endeavor. The "old" guy was likely Barney Welch, who after his retirement as Intramural Director, still played handball from time to time on the A&M courts. Burnett was intrigued by this new game and asked if he could come back and play again. He simply wanted to learn and experience more of this game at least to the point he could earn a few points playing an "old" guy. The author will call the "old" guy Barney, since the author is very familiar with the relationship between Barney Welch and Ozzie Burke. Welch told Burnett that if he would make 30 minutes each week available to be at the handball courts, he would have someone teach him the game. So, each week during his doctoral program, Burnett would show up at the courts and Burke taught him the game. Burnett obviously learned the game very well and ended up at then, Southwest Missouri State University, where he became the handball team coach. And, as they say "the rest is history." Southwest Missouri State University is now known as Missouri State University.

In the early '90s, Burke and Burnett brought their sons to play in the USHA National Juniors in Cincinnati, Ohio. While there, a doubles tournament was held for the adults in attendance. Burke and Burnett paired as partners and won the tournament by defeating Anna Engele and Kenneth Kane.

In Burnett's first 20 years of tenure at Missouri State University, he coached 21 All-Americans, nine of his alumni became professional handball players and his handball teams won nine USHA national collegiate titles. On 10 February 2008, he was inducted into the Missouri Sports Hall of Fame. He is also a member of the Springfield Area Sports Hall of Fame and the USHA Hall of Fame.

Burnett attended the 2020 USHA National Collegiate Handball Tournament where the author had another good visit with him. All of handball lost a great advocate and person on 22 July 2021 when Tommy Burnett lost his earthly battle of life.

All of this started because a great athlete couldn't score a point playing against an "old" guy in the game of handball at Texas A&M University.

Carpenter, David C., Jr., '57-The following letter was received from David:

29 September 2018

BG Don Johnson
11891 Great Oaks Dr.
College Station, TX 77845

Howdy Don,

Got your letter re handball at A&M. I am class of '57 and went by Carl Carpenter. I'm happy to give you what little I have about my handball experience. I grew up playing tennis and had never heard of handball. My freshman year, out of curiosity, I wandered down to the handball courts and a kind sophomore, whose name I do not remember, took me under his wing and taught me the basics. It was a pretty natural extension of my tennis, and I took to it quickly. I played when I had a chance, but never was a part of the handball club or any teams except the 1956 Squadron 1 team that won the Class A intramural championship and which consisted of Glen Rice, John Dillard, Allen Lee, Don Turbeville, Irv Ramsower and myself. I'm sure you knew Glen Rice and John Dillard who were both in the handball club. The only other time I played other than casually was in '57 when I teamed with John Dillard, who won the Open singles championship. We won the Open Doubles. John was an excellent player and beat me the couple of times we played each other, but I gave him a pretty good run.

I can't for the life of me remember if I took handball for PE, but I don't think so. I certainly have no memory of it. I remember three of my PE courses, but can't remember the fourth, so it's possible. I know there were several Carpenters at A&M, but I only knew Oscar, who was in my class, and none were relatives, to my knowledge. I did not know Bob.

Glad you're still able to play handball at this age. Amazing. I played some in the Air Force, but never played again after I got out. I did play racquetball a few times. I went back to my tennis and was a pretty good A club player up to age 63 when I wrecked my rotator cuff. During recovery from surgery, I somehow messed it up again. That, coupled with being caregiver for my wife who came down with a variant of ALS, ended my tennis. I had a recent hip replacement, which put me in great condition and enables me to get out and hunt with my boys without pain, but I don't think I could hack handball.

Take care, and best wishes with your book.

David C. (Carl) Carpenter, Jr.

Cole, Ricky A., '91-The following was received from Ricky and most likely sums up the experience that many of the handball team/club members had during their time at A&M:

I arrived at A&M in the fall of '87. My P.E. class was badminton. When registering for the Spring semester, I signed up for tennis. However, over the Christmas break, I was notified that one of my academic classes had been rescheduled for the same time as my tennis class. So, I had to find a new P. E. class to take. Unfortunately, everything I wanted was no longer available, so I settled for handball, whatever that was. Turns out, that was the best thing that could have happened to me. I took handball every semester for the next 5 years. I had been a point-guard for the basketball team in high school, but was way too small to play collegiately at a Division I school like Texas A&M. Handball gave me a new sport to carry me through my college years.

After my freshman year, I always had the perfect class schedule for Mondays-Wednesdays-and-Fridays. I had classes from 8-8:50, 9-9:50 and 10-10:50. Then I had handball on Mondays and Wednesdays from 11-11:50. The beauty in this plan was that there were no handball classes from 12-1 due to lunch. So, I was actually able to play an extra hour of handball every day. Then, on Fridays, I was through with class by 11, so I had plenty of time to get to whatever town was hosting a tournament-Austin, Houston, Corpus Christi, Beaumont, Dallas, or even College Station.

In the Spring of my sophomore year (1989), t. u. was hosting Nationals. With Nationals in Austin, Lance Lowy (Texas A&M's handball coach), chose to take just about anyone who was serious about handball and showed potential of someday being good. I don't know if he put the top players up in a hotel or not, but most of us just fended for ourselves just like any other weekend tournament. That year, the men finished 3rd, but the women finished 1st, and overall, we were team national champions. I am fairly certain that my efforts did not contribute in any way to our team success, but I was there on the team, and loving every minute of it.

With our top players being seniors, I wondered how good we would be the next year without them. To my surprise, that was not a concern for several years. Each time the top group graduated, the group below them stepped up the next year and we didn't miss a beat. I did not realize it at the time, but my "class" was absolutely loaded on the men's side.

In handball, the team score is based on the level reached by the top 6 finishers from that school. In 1990, Nationals were in Portland, Oregon. This was going to be an expensive trip. Lance decided that he could only take the top six men and the top six women. On the men's side, the top 3 or 4 were pretty much locked up, but there were quite a few of us that had a legitimate shot at those last couple of spots. Lance created a "Challenge Ladder." Someone lower on the ladder could "challenge" someone higher on the ladder. If the "lower" person won, his name moved just above the person he just beat. The "higher" person could not deny a challenge. Both parties did have to be respectful of each other's academic schedule and agree on a time to play. I had worked my way up to # 7, but still needed to get past Mark Rhodes. He was undeniably better than me, but not by much. I challenged him. I can honestly say I gave all I had, but it wasn't enough. When the match was over, my left hand was bruised so bad, that the top of my hand swelled about an inch. Even had I won I probably wouldn't have been able to go because it took a couple of weeks before I could use that hand again. By the way, I am left-handed. In Oregon, the team repeated 89's results. The women carried us by winning it all. The men finished 3rd. But as a combined team, A&M won the National Championship again. I did not get to go to Oregon, and I did not contribute to our victory, but I consider myself part of that team, and I claim that National championship too!

My being left behind in 1990 led to change in 1991. Lance asked his top players if they wanted to do the Challenge Ladder again or have each player pay enough out of pocket to allow all deserving players make the trip to Cincinnati, Ohio. Aaron Cooper immediately said everybody goes. When this idea was then shared with the rest of us, of course, we all agreed, 13 boys and 7 girls. My first plane ride was some little thing with one seat on each side of the aisle. We flew on it from College Station to Dallas. I swear, as we were landing, that plane was flying sideways. I am looking out my window right at the runway. Just before the plane touched down, it turned straight and landed smoothly. Of course, we caught a much bigger plane to Ohio. In Cincinnati, I was no longer a "bench warmer." I was a major contributor now. Sal SantaAna was eliminated in the quarterfinals and Aaron Cooper lost in the round of 16. Eight of us were eliminated in the round of thirty-two: myself being Ricky Cole, Shane Rothenberger, Vern Hegwood, Brian Carr, Kevin Hobbs, Mark Rhodes, Steve Naftanel and Chris Uren. I think a couple of guys went a little further in the "B" bracket, but I believe 6 of us lost again in the same round. So, I could have been considered anywhere from our 5th best finisher to the 10th Aggie. Not only did we do well for A&M, but we also eliminated a lot of players from other schools to keep their team points low. Of course, the Aggie women were National Champions again. It is important to note that the Aggie men getting 2nd place was the best that we could hope for. The Memphis State men were always the National Champions. They were recruited SCHOLARSHIP athletes. At A&M, we were a Club of individuals, most of whom never even heard of handball until we took the P. E. class at A&M. That made our championships even sweeter.

The spring of 1992 marked my 5th year of college and my last year to play handball. Nationals were in Palatine, Illinois, just outside of Chicago. For me personally, this was an emotional roller coaster. Sal SantaAna made it to the quarterfinals again. The rest of our top players were in the "B" bracket, and I was the last one standing. We had calculated that I had to beat Don Cottam (younger brother of Jeff Cottam) in the B semifinals in order for us to win the Men's 2nd place team. I battled the best I could, diving all over the place. The whole team was watching my match. By the end, every rally was followed by Cottam wiping up my blood from the floor while I sucked wind in preparation to do it all over again. When the match was over, I thought I had cost us the trophy. I went to Lance and apologized for letting the team down. He smiled and said, "Man, you're a f****** warrior." That made me feel a little better, but it didn't change the fact that I was unable to come through for my team. But that night, at the awards ceremony, Men's 2nd place team went to Texas A&M! Apparently, we had miscalculated. I only had to make it to the semi-final, not win it. Now I was ecstatic! I had come through for my team after all. So, the Men earned 2nd place, the Women ran away with their National

Championship, and Texas A&M was once again combined Team National Champions. That 1992 "B" semifinal trophy meant more to me than any 1st place trophy I ever won. I was one of the top 20 collegiate men's handball athletes.

I played handball for Texas A&M from 1989-92 and get to claim National Champions all 4 years.

The Texas A&M women just destroyed the competition during this span. The leaders I remember were Sharon Baylor and Betsy Boswell. When I first started the Smalley sisters were pretty dominant, but they graduated about the time I started. I don't remember them as well as I would like.

There was a handball tournament in Austin and one in College Station every semester. So, we saw a few of the Longhorns on a regular basis. I was quick and anticipated where the ball was going to go very well. This allowed me to get to a lot of balls that would have been winners against other opponents. A group of Longhorns nicknamed me the "Spiderman" because all they saw were arms and legs going every which way as I dove all over the court. They were the only ones who called me Spiderman, but I thought it was pretty cool.

I met my "dance partner" on the handball courts. It was a new semester, and I was just looking in on all the courts to see what kind of talent was in my class and check out the girls. Heather Helfrich caught my eye. We hit it off together and became friends. She liked to party, and I didn't know how to dance. So, she agreed to take dance lessons with me from the Aggie Wranglers. Country lessons were on Monday and Jitterbug lessons were on Thursdays. Then we hit the dance halls on Friday and Saturday. I went from never dancing in my life to dancing 4 nights a week. I remember us going to a tournament in Beaumont. Heather went 0-2. I went 1-2. It was very unusual for me to get eliminated that fast, but it happened. Then, Saturday night, the handball party was at a dance hall. The first time they played a jitterbug song, there were lots of people on the floor. After that, every time we headed for the dance floor, everyone else left. That weekend, we sucked at handball, but we kicked butt on the dance floor. It wasn't such a bad weekend after all.

Ricky Cole was born in Wills Point, Texas and attended several different schools growing up. He excelled in high school basketball, earning All-District honor 3 years, Academic All-State and Givins All-Star honors. After graduation from A&M with a BS degree in Computer Science and a teaching certificate in Mathematics and Computer Science he was hired to teach in Somerville, Texas. After 8 years in Somerville, he moved to New Waverly and as of his letter was still teaching there. At New Waverly he teaches Algebra 2, Pre-Cal, AP Calculus and is the Beta Club Sponsor, UIL math coach, and UIL Number Sense coach. His teams do very well in state competition, with the UIL math team earning fourth. In 2018, he was named the recipient of the Mirabeau B. Lamar Award for teaching excellence.

As for handball, he stopped playing after graduation from A&M. He never intended to stop and planned to play for the rest of his life. However, as a teacher, he was busy until late in the night designing lesson plans, so he didn't have a lot of time. But he also wasn't near enough to use A&M's Rec Center. As it happened, all of his friends graduated and moved away and he wasn't able to play on a regular basis anymore. He lives close to Conroe, Texas and their rec center, but has not been able to make contact with any handball players to return to the game that was so much a part of his life at A&M.

Collins, Phil-Phil grew up in Chicago, did not attend Texas A&M and did not reside here. Still, he has an important tie to handball at A&M.

In the early '50s, he entered the US Air Force as an enlisted airman and was stationed at the Bryan Air Base. His only chance to continue his handball locally was at the A&M handball courts. It was there that he asked late one September evening in 1954 if he could play with two members of the A&M handball team, Jim Mathis and Don Johnson. He continued to come to the courts and the two received some valuable lessons on the game of handball. Later, he brought a handball player from the Air Base and the two teamed up in doubles against Mathis and Johnson. Mathis and Johnson won one game of doubles against Collins and his partner. Collins basically became a spectator since all of the balls, serves and returns, were directed to his partner.

It was late in the fall semester that Collins suggested to Mathis and Johnson that they enter the National Collegiate Handball Tournament, to be held in his hometown over the Christmas holidays. The handball team went to Chicago and A&M's long history of participating in the national collegiates had its beginning.

Following are some extractions from several articles that have appeared in the USHA's *Handball* magazine:

> Teamed with fellow Chicagoan John Sloan, Phil Collins dominated the national doubles scene in the 1950s and 60s. In addition to his heralded right-side doubles play, Phil was ranked among the top four singles players in the country for almost a decade. Starting in 1952 Phil helped win 17 national doubles titles and one world doubles crown. He said, "I never won a national singles title because I would run out of steam. In my day, we'd have a field of 128 players in a singles tournament, and I preferred doubles. So, while I was competing, I always found myself trying to save some of my stamina for doubles. After all, we were being asked to play singles in the afternoon and doubles in the evening."

Phil Collins 1930-2011
(*Handball*, August 1989, page11)

> Phil came to handball through baseball and basketball. His father was a professional pitcher with the Cubs, Cardinals, and Phillies in the thirties. Phil himself tried pitching, but got a sore arm his first year out in Terre Haute.

> Phil said, "I well remember how I happened to get involved in handball, I was 18 and was at the Y watching four fellows whack the ball against a wall. It was obvious they were having a lot of fun. I concluded handball would develop strength in my left hand as well as my right. I felt having two strong arms would help me improve in basketball, my first love at the time. But it became sort of an entrapment. I became so enamored about hitting that ball against the wall that I forgot about basketball, and even baseball. I found handball particularly attractive because only one other player is needed to enjoy it. In basketball, you need a full team."

Playing all around the country in tournaments and as part of a barnstorming tour with Johnny Sloan, Collins met so many different people in important positions through handball that he knew it would help when he retired from handball. He met the chairman of Goodyear Tire and Rubber in Akron, a contact that brought him millions of dollars-worth of business in later years.

Bob Kendler, Chicago businessman and the person who started the USHA, started him in the construction business and he learned the basics there-getting building permits, carpentry, how to sell a job, etc. Later he went into the industrial side of the construction business. He wasn't educated as an engineer, but learned it in the field, and pretty soon was able to sell jobs to big companies like Coca-Cola. He built plants for Chrysler, General Mills, and Goodyear. He met all these contacts through handball. Collins retired from playing handball to devote his time to business. He did not remain in the Chicago area but established his very successful commercial construction firm in Florida. His long-time doubles partner, Johnny Sloan, moved to Hawaii after his retirement from handball.

In 1989, he was honored for his handball success when he was inducted into the Handball Hall of Fame.

Corrington, Dennis-Dennis came to Texas A&M in 1973 as a new hire to replace Les Palmer as the Director of Intramurals, sport club programs and manager of the recreational facilities. A graduate of Morningside College in Sioux City, Iowa, he never enrolled in a handball course, but started playing under the guidance of Pete Tyson while a Graduate Assistant at the University of Texas. Pete Tyson coached the University of Texas handball team to many national collegiate handball titles.

In addition to his primary responsibilities at Texas A&M, Corrington taught handball at A&M beginning in 1973 and through the 1979-80 school year. He continued his play in handball and as a testament to his playing ability, won the Intramural Open Singles Handball Championship over 37 other

players in his first year here. He encouraged women's participation in all intramural sports and, in 1976, organized the first women's intramural handball championship. The author and Corrington played many handball games over his time on the courts. He was very competitive and continued playing until 1995 when he had both knees replaced.

Corrington will be remembered much longer for his leadership in moving the intramural sports program forward to accommodate the continued expanding student body, and his vision and leadership in the creation and construction of the current Recreational Center at A&M. For 45 years, he provided the necessary vision and leadership in providing the very best possible recreational programs and facilities for A&M's students.

Crim, Brenda D., '83-The following letter, dated 13 August 2020, was received from Brenda:

> I founded a mission organization in Alaska and host 800 volunteers per year in a variety of projects all over Alaska-www.akmissions.com. Along with that, I've embraced the Alaskan lifestyle of self-provision, having harvested several moose and caribou. I also hunt bears in overpopulated bruin territory, and have taken down 2 grizzlies and 8 black bears. Just part of this great Alaskan life.
>
> In Alaska, I've enjoyed many adventures. Three years ago, four of us (2 Aggies) rode the Iditarod trail (1,049 miles through rugged terrain) by snowmobile. Our non-profit hosts projects concurrent with the race finish in Nome, AK.

I'm headed shortly, to a remote caribou hunt location. Today, I hope to catch silver salmon, as I live near the Kenai River.

Before my handball days at Aggieland. I was on the volleyball team (ranked 9th in NAIA nationally), worked full time, and held 18 hours course work per semester. Before Title IX, funds in women's sports were limited, and I received a half scholarship (only 6 scholarships for volleyball). Thus, my time and resources were limited. Nearing exhaustion, I resigned the scholarship so I could focus on work and school.

During that time, I signed up for an activity class with Lance Lowy in the Kinesiology Department. The hand-eye striking skills from volleyball transferred easily from volleyball, so I wound up playing men in the class ladder. At the end of the semester, we could gain extra credit by playing in the Aggieland Classic Handball Tourney. I signed up and played other women for the first time.

Lance seeded me at the top of B division/bottom of A division, so the first round, I faced the #1 seed in women's division. As a surprise to everyone, I won that match 21-0, 21-0. And, I blew through the rest and championed the women's A division. I was hooked. And my need for competition was satiated.

Lance quickly recruited me for the club team and I began competing and winning consistently. I remember Lance saying I had a "rocket right".

That same year (1982), I qualified for nationals; however, I had emergency gall bladder surgery the week of the tourney. Two weeks later, still with 8" of stitches across my abdomen, I played a pro divisional in Austin and won women's A. (Don't tell my mom.) (Disclaimer: Our dear Sue Oakleaf was not playing women's division-she had won women's so many times, she was playing men's. She's an animal on the court.)

The following year (1983) was full of tourneys and wins. The only tourney that Sue Oakleaf played women's division was at Nationals in Chicago. Sue took first place and I took third place.

I'll have to say that playing handball with a teammate like Sue Oakleaf certainly elevated the rest of us as competitors.

Lance Lowy deems honoring as well. He built a great intercollegiate program and was fully invested in us as a coach and friend.

Feel free to contact me any time.

Brenda Crim

Cumbie, Donovan R. "Don", Col USA (Ret), '68-Don took handball in PE, enjoyed the game and became a member of the A&M handball team. He did not continue playing handball after leaving A&M. He chose his life's career in the Army and loved flying so became an Army Aviator. He retired from the Army and moved back to College Station. His physical condition (knees) prevents him from playing handball.

Davidson, Robert "Bob"-Bob received his Doctor of Divinity Degree from Abilene Christian. The author met Davidson on the handball courts and played many games with him. He was always a fiery competitor and gave all he could to the game. His natural athletic ability-he had played college football-aided in his development into a good handball player. He was always enthusiastic and played with a passion for victory. He continued playing, although on a limited basis. until the current pandemic arrived in the local area. Due to his age, 90 plus, it is unlikely he will return to the courts after clearance was given to resume play on the handball courts.

Davis (Baylor), Sharon B., '92-The following letter and articles were received from Sharon:

Date: Wednesday, March 13, 2019, 08:56 PM CDT

Hello Donald,

What a great surprise and honor to receive your letter asking about the handball history at A&M. Playing for Lance and the A&M Handball team was a joy for sure.

I was born and raised in Austin, Texas since 1970 and still remain here. I went to Johnston High School in Austin and played volleyball, basketball, soccer, and softball. Back then, they did not make you choose one sport, so I had the opportunity to do it all. We were bused across town for high school, so I was able to experience people from all walks of life which has benefited me greatly through my adult life. My goal was to play basketball at t.u., but realized being 5' 6" was not what they were looking for, so I stuck with soccer and was recruited to play for A&M. I played soccer for A&M my first two years of school and enjoyed those days traveling throughout the Southwest Conference and the United States playing against teams from the Northeast, Southwest, and everyone in between. Our coach left the school my Junior year and the assistant took over, which at that point, I decided to focus more on school.

During my Freshman year at A&M in 1988, I had signed up for a racquetball class, but when I received my schedule, it showed handball as my choice. Back in those days, to change a class required standing in line for a long time to do so. Not having the patience to stand in line, nor the time, due to my soccer commitment, I decided to give handball a try. I remember those first few days of class were so interesting because it was a sport I had never tried and I loved the nuances of it. My hands took a beating and were so sore, but the pace of the game was right down my ally. It took a while for my left hand to catch up to my dominant right hand. We took the class in the old courts of DeWare. Talk about dingy compared to what the kids have today, but it was nostalgic since my father roamed the same areas during his time at A&M (class of'63). I think it was during this period of time that Lance may have seen my potential. I signed up for another handball class in the Spring and started to make progress. My sophomore year I made the team and continued to hone my skills. There was a set of twins that played on the team that continually beat me. My competitiveness was not going to allow that to continue, so I remember practicing so much that my skill set got to a point that I was able to win some one on one battles with them. They were great competitors and motivated me to get better.

We had fall and spring tournaments and I was able to start racking up wins. I remember how the one court that had the whole left side wall and back wall as glass which was so intimidating at first and it was hard to follow the ball down the left side of the court. Once the fear of playing on that court subsided, it was the only court I wanted to play on. Everyone was able to gather outside the court to root you on and watch your match. Otherwise, only one or two people could peer through a small window in the other courts to see the match. Again the courts they have built since, are so much more user/spectator friendly. During practice, I played against the boys which was a tremendous help due to the speed and power of their game. All of my teammates, both the men and women were fun and supportive. We had a fabulous time when we would travel and just sing/dance and tell stories about our childhoods.

In 1990 we went to Portland, Oregon for the National tournament and won the team title as well as the Women's title. My quarter final results were enough to help the team, but resulted in a learning experience that propelled me to much better things down the road.

In 1991, I continued to improve throughout the year, so when we went to Cincinnati for the National Tournament, I was able to make it to the finals, but came up short. My doubles partner, Betsy Boswell, and I placed second, and we defended the team title, as well as the Women's title again.

In 1992, we went to Chicago for the National tournament and finally, I was able to take first place in the individual competition, first place in doubles, and first in the team and Women's finals. It was a crowing year to finish off my career at A&M. My parents were able to make it to Chicago to see me win, as well as some relatives that lived in the area.

The friendships and camaraderie while playing for the A&M Handball team were exceptional. They are lessons and memories I carry with me in all my endeavors. I have not really played handball since due to my career, kids, and a lack of folks that play in the area. I have played racquetball with the kids a few times though.

After I graduated from A&M in 1992 with a Business Management degree, I went to work for State Farm Insurance Company and earned my CPCU designation in 2000. I am still with the company after 26 years. My husband, Keith, has been with them for 25. We have two children, Amesley (16), and Austin (13). Both of the kids are highly involved in school and select sports. About my second year at State Farm, a friend asked me on a Friday if I wanted to go to a movie or go play golf. I suggested golf since I had never played it. She belonged to a local country club and provided me with clubs to use for the outing. I did not know what I was doing and was just out there to have fun. Since I had injured my back and soccer was no longer an everyday option, I took up golf and taught myself the game. I still had a competitive nature that never left me, so I honed my golf skills, entered the Austin City Golf tournament, and beat the lady that had won it 14 years in a row. In fact, the mayor of Austin had sent a framed declaration that it was 'Beth Cleckler' day thinking she was going to win it for the 15th year straight. I proceeded to win the Austin City Golf tournament two more times and come in second place at least 10 times. I still play golf around my kids' activities and while on vacation. It is a sport I fell in love with and can play with a whole range of people. I have had two hole in ones, and am playing to a 2.5 handicap. I got to go to the Master's practice round on a Monday back in 2010 and was in Heaven. Needless to say, accidental sports have been my thing.

I have attached various articles of my handball experience as well as golf. If there is anything you need me to clarify, let me know. I will be out on vacation until March 25th, but will be back in the office after that.
Thank you again for reaching out to capture the wonderful moments we had at A&M.

Gig 'Em,

Sharon Davis '92

June of '90

C10 Thursday, October 4, 2001   SPO

T. Jones for American-Statesman

Women's city champion Sharon Davis has been hitting balls a long time, but not golf balls. She was an All-American handball player at Texas A&M and didn't take up golf until 1995.

City champ a relative newcomer to golf, but a veteran of pressure

Doug Smith
Austin golf

When Sharon Davis won the Austin Women's City Championship two weeks ago, naturally, people wanted to know more about this relatively unknown golfer who stopped Beth Cleckler's string of city titles at 14. During the tournament, Davis packed a Texas A&M golf bag that indicated she had played for the Aggies. That's correct. Sort of.

Davis, the former Sharon Baylor, was born and raised in Austin. In 1968, she graduated from Johnston High School, where she excelled at volleyball, basketball and soccer. But in high school, and later during her college career, she never even picked up a golf club.

Davis went to Texas A&M to play soccer and stumbled into handball because of a mix-up in a class registration.

"I thought I had signed up to take racquetball, but it turned out to be a handball class," Davis said. "It was just easier to stay with handball than try to go through making a schedule change."

Fate must have been at play in the mix-up. Davis played two seasons of soccer at A&M but went on to twice earn all-America honors in handball. As a senior she won NCAA titles in both singles and doubles.

Davis graduated from A&M in 1992 and returned to Austin, where she works today as an underwriter with State Farm Insur-

year she took up golf. During that period, she had trouble finding people her age to join her for handball or soccer.

"But it seemed like everybody was playing golf," Davis said. "I actually took up golf by accident. One day a friend asked if I wanted to go do something — either go to a movie or play golf.

"I had never played, but I thought I would give golf a try," Davis said. "I borrowed a set of clubs, and we played at Georgetown Country Club. Right from the start, I loved golf courses, just their natural beauty."

Davis was quickly hooked on golf. Considering her athletic background, it is not surprising what happened next.

"I have always been competitive. Golf takes a fair amount of time and money, so I decided if I was going to get into this game, I was going to do it right and get as good as I could," Davis said.

Davis never took a lesson, but taught herself by watching golf on TV and poring over instruction magazines. She entered her first tournament in March 2000, and 18 months later won the biggest women's amateur title in the city.

You don't usually think of golf and handball together, but perhaps there is a connection.

said teaching professional Will Stephens when told of Davis' handball background. "Her head is not filled up with too many swing thoughts. I imagine she just sees the ball and reacts. Just see the ball and hit it. And she is accustomed to competing in pressure situations."

Davis agrees that her athletic ability has taken her this far, and she acknowledges that her competitive background has helped.

"I played in a lot of very close handball matches in college, and in those situations you keep reminding yourself to stay focused and stay positive," Davis said. "It's the same in golf."

Davis plans to step up her competitive schedule next year by entering more regional and state tournaments.

Notes: Cleckler is the only area player to qualify for the U.S. Women's Mid-Amateur Championship, which begins Saturday at Fox Run Golf Club in Eureka, Mo. ... During last week's Texas Open, **Justin Leonard** was asked about players getting back to normal on the PGA Tour following the Sept. 11 terrorist attacks. Leonard's reply: "When you are on the golf course, it's fine. You are focused on your game. Otherwise we are like everybody else, and it's hard to think of anything else. One difference is that now guys go back to their (hotel) room and turn on CNN instead of ESPN."

14-year reign ends in City Golf

■ Former A&M handball player defeats longtime champ in 20-hole final

By Doug Smith
American-Statesman Correspondent

It took a former national handball champion to finally remove Beth Cleckler's 14-year hold on the Austin Women's City Golf Championship trophy.

Thirty-one-year-old Sharon Davis, a former NCAA handball champion at Texas A&M who also played on the Aggies soccer team, defeated Cleckler 1-up Friday in a 20-hole championship final at Morris Williams.

Davis was a student at Johnston High School in 1987, the year Cleckler began her 14-year victory streak. Cleckler appeared on the verge of making it 15 in a row Friday when she took a 1-up lead to the 18th hole, but Davis extended the match by sinking an 8-foot birdie putt on the par-4 18th.

Davis and Cleckler halved No. 1, their 19th hole, with bogeys. Davis then closed out the match on the par-5 second hole by dropping a 4-foot putt for bogey. Cleckler's 3-foot effort for bogey slid by the cup.

The pair dueled all day in a dramatic match. Cleckler took a 1-up lead with a birdie on the par-4 fourth, but her bogey on the par-4 seventh squared the match again. They halved the next six holes before Davis took a 1-up lead when Cleckler bogeyed the par-3 14th.

Cleckler won the next two holes to regain a 1-up advantage through 16 and took that lead to the 18th tee. On the par-4 18th, both players hit long drives and solid approaches. Cleckler just missed a 22-foot birdie putt and then watched as Davis extended the match with her short birdie putt.

"This is a great thrill. It was such a tough, close match all day," said Davis, who took up golf six years ago and has never had a lesson. "Beth is such a wonderful golfer and a wonderful individual. To have won 14 in row like she did is amazing. I mean, that's the type of thing not even Tiger (Woods) does."

"In a way I am relieved" the winning streak is finished, Cleckler said. "Every year that went by there was more pressure to win again. Next year I won't be so nervous at this tournament."

(Courtesy Sharon Davis)

Davison, Jeffrey T. "Jeff" Lt. Col, USAF (Ret), '83-Jeff started playing handball his freshman year in PE because racquetball was full. He fell in love with the game and continued to improve throughout his years at A&M. He was a gifted athlete who played football and baseball while growing up in Bryan. Early in his handball life, he quickly gained enough skill to be a member of the A&M handball team and played his way into the quarterfinals at the national collegiates in 1982. In 1983, he was the Class C national champion.

After graduation his calling was in the USAF where he served for 22 years as a pilot and during a great career, earned two top gun awards. After retiring from the Air Force, he became a banker and is still in that profession.

Davison continued playing handball in the Air Force and played until 2010. Two shoulder surgeries terminated his handball playing career.

One of his fondest memories in handball happened while he was a senior at A&M and taking a handball PE class. There were several freshmen in the class and one day the entire class was taking a test when all of sudden Lance Lowy, the teacher, grabbed the test from him and accused him of cheating and told him to leave the room. Davison did as ordered, went next door to an adjacent court and started practicing his shots. The freshmen were aghast at what happened. They were scared because of what they had just witnessed. Davison and Lowy had a great laugh afterward as the whole incident was to play a joke on the freshmen.

deLassus, Rene A., '86-Rene started playing handball as a freshman at A&M and quickly displayed her athletic ability. In her class were several Aggie football players. She figured out early in the semester that she could hit the ball to their off hand and frustrate them and, of course, at that point, win. Her teacher, Lance Lowy, quickly noticed her beating the male students in her class and invited her to join the handball team. deLassus continued her improvement and reached the All-American level before she graduated. Though she was not accorded the honor of All-American status, she had developed her handball game to that skill level. One year after her graduation, the USHA started recognizing players with the All-American honor. She was recognized as an All-American in another sport-soccer-where she was named second team All-American.

She stopped playing handball after graduation due to no available courts in her area. She credits the game of handball for helping her to be successful in the business world. Having played against men during most of her handball career, she developed a competitive spirit that helped her as she transitioned into the technology field, which was male dominated at the time of her entry into the business world. Having retired from Travelers as a Vice President of Information Technology, she now enjoys her time on the golf course and also playing pickleball.

DePasqual, Joseph D. "Joe," Jr., '65-Following are selected parts of a letter received from Joe:

> Second semester of my fish year, early 1962, new courts were ready for play and P. E. courses were offered in two tiers, beginners and advanced. I learned basic one-wall play in high school, so, started in beginners. Success there put me in the advanced section at the start of my second year.

> We had very little instruction, no coach and no "team." My impression was there hadn't been much activity in recent years. Gene Evans, a faculty member, was an excellent, experienced player and became the sponsor of the handball "Club." I don't know

anything of the club's genesis. A note was posted on the bulletin board at the courts inviting people to join and I responded.

Gene had us all amazed at part of his warm-up routine. He would stand about 3 or 4 ft. from a court wall and volley the ball, left hand vs right hand, for several minutes, never letting it hit the floor. He had unbelievably fast hands. Made him very dangerous in front court.

Rice had a very active club/team. We played them several times, in Houston and at home, and won all the contests in those years, '63, '64, '65.

The University of Texas had a coach, Pete Tyson, and a formal handball program. In 1964, they opened a state-of-the-art handball facility in Gregory Gym-12 courts plus a central, glass walled (3 sides) court with surround seating. Pete was a nationally ranked player and a great host. We traveled there several times for instruction and to pair off against his players. He was very good at matching us up for good competition as opposed to winning the day. He was also a terrific coach/instructor and his star pupil, Bob Lindsay, became nationally ranked in 1966.

In March 1965, Pete hosted the USHA National Collegiate Championships, which brought in players from across the nation. Playing in that event was a high point for us, even though we didn't advance very far. We did pick up a couple of trophies but don't remember what for. The coaching other schools had was very evident. Our "team" was: Bill Altman, Dave Engle, Hector Diaz, Bob Paulson, George Behrendt, and myself.

We did play in the Southwest tournament in Houston, but I don't have any results. Our activity just wasn't followed much, probably because it had no part in the school athletic program. P. E. and the club were it.

On the other hand, intramural competition was hot and heavy, driven by Army/Air force rivalries and Corps bragging rights. Tom Fine, Hector Diaz, and I were on the 3rd Brigade, Company C-3 team and won the Class A intramural championship for '64-65.

Early 1965 was busy because we wanted a good showing at the Nationals. We played Rice three times during the '64-'65 school year, once in Houston and twice at home. We also went to Austin once to get more time on the new courts and more pointers from Pete. The other players that show up in the clips (from *The Battalion*) were from the top P. E. classes to fill in brackets as needed for tournament play.

Handball never developed into a program while I was at A&M. We had no athletic department support for gear or travel. Sad fact was we could have been strong. Lots of occasional players were very good and cross-over players from baseball and basketball could have been terrific. Pete Tyson had been a star baseball player before joining the faculty at UT.

We did not have an instructor for P. E. A staff member explained we would play doubles only and the winning team would advance a court from #3 to #2, etc. Finishing the semester in court #1 got you an A grade, #2 Court a B and so forth. So, 4 guys got A's, 4 B's, etc. I don't know if anyone failed; the classes were small.

I continued to play regularly and in tournaments until 1983, when a badly jammed thumb, that was too easily re-injured ushered me out.

Regards,

Joe

DePasqual attended Jesuit High in Dallas and played handball with a tennis ball on a one-wall court which measured 20'x36'.

After graduation from A&M, he continued playing and normally made all the tournaments of the "Texas Circuit" which included Abilene, Amarillo, Austin, Big Spring, Corpus Christ, El Paso, Lubbock, Midland, Odessa and Waco. His strong point in handball was an effective serve to get a weak return and then kill it. He claims he was not great at volleying.

When he jammed his thumb, he quit handball and started dancing. He competed in dancing for about 10 years and reached a level that saw him as a finalist in the US Swing Championship in Anaheim, CA.

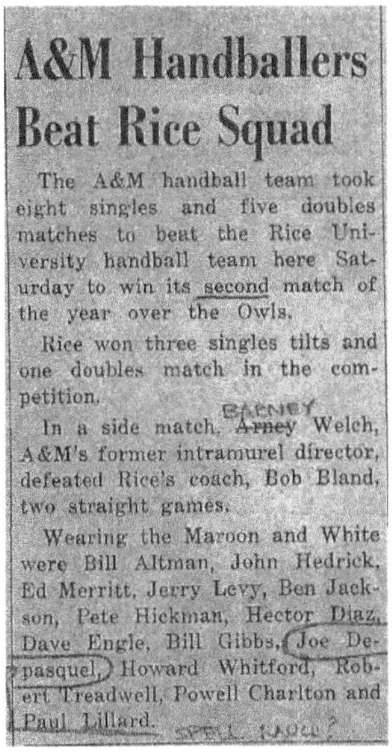

A&M Handballers Beat Rice Squad

The A&M handball team took eight singles and five doubles matches to beat the Rice University handball team here Saturday to win its second match of the year over the Owls.

Rice won three singles tilts and one doubles match in the competition.

In a side match, Arney Welch, A&M's former intramural director, defeated Rice's coach, Bob Bland, two straight games.

Wearing the Maroon and White were Bill Altman, John Hedrick, Ed Merritt, Jerry Levy, Ben Jackson, Pete Hickman, Hector Diaz, Dave Engle, Bill Gibbs, Joe DePasqual, Howard Whitford, Robert Treadwell, Powell Charlton and Paul Lillard.

The Battalion
Fall 1964
(Courtesy Joe DePasqual)

Ag Handballers Slaughter Rice

The A&M Handball Team won 17 out of 19 matches to defeat the Rice Owls Saturday in DeWare Field House.

In a separate match club advisor Gene Evans defeated the Rice team coach Paul Pfeiffer.

Playing for the Aggies were George Behrendt, Bill Altman, Dave Engle, Hector Diaz, Bob Paulson, Joe DePasqual, Lou Stout and Jim McAfee.

The team will travel to Houston Friday to compete in the Southwest Invitational Collegiate Tournament.

The Battalion
February 1965
(Courtesy Joe DePasqual)

Diaz, Hector, '66- The following is the information and handball stories received from Hector:

Austin Nationals

Discovered handball at the downtown YMCA in San Antonio, Texas. It was a great "singles" game that required many physical attributes. I became very, very good in a short period of time. As a 'fish' in the Corp of Cadets at Texas A&M in 1962, I enrolled in a handball PE Class (thought it was a good idea for grade points).

The handball courts were made of plywood. A well hit ball often put a hole in the lumber! I practiced twice a day, ran bleachers as often as possible, threw a ball against a wall with my left hand for an hour and walked away from football (my first love) as this sport left no time for anything, and I mean anything else in your life! It scared me that there would not be enough time for studies.

The handball courts at the University of Texas in Austin, TX were the best in the country! They were beautiful, well maintained and the National Doubles Champion, Pete Tyson, was the handball instructor. Every January I would leave A&M and stay at the athletic dorm with a friend from high school on a baseball scholarship. I would return to classes after only missing the first two weeks. I was in pre-med outfit in the Corp of Cadets and managing time was always difficult.

I was always broke and hungry!!! Especially the week that the nationals tournament started in Austin. Two matches were played on the first day. The biggest adjustment I had to make was playing the next match at least 10 pounds lighter than the previous match. My body moved further and quicker than anticipated as if I was overreacting! On the third day of the tournament, I was exhausted. I recall going outside of the building and walking to the curb of the street and sitting down. At this point I was delusional and oblivious to my surroundings! Somehow a car that was passing by thought I was hitchhiking and stopped to talk to me. They only spoke Spanish and I had already failed Spanish 101. I evidently got into the car and passed out. When I woke up, they were talking to me and I could not understand them. I was even more confused and lost and did not know where I was at. They said we were in San Antonio! So they basically dumped me on the corner and drove away. I looked around and thank goodness but there was a telephone booth right next to me. I found a dime in my pocket and dialed a number. To this day I do not know how I dialed the phone number of a girl friend I had known in high school. The mother of my friend answered the call and was completely surprised. I was delirious and do not know what I said but I relayed the street name that was on the corner street sign.

That evening I briefly awoke to find that I had perspired (sweat) so much that the mattress was soaking wet. It was ruined. The next thing I remember I was on an ambulance. Next thing I remember, I awoke the next day in a hospital with an IV in my arm and did not know where I was at! It was a hospital. The Doctor walked in and asked how I felt. Before I answered, I asked where I was!! Then I asked what was wrong with me..... the Doctor said it was not to serious.... He said I was suffering from exhaustion and malnutrition!!!

Scariest match ever!

Barney Welch was a legend at Aggieland. There was so much "campus ology" and so much history. We learned to respect and we learned to know as much campus ology as we could and it made us proud. Barney had scored the first touchdown in Austin and I believed and thought he was a god. I had seen him on campus several times and was not as big as I had imagined but still totally respected that he had played football for A&M. To me, he was a great athlete and in the Texas A&M books of history.

One day I heard about a football player coming to A&M that the whole world had tried to recruit. He was going to be the player we needed to win it all!!! I met him on campus and he was very calm, quiet and mild mannered. He was huge! I mean huge!! I watched him on the practice field and he was very quick and limber for his size. I could see how he would be a very strong addition to the football team. To me, he was also a great athlete!

I weighed 165 pounds. I was determined to be "ranked" at handball. I thought it was an excellent individual sport.... So I ran bleachers every morning at Kyle Field, practiced in the court at least once per day, had at least one match per day and then would throw a rubber ball against a wall with my left had every evening for at least an hour. (I was right handed, but after a year you could not tell if I was right or left handed)

One day, I saw a poster in Deware Field house about a campus handball tournament. So I entered the tournament. I entered the singles and doubles brackets. I remember the singles matches were of no consequence and was pleased with my performance. Then one day I found out that I would be playing Barney Welch and Mo Morman for the finals doubles match. Wow, I thought. I would be playing against a legend and an upcoming legend. I was so proud and so respectful of the situation and opportunity.

When I arrived at the court, Barney and Mo were warming up. They had been there for a while as they were soaking wet with perspiration. I walked into the court and approached Barney, extended my hand for a handshake and said "Good afternoon Mr. Welch, my name is Hector Diaz". He looked at me, up and down, like I was nobody and asked if I was the guy they were supposed to play. I think he was trying to psych me out. He asked if we were ready and I said my partner had not arrived yet.

Soon thereafter my partner showed up and the match started. Immediately I knew that Barney and Mo were there to win. The first service started and it was crazy. I could hear every step Mo took on the floor.They went after every shot no matter what! Mo was ferocious!! You could hear every thunderous footstep and I was very, very cautious and always knew where he was at. They were so very serious. We went back and forth in the match. Then they begin to try and hit every shot to the "other side" of the court where my partner was doing his best. So, I decided to move him to a defensive position (basically out of the way and let me take over). The match would be one of my most memorable performances. Every time I scored a point,

Barney would look at me with an angry look on his face. He would call time out and talk to Mo and set a strategy. I kept very quiet and very respectful. I said "yes sir" to him many times. What made the situation more tense was one particular shot. I moved over the entire court responding to shots intended for my partner. Barney made an excellent shot that should have been a point but I was able to react and make a saving shot right next to the floor. Then Barney hit the ball very hard and it was back directly at me at a very high velocity. The ball bounced directly in front of me and all I could do was spread my legs, the ball went between them, and I hit the ball behind my back and it made a kill shot and a point!!! What a fantastic shot. Barney exploded! He ran up right into my face and yelled at the top of his voice "you think you're pretty good, don't you"! I did not know how to react. Normally I would probably respond with a smart answer like—"yes, what was your first clue"! But I could not do that. This was the legendary Barney Welch. All I could do was to be respectful so all I said was "no sir". Mo walked up and I thought I was going to die with his fist down my throat. But Mo grabbed Barney and they moved back into position for the next serve.

When the final point was scored Barney was very mad. He made a couple of angry comments and walked out of the court. We did not shake hands, we did not say good game…. It was very awkward because I just stood there in disbelief and still respected the legendary Barney Welch!

Donaho, Glynn R. '66-The following letter was received from Glynn:

I am not going to be much help regarding the history of handball at A&M. I am having trouble remembering the names of people involved with handball, but you may already know some of those and you could probably jog my memory. There really was not much "history" of handball in the years I was at A&M.

I think the courts were pretty new during my stay at A&M 1963-1966. I actually graduated in January 1967. I heard that those courts no longer exist today, but I do not know that for a fact. When I came to A&M, I had played a lot of what we called handball in high school. (Bellaire High School, Houston, Texas) but it was a court set up in the corner of the gym (side and front wall) and we played with a tennis ball, bare-handed. Usually, the best kill shot won the game (closest to the floor). I was probably the best at the high school, and you had to beat me to take the court which didn't happen very often.

When I got to A&M I was amazed at the size of the courts, how responsive the walls were and all the things you could make a rubber handball do with so many walls. I loved putting on those handball gloves-very seldom did mine dry out. For physical education requirements you could take handball two semesters and we were required to take other sports the other two semesters. I took six semesters of physical education (PE), and I think I took four semesters of handball, but two classes were "electives." At that time, we played doubles most of our classes and you moved up a court if you won and changed partners. If you lost, you moved down a court and changed partners. In four semesters, I only lost one game in PE-had to be my partner's fault!

I cannot remember the name of the professor, but he was good and I could not beat him. He may have been a Hungarian refugee who taught fencing and several other sports. If it was him, I think he was a world champion in several sports-fencing, and pistol shooting for starters. There was another older guy who sold life insurance to us students who was very good as well, and I could not beat him. I just cannot remember his name and I kept in contact with him for years. Young people played with energy, agility and power. Old people play with patience, finesse, skill and intelligence. That is a hard combination to beat.

There was one student who played at A&M who was definitely better than me. I don't remember his name, but he was probably listed as president of the A&M club or team. I think he was ranked nationally during those years. My whole time at A&M, I may have won one game from him…maybe two when he let me win.

Regarding playing in the Southwest Conference, there was no structure to do that between 1963 and 1966 that I remember. If we played another school, it was because someone called the other school and our "club" played their "club." As I remember most other schools had more "school" sponsorship than we had at A&M. As I remember, only a few colleges had handball courts. It was not really a school sponsored sport that I remember. However, we did have the ability to take priority over the courts if another club was coming to play us (on the weekends). We did not have a school coach that I remember. We coached and taught each other. I also remember that the one student who I mentioned who was so good played in a lot of individual tournaments to get ranking. Some of those tournaments may have been sponsored by other colleges/universities. Most students did not have time for that. For a lot of us, just buying handball gloves and a ball was a strain on our budget. One ball would get you thru a year and everyone had a ball. You always played with the ball that bounced the highest when you dropped your ball and your opponent's ball together.

With regard to intramural handball, there was none that I remember. I taught a lot of guys to play so many of the best players were in Guzzlin G-3. One guy during my freshman year was from California and won honors in California as the best junior college quarterback. He became very good, but he did not come back to A&M after his freshman year. I played a few of the A&M football players of that era and they were just not very good at handball. Some were not all that good at football either. Most football players had strength but that was about it. They would stand in the middle of the court and hit the ball a hundred miles per hour, but that was about the extent of their ability at handball. There was a lot of pampering that happened to football players, but I did not pamper them when they played me. I would beat them like a drum so not many wanted to play me.

I would like to share with you a bit about one guy I taught to play. His name was Jack Blake. He was a vet student. He came to me one day and wanted to learn to play. Well, Jack was good at everything and mostly an A student. I took this as an opportunity to be better than him at something. He ended up being the best student I ever had. It was common for me to give guys 19 points to play me, but not Jack. I started with 12, then went down and within a month or two we were playing straight up handball. As a doubles team we could probably beat any other student team on campus. Jack made it thru vet school, took his commission after vet school and ended up in Vietnam where he died when his jeep hit a mine/booby trap. It was sad that the world lost a guy who was so good at everything. What a loss-one of those guys you expected to do great things during his life.

I loved a good handball volley but I could win a game on just the serve. I managed to perfect a serve that started in the right most corner of the service box and it arched up to maybe a foot from the ceiling toward the left rear corner, but it would not quite hit the rear wall but would hit the side wall one to three feet from the floor, (maybe a foot from the rear wall). The only way to play it was to hit it left-handed before it hit the wall which was usually a weak overhand shot if it was returned. I could usually put it away-kill it. I never perfected that serve for the right side for left-handers who usually had a weak right-hand shot. I just could not get the right spin on the ball. I would go to a court and spend hours just serving over and over. I also spent hours just hitting everything left-handed and trying to serve left-handed. I digress again.

When I got back from Vietnam, I was assigned to a Mechanized Infantry unit at Fort Hood and the day I got on post I heard about a post handball tournament, which I promptly entered. I had not played handball in almost three years and I placed 12th in the tournament, but the guy who won the tournament claimed that I was the toughest game he played. He won the tournament by only 4 points. He was one of the guys who ran the Sports Complex on post. The point is not that I was good, but that A&M put out some pretty good handball players and what is important is why. We viewed handball a manly sport fitting for the Corps-no soft racquetball. I don't know which ball goes faster but I know that sooner or later all handball players get hit by a hard, fast-moving handball that hurts but you don't blink and no tears are allowed. As our world became more soft, it would upset me when racquetball players started monopolizing courts that were designed for the manly sport of handball. I preach again.

One other thing I will say about handball is that we played it because we absolutely loved the sport. What a rush to make the perfect shot. What a motivator to see someone else make a perfect shot. What a tremendous workout. What a "high" to play a new player you have never seen on the court before and discover he is really good. What a "high" to serve aces. What a high to change strategy mid-way thru a game to beat a really good player. It is a great sport and we did not care if Texas A&M put all of its financial support and supervision in other forms of athletics. We loved handball. I would probably still play today if I had not snapped my Achilles Tendon on a court. It was put back together but never the same

Glynn Donaho

Donaho was commissioned into the Army as an Infantry Officer, received training as an Army Ranger and rose to the rank of Lieutenant Colonel. He has retired from the Army and is now living in Normangee, Texas.

Edwards, Kara M.-Kara came to A&M after earning her bachelor's in Kinesiology and Psychology and her M.Ed. in coaching, sport, recreation and fitness administration while attending Angelo State. Here she taught Kinesiology 199/handball and played handball during her spare time. She motivated some of her students to join the A&M handball team. All have graduated and moved on with their lives. Following are some of her stories in handball:

I started playing handball a little different than most. I grew up on a soccer field in which hand-eye coordination was not one of my true talents, but I enjoyed playing racquetball during the off-season of soccer. At one time, I was playing racquetball when a guy walked into the court asking if I wanted to play handball. I did my best to avoid him, but he was persistent. Finally, we decided to make a bet, racquetball vs. handball. The rules were as follows: 1) we would play three games to 21; 2) we would use a racquetball; 3) I would have a racquet; he would use his hand; and 4) all I had to do was get six points on him between the three games. (He did not mention he was ranked as one of the top 10 handball players in the nation). If I won the bet, he would never ask me to play handball again. If he won, I would have to play at the collegiate handball tournament in Oregon. After an hour, I was researching Catriona Casey, Tracy Davis and studying strategies on how to play this sport called handball. (NOTE: Kara earned 4 points in the three games.)

My first year at the collegiate tournament was the 63rd USHA Collegiate National Handball Championships in Portland, Oregon. Being my first collegiate, I started in the novice division and slowly ended in the Women's B. Though my goal was to finish in the Women's Open bracket, I did walk away with a Women's B Double's champion's medal that day with my partner, Angela Snow. The tournament highlights were when Daniel Cordova defeated Martin Mulkerrins in an epic Men's Open battle and Catriona Casey played her last collegiate before going pro. Watching these two games, really fueled me to work harder and be better.

The following year, Minneapolis, Minnesota hosted the USHA Collegiate National Handball Championships and that year I played some of my best games. Going in, I was ranked 15th and got to play the number 1 seed Ciana Ni Churraion. Honestly, she killed me score-wise; however, I walked away from that game knowing I put on a show and did my best. Then I was hit with a double whammy and played Mikaila Mitchell, the number 3 seed. That game was a little more intense and though I did not win, I still had the best time. I walked out of that tournament ranked 13th, playing the best handball of my life.

Some of my fun handball memories came on trips traveling with the University of Texas handball crew. Angelo State did not have a very competitive team at the time. We were not like most teams such as the University of Texas or Missouri State. Our "team" was more of individuals coming together every couple of tournaments. I became used to being the only player from Angelo State to play at tournaments. But I enjoyed the competitive side and wanted to play more. It seemed like every weekend I would drive to Austin, meet the UT crew, we would stuff ourselves in cars that were way too small, and go off to the next tournament. We went all over Texas, Florida, Missouri, Arizona and every year we would always go somewhere new.

I remember the road trips the most. During each trip, we required stopping at a restaurant with pancakes so we could have our pancake eating contest. I was never close to winning. We also had a tradition of connecting as many straws as possible. This served two purposes: 1) spitballs-minus the spit. We wanted to see how far we could get the ball of paper from one end to the other, and 2) to see how many straws we could connect and still be able to drink a drink. At one point we connected 37 straws and were able to put a glass of water on one side of the restaurant and drink the water through the straw from the other side of the restaurant.

Aggieland will always hold a special place in my heart. It was the first place my parents came to see me play handball. Later, I would get my first job in Aggieland, teach my first solo handball class, and meet a talented group of handball mentors.

Frisbie (Werner), Julia W., "Julie," '86-Julie has always loved and continues to love participating in athletics. With her business, raising a family and being an athlete, her days are always busy. Following is the letter she sent for inclusion in the book:

Don,

Thank you for your letter and I apologize for just getting back to you. I am so glad you reached out to me and appreciate Coach Lowy giving you my information. I would love to see him!

As for your interview sheet I thought it would be best to answer via e-mail if that's OK.

I was born in Iowa City, IA in 1964. My family moved to Austin, TX in 1969, which is where I attended grade school and High School.

I attended Texas A&M from 1982-1986 and graduated with a bachelor's degree in Business Administration with a concentration in Marketing. After graduation I moved to Chicago, IL and began working for Marshall Field's Department Store in their Management Training and Buying Program. I was there for just over 2 years, but moved back to Texas when the store sold to Federated. Had I stayed with them I would have had to move to Minneapolis, MN.

While in Chicago I competed in a few amateur/pro handball events, but because of the distances I would have to travel to play in tournaments, I gave up the sport and began playing racquetball. I had played years of tennis as a child, so racquetball came pretty easy to me and my skills in handball certainly helped as well. I competed in multiple state tournaments and was a top player for my age group.

As for how I started playing handball.... I was always an athlete as I played basketball, volleyball, and softball at A&M as well. My father played handball in the Navy and I knew how much he loved the game, so I actually selected handball as my required PE course at A&M. From there, my love for the sport grew and the rest is history. I competed in every local tournament and by the time I was a junior (1985) I won the National Championship in Austin, TX. We also won the national championship as a team so it was a special time. The following year I placed 3rd at Nationals in California Berkeley.

I currently own my own Sporting Goods store, Elite Sports Georgia in Atlanta, GA. I have owned it for 11 years and we specialize in team sports equipment and uniforms, screen printing and embroidery. I love working with young athletes just getting started in sports, which will always be a passion of mine.

I currently play league tennis in Atlanta (ALTA) and am an Orange Theory fitness enthusiast.

I have 2 adult girls Darby (23) and Chandler (24)l both of whom are athletes.

Thank you! I look forward to hearing back from you.

Julie Frisbie, Owner
Elite Sports Georgia

Gorrod, Herbert M. "Bert," '52-The author was surprised to learn that his freshman year Commanding Officer of Company 12 played handball. The author was on the A&M wrestling team, had a job in the Cushing Library and with classes, had little time to learn of what others in the unit were doing. However, "Mr. Gorrod, Sir" answered my request for information and the following is the letter received from him:

Dear General Donald;

I was both surprised and delighted to get your letter. I have not kept up with the many A&M friends that I had. Many of them have gone to meet Jesus and, of course, I did not have a close relationship with the 100 or so young men in Company 12. I was, also, glad that you were physically able to play and teach handball. Your book sounds interesting.

I title my story: "HANDBALL AT TEXAS A&M CHANGES MY LIFE"

I attended A&M with an Opportunity Award Scholarship honoring General Dwight David Eisenhower with the goal of serving a lifetime in the military.

Prior to my sophomore year at college, I had never played handball, but, if you remember during that period you had to take 2 years of PE. That year I chose handball and badminton as my electives. As I recall, Emil Mamaliga was the handball overseer, but he was also the diving coach.

ASA (Army Security Agency) had some very accomplished handball players but they needed "cannon fodder" for practices and warm-ups. That was me! I never played in a match during 2 years; however, I made most of the practices. A guy named, Hub, stands out. He was about 6'2" with very long arms. In fact, when he stood upright, his hands were at his knees. With his arm spread, he covered about ¾ of the court. Very few things got by him. During my senior year with Company 12, I played handball with several "fish" in the company.

On April Fool's Day 1952 about 9 PM members of Co. 12 were playing doubles handball. I took a step back and landed on someone's foot who was moving laterally. The torque on my knee caused my kneecap to slide on the underside of my leg. I popped it back in place and went to the hospital. The swelling went down but it was injured again so that by May 4, I had radical knee surgery. Therefore, I was on crutches during Final Review, Army Commissioning, Graduation and my wedding. Also, I was delayed in reporting to training at Fort Devens, Mass. Instead, I took a job with Humble Oil & Ref. Co. as a geologist. From that time, I had to take a physical, at the nearest military facility every 4 months. Finally, in January 1954, a doctor at Goodfellow Air Base in San Angelo, Texas rated me "fit for duty" so in January I reported for 18 months active duty with the Army Security Service.

However, comparing the time as a geologist with the time spent in the military, I chose being a geologist as the path of my life. Thus "HANDBALL CHANGED MY LIFE."

Gressett, Marion J. "Jack," '76-Jack is the son of a Chamber of Commerce executive director and they moved every two to four years. At age 11 he would ride the city bus after school to the downtown Y in Omaha, Nebraska and take swimming and Judo lessons. His father and he were introduced to handball through an associate who had a son about Jack's age. They started playing father/son doubles about once a week. Jack and his dad enjoyed the sport so much they began playing singles on other evenings and Saturdays.

From Omaha they moved to Billings, Montana where Jack taught several fellow YMCA members the game of handball. There was a handball ladder and they started challenging and being challenged based on the rules of the ladder. One old timer named Smokey was known well for his ability to kill shots off the back wall.

In 1969 the family moved to Abilene, where Jack continued his handball by playing the locals and personnel from Dyess Air Force Base.

After graduating from high school, Jack attended Texas A&M and he continued his favorite sport, handball. He credits Stan Lowy, Glen Williams, Jeff Bronson, Tom Kozik and Ozzie Burke for teaching him so much about the game of handball. He traveled to many tournaments with Jeff Bronson. After graduation, he moved away from College Station; however, four years later he moved back and is now a very successful businessman. In 2014, he started assisting Ozzie Burke, Charlie Bokelman and Don Johnson in coaching the A&M handball team.

Harris, Marvin K. PhD., Professor Emeritus of Entomology-Marvin is an unusually gifted athletic and intellectual individual. The author first met him at the handball courts at the Texas A&M Recreation Center. I was asked to join him and others in doubles competition. As time went on, we soon started playing singles. Harris is first of all, a teacher/professor, a fact I learned as we progressed in our singles play. It did not take me long to realize that he was showing and doing only what it took to get to 21 first. It may have been six months-maybe a year or more-before I learned all aspects of his handball ability, strategy and his "chicanery", as he calls it. I can speak only from my standpoint but he and I had many great afternoons on the handball courts. He has provided the following stories, which those in the handball world will fully appreciate:

Stan Lowy's Broken Finger

I spent my 30's and 40's just developing some largely self-taught skills by playing with opponents much better than me. I had a few skills before I played much with Stan Lowy and Glen Williams who were on the faculty at A&M. Stan was a diminutive man, half my weight and a foot shorter in height. Glen was built like a standup freezer, just over six foot and could hit a fist shot harder that most players to return it on any place on the court. Stan and Glen were almost always Doubles partners. They took me in and we normally played about 2 hours of handball three times a week after work for many years. They took me back to school again and it was several years more before I offered them much competition but I benefitted from the exercise and their friendship. I also had evil plans for them on the court if I ever could gain such skills.

One day between games during a water break the subject came up of injuries that the sport might pose to players. I had found it rigorous but with a little protective equipment like eye protection, there seemed minimal risk of serious injury. On that occasion, I asked Stan, given his many years of play, whether he thought there was much danger in the sport. Initially he just shook his head "no." But then paused for thought as the three of us were now ready to resume play when he said "I guess I did break a finger once." I was a bit surprised that this answer had not been shared right up front given that seemed serious enough of an injury to a pool player like me at least. I continued my inquiry and asked him what he did then. "Nothing really" he said, "I just kept playing." Now I was totally confused and inquired further asking "Didn't it hurt at all to do that?" Stan cryptically answered again "I don't know." Now I was totally confused and just had to ask the obvious: "Why don't you know?" Stan gestured at our standup freezer friend Glen, who had stood silent during this colloquy, but now had a smile that said he knew something I did not. Stan then said "It was Glen's finger." Glen, it turns out, just taped it up tightly and continued play as well. Handball seems to build character and I feel I am better because of the game too.

Marvin's Handball Virgin

My regular 5-7pm M-W-F time on the Rec Center handball court was usually spent with regular opponents but if aspiring TAMU handball club players showed up wanting more experience, we all would try to accommodate them. My unconventional game that included tactics they had not seen or had to counter before, were challenging to overcome to those at B+ level or lower divisions. I helped many get some coping skills. The handball coaches of the club, trying to teach the players the solid, time-tested skills needed to really be competitive at all the upper levels, were responsible for keeping their students from adopting too many bad habits from me. Things seemed to work out. I had fun with all who played, and exercised, if forced into that.

Sometime in my last decade of play there was a student that began to seek me out. I could see he had potential but was still learning and needed to work at it. The first year we played off and on. He had developed a fair game by the time summer break came. The fall semester found us playing a great deal. His skills continued to improve. By Halloween I knew he had the physical ability and minimal skills to beat me but still lacked the self-confidence and strategic planning to make that happen. My primary role was not to tell him all this. My role was to remain as a formidable opponent he must learn to defeat on his own and with the aid of his coaches and other mentors since "real" opponents in serious competition with him would do precisely that as well. Thus, he would "own and deserve the victory" not just over me but be even better prepared to face unknown opponents in the future and what was required to overcome them, too. We continued to battle. I was often getting more exercise than I wanted as many games increasingly were fought where I had to come from behind to prevail. Trying to add a little more incentive to do so, about Thanksgiving I began to refer to him as my 'Handball Virgin' just in fun, but I knew that was pushing things a bit in trying to inculcate more grit and determination into his effort and also sweeten the pot for him when he surely would prevail no matter how hard I tried to prevent it. By the close of the fall semester, despite several extended games that required breaking the tie, he still had not won. I was certain by then that my hegemony would be in ruins before Spring Break.

However, the beginning of the spring semester did not find the shadow of my Handball Virgin darkening my small handball court door. I asked the current coach and past National Collegiate Doubles Champ, Ozzie Burke, what had happened to him. He informed me that the student was doing an internship in Dallas and would not return for some time. I felt bad and related the above to Ozzie since I now was concerned that my unconventional mental approach program to character build a little may not actually benefit the student as I had intended it to in the end. Nothing more was said about it. I put the matter on the back burner for the rest of the spring. The end of spring TAMU Invitational Handball Tourney dates of play conflicted with unavoidable duties elsewhere. I told Ozzie early on that I could not compete beyond the first day and would not enter so as not to mess up the brackets. During the week before the tourney just after entries closed Ozzie sought me out on the court and asked me to play a match on my open day because he needed my help in a matter that had just come up. It was easy to say yes since I want to help the team in such matters so I agreed, not thinking much about it.

I show up for my scheduled match and warm up with no opponent in sight. Moments before the start I seek out Ozzie. He informs me he is on his way. Moments later out of a nearby but out of sight court emerges the Handball Virgin with a big smile. I am surprised alright. We commenced play and I am quickly behind by 5 points or so before it really dawns on me that the internship had also included some serious handball play. I was in deep trouble. This, at least for a last brief moment, was still my Handball Virgin. While he now had the raw skill to really prevail, he still had to contend with my chicanery, as well as his mental state where the actual taste of my blood had never been enjoyed. He had really improved his strong side right hand in particular but I did make note in that early start he got that his left hand was not as improved as his right. I finally got a couple of opportunities to try some serves to the left that might cause a little trouble. We were playing in Court One with the glass side on the left wall that allowed spectators to see into the entire court and make for a wall that had different proper-ties of depth perception and occasional tracking of the ball a little more problematic in shots to that area, particularly deep into the back left corner. I found my very high arced slow spin serve deep into that back left corner, if correctly placed, caused real problems for him.

My entire strategy for the remainder of the match was established at that moment. I would make him play with only his left hand as often as possible, even if seemingly 'gimme' passing shots to the right were available. All serves went highly arced with spin deep into that back left corner. Passing shots and attempted wrong footed kill shots went down the clear left wall or to the front left corner. My Handball Virgin scrambled and dug out many shots. I had to fight hard for most points and lost about every one where his right hand had been allowed to come into play. I barely edged out that first game. He took a break before starting the second "must-win" game for him to force a tiebreaker match to 11. I took the opportunity to grab some handballs to work more on my high serve to the back left 3x5 "Coffin Corner" which I knew was essential for me to have any chance. I definitely did not want this to go to a tiebreaker game since I was already feeling our approximately 40-year age difference and did not want to find out how long I could extend a break just to remain vertical. If the match got to that point, he would likely breeze through the tiebreaker. We played the second game with most of his time spent in that Coffin Corner. I won with what I dimly recall, him at 18 on the scoreboard and me as tired as I have ever been on a handball court.

Ozzie had set me up. In addition, my Handball Virgin really should have prevailed. My skills were far below his. Only chicanery saved me that last time. I have one truly great joy in all of my decades on a handball court. This was when I partnered with Stan Lowy when he was over 80 in a B Plus division of an Aggie tournament. We placed 2nd after losing a close tiebreaker to a father/son team. No doubt they still enjoy that win more than Stan and I ever would-and they deserved it. My bitter-sweet regret is that my Handball Virgin never got to enjoy what would have been well deserved revenge given my goading. I tried with my unconventional game and unconventional mentoring to set him up to enjoy the real thrill of victory. Maybe fate intervened with my intended outcome and opted instead to leave someone so young with a fire still burning in his gut so he still had something to prove to the world to make getting up each day count for something. We could all do with a little more of that too since one in the real world is only as good as their next game.

Charlie Cole Beats Marvin 21-0

Charlie Cole was among many entomologists who also played handball for various periods of time. He was a small fellow and awesome on the court with his left hand. He was so committed to using his left that he would scrunch into the right wall however he could do so. I had already played more than a decade before we first played. My game was not accustomed to his kill-everything style or an opponent who could do so from about anywhere if his left hand could be used. We played about 4 games which he won easily including one stinging loss I took 21-0. He was a good and respected friend but I wanted revenge. He worked at an off-campus center. He infrequently came to the main campus and would play handball after work on days when he was spending the night. I ducked him for 3 years and worked especially hard at improving a game developed specifically for him. My normal skill progress also improved. I think Charlie helped me focus my attention. I'd been ready for a few months by then to try Charlie Cole again at the next opportunity. Learning he was scheduled to come to town I asked for and got a match scheduled.

I played with my normal but improved game for the first two just to warm up good and see his game again when he could play his way. His left hand was as awesome as I remembered but tested his right once in a while to refresh my memory. It was as wooden as a post. He would rather extend his left hand across his chest palm outward and swipe the ball that way rather than use his right hand at all. Either of my hands by then were far superior than his right hand. Nevertheless, he beat me both games using just his left hand.

The third game was a little different. Every time I had any control of the matter Charlie got to scrape things off the right wall. Sometimes he would face the back wall in the process and use a reverse swing with his left hand to contact the ball while peeking back over his left shoulder to find it coming. I used the high arching serve with spin that stayed within inches of the right wall and stayed there even if it bounced back out of the corner from the back wall down the court again. Charlie was not coping well at all with my improved game that used very little of the large court he preferred to play and excel in. I won that game 21-0. I had my revenge and played future games in later matches more for the exercise we both needed than the score. Even years later Charlie's right hand remained weak. I did not rub that in either. We were even after all and still friends for many years to come. Handball is more than just a game.

Marvin Harris no longer plays handball. He had to stop playing due to hand cramps. The cramps gradually worsened and became persistent to the point of continuance. Fortunately, the cramps have abated almost entirely but at a price of lost exercise and playing handball with good friends. He still plays billiards locally and excels in that game. He has remained the best, at least near the top, of all the billiards players in the area. Harris made a cogent point in his last story- "Handball is more than just a game." Friendships developed through sharing a court hitting a handball to reach 21 points first last a lifetime.

Harrison, Richard Henry "Dick" III, MD, '47-Dick was one of the local handball players who would meet over the lunch hour during weekdays and always find a game. He was not one of the top handball players of that group; however, he always gave his top effort, was a life-long friend to those who played with him, and, he absolutely loved playing the game. Harrison passed from this earth and handball at the age of 78 on 5 September 2005.

House, Randolph W., "Randy" LTG, USA (Ret), '67-The author played with Randy on the handball courts at A&M. He is slightly shorter than average in height and reach but he always covered the court with speed, anticipation and desire. He is another one of the handball players who never gives in and is a "fighter" to game and match point. Following are the stories he forwarded for inclusion in this book: Photo courtesy House.

I began playing handball at Texas A&M in the fall of 1965. Then we were required to take 4 different sports as part of our curriculum. I became hooked on handball from the first day and played for 40 years. At A&M I joined the Handball Club and played with the team against other University teams to include the University of Texas team in Austin. Our courts were in the old field house over the indoor swimming pool where Kyle Field's Zone sits today. They were constructed out of plywood so you had to learn how the ball bounced differently depending on how far away it hit from a 2x4 stud. And you learned to really keep your eye on the ball…not a bad life lesson. Our courts were regulation size, but no AC so you had a great workout just from the heat and humidity. I played several times a week from 1965 to graduation.

At the time I was in the Corps of Cadets, but my last two semesters I lived in a small shell camper in the back of my pickup parked behind Guion Hall. My shower was the handball courts showers. Randy Matson, Class of '67 and an Olympic gold medal shot putter, worked out in a small weight room near the courts. When he needed a break from pumping iron, he would join us in handball. I am still in wonder how such a huge man could be so quick. He was hard to beat. And is still a wonderful classmate.

My first tour of duty in Vietnam I flew helicopters. I talked a US Navy Sea Bee unit into building a handball court at Camp Evans, RVN. It had a concrete floor and 4 concrete walls without a ceiling or a door. We entered and exited the court by rope ladder. If the ball hit the ladder, we played the point over. I taught many a helicopter pilot how to play handball. One day the NVA mortars tried to hit our parked helos and a round landed in the middle of our handball court causing a crater in the floor and knocking down all four walls. I jumped in a gunship and went after the NVA mortar crew. They made the war real personal. You do not mess with a handball player's court.

I played a lot of handball while at Ft. Knox. While at Knox I had the opportunity to attend a handball clinic taught by Paul Haber, multi-year National USHA singles champion. At the time many sports were adding strength exercises to their programs. Paul was asked if he did any extra training. He said "No, I just play a lot of handball."

After my second tour in Vietnam, I was posted to Clemson University where I learned to play one- wall handball in a big gym with Professor Ernie Rogers, an Aggie Class of '52. You really learned the cut off game because if the ball got past you, it rolled to the end of a big gym. I recruited my 4-year-old daughter to shag missed balls. To this day she still remembers chasing those handballs.

In the early 80s I played a lot of handball at Ft. Hood. I was fortunate to play a very good handballer, LTC Don Johnson, who had a wicked serve that dropped into the back, left corner. He won many a game from me on that serve alone.

In DC, I played handball at 5:30 in the morning at the Pentagon fitness center against some really talented players to include four-star Generals Glenn Otis and John Tilleli. Both are outstanding Generals and handball players.

As the 8th Army Commanding General in Korea, I was able to play some handball at the Yongsang military post in Seoul, but because of the mission and the environment I had to be in contact with my command post 24x7, so I had to play with a pager on my waist. That was a first.

House had his right shoulder totally replaced, the results of a Vietnam War injury in March 1970 when the helicopter he was piloting was shot down by an enemy RPG. He made a successful autorotation, but the aircraft was in flames. By the time his crew got out of the only fire free door, flames forced him to exit through the emergency green plexiglass cover above the pilot's seat, where his right shoulder was severely injured. He was young so he dealt with the injury for years, but as time went on the shoulder pain became unbearable and required major surgery. Today, the new shoulder is relatively pain free, but he has also had both knees replaced. He replaced both knees at the same time, which required several days in the hospital and hours and hours of rehab. All of these body replacements have terminated his handball playing days and as all of us know who love the game so much, the camaraderie, exercise and fun are great memories to be reflected upon. He is far from finished with life as he now runs cattle on the ranch near Navasota where he grew up. Almost every day he gets up on his favorite steed and rides the ranch to check that all is well.

Hummel (Motal), Glorian A. "Peanut," '79-Arguments can always be made as to who was the best handball player to graduate from A&M. I will not go there with this book, but Peanut's record leaves no doubt as to her athletic prowess. Her story follows:

> Through high school our basketball team achieved state finals 3 years in a row. My sophomore year we were runner-up champs and personally receiving All district and All state honors. My junior and senior year we won the state championships. In addition, ran track and played softball and received all conference honors.
>
> After high school I attended the University of Houston for three years and played on the University of Houston women's basketball team. Being 5'-4', I rode pine a lot but that was OK. It was a great experience. I was studying Mechanical Engineering. During those years, I played on the premier women's fastpitch softball team in Houston of which we attended nationals every year representing the Texas region.
>
> Between my 3rd and 4th year at U of H, I was approached by one of my fellow softball players to play softball for Texas A&M. At that time, women sports were part of AIAW and not NCAA. The AIAW women's eligibility rules stated that you were limited to playing 4 years of any one sport and there was not a time limit on it. Thus, I was able to drop my basketball scholarship at U of H, and pick up a limited softball scholarship at Texas A&M. Playing softball was a two season sport. We played in the fall and spring. Most of my credits transferred from U of H to Texas A&M, so entering my fifth year at A&M, I only needed 22 more credits to graduate.
>
> Thus I added a PE class my fall season of my 5th year. My plan was to sign up for racquetball; however the classes were full, and then there sat Lance Lowy convincing me that handball was very similar to racquetball – my handball career started! During that fall season of 1979, my softball coach was disappointed with our team as we place 2nd in the fall. He made an edict that all players had to show for practice from 4-7PM everyday or they lose their spot on the team. Unfortunately, I only had lab classes left for my degree and they were from 2-5PM. So I had to make a decision to graduate on time and not play softball, or delay my graduation and play softball. At that time our team was ranked #1 in the nation.

Thus, I chose my profession and quit softball. I filled my time playing handball about 4 hours out of the day. In the mornings, I would go to Jepsen and Lance would put me in classes whenever some of the students didn't show up. Then there was open handball play from 5-7 where Sue Oakleaf and I would play doubles against the guys. Then from 10 to midnight the courts were always open and I could work on shots. Handball filled my time. From there, the state championships were held in Austin and I won Consolation against my good friend Beth Rowley(Texas A&M). While there I met Pete and Leann Tyson(Texas).

Sue convinced me to go to collegiate nationals. A funny (scary) story ensued. We were poor college students and thus tried to make this the cheapest flight possible. There were 3 women and 1 man. We drove to Houston to get a red eye to Los Angeles. When we got there at 2AM, we were to drop off our fellow male handball player at USC where he was going to stay with a friend. Back then, there were no cell phones. It was the guys responsibility to guide us to USC. We drove close to there and then the neighborhoods started to get worse and worse. Finally we stopped at a phone booth and the USC student asked us where we were. We looked at the street signs and were at the corner of Executioner and another street. Immediately the USC student said, "Get the hell out of there". It appears we were in the heart of Watts, one of the worst neighborhood of LA at 2AM. Needless to say, we escaped and everything went well after that.

All these people mentioned were instrumental in my handball career. I graduated in May 1980. Women's handball was developing at these times. In tournaments, the men played with the normal Red Spaulding handball (referred to as the hardball) and the women played with a newly developing soft ball. If was difficult because many nationally ranked women would practice against men with the hardball and then have to changed their game when approaching nationals.

After college I went to work for Dow Chemical as a mechanical engineer in Houston. I practiced handball at a club close to work but there were not any other handball players there. To help out, my good friend Ron Emberg at the Houston YMCA would help me in to get into the open play courts there. At that time the Houston YMCA was all men. To get into the open courts you needed to go through the men's locker room. Ron would put a towel over my head to get in! Finally, the YMCA changed their rules and women were accepted. I changed my membership then to the Downtown Houston YMCA.

During these initial years, Sue Oakleaf(Texas A&M) was my teacher/nemesis in Texas. I would finish 2nd to her on many occasions. Then in 1981, USHA nationals came around and Sue convinced me to go. I asked Sue to be my doubles partner. Unfortunately, the number 1 ranked woman in the nation, Rosemary Bellini had already asked her. Thus, Sue got me in contact with Allison Roberts. That first year I finished in the quarter finals singles against Rosemary Bellini and finished 2nd in doubles with Allison, only loosing to Rosemary and Sue. From that point on, I was hooked.

In 1984, Dow Chemical moved me from Houston, Texas to the Bay Area near San Francisco. My handball club changed to the Big C in Concord, CA. During my time in Texas and California, I won many tournaments in statewide and nationally. The most notable national 1st and 2nd finishes are below:

1981 –USHA women's double runner-up champion with Allison Roberts
1982 - USHA women's double champion with Allison Roberts
1983 - YMCA women's double champion with Allison Roberts
1983 - USHA women's double champion with Allison Roberts
1984 - USHA women's double champion with Allison Roberts
1985 – Bud Light women's singles invitational champion
1985 – USHA women's singles champion
1985 - USHA women's double runner-up champion with Allison Roberts
1986 – USHA women's singles champion
1986 - USHA women's double runner-up champion with Allison Roberts

Then in 1987, I married my good friend Jim Hummel and my focus changed to family life.

In 1988, at the USHA nationals in Berkley, CA, USHA offered two divisions for women – the hardball division and the softball division. Leann Tyson called and asked if I would be her partner for the softball division. I accepted even though I was not in tournament shape. We won nationals but basically she carried me.

My gloves were hung up after that, and the family expanded with three wonderful children.

The other notable sports honor occurred in 1983. While in Houston after college, I continued to play fastpitch softball through the summer. In 1983 at Salt Lake City, I was awarded an All-American honor.

I owe many things to handball. It was my rescue my final year of college when I have to give up softball. It built confidence and strength of character facing many challenges in life. After handball, I knew I was a winner and enjoyed life without having to compete.

Professionally handball gave me the ability as a woman to survive, and excel in a man's world of engineering. After 38 years at Dow, I just retired as a senior project engineer. During that time, I have led multiple projects with the largest being around $50 million

I do want to thank Lance Lowy for introducing me to handball, Sue Oakleaf and Beth Rowley – fellow TAMU handball players, Pete and Leann Tyson for their knowledge and friendship, Ron Emberg for the YMCA help, and all the handball players at TAMU, Houston Downtown YMCA and the Big C club in Concord, CA.

Following article has been taken from the November-December 1984 issue of the USHA's *Handball* magazine.

Feature

Three-Time Women's Doubles Champion, Peanut Motal

by Marla Higgins

Peanut Motal with one of her many first-place trophies.

You would be hard-pressed to find a more enthusiastic handball player than Peanut Motal. It would be equally difficult to find a player with a more positive and contagious attitude. The first thing I noticed about Peanut is that she is the same person both on and off the court. She takes her life and handball seriously, while leaving room for herself to have fun at both. I suppose that's why this pint-sized lady rates so high on my list of extra special people.

Peanut is among the top four female handball players in the country, losing in this year's semifinals. For the last three years, she has teamed with Allison Roberts to win the Women's national doubles title as well. I recently had the opportunity to talk with Peanut while she was enroute from Houston to Northern California. During the talk, I tried to get her to reveal all of her secrets for success on the court.

Peanut was born in Houston in 1957 and has lived there her entire life. However, as of October 3, she was transfered to Martinez, Calif., through her job with the Dow Chemical Company. Too bad for Texas, but great for Northern California. She grew up the middle child of five with two older brothers and two younger sisters. Of course, her family expects her to bring home nothing but first-place trophies. Peanut earned her degree in Engineering from Texas A&M and has been working for Dow in Houston as a vessel engineer since graduating.

Sue Oakleaf is the person who introduced Peanut to handball while they attended Texas A&M in the Fall of 1979. Peanut got instruction from Pete Tyson and Ron Emberg as well as Oakleaf who was the Collegiate champ at the time. She started to play with the Spalding Ace since the family ball was still just a thought. Peanut still plays with the Spalding ball except when she's competing in

Women's tournaments. She said that she prefers the hard ball and enters Men's C divisions as well as the Women's events. It's not that she doesn't get enough competition from the women, but that she feels playing in the Men's divisions has helped her game progress. She is an avid supporter of Women's handball and is always willing to help get more women involved.

It was defending champ Diane Harmon who squeaked past Peanut in two close games at the Baltimore Nationals in the semifinals. During Motal's matches, one of the most outstanding things about her game was her use of her left (off) hand. Not many of us are able to use a smooth sidearm stroke with our off-hands, but Peanut is very close to being ambidextrous. She says it's taken hours and hours of practice to develop her left side, which brings up what she does to train.

For weeks before the nationals, Peanut sets aside her other interests (karate, basketball and softball) to devote more time to the regimented training program she uses to get ready for the big event. Her "get-ready-for-the-nationals" program is a three-hour-per-day, six-days-per-week regimen. She starts with 30 minutes of stretching and then 90 minutes of actual playing time. After playing, she

alternates lifting weights with practicing specific shots on a daily basis. She emphasized her belief in the importance of playing as hard as possible during her training period. She likes to simulate the intensity of a tournament match as much as possible during her workouts.

Of all her training secrets, most intriguing was her discussion of the "perfect mechanics" of the sidearm stroke. She recommended that throwing the ball is the best way to get a feel for the proper stroke. You should be aware that when you are striking the ball, you are transfering energy from the floor to your hand, to the ball. To maximize your potential and minimize your energy output, a sequence of movements should be followed. The stroke should start with the proper footwork of moving into the ball and your shot. The hips and shoulders generate a lot of power and should be rotating forward as you stride into your shot. Leading your arm with the elbow will help you use your entire arm as a pendulum and snap the wrist upon completion of the stroke. Of course, her No. 1 rule is, "Always watch the ball."

Whenever time allows, Peanut likes to start her stroke six feet behind where she thinks she will actually make contact (another Tyson tip). She's always moving into her shot, keeping her hands cupped so the ball will have some hop on it. Peanut feels that using the hard ball enforces these habits since if you don't move into the hard ball when you hit it, it doesn't reach the front wall. Also, if you don't cup your hands, you get bruises. The hop that Peanut tries to impart to the ball is not to score points, but merely make it harder for her opponent to set up for the return. Peanut practiced these stroke mechanics until they became automatic and suggests that all beginners do the same.

In addition to being a handball fanatic, Peanut is an exceptional softball player. Her experience in softball as a team player has helped her in her handball doubles, especially since she plays the right side. In 1983, Peanut was named First-Team All-American and the Houston-based team she played on placed seventh in the national tournament. She noted that the main difference between softball and handball is the margin for error. In softball, when it's your turn at bat or to make a fielding play, you have to make the play. Rarely does one get 21 chances in a softball game to make a play or get a hit. Peanut believes that softball has helped her with her concentration and team skills for playing the right side in doubles. Because of her experience, she feels more comfortable playing doubles with Allison Roberts than singles. Her winning doubles strategy is simple. She only takes the shots that she is in position to hit well. Peanut and Allison communicate on every shot as anyone who has watched them play would surely note. Besides their well-rounded skills, Peanut and Allison merely make sure that they don't miss when playing doubles, thus keeping the pressure on the other team.

In the national final this year, Motal and Roberts defeated the two best singles players, Diane Harmon and Rosemary Bellini, in two straight games. Although Bellini and Harmon had defeated Roberts and Motal, respectively, in singles by forcing the play and moving them out of center court, they couldn't do it in their first attempt against the excellent teamwork of Peanut and Allison. Peanut knows that the right side is not the glory position in doubles, but she is more than happy to play her role as long as the team wins. That particular match was a showcase of Peanut's gutsy play and tremendous desire to win.

Peanut lost to Diane Harmon in this year's national semifinals, but got a little revenge with the final doubles win over Harmon and Bellini.

Peanut stated that she didn't see any reason to add a hard ball division to the national tournament. "It would just be the same people and the final scores would be just about the same," she added. She predicted a 50 percent increase in participation of female handballers in the near future. "The only deterrent to a bigger increase is the dedication it takes to become a handball player. I just wish that people would stick to it and play regularly to avoid the hurting hands and frustration that comes with sporadic play," Peanut explained.

Before Peanut resumed her journey to California, she mentioned that she would like to see more Women's tournament results in the magazine. "It would be easier to scout my opponents and know whether I could enjoy myself the night before or lay awake in nervous anticipation." Of course, she would like to see her name in print more often, too. So, we'll try to oblige her if you tournament directors will send in the results.

Lastly, it's time for the scoop on the name of Peanut. "Is it really Peanut?" I asked. "No," she replied, "my real name is Glorian." It seems that when she was in the first grade and just a tiny little tot, her family nicknamed her "Peanut." The name has stuck and she's been called Peanut ever since, even though she's grown into an "enormous" 5-foot, 3-inch, 100-pounder.

Peanut has worked hard to develop her smooth and powerful stroke.

Jackman, John A., PhD.-An Entomologist who came to AgriLife Extension at A&M in 1976, John was also a fly-tying expert but started playing handball late in life. Unfortunately, his handball playing was cut short when he lost his earthly life battle on 28 December 2008.

Johnson, Donald "Johnny" "Don" J. BGen, TXSG (Ret), '55-Following is the talk that I gave to the participants at the fall 2014 Aggieland Classic banquet. Jim Mathis and I were being honored at the Classic on the 60th anniversary of our National Collegiate Handball Doubles Championship:

A Handball Experience

Don "Johnny" Johnson

In 1951, my freshman year at Texas A&M, all new students had to take a physical proficiency test. Being athletic I passed the test easily so was able to choose which required PE (now Kinesiology) course I wanted to take. Wrestling around with other boys growing up was always fun so I choose Wrestling. I became the University (then College) 157-pound weight champion and was on the wrestling team. In the fall semester of my sophomore year during practice I had a blood vessel burst in my ear lobe causing a great deal of swelling. The doctor drew a lot of blood from my ear. The blood that remained became hard and I still have a bump, not large, in my ear. While recuperating I noticed those rectangular, enclosed courts where a game called handball was played. I became interested and took handball in a PE course. My skill in handball progressed rapidly and I soon joined the handball team. I was elected the team captain for my senior year.

One of my classmates that I met on the handball team was Jim Mathis. He and I became the two best on the team. During our senior year he and I played 80 games against each other. If you talk to him, he will tell you that he won one more game than I. I'm not so sure of that. I believe I won one more than he. Obviously, we were very evenly matched. Early in the fall semester of our senior year during one of our matches we were playing late at night when we heard a knock on the door. We looked out the only window in the court. The window was no more than a 12-inch square. It was just large enough for anyone to look inside and be able to determine who and how many might be playing. I do not remember the size of the courts but they were shorter in length than the normal 20'x40' handball court of today. As I recall the courts were essentially the same width as the courts of today. The ceiling was entirely different. It may have been 10 feet in height, maybe slightly higher, but was made up of "chicken wire." The ball could not go up into the ceiling above the wire because the mesh was too small and may have been doubled. I don't remember how far back that plywood extended from the front wall but ceiling shots were not a big part of the game on those courts. The lights hung from the rafters above the wire mesh. The courts had enough light to play but were, essentially, dimly lit. The handball in use at that time was black. The quality was not that of the handball in use today but was still a very good ball. The balls would not last as long (without breaking) and the "bounce" would deteriorate much quicker than the ball of today. NOTE: I passed one of the old black balls around so all could see.

Back to the knock on the door. Jim and I opened the door and looked at the very unimposing figure of a man. He was very slender and his arms and legs were thin. His glasses were very thick. He said his name was Phil Collins and he asked if he could join us. Jim and I looked at each other and I could tell that Jim and I were thinking the same thing. I don't really think this guy would be able to play at our level. However, we knew that no one else was in the other courts so we invited him in to play. We gave him the ball to warm up. He threw it a couple of times with each arm and said he was ready. Our game was "cut throat" with two playing against one and rotating so each of us would have the opportunity to be the server. We told Phil to serve first. His first serve went to me and I didn't even touch the ball. He then served to Jim with the same result. This went on for four or five points until we said, "Time out. Show us what you are doing." If I remember correctly, Phil was the number four ranked handball player in the world. Phil showed us how to put "hop" on the ball. He could make it hop in either direction. Phil came many times after that and continued to mentor and coach Jim and me in the game of handball. One night later in the fall semester, he brought another handball player and Jim and I played doubles against Phil and his partner. Jim and I kept the ball to Phil's partner all of the time and won the game.

Phil was stationed with the United States Air Force at Bryan Air Force Base. He was an enlisted airman and had been on active duty a very short period of time. The playing partner that be brought was also in the Air Force. Bryan Air force Base was closed long ago but I can remember seeing a lot of planes flying to and from the base.

After Phil saw that Jim and I could play doubles well together he told us about the National Intercollegiate Handball Championships to be played in his hometown of Chicago, Illinois. The date of the tournament was after Christmas but before we returned for the end of the fall semester. Back then, the fall semester ended about one to two weeks after the Christmas/New Year's holidays. We basically came back from Christmas for finals. There was one week off before the spring semester would start.

Phil gave us all of the information about the tournament and what to do to enter a team from Texas A&M. Since I was the Captain, it was my responsibility to get a team together. Dave Korry, who was very close to Jim and me in ability, could not go, and neither could Gary Leslie and Charlie Johnson. All were very close to Jim and me with their handball game. Don Grant, a graduate student. and Paul Meiners were available and wanted to go. Both were very adequate players with Don usually winning. Since Jim and I had played so much together and had learned so much from Phil we wanted to be the doubles team. Don would play in the number 1 singles position and Paul the number 2 singles position. At that time four handball players made up a handball team at the collegiate level.

I volunteered to drive my car. We met in Dallas and then drove to Chicago without stopping overnight. We took alternating turns at driving and sleeping. We traveled in my 1950 Plymouth sedan that I bought from my banker in Cranfills Gap for $200. I bought it for my senior year at A&M. Being after Christmas it was very cold. We were lucky that the weather cooperated. We had no rain or snow on the way but did see some snow on the ground after we got into Illinois. The closer we got to Chicago the more snow there was on the ground. All of the snow had been cleared from the road so there was no problem. I cannot recall any difficulty in finding the handball courts or the place where we stayed.

When we saw the handball courts, we were absolutely amazed. They were the normal 20x40 foot and a ceiling of 20'. The courts were also very well lit. We thought the courts were cavernous compared to those at A&M. Coming from our courts we knew nothing about ceiling shots or of using our fists to hit the ball. We had no idea of the quality of the competition we faced. Jim and I adjusted to the courts very quickly although we did not use any ceiling shots in our doubles competition. Jim and I won 6 matches on the way to winning the championship. I do not remember the scores but we never lost a game in any of the matches. I do remember the scores of the last match. The match was against the University of Detroit doubles team and the score of both games was 21-20. Jim and I had become the National Intercollegiate Handball Doubles Champions. As for the team competition, we won 3rd place with a total of 8 points. The second-place team nosed us out by one point. The winning team had a total of 11 points.

After graduating from Texas A&M while at the Basic Air Defense Artillery Course at Fort Bliss, Texas, I saw one of the University of Detroit doubles teammates that Jim and I had played against. We were not in the same class but we happened to meet one day and had a good conversation.

While preparing what to say at the Aggieland Classic dinner I located both Don Grant and Paul Meiners. Don had a great career with General Electric. He is retired and living in Kentucky. He no longer plays handball due to physical limitations (knees) but now enjoys golf. Paul was in the USAF for 30 years and retired with the rank of Colonel. He is now in a retirement home in Colorado. He is in the home due to Parkinson's Disease.

After starting the spring semester in 1955, Phil told Jim and I that we should play in some of the Texas handball tournaments to be held that spring. Our first handball tournament was at the Dallas Athletic Club. As we were on the way to Dallas, Jim and I stopped for a cup of coffee. Jim picked up a newspaper and started reading while we enjoyed our coffee. All of sudden Jim burst out in laughter. I said, "What is going on?" He said that our first match would be against the current World Handball Doubles Champions, Ken Schneider and Sam Haber. Obviously, we were no match for them but I will always remember serving 3 or 4 shots to Haber that were aces. We enjoyed watching Phil and others at the tournament. We suddenly became aware of how good the world's best were. Our second tournament that spring was at the Houston YMCA handball courts. Our first match was against Jimmy Jacobs and his partner. I cannot recall his partner but do remember how good Jimmy was.

Having the opportunity to play against the best in the world was an eye-opening experience and was a great honor for Jim and me. All of this was because we opened the door to a knock late one night at the A&M handball courts and met Phil Collins. From that meeting came some very memorable experiences but maybe the most important lesson of life was to never ever judge an individual just by outward appearance.

I graduated from Texas A&M that spring and was commissioned a Second Lieutenant in the US Army. At the age of 26 I was stationed at Fort Wolters, Texas, home of the Primary Helicopter course. We welcomed a new Commander of the Post who was an Infantry Officer named Jack Norris. Within a month he had all of us doing physical exercises at 6am. After approximately a month I felt so much better that I made a commitment to myself that I would never be in that poor physical condition again during my lifetime. To this day, at the age of 80, I have kept that commitment. It is my strong recommendation that each of you commit the same for yourself. You will enjoy a better quality of life and will be more successful in whatever endeavor you choose. A big part of maintaining a reasonably good physical condition has been playing handball. Handball is a sport that can be enjoyed for years and years and is the "perfect" game for keeping the overall body in excellent physical condition.

I opened the talk to questions and there were some very good questions. I ended by thanking Jeff Wall, Southwest Region Handball Commissioner, Ozzie Burke, coach of the Texas A&M University handball team and the Texas A&M handball team members for recognizing Jim and me on this very special occasion.

Johnson, John Drake "Johnny"-Yes, Johnny and the author have enjoyed (my opinion) many games on the handball court. Following is his story:

I grew up in Bryan, Texas the epicenter and pinnacle of both national and international handball play. Just kidding. The mention of handball elicited nothing save blank stares and cricket chirps down dusty hallways of the local gyms. No one knew what a handball court was. If the person knew a bit of the game, it's almost guaranteed they'd refer to it as "that game they play in prison" and always framed it as a question, as they're still not entirely sure. Sorry, do you have any courts they play racquetball in…

With no external avenues, my exposure to the sport was ultimately sown thirty years prior to my birth-a matter of fate I suppose. My dad started playing in college, with him and his doubles partner, Jim Mathis, winning the 1954 Intercollegiate National Doubles Championship. Handball resonated with my dad far beyond the pass line of higher education, through the years, and eventually served to his youngest son.

My formal introduction came watching my dad compete annually at the Mathis Handball Invitational held in Waco, Texas-as you might've guessed, it was Jim Mathis' gig. As a young boy, I'd sit in the gallery overlooking the courts and watch the matches with as much curiosity as a kid could muster at that age. It's only fitting the first time I stepped on the court was in preparation to play in the Mathis Invitational. Even though the name suggested exclusivity, it was a welcoming and supportive event open to anyone foolish enough to undertake a one-day tournament where you could play six matches in an 8-hour period. Whew! The tournament wasn't marketed and didn't have an open registration, so labor came from a group of regulars and their friends. The regulars were a motley bunch, robust with diverse characters.

There were people like Jim High, who was a white guy with an Afro and wore knee pads (he needed them for all of the time he spent scooting across the floor to make a shot) and garden gloves, and elite players like stoic Don Cunningham and Ken Delaney who'd yell out "AW, KEN" every time he missed a shot. After a few years, I was inducted into the inner circle, and the whole troop was bookended by Jim Mathis and my dad.

The divisions were named after extinct or endangered species. Ever the tacticians, the old guard created the Geezers division as a perfect strategy to out-flank the cardio-circus of younger men. The Bison were strong, seasoned players in their prime destined for greatness while stampeding towards the frontier's indelible twilight. The T-Rex and Dinos were the amateur divisions, extinct but still discussed, and the beginners were aptly labeled Unicorns since they never existed. After play was over, everyone and their families would meet at a local restaurant for good food, great friends, and the typical shenanigans. The whole spectacle was a fitting tribute to the eccentric, waning community of Texas handball.

What a grand show it was. The matches were epic, full of top ten plays and hall of fame performances. Every year, a regular would invite the hottest new players, hoping to dethrone the Bison kings, only to watch helplessly as Cunningham and Delaney sent them home crying to their mommas. The division championship matches always went overtime and were won by small margins. I even shared in the action becoming the only player to win all non-Geezer divisions. Of course, the largest crowds would gather when Jim and Dad would play. Their matchup seemed to perfectly illustrate the essence of the game in that this sport is not made by the simple act of competition but in the camaraderie and character of those who compete.

Johnny played many games of handball at the A&M Recreation Center and was a member of the handball club. Currently, he is living in an area without local handball courts so his physical activity is through his mountain bike and physically demanding distance racing.

Jones, Kayla D., '09-Kayla has always loved participating in athletics and, as a result, majored in Kinesiology to earn her bachelor's degree, then went into Sports Management to earn her master's. She provided the following for inclusion in the book:

I started playing handball in the spring of my freshman year. I chose handball for several reasons. There were not a lot of options left for KINE classes, but both handball and racquetball were available. I already knew how to play racquetball and wanted to learn something new. I was told by several people that I would be the only girl in the class and that if I did not win games in the tournament, that I would fail the class. I decided to take the risk, because 1-hour Q drops did not count against you. I did end up being the only girl in my section, but quickly realized that I would not fail the class because of this.

One of my memorable handball stories was my first collegiate tournament in Los Angeles. Charlie Bokelman was already in town (I think for a conference) and had a rental car. Charlie, Ozzie, Ashley Gregg and myself snuck away from the hotel to go site-seeing. Charlie did not have just any car; he had rented a Mustang convertible! We drove all over the city that day, ate lunch on the Santa Monica Pier and then walked up and down boardwalk at Venice Beach.

Another story from the summer of 2010, when the USHA hosted a collegiate 1-wall tournament in Queens. Krystin Deason, Melissa Roberson (Longhorn) and I decided to go play in this tournament. We were supposed to fly from Houston to Atlanta to New York. Our flight out of Houston was delayed due to bad weather. This happened at the last second, so Krystin was already on the plane and was not allowed off and Melissa and I were still in the terminal. We finally made it to Atlanta, but our flight to NY took off as we were landing. After sprinting through the airport in a desperate attempt to catch the flight, we were stuck trying to figure out how to get to New York. The next flight on our airline was not until the next afternoon which would have caused us to miss the tournament. The airline suggested flying us to Philadelphia where we could rent a car and drive to New York. There were other people in the same situation as us and we were trying to go in on a car with this lady and her daughter. The plan was not going to work for them, but worked for another man standing there who I had incorrectly assumed was with her. Manuel, affectionately known as the Colombian Cowboy, agreed to rent a car with us. Obviously, our parents were not thrilled with the thought of us driving across the Northeast in the middle of the night with a stranger, but we figured 2 things: 1. We were in an airport, so he did not have weapons and 2. that it was 3 athletic girls against a small man. We could take him! I did tell him that I had to drive or I would get car sick so that we were always in control of the vehicle. We landed in Philadelphia at 1:00am where Manuel went into the bathroom and changed into a Texas state flag pearl snap shirt. We rented a car and started driving through the night. We made it to NYC around 6:00 the following morning, dropped Manuel off at LaGuardia and then proceeded to our hotel. The hotel was nice enough to give us a room to crash in for a few hours before we had to be at the courts. After a short nap, we spent the rest of the day attempting to play 1-wall. We definitely did not win. I think half of my shots sailed over the wall, but it was quite an experience and a great memory.

Handball has given me the opportunity to continue to compete and be an athlete in adulthood. I won the Collegiate A division at Nationals in 2010 and 2nd place in the A division of the USHA National Championships in 2015. I was the Texas State Champion in 2016 and 2017. While continuing to compete, I am also trying to introduce a new generation to the game through the classes offered at A&M.

When Coach Ozzie Burke lost the services of Joel Rice and Sally Kenworthy as co-presidents of the A&M handball club in the fall of 2009, Kayla Jones stepped forward, as did Dustin Van Brunt, to accept co-chairmanship of the club. Jones's work started immediately as the new Aggie executive team had a lot of work to do to prepare for the 2010 National Collegiate Handball Tournament, which was to be hosted by Texas A&M. Through Herculean efforts on their parts, the tournament was highly successful even though it was held in the Houston YMCA, which was 90-100 miles from Texas A&M University.

Jones received her degree, then moved to Houston where she taught and coached at Westbury Christian High School. Her coaching duties included varsity softball, JV basketball and middle school volleyball. While there she continued playing handball downtown with the Houston club. She was in Houston for four-and-a-half years before returning to A&M. In 2016, she accepted the responsibility as faculty advisor to the A&M handball club. This was a key decision on her part as it helped the club interface with vital parts of the operational aspect between the handball club/team and the university.

Since none of the handball team coaches are full time A&M employees, Jones plays a vital role in the success of the handball team.

She has been rehabilitating injuries that required surgery and plans to start playing again on a regular basis.

Kennerly, Kenneth D. "Dan," '68-Dan became an excellent handball player through a lot of hard work and persistent play. Not all handball players have the opportunity to step on the court and compete with some of the nation's best. He relished the opportunity and benefited greatly from the experience. Competing with the best handball players results in lifetime memories that are carried in a part of the memory bank that can easily be recalled when the perfect occasion presents itself. Kennerly's memory bank opened up when asked to recall some of his handball stories, which follow:

Thanks for your interest in handball during my attendance at A&M from 1964 to 1968. I believe that you are the first person to ask me about it. I don't know whether I can add anything that my old doubles partner Ozzie Burke hasn't related, but I write whatever I can recall. Meanwhile, I wonder about your experience with handball. Whether you got to see or play any of the greats of that time. I remember only two names from the pre-'60s era, Joe Platak and Vic Hershkowitz, who Jimmy Jacobs beat in a filmed match around 1960. There also was a filmed match between Jacobs and Paul Haber several years later. I believe Jacobs was ahead when Haber separated a shoulder against a wall and had to retire. Early '70s I played against Jacobs and Marty Decatur in the finals of a doubles match in New Orleans, and we were satisfied to score 6 and 11. I had a lefty partner and played right side, not really well.

There was no organization whatever among the better players I knew at A&M, and with one small exception (later), there was no interest from the university. It never occurred to me that it could be of any help. There was a PE handball coach whose name I don't recall, but the PE class was irrelevant to us better players. I never saw him but at his PE classes, which was an elective course, taken by me mostly for the easy A. He was an older man, maybe 55, short, not spry and I doubt he played the game then, or maybe ever. He gave no instruction aside from rules. I never met or heard of an Intramural Director, but I did play intramural handball one year, which I hardly remember at all, the matches not being competitive.

I recall only the names of Ozzie and one other serious player, Hector Diaz. He was a good player, the best there in 1964, but I believe Ozzie and I both overtook him by my junior year. I'm not sure why Ozzie and I started playing doubles, but we did well together and probably had a better chance of snagging a trophy than in open singles. Before and after graduating I played in tournaments in Austin, Dallas, Houston, Odessa, Victoria and New Orleans, but I recall mostly playing singles but sometime probably played doubles with Ozzie. He was always on the right side. I don't believe we played together after I graduated. I'm right-handed but Ozzie's right was better and my left was harmless but somewhat reliable defensively. Right side is harder to play. Left side plays most of the balls. I now recall another fair Aggie player whose last name may have been Fine. He was two or three years ahead of me. Hector Diaz played singles in one tournament in Houston but no other that I remember. I don't believe Hector was in the Corps. Fine was.

I would be remiss if I didn't tell you about Ozzie's kill shot, which he did with either hand. It rolled out flat, no bounce whatever. I only saw one other player ever who could do it several times in a game. He was Bill McGreevy out of St. Louis. One referee had never seen Ozzie's rollout kill shot and called all of them skips. Early round, so it didn't much matter. We didn't argue after pointing out the error. Ozzie played most of our back-wall setups coming down the middle with his left.

We did get some invaluable coaching from Pete Tyson. He was the handball coach at UT Austin. He and Bob Lindsay won the National Open doubles championship mid '60s. We benefitted from his experience and generous advice every time we saw him at tournaments, and he drove down to College Station once or twice to give a handball clinic at Ozzie's request. He knew strategy and tactics I had never thought of.

We decided to try our luck in the collegiate division of the nationals in St. Louis in 1968, so four of us piled into Ozzie's car and took off. Ozzie allowed that the university had given him $50 for gas. I can't recall the names of the other two players. One had an Irish last name beginning, I think, with B-maybe Bradley. I believe that they flipped a coin and the loser played Open division, the winner Class B. There was a better chance of a trophy in Class B. It's a two-day drive and one of us knew someone who had a vacant cabin somewhere in Missouri, so we stopped there on the way up. It was so Spartan and disordered, and no bed that I recall, that the four of us slept in the car. It was freezing, and we had to open windows for oxygen. One of us (Bradley?) knew Bill Bradley's parents in Crystal City, Missouri, and we stopped and met them and saw his full trophy room, framed cover of Sports Illustrated with his picture on it and all. On the way back, I think, they gave the four of us a ride in their Rolls Royce that I imagined Bill had given to them.

I remember playing only the finals' match in St. Louis against Pete Tyson's UT doubles pair. Pete confided to Ozzie and me that he wasn't sorry that we won. Maybe we paid him more attention than his own players. Maybe that's why we beat them. The previous matches must not have been too difficult.

I recall seeing Stuffy Singer beat Ray Neveau there in the Open Singles finals. I got to play Stuffy a game in the middle `70s in Virginia-lost. He said he had received flak about his choice of shot that finished the match, a fly shot rollout from about 27 feet out. I remembered it exactly and agreed that any player who can hit a fly kill should use it with an opponent in back-a no-brainer. You can see that match on YouTube. Singer was national junior table tennis champion, Los Angeles tennis champion having not played tennis until two weeks before the tournament, all-league quarterback in high school (maybe La Jolla) at 135 pounds and played semi-pro baseball. I learned that from reading. He never mentioned any of it.

Aside from Jacobs, Decatur, Singer and Lindsay, I have also played Freddie Lewis, Dave Graybill, Dr. Claude Benham, Dr. Steve August and John Sabo. Never won a game except for eliminating Sabo in a tournament and taking one game off Benham at a major tournament at his own club in Norfolk. They said it was the first game he had lost in six years, but he was about 40 years old when we played. You may also know the name of Roger Berry, who won several Masters trophies. We played in Arlington, Virginia when he was starting out early '70s. We drove over together to Penn State about 1974 and he won Class B and I the Open division. The Nittany Lion statue trophy is the only one I have kept and it sits now on the desk of a Penn State professor, who is our daughter. Berry played ice hockey at Maryland and afterwards. I never once saw him breathe hard during a match although he won mostly by dogged pursuit of the ball at that time. I wonder whether you may have met Benham. He was a physician at Fort Campbell and a jumping medic with the 101st Airborne Division.

You asked about a possible team competition at a Houston Southwest tournament. I never knew of any collegiate division or team competition anywhere except at the nationals. Ozzie and I may have played Open Doubles at one of those Houston tournaments at their YMCA. I can't recall. I do recall that my first match in my first tournament was played there about 1965. It was singles against Bob Lindsay. He was the number 1 seed and I was last. I don't think Ozzie entered. I mostly remember stuffing my tongue back into my mouth and sweating profusely in the court at 64 degrees, where they had to keep the temperature so the walls didn't get wet and the ball skid off. I scored 11 points total and was generously told I did well. I won my share of regional tournaments after relocating to the Mid-Atlantic area in 1971, but I don't recall winning any in Texas. Maybe I won one in Victoria. After two or three moves, I chucked my trophies but the one. The heads and arms kept coming off and they were always in the attic, anyway. I don't remember the collegiate trophy, if there was one. There was never really any handball team at A&M or sponsor that I knew of.

If you played at DeWare Field House, then you will remember that the courts were murder, no air-conditioning with temperature and humidity around 85-95 most of the time.

If you were stationed in Europe in the very early '70s and at the American European military handball championships in Bitburg, then we may have met. There was a Signal Corps Major stationed in Frankfurt who played there and at military tournaments, Art Wilshire, born about 1943, tall and dark. The fellow I beat in the finals at Bitburg was a short red-headed sergeant stationed there, I believe.

Following back surgery in 1980 I had to switch to racquetball and became a good club player but not good enough to compete in regional tournaments.

This is way more than you want to know, but it is always fun recounting handball stories.

Best wishes to you and yours this Christmas and to Ozzie.

Kojin, Priscilla (SEE: Shumate)

Kozik, Thomas J. "Tom," PhD-Tom was born in 1930 in Jersey City, New Jersey. Somewhere along the way he learned about the game of handball. It was likely before he was hired by Texas A&M in 1963 to the faculty of Mechanical Engineering. When the author played him in the '70s he was already an accomplished player. At 6' 6"-he seemed that tall, or maybe more, to the author-he could cover the court side to side with ease. Kozik was always there for anyone who asked for advice and many give him credit for providing them with sage advice on the game of handball.

Lowe, Robert F. "Bob," DVM, '61-Bob started playing handball at the YMCA in Waco while attending Waco High. Naturally, after matriculating to A&M he chose handball as one of his required PE courses and remembers that Spike White was his teacher. After serving four years in the Army, three of which were served in Germany, he settled into his lifelong calling of veterinary practice, eventually retiring in Green Mountain, Colorado. He continued playing handball until 2017 when back problems forced him to stop. He played at the handball courts in Colorado Springs and at that time there were five to six players over 80 years old that would meet every Tuesday and Thursday for doubles competition. After handball they would stop by at one of their favorite spots for beer.

He recalls that previously there was a woman who had been on the A&M handball team and at that time played with them in Colorado Springs. He could not remember her name; however, no one there could come close to beating her. It is possible the woman might have been Priscilla (Kojin) Shumate.

Every Christmas, the handball group meet at Jerry White's home for a get together of handball nostalgia, camaraderie and just good fellowship. Jerry White is a well-known handball enthusiast and retired USAF Major General.

Lowy, Gabe W. "Dutch," '05-Dutch Lowy was born into a handball playing family so started playing at a young age. Dutch tells the following story:

> Hi Don;
>
> I thought I would start out by just talking about how Texas A&M Handball impacted me and my life. In case it's not obvious, the three of us (Zach, Marshall and myself) have been around the sport for a long time. I have vivid memories of chasing a ball around the courts in the old READ building. We spent many hours in that dungeon roaming the halls and playing all sorts of games.
>
> Through the years playing handball taught me many lessons and most of them off the court. We played against the team members during their practice times MWF between 5-7 but we had to call and set up games with them to make sure we had someone to play. We worked off the team phone list and would have to call these college kids and leave messages or ask them if they wanted to play at a certain day/time. In hindsight it was a big responsibility and I learned a lot about how to manage time, communicate effectively and create long term relationships. Surely now a days they just text each other.
>
> Aggieland Classics were major events with entries over 300 most years. Coach (dad) would spend hours creating systems and double checking them to make sure everyone got their fair share of playing time. He accommodated the guys that wanted to play singles and doubles by adjusting schedules on the fly. I remember when he handed that off to me one year and how overwhelming it was. He showed me how important it was to create an environment where people had fun and got to play as much as they wanted. Now when I run events, I remember how those experiences affected people and try to make our events equal.

The transition out of the READ building and into the new REC Center was a massive undertaking and very cool to watch come together. Coach was heavily involved in the development and layout of the courts. It seems like they are almost a focal point at the rec and I don't think that was by accident. They very easily could have stashed them on the third floor. Coaches' involvement and time spent at the rec was massive. We spent a lot of time there and I remember that he knew everyone by name. Even the kids working the front desk. Again, another lesson in how to communicate with people and create relationships.

I played consistently through middle school and high school with some fair results at national events but my main focus was soccer.

My college years at A&M were fragmented. I started college in North Carolina at ECU playing soccer but after two years I returned to College Station and started paying handball again. I played for a year, then moved to San Marcos for a year. When I returned, I picked up handball more seriously in conjunction with starting a business and finishing school. I played 2-3 times a week and we had a great crew to play with. I gotta be honest, I don't have the recollection of national meets quite as strongly as I do the daily grind. Playing at practice and of course taking class. I couldn't tell you who I played at nationals, or where I placed, or even where each of them was like Coach can. I think I enjoyed the process as much as the competition and it was always fun to play then hang out in the lobby with teammates.

Dutch

A future star in the making. At 11 Dutch won the 1993 USHA National Junior title for 11-and-under. In his four matches, his opponents only could muster a total combined score of 20 points. At age 11, he began playing, when possible, with members of the Aggie handball team. Playing with college players helped him develop a highly skilled game well before reaching college age.

A further testament to Dutch's athletic ability is that he did make the soccer team at East Carolina University and then after graduating with a bachelor's degree in Health from Texas A&M moved to Crossfit. At Crossfit, he was one of 250 entrants for the world-wide games. He finished seventh in those games. He moved from Crossfit games to Olympic Weightlifting where his last finish was third in his weight class in the 2015 national tournament.

(*Handball*, February, 1994, page 16)

Lowy, Lance K.,'78-To thousands of Aggie handball players, he will always be known as "Coach."

He has left his mark on handball in many ways, but most of all his drop-down format that insured fair play at each individual's level and also guaranteed a minimum number of games to be played at each handball tournament. Lowy developed that format, which is still being used today and there is no reason for change in the foreseeable future. Pages could be written, but the author will defer to him for the following stories:

When I started at TAMU in the fall of '77 as a graduate assistant, I had 6 classes, all handball, with 44 people per class. I recognized that we had some talent and needed to develop it. By the end of the semester, I thought we needed a way to compete to determine who were our best players. So, I started the Aggieland Classic handball tournament to do that and to make some money for travel in case we had players who wanted to attend the National Collegiate Tournament. It turns out that we did and it was apparent that we should grow our program and our tournament so we didn't have to rely on someone else to fund our travel and get better skill wise to compete with the best schools in the country.

Once we determined that we were going to go for it, certain changes to the National Collegiate rules were necessary. Since its inception in 1953, a collegiate handball team consisted of 1 A player, 1 B player and a doubles team, all males. I had some good women so I began pushing for a women's division which passed and was installed in 1980. Another change was to make teams bigger and add a C division for players just starting out to appeal to more schools to compete. In 1983, a C division was added and teams consisted of 6 people with 1 or more women in that 6. In 1986, we added a B and C division for women and in 1987 we switched to a men's team of 6 and a women's team of 6 to form a combined team championship of 12 players. In 1987, we started the system or format where you didn't enter a division but rather played into a division by whether you won or lost. Points were awarded according to what division and in what round that you finished. For instance, the higher division you finished, the more points you earned for your team. Further, finalists earned more than semi-finalists within a division, etc. I developed this format that guaranteed every player a minimum of 3 matches and is generally referred to as the drop-down format. Participation in the National Collegiate Tournament went from dozens of players to hundreds of players and this format is used to this day. We moved to a 5 division drop down in 1992 and have expanded to 7 and 9 divisions as the tournament grew.

If you look thru past national champions, you will notice that the Irish schools are well represented. They began coming over for the National Collegiates in 1997 when we hosted our first time at TAMU in the Recreation Center. We hosted two more in 2002 and 2006. The best players from Ireland were some of the best in the world and they sent large teams because they liked the format. I went to Ireland many times and helped install this format for the Irish National Collegiates that are called Intervarsities and it is used in Ireland to this day.

TAMU won 13 national championships during my tenure from 1978 thru 2007. The gold standard was to make the top 16 or better in the National Tournament which meant you were in the top 16 players in the entire tournament. For men, it was more difficult as other teams recruited the top junior players in the country and 99% of our players started playing handball at TAMU. For women, 99% of all women playing in college started playing in college. It was quite a special accomplishment for our men and women.

Lance Lowy could tell handball stories for hours but the following are special memories:

1) In 1988, in Chicago, our best player Todd Bryan was playing a very accomplished player from the University of Illinois in the Open/A round. Todd lost the first game and was losing the

second game handily. I thought, being somewhat superstitious, that if I quit watching maybe he'd do better. So, I started watching other matches and saw Todd about half an hour later. He asked if I knew when he played again and I said that depends on whether you won or lost. With a straight face, he said, "Oh, I won. I came back and won the second game and the tiebreaker." Todd had just become the first Aggie man to win his way into the top 16 of the Open division during my time as coach.

2) In 1994, in Portland, Oregon, Sal SantaAna was playing Tyler Hamel of Southwest Missouri State in the men's Open semifinals. Tyler had just finished playing a tough doubles match so our strategy was to move him around and try to tire him out. Sal was a master at this and worked our game plan to perfection. Early in the second game after Sal had won the first game, Tyler called timeout, went outside the court and sat down. The ref told him his time was up and he called another timeout. Same thing happened after another minute. This was the only time I have ever seen someone call 3 timeouts in a row. Sal won and became the first Aggie man to ever make the finals in men's Open singles.

3) In 1999, in Chicago, Morris Libson had a disappointing National tournament finishing in the middle of the pack in the C division. Morris worked extremely hard all year prior to our next one. In 2000, in Springfield, Missouri, Morris narrowly lost in a tiebreaker in the Open/A round. Not to be deterred, he ended up in the finals of the A division. Kevin Price, a fine player from Arizona, beat Morris in the first game before Morris caught fire and won the second game. The tiebreaker was close until Morris made a run. Price turned to the ref and asked for a timeout but the ref informed him that he didn't have any timeouts left. The look on his face told the story. He knew he was about to get run over by a train named Morris Libson. Morris completed his national tournament with a win in the A division and made the biggest improvement from one year to the next of any Aggie man ever during my time as coach. He made the top 16 in the Open division his final year in 2001 in Minneapolis to cap a stellar college career.

4) In 2001, in Minneapolis, Brad Alesi was playing one of the top Irish players, Dessie Keegan, in the men's Open semifinals. Brad was not his usual self and took a timeout. He said in losing the first game, he could barely swing his right arm. We went to a plan to lob underhand serves to Dessie's left and shoot the return with Brad's left hand. It is a risky strategy to go to the 3 shot drill of serve, return, the pass or kill but we had no choice and Brad's left was as good as his right. It worked. Brad executed like a champ and he was in the finals the next day. He didn't win that one and when we got home and had his right arm examined, it was a torn right bicep tendon that required surgery. A total gutsy performance. He came back the next year and made the finals in Open again leading his men's team to our first men's National Championship.

5) In 2007, in Los Angeles, Kelly Arunski was in the Open/A round and had lost the first game badly and was getting beat 18-0 in the second game. Kelly suddenly decided that she was not going to lose. She started executing and playing flawlessly. She came back and won the second game and tiebreaker in the best comeback I have ever seen. She played her way into the top 8 in the Open division.

6) Jason Green was a freshman playing in his first Aggieland Classic. He was in the 128 player C division so he had to win 6 matches over a day and a half period to make it to the finals on Sunday. He reported in Sunday and went to the court where he thought he was supposed to play. His opponent was there so they played and an hour later he came up and told me he lost

in a tiebreaker. We took a look at the draw sheets and determined that he played the B finalist in the wrong court. He got straightened out and played his C finalist opponent, beat him and that was the beginning of a productive 4-year career on the TAMU handball team.

Lance Lowy served on the Collegiate Commissioners Board for many years and during 1983-85, chaired the Board. The Board ensures that the National Collegiate Handball Tournament is always within the established rules that govern the tournament and makes suggestions and decisions for the betterment of the tournament and the game of handball.

Even though Lowy's dad, Stan, had played handball most of his life and moved often, growing up Lowy enjoyed baseball and played that very well-four-year letterman, two years All-District at A&M Consolidated High School. He did not start playing handball until 1970 during his undergraduate years at the University of Texas. In handball, he played many tournaments at the Open level; however, his enduring legacy will always be as a teacher and coach of handball at Texas A&M. Lowy played handball for 30 years and was forced to stop due to a ruptured disc in his back.

In addition to teaching and coaching, Lowy took the time to write a book on handball-*The Handball Handbook: Strategies and Techniques*. He has also had a Second Edition published. Though Lowy is no longer playing or coaching, he monitors all of the pro tournaments and the collegiates. Handball has been his life and will continue to be so; however, he still must make time for his kids and grandkids.

Lowy, Stanley H. "Stan"-Stan Lowy was born in New York City and grew up playing one-wall handball in the Bronx and continued playing until he was over 80 years of age. When he turned 80, he told his playing partners that he now gets two bounces.

Stan Lowy was not large, perhaps 5' 7" or at approximately that height, was not slender, and had no excess weight to carry around. Over the years, he had developed a formidable game. Lowy's speed and agility to be in position to contact the opponent's return of serve or volley gave him the ability to gain control of the court. This compelled the opponent to scramble to make returns followed by his placing the next ball into a tougher part of the court for the opponent to reach. Experienced opponents knew a weak return that bounced in the front court would likely end the volley since Lowy would hit a kill shot that normally was unreturnable. He was a master of putting the correct hop on the ball to create difficulty for an opponent's return.

With a bachelor's degree from Purdue and a master's of science from the University of Minnesota, he made a few moves before coming to Texas A&M in 1964. Soon after his arrival, he searched out and found those who usually ended up on the handball court more than once per week. Not only did he possess a formidable game, he was also a great teacher. Many credited Stan Lowy with great improvement of their own game from his teachings. He also became very active in the handball club and some say he revived it. There can be no question that the club began to grow and become more active after his arrival.

Stan Lowy also made his mark with the Aerospace Engineering Department as he rose to Department Head and then to Associate Dean of Engineering. Handball player, professor and a father to Lance, there can be no question as to the great impact Stan had on the handball program at Texas A&M.

MacManus, Gerald R. "Jerry," '49-The following story was received from Jerry:

> Johnny!
>
> Good to hear from you, especially about handball. My roommate did well in the game and he carried the team. We played intramurals only-no coach. We were instructed on rules and got with it. I don't remember much about who played, but I was in A Inf in the Corps and we kept the flag a long time. Leslie Layne and Jewell (McDowell) were

hard to beat. I took handball for PE but don't remember the professor. I also wrestled Heavyweight. My roommate and I were both on the Rodeo Team-Bull Riding and Mule Riding.

I did not touch a ball till I was 50 years old and switched to racquetball. I quit when I was 68 years old. I am now 90 and do good to keep from falling.

Marchbanks, Miner P. "Pete," Jr., D CPSC '69-Pete started his handball playing at A&M and continued until the current pandemic closed down the handball courts in March 2020. Pete and the author had many games together during the lunch hour. He thoroughly enjoys the game and will continue playing when the courts open again for play.

Martin, Frederick B. "Rusty," LTC, USA (Ret) '75-The following letter was received from Rusty:

Dear Don;

I am Frederick Martin, '75 Texas A&M. I am responding to your letter of inquiry to me dated 30 April of this year. Yes, I am the Rusty Martin you seek. Indeed, I was very active in many intramural sports while at A&M, not the least of which was handball (and later racquetball). I enjoyed them immensely and continued racquetball for many years thereafter.

As I recall, over the four years at A&M, I gradually gravitated towards racquetball as my more preferred sport as opposed to handball for a couple of reasons. First of all, handball was taking a toll on my hands which I needed to be injury free due to my major-Architecture. It's difficult to draw, draft and build architectural models with sore and swollen hands and my seasonal participation in the sport hindered the toughening process. Second, it seemed to me that the interest in racquetball was growing and that handball was being left behind a bit. That was merely my impression at the time and was probably inaccurate. I enjoyed both and kept up both sports until I graduated. I played racquetball without interruption in the Army, but when I retired, I stopped-mainly due to lack of courts. To me the best thing about handball and racquetball was the irrelevance of the weather. Much of my Army time was in Germany and with racquetball, I could always get a great workout in all year. The camaraderie aspect goes without saying.

Good luck with your project and I do indeed remember you. Thanks for what you did for us in the Corps.

Mathis, James R. "Jim," CLU '55-Jim is a multi-talented athlete. If the author's memory is correct, he won intramural championships in badminton, golf, ping pong, tennis and handball. He probably would have won at horseshoes if he had ever tried the game. He definitely was the one person the author wanted on the right side of a doubles match when he and I played against others. Mathis' right would roll out ball after ball. The author's left was a little better than his.

It was with regret that he could not make the 60th anniversary of his and the author's collegiate doubles championship which was recognized at an Aggieland Classic handball tournament. Following are the remarks he had planned to make that evening but unfortunately was unable to attend:

At A&M we played in a barn like structure where the north part of Kyle Field is now. There was a hallway down the middle between the courts. The two courts on the right side were about 16x36, with chicken wire ceilings. The two on the left were about 14x34. We once played a doubles match on the left court against Baylor football players Wayne and Bill Luck. We could hardly see the front wall, so just hit everything as hard as possible. Their legs had lots of red spots. We won the match.

I remember Phil Collins who was stationed at Bryan Air Force Base. He was a nationally ranked player for many years from Chicago. We were playing one night and he knocked on the door and asked to play. I thought about asking him if he was any good and am thankful I did not ask. He gave us lessons from then on. Don and I played many games with him-singles against doubles-and we never got into double figures against him. He invited us to Chicago to the Town Club for the National Collegiate. If not for Phil Collins, we would never have known about the tournament. And, of course, never become national doubles handball champions.

I remember the tournament was over the Christmas Holidays. Then we had fall semester finals when we returned from Christmas and New Year's break. To make the trip I rode the train from San Antonio to Dallas. From there we traveled in Johnson's car. There were four of us. We nearly froze until we got inside the Town Club for the next 3 or 4 days. We beat every team there in round robin. The finals were against the University of Detroit team. We beat them 21-20, 21-20. I saved Johnson once or twice. He saved me 10 times.

Don and I played 81 matches by my count against each other. I won 41, he won 40. When he and I discussed this recently, he said he remembered he had 41. He may want to comment on this.

Thanks for remembering us.

Mathis was commissioned into the Air Force where he was a pilot and stationed at Connally Air Force Base, Waco, Texas. He finished his military commitment there and never moved from the Waco area. He continued to play handball, became mayor of Waco and started an invitational handball tournament. Being an invitational tournament, he and his handball friends decided they would also hold a golf tournament on Friday before the handball tournament on Saturday. Those who wanted to play in the golf tournament, each had to make a commitment to play in the handball tournament on Saturday. The author remembers partnering with Mathis on more than one occasion, but also remembers partnering in the golf tournament with an excellent golfer (whose name can't be recalled), but who played handball the first time on a Saturday in the tournament. He would play handball once each year just to be able to compete in the golf tournament. Unfortunately, he met with an untimely death before the next year's golf and handball tournaments.

The Mathis Invitational Handball Tournament became an event all anxiously anticipated each year. Each year there were some great contests and new faces of those who had just started to play. Players came primarily from Texas, but an occasional player from out of state would enter the tournament. He put on the tournament for 25 years and then said *I have done enough* and stepped down from the directorship. The tournament continued for a couple of years, but without the leadership of Mathis, faded out of existence.

Matson, James R. "Randy," '67-It is not often a handball player can step onto the court and play handball with an Olympic Champion. During the mid-'60s, it was an often occurrence during the fall semesters. Randy gained his worldwide sports fame primarily by holding the world record in the shot put. He was also a champion discus thrower and played basketball on the A&M team.

Matson started playing handball at the encouragement of his strength coach. It would be a break from his continual weight training and also might be of help athletically in his overall physical prowess.

Matson claims he never excelled at handball but it was a lot of fun and was a great diversion from his training regimen. According to Randy House, a classmate, Matson had a long reach and it was very hard to get anything past him. He did not continue playing handball after his college days.

McKean, Sherman M. "Mike," '70-Follwing is the letter I received from Mike:

Howdy General: Your recent letter arrived while we were out on a last of the year vacation to the Texas Hill Country. Lots of water under the bridge since 1970. We played handball at DeWare field house. I usually played at least twice a day-7am and 4 pm. I was a non-Reg and the Head RA at Keithley Hall. I think Les Palmer was the Director of Intramurals and I think he may have been the faculty sponsor of the club. I do not recall any tournament at Houston. I played HB regularly from 1969-1971-I squeezed 4 years into 5-and graduated May 1971 and in 71-72 I started my Masters for a year…ran out of money then went to work. I moved to Amarillo to work with Mobil Oil and continued to play with my A&M roommate at the Amarillo YMCA where there were only a couple of courts.

Remembrance: While at A&M, I was the #2 singles player and a member of the #1 doubles team. During the afternoons and weekends, we would hang out at DeWare to pick up games. Being the top players during those years, we were dressed out in the finest Adidas shoes, Champion gloves, and all the rest. We accepted a challenge game from a couple of professors who looked rag-tag..dressed in faded swim suits, black tennis shoes with brown laces, holey t-shirts, one blue sock and one red one … all I can say. My partner and I sure looked good while those rag-tags pounded us 3 games to 2. Needless to say, never judge a book by the cover.

I did not take handball as a PE class. I took badminton (loved it), tennis and golf.

I quit playing in 1974 when I began my career with FAA as air traffic controller, married and our first child. My responsibilities had changed. I worked 36 years as an air traffic controller, operations supervisor, operations manager and then facility manager … 29 of those years were at DFW.

I retired in 2010, had a small ranch, sold it to live in a subdivision and RV travel. I married one of the first female Aggies (from Bryan). Sue is class of '71. Our son was on the football team and class of '98 and our daughter was class of 2000. She served on the Women's Former Students Board of Directors for 3 years.

Mike McKean '70

Motal, Peanut (SEE: Hummel)

Mulkerrins, Martin-Martin chose Texas A&M for his study abroad program as part of earning his bachelor's degree in Animal and Crop Production from University College Dublin, Belfield, Dublin, Ireland. He continued his education to earn his master's in Agricultural Innovation Support. His study abroad at A&M was during the 2013 fall semester. While here he made extensive use of the handball courts at the Rec Center. Most of the regulars knew who he was and his skill level before his first day on campus. He was the current reigning National Collegiate Singles Handball Champion. One day when the courts were basically empty, the author saw Mulkerrins practicing by himself. I knocked on the door and went in to say Hello. After conversation he asked if I would retrieve his serves while he practiced. No problem. He would serve and I would catch the ball and give back to him. A win-win situation for the two of us. He didn't have to chase the balls down and I had the opportunity to see all of his power serves.

I knew then that I wanted to have my usual playing partner, Marvin Harris, get on the court with Mulkerrins so it was set. Harris and I would play Mulkerrins in a game to 21 with the two of us against one. After the game, Harris and I thanked him for the opportunity and we were happy that we were able to score four points especially since earlier Charlie Bokelman and his partner (can't remember if it was Jack Gressett or Ozzie Burke) had ended up on a short end of a 21-3 score against him. All of our Aggie team and local players benefitted greatly from his semester at A&M.

Mulkerrins continued to improve his game and is currently ranked number two in the world. He provided the following for inclusion in the book:

Handball Championships/Role of Honour

I started playing handball in 2004 and have won numerous National, International and World Championships since then. Winning the 2018 men's Open 40x20 Singles Championship in Ireland in March has been the pinnacle of my career which also earned me the right to Captain Ireland at the 2018 World Handball Championships at the University of Minnesota where I won a silver medal in the main event, the men's Open singles, I regularly compete on the United States WPH Race 48 Professional Handball circuit.

2019 *Men's Open is the highest/top division in the sport

> *Irish Nationals 60x30 Men's Open Singles Champion
> *Irish One Wall National Men's Open Singles Champion
> *United States Handball Association (USHA) Men's Open Silver Medalist
> *Irish Men's Open 40x20 Doubles Championship Silver Medalist

2018

> *Irish Men's Open 40x20 Singles Champion
> *World Championships Men's Open Singles Silver Medalist
> *Irish One Wall Nationals Silver Medalist
> *Captain of Team Ireland at the World Handball Championships at the University of Minnesota
> *No. 1 Ranked Player in Ireland and Irish Male Handball Player of the Year.

World Championships

*2018 Men's Open Singles Silver Medalist (Minnesota, USA)
*2015 Men's 23 and Under Gold Medalist (Calgary, Canada)
*2012 Boys 19 & Under 40x20 Doubles Gold Medalist (Dublin, Ireland)
*2012 Boys 19 & Under 40x20 Singles Silver Medalist (Dublin, Ireland)
*2012 Boys 19 & Under One Wall Doubles Silver Medalist (Dublin, Ireland)
*2009 Boys 17 & Under 40x20 Singles Gold Medalist (Portland, Oregon)
*2009 Boys 17 & Under 40x20 Doubles Gold Medalist (Portland, Oregon)

United States National Championships

*2019 USHA Men's Open Singles Silver Medalist
*2018 USHA Men's Open Singles Silver Medalist
*2015 USHA Collegiate Nationals Men's Open Doubles Champion
*2015 USHA Collegiate Nationals Men's Singles Silver Medalist
*2014 USHA Collegiate Nationals Men's Singles Champion (first non-American to win 3 consecutive Collegiate Men's Open Singles Championships)
*2013 USHA Collegiate Nationals Men's Singles Champion
*2013 USHA Men's Open Singles Silver Medalist
*2012 USHA Collegiate Nationals Men's Singles Champion

Irish National Championships

From 2008 to 2019 I have won over 20 Irish National Championships from U16, U18, U21, Intermediate (Men's A) and Men's Open. The most notable of these, as mentioned previously, was winning the highest honour possible in Irish handball in 2018, the Irish Men's Open Singles National Championship. I have also equaled the all-time record of Irish Collegiate Men's Open Singles titles winning 5-in-a row from 2013 to 2017 inclusive.

Other National/International Achievements and Awards

*Australian One Wall Nationals Men's Open Champion 2016
*Texas State Men's Open Singles Champion 2013
*University College Dublin Ad Astra Elite Athlete Academy Member 2013-2015
*University College Dublin/Dr. Tony O'Neill Sports Person of the Year 2012-2013

Ozzie Burke and Don Johnson made arrangements for Mulkerrins to travel to A&M and give a handball clinic during the 2019 fall semester. He was in the US for a pro handball tournament. While here, he interviewed for a job at Texas A&M to join the Physical Education Activity Program (PEAP), teach Kinesiology courses and also to coach the A&M handball team. He was accepted and was to be hired at an agreed salary and certain other conditions. The plan was for him to start with the fall 2020 semester. Enter the COVID-19 pandemic. He has not been able to come due to the pandemic and other reasons; however, as of this time, May 2022, is scheduled to be at Texas A&M to begin teaching various Kinesiology courses and assume the duties as handball team coach beginning with the 2022 fall semester.

Oakleaf, Sue (SEE: Sellars)

Oshlo, Eric L. "Rick," '69-I received the following letter from Rick:

Don

I apologize profusely for not responding more promptly to your 12 November letter regarding the history of handball at Texas A&M. No excuses worth mentioning.

I was Class of 1969 but graduated in May 1970 as a result of being on the Electrical Engineering Co-Op program where I alternated semesters at school with semesters working in Dallas for Square D company. Another student was on the opposite schedule so that the company always had a student employee. It was a trimester schedule with summers being the 3rd semester. As such, other than my freshman and senior years, I was never on campus two consecutive traditional fall/spring semesters, so my involvement with TAMU handball was a bit fractured and sporadic.

I do not remember exactly when I became involved with handball at A&M. I was not acquainted with the game prior to at least my sophomore or more likely one of my junior semesters on campus. It likely was out of curiosity, perhaps needing a PE elective class and my roommate, Wes Rogers' involvement in handball during that time. I don't recall playing any structured intramural handball, perhaps due to my odd on campus schedule. My recollection is that it was more of a club or somewhat structured group of guys who enjoyed the game, workout and each other.

The key individual drivers were Dr. Jeff Bronson, a Physics professor and Ozzie Burke, whom I believe was an athletics staff member rather than a full-time student. (NOTE: Ozzie Burke was a full-time student and President of the A&M handball club) They were our primary interface with TAMU Athletics and organized our participation in area tournaments as well as the occasional trip to Austin for weekend "tournaments" so to speak at UT. It was quite an experience to play in their glass center court.

Our primary competition came from regional tournaments rather than intramural or organized intercollegiate play. I recall playing tournaments in Austin, Houston and Corpus Christi. Those are the ones I remember, but have no doubt there were others. I often played doubles in the tournaments with Walter "Zach" Zacharias as my partner. Given that I'm left-handed, we made a good doubles team and had some modest tournament success.

One memorable item was that even though there was no formal conference or intercollegiate competition, Ozzie, Jeff or someone convinced the Athletics Department to recognize and award a number of us TAMU Athletics letter sweaters in the 1969-70 school year as a result of our tournament play. It was a surprise and an honor.

I did continue to play handball sporadically after graduation but never like when I was at A&M. The primary issue was finding good competition. I lived in Houston for 18 months post-graduation, worked downtown and could play at the downtown Y after work-plenty of good competition there. Following that, I moved 6 times over the next 8-9 years (all with the same company-Conoco) and rarely found good opportunities other than a couple years in Corpus Christi where I worked near the YMCA. After that, racquetball was coming into vogue and popularity; however, it's just not the same game in my view. Regardless, I have always remained active, first primarily as a runner and then following retirement to Colorado as an avid road cyclist, logging upwards of 7,000 miles per year here and in Europe to this day.

I doubt there is much notable history here, but it is the best of my recollection. Hope it helps.

Regards,
Eric (Rick) Oshlo

Penberthy, Walter L. "Penny"-Did Penny ever play a game of handball? A rhetorical question; however, it does not matter whether or not he ever hit a ball on the court. He needs to be included here for the impact over the years he had on the game of handball at Texas A&M. It was Penberthy who established the team concept of handball play within the Corps of Cadets soon after he became the Director of Intramurals. Playing as a team of six (three doubles teams) each company was required to enter a team which would gain points to an overall championship. Then, to get more cadets involved, the play was divided into Class A and Class B divisions, with Class B being the freshmen in the Corps. Having been a member of the Corps at Texas A&M, the author understands that basically all freshmen in each outfit would be required to display their athletic ability to learn and play handball to represent the outfit in League play. Whether or not any freshman ended up being on the handball team, essentially 100 per cent of all Corps members would have had their try at handball. And, as they moved into their upper-class years those who made the team or just enjoyed the game would continue to play. The total number of cadets involved in league play reached 1,796 in 1941-42; however, that number was only those involved in league play. There are untold numbers who played at some point in their undergraduate years in Aggieland. So, it does not take a mathematician to quickly compute that Penberthy influenced more Aggie students to the game of handball than anyone else in the history of Texas A&M. Lance Lowy definitely would be among those who introduced great numbers of students to the game; however, the two cannot be compared. Penberthy provided the means and requirement for introduction to the game while Lowy taught and coached the game.

Texas A&M lost the "Father of Intramurals," as he was affectionately known, on 19 December 1988.

Randolph, Douglas, E. "Doug"-Doug did not attend Texas A&M nor did he learn to play handball here; however, based primarily on his million-dollar gift to Texas A&M for the purpose of continuing handball at A&M well into the future, it would be absolute negligence to ignore what he has done. To better understand a person such as Randolph, one has to peel some of his layers of experience back to his childhood and early years of adulthood. He provided the following for inclusion in the book:

So, his story begins in Roswell, New Mexico at birth "when he was discovered by his parents Velma L. and Troy D. Randolph on 8 April 1949". He was a curious and energetic child. At 2½ he left his mother in a Roswell department store and walked over a mile through downtown to his grandmother's house for cookies. His mother thought he was lost.

He would walk through 2 sections of cotton fields, crossing irrigation ditches, on his way to his Aunt Maggie's house. Aunt Maggie had long, braided hair and chewed tobacco, which she shared.

Not quite as tall as the cotton, accompanied by a small grey cat named Ringworm, Doug roamed the New Mexico countryside to the dismay and exasperation of his parents. In an act of anger, his mother tied him to a tree to restrict his movements. When she returned, he had escaped, cutting down the tree using the serrated edge of the lid from a can of Baked Beans.

Navigating down the crop rows, one section to the West, Doug would visit his neighbor who drove a beer truck. The neighbor would share the beer. Ringworm loved beer especially after a long walk through the hot cotton. Ringworm would sometimes go to sleep on the trip back home. The neighbor said "If you drink beer, you will get worms." Then he pulled a large green caterpillar from behind his ear.

At age four his operating privileges were revoked when his parents found him playing Doctor with a neighbor girl on a wooden table in the driveway. From humble beginnings Doug learned to use what he could find and befriend, filling his childhood with experiences that would last a lifetime.

At the age of 5 the Randolph family moved to Lubbock where Doug attended 1st grade in Bozeman Elementary. During the year he was sent home for allegedly kissing a girl in the restroom line. The accusations were dropped. His frustrated parents enrolled Doug in a private school and in due time he graduated from Lubbock Christian High in 1967 and then attended Lubbock Christian College for 2 years.

Doug obtained his first loan in 1969 from Lubbock National Bank and has been a customer for 49 years. He currently serves on the Advisory Board of Amarillo National Bank.

Doug worked in the family business (Randolph Manufacturing Co.) until 1980. He has formed 11 companies, acquired 2 competitors and has partnered in 2 additional companies. The most significant of which was the formation of The Randolph Foundation for Higher Education Inc. in the fall of 2013 (Randolph-Foundation.Com). The Randolph Foundation has funded the following Handball Endowments and activities to date:

> $1,000,000 Handball Endowment to the University of Texas, 2014
> $1,000,000 Handball Endowment to Texas A&M University, 2018
> $500,000 Construction of 3 Handball Courts and Renovation of Rhodes-Perrin
> Recreation Center at Lubbock Christian University, Summer 2020
> $1,000,000 Handball Endowment to San Angelo State, fall 2020

As part of this writing Randolph made the following statement. "I always felt that my lack of education has held me back." The author wonders what amazing things he could have accomplished had he attended Texas A&M. Of course, that is written with the same levity as he when he made his statement.

Randolph started playing handball at the age of 21 and has continued for the last 49 years. While the handball courts at A&M and many other places have been closed due to the current pandemic, he continued to play because some time ago he constructed

2 glass-back handball courts at his office building. Obviously, he can open and close the courts as he sees fit. He has won many Consolation trophies in his age group. He states "the Consolation trophy is a trophy for the best of the worst players at the tournament. Primarily a **support player** at tournaments. The support players give the winners someone to step on to get to the top. Without the support players there would not be a tournament."

The author can attest to the fact that Randolph is not just a support player since he won his-and my-age group tournament in the last tournament I played. He also paired with Charlie Bokelman to take the Doubles championship at the last Aggieland Classic.

Why do I give? The short story is "I have been blessed. God has been good to me and my family. I worked, saved, invested, and invested again. When I started working, I wanted to earn enough money so that I could order the most expensive steak at a restaurant and pay for it. Now that I can buy the steak house, the doctor says I can only eat salad and watermelon. So, at 70, I cannot wear any more clothes, or eat any more than I do, so now I give."

Why did I give to TAMU? I love handball and have participated in the sport since I turned 21. As far as playing goes. I have 1 year of experience 49 times. TAMU has hosted many tournaments and I have made life-long friends playing here. TAMU has a great handball history and a better handball future. Playing handball gives the opportunity to compete in a game where YOU are in charge-win or lose. You surround yourself with people who do not quit and are not afraid to lose. Handball players are achievers in life. Even in the face of failure, they will try again and again until they win. Handball reduces the stress of everyday life, is healthy, mentally challenging, and rewarding. **I give so you can play handball for life.**

Reeh, Robert A. "Bob," '60-The following letter was received from Bob for inclusion in the book:

Don;

My handball experience started in New Braunfels Junior High when our coach, Frank Heffner, converted a couple of under-sized rooms in the basement of the gym into handball courts. He taught us the rules and after that we were hooked.

I did take handball at A&M as a freshman or soph, but I do not remember the name of the instructor, obviously a PE instructor. My intramural partner was Tom Wallace (deceased) who also learned handball in junior high. Tom was a good athlete and played freshman basketball for A&M. We were friends, hometown buddies, and, together, we were a pretty good handball team. Our outfit won the Intramural championship in our junior year as SQ 17 and in our senior year as SQ 12. The outfit number changed several times, but the usual suspects were the same each year.

I remember the old wooden courts at the end of the street where expanded Kyle Field now sits. We would go there late at night so we could get an available court—you probably fought the same battle given the scarce court situation.

I continued to play a little in the Air Force and for a few years after, but my hand and body could not take the pounding, plus I got into a crowd that played better than I did even though they were older. Probably my pride really made me give it up rather than the sore hands.

I think you and I have crossed paths at the Corps golf tourney. I have lost my partners and have not been at the tournament for a few years.

Thanks for your effort and if not too difficult, I would like to read your handball history when finished. Maybe you can e-mail it to me or point me in the right direction to get a copy.

Best to you and Gig 'Em,

Bob Reeh

Reesing, Ernest O. "Ernie," Jr. '56 DVM - The following was received from Ernie for inclusion in the book:

Ramblings and Recollections of an old man

I think that I started playing handball during the fall semester of 1954 at A&M, my sophomore year. I don't think that I ever took the handball class for PE. We played in the old white barn, next to the Natatorium. There were three courts on the east side and two smaller courts on the west side. This made up the east half of the building and the west half was used for gymnastics, wrestling, and other PE classes. G. Rollie White was under construction.

The courts were open 24 hours a day, and you could find guys playing at 2 AM sometimes. I often played at night and then slept in classes the next day. I don't remember the names of many that I played with. I do remember a guy named Grant that was good. I remember when you and another guy went to Chicago and won the doubles tournament.

During the summer of '54 I played at the YMCA in Dallas. Those were the first "Official" courts on which I played. I was working as a milk tester for the USDA that summer. I played on the old courts at A&M until I graduated in May 1956. I was in the Army from 1956 to 1958 in Germany and did not have a chance to play until I returned from Germany.

When I went back to Veterinary School, the new courts had been built in the old DeWare field house. I played a lot during my years in Vet school. My close friends that I played with were Ed Merritt and Ray Allen. Both were in Vet School. Ed, who passed away several years ago, was a big, quick man who had been a tight end at Rice under Coach Jess Neely. He was left-handed, and the unofficial leader of our bunch. He set up tournaments at Rice and UT a number of times. I remember one time Ed played singles against the UT coach, Tyson or Tyree-don't remember his name. Ed lost but it was a good game.

Ray Allen was in a veterinary practice for a number of years with Delbert Davis. You may remember Delbert as he was a heavyweight wrestler. He was a junior in our "jock" outfit during my freshman year. I took wrestling for PE and remember the instructor, who was also the wrestling coach, talking about you. He laughed when he said that you were from Cranfills Gap. Said that you didn't really live in Cranfills Gap, but several miles out of town. I was probably the only one in the class that had been to Cranfills Gap or knew where it was located.

I remember playing one evening in the courts at DeWare with three others. Two were pro football players, San Francisco I think, and one who was a younger brother and an A&M player. I believe his older brother had been an All-American lineman at A&M, but I don't remember his name. The younger brother and I played the two Pro's and whipped up on them. The older brother didn't take it well, especially getting beat by a younger brother.

I have played on some "make shift" courts. A doctor in Missoula, Montana made a court in his garage. The floor was cement and really got slick when we sweated. The courts in the YMCA in Butte, Montana had a chicken wire ceiling.

I continued to play until about 5 years ago when my back started giving me a lot of pain. My neighbor across the canyon is a really good player. Harry A. (Hat) Turner is his name, and I think that he was nationally ranked at one time.

I am 83 now, and doubt if I can ever get on the court again. I envy you, Donald, if you can return to the courts. You must be around 85 now.

Ernest O. Reesing

AUTHOR'S NOTES; The UT coach that Ed Merritt played is named Pete Tyson, and is still very much alive. I visited with him at the National Collegiate Handball Tournament in late February 2020. I knew Reesing's uncles very well, who lived a couple of miles south of the "bustling metropolis" named Cranfills Gap, population less than 400. I was on the wrestling team at A&M with Delbert Davis and remember him very well. A wrestler in the 157 lb. weight class did not take on the heavyweights, especially Delbert Davis. I also remember Coach Griffin, the wrestling coach, very dearly.

Ridings, Holly E. '96-From All-American in handball (doubles with Priscilla Kojin) to Flight Director at NASA is an impossible dream; however, for Holly, impossible is not a part of her character. Today, handball is a part of her past and she is living a challenge she formed early in life. The following quotes and photo (Ridings) are from pages 28 and 29 of March-April 2019 issue of *Texas Aggie* magazine:

"I was in sixth grade when the Challenger explosion happened. We watched it in the cafeteria live." Ridings said her generation reacted to the tragedy with a fight-or-flight response. For her, there was no question that a career in space was the right path.
"I was like, OK, I'm going to figure out: How do I help, how do I make that better, how does that not happen again?"

Once she knew what she wanted to study, Ridings needed to choose a school that could launch her to her dream career. "When I was looking for a school, part of it was practicality. I needed a rock-solid engineering school, and staying in Texas was much better than going out of Texas. I needed something that was affordable but had a really good engineering reputation."

During Ridings' first semester at Texas A&M, the US Senate considered reducing the budget for what would become the International Space Station by $1.6 billion. American scientists, frustrated by a lack of research breakthrough, similarly debated the value of spending money on space missions. These developments led Ridings to pursue a degree in mechanical engineering rather than aerospace engineering.

"Me going into an aerospace field, that seemed concerning at the time. I thought, 'OK, well, I better do mechanical engineering so I have a backup plan,' and I loved it. It was awesome."

After graduation, Ridings went to work for NASA and found a culture similar to what she experienced at A&M. Teamwork, which was so important to becoming handball doubles champions, was very much a part of her life. And, she wasn't a lone Aggie at the Johnson Space Center. One day a call was sent out for all Aggies to wear maroon. The next day there were 224 Aggies wearing maroon.

Rowley, Beth J., '82-The author has had the honor of playing Beth in handball. It has been a number of years since and was on a limited basis. Rowley is a handball legend in Texas and has been involved in the game for many years. Her letter to me follows:

Hi Don-

Thanks for your letter on December 8th.

I was born in 1960 in Ft. Worth, TX and grew up in Dallas (plus 3 years in Japan 1967-1971). I moved back to Dallas after graduating from TAMU and lived there until moving to Austin in 2004 where I remain.

(*Handball,* October 1992, page 60)

I graduated from TAMU in 1982 with a BBA in accounting and subsequently got my MBA.

I have been in the accounting field since graduation and have held 5 jobs, including 15 years at Trammel Crow.

I started playing handball at the beginning of my sophomore year at A&M (fall 1979). I took a handball class and have been hooked since. I played on the A&M handball team from 1980-82. I played for 32 years and finally gave it up in 2012. I had to stop because my knee got so bad it just wasn't fun anymore (4 knee surgeries finally took its toll on me). In those 32 years, I played in about 325 tournaments locally, throughout the US and the world. I had a very successful handball career winning approximately 30 state and regional tournaments, 8-10 national titles and 3 world titles as well as many local tournaments. I played on what was considered the women's pro tour.

I am currently the first and only woman in the Southwest Handball Hall of Fame, earning the recognition in 2002 in my first year of eligibility. I went in as a player but it was noted that I could have also gone in as a contributor because of all the contributions I made to handball through the years. Such contributions include being women's commissioner on the national level (USHA Board) for many years and running many tournaments in Dallas and Austin. I also coached the Southwestern handball team in Georgetown, TX for 5 years as well as taught a handball class. I have worked with many collegiate women over the years trying to keep our sport from dying.

This is making me uncomfortable…I am not usually a bragger but I am proud of my accomplishments and what handball gave to me in return. Such returns include many long and lasting friendships which I will forever cherish.

While I am proud of the "trophies won", I am equally proud to be the recipient of several sportsmanship awards. To me, this means my peers recognized that I played the game the right way and had respect for our wonderful sport.

Thank you for reaching out to me. If you have any further questions, please let me know.

Merry Christmas,

Beth

When offered the position of Women's Commissioner of handball, Rowley did not hesitate to accept. Her first article as Women's Commissioner was published in the USHA's *Handball*, April 1992, page 28. At that time, tournament handball for women was in its infancy. At that time, most tournaments offered play in an A and B division. Women who lacked the skill to play at that level were basically shut out of tournament play. Rowley worked hard to promote the game for women and at one point organized and held a tournament in Dallas that included 64 players from the US and Canada. It was very successful and a pattern for other clubs to use. With the position as Women's Commissioner also came the requirement to attend USHA Handball Board meetings as a voting member. After essentially living handball for four years, she stepped down in 1996. Her parting words to all handball players are found in her last article as Women's Commissioner in the USHA's *Handball,* August 1996 issue, page 71:

> Although my term is over, I vow to continue to promote women's handball, especially at the collegiate level, where I believe the future of women's handball lies. I believe our great, lifetime sport is one that can build confidence and initiative in young players. I encourage everyone, especially we "seasoned veterans," to continue supporting participation by young women. Because of the current emphasis on "super-star" athletes, many girls (and boys) who are not "superstar" material are not encouraged to play sports or even participate in fitness activities. Your support of women just starting out in athletics can make a critical difference in their future. I challenge you to invite high school and/or college-age women to participated in clinics in your area, and invite them to watch you play. Encourage them to see themselves as handball players, and offer them advice on how to get started in handball.

True to her word, Rowley continued to actively support the game of handball and became an "ambassador" of handball in the state. For over ten years she has been the "Texas chair" for USHA, and as of May 2022, still maintains that responsibility. The Texas chair reports to the Regional Commissioner (Arkansas, Louisiana, Oklahoma and Texas) and assists and coordinates USHA activities for the state of Texas.

Alvis Grant, Texas handball legend and charter Hall member, sponsored Rowley's induction into the Southwest Handball Hall of Honor as a player. She is the first and only female handball player to be inducted into the Hall and joins 10 others (all male) who were previously inducted. The ceremony was a part of the 56th George Lee Invitational Handball tournament held in Dallas. Making the presentation was Alvis Grant (left) and Mike Driscoll, Regional Commissioner, who was holding the bouquet of flowers to be presented to Rowley.

(*Handball*, April 2002, page 49)

SantaAna, Marla T. "Terry," '92-I was sitting at my desk working on this book when the phone rang. I answered the call and it was Terry SantaAna. She was on the way home (driving) from playing handball. She is still actively playing and was practicing for the following week's tournament in Tucson.

Terry claims she was the one who taught her brother, Sal, the "Sal serve". The serve will be described under Sal's personal. Terry was at A&M and played on some of the best women's teams the Aggies have ever had. Although she never achieved All-American status, she was a very important point producer for the team.

SantaAna, Salvador "Sal," '94-According to his coach, Lance Lowy, Sal SantaAna was one of the hardest working handball players he ever coached. He sought out training routines that would help develop his strength, flexibility and coordination-all to become a better handball player. He was always seeking, and wasn't afraid to experiment new shots, all to improve his game. He started using the "Sal serve" in the USHA National Collegiates and, since it had not been seen by the collegians, they started calling it the "Sal serve." Done correctly, served from the right server's box, softly and high to the ceiling and coming down just touching the left wall about three to four feet from the floor and just in front of the back wall, the ball will come out almost parallel to the back wall and is very difficult to return. (NOTE: The serve is not new. Glynn Donaho practiced it over and over again to almost perfection-see Donaho Personal. The author has had it used against him many times in the Mathis Invitational and has used it.) While it was not a new serve in the handball world, it was new to the collegians, who, as young people do, came up with a name.

SantaAna grew up playing three-wall in El Paso and Juarez, and developed a unique skill of taking the ball out of the air or on the fly from the front or side walls. This is an absolutely necessary skill to have in three-wall but is not seen as much in four-wall. When he came to Texas A&M, he had no experience in four-wall so he had to learn the skills, e.g., a back wall shot that he had never used, but he had those three-wall skills with his deft touch on the fly shots that made him very difficult to defeat. Once he learned the nuances of four-wall, he became one of the best players in the country evidenced by his collegiate results as well as his professional career.

SantaAna played on the pro circuit for a time; however, he is now, based on the phone call with Terry, limiting his play to his local area. The last time he played professionally was in Tucson, where he ended up in the top 4.

He is a legend in El Paso, his home town, and still gives advice to the local youngsters on the game of handball. Handball is "alive and well" in the El Paso school system where students play the game on a regular basis-and, when asked, he is always available within the constraints of his business.

Scherrer, Dr. Donald G. "Don," HPED, '71-Both Scherrer and Dr. Tommy Burnett (See Burnett-this chapter) came to Texas A&M for the same purpose: to earn their Doctorate in Health and Physical Education.

Following is the letter received from Don:

> Thank you very much for your letter dated November 12, 2018. Because we changed addresses in April of 2017, your letter did not find its way to us until last week.

> I would like to provide you with a summary of my experiences playing handball. I hope that some of the details will not bore you.

> I learned to play handball as an undergraduate student at the University of Illinois in Champaign, Illinois. Upon graduation I joined the faculty at the University of Illinois in Chicago for 3 years (1965-1968). I was also the golf coach. UIC had 6 handball courts, so I continued to play and try to improve my game.

(Courtesy Dr. Scherrer)

> I then was offered an opportunity to enter a PhD program at Texas A&M with a half-time teaching assignment for 2 years and then a full-time appointment for 1 year. The years were 1968-1971. I may have given you the wrong dates in our phone conversation. It was during this time that I had the opportunity to play a lot of handball at DeWare Gymnasium. The names of those that I played with were Jeff Bronson, Pat Patterson, Ozzie and Cyril Burke and a few others. I remember going over to UT and playing against their club.

> After graduating, I took a faculty position at Missouri Western University in Saint Joseph, Missouri. While there I won the Saint Joseph City handball title and played in tournaments in Kansas City and Ames, Iowa. As an additional bit of info, I took 2nd in the Saint Joseph City Amateur Golf tournament.

> I only stayed at Missouri Western for 1 year. I accepted a position back at the University of Illinois in Chicago. We moved to the Chicago area in the summer of 1972. I remained at UIC until I retired in 2001. During those years I sponsored the student Handball Club and also the UIC Handball Club that included students, faculty, alumni and staff. We participated in a very competitive Chicago Metro Handball League. The league included other universities, YMCAs, Health Clubs and Court Houses. It gave me the opportunity to get beat by the very best, with a big win every now and then. You may have heard of such players as Hofflander, Dohmann, Roberts, Yee, Dema, Ardito, Kendler and others that I can't recall.

> One highlight that I will never forget is when my doubles partner and I were asked to play an exhibition match at the College Intercollegiate handball tournament at Lake Forest College against Paul Haber and a partner. Paul was well past his prime and my

partner, David Krantz, and I won the match taking 2 straight. Needless to say, Haber was not very happy, but it sure made our day.

I gave up handball around 1992 when I was experiencing numbness in my right forearm and hand. I tried to make a comeback but the same problem came back. I then switched to racquetball for about 10 years and then a rotator cuff problem occurred, and so I gave that up. I did not want to endanger my golf game which I still play reasonably well.

So that's it. My wife and I have 2 daughters, (the oldest born in Bryan in 1968) and 4 grandchildren which we enjoy immensely. I would also mention that I am an avid duplicate bridge player. These are long winters in Chicago.

Thanks again for your letter. It was fun to recall the A&M experience. I hope to hear back from you. Gig 'Em!

In addition to providing the author with this letter and photo, it was Dr. Scherrer who provided me with the name and photo of Ray Fletcher, Texas A&M Intramural Director, 1965-1971. The Intramural Director during this time period was not known to the staff of the Recreation Center and was not listed in any *Aggielands* during that time period.

Scott, Patrick J. Lt. Col., USAF, (Ret), '69-Follwing is the letter I received from Scott:

Don,

I must admit, your letter was a surprise and an opportunity to reflect on some ancient history. I'm not going to be able to help you much because after being introduced to handball as a freshman (not as a PE requirement) and playing for three years, I finally joined the handball club, promptly developed tennis elbow, and was never able to participate in any club events. As I recall, the club secretary, Eric Oshlo, was a key figure in the club and could likely give you some of the information you need.

I did play handball in the Air Force for a few years after graduation but switched to racquetball since fewer and fewer handball players were available. One technique that I used with beginner racquetball players was to play handball against their racquetball game to even up the competition. A racquetball is softer on the hands, too

You asked for handball stories that might be considered in the history and here's one anecdote that might apply. In 1985, I was playing in a racquetball tournament and my opponent returned a ball that hit the front wall, the floor, the back wall, a side wall and back to the front wall without bouncing a second time. You can imagine that that event would be even rarer in handball and for some reason, I considered it to be a dead ball and didn't return it. My opponent disagreed and we went to the club's front desk for a ruling. The young lady there concurred with my opponent saying that because it had only bounced once, it was still in play, and I (somewhat emotionally) responded with "I've been playing handball and racquetball since 1965 and have never had this happen." Her young, breathy response was, "1965? That's when I was born!"

Needless to say, that was not the response I was really expecting or looking for and didn't play my best after that.

In Los Angeles, my wife and I took up Paddle Tennis which seems to have a mostly West Coast base since I've not seen it elsewhere.

So, now, in Alabama, I'm taking up Pickleball which seems to be OK on my elbow, we have a local club, and our public park has striped the tennis courts for Pickleball, too. Some friends in Florida say that it has really caught on with the retiree set there.

Well, that's about all I've got for you regarding my experiences relating to your quest. Good luck with it. BTW, there was a fiction book years ago called "Killshot" by Tom Alibrandi, about a black-market handball gambling operation with world class players who could literally maim or kill you with a well-placed handball return. Might be good backdrop for your history…or not.

Patrick

Sellars (Oakleaf), Susan E. "Sue," '83-Sue arrived at Texas A&M from West Hartford, Connecticut with little or no fanfare. It did not take long for her to become a trailblazer in Aggieland for women who wanted to be a part of the handball program and the Aggie handball team. When the opportunity opened for women to participate in the National Collegiate Handball Tournament in 1980, Oakleaf was ready. She and her good friend "Peanut" Motal had been practicing by playing doubles against the men on the handball team.

The March 1980 National Collegiate Handball Tournament, hosted by the University of California in Irvine, became a historic event when, for the first time ever, women were allowed to compete in the tournament. Equally important, especially to Aggies, Sue won the women's National Collegiate Handball Singles Championship. Motal won third and was there only because Sue convinced her that she should go. Sue added another National Collegiate Singles Handball Championship in 1981.

When her playing days were over, Sue had collected many other handball titles. Included were National USHA women's titles, Texas women's singles championships and many others at various levels. Texas is now her home state.

Sheffield-Moore, Melinda S. "Missy," Ph.D., '87-When I started this book, among one of my first contacts was former Aggie handball coach and teacher, Lance Lowy. During our conversation Lance told me that one of this former students and handball players, Dr. Melinda "Missy" (nickname given her by Coach Lowy) Sheffield-Moore, had recently been hired to fill the position of Department Head of Health and Kinesiology. I instantly thought what a great opportunity to have someone available who could relate her experience as a student and handball team member during her student time at Texas A&M. So, a call was made to set up an appointment to meet.

During our meeting, it became evident that her love for the game of handball had not waned, but had been put in her memory bank to be recalled as needed. Also, her love for Texas A&M was expressed, not only to me in our meeting, but her willingness to uproot herself and family routine to accept and move to become department head. There was no way to predict the challenges she would face. The normal challenges of department heads are an everyday routine; however, when the COVID-19 pandemic hit in the middle of the 2020 spring semester, virtual learning became reality for ALL A&M students and the faculty that taught them. The subsequent meetings to establish the process for semester completion, the summer sessions and follow-on preparation for the fall 2020 and spring 2021 semesters, both which included face-to-face and virtual learning, essentially became a daily routine. An added challenge, resulting from the pandemic, was a short fall in money. With a sizable cut in the budget, difficult and hard decisions had to be made. Dr. Sheffield-Moore handled all of the problems with the leadership skills she had developed throughout the years. No doubt some of her skills, determination and never quit attitude were developed during her years on the handball court.

During all of this turmoil, she never backed down from wanting to provide me with the Foreword and her story. She just asked that I be patient.

The following letter was received from Melinda for inclusion in this book:

Dear Don-

Thank you for the opportunity to write the foreword for the history of Texas A&M handball. It is also a pleasure to be able to share a few memories of playing on the handball team from 1983-1987 – or at least what I can remember from that exciting and life-changing time. It's funny how particular memories stick and others simply fade. I played handball during the days of the Read building and Deware, and I also remember many nights closing Deware at 2:00 am as an intramural supervisor. The courts were my home away from home, and the team was my family. My time as a member of the handball team was truly the highlight of my time as a student at Texas A&M. I particularly remember the many wonderful tournaments Lance Lowy held at A&M, the trips we made to Austin for tournaments, and also the bus rides and team events at nationals at UT, Memphis, and UC Berkley. I more readily remember spending hours with my teammates singing in a piano bar on Austin's 6th street after having played the sport we love. I also remember the many hours that Lance Lowy spent helping us all improve, as it was frankly a little humbling for many of us (athletes from other sports) to come in and realize how challenging the game of handball could be. I have to admit that I loved that it was a co-ed sport, and that the guys were always willing to play against us so that we could improve. Memories, of course, can be both positive and negative. I also remember that during one of the A&M tournaments, one of my Aggie teammates and I were playing against each other, and I remember she had a long reach. When she swung with her right hand, I closed in on her from the left. She followed through on her swing, and hit me on the left side of my nose. She broke my nose, and my nose broke her hand. I continued playing in the tournament, and she was unable. Fun times…

Because I was always in the Read building for classes and work, I have many fond memories of hanging out in Lance's office in between classes, following hours of practice, and before evening work at intramurals. He was always very supportive, and had a tendency to call me "Misty" to be funny (apparently, he liked the movie *Play Misty for Me)*. Of course, I have still never seen the 1971 thriller… When I returned to campus as department head, Lance was one of the first people I met up with to say hello and catch up. We also met in 1998 when my current department and the department head at the time, Bob Armstrong, invited me to give a talk. I flew up in a small plane and Lance drove me to the airport when I was done giving my talk. We struck up a conversation like old times, and like time had not passed.

Fast forward 30 years later, and in 2017 I returned to TAMU as the Department Head of Health & Kinesiology. In fact, at my first graduation in Reed Arena in August 2017 as a department head (while I was sitting on the stage and looking at the graduation booklet), I realized that it was exactly 30 years to the month from when I graduated in August of 1987. Before coming to TAMU, I spent 20 years working as a Professor of Medicine at the University of Texas Medical Branch teaching medical school, and studying diseases such as cancer as a physiologist and muscle biologist. Now I'd come full circle and was once again a part of Texas A&M handball.

My job now affords me the pleasure of working with you and others to support and enhance the handball team through offering KINE 199 handball classes, player scholarships, and generous donations and endowments from a number of key individuals (including you) who simply love the game. When we first met, we discussed our days of playing handball, the individuals that we both knew who played 'in my day' (the likes of Lance Lowy, Stan Lowy, Charlie Shea, Dennis Corrington, Ozzie Burke, Pete Tyson and many others), and discussed how you would like to chronicle the history of the game. Interestingly, Kayla Jones (Class of 2009) is now one of my department staff members, and she too has been paramount in continuing the tradition of handball at TAMU. You also asked if I would be interested in helping to re-invigorate the game and grow the handball team so that it could once again regain its national championship form. You and others knew a handball player named Doug Randolph, who lived in Lubbock, but loved the game so much he donated a significant endowment to support the UT Handball team. You shared that Doug wanted to do the same for Texas A&M, and asked if I would help pull together the group in my department and at A&M that could make that happen. Thanks to you and a handful of others, we made that happen in 2019 as Doug generously donated to Texas A&M on behalf of my department and the handball team. These monies help fund faculty to teach handball classes (including you, Don), support the team, and also provide scholarships to students who play the game.

Finally, I'm certain that there are many more memories about handball that I could share, but frankly none will be better than others have shared in this book. The wins and losses are fading, as are some of the fond memories, but this book will ensure that at least some of the important stats and memories are documented for the ages.

Thank you for your tremendous contribution to the sport of handball at Texas A&M, and thank you for undertaking this monumental task to show those in the present and future, the significant impact that the sport of handball can have on one's life.

Warm wishes and Gig 'em,

Melinda

Shumate (Kojin), Priscilla R., '97-Matriculating to Texas A&M from her home in Brazil, Priscilla registered in a Kinesiology class called handball. Having played handball growing up and being very good at the game, she thought this would be an easy course and could "teach the Americans a thing or two about the game." When she went to her first class she was totally confused because this was not "team handball" which she had been playing. However, she did not drop the class and decided to learn "American handball". As the saying goes, "The rest is history."

She fell in love with the game of handball and would spend many hours on the courts playing her "new" game. With her endowed athletic ability and drive, she quickly developed past a good player stage into one of the top collegians and, in her sophomore year, became an All-American handball star. Not content with just being an All-American, she would find any of the male handball players who would agree to get on the court with her and promptly show she was a force hard to handle. There is enough coverage of her handball playing days to write a book; however, the following articles and photos will make the point of her handball achievements.

Women's Classic champion Priscilla Shumate flashes a winning smile.

With Priscilla Shumate defeating Jennifer Schmitt in the final and veterans Anna Christoff and Lisa Fraser relegated to semifinal status, it was ...

New students at the head of the Class(ic)

The Women's Classic has been dominated in the last decade by two outstanding players, Lisa Fraser and Anna Christoff.

In the 1999 Women's Classic the third weekend of April at the Multnomah Athletic Club in Portland, Ore., history repeated--sort of. These two veterans battled again at the end of the tournament, but this time they were playing for third place.

That's because both stars met their surprising undoings in the semifinals as Priscilla Shumate trounced Christoff and Jennifer Schmitt edged Fraser in a tiebreaker.

Thus, the finals of the 1999 Women's Classic had an entirely new look.

Shumate raced to an early 16-6 lead in the first game. But that failed to discourage Schmitt, who regained control of the game and scored the next 12 points with incredible passes down the wall and long kill shots, leaving Shumate behind at 18-16.

From then on it was a point-by-point thriller. Both players had a chance at 20-20, but·Shumate closed it out to win 21-20.

Shumate's early second-game lead held up as she pressed hard until the end. Luck helped as she fired several cracks early on, which made it hard for Schmitt to rely on her impressive defensive skills. The 6-foot Shumate also was aided by her extensive reach, and she cruised to a 21-10 victory for her first Women's Classic crown.

The semifinals had produced true shockers. Schmitt and Fraser engaged in a long battle in Game 1, but the Winnipeg resident used her finesse to escape with a 21-19 de-

Schmitt had a wonderful tournament that ended with a defeat in the open final.

cision. Since Fraser is pregnant with twins, she "had to focus on anticipation" and be as precise as possible. But the Tucsonan rebounded, using her speed and sharpness to squeeze out the match 21-20 and 11-9.

Shumate, of Houston, had finished in the top four in the last two Classics and was determined to improve this time around. And she did in her semifinal against Christoff, of St. Paul, Minn. Shumate displayed more mental maturity than ever in the face of Christoff's awesome power and agility. The Texan won a tight, intense first game 21-18 by "remaining calm and confident to finish up that game and cross that milestone." The second game was 21-3.

When Fraser and Christoff met again, though for third place, it was another display of incredible talent. A still-fresh Fraser dominated Game 1 with precise shots and won 21-8. But Christoff began to force her opponent to move around in the second game, winning 21-13 and carrying that momentum to a third-place triumph 11-4.

As in every Classic, the women in the round of 16 compose the open division, competing for the top eight spots in the female handball world. And of the final eight, only 10th-seeded LeaAnn Martin of Bellingham, Wash., upset the seeding.

The quarterfinals went almost by the book as No. 1 seed Fraser defeated No. 8 Stephanie Lowe of Los Angeles. The "Energizer Bunny" hung tough, though, and stole 12 and 16 points from last year's champ. Third-seeded Shumate defeated No. 6 Amber Rounseville, of Springfield, Mo., with Z-serves to the left, and second-seeded Christoff beat Martin with powerful passes.

The surprise of this round came when No. 5 Schmitt took down No. 4 Sydell Smith of Brooklyn in two straight, 21-13, 21-1. Schmitt played extremely well, making great use of her ceiling and fist shots.

Women who come up short in the quarters play off for fifth through eighth. Smith's one-wall power and fly-kill game were too much for Lowe. Martin and Rounseville had a roller-coaster match, Martin prevailing 7-21, 21-9, 11-8. The only collegian in the top eight had defeated Martin in the last Classic, and the women's commissioner was out for revenge. Due to her intense perfor-

WATERFORD CRYSTAL WORLD CHAMPIONSHIPS: WOMEN'S FOUR-WALL OPEN SINGLES

Simple adjective for Shumate: Best

By Jennifer Schmitt

Priscilla Shumate has stormed into dominance of women's handball in a way that has never been accomplished until now. She proved her amazing versatility in winning the national four-wall title, followed by the national one-wall and three-wall. This was a first in Women's open play in the same year.

What could possibly top this? Well, the World Championships, held every three years, completed this incredible year for Shumate.

She started the tournament cautiously, thinking maybe this dream couldn't come true. She hadn't cut her hair in a long time, thinking it had brought her luck. She was also nursing a shoulder that had been nagging her all year.

But no one could detect uncertainty from watching her play. She displayed crisp, clean shots, few emotions, and the same steady tenacity, regardless of the score.

Shumate said she had come to the tournament thinking: "I've had a great year. It's OK not to win this." She thought this was a good attitude, putting no pressure on herself and playing relaxed all the way to the final. But when the final came and she stepped into the court to play Anna Christoff for the world title, she realized: "It's not OK to lose. I do care, and I'm going to win this title."

Then the pressure was on. She said she had never been so focused as in this match.

Christoff started strongly and repeatedly passed her opponent on the tough left glass wall, going up 14-10. But nothing seemed to affect Shumate, who started chipping away at the deficit.

When Shumate closed within a point at 16-15, it was Christoff who started to get flustered and called time out. After Shumate delivered some great power serves to go ahead 19-16, her foe called time again. Then Shumate pounded another awesome serve for 20 before struggling through a tough rally, which she ended with a decisive right-side kill to win Game 1.

Shumate later cited her comeback as the turning point in the match. She was confident in the second game, even as Christoff got off to an early advantage. Trailing 7-6, Shumate called time to regroup, and she returned with a well-timed ace. It tied the game and restored her momentum as she forged ahead 17-9. Though Christoff flurried with a surge of flat kills, all she could muster was 13 points before Shumate closed out the match.

Brian Shumate couldn't wait to congratulate his wife, and he quickly entered the court. Priscilla said he had played her with the White Label to train for the tournament, even though he had to prepare for his events too. Now, that's love!

Christoff and Lisa Fraser Gilmore, who had met in the two prior world finals and in many other finals over the last 10 years, collided in one semifinal. Though Christoff led most of the first game, Fraser rallied to win 21-18. But Christoff rebounded by blasting to a 21-7 Game 2 win. Helped by some unusual Fraser errors, Christoff came out on top in the tiebreaker 11-4.

December 2000

On her feet or from her knees, Shumate wasn't shy about shooting against Christoff ... though some of the play did tend to take place in rather close quarters in the women's open four-wall final on the glass court.

In the other semi, Shumate defeated Fiona Shannon, Ireland's national champion. Shannon played well through the first half of Game 1, but then Shumate turned on her power serve and Shannon was left scrambling. The second game was more of the same.

The Irishwoman was the only semifinalist who was thoroughly pushed in the quarters, outlasting Jennifer Schmitt 11-4. The biggest first-round match was the Amber Rounseville-Jessica Gawley duel. This time Gawley came out on top 11-5.

Some new talent of note in this division:

■ Courtney Peixoto continues to improve and should be pushing the top players in no time.

■ This year's national B champion, Vanessa Kamp, gave Schmitt a bit of a struggle in the first round.

■ Ireland's Roisin Faulkner played well against Rachel Kos.

First round: Priscilla Shumate (Albuquerque) d. Courtney Peixoto (Watsonville, Calif.) 4, 6; Lavonah Madden (Antigonish, Canada) d. Julie Long (Dublin) 5, 4; Jennifer Schmitt (Tucson) d. Vanessa Kamp (Bloomfield Hills, Mich.) 15, 4; Fiona Shannon (Antrim, Ireland) d. Sabrina Zamora (Pasadena, Calif.) 4, 7; Lisa Fraser Gilmore (Winnipeg) d. Marla Higgins (Albuquerque) 4, 5; Rachel Kos (Round Rock, Texas) d. Roisin Faulkner (Cavan, Ireland) 9, 9; Jessica Gawley (Regina, Canada) d. Amber Rounseville (Sioux Falls, S.D.) 15, (10), 5; Anna Christoff (St. Paul, Minn.) d. Cherylann Mendonca (Sacramento) 2, 1.
Quarters: Shumate d. Madden 5, 16; Shannon d. Schmitt 10, (14), 4; Fraser d. Kos 4, 5; Christoff d. Gawley 7, 4.
Semis: Shumate d. Shannon 13, 4; Christoff d. Fraser (18), 7, 4.
Final: Shumate d. Christoff 16, 13.

(*Handball*, December 2000, cover)

Smith, Manning D. "Dee" Lt. Col., USAF (Ret), '64-Following is the letter received from Dee:

Don,

I'm happy to shed whatever light I can on Dad's handball playing, but I can only remember a little of what he told me back in the mid 50's.

I vaguely remember him telling me about playing some of the other staff members at A&M when he was coaching. They must have played often. Handball had to have been a favorite sport for some important people back then, because there was apparently enough pull to get the old DeWare Field House (adjacent to Kyle Field) converted into all those beautiful handball courts. That's where Dad initiated me, and I loved playing there for a good many years.

We played a number of times on those courts, but when I got almost good enough to beat him, he left the playing to me and my best friend. We were totally hooked. Though we were at A&M Consolidated at the time, my friend and I would spend our weekends playing handball in those courts at A&M, day or night! Subsequently, we both went to

A&M ('60-'64) and continued playing a lot, at least in the first two years. We even took handball in P.E. because it was an easy "A" for us! No intramural activity though.

Sorry if I couldn't give you more specifics about Dad, but that was a long time ago! I did look in some of the old "Longhorn" yearbooks and noted that intramural handball was included even as far back as 1931, but you probably already knew that. If I can be any help to you, just email me.

Regards.
Manning "Dee" Smith

Smith, Steven "Steve" M., PhD -Blessed with great physical attributes and a mental capacity equal or better, it was inevitable he would excel in sports. Growing up in the St. Louis area where the winters are long and cold, and handball was played by many, so it was a natural growing process for youngsters to be introduced to the game of handball. For young Steve, handball was not a choice but a requirement. His dad's idea of babysitting was to give him and his brother a handball and send them off to the courts.

(Courtesy Steve Smith)

His father and theses advisor wrote the Sports Illustrated (Lippincott) book on handball. Smith's brother, David, and best friend are pictured on the cover. Smith, to this day, claims that he was not on the cover because the publishers did not like his long hair. Wow! By viewing the photo, questions arise on the length of his hair at the time.

Smith's dad coached a number of young handball players, including he and his brother. He also coached racquetball-including 4 world champions. Steve Smith was a quick learner and, by graduation from high school, had received a handball scholarship to attend Lake Forest College. Though his brother attended and played handball at Lake Forest, it was not enough to entice him to attend. He felt his life's future plans would be better served elsewhere. He received his Bachelor of Arts degree from the University of Michigan. He then attended the University of Wisconsin-Madison for his MS and PhD, the latter of which was completed in 1979.

Was it to transplant to a warmer climate, or to accept a new challenge, that he answered a call to a relatively unknown university (at least in the St Louis and upper Midwest area) named Texas A&M University? Hired in 1980, he thought he had left handball behind. Instead, he arrived at A&M when handball was really beginning to flourish. Happily, he continued with his game of handball as well as adjusting to the new environment. At A&M, he challenged his students that any student who won two out of three handball games from him would get an automatic "A". However, the other side of that coin was that any student not winning the challenge would receive an "F". A testament to the Aggies mental sharpness is: there were no challenges.

The author was not a regular on the handball courts with Smith; however, we did play a number of times. I could never get to 21 first, but I felt that his sweat was somewhat induced by my game. Though he seldom ventured away from the local area to participate in handball tournaments, he showed his level of skill and competitiveness by participating in the Aggieland Classics.

In the ninth Aggieland Classic, Steve played his way into the Open final to face John Bike. At the time, Bike was the number nine ranked handball professional. Yes, professionals and anyone who wanted to enter, were welcomed to play in the Classic. The score of 21-10, 21-16, with Bike winning, was proof enough that Smith could have played professionally had he chosen that direction. He later won the Open Singles title at the Aggieland Classic three years in a row and in the process would dispatch the Texas State handball singles champion to runner-up status. Smith's incomparable winning record beginning in the 1982 Aggieland Classic-and he did not play after winning his last year's play in the Open championship of 1996-is 11 Open singles championships, six Open singles second place finishes, one Open doubles championship and two second-place Open doubles. No one who ever played in the Aggieland Classic is even close to that astounding record.

Other notable handball achievements were his third place finish in the USHA National Junior tournament in 1969, winning the 1972 Midwest Collegiate Championship by taking down Wes Yee, the reigning national collegiate open singles champ, and while at the Universities of Michigan and Wisconsin, he was the campus handball champ.

Despite Smith's mental capacity, physical prowess and healthy lifestyle, in 1996, the dawning of time and age had taken their toll and he had to have a hip replacement, thus ending his time on the courts and playing of the great game of handball. He still maintains good physical conditioning and enjoys rock climbing at A&M's Recreation Center.

Splittgerber, Tommy R., '49-Tommy enjoyed the game of handball while a student at Texas A&M. He did not write a letter for inclusion in this book; however, he did call me and discussed his time here. He was born in Mason, TX on 8 December 1927, lived in several places and returned to live in Mason until he died 3 December 2018. What makes his story interesting is what he did after graduation. Although a Business major, he went into the movie industry as an actor. His first break came in *Tora! Tora! Tora!* In that (1970) movie, he was a telegraph operator. That followed with *The Getaway,* where he played a train station agent (1972), *Hernandez* as a gun club member (1973), *Attack on Terror: The FBI vs. the Ku Klux Klan* as a redneck (1975), *Race with the Devil* as a shop foreman (1975), *Outlaw Blues* as Tiny (1977), *Where's Willie?* as school principal (1978), *Resurrection* as a man in dance hall (1980), *Dallas,* the TV series (1981) and *Getting Even* as Calvin Deats (1986). He was best known for *Resurrection, Getting Even* and *Where's Willie?*

Sullivan, James E. "Sully"-Sully may have never hit a handball at Texas A. and M.; however, he deserves recognition in this book of handball history. It was Sullivan who built Memorial Gymnasium and later (1926) the first handball courts (two) in Memorial to support the intramural handball program installed by Penberthy. With the rapidly increasing number of students and the gaining popularity of handball, the two courts and other athletic facilities in Memorial were not large enough to support required Physical Education, so Sullivan had the Auxiliary gym built (1929), with five handball courts and other athletic facilities. Those five courts were still in use when the author was an undergraduate at A&M.

Sullivan was a financial genius. He accepted the job of Business Manager with the athletic department on 1 June 1919 when the department was $17,000 in debt. At the end of his first fiscal year, he paid $10,000 toward retiring the debt. At the end of the 1921 fiscal year, the remaining $7,000 was paid along with the erection of a steel football stand at the cost of $17,000. His tireless efforts and impact at Texas A&M cannot be adequately addressed here; however, the following writeup found in the Texas Agricultural and Mechanical College, *Longhorn,* page 330, helps:

There are few students who do not know Sully. He is everyone's friend. Anyone can walk into the Athletic office and get him to grant a reasonable request, even though it may inconvenience him personally. Sully has touched human nature in many walks of life and he is a keen student of human wants. He has been a baseball umpire, an office secretary, and now he is a married man. He will be a fixture at A. and M. as long as he desires to stay, and we hope that when we return to see the Thanksgiving game in 1948 Sully will be standing at the gate.

The 1929 Texas A&M *Longhorn*, page 229 adds more to Sullivan's performance and presence:

The best way to know a man is by what he has done: Mr. Sullivan has built what is acclaimed the finest athletic unit in the Southwest, three football fields, a baseball diamond and grandstand, a stadium, and a gymnasium-and that-is Mr. James E. Sullivan.

Mr. Sullivan left his job and Texas A&M in 1931, but in his short time here, left a legacy that should never be forgotten, and earned a right to have a footprint on the pages of A&M handball history.

Tew, Clyde A. '59-Following is the letter received from Clyde:

Hi Don,

Sorry to take so long to respond. Have tried to answer your questions below.

My company, B Infantry, was the freshman intramural champion in 1955. My handball partner, Samuel Stephen McKenney, and I were part of the B Infantry team that won the handball title.

Another B Infantry freshman, Jim Sonnier, and I played a couple of tournaments together in Houston and placed second in one tournament. I can't remember if it was 1955 or 1956.

I did not take handball for PE nor did I belong to the handball club.

I played all 14 sports and B Infantry was the freshman champion in 5 or 6 of the sports. In addition to handball, we won cross country, wrestling and rifle shooting-don't remember the others.

Know I did not help much with your book but wish you good luck on it.

Gig "Em.
Clyde Tew

Tuttle, Stacey K., '97-The following letter was received from Stacey:

I am so sorry for the delay. I was traveling a lot this fall and your request for help got buried...and then the holidays hit...sorry!

I don't have much I can help you with, unfortunately. Any pics or articles, etc. I might have are all somewhere in storage right now. I won't be able to dig for any of those things at this time.

I was born in Lubbock, TX in 1975 but grew up in Dallas. Went to TAMU literally because it was far enough to leave home, but close enough to come home. I wanted to ride my horse and watch my little brother play football. I ended up playing handball because the volleyball class was full, and my dad played handball, so I was familiar with it. If that volleyball class had been empty, I probably would never have played handball but I fell in love with it!

I've finally started playing handball again-just recently found a few people in CO to play with. (I've struggled to find people to play with-which is why I stopped). Not as competitive as I would like, but it's good to be playing again. I also play walleyball (volleyball in a racquetball court-you play off the walls) and indoor soccer regularly.

My only tournaments were when I was at TAMU… and I don't remember any accomplishments/awards, etc. Priscilla Kojin Shumate may remember more-we were doubles partners. I remember that Bryan Holmes and I planned a few fun get togethers for the team-most notably a weekend at his parent's lake house. We all bunked on the floor of the garage like sardines and stayed up late playing volleyball on the beach and watching the stars out on the boat. It was a no-alcohol event and I remember one of the guys telling me that it was the first time he remembered having fun in ages, because he was usually too drunk to remember it.

And many of us would take 2 handball classes/semester-a Mon/Wed class and a Tues/Thurs so we would know we were playing 4 times a week…and stack it so it was the last class so we could stay and play longer after. We lived at the gym! And I made so many wonderful friends through that sport...both at TAMU and at other schools that I met via tournaments.

I have some memories of an opened can of sardines that got hidden in the back of one of the vans coming back from the SMSU tournament. Every bathroom break someone was looking for what stunk in the back of the van…and then trying to slip it onto another van without being noticed. And, I probably shouldn't share this, but on that same trip, I do remember some handballs being thrown from van to van (via open windows) going down the highway (obviously an empty highway) or at least we ATTEMPTED to. I am pretty sure the roads are littered with handballs because of us.

Thanks-I can't imagine what a challenging project this will be!

Stacey

Werner, Julie (SEE: Frisbie)

Williams, Glen N., PhD, '60-It is not known when Glen started playing handball; however, it is important that he did start playing and thoroughly enjoyed the game. He was always a good athlete and excelled as a fast pitch softball pitcher. That was always evident during his warm-up on the handball court and many times during his underhand stroke of the ball.

Earning his PhD in 1965, it was four years before he was hired at Texas A&M to teach Computing Science and Industrial Engineering. Whether he had started playing handball before that time is a mute-point. Being a part of the College of Engineering, he would have been an acquaintance with Stan Lowy. Stan Lowy grew up in the Bronx playing one-wall handball and played all of his life. It would not have been long after Williams' hire that he became a part of the handball group with Stan Lowy. It is a claim that Lowy broke one of his fingers-see Marvin Harris in this chapter-during a match and he just taped it up and continued playing.

The author did not have the opportunity to play with Lowy's group for many years-I always played at a different time. However, when I joined the group, it was always a pleasure to partner with him in doubles play.

Health issues prevented him from playing in the last days of his time.

Winans, Robert C., "Bobby," MD.,'85-Bobby was born in Gallipolis, Ohio 19 July 1963. His dad was a Navy doctor, so the family moved several times during his youth. They settled in Garland, Texas where Winans went to high school, then to A&M and later Medical School.

Winans played tennis in high school so he opted for racquetball his first semester. The class was full so he decided on handball. Coach Lowy saw potential in him to become a good handball player so took him under his wing. Winans played all four years while at A&M. He played in many tournaments including the USHA National Collegiates at Lake Forest, the University of California-Berkeley, United States Air Force Academy and the University of Texas-Austin. His greatest thrill was winning the team national championship in 1985 at the University of Texas. Then another thrill was when he brought his family (wife and three boys) to the Rec Center and showed them the banner of the National Championship.

One of his favorite handball memories at A&M was the opportunity to play John Bike who would later become Number 1 in the World. Winans took the first game and Bike won the second. In Winans' words "He got tired of me and crushed me in the tiebreaker 11-1." John Bike was a very nice person and they had a good friendship through the four years at A&M.

Winans remembers his relationship with Coach Lowy very fondly. Winans said, "He and his wife, Susan, were always so hospitable to me and the other players. They had me to their house on numerous occasions for dinner and/or drinks. We spent one fun weekend together at my parents' 130-acre farm in Big Sandy, Texas four-wheel riding, fishing and sitting by camp fires."

Winans stopped playing handball when he went to medical school. There wasn't enough time for both. He now lives in Tyler and is playing tennis again. He has been rated as high as 4.5 in tennis. He recently started playing racquetball and occasionally gets on the golf course.

APPENDIX A
Texas A&M Handball Club Presidents and Officers

Athletic teams and student clubs/organizations always appoint, elect, vote or determine in some manner who will be the captain, president or individuals who direct, organize, make decisions or in some manner assist in running of the team, club or organization. From the beginning, the A&M handball club/team has been fortunate over the years to have had very capable individuals to be in leadership positions. Following are those individuals listed that can be confirmed to have held leadership positions. Obviously, there are many years in which the leadership could not be confirmed so those years are not listed.

1052-53 President----------------------------John Centilli

1953-54 President----------------------------John Centilli

1954-55 President----------------------------Donald "Johnny" Johnson

1956-57 President----------------------------John A. Dillard, III

    Vice President-----------------------Charles S. Saxe
    Secretary-Treasurer------------------Fred L. Huttanus

1960-61 President----------------------------Gary E. Staley

1967-68 President----------------------------Ozzie Burke

    Vice President-----------------------Cyril Burke
    Secretary-Treasurer------------------Dan Kennerly

1968-69 President----------------------------Ozzie Burke

    Vice President-----------------------Tommy Patrick
    Secretary-Treasurer------------------Eric Oshlo

1969-70 President----------------------------Ozzie Burke

!970-71 President----------------------------Ozzie Burke

1971-72 President----------------------------Roger Duelm

    Vice President-----------------------Gary Sheffield
    Secretary-Treasurer------------------Max Rogers

1973-74 President----------------------------Jack Gressett

1974-92 President----------------------------Charles Bokelman

1992-93 President----------------------------Steven Soto

1993-94 President----------------------------Tiffany Precht

1994-95 President-----------------------------Tiffany Precht

1995-96 President-----------------------------Priscilla Kojin

1996-97 President-----------------------------Andy Bailey

1997-98 President-----------------------------Ryan West

1998-99 President-----------------------------Ryan West

1999-00 President-----------------------------Ryan West

2000-01 President-----------------------------Richard Reynosa

2001-02 President-----------------------------Richard Reynosa

2002-03 President-----------------------------Veronika Libson

2003-04 President-----------------------------Veronika Libson

2004-05 President-----------------------------Josh Smith

2005-06 President-----------------------------Josh Smith

2006-07 President-----------------------------Dustin Delay

2007-08 Presidents (Dual)--------------------Jessica Gray/Dustin Delay

2008-09 Presidents (Dual)--------------------Sally Kenworthy/Joel Rice

2009-10 Presidents (Dual)--------------------Kayla Jones/Dustin Van Brunt

2010-11 Presidents (Dual)--------------------Kayla Jones/Dustin Van Brunt

2011-12 President-----------------------------Dustin Van Brunt

2012-13 Presidents (Dual)--------------------Ashley Burney/Austin Acosta

2013-14 President-----------------------------David Bood

2014-15 President-----------------------------Marshall Strain

2015-16 President-----------------------------Marshall Strain

2016-17 President-----------------------------Marshall Strain

2017-18 President-----------------------------Chris Hitch

2018-19 President-----------------------------Logan Call

      Secretary-Treasurer---------------- Michael Guillen

2019-20 President-----------------------------Logan Call

      Secretary-Treasurer------------------Michael Guillen

2020-2021 President---------------------------Logan Call

2021-2022 President---------------------------Jason Buley

      Secretary--------------------------------William Henry, IV
      Treasurer--------------------------------Ethan Fritzsche

APPENDIX B

USHA National Collegiate Handball Championship

Texas A&M University Handball Team Record

Year	Men	Women	Combined Team	Host Team/Location
1954	3rd	n/a	n/a	USHA/Town Club in Chicago, IL
1955-80	n/a	n/a	n/a	Various hosts and locations
1981	3rd	n/a	n/a	University of Colorado/Boulder, CO
1982	3rd	n/a	n/a	Memphis State/Memphis, TN
1983	3rd	n/a	n/a	Lake Forest College/Pallatine, IL
1984	2nd	n/a	n/a	Air Force Academy/Colorado Springs, CO
1985	1st	n/a	n/a	University of Texas/Austin, TX
1986	2nd	n/a	n/a	University of California/Berkeley, CA
1987	3rd	2nd	n/a	Memphis State/Memphis, TN
1988	3rd*	1st	3rd*	Lake Forest College/Pallatine, IL
1989	3rd	1st	1st	University of Texas/Austin, TX
1990	3rd	1st	1st	Pacific University/Portland, OR
1991	2nd	1st	1st	University of Cincinnati/Cincinnati, OH
1992	2nd	1st	1st	Lake Forest College/Pallatine, IL
1993	4th	2nd	2nd	University of Texas/Austin, TX
1994	3rd	1st	2nd	Pacific University/Portland, OR
1995	2nd	2nd	2nd	Southwest Missouri State/Springfield, MO
1996	3rd	2nd	2nd	University of Cincinnati/Cincinnati, OH
1997	3rd	3rd	3rd	Texas A&M/College Station, TX

1998	3rd	2nd	3rd	University of California/Berkeley, CA
1999	2nd	3rd	2nd	Lake Forest College/Pallatine, IL
2000	3rd	3rd	3rd	Southwest Missouri State/Springfield, MO
2001	2nd	2nd	2nd	University of Minnesota/Minneapolis, MN
2002	1st	2nd	2nd	Texas A&M/College Station, TX
2003	1st	3rd	2nd	Pacific University/Portland, OR
2004	4th	3rd	3rd	Southwest Missouri State/Springfield, MO
2005	6th	2nd	3rd	University of Minnesota/Minneapolis, MN
2006	4th	3rd	3rd	Texas A&M/College Station, TX
2007	5th	3rd	3rd	University of California/Berkeley, CA
2008	3rd	3rd	3rd	Missouri State University/Springfield, MO
2009	3rd	7th	6th	University of Minnesota/Minneapolis, MN
2010	5th	2nd	3rd	Texas A&M/YMCA in Houston, TX
2011	7th	10th	7th	Arizona State University/Tucson, AZ
2012	3rd	n/a	12th	Missouri State University/Springfield, MO
2013	12th	16th	13th	Arizona State, Tucson, AZ
2014	9th	16th	9th-Div II	North Carolina State University/Raleigh, NC
2015	2nd	2nd	1st-Div II	Pacific University/Portland, OR
2016	1st	8th	7th-Div A	University of Minnesota, Minneapolis, MN
2017	7th	12th	10th-Div A	Arizona State University/Tucson, AZ
2018	n/a	n/a	n/a	Missouri State University/Springfield, MO
2019	1st	12th	10th-Div B	University of Minnesota, Minneapolis, MN
2020	4th	n/a	4th-Div A	University of Texas/ Austin, TX
2021	**	**	**	
2022	2nd	2nd	1st-Div A	Missouri State University, Springfield, MO

*- The men and combined team's place finish is not available. Coach Lowy, as best he can remember, provided the place finish. The record from the other years would support his memory.

**-The National Collegiate Handball Tournament was not held due to COVID-19.

n/a - Did not exist, information not available, or not enough Aggies participating to compete as a team.

APPENDIX C
Aggie All-Americans in Handball

It was not until 1987 that the USHA began recognizing and naming the top collegiate handball players to All-American status. Even though some earlier Aggie handball players never received the All-American honor, these top Aggie handball players should be recognized: players like Sue Oakleaf, who was the first female collegiate singles handball champion, and others who achieved the level of those who later received the honor. These players will be listed in this chapter with asterisks (**) by their name and with the title/titles won.

James R. (Jim) Mathis '55**
Personnel
Administration
San Antonio

(1955 *Aggieland*, page 167)

Donald J. (Don) (Johnny) Johnson '55 **
Wildlife Management
Cranfills Gap

(1955 *Aggieland*, page 163)

1954 National Intercollegiate Handball Doubles, champions

O.T. (Ozzie) Burke '71**
Physical Education
College Station

(*Handball*, May 2016, page 6)

Kenneth D. (Dan) Kennerly '68**
Mathematics
Odessa

(1968 *Aggieland,* page144)

1968 National Collegiate Handball Doubles, champions

Susan G. (Sue) Oakleaf/
Sellars '83**
Chemistry
West Hartford, Connecticut
1980 Singles, champion
1981 Singles, champion
1982 Singles, 2nd
1983 Singles, 2nd

(*Handball*, September 1982, page 62)

Glorian A. (Peanut) Motal/
Hummel '79**
Mechanical Engineering
Houston
1980 Singles, 3rd

(Courtesy Glorian Hummel)

**NOTE: Beginning in 1987, All-American recognition would go to all who reached the semifinals in singles and finals in doubles. For purposes of recognition, the same criteria have been used to recognize those who reached the same level prior to 1987.

Brenda D. Crim '83**
Physical Education
Caldwell
1983 Singles, 3rd
(Cushing Archives)

Renee A. DeLassus '86**
Business Analysis
Lake Kiowa
1984 Singles, 3rd
1985 Singles, 3rd
(Courtesy Renee DeLassus)

Julie W. Werner/Frisbie '86**
Marketing
Austin
1984 Singles, 2nd
1985 Singles, champion
1986 Singles, 3rd
(Courtesy Julie Frisbie)

NOTE: With the drop-down format, which began with the women's competition in 1987, the playoff for third and other places became past history. To reach All-American status, each player would have played three or more matches so it was felt there was no need to determine third or fourth place since both would be listed as All-Americans.

Gloria A. Smalley '91
Kinesiology
Richardson
1987 Singles, 2nd
1989 Doubles, 2nd
1990 Singles, 2nd
1990 Doubles, 2nd
(Courtesy Lance Lowy)

Wendy L. Smalley '91
Kinesiology
Richardson
1989 Doubles, 2nd
1990 Singles, semifinalist
1990 Doubles, 2nd
(1987 Aggieland, page 692)

Gloria and Wendy were partners in Doubles

Kimberly (Kim) D. King
'90
Accounting
Cypress
1989 Singles, semifinalist
(1987 Aggieland, page 760)

Audrea L. Stork/Crane '92
Kinesiology
Rockdale
1991 Singles, semifinalist
(Handball, June 1990, page 12)

Sharon B. Baylor/Davis '93
Management
Austin
1991 Singles, 2nd
1991 Doubles, 2nd
1992 Singles, champion
1992 Doubles, champion

(1991 *Aggieland*, page 675)

Betsy L. Boswell '93
Petroleum Engineering
Houston
1991 Singles, semifinalist
1991 Doubles, 2nd
1992 Singles, semifinalist
1992 Doubles, champion

(*Handball*, June 1991, page 35)

Sharon and Betsy were partners in Doubles

Kimberly (Kim) F. Harris/
Bowers '93
Interdisciplinary Studies
Dallas
1992 Singles, semifinalist

(1992 *Aggieland*, page 647)

Salvador (Sal) SantaAna '94
Management
El Paso
1993 Singles, 2nd
1994 Singles, 2nd

(Courtesy Lance Lowy)

Tiffany M. Precht/Good
'94
Petroleum Engineering
Waco
1994 Doubles, 2nd
1995 Doubles, 2nd

(*Handball*, June 1944, page
35)

Cassandra C. (Cassie) Tijerina
'94
Mechanical Engineering
Arlington
1994 Singles, 2nd
1994 Doubles, 2nd
1995 Doubles, 2nd

(*Handball*, June 1944, page 35)

Precht and Tijerina were Doubles partners in 1994 and 1995

Priscilla R. Kojin/Shumate '97
Marketing
Sao Paula, Brazil
1996 Singles, 2nd
1996 Doubles, 2nd with Holly Ridings
1997 Singles, champion
1997 Doubles, champion with Stacey Tuttle
1998 Singles, champion
1998 Doubles, champion with Stacey Tuttle

(*Handball*, June 1999, page 4)

Holly E. Ridings '96
Mechanical Engineering
Amarillo
1996 Doubles, 2nd with
Priscilla Kojin

(*Handball,* June 1996, page 27)

Stacey K. Tuttle '07
Interdisciplinary Studies
Frisco
1997 Doubles, champion with Priscilla Kojin
1998 Doubles, champion with Priscilla Kojin

(*Handball,* June 1997, page 5)

Bradley D. (Brad) Alesi '02
Marketing
Des Plains, Illinois
2000 Singles, 2nd
2001 Singles, 2nd
2002 Singles, 2nd

(*Handball,* April 2000, page 4)

Lynn M. Alesi '04
Marketing
Des Plains, Illinois
2001 Singles, 2nd
2002 Singles, 2nd
2003 Singles, 2nd,
Doubles, 2nd
2004 Singles, semifinalist

(Courtesy Christina Luther)

Christina L. Matthews/Luther '07
Nutritional Science
Austin
2003 Doubles, 2nd

(Courtesy Christina Luther)

Alesi and Matthews were partners in 2003

Katie Nieswiadomy
Animal Science, Masters
Burleson
2017 Singles, top American female,

(*Handball,* May 2016, page 12)

NOTE: In recent years the Irish handball players at the National Collegiate Handball Tournament have dominated the All-American honors. The USHA Collegiate Commissioners agreed that the All-American honors should rightfully only be awarded to American handball players. Beginning in 2017 and forward, the All-American honors will go to the top four American players of each gender. A new designation called the All-Tournament Team will honor all entrants who earn the same level as previous All-Americans.

APPENDIX D
Top 16

Handball players initially begin this great game by learning to hit the ball and then developing their off hand to be able to keep the ball in play. Then comes the learning of strategy and how to use the strongest part of your individual game to get to 21 first. For those in college and members of a college/university handball team, working hard to earn a top 16 ranking worldwide among the collegiate ranks is obviously not an easy task; however, to reach that point, the rewards for team and individual recognition are at the highest level. The highest number of team points earned toward a team championship is in the Open division which is comprised of the top 16 players. The best individual champion from the collegiate ranks is always from the Open division. Team championships can be won without a player in the Open division, but the team has to perform extremely well, especially in the A division to earn a team championship. Many Aggies through the years have achieved the skill level to play in the Open division and this Chapter will recognize those Aggies.

There will be no player listed in the top 16 before 1983, although some would have earned that honor had there been such a ranking in collegiate handball. College handball teams were made up of 4 players and were male only for many years, so the top 16 ranking was not important. I have chosen 1983 as the starting point because it was that year when there were enough women entrants for the top 16 to become more meaningful. As for the men, the top 16 did not mean much until the drop-down format was instituted for men in 1988. Also, during the time frame 1980-1988 there were no Aggie men handball players who would have earned that ranking.

Without a doubt, Sue Oakleaf and Glorian Motal would have earned that ranking in 1980, and Sue Oakleaf in 1981 and 1982, Beth Rowley in 1982 and Ozzie Burke in 1971; however, those years were not significant for a top 16 ranking.

National champions and All-Americans listed in this chapter will only be recognized as being in the top 16. Titles, name changes, and other name differences are not all known so each will be listed as they were known when on the A&M handball team.

1983	Brenda Crim, Sue Oakleaf
1984	Renee deLassus, Julie Werner
1985	Cissy Burns, Renee deLassus, Julie Werner
1986	Dawn Bell, Renee deLassus, Julie Werner
1987	Dawn Bell, Tanya Brackeen, Ana Griffin, Julie Hutchinson, Melinda Sheffield, Gloria Smalley, Wendy Smalley, Caryn Stallings
1988	Todd Bryan, Dawn Crane, Ana Griffin, Julie Hutchinson, Kim King, Gloria Smalley, Wendy Smalley, Francis Woodcock

1989   Dawn Crane, Anna Griffin, Kim King, Gloria Smalley, Wendy Smalley, Lisa Smith, Francis Woodcock

1990   Sharon Baylor, Anna Gonzalez, Mollie Huber, Kim King, Gloria Smalley, Wendy Smalley, Audrea Stork

1991   Sharon Baylor, Betsy Boswell, Aaron Cooper, Katie Hutcheson, Tammy Reyes, Sal SantaAna, Audrea Stork, Leigh Ann Williams

1992   Sharon Baylor, Betsy Boswell, Anna Gonzalez, Kim Harris, Katie Hutcheson, Sal SantaAna, Terry SantaAna, Terry Slusarek, Audrea Stork, Cassie Tijerina

1993   Michele Alton, Anna Gonzalez, Becky Pinkard, Tiffany Precht, Shane Rothenberger, Sal SantaAna, Cassie Tijerina

1994   Michelle Alton, GeorgeAnn Kidd, Kim McKinney, Becky Pinkard, Tiffany Precht, Jaime Rupple, Sal SantaAna, Cassie Tijerina

1995   Eric Fields, Joanne Jackson, Jeff Jeffers, Jeff Jones, Priscilla Kojin, Kim McKinney, Tiffany Precht, Cassie Tijerina

1996   Priscilla Kojin, Kim McKinney Jennifer Powis, Holly Ridings, Stacey Tuttle, Jeff Walsh

1997   Priscilla Kojin, Jennifer Powis, Stacey Tuttle

1998   Priscilla Kojin, Jennifer Powis, Stacey Tuttle

1999   Brad Alesi, Janna Althaus, Ben Barbour, Ryan West

2000   Brad Alesi, Ross Burke, Christina Matthews, Ryan West, Karla Wray

2001   Brad Alesi, Lynn Alesi, Morris Libson, Christina Matthews

2002   Brad Alesi, Lynn Alesi, Ross Burke, Carrie Lucas, Meagan McDuff

2003   Lynn Alesi, Ross Burke, Carrie Lucas, Christina Matthews

2004   Lynn Alesi, Carrie Lucas

2005   Michelle Cochrane

2006   Kelly Arunski, Dutch Lowy, Marshall Lowy

2007   Kelly Arunski, Dutch Lowy, Marshall Lowy

2008   Dutch Lowy, Marshall Lowy

2010   Angie Burrer, Krystin Deason, Kayla Jones, Dustin Van Brunt

2016   Katie Nieswiadomy

2017   Katie Nieswiadomy

APPENDIX E

USHA National Collegiate Handball Tournament

Top Aggie Men by Division

The listing of the men who have achieved the same level of play as that listed for the women will follow the same pattern. For more than the first quarter century (1953-1981) of the USHA National Collegiate Handball Tournament a handball team consisted of the number one singles player, the number two singles player and a doubles team. Individuals could compete as individuals if there were not enough players entered in the national competition from their respective colleges or universities to make up a handball team. Typical of any USHA Collegiate National Championship Tournament, there were greater numbers of men competing than women so the competition to earn the same distinction as the women required greater skill. With the drop-down format that was solved. The drop-down format was great for many reasons but it also was designed to accommodate more divisions to be established based on the number of participants. As was the case with the women, matches in some years/tournaments went unreported. It is acknowledged that the following list is not 100 per cent complete.

1954	Jim Mathis and Don "Johnny" Johnson- Doubles, champions	
1968	Ozzie Burke and Dan Kennerly- Doubles, champions	
1974	Charles Bokelman and Jack Gressett- Doubles Consolation, 2nd	
1982	Raymond Walkup-C, 3rd	
1983	Jeff Davison-C, 1st Bobby Winans-C, 2nd	Brent Bertrand-C, semifinalist
1984	Mark Pokryfki-B, 2nd Brent Bertrand-C, semifinalist	Kevin McIntosh-C Consolation, 2nd
1985	David Allen-C, 2nd Randy Pullen-C, semifinalist	Tim Sutton-C, 2nd
1986	Todd Bryan-C, 2nd	Larry Wisdom-C, semifinalist
1987	Mike Forbes-C, semifinalist	

1989   Wayne Crouch-B, semifinalist

1990   Mark Rhodes-B, semifinalist

NOTE; In 1991 those who lost in the round of 32 of A division were placed in a specially created division called the Second Flight A division. It is the only time this type of new designation was used. This designation was eliminated after one year and has not been used again during the coverage of this history.

1991   Vern Hegwood-Second Flight A division, semifinalist

1992   Ricky Cole-B, semifinalist   Dusty Davis-Contenders, 2nd
              Vern Hegwood-C, 1st

1993   Sal SantaAna-Open, 2nd   Warren Ferguson-Novice, 2nd
              Colin Errington-C, semifinalist   Jeff Townsend-Novice, semifinalist
              Ryan Isenberg-Contenders, semifinalist

1994   Sal SantaAna-Open, 2nd   Ryan Isenberg-Novice, 2nd
              Ricky Reynolds-Contenders, semifinalist

1995   Jeff Walsh-B, 1st   Andy Bailey-C, semifinalist
              Noel Keen-B, 2nd   Joshua Ely-Novice, 1st
              Scott Korth-C, 1st   Chad Lucas-A, semifinalist

1997   Bryan Holmes-B, semifinalist   Ike Haines-C, semifinalist
              Jason Green-C, 1st   Joel Petershagen-C, semifinalist
              Mike Cox-C, 2nd

1998   Ben Barbour-A, 2nd   Mark Hill-C, semifinalist

1999   Ryan Miller-Contenders, 1st

2000   Brad Alesi-Open, 2nd   Chad Lucas-B, semifinalist
              Morris Libson-A, 1st   Bill Phillips-C, 2nd
              Jeremy Doege-B, 1st   Ryan Miller-C, semifinalist
              Danny Knapp-B, semifinalist

2001   Brad Alesi-Open, 2nd   Zach Lowy-A, semifinalist
              Jeremy Doege-A, 2nd

2002   Brad Alesi-Open, 2nd   Lance Hoffman-C, semifinalist
              Zach Lowy-A, semifinalist   Grant Potter-Contenders, semifinalist
              Richard Reynosa-A, semifinalist   Ryan Collier-Challengers, 2nd
              Chad O'Neal-B, 1st

2003   Juan Zavala-A, semifinalist   Randy Key-Intermediate, semifinalist

2004	Dutch Lowy-A, 2nd	Clint Alexander-Challengers, semifinalist
	Ross Burke-A, semifinalist	Cain Kohutek-Novice, 2nd
	Hap Potter-C, semifinalist	
2005	Clint Martin-Intermediate, semifinalist	Grant Rybak-Challengers, semifinalist
2007	Matt Acker-C, 1st	Miguel Garza-Intermediate, semifinalist
	Dustin Delay-C, semifinalist	Joel Rice-Contenders, semifinalist
	Chris Patton-Intermediate, 1st	
2008	Matt Acker-C, 1st	Josh Gavin-Contenders, 2nd
2010	Jared Beirmann-Consolation, semifinalist	

The Commissioners of the USHA Collegiate Handball Tournament voted to divide the men's competition into Division I, Division II and Division III. Any team with a Division I men's entrant would compete for the team national championship in Division I. All other college/university teams would compete for the National Team and Combined Team Championships in Division II or Division III. It is very unlikely that any college or university team would have a team of six Division III male handball players.

2012	Zachary Smith-Challengers, Division II, semifinalist	
2013	Enrique Clarke-A, Division III, semifinalist	
2014	Tyler Isenhart-B, Division III, 2nd	Michael Henrietta-C, Division III, 1st
2015	Marshall Strain-A, Division II, semifinalist	Bill Foran-A, Division III, 2nd
	Mark Munson-Intermediate, Division II, semifinalist	

Beginning with the 2016 season the new divisions are Open, A, B for the men and Open, A for the women. Divisions C for the men and B for the women were added in 2017.

2016	Marshall Strain-A3, semifinalist	Mark Munson-B1, 1st
2017	Chris Hitch-B2, semifinalist	
2019	Michael Guillen-B2, semifinalist	Marcus Shanaa-B3, semifinalist
	Logan Call-B3, semifinalist	
2020	Logan Call-B2, semifinalist	Logan Call and Marcus Shanaa-B
	Michael Guillen-B3, 2nd	Doubles, 2n
2022	Phillip Barrett-B2, 1st	
	Andrew Applewhite-B2, semifinalist	
	William Henry, IV-B3, 2nd	

APPENDIX F

USHA National Collegiate Handball Tournament

Top Aggie Women by Division

From the very beginning of the USHA college handball competition in 1953, one of the goals was to determine individual champions. As the numbers of competitors and college/university entrants continued to grow, it became necessary to add champions at different skill levels to recognize hard work and encourage continued improvement. The purpose of this writing is to recognize those Aggies who have finished at the semifinals or higher level in singles and finals in doubles within their respective divisions. The first-year women were allowed to compete in the USHA National Intercollegiate Handball Tournament was 1980. The division of competition by individual is provided after their name. All listings are in singles play unless identified as partners in doubles. The first-year women were allowed to play the top division was referred to as the A division. I have used the term Open division, since that would be the term used, beginning in 1987 when the drop-down format became the yearly way to determine the exact division of play based on individual talent. Those losing their first-round match in the Open (A) division would then compete in the B division. There were some years/tournaments when the matches were not reported; consequently, this listing is only complete for the matches reported.

Year

1980	Sue Oakleaf-Open, champion	Jill MacAluso-Open Consolation, 1st
	Glorian Motal-Open, 3rd	
1981	Sue Oakleaf-Open, champion	
1982	Sue Oakleaf-Open, 2nd	Beth Rowley-Open Consolation, 1st
1983	Sue Oakleaf-Open, 2nd	Caroline Henning-B, 3rd
	Brenda Crim-Open, 3rd	
1984	Julie Werner-Open, 2nd	Caroline Henning-B Consolation, 1st
	Renee deLassus-Open, 3rd	Kay Kern-C, 1st
1985	Julie Werner-Open, champion	Renee deLassus-Open, 3rd
1986	Julie Werner-Open, 3rd	Melinda Sheffield-B, semifinalist
	Debbie Daks-B, 2nd	

NOTE; In a few short years the number of women handball players had increased to a number that more divisions were needed. Also, in 1987 the drop-down format was first tried in women's competition. The available divisions for play were the Open, A, B, C, Novice, Contenders and Open doubles. With the drop-down format the consolation bracket of any division no longer served a purpose and was discontinued. As the tournament continued to get bigger and bigger with each passing year new divisions were added. The rank order of the divisions can be determined by the yearly listing. The highest finisher is always listed first and then others in descending order. Semifinalists are listed alphabetically.

1987
Gloria Smalley-Open, semifinalist
Anna Griffin-A, 2nd
Dawn Bell-A, semifinalist
Tracy Johnson-B, semifinalist
Dawn Crane-C, 2nd
Susan Owens-C, semifinalist

1988
Francis Woodcock-B, 1st

1989
Kim King-Open, semifinalist
Diane Purinton-B, 2nd
Gloria and Wendy Smalley-Doubles, 2nd

1990
Gloria Smalley-Open, 2nd
Kim King-Open, semifinalist
Wendy Smalley-Open, semifinalist
Audrea Stork-B, 1st
Gloria and Wendy Smalley-Doubles, 2nd

1991
Sharon Baylor-Open, 2nd
Betsy Boswell-Open, semifinalist
Audrea Stork-Open, semifinalist
Katie Hutcheson-B, 1st
Leigh Ann Williams-B, semifinalist
Laura Gross-C, 2nd
Sharon Baylor and Betsy Boswell-
Doubles, 2nd

1992
Sharon Baylor-Open, champion
Betsy Boswell-Open, semifinalist
Kim Harris-Open, semifinalist
Audrea Stork-B, 2nd
Katie Hutcheson-B, semifinalist
Terry SantaAna-B, semifinalist
Anna Gonzalez-C, semifinalist
Cassie Tijerina-C, semifinalist
Sharon Baylor and Betsy Boswell-
Doubles, champions

1993
Anna Gonzalez-B, 2nd
Becky Pinkard-B, semifinalist
Kelly LeWallen-C, 2nd
Joanne Jackson-Contenders, semifinalist
Georgann Kidd-Novice, 2nd
Joan McDowell-Novice, 4th

1994
Cassie Tijerina-Open, 2nd
Tiffany Precht-B, 1st
Georgann Kidd-B, 2nd
Michelle Alton-B, semifinalist
Kim McKinney-C, semifinalist
Becky Pinkard-C, semifinalist
Jill Emerson-Contenders, semifinalist
Tiffany Precht and Cassie Tijerina-
Doubles, 2nd

1995
Cassie Tijerina-Open, semifinalist
Tiffany Precht-B, 1st
Tiffany Precht and Cassie Tijerina-
Doubles, 2nd

1996	Priscilla Kojin-Open, 2nd	Priscilla Kojin and Holly Ridings-
	Jennifer Powis-B, 1st	Doubles, 2nd
	Kim McKinney-B, semifinalist	
1997	Priscilla Kojin-Open, champion	Jennifer Bailey-Novice, 2nd
	Ashley Kuehn-C, semifinalist	Priscilla Kojin and Stacey Tuttle-
	Nicole Nelson-Contenders, semifinalist	Doubles, champions

NOTE: Prior to 1998 there was no A division. The highest division was Open and the next lower was B division. The A division was added in 1998.

1998	Priscilla Kojin-Open, champion	Carolyn McCrary-Challengers, 1st
	Jennifer Powis-A, 2nd	Priscilla Kojin and Stacey Tuttle-
	Nicole Nelson-B, 2nd	Doubles champions
	Ryan West-C, semifinalist	
1999	Sandi Bruner-C, semifinalist	
2000	Karla Wray-B, 2nd	Meagan Head-Challengers, 2nd
	Jennifer Minarcik-C, semifinalist	
2001	Lynn Alesi-Open, 2nd	Kirsten Bode-B, semifinalist
	Meagan McDuff-B, 2nd	Jennifer Minarcik-C, 2nd
2002	Lynn Alesi-Open, 2nd	Courtney Gordon-B, 2nd
	Meagan McDuff-A, 1st	Dara Crain-B, semifinalist
2003	Lynn Alesi-Open, 2nd	Wendy Ridings-C, 2nd
	Christina Matthews-A, semifinalist	Lynn Alesi and Christina Matthews-
	Courtnee Gordon-B, semifinalist	Doubles, 2nd
2004	Lynn Alesi-Open, semifinalist	Michelle Melton-Intermediate, 1st
	Wendy Wheeler-B, 1st	
2005	Michelle Cochrane-A, 2nd	Heather Sablutura-Challengers, semifinalist
	Jessica Kelly-C, 2nd	
2006	Kelly Arunski-A, semifinalist	Sarah Wood-Intermediate, semifinalist
	Jessica Kelley-A, semifinalist	
2007	Pam Early-B, 2nd	Sally Kenworthy-Intermediate, 1st
	Jessica Gray-B, semifinalist	Hope Pond-Intermediate, 2nd
2008	Jessica Gray-A, semifinalist	
2009	Jessica Gray-A, semifinalist	Sally Kenworthy-B, semifinalist
2010	Kayla Jones-A, 1st	

2014   Ashley Burney-1 B, semifinalist

2015   Macie Morris-1 C, 1st   Emily Seyl-1 C, semifinalist

2016   Katie Neiswiadomy and Sarah Lehman-A
              Doubles, 1st

Note: The Commissioners of the USHA National Collegiate Handball Tournament made the decision that the All-Americans honors would no longer be awarded to international players but only to those playing in the tournament from American colleges and universities. As indicated below, Katie Nieswiadomy earned the honors under the new ruling.

2017   Katie Neiswiadomy-Open top   Marilyn Delgado-A 1, 1st
              American woman to play-earned All-
              American honors

2019   Lauren Waters-1 B, 1st
              Bethany Butler-1 B, 2nd

2020   Lauren Waters-A 2, 1st
              Lauren Waters and Briley Buchanan-
              B Doubles, 1st

2022   Faith Kucera-A 2, semifinalist

INDEX

NOTE; Only Aggies, those who regularly played in the Texas A&M handball courts or individuals who have had a significant impact on the game of handball at this University are listed in the index. Some exceptions are students from other colleges/universities who played in the Aggieland Classic. Except in the chapter on PERSONALS, individuals are listed as they were known during their student/playing years. It is likely that some individuals may be listed more than once; however, the names here are as listed in print. Foreword and Preface are not included.

Lightning Source UK Ltd.
Milton Keynes UK
UKHW050619070223
416551UK00003B/323

9 781039 149892